MARRIAGE, DOWRY, AND CITIZENSHIP IN LATE MEDIEVAL AND RENAISSANCE ITALY

Through his research on the status of women in Florence and other Italian cities, Julius Kirshner helped to establish the cross-disciplinary study of social and legal history in late medieval and Renaissance Italy, and challenged the idea that Florentine women had an inferior legal position and civic status.

In *Marriage, Dowry, and Citizenship in Late Medieval and Renaissance Italy*, Kirshner collects nine of his most important essays that address these issues in Florence and the cities of northern and central Italy. Using a cross-disciplinary approach that draws on the methodologies of both social and legal history, Kirshner's research presents a wealth of examples of daughters, wives, and widows acting as fully fledged members of society.

Revised and updated to reflect current scholarship, the essays in *Marriage, Dowry, and Citizenship in Late Medieval and Renaissance Italy* appear alongside an extended introduction which situates them within the broader field of Renaissance legal history.

(Toronto Studies in Medieval Law)

JULIUS KIRSHNER is a professor emeritus in the Department of History at the University of Chicago.

Marriage, Dowry, and Citizenship in Late Medieval and Renaissance Italy

JULIUS KIRSHNER

UNIVERSITY OF TORONTO PRESS
Toronto Buffalo London

Toronto Buffalo London
www.utppublishing.com

ISBN 978-1-4426-1421-5

Toronto Studies in Medieval Law

Library and Archives Canada Cataloguing in Publication

Kirshner, Julius, author
Marriage, dowry, and citizenship in late medieval and Renaissance Italy / Julius Kirshner.

(Toronto studies in medieval law)
Includes bibliographical references and index.
ISBN 978-1-4426-1421-5 (pbk.)

1. Marriage law – Italy – Florence – History – Medieval, 500–1500. 2. Dowry – Italy – Florence – History – Medieval, 500–1500. 3. Citizenship – Italy – Florence – History – Medieval, 500-1500. 4. Real property – Italy – Florence – History – Medieval, 500–1500. 5. Women – Legal status, laws, etc. – Italy – Florence – History – Medieval, 500–1500. 6. Law, Medieval – Italy – Florence. 7. Renaissance – Italy – Florence. I. Title. II. Series: Toronto studies in medieval law

KKH542.K57 2015 346.4501'60902 C2014-908167-7

University of Toronto Press gratefully acknowledges the financial assistance of the Centre for Medieval Studies, University of Toronto, in the publication of this book.

University of Toronto Press acknowledges the financial assistance to its publishing program of the Canada Council for the Arts and the Ontario Arts Council, an agency of the Government of Ontario.

University of Toronto Press acknowledges the financial support of the Government of Canada through the Canada Book Fund for its publishing activities.

Contents

Acknowledgments

In researching and writing the studies in this volume, I have benefited from the innumerable acts of generosity – smoothing the way for me to gain access to local archives, providing archival and manuscript references, sending copies and scans of texts that were unavailable in Chicago, providing bibliographic leads, and commenting on drafts of early versions of the studies – of friends and colleagues. Warm thanks to all: Harvey Adelstein, Lawrin Armstrong, Mario Ascheri, Nicola Lorenzo Barile, Gabriella Battista, Kees Bezemer, John Cochrane, Vincenzo Colli, Gino Corti, Angela De Benedictis, Constantin Fasolt, Robert Fredona, Orsola Gori, Maria Teresa Guerra Medici, Linda Guzzetti, David Herlihy, Alexander Kirshner, Susanne Lepsius, Michele Luzzati, Christine Meek, Sara Menzinger, Maria Grazia Nico, Diana Robin, Rodolfo Savelli, Justin Steinberg, Claudia Storti Storchi, Francesca Trivellato, and Alan Watson.

Special thanks are due to Elena Brizio of the Medici Archive Project, who verified archival and manuscript references in Florence; Daniel Jamison, who skillfully transformed the PDF files of the published studies into clean MS Word files and compiled the first draft of the comprehensive bibliography; Erik Carlson, who meticulously edited the manuscript; and my coauthors Osvaldo Cavallar and Jacob Klerman, who agreed to the republication of chapters 1 and 5, respectively, in this volume.

The research on the records of the Monte delle doti and Monte delle Graticole, which supplies the basis for the findings in chapters 4 and 5, was undertaken in collaboration with Tony Molho. Our collaboration has been fruitful, resulting in a number of publications, written together as well as individually. I want to express my appreciation for Tony's hospitality, first in Providence and then in Florence, intellectual engagement, and readiness to share his incomparable knowledge of Florentine public finance in the Renaissance. Tom Kuehn and I have been commenting on each other's drafts and exchanging ideas since the 1970s. I have come to rely on his sound judgment and have profited immensely from his substantial and farsighted sociolegal contributions. I am beholden to Osvaldo Cavallar, friend, coauthor, and indefatigable decipherer of medieval legal texts, who over the past twenty-five years has patiently read and critically commented on draft after draft of my work. It was Lauro Martines who urged me to publish a volume of my studies. I hope the volume measures up to his high scholarly standards.

I am indebted to Paolo Grossi for his welcoming friendship and for making available the resources of the Centro di Studi per la Storia del Pensiero Giuridico Moderno at the University of Florence, when he was its director and before his appointment to Italy's Constitutional Court. Many of the legal works cited in the volume are found at the remarkable Robbins Religious and Civil Law Collection, School of Law (Boalt Hall), University of California at Berkeley. I am grateful to its director, Laurent Mayali, and staff for making my visits to the "Robbins" both pleasurable and productive. I am also grateful to the personnel of the Archivio di Stato and Biblioteca Nazionale Centrale in Florence and the Biblioteca del Senato in Rome for their efficient and courteous assistance.

I wish to acknowledge the support of the Centre for Medieval Studies, University of Toronto, and particularly its sometime director, John Magee, who generously allocated a subsidy from the departmental publication fund for the production of this volume; and Lawrin Armstrong for his abiding enthusiasm for this project and encouraging me to publish the volume in the Toronto Studies in Medieval Law, of which he is the editor.

Much more than formal acknowledgment can express, my deepest debt is to my family, and above all to Judith, whose loving support sustained me during the years of research and writing, and finally and happily I dedicate the book to her.

MARRIAGE, DOWRY, AND CITIZENSHIP IN LATE MEDIEVAL AND RENAISSANCE ITALY

Introduction

The nine studies gathered in this volume appeared over a twenty-six-year period, from 1985 to 2011. Originally, they were published as contributions to volumes honoring the research and careers of colleagues and to the proceedings of conferences held in Europe. Allowing for their diverse origins, the studies share a common focus on three interrelated subjects: marriage, women's property, and citizenship in medieval and Renaissance Italy (1200–1550). While the primary geographic locus is Florence, comparative attention is paid to the laws and customary practices of other cities, including Siena, Lucca, Perugia, Pisa, and Venice, in central and northern Italy. The approach taken in each study cuts across conventional boundaries, drawing on the techniques and sources employed by scholars of both medieval legal and social history. A cross-disciplinary approach makes it possible to illuminate the mutual interactions between social practices and the juridical constructions of persons, kinship, and property. My studies contrast with the narrow textual analysis of legal sources, which disregards the fluid interplay of choice, chance, and legal norms, leaving us with a hermetically sealed world where thought never bursts into life. They also contrast with purely social history methods, which treat law as an alien intrusion, resulting in simplistic and reductionist misreadings of the sources.

Sources

For these studies, the archival, manuscript, and printed sources are as superabundant as they are varied. The legal sources cited in the volume are often divided by scholars into two broad categories: the *ius commune* and *iura propria*.[1] By the late Middle Ages, the *ius commune* referred to a constantly changing and expanding body of Roman civil, canon, and feudal law, with transterritorial applicability. This body encompassed the *Corpus iuris civilis* promulgated by Emperor Justinian and the *Corpus iuris canonici*, each with its own glosses, the principal sources of medieval civil and canon law; and disputations, *summae*, commentaries, treatises, and opinions called *consilia*. The large majority of these works were produced by jurists hailing from northern and central Italy. After receiving their university degrees at Bologna, Siena, Perugia, Florence, Padua, or elsewhere, the most talented jurists became professors. The authoritative and innovative works of these professor-practitioners – for example, Azo, Accursius, Pope Innocentius IV, Hostiensis, Gulielmus Durandus, and Dinus Mugellanus, in the thirteenth century; Cinus de Pistorio, Johannes Andreae, Bartolus de Saxoferrato, and Baldus and Angelus de Ubaldis, in the fourteenth century; Paulus de Castro, Alexander Tartagnus, and Bartholomaeus Socinus, in the fifteenth century; and Philippus Decius and Jason de Mayno, in the sixteenth century – prevented the *ius commune* from degenerating into a sterile and rigid academic tradition.

The *iura propria* referred to the laws of specific places, from metropolitan cities like Florence and Milan to small towns like Gubbio in Umbria and Castiglion Fiorentino in Tuscany.[2] These laws took the form of comprehensive volumes of statutes (*statuta/statuti*), ad hoc legislative enactments (*provvisioni*, *riformagioni*), ordinances, and customs. Statutes and individual enactments were ordinarily drafted by jurists and public notaries with legal training in the same technical juridical language as the *ius commune*. Jurists, in their glosses and commentaries on the statutes[3] and in works explicating Roman civil law, sanctioned local practices and procedures to the extent that they could be justified within the broader normative framework of the *ius commune*. The differences between the *ius commune* and *iura propria*, though well documented, should not be exaggerated. As it turned out, there was a symbiotic relationship between the two seemingly disjunct and rivalrous domains. Absent a unified and hierarchical legal system capable of issuing determinate decisions enforceable across myriad jurisdictions, local officials looked to the jurists to resolve on an ad hoc basis conflicts between the *ius commune* and the *iura propria*. The same process applied to statutory gaps and flaws. Filling gaps and correcting flaws from *ius commune* sources, jurists moved the law.

Other sources include records of Florence's property tax census (*catasti*), government-sponsored Dowry Fund (*Monte delle doti*) and its offshoots, and the proceedings of the *podestà*'s court; notarial manuals and legal instruments, such as powers of attorney, betrothal, marriage, and dowry contracts, gifts, property transfers, discharge of obligations and debts, and last wills, all drafted and authenticated by public notaries; *libri di famiglia* or *ricordanze* ("things to be remembered") – an informal, fluid record of domestic and business accounts, notable life-cycle events, first-person observations, with discrete entries arranged by date – compiled and preserved mainly by the heads of Florentine merchant families; the reality-saturated and darkly comedic short prose tales (*novelle*) of Franco Sacchetti of Florence and Giovanni Sercambi of Lucca; and, finally, the vividly immediate sermons of San Bernardino of Siena, along with impersonal but instructive handbooks for confessors (*summae confessorum*).

Themes

Two overarching themes connect chapters 1–6. First is the reciprocal interplay between legal and social norms and practices during our period. Chapter 1 demonstrates how betrothal contracts, with their detailed specification of performance contingencies – principally large amounts of compensation and automatic judgment against the breaching party – succeeded in minimizing the occurrence of broken promises to marry. Betrothal contracts attest to the instrumental know-how of Florentine families to contract alliances from which neither party could withdraw with impunity. Chapter 2 examines the legal remedies and financial arrangements available to newlywed – but disgruntled – husbands who, having spent lavishly on nuptial gifts had received partial payment of the promised dowry or nothing at all. It was the desire to preserve their honor as well as the fragile bonds with their in-laws, I maintain, that motivated husbands to seek remedies other than litigation to collect the dowries promised them. Chapter 3 explores the ramifications arising from the legal distinction between dotal and nondotal assets and the ways in which such distinctions informed patrimonial strategies. What was happening in Florence conformed to a wider pattern across northern and central Italy in which lawmakers were granting husbands broad control over all the wife's property. Chapter 4 analyzes in detail the requirements the newlywed husband, often in tandem with his kin, was asked to satisfy before he could receive payment of his wife's dowry from Florence's Dowry Fund. As I show, the chief requirement, which only the husband himself could perform, was consummation of his marriage. The requirement, ostensibly related to the Florentine government's attempt to promote child-bearing families, raised the oft-debated question of whether consummation was a necessary condition for a valid marriage, and, by extension, for the husband's ability to lay claim to the promised dowry. Chapter 5 presents a quantitative analysis of the sophisticated use of legal proxies and assignment by the husband and his in-laws in managing, encumbering, and transferring rights to the interest-bearing unpaid portion of the Monte dowry lodged in the Seven Percent Fund, an offshoot of the Dowry Fund.

The second theme concerns the depiction of women as powerless. The too-common view is that owing to cultural and legal barriers women lacked the capacity to act on their own behalf and that of family members. Against this view, I provide a wealth of resonant examples of daughters, wives, and widows performing as full-fledged social and legal actors. Their actions were fundamental to the maintenance and transmission of a family's patrimony. And in contrast to the depiction of the male heads of families (*capi di famiglia*) as almost despotic figures, I show that fathers provided for the material welfare of their daughters, while husbands generally sought to ensure the welfare of their widows. Chapter 5 also reveals the role of legal guarantees and precautionary encumbrances in safeguarding the dowry during marriage. Chapter 6 was the first and remains the only study published on the reaffirmation, enhancement, and widespread enforcement of the Roman law remedy permitting a wife to sue for the return of her dowry from a husband teetering on the edge of insolvency (*vir vergens ad inopiam*).

Reappraisals

Chapters 1–6 build on the field-shaping research of David Herlihy and Christiane Klapisch-Zuber; they also critically engage the work of Manlio Bellomo, a distinguished historian of medieval law. Below I briefly summarize and evaluate the main findings of these scholars as they relate to the arguments developed in the first six chapters.

Herlihy and Klapisch-Zuber's landmark and monumental *Tuscans and Their Families* appeared in French in 1978 and in a handy abridged English translation in 1985. In their quantitative analysis of the *catasto* of 1427–30, a wide-ranging census conducted by Florentine officials covering more than 260,000 persons in about 60,000 households in the city and its subject territory across two-thirds of Tuscany, the authors furnished a comprehensive portrait of the region's demographic characteristics, types of property and their distribution, and economic activities. They contrasted the marriage patterns of Tuscany with that of the "West-European pattern of marriage." The identification of a distinctive marriage pattern in Tuscany is, in my opinion, their most significant finding. According to John Hajnal (1965) the marriage pattern of modern western European societies that emerged in northwestern Europe during the fifteenth century was unique.[4] Hajnal discovered a "relatively late age at first marriage for men (age 26 to 27 or older) and women (age 23 to 24 or older) and high proportion of both men and women in the population who never marry at all."[5] Instead of arranged marriages, men and women tended to choose their own spouses, and, because of employment patterns, newly married couples tended to establish their own independent households. In stark contrast, the Tuscan marriage pattern was characterized by early age at first marriage for women and late age at first marriage for men. In the city of Florence, in 1427, women at first marriage were around eighteen years old; men around thirty years old. Marriages in Florence were arranged by fathers, older brothers, or other male relatives. Apart from nuns, nearly all women married, as did men. Lifelong bachelors were rare. Patrilocality was the norm, with the couple commencing married life in the household of the husband's father. Only rarely did sons-in-law reside in the wives' natal households. Of critical importance for the transmission of property between generations and the disposition of the wife's dowry and nondotal properties was the twelve-year age gap between spouses, which assured that a large proportion of husbands would predecease their wives, leaving one-fourth of the adult women in Florence widows.

The average size of the Tuscan household in 1427 was about 4.50 persons, falling to about 3.80 persons in Florence. The size and composition of households in Florence were positively correlated with social rank, profession, and wealth. The largest households, claiming at least six persons, were typically identified by a surname and reported assets above 3,000 florins. Nuclear conjugal families predominated, however, amounting to nearly two-thirds of Tuscan households. These percentages suggest that the large extended families or patrilineages that had dominated Florentine social and political life in the twelfth and thirteenth centuries had disappeared or fragmented into nuclear conjugal families by the beginning of the fifteenth century. This process of fragmentation was encouraged by a system of partible inheritance, in which each son upon the father's death received an equal share of the patrimony. In fact, this thesis was famously put forward in Richard Goldthwaite's study *Private Wealth in Renaissance Florence* (1968). The ineluctable disintegration of the family in fifteenth-century Florence, he confidently concluded, "reached the point at which each man established his own independent household and possessed his own property privately."[6]

William Francis Kent, in his *Household and Lineage in Renaissance Florence* (1977), roundly rejected Goldthwaite's discovery of protomodern autonomous nuclear families. Confusion over Florentine kinship terminology, he contended, had resulted in a gross misinterpretation of the relationship between households and lineages. For Kent, Goldthwaite's discovery derives from erroneously inferring that transitory life-cycle events occurring *within* durable patrilineages – in particular, the creation of a new household by a married couple or by brothers after dividing a common patrimony equally – were indicators of family fragmentation and the triumph of the individual. In Kent's formulation, "the household, whatever its structure at a particular time, was the principal property-owning family group, though often a father and his adult son, or brothers who had 'divided,' kept up close economic ties ... It followed that men almost always named as heirs their sons, brothers, uncles, nephews, great-nephews, or grandsons."[7] Although one branch of a lineage may have been obviously superior in wealth, marriage alliances, and politics, lineages were never segmented into major and minor branches.

There is no need to rehearse the methodological shortcomings of both books pointed out in the reviews and scholarly literature.[8] Suffice it to say, generalizations flowing from the records relating to a handful of patrician families are hazardous at best. After reading both books, I was struck by the omission of reference to the legal rules and institutions which simultaneously enabled and circumscribed the decisions of the "men" admiringly portrayed by the authors. Even more striking to me was the absolute indifference to the roles, either backstage or onstage, that women played in Goldthwaite's autonomous nuclear families or Kent's patrilineages. The exclusion of women from Kent's "selected genealogies" is an extreme expression of a patrilineal ideology that renders wives, mothers, and daughters mute and invisible and therefore nonexistent.[9]

Although Herlihy and Klapisch-Zuber steered clear of the debate between Goldthwaite and Kent, they did address the issue of the relationship between ever-changing, small households and enduring lineages. Echoing the views of Manlio Bellomo, they explained that the agnatic lineage, which made its emergence in Tuscany in the eleventh century, is linked to the control of patrimonial property by simultaneously providing dowries for daughters and excluding them from further inheritance. In a nutshell, "the inheritance right, which, *ex patrimonio*, a male relative possessed, becomes the principal criterion of lineage membership."[10] They shared Jack Goody's insight that "the fact that the 'family' or 'household' is always small does not say anything about the importance attached to kinship ties in a more general sense."[11] They agreed with Kent that variations in the size and composition of individual households forming a lineage do not alter its permanence and unity centrally evinced by a common surname, coats of arms, patron saints, communal chapels, funeral processions, and *ricordanze*. In contrast to the practices of northern Europe, marriage did not necessarily entail the formation of a new household. As Klapisch-Zuber would insist, "lineage ties and domestic configurations evolved independently of one another, each according to its own logic, the latter much more sensitive, apparently, to the demographic conjuncture."[12]

The rituals attending betrothal and marriage, dowries, the relationship between the wife and the husband's family and the husband and his in-laws, the capital role played by relatives (*parenti*) generated through marriage, the naming of children, and the dynamics of widowhood are among the subjects of Klapish-Zuber's groundbreaking, richly woven historical-anthropological studies.[13] Quantitative data are supplied where appropriate, but the focus is on the identification of underlying collective attitudes and beliefs that organize and condition individual behaviors and everyday routines.

Klapisch-Zuber's Florence is a male-dominated society, with the *paterfamilias* a veritable lord in his household, making all the decisions on the use and disposition of the household's resources, including his wife's dowry during marriage. He chose the names of his children, with the sons normally named after departed paternal kin, selected their wet nurses, directed their education, and before his death arranged his daughters' and sons' marriages. Women are portrayed as marginal figures subject to lineage strategies. These strategies constricted female lives from the cradle to the grave, allocating the largest share of the paternal estate to sons and paternal kin and favoring the continuity of the husband's patrilineage over the relationship between mothers and their children. Accompanied by the husband's kin, the ceremonial transfer of the bride from the father's household to the husband's symbolized the prevailing patrilineal ideology.

In theory, the dowry represented the bride's contribution to the expenses of the common household (*dos sustineat onera matrimonii*) and after the husband's death would provide support for the widow or facilitate her remarriage. This normative schema, Klapisch-Zuber maintained, hardly matched the way the dowry system actually worked in fifteenth-century Florence. By law, the husband was designated master of the dowry and was required to apply it for the benefit of the married couple and their children, yet his ability to employ the dowry for this purpose was stymied by delayed and partial payments. As the size of dowries increased, it became increasingly more difficult for the bride's family to pay the full amount in a timely lump sum. The evidence from *ricordanze* reveals that while the bride's trousseau was usually conveyed to the husband on the day of the wedding, with an initial cash payment around the time of the consummation of the marriage, the major portion of the dowry (in cash or from Florence's *Monte delle doti*) was paid in installments, "sometimes occurring many years after the wedding."[14] This initial cash payment was not applied to ordinary household expenses, as "judicial theory" required, but was diverted to pay for nuptial gifts to adorn the bride. The diversion of the dowry into the ritual "dressing the bride" strongly militates against an economic interpretation of the role of dowries in Florentine society, specifically that dowries supplied husbands with the necessary capital to invest in commerce. For Klapisch-Zuber, the significance of the ritual role played by nuptial gifts far outweighed their material worth.

While mindful of Klapisch-Zuber's prolific contributions to the historiography of Renaissance Florence, several scholars have taken issue with what they reckon to be an overreliance on *ricordanze* for reconstructing family history. Their argument is this: centered on the activities and relationships of the male head of the household, *ricordanze* inevitably offer a skewed vision of families in Renaissance Florence as overly patriarchal and patrilineal.[15] Sharon Strocchia, in a study of Florentine funeral and mourning rituals, protests that the debate over "household and lineage, has done little to include women as historical actors. Even in the work of Christiane Klapisch-Zuber, who has done so much to recover the texture of Florentine domestic life, women emerge as displaced and disempowered."[16] Notwithstanding their subordination, Ann Crabb argues, Florentine women affected "outcomes through their activities as interveners, advisers, and mediators" in the public as well as private sphere.[17] Even though women were barred from holding public office and wielding formal political power in Florence, Natalie Tomas establishes that Medici women negotiated "significant space for themselves within the Florentine *sottogoverno* [an informal system of political patronage] through an alternative feminine model of patronage by intercession, which was premised on their authority as wives, widows and mothers."[18]

That Florentine families were scarcely bastions of male privilege and that wives and widows, not just at the apex of Florentine society but across the social sphere, actively asserted their rights to dotal and nondotal property and disposed their properties via transfers, donations, and last wills is now persuasively documented. To achieve their objectives, Florentine women, like their counterparts throughout northern and central Italy, turned to notaries and jurists for assistance. In separate studies, Thomas Kuehn and I have analyzed the actions of wives and widows who, by employing notaries and jurists and calling on male relatives, were able to manipulate to their own advantage ambiguous local statutes and the paternalistic principles underlying Roman and canon law jurisprudence touching women.[19]

Klapisch-Zuber's core assumption was that sons received a disproportionately larger share of the paternal inheritance than daughters, who, after being provided a dowry, were legally excluded from inheritance. This was disputed by Maristella Botticini and Aloysius Siow in an analysis of intergenerational wealth transfer in Florence.[20] Their statistical analysis of four thousand dowry contracts, together with testamentary bequests, and wealth data culled from the *catasto* of 1427, shows that in Renaissance Tuscany a daughter's dowry on average corresponded to about 55–80 percent of a son's inheritance. They argue that married sons – who regularly followed the father's occupation and continued to reside in his household even after they married – were motivated to contribute, by their own labors, to the paternal estate that they expected to inherit. If married daughters had equally shared the paternal inheritance, their brothers would not have reaped the fruits of their labors in extending the paternal estate. "Thus, in order to mitigate the disincentive for their sons, parents will want to assign large dowries and consequently small [testamentary] bequests to their daughters."[21] In this scenario, both sons and daughters are better off in economic terms, by definition, an efficient outcome. Yet this suggestive analytic narrative fails to account for the inherent limitations of last wills for calculating the net monetary value of the testator's estate. Nor does it consider that in fifteenth-century Florence sons regularly turned down a burdensome paternal inheritance.[22] An issue overlooked in their explanation of the willingness of sons to remain in the father's household and contribute to his estate is that the legal capacities of unemancipated sons were limited, as was their freedom to live independently. So long as the father was alive, married as well as single sons, no matter how old, were legally bound by the father's power over the family (*patria potestas*) and therefore generally subject to his veto power.

Klapisch-Zuber's contention that Florentine husbands enjoyed minimal, if any, economic benefits from dowry payments, which were, first and foremost, translated into nuptial gifts, was as salutary as it was provocative. For a long time, the assumption that merchant husbands in Florence invested cash dowries in business enterprises went unquestioned, but the substantiation of such investments, either in the *ricordanze* or the records of the *catasto*, is hard to pin down. On the other hand, the evidence that husbands in mid-fifteenth-century Florence experienced debilitating delays in collecting the dowries they were promised is extensive.[23] That said, the husband's predicament was not as grim or one-sided as Klapisch-Zuber contends. As Jacob Klerman and I show in chapter 5, by the 1440s, Florence's Dowry Fund no longer paid dowries as they came due, and beginning in the 1450s, it made payments in periodic installments. But from 1478 onward husbands received a partial lump sum payment, plus a dependable stream of interest income until the *Monte delle doti* dowry was fully paid. A raft of husbands used the unpaid portion of the Monte dowry as collateral for other transactions or sold their claims to the interest-bearing unpaid portion to third parties in the secondary market. Although they no longer expected to receive the full Monte dowry originally promised, husbands were in possession of a fungible asset that was valuable, negotiable, and in demand.[24]

As I point out in chapter 2, husbands intent on receiving their dowries immediately demanded advance payment from their in-laws, to whom, in return, they assigned their claims to the Monte dowry. In other cases, they opted to receive temporary consignments of property. In still others, they received annual interest (9–10 percent) from their in-laws on the unpaid portion of the Monte dowry. Eventually, having received the whole dowry or a substantial portion, an uncertain number of merchant husbands did invest dotal capital in business.[25] Did Florentine husbands occupying the lower social rungs use cash dowries to purchase foodstuffs, clothing, furniture, to pay off private debts, including the redemption of pawned goods, and to pay rent and wet nurses, as happened in eighteenth-century Turin?[26] It is conceivable that they did, but we currently lack evidence to support this hypothesis. My observations on the potential economic benefits accruing to Florentine husbands admittedly derive from a cluster of examples that are meant to be indicative only. The economic function of dowries in northern and central Italy is a subject that demands systematic and comparative study.[27]

No scholar has contributed more than Manlio Bellomo to an understanding of the legal framework for the dowry system in medieval Italy, from the dowry's constitution in anticipation of marriage, to its transfer to the husband, to its management and function during marriage, and, finally, to its disposition upon the marriage's termination. His monograph *Research on Property Relations between Spouses: A Contribution to the History of the Medieval Family*,[28] published more than fifty years ago, remains fundamental. Bellomo began by rejecting the explanation that the reappearance of Justinian's *Digest* in the late eleventh century, which spurred a renewal of Roman jurisprudence, was directly responsible for the resurgence of the Roman dowry in the twelfth century. Similarly, he dismissed the argument that the resurgence of the dowry expressed a cultural preference for Roman over Germanic mores and tradition. Reasonably enough, he offered an explanation stressing the transformation of a rural world enmeshed in feudal relations to an urban society in which warring families engaged in competition for power and prestige. In Bellomo's telling, the dowry became a capital asset that husbands deployed in their quest to advance their family's position in the rough-and-tumble universe of communal politics. Their quest was buttressed by jurists and municipal legislators, for whom control of a woman's personhood and property, by her father, brothers, and kinsmen, and then by her husband, was crucial for the continued existence of patrilineages.

For Bellomo, this socioeconomic transformation entailed a sweeping change of spousal property relations, which became heavily tilted in favor of husbands and their families. The Lombard *Morgengabe* and nuptial gifts (*meta* or *meffio*) from the husband and his family to the bride were replaced, for the most part, by a truncated Roman counterdowry or *donatio propter nuptias*.[29] By the early thirteenth century, the husband's *donatio propter nuptias*, which under Justinian equaled the dowry, was reduced to a trifling sum that the wife could claim on her husband's death. No longer did widows have an automatic claim on their husbands' estates – a quarter share under Lombard law, a third under Frankish law. The conception of the dowry as a gift necessary for the validity of the marriage gave way to a conception of the dowry as a capital asset. The regulations governing dowries set forth in Justinian's *Corpus iuris civilis*, which served to protect the rights of the wife and her family to dotal property, were altered in principle and thwarted in practice. Under Justinian, a father who provided a dowry was entitled to reclaim it from his son-in-law when his daughter predeceased her husband. Now, the son-in-law, in accordance with the laws of the locality in which he claimed legal domicile or citizenship, was permitted to retain a part of or even the whole dowry upon his wife's predecease in the absence of surviving children. The husband was also granted leeway to transfer dotal property consisting of movables to third parties, so long as its cash value was appraised, while the protections afforded the wife under Justinian were suppressed and sidestepped.

Two features of the new dowry regime stand out. First, unlike daughters in imperial Rome, daughters provided with dowries in medieval Italy were excluded from sharing in the paternal inheritance that was reserved for sons and, in their absence, paternal male relatives. Second, a widow's ability to reclaim her dowry, to which she was legally entitled upon her husband's predecease, was routinely denied by the husband's heirs, because they viewed the obligation to restore the dowry to the widow or her heirs as a burden on the paternal estate.

Consistently informative and carefully documented, Bellomo's characterization of the transformation of property relations of married couples in twelfth- and thirteenth-century Italy is still accepted by both historians of law and social historians as the gold standard.[30] While I share the admiration for and have benefited from Bellomo's scholarship, his study is vulnerable to objection on specific interpretations in light of the research published over the past thirty years devoted to dowries, inheritance, and last wills, and the economic activities of women from all social sectors in medieval and Renaissance Italy. Along with other scholars, Bellomo presupposes, rather than demonstrates, that sons received a lopsided share of the paternal estate. Needless to say, the sources, primarily last wills, for testing this assumption before 1250 are few and far between, with Genoa a notable exception. In a study of Genoese last wills for the period 1150–1250, Steven Epstein observes that "testators, male and female alike, usually divided their estates evenly between sons and daughters."[31] As I have already noted, the ability of the husband to enjoy the dowry fully was impeded by delayed and partial payments, a material circumstance that must be taken into consideration in appraising the dowry's value as a productive capital asset.[32]

Bellomo's relegation of women to the role of lifelong spectators in a male-dominated society and economy and his insistence that women lacked effective ability to exercise their property rights collides with evidence presented in these studies.[33] Urban women, in addition to working as caregivers in hospitals, orphanages, and asylums for widows, participated in the economy as artisans in the wool, linen, and silk industries, as itinerant vendors of used goods and clothing, and as purveyors of food and drink; as creditors in private commercial activities and investors in the public debts in Florence, Venice, and Genoa; and as capable administrators of the estates left by predeceased husbands. In the following chapters, we will encounter wives and widows exercising their rights to dotal and nondotal property and freely disposing of their property via gifts and testamentary bequests to their own daughters and female kin. I also examine the measures taken by the wife's father and brothers by means of dotal pacts and encumbrances and by paternalistic public authorities to restrict the husband's control of the dowry during marriage and to require the husband and family to provide both surety and security for its return to the widow or her heirs.[34]

Further evidence of husbands who afforded their widows with a material safety net is presented by Isabelle Chabot in a series of studies on lineage strategies in Renaissance Florence. Husband-testators with direct male descendants provided habitation and annuities for their widows, while husband-testators without direct male descendants "left their heirs precise instructions" for the repayment of the dowry to their widows.[35] The extent to which widows were able to retrieve their dowries has not yet been satisfactorily explored. Fortunately, copious documentation exists for addressing this wide-open issue, in particular, court records and legal opinions. Recent research indicates that in Bologna and Venice properties roughly equal to the value of the dowry were restored to widows by their husbands' heirs, either voluntarily or through adjudication.[36]

Curiously neglected by Bellomo is the frequency with which women engaged the services of notaries and jurists, who had no reservations whatsoever in managing and defending the claims of daughters, wives, and widows to dotal and nondotal properties. Far from being self-explanatory or self-implementing, the municipal statutes and the stream of ad hoc laws regulating women and their property were mired in insoluble ambiguity and self-contradiction, an endless source of disputes. The application of these laws to a broad range of factual situations that were not expressly foreseen by lawmakers, including the gap between hallowed rules and new, unfolding circumstances, was thoroughly dependent on the interpretations rendered by *ius commune* jurists in their *consilia*. The immense value of *consilia* for historical research was demonstrated by Lauro Martines in his pioneering book *Lawyers and Statecraft in Renaissance Florence* (1968), and *consilia* are a principal source for the sociolegal studies in this volume. For historians, they occupy a unique vantage point for studying real-world disputes over women's legal rights, obligations, and property (*bona mulieris*) that occurred in Italy in the period 1300–1550. What is more, *consilia* are often the only concrete evidence we possess that these disputes actually occurred. Although no attempt has been made to estimate the number of *consilia* touching on women and their property, it safe to say, proceeding from a familiarity with manuscript and published collections of *consilia*, that it runs into the thousands.

Gendered Citizenship

Chapters 7 and 8 explore the transformation upon marriage of women's civic status. Although considerable attention has been paid to the conceptual foundations and practice of citizenship in medieval and Renaissance

Italy by historians of law, political philosophy, and institutions, only meagre and sporadic attention has been devoted to women's status as citizens. The cause for this pervasive neglect has nothing whatsoever to do with lack of documentation. The sources documenting women's citizenship are, as a matter of fact, plentiful. Rather, the failure to take seriously women's status as citizens has everything to do with an ancient bias of reflexively equating really real citizenship with the capacity to engage actively in the public life of one's community. It is, of course, undeniable that in Italian cities women were prohibited from exercising power and authority as public officials. Legally excluded from public and judicial office and the *palazzi* in which public power was wielded, and subordinate to their fathers, senior kinsmen, husbands, and male authority generally, the female inhabitants of towns and cities have been treated at the very most as nominal citizens.[37]

Such a view is skewed. A comprehensive, internally consistent theory of citizenship did not exist in this period. Nor was there a coherent, one-size-fits-all category of "real citizenship" or "real citizen." The grammar of citizenship was elusive, constantly evolving, and inflected by local variations. For the jurists, the primary arbiters of definitional meanings, the neologism *civilitas* (citizenship) and *civis* (citizen) were semantically polysemic. They had meaning insofar as they were qualified by prepositions, nouns, adjectives, and conjunctions. For instance, a daughter as well as a son automatically assumed citizenship in the place where her father was a citizen and was accordingly designated as *civis originaria*; one could become a citizen by statute (*civis ex privilegio* and *ex statuto*); and through the magical power of legal fiction a wife was treated as if she were a true and original citizen (*tamquam vera et originaria civis*) in her foreign husband's place of origin (*origo*). That a woman was a citizen in her father's *origo*, and had the ability to enjoy the public rights and privileges (especially the ability to bring suit in the city's courts) and undertake obligations (especially the obligation to pay taxes) appertaining to all citizens, was taken for granted. As I demonstrate in chapters 7 and 8, a woman's marriage to a foreigner profoundly modified her civic status, compelling jurists and lawmakers in Italy from the late Middle Ages down to the late twentieth century to address intricate questions arising from the gendered character of citizenship.

Consilia are central to the final three chapters, in which I explore the legal puzzles arising from marriage between foreigners, that is to say, between citizens of different cities. The protagonist of chapter 7 is the "woman married elsewhere" (*mulier alibi nupta*). Her story begins in the late Roman Empire, where a free Roman woman born legitimately was regarded as a citizen of the common fatherland (*communis patria*), Rome. She also enjoyed citizenship in the city of her origin, which derived from paternal descent rather than from her physical birthplace. Upon marriage, she automatically adopted her husband's domicile (*mulier sequitur forum viri*), while she retained her original citizenship. This paradigm was upended in the early thirteenth century by the Bolognese jurist Accursius, in his *Glossa ordinaria* to the *Corpus iuris civilis*. A woman who marries a foreigner, Accursius opined, simultaneously becomes a citizen in his place of origin and ceases to be a citizen in her own. In effect, she loses access to the valuable rights and privileges reserved to citizens in her place of origin. The transformation of the "woman married elsewhere" into a citizen of her husband's place of origin was treated as an exception to the tenet that the attachment to one's place of origin, because it is an artifact of nature, is therefore permanent and cannot be denied or withdrawn.

About a century later, the preeminent jurist Bartolus modified Accursius's opinion. He accepted the determination that a wife becomes a citizen in her husband's place of origin but objected to the loss of rights and privileges she formerly enjoyed as inequitable. In remedy, Bartolus postulated that the wife retains her original citizenship insofar as the rights and privileges that citizens ordinarily enjoy are concerned, while she is excused, apart from a few exceptions, from the burdens that all citizens are required to shoulder. Bartolus's remedy was quickly and widely endorsed but was never a panacea, owing to statutory provisions that differed from city to city and jurisdictional conflicts. Specifically, did the laws of the husband's place of origin or legal domicile or those of the wife's place of origin apply in disputes over the payment of the dowry, its restoration, and the husband's claim to part of the whole dowry upon the wife's predecease? Similarly, which laws applied in determining whether the wife could make a contract and last will without first obtaining the consent of her husband? To address these questions, I discuss in detail three *consilia* by Baldus, also Bartolus's pupil, who combined a quicksilver intelligence, an exceptional mastery of civil and canon law, Aristotelian philosophy, and a dialectical method of reasoning to unravel knotty jurisdictional conflicts over citizenship and domicile.

Further confounding matters was a patchwork pattern of jurisdiction within the territorial states that emerged in the late fourteenth and early fifteenth centuries.[38] Chapter 8 analyzes a single dispute pitting a surviving husband against the heirs of his wife, who predeceased him. The wife was a citizen of Florence, the husband a citizen of Pescia (located about 30 miles northwest of Florence), also his place of legal domicile. The statutes of Florence awarded the surviving husband the whole dowry, the statutes of Pescia one-half. Under the *ius commune*, the applicable statute in such cases was that of the husband's domicile. Yet Pescia was subject to Florence's overlordship, making the husband a subject of Florence. In addition, his lawyer argued, he should be regarded as a citizen of Florence, entitling him to claim the whole dowry. The argument was a stretch, but it illustrates how *ius commune* jurists nimbly manipulated jurisdictional asymmetries to the client's advantage.

Chapter 9 examines three multijurisdictional disputes over the contract tax that Pisan husbands were required to pay on the amount of dowry they acknowledged having received in a legal instrument called a *confessio dotis*. In all three cases, the husbands were Pisan citizens who had married in foreign cities (Lucca, Genoa, Venice) with independent jurisdictions, where they concluded *confessiones dotium* and paid the local contract taxes. This was all perfectly in accordance with the *ius commune* rule that the contracts were subject to the laws of the locality in which they were concluded. But Pisan authorities nevertheless sought to collect the contract tax, on the grounds, first, that its statutes extended to all citizens residing within fifty miles of Pisa; and second, that the laws of a husband's native city were said to have priority over the laws of the foreign jurisdictions in which the *confessiones dotium* were concluded. The upshot was that no matter where these husbands resided or how distant from their native city, they must comply with Pisa's laws and pay the tax by virtue of being original Pisan citizens. An intuitively appealing argument that *ius commune* jurists commissioned to settle such disputes resisted vigorously.

The studies republished here differ from their original versions in a number of ways. I have corrected mistakes, eliminated extraneous and repetitious passages, revised translations for the sake of clarity as well as precision, and attempted to bring intelligibility to the parsing of technical terms and concepts. I have taken advantage afforded by republication to update the studies with subsequent scholarship in legal and social history relevant to the questions under investigation. The discussion of notarized betrothal contracts in chapter 1 has been revised in view of Tovah Bender's doctoral dissertation on the marriage of artisan women in fifteenth-century Florence. In chapter 7, drawing on Emanuele Conte and Sara Menzinger's magnificent critical edition of the *Summa Trium Librorum* of Rolandus de Lucca, published in 2012, I was able to round out the treatment of married women's citizenship before the Accursian *Glossa ordinaria*. Similarly, drawing on Laurent Mayali's research canon on legal fiction and marriage in the canon law, I revised my analysis of the legal fiction underpinning the joining of husband and wife into one flesh and a common citizenship. The conclusion of chapter 7 now reflects significant developments in Italian citizenship law and procedures from 1992 to 2009. In other studies, as in chapter 3 on nondotal assets and chapter 6 on wives' claims against husbands approaching insolvency, I have incorporated supplementary archival research to flesh out several arguments.

For the sake of uniformity and to avoid duplication, the citations of primary and secondary sources in the notes have been abbreviated to short-title references. Full references are given in the comprehensive bibliography. In the original versions, the names of medieval jurists and theologians were cited both in Italian and Latin. Here all the jurists' names are rendered in Latin to avoid misidentification. A select list of the names of jurists and theologians is provided in appendix 6. All other names are given in Italian, unless I am referring to names as they appear in a Latin source.

The Florentine new year began on 25 March, the Feast of the Annunciation. For the sake of readability, all dates between 1 January and 25 March cited in the text have been modernized. To facilitate tracking down references, all the dates of Florentine documents cited in the footnotes are given according to both Florentine and modern conventions. I have also modernized all dates in the text originally recorded in Pisan style (*more Pisano*), which was one year ahead of modern (and Florentine) usage for the period 25 March–31 December.

1 Making and Breaking Betrothal Contracts (*Sponsalia*) in Late Trecento Florence

Contracting Betrothals

Ideally, couples in late medieval Italy contracted a valid Christian marriage in three stages: betrothal (*sponsalia*) through words of future consent (*consensus per verba de futuro*); marriage (*matrimonium*) through words of present consent (*consensus per verba de presenti*), which alone sufficed to establish a valid, indissoluble union; and consummation through sexual intercourse, which transformed a *de futuro* marriage into an indissoluble union, while it brought to full perfection a *de presenti* marriage. The minimum legal age for giving *de futuro* consent under canon and civil law was seven years; for *de presenti* consent, the couple had to have attained puberty: as a rule, twelve for girls, fourteen for boys. Puberty was not strictly determined by reaching the threshold ages, twelve and fourteen, but occurred when males could generate and females could become pregnant. Making the physical capacity to engage in procreative sexual intercourse the defining feature of marriageable age made sense given the difficulties of ascertaining someone's precise age in this period.[1]

Previous studies of *sponsalia* in medieval Europe have generally focused on canon law doctrines and the disputes adjudicated before ecclesiastical courts.[2] Our study differs in that it also highlights the varied ways in which betrothals were actually contracted and the municipal law procedures and civil law regulations and doctrines that applied to betrothals. In particular, we focus on betrothals contracted by merchant families in late Trecento Florence. To that end, we examine two opinions (*consilia*) of the distinguished Perugian jurist Angelus de Ubaldis, which offer valuable insights into the making and breaking of Florentine betrothal contracts.

Apart from presenting new documentary data, our study offers new entry points for the study of betrothal contracts in late medieval Italy.

Knowledge of Florentine betrothals derives from two principal sources: private *ricordanze*, or *libri di famiglia*, and betrothal and marriage contracts drafted by public notaries. Compiled by the heads of merchant Florentine households, *ricordanze* constitute a unique record of business and financial transactions, vital events (births, marriages, and deaths), and observations on contemporaneous social and political events and personages.[3] Even though references in *ricordanze* to prenuptial, nuptial, and postnuptial acts and rites were as a rule formulaic, they nevertheless provide invaluable details on the circumstances engendering new unions. The leader among the historians employing *ricordanze* for family history is Klapisch-Zuber, whose essay "Zacharias, or the Ousted Father," has brilliantly illuminated the sequence and meanings of the rites culminating in a legally valid marriage in Florence.[4]

The Florentine prenuptial scenario was premised on the primacy of the family – on the cultural conviction that marriages are generated by families, in contrast to today's prevailing conviction, at least in the West, that families are generated by marriages. By convention the scenario began when a household head (father, widowed mother, senior male kinsman) enlisted the services of a marriage broker (*sensale*) to find a spouse for marriageable daughters and sons. Not only were marriages arranged for girls, who were customarily thought of as weak-minded; it was legally and morally incumbent on a *paterfamilias* to arrange marriages on their behalf with men whose social worth approximated that of his own family. A marriageable son, who would become a household head on the death of his father, also relied on marriage brokers. Other intermediaries (*mezzani*), normally immediate kin and friends, were enlisted to assist in the negotiations. A private meeting between the parties and their kinsmen followed successful preliminary negotiations. At this meeting the representatives of the prospective spouses concluded an alliance between the two families (*fermare il parentado*), which was emphatically affirmed by a ritual handclasp (*impalamento* or *toccamano*).[5] It was common for the parties, often after wheeling and dealing, to settle on the amount of the dowry the future bridegroom would receive upon marriage. From the fifteenth century on, prenuptial arrangements were normally recorded in a *scritta*, a private written agreement safeguarded by the intermediaries. There is no hint that Florentines cast horoscopes, as is done in India today, to determine the compatibility of the prospective spouses and the most auspicious time for the wedding.

The expression *fermare il parentado* was the social equivalent of *fermare una compagnia*, the expression for forming a business company.[6] The commercial component of alliance making and matchmaking became a convenient target for moralists and was satirized by the *novellieri* Franco Sacchetti and Giovanni Sercambi and the poet Antonio Cammelli of Pistoia. In referring to prenuptial negotiations as *la mercanzia* Sacchetti meant to underscore that matchmaking in Florence was little more than a commercial venture.[7] Cammelli (1436–1502) was critical of the social script in which nubile girls were loveless pawns of venal parents and grubby marriage brokers. One of his sonnets depicts a widowed mother as reprehensibly impatient to find a husband for her daughter.[8] Pietro, the marriage broker, informs her that he has found a suitable groom who is not only rich but also "virtuous, polite, and well attired, and has never uttered a bad word." She tells Pietro "he will have in exchange a charming girl. She can do what he wishes and in her behavior is chaste, respectable, docile, and beautiful." Her mother promises a dowry of 1,000 gold ducats, half of which she agrees to pay in advance. Eager to conclude the match, she instructs Pietro to see to it "that the young man be informed. Act in earnest! Conduct the deal and let the contract be signed." In order to be paid, Pietro quickly arranges the business, and the parties conclude the contract at breakneck speed ("in un punto il col scavezza").[9] Cammelli's disapproval of the marriage market most likely amused his knowing audience, yet, as we argue below, there were sound reasons for the rush to marriage.

Soon after the agreement to *fermare il parentado*, the couple was solemnly betrothed or espoused (*giuramento*, *compromesso*) in church and in the presence of witnesses. It was the *sponsa*'s (future bride's) legal and moral protector – father, widowed mother, brother, or kinsman – who publicly promised that he or she would ensure that the absent bride-to-be would give her future consent to take the *sponsus* (bridegroom) as her lawful husband, to contract marriage with him, and to receive from him a ring signifying the legitimate union of the couple. Faithfully reflecting practice, *sponsae* were typically absent in literary representations of prenuptial negotiations and the *giuramento*. Florentines would have undoubtedly endorsed the admonition of the canonist Petrus Ancharanus that it was unnecessary for the prospective bride and bridegroom to know each other personally for the purpose of contracting betrothals or marriages.[10] Indeed, canon and Roman law sanctioned betrothals and marriages contracted between people who were absent (*inter absentes*).[11] Marriage by proxy still remains a possibility in contemporary Italy. Courts have permitted them to occur when one of the parties lives abroad and compelling reasons exist for the marriage to proceed.

No indication is given in *ricordanze* or other sources that Florentine couples, as other couples in Europe, treated "betrothal as a trial marriage and normally slept together once they had exchanged future consent."[12] While marriages *per verba de futuro carnali copula subsecuta* were fairly common throughout Europe before the Council of Trent in the mid-sixteenth century,[13] Florentine merchant families intent on preserving their honor were successful in keeping contact between *sponsae/sponsi de futuro* to a minimum. The constraints on the sexuality of upper-class unmarried women, on the other hand, contrast with the lack of constraints on low-status rural and urban youth, for whom "premarital intercourse was evidently accepted and widespread, as long as relations were initiated with an intent to marry, or at least create a stable bond."[14] High-status male predators, however, habitually seduced gullible low-status girls and women with promises to marry at a future time, which they had no intention of keeping.

In his turn, the *sponsus* promised that he would take the *sponsa* as his lawful wife. If the *sponsus* could not give his *de futuro* promise to marry, because he had not yet reached the age of fourteen, the promise would be made by his father or close kinsman. When a *sponsus* of legal age was absent from the city, the promise to marry at a future time would be given by a duly appointed agent, which was how the Florentine lay canonist Lorenzo d'Antonio Ridolfi (Laurentius de Ridolphis) was betrothed. On April 2, 1388, Niccolò Ridolfi, acting as Lorenzo's agent, made an agreement with the Barucci family committing his brother to future marriage with Caterina Barucci. At the time, the twenty-six-year-old Lorenzo was in Bologna, having just passed his doctoral examination in canon law at the city's university. The *giuramento* took place on April 20, with Niccolò again acting as his brother's agent, promising that Lorenzo would take Caterina as his lawful wife (*per verba de futuro*). The following July, having returned to Florence, Lorenzo met his wife for the first time.[15] The *giuramento* customarily included an agreement on the date of marriage and the composition of the dowry – namely, cash, credits in the public debt (*monte comune*), goods, and real property. If the betrothed had not yet reached puberty, the parties agreed to entrust mutually acceptable intermediaries (*prudentes et discreti viri*) with the decision of establishing the date of marriage and the composition and amount of the dowry (as in Angelus's *consilium* II, in appendix 3).

The *sponsus* was not required to pledge his fidelity by placing a ring on the *sponsa*'s finger. Nor was the exchange of a kiss obligatory.[16] In Florence, the absence of the *sponsa* at the formal betrothal made the betrothal ring and kiss moot. The Roman law prohibition still in force against interspousal gifts did not apply to gifts exchanged by a couple betrothed but unmarried. After the *giuramento* was concluded, it was customary for the *sponsus* to pledge his fidelity by sending to his betrothed a chest (*forzerino*) containing rings, precious stones, belts, and other goods, and by celebrating the betrothal with a dinner at his future in-laws' house. A *sponsa*'s acceptance of gifts in anticipation of marriage established a presumption, unless contrary proof was produced, that she had given her consent to the betrothal made on her behalf.[17] Betrothal gifts were treated neither as the Roman *donatio propter nuptias*[18] nor as the Germanic *Morgengabe*,[19] nor even as earnest money or a pledge, which the *sponsus* would forfeit in the event he failed to fulfill the betrothal contract. The betrothal gifts belonged to the husband, and he could demand the return of them at any time.[20] The 1372 statutes of Lucca likewise emphasized that ownership of both prenuptial and nuptial gifts was not transferred to the wife ("non intelligantur esse mulieris nec intelligatur translatum dominium a sponso in sponsam"), and thus, apart from nuptial rings, they had to be restored upon demand to the husband or his heirs.[21]

Later – sometimes a few days, more often months, and, on occasion, years later – the couple contracted marriage through an exchange of words of present consent, followed by the *annelamento*, the ringing of the bride. According to Florentine jurists, the groom's giving of the ring and bride's reception constituted extrinsic signs (*signa extrinseca*) or presumptive evidence of marriage.[22] Marriage vows were almost always performed in the bride's home. *Ricordanze* include details about the wedding festivities; the composition and exchange of nuptial gifts; the transfer of the dowry, in part or whole; the husband's acknowledgment of the dowry in a notarial instrument called *confessio dotis*; the time and place of the marriage's consummation; and the introduction of the bride into the husband's household (*ductio*).

As Klapisch-Zuber has observed,[23] before the decrees of the Council of Trent, which made the validity of the nuptial rite dependent on the presence of the priest and his blessing, it was the notary who officiated at the betrothal and marriage and who attested to the solemn exchange of consent between the parties.[24] As canon law validated not only the substitution of public notaries for priests at betrothal and marriage ceremonies, but also the legal effects of these solemn exchanges of consent, it is anachronistic to treat these ceremonies as civic and secular and distinct from religious rites. In contrast to the private setting of the ceremony of marriage, betrothals among upper-level families in the late Trecento and early Quattrocento were customarily celebrated in church and typically presided over by a notary and attended by lay witnesses.[25] The betrothal of Lena di Bernardo Sassetti to Lodovico di Filippo Fabrini Tolsini, in 1384, for example, was performed in the church of the Cistercian Badia Fiorentina, the city's richest monastery (appendix 1). During this period, public notice of the impending marriage was not given. And objections to the marriage were seldom interposed, probably because betrothals violating the church's prohibition against consanguineous marriages, at least among Florence's merchant families, were rare.[26] The public and solemn setting of the Florentine betrothals, however, was designed to accomplish two critical tasks. First, the public betrothal announced to the community that a socially and politically consequential alliance between the two families had been sealed. Second, it announced that the betrothed were spoken for and that they had exited the marriage market. It was now difficult for one of the parties to unilaterally or arbitrarily abandon the betrothal without losing honor and without inflicting dishonor on the aggrieved party.[27]

In his study of Florentine betrothal and marriage contracts in the fourteenth century, Cohn found that contracts of marriage far outnumbered betrothal contracts, by nine to one.[28] What explains the large difference? Families in late medieval Italy, with some exceptions, practiced informal betrothals or simply married without prenuptial formalities. The large majority of individuals who married did not grasp (as Angelus observed in *consilium* II) the subtle and consequential distinction between *verba de futuro* and *de presenti*, on which medieval jurists and theologians concentrated their attention.[29] In the previous version of our study, we agreed with Cohn that notarized betrothal contracts were commissioned "almost exclusively" by the wealthy and by families with surnames, a badge of prominence. We also discussed sixteen Florentine *sponsalia* contracts recorded in the register of the notary Francesco di Piero Giacomini, spanning four years, from March 1418 to March 1422, that supported Cohn's findings.[30] All the betrothals were celebrated in churches, including Or San Michele, Santa Trinita, San Pier Scheraggio, and Santa Maria sopra Porta, where the prenuptial negotiations satirized by Franco Sacchetti took place.[31] The betrothed, as their surnames (Bardi, Strozzi, Tornaquinci, Manelli, Del Caccia, and Guidetti) indicate, were members of upper-level families. Among the future bridegrooms we find the jurists Bartholomaeus Iohannis de Montegonzi, and Franciscus Iacopi de

Empoli.[32] Jurists, including Laurentius Ridolphis, Stephanus Iohannis de Bonaccursiis, and Petrus Leonardi Beccanugiis, appeared as witnesses.[33] Curiously, none of the betrothal witnesses belonged to the clergy, who appear as witnesses in testaments and other transactions.

It turns out that Cohn's findings are open to question and that our concurrence was made in haste. In a recent study of artisan betrothals and marriage contracts made in Florence from 1425 to 1429, Bender finds that Florentine notarized betrothal contracts "were neither rare nor limited to the elite." In fact, about one-third of 387 marriages sampled for these years are preceded by a betrothal. Only one-third of the brides and grooms carried surnames. Significantly, slightly more than 20 percent of the grooms are identified as skilled laborers in the cloth and clothing sectors, while 23 percent of the brides are connected to family members belonging to minor guilds or otherwise identified as skilled laborers.[34] As valuable as Bender's research is, expanded archival research on contracting *sponsalia* remains necessary to gain firmer understanding of the social dimension of betrothals in fourteenth- and fifteenth-century Florence.

Our evidence somewhat differs from Cohn's finding that the acts of betrothal, marriage, and dowry acknowledgment were separated by a few days and seldom by more than a month. His finding is more applicable to the occurrence of marriage contracts and *confessiones dotium*, which were frequently recorded on the same day in Florence and its *contado*,[35] and less applicable to the interval between betrothals and marriages. For thirteen of the sixteen *sponsalia* contracts in our admittedly tiny sample, Giacomini recorded subsequent marriages. It is likely that the three remaining marriages were recorded by other notaries, or that conceivably the marriages did not occur owing to the death of a future spouse. Three betrothals and subsequent marriages occurred within one day,[36] all the rest within a matter of months.[37] The year-and-a-half lapse between the betrothal and marriage of Agostina di Zanobi de' Bardi to the banker Roberto di Buoni was unusually long and risky.[38] In Florence and other Italian cities, especially during this plague-infested period, the rush to marriage was prompted by fear that the longer the interval, the greater the possibility that the marriage, and therefore the family alliance, would not take place owing to the death of the *sponsa* or *sponsus.* But there were other good reasons for not waiting to contract marriage. The *sponsus* wanted the dowry promised him, which was customarily conveyed at the time marriage was contracted. To dampen suspicions invited by a long interval that the betrothed were behaving dishonorably, it was in everyone's interest to conclude the marriage in measured haste.

Breaking Betrothals

Helmholz reminds us that canon law departed from Roman civil law by making a "contract by words of future consent ... specifically enforceable in church courts. Even where the espousals were entered into without the force of an oath, where the contract was a *nudum pactum*, the canon law granted an action to secure its enforcement."[39] The proof text authorizing compulsion was the canon *Ex litteris Silvani* (X 4. 1. 10), in which a breaching party, under threat of ecclesiastical censure,[40] is compelled to fulfill the betrothal promise. If the breaching party disobeys the order to marry, he and his father are to be excommunicated, unless it can be shown that a legitimate cause exists impeding the marriage. Because of these conditions, we have deliberately avoided employing the terms "engagement," "fiancé" and "fiancée," and "fidanzamento," which in recent and current usage lack the binding force carried by medieval *sponsalia*, *sponsus*, and *sponsa*.[41]

Determining whether a breach of contract was committed when marriage did not follow the betrothal was a matter for legal experts and church authorities. No breach of contract ensued, the canonists agreed, where the *sponsa* and *sponsus* voluntarily and mutually consented to withdraw from the betrothal with authorization from their bishop, or where the death of a party made marriage an impossibility, or where a party proved that the betrothal promise was coerced.[42] A prominent case in point was decided by Pope Urban III (1185–7). He adjudicated a Pisan dispute in which a twelve-year-old girl was betrothed to a boy of age nine or ten. She alleged that her parents had installed her against her will in the home of the boy's father, that she was forced to stay there for about a year until she eventually returned home, and that despite her mother's threats, "she [did] not want to have the boy as her husband." The archbishop of Pisa reported that the boy had neither reached the threshold age of fourteen nor had had sexual relations with the girl. Urban instructed the archbishop to counsel the girl to wait for the boy to complete his fourteenth year. Should she decide not to wait, she was permitted to take another man as her husband (X 4. 2. 11, *Ex litteris*). These and other papal decretals sought to reconcile the requirement that children's consent to betrothal and marriage be freely given against the children's natural obligation to obey the wishes of parents and kinsmen.[43]

A party's subsequent serious physical or mental infirmity or entrance into a religious order also constituted legitimate reasons for dissolving the betrothal contract. Recall that after his conversion to Christianity,

Augustine withdrew from the betrothal that his mother Monica had arranged on his behalf with a ten-year-old heiress.[44] In other cases, a marriage might become impossible when a party had not yet reached puberty on the agreed-upon date of marriage, when the parties were related to each other within prohibited degrees or when they came to be related by affinity, or when one of the parties was already betrothed or married.[45] A future marriage might be derailed if one of the parties was declared infamous or committed fornication with a third party, or if the future bridegroom was absent from the city for a protracted period – conventionally, two years.[46]

In theory, ecclesiastical courts, operating under the assumption *matrimonium gaudet favore iuris*, should have been inclined to grant the petition of the party seeking to enforce the betrothal contract. In practice, church courts were disinclined to compel an obdurate party to marry, which would have undermined the sacred principle that choosing a spouse must be ultimately grounded in consent given freely with a clear mind.[47] Church courts in Paris and Regensburg permitted the dissolution of betrothals where one party repudiated the betrothal contract, but they ordered the breaching party to compensate the other party for expenses incurred in anticipation of marriage.[48] The available published evidence suggests that adjudication of disputes in Italian church courts on the validity and performance of betrothal contracts occurred infrequently, before and even after the Council of Trent.[49] Only a handful of cases involving betrothal contracts were adjudicated before the diocesan courts in fifteenth-century Florence and Fiesole.[50] None of the litigants belonged to families of high social standing.

In the middle of the fifteenth century, statutes enacted in Bologna, Carpi, Modena, and Piombino imposed penalties on parties contracting and breaking multiple betrothals.[51] These statutes were aimed at the chronic problems caused by clandestine betrothals and marriages. Incensed that their children were betrothed and married without parental and family approval, parents and relatives pressured the *sponsae* and *sponsi* to break their promises, so that they could be married to other persons who had received the family's approval. The statutes also refer to violent reprisals undertaken by the jilted parties. As far as we know, Florentines who were victims of broken betrothal promises in the late Trecento and Quattrocento resorted to legal remedies rather than to violence.[52]

Long gone were the days when the Florentine knight Buondelmonte de' Buondelmonti was murdered for breaking his solemn pledge to take as his wife an Amidei girl. Like many marriages among warring noble families in the early Duecento, Buondelmonte's marriage had been arranged to keep peace between the two families. However, he was enticed by Forteguerra Donati's wily widow to break his betrothal and marry instead her daughter, whose singular beauty captivated him. As an inducement, the widow promised that she would pay the penalty (*pena*) for Buondelmonte's repudiation, which, as we know, did not quench the Amidei's and their allies' thirst for revenge. According to Florentine tradition, the dramatic murder of Buondelmonte at the foot of Ponte Vecchio beneath a statute of Mars on Easter Day 1216 ignited the Guelph-Ghibelline conflict, which devastated the city for generations.[53] The lesson of Buondelmonte's ill-fated betrayal was immortalized by Dante (*Paradiso*, XVI, 140–1): "o Buondelmonte, quanto mal fuggisti / le nozze sue per li altrui conforti" (Oh, Buondelmonte how ill you fled those nuptials at the incitement of others).

In Florence, the name Buondelmonte became synonymous with a groom who could not be trusted to fulfill his betrothal contract. The lead character in Giovanni Sercambi's satiric depiction of betrothal practices among noble Florentine families was purposefully given the name messer Renaldo de' Buondelmonte. He wants to marry Ginevra, the daughter of messer Lanfranco Rucellai, and after the standard preliminaries, the two families come to an agreement on the betrothal and marriage. Lanfranco's wife is delighted with her daughter's betrothal to Renaldo but wants them to marry immediately, for she is alarmed that he will change his mind. Sercambi's audience, familiar with the story of the nonfictional Buondelmonte, would have instantly appreciated the wife's shrewdness. Relating her fears to her dull-witted husband, she urges him to find the notary who had come with Renaldo and who had prepared the *sponsalia*, so that he can draw up the marriage contract. Lanfranco finds Renaldo who is agreeable to the wife's plan. Soon afterward Renaldo arrives with his kinsmen and his notary at Lanfranco's house. The couple then exchange words of present consent and the bride is given a beautiful ring, all of which is attested by the notary in the contract of marriage.[54] Later, Renaldo, amid pomp and circumstance, introduces Ginevra into his household.

Arrhae Sponsaliciae

Breach of promise to marry in Roman law, unlike English common law, was not actionable. Under Cod. 5, 1, 1, *Alii desponsata*, a *sponsa* was free to withdraw from her betrothal promise to one person and marry another. At the same time, Roman emperors and their jurists sought to deter breach of betrothal promises by requiring the *sponsus* or his family to put up *arrhae sponsaliciae* (earnest money), which became a standard feature of betrothal contracts in the late Roman Empire and of the notarized contracts in the Middle Ages. The standard Roman law model required the *sponsus* to consign the agreed-upon *arrhae* to the *sponsa.*[55] If he breached the betrothal, the *sponsa* would simply retain the earnest money. In the event the *sponsa* was the breaching party, she or her family was obligated to indemnify the *sponsus* with double, or quadruple, the amount she received from the *sponsus.*[56] The chief purpose of *arrhae* was to compel contractual performance by preventing a party from withdrawing from the betrothal contract with impunity. In contrast to the standard Roman law model, the Middle Ages saw the introduction of a consequential practice: the *arrhae* came to be simply promised, not given, by both parties. In the model betrothal contract included in the 1391 Florentine formulary of ser Iacopo Toschanelli (appendix 2), both parties affirm and acknowledge receipt of 200 florins as *arrhae*, with the stipulation "that the violating and breaching party will give, pay, and restore double this amount to the aggrieved party." The clause for the reciprocal and simultaneous exchange of *arrhae* had been a standard feature of Florentine and Tuscan betrothal contracts since at least the middle of the thirteenth century.[57] More important, it was a legal fiction, since obviously the parties did not exchange anything.[58] The common practice of setting the *arrhae* at the same amount as the agreed-upon dowry and of not conveying them was a custom affirmed by the Florentine canonist Laurentius de Ridolphis.[59]

In Florence, the fictional exchange of the same amount of *arrhae* seems, at first glance, illogical. Yet upon closer inspection the *via fictionis* taken by our merchant families was, in fact, an effective way of managing risk. Florentine merchant families – fearing loss of *arrhae*, no matter which party defaulted – were wary and often incapable of transferring large sums to another party. Nor was it feasible for them, even if they had the cash on hand, to tie up large amounts of capital that were indispensable for business undertakings. Just as the size of the dowry increased in the fifteenth century,[60] so did the amount of *arrhae* that was required to secure the performance of betrothals contracted by the wealthy and prominent. We were able to match *sponsalia* and dowry contracts of eight couples in the register of Francesco di Piero Giacomini cited above. In four cases, the amount of *arrhae* slightly exceeded the amount of the dowry, in three cases the amount was slightly lower, and in one case the amount was identical. By way of illustration, in a betrothal contracted between the Lipacci and Alessandri, the amount of *arrhae* was 1,500 florins, while the corresponding dowry was 1,600 florins.[61] In the betrothal contracted between the Carocci and the Barucci, the amount was 800 florins; the corresponding dowry 720 florins.[62] In a late-fifteenth-century Florentine formulary, the exemplar *arrhae* were set at 1,000 florins.[63]

To more fully appreciate the doctrinal context in which Angelus de Ubaldis rendered his two *consilia*, it is necessary to complement our brief account of *arrhae sponsaliciae* in Florence with a summary of the debate that erupted in the Middle Ages over the validity of attaching penalties to *sponsalia* contracts. From their Middle Eastern or Semitic origins to their incorporation into Justinian's *Corpus iuris civilis*, *arrhae sponsaliciae* have attracted considerable attention from historians of ancient and Roman law. Koschaker, Cornil, Volterra, Brandileone, and Astolfi have focused on the reception of *arrhae* by Roman society, the efforts of legislators to include them in the system of Roman law, and the subsequent legislative developments, including the legislation of the Eastern Empire.[64] Anné produced a nuanced study of their origins and diffusion, first in the eastern and then in the western part of the empire, and of the influence of Christianity on them.[65] In contrast to this profuse attention, *arrhae* under the *ius commune* remain a largely uncharted territory.

For the Middle Ages we focus on a few broad issues gravitating around both doctrine and practice. From a theoretical point of view, one of the first issues jurists had to face was that of determining the differences between *arrhae* and a penalty. Next, especially in view of canon law, came the problem of the compatibility of *arrhae* with the sacred principle that marriage should be based on the free will and consent of the contracting parties. The custom of promising and acknowledging the fictitious receipt of substantial *arrhae* made the jurists examine not only whether the promise and acknowledgment of *arrhae* were legally valid, but also whether the amount should be limited to a token whose loss would be financially negligible. If, instead of a cash transfer, the *arrhae* consisted of a pledge (*pignus*), how should the pledge be construed in view of the imperial legislation on *arrhae*? With regard to the so-called Romano-canonical procedure, jurists had to face the question of what action could be granted to the aggrieved party when the *sponsalia* were unilaterally broken.

The chief piece of legislation regulating the system of *arrhae* was *l. Mulier* (Cod. 5. 1. 5) – a constitution originally promulgated by Emperor Leo in 472 and then inserted in the Codex.[66] Classic Roman law recognized that the stipulation of a penalty for the party who unilaterally withdraws from the *sponsalia* violates the customary principle of free marriage. While endorsing this principle, *l. Mulier* permitted *arrhae* and regulated their restitution.[67] Since both *arrhae* and a penal stipulation violate the principle of freedom of marriage, a coherent piece of legislation would require the prohibition of both.[68] The inconsistent treatment to which *arrhae* and a penalty were subjected by imperial legislation became a conundrum for civil and canon lawyers in the Middle Ages.

In *c. Gemma* (X 4. 1. 29), the *locus classicus* for discussing *arrhae*, Pope Gregory IX reiterated the principle of freedom of marriage and prohibited forcing an unwilling partner into marriage by the threat of a penal stipulation. In his decretal, the pope prohibited the future groom's father from extorting (*extorsio*)[69] an agreed-upon penalty from the future bride's mother (*Gemma*) on grounds that the marriage had not been contracted after the *sponsalia* had been made. The case and the papal response are patterned after *l. Titia* (Dig. 45. 1. 134). According to this fragment, when either spouse refuses marriage, a penal stipulation attached to the betrothal contract is invalidated, because the penalty runs counter to the commonly accepted standards of a community (*boni mores*) requiring that marriages, present and future, not be secured by the threat of a penalty.[70] The text of the decretal has nothing specific to say on *arrhae*, and *sponsalia* are mentioned as a fait accompli. Note that, even without papal intervention, a reason existed for invalidating the suit, as both the *sponsus* and *sponsa* had not yet reached the minimum legal age of seven years for contracting lawful *sponsalia*.[71]

While the pope looked ahead to marriage, Bernardus of Parma in his gloss to *c. Gemma* looked back to *sponsalia*, asking whether or not *arrhae* are compatible with the principle of freedom of marriage. Torn between a theological principle and an institution sanctioned by Roman law, and compelled to take into account the custom of giving *arrhae*, his gloss is a conceptual jumble and amounts to little more than a convenient repository of opinions that could be helpful to canonists.[72] "Attaching a penal stipulation to *sponsalia*," he wrote, "makes that stipulation invalid for the reason given in the text." Shifting to a series of Roman law texts, he went on, "*Arrhae* given at *sponsalia* are lost, if the giving party withdraws without producing a just reason." "Since the reason for giving the *arrhae* and establishing a penalty is the same," he observed without supplying the reason for treating them in the same fashion, "both should be subjected to the same prohibition."[73] The two laws, civil and canon, were on a collision course. In an attempt to avoid the conflict, Bernardus sought another reading of *arrhae*: they may be understood as an incentive (*res favorabilis*) to marriage; penalties were not. Worse, penalties were hateful.[74]

How Bernardus worked was immaterial; it mattered how he was understood. For civilian jurists, including Angelus de Ubaldis, the glossator, by treating *arrhae* as if they were a penalty, had misunderstood their distinctive character. Jurists loudly lamented his misunderstanding,[75] and canonists, too, reprimanded the glossator.[76] An unexpected helping hand came from Sinibaldo Fieschi, later Pope Innocent IV. In his commentary to *c. Gemma*, Innocent turned out to be more Romanist than the Romanists. Although he addressed the delicate theological issue of freedom of marriage, he disregarded the *Glossa*, piling up citations of Roman law without a single reference to canon law.[77] On grounds of *l. Titia*, penalties are forbidden but *arrhae* are permitted. On grounds of *l. Mulier*, the party who gives the *arrhae* loses them if, because of the party's fault, the marriage is not contracted, while the party who receives them must return double or fourfold if likewise the marriage is not contracted. On grounds of *l. Si quis*,[78] if a pledge (*pignus*) is given, it should be treated like *arrhae*. On grounds of *l. Si is, qui* and *l. Saepe*,[79] if within two years after the *sponsalia* marriage is not contracted, the dispositions on *arrhae*[80] become ineffective and the *sponsa* is free to marry another. Similarly, on grounds of *l. Arris*,[81] if marriage is prevented by the death of one of the parties, the dispositions on *arrhae* are inapplicable. On grounds of § *Hoc quoque* and § *Sin vero*,[82] the same applies if there is a lawful impediment to marriage.[83] It is no wonder that Bartolus de Saxoferrato counted Innocent IV among the *nostri* (civilian jurists) who recognized that a cardinal difference existed between *arrhae* and a penalty.[84]

The equation Bernardus of Parma made between a penalty and *arrhae*, coupled with the canonists' suspicion of *arrhae* as a possible peril to the freedom of marriage, prompted both civil and canon lawyers to dwell on the difference between giving *arrhae* and promising to pay a penalty. Their task was not easy and, as Petrus de Bellapertica aptly noted, "jurists have their hands full" in searching for a convincing difference.[85] For Odofredus, the difference was plain: *arrhae* constituted a cash payment, distinguished from a penalty, which constitutes a promise to pay. When one promises to pay a penalty if the marriage is not contracted, the promisor has not drawn anything from his purse (*non extrahit aliquid de marsupio*). As Odofredus quipped, human beings are generous when handing out mere words. In a worst-case scenario, one would take a blind wife rather than pay the 1,000 pounds he promised on breach of contract, which was tantamount to forcing the promisor into a marriage he would not have otherwise contracted. Moreover, since in the case of *arrhae* only a small amount of money is disbursed to a mutual friend of the parties, it is unlikely that one would unwillingly contract marriage out of fear of losing it.[86]

Jacobus de Arena also distinguished between a penalty that obligates one to give something, which is permitted, and a penalty that is merely stipulated, which is invalid. The reason behind the distinction is that "it is easier to make a promise [to pay] than to make an actual cash payment."[87] Petrus de Bellapertica concurred and thought that the stipulation of *magnae arrhae* was invalid. Yet he permittted a significant exception to *l. Titia*. Instead of giving *arrhae*, kings may promise a substantial penalty, for the fear of a loss would not force these potentates into marriage.[88] In general, jurists recognized the essential difference between a stipulation consisting of words and a cash payment (*facto bursali*).[89] Arguments about the validity of small amounts of *arrhae* were not entirely convincing, since any amount paid in case of withdrawal from the betrothal contract is after all the functional equivalent of a penalty. That civil and canon lawyers referred to *arrhae* as a "penalty" is an indication they realized that both were an obstacle to freedom of marriage.

Canonists likewise found nothing in the body of decretals and canon law forbidding an aggrieved party from asking the counterpart to return double or fourfold the amount of *arrhae.*[90] In particular, for Hostiensis *arrhae* were tacitly permitted, a penalty explicitly forbidden. The reason to treat *arrhae* and a penalty differently was that *arrhae* are actually conveyed and upon conveyance one may make an agreement that the receiving party may retain them if marriage is not celebrated.[91] But in a penal stipulation nothing is conveyed and, since there is no conveyance, no agreement may be made as to the penalty's disposition. Accordingly, in the case of a penalty, if marriage is contracted, there is no gain (*lucrum*) or hope of retaining something. If marriage is not contracted, there is the fear of having to restore the agreed-upon sum or the pledge to the aggrieved party. The *arrhae* serve as an amicable incentive to contract marriage; the penalty induces fear, which abolishes free consent (*liber consensus*). In a doubtful case, he held that the hope of a gain rather than the fear of a loss was the reason prompting the parties to enter into marriage. Yet Hostiensis thought that not only giving but also asking for the restitution of the *arrhae* was favorable (*favorabilis*) to marriage.[92] His ingenuous explanation works only if marriage follows the *sponsalia*, for then the law presumes that the parties are induced to contract marriage by the hope of gain and fear of loss.

Hostiensis's construction pleased neither Johannes Andreae nor Antonius de Butrio. The fear of losing *arrhae* and the onerous restitution of double or fourfold the amount were obviously a penalty and an impediment to a free marriage. "I have seen," Andreae wrote, "*arrhae* of four thousand pounds." His solution, therefore, was to cut short legal speculation and fix *arrhae* to the social status of the persons contracting *sponsalia* (*qualitas personarum*). "Who doubts," he asked, "that it is an impediment to marriage if a poor person gives big *arrhae*." Since "gives" meant "promises," Andreae alleged that such a promise was invalid. Conversely, wealthy persons or magnates may stipulate a small penalty, for the loss would be negligible. Though the canonists attributed this opinion to an unidentifiable[93] group of jurists (*dicunt quidam*), Andreae endorsed it on grounds that *l. Mulier* was based on frequently occurring cases and applied to ordinary circumstances; kings, nobles, and very rich people may be treated differently and permitted to stipulate a small penalty if a party broke the betrothal contract.[94] Abbas Panormitanus, too, approved of the two criteria (status and amount) proposed by Johannes Andreae.[95] Canonists were willing to gloss over the prohibition of inserting any penalty, for they thought that a small penalty would not force a person with means into an unwanted marriage. The rationale of the law (*ratio legis*) was to safeguard the freedom of marriage; its literal interpretation (*verba legis*) was the prohibition of attaching a penal stipulation to a betrothal contract. For them, the *ratio* was preferable to the *verba*.

In the end, neither civil nor canon lawyers succeeded in producing a persuasive analytical distinction between *arrhae* and a penalty. Toward the end of the fifteenth century the Milanese jurist Jason de Mayno neatly summarized the impasse. He found that jurists had devised five basic reasons but, on close inspection, none of them was convincing.[96] The Florentine jurist Petrus Aldobrandinus echoed him: "there is a big dispute among doctors on the differences ... and none of them is conclusive, if they can persuade at all."[97] In short, jurists elaborated a distinction without difference, and that distinction could be supported only by persuasive, not convincing, reasons.[98] Despite the impasse, we can neither deny the jurists' efforts to establish a real difference nor accuse them of being mere nominalists. Roman law had bequeathed them an inconsistent set of norms, and they had to make the best of it.

Jurists required actual conveyance (*traditio corporalis*) of *arrhae*. The wording of *l. Mulier* made clear that the mere acknowledgment (*confessio*) was insufficient to ground a future claim. The expression "received" (*accepit*), which recurred several times in the fragment, meant that a thing had been actually conveyed to the other party. The term "to receive" was understood to signify reality (*veritas*) not fiction.[99] The standard formula regularly used in betrothal contracts, "I promise you that I will ensure that A will take B as his wife and, if I do not do so, I promise 100 as *arrhae*," was plainly invalid, for this was a promise to pay a penalty, and *arrhae* had to be actually transferred. Reciprocal acknowledgment of *arrhae* between *sponsus* and *sponsa* was also invalid, Bartolus declared, for one acknowledgment caused the other and no actual payment occurred.[100] Unilateral acknowledgment of *arrhae*, on the other hand, was considered valid and sufficient, unless fraud was proved, on grounds that any *confessio* is prejudicial to the person who makes it but not to a third party.[101] The reciprocal acknowledgment of any actual cash payment (*numerata pecunia*) made between the parties contracting *sponsalia*, Bartolus insisted, was a fraud.[102]

The breach between Bartolus's doctrine and the entrenched practice of the reciprocal acknowledgment is strikingly revealed in the betrothal contract that he himself concluded for his daughter Paola. When "Bartolus Cecchi Bonaccursi de Saxoferrato," on 3 March 1354, betrothed his daughter Paola to Niccolò di Alessandro di Tancredi, he set the dowry at 750 gold florins and authorized his colleague and trusted friend and colleague Francesco Tigrini to establish the terms of payment. Concomitantly, both parties "put up" 750 florins as *arrhae* – the same amount as the dowry – and, in front of three witnesses ("Ufredutio domini Petri," doctor of law, "Agnolino Ceccoli," and "Pellino domini Ranutii"), declared that they had had and received ("habuisse et recepisse") that amount. On 6 August 1358, Tigrini fulfilled his mandate. The dowry had to be paid in three installments: the first when the marriage contract was drafted, the second at the moment of Paola's "traductio" (when she was introduced into her husband's household), and the last one within eight months after the "traductio."[103]

For Baldus de Ubaldis, in a doubtful situation, the reciprocal acknowledgment was valid only if the parties renounced their right to raise an *exceptio non numerate pecunie* – that is, in court they would not raise the objection that the payment had not been made.[104] Angelus de Ubaldis found an additional reason to distrust the reciprocal acknowledgment: the *confessio* occurred between two parties who by law were barred from making such a declaration.[105] In one of his opinions, Honofrius de Bartolinis of Perugia maintained that since the fictional exchange of *arrhae* was invalid, the aggrieved party had no basis for suing the breaching party.[106] Paulus de Castro granted that cases where both parties make a reciprocal acknowledgment of *arrhae* occurred daily, but the legal presumption was that the transaction was fraudulent, even if cash was actually transferred from one party to the other. That a presumption of fraud existed was the advice he gave in one of his *consilia.* "To any persons endowed with discernment," he asserted, "it should occur that this [meaning Bartolus's view] is the sounder view."[107] Canonists, too, sided with Bartolus. Abbas Panormitanus wrote that "on this matter, I have seen *consilia* against Bartolus, but I did not endorse them, for, then and now, I believe that his opinion is truer."[108]

The intricacies of a reciprocal acknowledgment of *arrhae* transferred figments of the court debate into the classroom. Suppose, Baldus told his students, "the *sponsa* acknowledges a hundred as *arrhae* and the *sponsus* does the same." "You answer," he went on, "that obviously nothing has been received."[109] But for the jurist things were not as they appeared at first sight. "If I give you a hundred as a loan," he argued, "and you give me a hundred as a loan, there are undoubtedly two loans. Here we have two contracts and two causes."[110] It was like the case of a gift made in anticipation of future marriage (*donatio propter nuptias*) and the dowry; though according to *ius commune* the amount of both must be the same so that they may not be confused.[111] Again, Baldus asked, "Suppose that two parties reciprocally acknowledge that they have received a hundred for the *sponsalia* and then one party withdraws. What is the effect of this transaction?" For the jurist, the party in default may be summoned on grounds of having given *arrhae* but not on their acknowledgment. Once in court, the defendant argues, "I compensate you by losing the hundred I gave, as it appears from the acknowledgment." The other party replies, "You lost those hundred because you withdrew from the *sponsalia.* And you deserve a double penalty. Because of the reciprocal giving of the *arrhae*, you lose what you gave and must return double of what you received." Baldus called attention to this case, for questions of this kind were raised time and again.[112] The "reply" of the aggrieved party shows how risky the reciprocal acknowledgment of *arrhae* in cash was. The question whether or not a double penalty – that is, the loss of the given *arrhae* and the obligation to return double or fourfold the received *arrhae* – may be imposed in the case of a reciprocal acknowledgment of *arrhae* attracted the attention of speculative jurists.[113]

The increase of the amount of *arrhae* also preoccupied the jurists. The most sustained and coherent effort to reduce them to a "token" was made by Bartolus. He started with the presumption that *sponsalia* and *matrimonium* do not have the same importance. Consequently, the penalty imposed for unilaterally withdrawing from a marriage should not be the same as the one for withdrawing from *sponsalia.* The established penalty for breaking up a marriage was the loss of the dowry and the gifts given in anticipation of marriage (*donatio propter nuptias*). No penalty was imposed for withdrawing from *sponsalia* where the *arrhae* had not yet been given. If they had been given, the penalty was that established by *l. Mulier*. "It is an absurdity," he argued, "if the law penalizes more severely the breaking of *sponsalia* than *matrimonium*." Hence, the amount of *arrhae* ought not to exceed that of the dowry or the gifts given in anticipation of marriage, which, as we have noted above, sometimes occurred.[114] Dissenting, Angelus pointed out that Bartolus's argument was unacceptable, for Roman law did not establish any limit on the amount of *arrhae*.[115] Though Bartolus's opinion remained isolated, jurists agreed that an actual cash payment could be the effective way to stop the inflation of *arrhae*: any person can make a big promise but things change drastically when one has to spend money from his or her purse.

Sometimes *arrhae* were constituted as a pledge (*pignus*), such as an immovable, like a house or a piece of land, or a movable, like jewelry.[116] In case of default, what were the rules for the restitution of a pledge, and was one bound to restore double or fourfold? Among medieval jurists these questions became the object of dissenting opinions,[117] especially between Bartolus and his student, Baldus. Bartolus asked: "What is the law if I give you a piece of land as *arrhae* and appoint myself as its owner on your behalf?" Done in this form, the transaction is invalid, for actual conveyance of the property is required, just as in the case of money.[118] Furthermore, he asserted that when a piece of land or an individual thing (*species*) is given, the dispositions of *l. Mulier* do not apply, for the text spoke of things that can be doubled or quadrupled. A sum of money or, more precisely, its numerical equivalent, can be doubled or quadrupled; an object in itself, never.[119] Though movables and immovables have a value, this aspect was immaterial for the jurist, because it was the object itself that constituted the pledge.[120]

Baldus strongly dissented. "Suppose that not cash but a movable or immovable is given as *arrhae*," he asked, "does the penalty of the double or fourfold apply?" Pledges given as *arrhae*, being quantifiable, increase (*crescunt in certo corpore*).[121] When money is given as a pledge, money is traded not as a *genus* but as a fixed thing, and pledges exist not as a *genus* but as a fixed thing.[122] "Supposing that Bartolus's view is true," Baldus went on, "in a sum given as a *species* there is no duplication, which is false." When considered as an object or individual body, a sum of money cannot be multiplied. Yet its value (*estimatio*) may be doubled. "On this point," he concluded, "my master [*doctor meus*] was wrong."[123] Baldus's reductionist approach was not entirely convincing. His brother Angelus, endorsing Bartolus's view, stated that things that cannot be doubled or quadrupled fell outside the purview of *l. Mulier.*[124] Paulus de Castro, on the other hand, qualified Bartolus's view. If Bartolus thought that one giving an individual thing as *arrhae* might not lose it where the marriage was not contracted owing to the fault of the giver, he was wrong, because the loss of the thing applied to both quantity and the individual thing itself. If he thought that the person receiving the pledge was bound to return the thing itself rather than double its value, if he or she withdrew from the marriage, Bartolus's opinion is plausible (*habet colorem*).[125] Yet Paulus was forced to admit that individual things can be quantified.

Canonists, too, admitted that a *pignus* was a difficulty-ridden issue around which contrasting opinions swirled. Abbas Panormitanus, following Bartolus, accepted the view that a pledge cannot be multiplied. If so, it could not be treated like *arrhae*, which could be doubled, tripled, or quadrupled. Furthermore, *l. Mulier* did not contemplate the case of a pledge, but only the transfer of money from one party to another. Accordingly, pledges could not be used, unless their value was supplemented in case of default (*pro interesse prestando*).[126] Women in Italy today who, upon breaking their engagement, opt to keep the engagement ring and restore its monetary value, while welcoming Baldus's opinion, would nonetheless be receptive to Bartolus's insight into the uniqueness and symbolic value of things.

Without examining a large sample of notarial *sponsalia*, it remains difficult to assess how frequently pledges were used. Indirect evidence that they were used can be gleaned from the commentaries of jurists and model notarial *sponsalia* contracts. Odofredus reported that upon contracting *sponsalia*, giving pledges to a commonly trusted friend was a Bolognese custom.[127] This custom bears a resemblance to Jewish customs, which required the betrothing parties to consign equivalent amounts of earnest money to a third party. Upon breach of contract, the earnest money would be duly conveyed to the nonbreaching party.[128] Moreover, according to Odofredus, canon lawyers counseled people to give pledges instead of *arrhae.*[129] For other jurists, there were no basic objections to giving pledges, provided that they were in fact transferred, not just promised.[130] After all, since Roman law did not prohibit them, they were permitted.[131] Among the notaries, Rolandinus furnished a model *sponsalia* contract in which *arrhae* consisted of a house and a piece of land. He also explained why and when the parties opted for immovables or cash. If the interval between *sponsalia* and marriage was long, the parties opted for immovables such as land or houses. If the two events were close in time, the parties opted for cash. But in an explanatory note to his *Ars notarie*, the author qualified this view as a "personal view, not a necessary one" (voluntarium dictum non autem necessarium) and asserted that the parties could not be forced to choose a particular option.[132]

In contrast to the dowry, where an action (*actio rei uxorie*) for the recovery of the dowry lay against the husband, Roman law did not grant any specific action to enforce a penal stipulation attached to *sponsalia.*[133] The rules regulating *arrhae* probably sufficed. The progressive importance *sponsalia* assumed in the Middle Ages stirred jurists to consider the question of whether an action for breach of a promise to marry may be granted. Their quest faced an insurmountable obstacle in *l. Mulier*, which prohibited inserting any penal stipulation, except the *arrhae*, in *sponsalia* contracts, since no one could enter marriage under the threat of penalty. Azo searched the *Corpus iuris* for an answer to the question, but in the end was forced to admit: "I cannot find one" – thereby indicating that Roman law did not recognize a specific action in cases of broken betrothal promises.[134] Accursius thought that an action *ad interesse* – that is, for damage – might be granted to the aggrieved party.[135] While leaning toward Azo's view, Odofredus thought that Accursius's concession required qualifications. Ordinarily, an action *ad interesse* was out of the question, for it was tantamount to stipulating a penalty. But there was one exception to withholding the *actio ad interesse*: when a poor young man contracts *sponsalia* with a rich widow and she refuses to marry him, he may sue for *interesse.*[136] Petrus de Bellapertica flatly rejected Accursius's view. If an action is granted, he stated, "marriages would be contracted on the basis of *interesse*." Just as stipulating a penalty was forbidden, so granting an action *ad interesse* amounted to permitting the parties to do in one way what was forbidden by another.[137]

Dinus Mugellanus made the telling distinction between an action directed at recovering *lucrum* and an action directed at recovering *damnum.*[138] An action for the recovery of any loss directly resulting from the broken promise was not a penalty but a *rei persecutio* – an action by which a thing is sued for. An action aiming at a future gain (*lucrum*), or the future advantages marriage might have brought to a party, is prohibited, on the grounds that the marriage was not yet contracted and granting the action would be comparable to a penalty. The challenge medieval jurists faced was aptly presented by Cinus de Pistorio. Granting an unqualified action *ad interesse*, as Accursius thought, meant that an action for a penalty was available to the aggrieved party, which was forbidden by *l. Mulier*. At the same time, it was difficult for a jurist to think that a stipulation bereft of force could exist, as such a stipulation was utterly useless. But the truth was that an unenforceable stipulation indeed existed, because by law a penal stipulation in *sponsalia* contracts worked only with regard to the *arrhae.*[139] The distinction between a future *lucrum* and a past *damnum* enabled jurists to overcome the impasse.[140] Canon lawyers, as well, accepted the distinction and recognized that the aggrieved party could bring an action to recover the loss.[141]

The always-imaginative Baldus recast the debate. Suppose that there are two *sponsae*, one rich and the other richer, and both are willing to contract *sponsalia* with me by words of future consent. I choose the richer, who promises me thousands as *interesse* in the event she fails to marry me because of the loss I suffer for not marring the rich one. May the aggrieved party legitimately bring an action ad *interesse*? Baldus proposed that if the promise reflects an actual loss suffered, the *sponsus* can bring an action for compensation, where, for instance, he expended a great amount of money in preparation for the impending marriage. If the promise reflects a future gain conditional on the marriage, the *sponsus* cannot bring any action, since that would be a condition forcing one into marriage. An action claiming that the richer party had committed fraud (*dolus*) was also available to the *sponsus*. But if an agreement violated the ethical standards of a community (*boni mores*), as in *sponsalia* carrying a penal stipulation, one who disregards it does not incur *dolus*. A finer distinction was needed. Clearly, if the agreement is construed as a penalty, it has no validity. If, on the other hand, the agreement is construed as true *interesse*, it is considered just and reasonable and does not violate the ethical standards of the community. Its purpose, Baldus asserted, was not "ad impediendum matrimonium" but "ad impediendum calumniam" – that is, to prevent dishonor. With an eye to practice, he advised against construing *interesse* in a formalistic way or in strict accordance with the agreement and in favor of proving its validity in court by presumptive evidence (*verisimiles coniecturas*). The grounds for suing for *interesse* did not rest on the unwillingness to contract marriage but on the agreement and the damage one suffered because the other party broke the agreement without legitimate cause.[142]

Baldus's doctrine stressed the need to penalize the party whose breach of the *sponsalia* served to humiliate and shame the jilted party. The breaching party was not only liable for causing damages, but also incurred *infamia*. The action *ad interesse* was the basis on which ecclesiastical courts in the fourteenth and fifteenth centuries compelled the breaching party to compensate the jilted party for expenditures made in connection with the marriage and litigation. The action *ad interesse* remains behind the *articoli* of Italy's *Codice Civile* of 1865 and the present *Codice*, which grant an action to the aggrieved party to sue for the recovery of the expenditures in preparation of marriage (see below, n. 168). It also remains behind the Japanese Civil Code, which leaves to custom the field of engagement (*konyaku*) but permits a party to recover the gifts (e.g., rings and expensive items) given in anticipation of marriage. In contrast, the French Civil Code ignores altogether the "promise of marriage" and protects the party who suffers loss because of an unjustified breach of the *sponsalia* by granting an action grounded in Aquilian responsibility. It has been pointed out that this approach opens the way to suing for unreasonable damages.

Preceptum Guarentigie

Under Florentine law, the obligation to pay even large sums of *arrhae* was enforceable and served as an effective deterrent. Since the early thirteenth century, Florentines and other Tuscans had placed their confidence in the summary procedure known as *preceptum guarentigie* to compel the defaulting party to pay *arrhae*. As Briegleb and Campitelli have remarked, this popular procedure, which derived from Germanic law, was used to compel the timely payment of debt obligations in myriad commercial and credit contracts without undergoing time-consuming court proceedings.[143] Municipal statutes sanctioned this institution and made it into a powerful tool in the hands of merchants and bankers. Widely utilized, it was attached to contracts and transactions to ensure the prompt execution of the clauses therein contained, including the payment of *arrhae*. The procedure worked as follows: the parties acknowledged to a public notary that they willingly submitted to summary procedure, and their acknowledgment was duly inserted in the contract. In effect, they promised, as if in a court of law, to accept full liability in the event of any future breach of contract they might commit. Further, they simultaneously agreed to waive their right to contest the entry of judgment ordering them to pay the *arrhae*. In a betrothal contract the breaching party was treated as the debtor, who had to indemnify the damaged party, the creditor.

What the parties wished to accomplish with such betrothal contracts containing a *preceptum guarentigie* is aptly described by Odofredus. "Everyday citizens of this city [Bologna] and of all the world," he stated, come to a jurist wishing that "one's son would contract *sponsalia* with the daughter of another. And both children are minors." The parties, then, ask the jurist "to make the *sponsalia* between my son and the other party's daughter and bind us in such a way that we cannot withdraw from the contract with impunity." He advised his students to avoid such arrangements and forthwith to explain to the parties that their wishes could not be executed, because the insertion of a penal stipulation in a betrothal contract violates the principle of the freedom of marriage. Yet, if the parties persisted, Odofredus offered a solution: in contrast to the canonists "we, the civilian jurists, handle the situation in the following way."[144] He recommended *arrhae*, to which an oath could be added, as it was "customary in Pisa and all Tuscany," as an effective legal device for binding the parties in such a way that neither one could break the carefully planned strategic alliance between the two families.[145] A century later, Baldus continued to refer to the widespread custom confirming the (fictitious) acknowledgment of *arrhae* and to the statutes sanctioning that custom by making available to the parties the *preceptum guarentigie*.[146]

Consilia

In truth, the large majority of notarized Florentine betrothals, propelled forward by social pressures and the prospect of losing *arrhae*, culminated in marriages. Where marriage did not follow, the death of a party or other uncontrollable circumstances were usually responsible. Still, a small, and probably unquantifiable, number of cases involving alleged breaches of notarized betrothal contracts were adjudicated in the court of the *podestà*. At issue was the operation of the *preceptum guarentigie* and payment of *arrhae*. Given the hodgepodge of conflicting rules on betrothals, civil law judges and litigants routinely asked local jurists to present *consilia* addressing and resolving the issues of fact and law that had caused the dispute. We examine two such *consilia* composed by Angelus de Ubaldis, which we have edited and included in appendix 3. Citations of Angelus's *consilia* below refer to the texts edited in appendix 3. From internal evidence, it is almost certain that the two *consilia* were rendered during the period when Angelus was teaching at the University of Florence from 1387/8 until the beginning of October 1391, when he left to teach at Bologna.[147] In 1398/9, he resumed his chair in Florence, where he taught until his death in 1400. During his Florentine years, Angelus was an active consultor, rendering opinions on cases in both the city and its territory and lending his endorsement (*subscriptio*) to *consilia* penned by colleagues.[148]

Consilium I

The facts provided in the *punctus*, along with the terms of the *sponsalia*, which both notaries and jurists knew by heart, were, as a matter of course, abbreviated. Male and female ascendants of two families promised each other to see and ensure (*facturos et curaturos*) that the son of one would take as his wife the daughter of the other. Since the instrument was a *sponsalia*, it is obvious that the *sponsus* and *sponsa* were more than seven years old but had not yet reached the canonical age for contracting a legally valid marriage. In the same instrument of betrothal the parties reciprocally acknowledged that they had received 1,000 florins as *arrhae* with the understanding that, in the case one of them failed to fulfill the terms of the contract, the breaching party would return to the. aggrieved party double the amount of *arrhae*. It happened that one party unilaterally broke the contract. The aggrieved party sued for the simple amount of *arrhae*. Since the parties had attached a *preceptum guarentigie* to the contract, the court official who drafted the *punctus* also transcribed part of the relevant rubric of the Florentine statutes on the *preceptum guarentigie*. The *punctus* ends with the question of whether or not the *preceptum guarentigie* is enforceable.

We are left in the dark about the precise ages of the *sponsus* and *sponsa*, the names of their families, the reason for breaking the contract and who broke it, and why the aggrieved party sued only for the simple amount of *arrhae* and not double, as originally stipulated. The court official was obviously puzzled, too, because the reciprocal stipulation on *arrhae* was inserted in the instrument. Was that Florentine practice? Did the reciprocal acknowledgment mean that both parties had exchanged 1,000 florins or had deposited them with a trusted person? Or was the reciprocal acknowledgment a mere promise to pay a penalty in the event a party breached the contract? The skeletal outline of the *punctus* and the lack of information were no obstacle to Angelus, an expert on disputes in which the competence of civil law, canon law, and statutory dispositions overlapped. The structure of the opinion follows the pattern of arguments *pro-et-contra*. Judging from the style of the argumentation, we regard it as a *consilium sapientis*, an impartial opinion commissioned by the court, not an opinion written at the request and on behalf of one of the parties.

The technical question on enforceability did not at all prevent Angelus from casting his net wider than the immediate issue of whether or not one party should be compelled to pay 1,000 florins. Theoretically, the *preceptum guarentigie* could be attached to a stipulation for performing acts prosecutable under criminal law – for example, hiring someone to commit homicide or steal, or to commit a sinful and immoral act like sacrilege. Since municipal legislation made the *preceptum* unconditionally executable, was it enforceable even in the case of an immoral act or a crime? And, if not, why? In view of the principle upholding the freedom of marriage, are *arrhae* permitted, or should they be treated as a penalty? Lastly, what distinguishes *arrhae* from a penalty?[149] "At first sight," Angelus began, "it seems that the said instrument containing a *preceptum guarentigie* deserves no implementation at all, for the contract violates the commonly accepted standards of a community [*boni mores*] requiring that present and future marriages not be secured by the fetters of a penalty." More generally, all contracts and agreements violating the accepted community standards have no force, do not entitle either party to bring an action or raise an exception, and do not create even a natural obligation.[150] Such agreements may not be secured by taking an oath. In short, the standard doctrine on agreements, by which any agreement involving illegal and immoral matters was voided by law, made the betrothal contract invalid and unenforceable.[151]

Next, Angelus considered an objection grounded in the unconditional enforceability of instruments containing a *preceptum guarentigie*. On details, one may argue that, since the statute aimed at expediting the payment of debts, a betrothal contract falls outside the statutory dispositions. More substantially, a rigid application of the statute produces absurd consequences. Paradoxically, if the *preceptum* is attached to a contract, no matter how shameful and wrong its content may be, it follows that the contract must be implemented. Perversely, marriages between ascendants and descendants would be permissible, a sacrilege or a crime would be permitted, and detestable deeds would be performed, as they were all secured by the *preceptum*. But this was an absurdity violating divine and human law, as well as canon and civil law. A literal interpretation and application of the statute would lead to impermissible consequences.[152]

Reversing course, Angelus now argued in favor of enforcing the betrothal instrument. He conceded that, as a matter of general principle, attaching a penal stipulation to a betrothal or marriage contract is prohibited by civil and canon law alike. Yet, "though we may call *arrhae* a penalty, nonetheless they do not have the same effect as a penalty." What distinguished *arrhae* and a penalty was "the reason for which *arrhae* were not given" – that is, they were not given as a penalty. If they had the same effect, *arrhae* would have been prohibited by canon and civil law. But civil law established that *arrhae* could be lawfully retained when, by fault of the giving party, marriage was not contracted, whereas they must be restored, doubled or quadrupled, when the receiving party was at fault. In contrast to Roman law, however, Angelus held that the breaching recipient was responsible for returning double, not quadruple, the amount of *arrhae*.[153]

Adhering to mainstream doctrine, Angelus stressed that the reciprocal acknowledgment of *arrhae* made in the same instrument was invalid. Yet its invalidity could not be raised as an exception, for the statute on the *preceptum* forbade ipso iure the defendant from presenting any exception whatsoever. "There are many deeds," he insisted, "that are utterly invalid by law; nonetheless, their nullity may not be produced, for the statute or municipal legislation shuts the mouth of one who wishes to allege their nullity." Similarly, the statutes may prohibit the judge from hearing such defenses. Municipal legislation enacted against the magnates and the dispositions on contumacy was a case in point. If a statute establishing that one may not be heard in court is valid, "it becomes invalid when worded in the following way: that justice should be denied to one person, for in this case it would be in violation of the law of God."[154]

Now Angelus answered the objections. To the argument that a *preceptum* attached to an agreement may validate any deed, such as marrying an ascendant or descendant, permitting marriage within prohibited degrees, or perpetrating a crime, he readily acknowledged that immoral deeds are forbidden by all the laws. In these instances the laws deny tout court the capacity of persons to enter into such immoral agreements. Yet there are deeds "in conflict with the commonly accepted standards of a community," he went on, "only because of a civil law disposition." Where conflict between deed and norm arises because of a civil law disposition, municipal statutes may be enacted contrary to civil law standards. In short, practices that are not in conformity with the *ius commune* may be permitted solely on the basis of the authority of municipal statutes. The logical conclusion was that the instrument on the reciprocal acknowledgment of *arrhae* must be enforced regarding the simple amount. Even the doubts the court had entertained on the proper form of the notarial instrument served as an additional argument supporting Angelus's main thesis. If the wording of the instrument conformed to Florentine notarial practice, it was valid and must be enforced. Different communities have different customs and standards, and notarial practice, as one would expect, reflects local customs. Consequently, one has to follow local customs, for where the conflict is between two customs, there is no compelling reason to prefer one over the other.

This case reveals that Florentine practices of betrothal among upper-level families were an exercise in risk management. Legal devices – such as the high amount of *arrhae*, their reciprocal acknowledgment without actual transfer of cash, and the attachment of a *preceptum guarentigie* to the betrothal contract – bound the two families with an ironclad contract, and, if no impediment occurred between betrothal and marriage, the alliance was secured. Though we do not know how the court ruled, Angelus's *consilium* underscored the high risks involved in the Florentine strategic management of betrothal contracts. At the end of Trecento, a loss of 1,000 florins was a substantial amount, as one can surmise from the amount of the dowries we have cited above. It comes as no surprise that jurists insisted on the actual transfer of money for a valid stipulation on *arrhae* to avoid an unhappy outcome in which the breaching party became a victim of his or her own fiction.[155]

Consilium II

The facts of the second case centered on an agreement concluded between Lady Massina, with the consent of her guardian (*mundualdus*),[156] and Eusepio on the future betrothal and marriage of their minor children. Under the agreement, Massina's daughter Sera, immediately after the month of February, 1390, upon the completion of her twelfth birthday, would consent to take Pellegrino, Eusepio's son, as her lawful spouse and husband (*sponsum et virum legitimum*). Next, Sera would contract lawful marriage with Pellegrino and accept from him wedding rings. Massina herself would pay Pellegrino Sera's dowry, a certain amount consisting of cash and things. It was stipulated that Sera and Massina would fulfill all these promises at a future time and in a way that would be decided by the arbiters, a certain Antonio and Lorenzo, selected by both parties. More specifically, it was left to the arbiters to fix the dates of betrothal and marriage, the exact amount and composition of the dowry, and the method of payment. For his part, Eusepio promised that Pellegrino, immediately after the month of May, 1391, upon the completion of his fourteenth birthday, would reciprocate Sera's consent to their betrothal and marriage.[157]

The abbreviated format of the *punctus*, however, leaves us in the dark regarding the social identity of the parties and the place where the agreement and dispute took place. Although Massina was not identified as a widow, it is almost certain that she was, for her husband was duty bound to marry off his *filia familias*, which he would have done had he been alive. The omission of surnames, which was usually done for the sake of brevity, prevents us from gauging the contracting parties' social standing. In the absence of toponyms or any mention of place, we cannot be certain that the parties were Florentine or that the dispute occurred in Florence. Nor can we say with certainty whether *consilium* II was solicited by the court or one of the parties to bolster its case. It is apparent from Angelus's *consilium* that the dispute occurred in Tuscany, but not necessarily in Florence. Similarly, the presence of a *mundualdus*, a Florentine institution, with dates in Florentine style (*ab incarnatione*), were practices shared by nearby communities in the *contado*, *distretto*, and other parts of Tuscany. If not definitive, Angelus's linking of *consilium* II with *consilium* I, discussed above, is yet another piece of indirect evidence suggesting that the case was being litigated in a court under the jurisdiction of Florence and subject to its statutes.

To avoid confusion, it should be remembered that in Florence the new year began on 25 March, the day of the Feast of the Annunciation, making Pellegrino's fourteenth birthday fall in May 1391, rather than May 1390, in accordance with the solar calendar, in which the new year begins on the first of January. The salient point here is that, based on the facts provided in the *punctus*, Pellegrino would have reached the legal age for marriage only two months after Sera had completed her twelfth birthday, rather than fourteen months later. In his *consilium*, however, Angelus never used the expression *ab incarnatione*;[158] he used only *anno domini*, which referred to the solar calendar. Inexplicably, perhaps unconsciously, and we believe in error, Angelus seemed to have reverted to the solar calendar of his native city, Perugia. In Angelus's reckoning, or as he said, according to the facts furnished him, Pellegrino was fourteen months older than Sera. It may be objected that Angelus had not erred, because he also used the expression *recte calculo computato*, together with *anno domini*, thus calling attention to a subtler way of counting years. Yet, in context, the expression meant "counting more precisely," that is, counting down to the months.

Consilium II opened with a reaffirmation of *consilium* I: "Just as I advised in the above-mentioned case," Angelus declared, "so likewise here I approve once more all that is stated in the above *consilium* and affirm that it was consonant with the law and well advised." Angelus's reaffirmation suggests that the judge who commissioned *consilium* II may have been familiar with *consilium* I and the case which it addressed. If so, the reaffirmation released Angelus from repeating or summarizing the tenor of the earlier *consilium*. It is also conceivable that Angelus felt that the reaffirmation was necessary to forestall any inference that his opinion in the present case contradicted *consilium* I. The present case differed from the earlier one in that here one of the arbiters had died before declaring the date on which the marriage was to occur, therefore terminating the agreement. The arbiter's premature death, however, did not discourage Pellegrino's father from formally notifying Massina, immediately after Sera's twelfth birthday in February, that the time for marriage was at hand or had passed. Formal notification was necessary when the date for fulfilling an obligation was uncertain, thus placing the other party in default. The concrete issue Angelus was asked to resolve was whether Massina and Sera had broken the betrothal contract.

Angelus responded: "At that time, unless fraud had altered his age, Pellegrino was incapable of contracting marriage, although he could enter into a contract of betrothal [*sponsalia*]."[159] While this was technically true, the two-step sequence, betrothal followed by marriage, was not stipulated in the contract. The convoluted wording of the contract, as Angelus construed it, stipulated that the betrothal, the ringing of the bride, and the marriage would all take place at the same time:

> The agreement was conceived as follows – namely, that the said girl will consent to take Pellegrino as her lawful spouse and husband; and that she will accept from him wedding rings; and that she will contract lawful marriage with him. Therefore, the words, "spouse" [*sponsus*] and "husband" [*vir*] are interchangeable, as is customary among the Tuscans, for whom women are espoused by having rings placed on their fingers [*subharatio*]. For then, reciprocally and in mutual agreement, one to the other and vice versa, the bridegroom [*desponsans*] gives his consent to the bride [*desponsatam*] to take her as his lawful spouse [*sponsa*] and wife [*uxor*]. And she gives her consent to the bridegroom to take him as her spouse and husband. And then, as is customary, the notary will ask the bride if she consents to take him as her spouse and husband. Likewise, the husband is asked if he consents to take her as his lawful spouse and wife, and both answer that they will. Therefore, the parties to this agreement did not intend that betrothal should occur first and marriage afterwards, but that both should occur at the same time. However, since betrothal and marriage could not happen, as a matter of law, default was not incurred.

Angelus's foregrounding of the temporal unity of Tuscan betrothal and marriage rites was roughly consistent with practice, for, as we have observed, the betrothal and marriage of a couple on the same day did occur in late Trecento Florence.

Next, Angelus pronounced that on grammatical grounds the clauses in the agreement supported his argument that Massina and Sera would not have to fulfill their obligations until after the month of May, when Pellegrino would be legally capable of contracting a present-consent marriage. He concluded that it was impossible for default to have occurred, since the time for contracting marriage had not been declared by the arbiters: "If, therefore, the time for contracting the marriage, paying the dowry, and determining its amount, as well as the means by which all this should be carried out, were unconditionally placed at the discretion of the arbiters, there can be no default whatsoever before a declaration is made by the said arbiters concerning the time when and the means by which all this should be carried out, provided the facts are as they were disclosed to me." Finally, under a bilateral contract carrying reciprocal obligations, as in this case, the defendant cannot be placed in default unless the plaintiff first fulfills his obligations. Since it was legally impossible for Eusepio and Pellegrino to fulfill their own contractual obligations, there were no legal grounds for suing Massina and Sera for nonperformance.

We have no idea what motivated Massina to withdraw from the contract after the arbiter's death. Perhaps she had found a better match for her daughter. Whatever the motives, it seems that in contrast to the first case, the parties resorted neither to the fictitious acknowledgment of *arrhae* nor to the *preceptum guarentigie* to cement the contract. Again, in the first case, the *sponsalia* had been unilaterally broken, and the issue was whether the agreed-upon penalty could be lawfully imposed, whereas in the second the issue was whether Massina's decision itself constituted a breach of contract. In *consilium* II, Angelus rehearsed, but then moved beyond, time-honored doctrines regarding the differences between *sponsalia* and *matrimonium* and the invalidity of marriage vows owing to an impediment of nonage. As in *consilium* I, he accented the wishes of the parties as instantiated in their mutual agreements and the constitutive role of municipal law and local customs in the construction and the operation of betrothal contracts.

Highlights and Contrasts

Our study is the first to highlight the interplay of Roman and canon law jurisprudence, together with municipal law and local customs, in making and breaking betrothal contracts. Although notarial manuals regularly featured model contracts of *sponsalia*, preliminary archival research indicates that betrothal contracts, if not rare, were far less common than marriage contracts. The short intervals between betrothals and subsequent marriages, it seems, inhibited the widespread use of notarized *sponsalia* contracts. Florentine families tended to rely on betrothal contracts for arranging the future marriage of minor children, when the interval between betrothal and marriage might be a year or longer. Above all, betrothal contracts attest to the strategic competence of Florentine families to contract alliances from which neither party could withdraw with impunity.[160] The cases we have discussed, along with the *novelle*, point to the instrumental role that widows played in arranging betrothals and marriages. *Arrhae* were one of the devices employed to construct an ironclad contract. Although *arrhae* were necessary, they proved insufficient, so that an oath and the *preceptum guarentigie* were required, as well, to ensure performance.

The process of identifying the crucial differences between *arrhae* and a penalty was laborious, and the distinguishing traits, as elaborated by the jurists, were ultimately problematic. Similarly, the custom of giving a pledge (*pignus*) instead of cash posed a dilemma: should the value of the object pledged be treated symbolically or materially? While in the second case the pledge may be considered an equivalent of *arrhae* given in cash, in the first it may not, and thus it falls outside the dispositions of *l. Mulier* on *arrhae*. Additionally, the reciprocal exchange and acknowledgment of *arrhae* called into question the neatly devised system medieval jurists inherited from Roman law. Nonetheless, jurists succeeded in unmasking frauds, especially in the form of the fictitious and reciprocal acknowledgment of *arrhae*. Since the value of *arrhae* corresponded approximately to that of dowries, the jurists failed in their attempt to limit *arrhae* to a small amount of cash actually transferred from one party to another. Of long-lasting significance was the jurists' effective defense of an aggrieved party's ability to mount an action *ad interesse* against the breaching party in order to recover expenditures made in anticipation of marriage.

The multiple and varied sources of law of the late Middle Ages constituted a sociolegal reality far removed from contemporary regulations governing premarital procedures across Europe and the United States.[161] Today, civil law regulations are almost always based on the monopoly of codes and statutes uniformly applied within the jurisdiction of each country and within each of the fifty U.S. states. Depending on the domicile of the parties, compulsory premarital procedures in Europe and the United States usually consist of premarital counseling, attestation of residence, the production of a birth, divorce, or death certificate (of a former spouse), and the procurement of a marriage license. In Italy, notice of the future marriage must be posted for a minimum of eight days in the town hall of the locality where the couple resides in order to permit interested parties to raise impediments. In addition, all civil marriages must be recorded in a public registry.[162] These compulsory procedures were introduced by governments over the course of the nineteenth and twentieth centuries for the purpose of regularizing and controlling the formation of marriage. One important result of these procedures is that present-day suits resulting from both broken promises to marry and divorce largely concern claims over property, rather than challenges to the validity of the marriage itself. By contrast, the ease by which betrothals and marriages were contracted in the late Middle Ages inevitably resulted in myriad disputes over the very validity of betrothals and marriages.

A persistent theme in the broken-promise-to-marry scholarship and in fictional literature is that from the Middle Ages to the present unscrupulous men have tricked credulous women with sex-motivated promises to marry.[163] In the late Middle Ages, paternalistic church and secular courts consistently sought to compel male seducers to marry their victims. Such suits typically involved low-status families and individuals. At the same time, church courts favored plaintiffs, regardless of gender, seeking to enforce informal betrothal and marriage vows. In the absence of an action at civil law to initiate a suit over a broken promise to marry, high-status families, like the merchant families of Florence, tended to rely on notarized betrothal contracts to avoid the suits and troubles attending informal promises to marry. Our research indicates that betrothal contracts, with their detailed specification of performance contingencies – principally large amounts of compensation and automatic judgment against the breaching party – succeeded in minimizing the occurrence of broken promises to marry.

The experience of Florence differed from that of nineteenth-century England and the United States, countries in which a common law action for breach of promise to marry was well established and was used to launch thousands of suits. The large majority of plaintiffs were lower- and middle-class women seeking pecuniary compensation from ex-fiancés who, they asserted, had failed to keep their promises to marry. As Frost has shown, jilted women in Victorian England easily persuaded sympathetic judges and juries that they were deserving of compensation for unwanted pregnancies, lost jobs, careers forgone, humiliation, and emotional wounds. Compensation was especially needed for women who had already invested in costly wedding preparations. Frost appropriately admires these jilted women for asserting their rights.[164] Yet there is also a paradox that in doing so they had to portray themselves as passive victims, and as Coombs observes, this portrayal was "contradicted by the very action of bringing suit."[165] It is not surprising that these women became the objects of caustic criticism from legal and moral pundits and social critics like Charles Dickens (*The Pickwick Papers*, 1836) and Gilbert and Sullivan (*Trial by Jury*, 1875). For them, female plaintiffs were heartless gold diggers and extortionists. Despite objections, the common law action of breach of promise to marry continued to be used by women to repair their lives well up until 1945. Only in 1970 did Parliament abolish the action.

U.S. state courts and legislatures in the twentieth century have significantly curtailed the ability of jilted women to win suits over broken promises to marry. According to Tushnett, "the idea of pure, romantic, nonmaterialistic love became so powerful over the course of the twentieth century that courts could no longer fully analyze the ways in which the economics of marriages and planned marriages were linked to the emotions surrounding them. This shift in understanding worked against many women's material interests, as once-common and oft-successful female plaintiffs disappeared from the case reporters."[166]

There is yet another contrast. In the late Middle Ages a sworn promise to marry was enforceable under canon law and the breaching party was held at fault and compelled to pay compensation. The promise importantly entailed a change in the promisor's legal status. It was unlawful for the party already betrothed to make a promise of future marriage to another party. Today, in Europe and the United States, an individual's legal status is not at all altered upon the exchange of promises to marry or upon the performance of premarital requirements prescribed by law.[167] Under Italy's *Codice Civile* (1865), a mutual exchange of a promise to marry in the future is not binding (art. 53). The breaching party, however, may be liable for compensation, where the promise was rendered by a party of legal age, or a minor with proper authorization, in an *atto publico* (a declaration made before a public official attested by a sealed document, or a document redacted by a public notary), or in a *scrittura privata* (one drafted by the parties themselves). In that event, the party who declines, without a sound reason, to fulfill the promise must compensate the aggrieved party for expenditures made in preparation for marriage (art. 54). The amount of damages must be limited to actual prenuptial expenditures. These provisions on prenuptial procedures, with minor modifications, remain in force (*Codice Civile*, art. 79–81).[168] Further, a standard textbook on contemporary Italian family law, echoing medieval doctrines, stresses that a penal stipulation attached to a "promessa di matrimonio" has no legal force or effect.[169] In addition, either party, having exchanged promises of future marriage, may demand the return of gifts (including love letters, photographs, and jewelry) given in anticipation of marriage, except where other arrangements for the disposition of the gifts had been made by contract (*Codice Civile*, art. 80).

State legislatures and courts in the United States take a minimalist approach and are no longer willing to assign fault to the party breaking a promise to marry or to grant compensation to the aggrieved party, even for expenditures made in anticipation of future marriage. Under current U.S. legal doctrines and case law, the value of a promise to marry may not be assigned a price. The engagement ring is also treated as a conditional gift that the fiancée must return when the engagement is not followed by marriage. American women think otherwise. According to recent surveys, women overwhelmingly consider the engagement ring, an object on which Americans of all classes lavish extravagant devotion, a down payment that they should be allowed to retain when a fiancé breaks his promise to marry.[170] In most states, however, an ex-fiancé may recover any tangible gift (or its equivalent monetary value) given to a woman in anticipation of marriage, particularly the engagement ring, which today frequently costs thousands of dollars.[171] "It does not matter who broke the engagement," the courts in New Jersey declared. "A person may have the best reasons in the world for doing so. The important thing is that the gift was conditional and the condition was not fulfilled."[172]

The contrasts we have pointed out must not mask the robustness, through the centuries and in radically dissimilar historical settings, of promises of future marriage. In fact, betrothal promises, which have been the exclusive preserve of heterosexual couples, are now made by same-sex couples in Europe, the United States, and Canada. In Italy, the cities of Florence and Pisa have led the way in permitting same-sex couples to register as domestic partners. With regard to medieval Italy, further exploration of archival and legal sources is necessary to better understand the function of *sponsalia* among diverse social groups and regions. The basic questions of who contracted betrothals and where, when, and how they were contracted remain to be answered. The different and conflicting material and emotional meanings attributed to betrothal promises by communities, legal authorities, yesterday's patriarchal families, and today's autonomous and self-fashioning individuals constitute a fascinating, ongoing chapter in comparative sociolegal history.

2 *Li Emergenti Bisogni Matrimoniali* in Renaissance Florence

Li emergenti bisogni matrimoniali[1] – namely, the urgent necessity at the outset of marriage to adorn brides with extravagant clothing and jewelry, to decorate the nuptial chamber, and to arrange wedding festivities – entailed sizable expenditures of capital on the part of new husbands and their kin in Renaissance Florence. In a legal opinion written in 1400, the Florentine jurist Philippus de Corsinis observed that "even before sexual intercourse, it is necessary for the husband to shoulder the expenses for his wife's clothing and other accessories, as well as other expenses related to the wedding."[2] In another opinion, Paulus de Castro, who taught and practiced law in early-fifteenth-century Florence, emphasized that in both Florence and Bologna the outfitting of the bride and expenses for the wedding consumed the whole dowry even before the couple had exchanged marriage vows and rings.[3]

By law, husbands retained ownership of all the nuptial gifts they personally transmitted to their wives, with the exception of ordinary apparel for everyday wear.[4] In the estimation of contemporaries, however, the financial demands that marriage imposed on new husbands made them forlorn figures who would derive marginal, if any, benefits from the dowries they were promised. Planning for the marriage of her sons, Alessandra Macinghi Strozzi despaired that "the world is in a sorry state, and never has so much expense been loaded on the backs of women as now. No dowry is so big that when the girl goes out she doesn't have the whole of it on her back, between silks and jewels."[5] With righteous indignation, San Bernardino of Siena reproved wives with small dowries who demanded from their husbands a precious woolen cloth (*rosado*) in return.[6] He also reproved brides with large dowries (*le grandi dote*) who sought parity by cravenly demanding from their husbands expensive clothing, adornments, and jewels.[7] And he directed his biblical fury at wives who kept the whole dowry in a chest yet forced their husbands to resort to credit on unfavorable terms in order to afford things beyond their meager resources.[8] Giovanni della Casa, in his misogynistic screed *An uxor sit ducenda*, protested that taking a wife reduces a man to poverty, "for he must support, clothe, and adorn her at tremendous expense" (ali, vestiri ornarique maximo sine impendio).[9] Machiavelli cast as his central character in *Belfagor* a husband ruined by his new wife's extravagant demands, among which were "dressing her in the newest fashions and keeping her in the latest novelties which our city habitually changes."[10] Renaissance audiences responded with familiarity to the figure of the nagging wife in Plautus's *Aulularia*, who expected a quid pro quo for her dowry: "I brought you a dowry far bigger than the money you had; so it is fair that I should be given purple clothes, gold jewelry, slave girls, mules, grooms, footmen, pages, and a carriage."[11]

It would be easy, but fruitless, to multiply contemporary denunciations making women's unappeasable greed and Venus envy directly responsible for the ills of their husbands and society, a well-known topos of the European misogynist imagination.[12] These denunciations raise questions whose answers are critical to any assessment of the role played by dowries in Florentine society. First and foremost, what sociocultural logic made dressing nubile women and young brides a duty that fathers and husbands could not fail to perform? Second, should we take at face value assertions that uxorious husbands spent sums equivalent to the entire dowry or the dowry itself on the wedding and the dressing of vain and mercenary wives? Put another way, was the promise of a dowry simply a promise to compensate husbands for expenses already incurred at the time of marriage and for indulging their wives in the latest fashions during the course of an ongoing marriage? Third, what legal remedies and financial arrangements were available to husbands who received only partial payment of the promised dowry or nothing at all? Finally, did husbands violate the usury prohibition by demanding and accepting compensation or interest payments on dowries promised but not paid?

(In)vestments in Auspiciousness

An indispensable requisite for the sumptuous weddings and indulgent craze for luxuries, scholars agree, was the conspicuous affluence of the Renaissance city-states, especially Florence.[13] Affluence, in turn, triggered competitive displays of wealth for the purpose of signaling family rank,[14] an enduring social dynamic brilliantly analyzed by Veblen, Simmel, and

Bourdieu.[15] As dress was employed as a primary visual means by medieval and Renaissance elites to manifest rank and magnificence publicly, sociocultural logic dictated that Florentine fathers and husbands, independently of their personal wishes, invest considerable sums in adorning their daughters and wives. Sociocultural logic also dictated that a wife existed as an appendage of her husband and his family, whose image of prestige and power was reflected in her dress. In the idiom of the period, they were pursuing honor, a heartfelt quest made strikingly tangible by the wife's clothing and ornaments and dramatized by nuptial festivities. As the jurist Angelus de Ubaldis of Perugia explained, the husband conveys precious clothing and accessories to his wife, "so that she may appear in public proudly and honorably."[16]

In his treatise *Wifely Duties*, dedicated to Lorenzo di Giovanni de' Medici, Francesco Barbaro urged wives to dress with moderation but advised that "if they are of noble birth, they should not wear mean and despicable clothes if their wealth permits otherwise."[17] What alarmed Barbaro and like-minded contemporaries was the ostentatious display (*pompa*) of wealth by aristocratic elites, which wasted patrimonies, and the unrestrained use of expensive clothing and adornments by upwardly mobile commoners seeking to rise beyond their inferior status. Spurred by these fears, lay and ecclesiastical authorities in Florence and elsewhere had attempted repeatedly, but in vain, to legislate modesty and regulate social competition by curbing nuptial pomp and vestimentary excess.[18] Despite recurring bouts of invasive moralism, sumptuary laws were ultimately doomed to failure because social competition, an insatiable appetite for luxuries, and ostentatious display had taken deep root in the psyche of fourteenth- and fifteenth-century Florentines. By the late fourteenth century, the statutory penalties imposed on conspicuous status wearers for violating sumptuary laws were mitigated and transformed into excise taxes or fees. By paying fees, fathers and husbands were able to purchase immunities from sumptuary regulations, enabling their daughters and wives to dress as social necessity demanded.[19]

An alternative thesis, rejecting this totalizing conception of social competition and the sociopsychological conception of conspicuous consumption, was advanced in 1982 by Christiane Klapisch-Zuber to explain the behavior of the bridegroom and his family.[20] Applying the insights of the ethnologist Marcel Mauss to the relationship between gifts and social cohesion in archaic societies, she explains that gifts exchanged between families at the time of marriage were not weapons in the battle for social prestige but, on the contrary, part of a system of compulsory reciprocities that secured peace among neighbors and maintained the stability of the social structure. With the demise of the Germanic *Morgengabe* and the reduction of the Roman *donatio propter nuptias*, or counterdowry, into a token gift by the opening of the thirteenth century,[21] "the reciprocal and almost equal exchange" that had existed for over half a millennium between the families of the bridegroom and bride disappeared. However, the gifts given to the bride by the bridegroom and his family served to perpetuate the function that *Morgengabe* had once fulfilled:

> Even more important than the material worth of these gifts, in fact, was the need that people engaged in the process of alliance felt – on all levels of society – to make such offerings. They took great pains to reestablish an equilibrium perturbed by the official modalities of the dowry system when an alliance was made and a new couple set up housekeeping. The obligation honored by the husband to "dress" his wife thus *acted* as a countergift. It reestablished equality between the partners, an equality that had been destroyed by the initial gift [the dowry] and by the superiority that it momentarily conferred to the giver over the receiver.[22]

Beyond reciprocity, matrimonial gifts, like linens and rings, had symbolic attributes that gave meaning to the passage of the bride from her own household into her husband's.[23] The bridegroom's adornment of his bride-to-be, in particular, with articles of clothing and jewels bearing his family's coat of arms, signaled that this woman was spoken for and that her initiation into married life had begun. Similarly, the gifts he gave to her on the morning after the consummation of the marriage signaled the husband's claim to sexual rights over his wife. Other gifts provided by the husband's relatives marked the acceptance of the bride into the husband's kin group and brought into relief new ties of *parentado*. A year or two after the right of passage of marriage was completed, it was expected that almost all nuptial gifts would be returned to their donors, which, for Klapisch-Zuber, shows that their primary role was to give symbolic meaning to ritual action. Since the husband remained the owner of all nuptial gifts that he personally gave his wife, with the exception of ordinary apparel for everyday wear, he had the right to dispose of them as he wished. Husbands in need of cash could sell them or lend them for a premium to other new husbands in need of nuptial gifts. Far from causing the diversion of productive capital into wasteful nuptial gifts, according to Klapisch-Zuber, Florentine wives were pitiable creatures, relegated to the role of passive agents of social solidarity and equilibrium, and ultimately sacrificed on the altar of patrilineal interests. Like Boccaccio's Griselda, they were victims of a ritual process stripping them of their clothing and adornments. Her image of men dressing and undressing women becomes a searing metaphor of the emotional bondage and dismemberment of women fated to live in a heterosexist, patriarchal society. And far from facing financial ruin caused by the obligation to dress their wives, husbands not only recouped their initial investment but could also turn a profit, as nuptial gifts shuttled back and forth between the sphere of ritualized generosity and self-interest and the sphere of commodities.

Klapisch-Zuber's illuminating and evocative analysis grounded in empirical evidence and ethnographic theory marked a watershed in our understanding of the role played by nuptial gifts in Florentine society and deservedly became the starting point for all subsequent studies of nuptial expenditures in Renaissance Italy. Nonetheless, I remain unpersuaded by the view that Florentine husbands and their families, responding to a deep-seated cultural predisposition, were compelled to spend large sums on nuptial gifts and festivities for the *almost exclusive* purpose of counterbalancing incoming dowries, thereby engendering social solidarity. This view, predicated on the assumption that rituals of exchange in medieval and early modern societies function to promote social equilibrium, slights the prevalence of social competition in Florentine society. It also ignores an outstanding feature of nuptial gifts, crucial to any explanation of why husbands and their families felt obliged to give them: that gifts of gemstones, pearl-studded garlands, richly decorated silver belts or girdles, clothing, and marriage chests were primarily regarded as investments in auspiciousness.

The magical powers attributed to nuptial gifts were believed to ward off evil spirits, to mediate the emotional and sexual relationship of the betrothed couple, and to create circumstances favorable to the successful consummation of their marriages.[24] Medieval and Renaissance lapidaries informed their readers that rubies dispersed poison in the air and guaranteed love and good fortune. Their fiery color, the humanist and Roman noble Marco Antonio Altieri explained, signified the body, repository of the heart, which was burning with the flame of love. The bridegroom who gave his bride rubies (*balasci*) had symbolically given her his heart. His soul was tenderly conveyed by gifts of sky-blue sapphires.[25] Besides the medicinal value of emeralds to repel poison, pestilence, dysentery, evil dreams, madness, and witchcraft, it was also believed that they preserved the chastity of the wearer and assisted women at childbirth. Gifts of diamonds and pearls showered on Florentine brides were considered antidotes to assorted ills. Such gifts were not restricted to members of patrician and wealthy families,[26] but were also given by shopkeepers and weavers,[27] and even *contadini*.[28]

Among the talismanic gifts traditionally given by the bridegroom, none carried more meaning than the erotically charged nuptial belt (*cingulum*, *zona*) or girdle molding the bride's breasts.[29] A fine example of a nuptial belt is depicted in an early-fourteenth-century miniature illustrating the title, *De donationibus inter virum et uxorem*, in Justinian's *Digest* (24. 1). Here the pledge and the counterpledge to marry (*sponsalia*) are sealed by the fiancé, who gives his fiancée a belt with a purse and in exchange receives a ring (figure 2.1). Sanctified heteroeroticism is symbolized on a Quattrocento nuptial belt depicting a maiden embracing a youth and a girl holding a carnation, the symbol of marriage.[30] Known as the girdle of Venus (*cesto*), the nuptial belt was believed to endow the bride with the graces of beauty and love. It was also a symbol of the bride's virginity, which she preserved for her husband and which remained intact until the consummation of marriage. Boccaccio informed readers of his *Genealogy of the Gods* that "some have asserted the girdle which binds the bride affirms the marriage's legitimacy."[31] Marco Antonio Altieri related that among his contemporaries brides were formally girded in memory of the *cesto* given by Vulcan to Venus. Without the performance of this ritual, it was generally held that the marriage was neither legitimate nor true, but impure (*incesto*).[32] A valid marriage was linked to the couple's ability to perform sexual intercourse,[33] which began, Sextus Pompeius Festus maintained, when the husband unfastened the bride's girdle in bed. Indeed, "the beginning of marriage occurs with the unfastening of the girdle, by which brides were bound."[34] Dressing and undressing the wife was thus a necessary prelude to legitimate sexual intercourse and procreation.

In the conventional medieval psychophysiology of love, the eyes were the opening through which the image of the beloved entered the heart, the seat of the sensitive soul and the appetites. Andreas Capellanus famously defined love "as an inborn suffering which results from the sight of, and uncontrolled thinking about, the beauty of the other sex."[35] A wife dressed to attract her husband's gaze would naturally give him pleasure and excite his sexual desire, leading him to bed her. From a Freudian perspective, the husband's visually derived libidinal pleasure was predictable. "Visual impressions," Freud posited, "remain the most frequent pathway along which libidinal excitation is aroused."[36] Indirectly confirming and extending Freud's insight, recent eye-tracking studies of love and sexual desire show that "eye gaze shifts as a function of his or her goal (love vs. lust)

Figure 2.1. Miniature: "De donationibus inter virum et uxorem." Tübingen, Universitätsbibliothek, Ms. 293, fol. 315r. Courtesy of the Universitätsbibliothek.

when looking at a visual stimulus."[37] Small wonder, then, that a husband was moved to transform his wife into an erotic object, just as her parents had done in order to attract potential husbands. Even San Bernardino, the apostle of conspicuous parsimony and uncompromising preaching, grudgingly admitted that it was acceptable for wives to deck themselves out in fineries within the confines of the *casa* to please their husbands, but only if they behaved discreetly and decently and without lascivious intention.[38]

The large majority of married couples, Bernardino believed, were actually incapable of exercising the self-restraint necessary to limit themselves to the three legitimate ends of sexual intercourse: procreation, rendering the marital debt, and avoidance of fornication. He assumed that the eroticized wife would inflame her husband to love her too ardently and therefore sinfully, and worse, that she would attract lovers outside matrimony.[39] No *meretrix* was as meretricious as the eroticizcd bride. He recounted the arrival of a bride at the house of her husband, adorned with a garland of silver acorns, her fingers laden with rings, glittering with gold, her face painted. She was greeted with joy, and after three days of feasting, "it seems that her husband has fallen madly and fiendishly in love with her" (che <’>l marito sia impazzato e indiavolato di lei).[40] As for wives who tell confessors that they dress sumptuously and paint their faces "to please our husbands," Bernardino replied, "You're blatantly lying. And the confessors are fooled by you if they believe it, and they are fooled by their generosity to you."[41] Leon Battista Alberti also pointed his accusatory finger at fickle women who "take great pains to please the public eye, and great pleasure in being admired. By nature, a woman can't help loving and respecting whoever admires her. When a woman is looked at, she thinks that you desire her beauty, and she regards your gaze as a sort of tribute."[42] Alberti, to apply the words of Maria Wyke, "operates as a hyperbolically normative male who has the power to dismantle the mask that constitutes the deceitful female."[43]

Other moralists, however, openly approved the behavior of a wife who adorned herself in sexually alluring, formfitting dress to capture her husband's wandering libidinous eye, even if it caused other men to sin by desiring her body.[44] Here transgressive sexualized voyeurism was considered morally acceptable because it was principally intended to incite the husband to perform the "duties of the flesh," not as a provocation to lust.[45] The Dominican moral theologian Antoninus of Florence, named archbishop of his native city in 1446, advised that if a wife dresses to please her husband, lest he abandon her for other women, or because he directs her to wear seductive dress, she does not commit a sin.[46] Contemporaneously, Antonius de Rosellis of Arezzo, who taught canon and civil law at the University of Florence and the University of Padua, enlisted the *Digest*, the *Decretum* of Gratian, Aristotle, Augustine, Thomas Aquinas, and above all the biblical models of the virtuously adorned Judith and Esther to support his contention that adornment in dress is not evil of its own nature but only in its abuse. Against the validity of an episcopal ordinance imposing limitations on women's dress and adornment, he argued that the civil law "permits men to provide potions and ointments to their wives, so that they may appear more beautiful." It permits them to send their wives gold and silver ornaments, gems and stones and toiletries, especially when such gifts and practices are sanctioned by regional custom. For Antonius de Rosellis, "in these matters no one can rule the wills of wives except their husbands, to whom God wished females to be subordinate."[47] Consequently, there is nothing cupidinous or sinful about married women who, at the command of their own husbands, adorn themselves with expensive garments and ornaments with the intention of pleasing them and stimulating their desire for sexual intercourse (*proprios maritos ad coitum provocent*).

Images of the wife's acquiescence to her husband's authority over her body and her will were customarily inscribed on the pair of marriage chests (*forzieri*) packed with the gifts the bridegroom sent his bride before the wedding ceremony. Marriage chests illustrated the classical virtues that the bridegroom wished to associate with his family: generosity, magnanimity, and prudence, as well as the selflessness and sacrifices expected of his bride. Among the most popular images depicted were the figures of the submissive Griselda dressed and undressed by her lord and husband; humble Esther, who appeared before King Xerxes dressed in her finest robes; and the queen of Sheba rewarded with royal bounty for journeying far to hear the wisdom of Solomon.[48]

The power of *forzieri* and *forzerini* (jewel boxes), as well as the gifts they contained, to convey moral and spiritual allegories was seized by the Florentine Dominican friar Giovanni Dominici. Like his contemporary Bernardino of Siena, Dominici was a master of performative rhetoric, leavening his devotional writings with the imagery of lived experience to establish a rapport with his largely lay female audience.[49] In Italy of the late Middle Ages and the Renaissance, the convention of arranged marriages coupled with the taboo against courtship precluded the romantic, passionate attachments and the drama of the flesh that have become a precondition of modern Western marriages. For Florentine girls the prospective husband was necessarily a stranger, and for many an overbearing imaginary figure.

In a rapturous passage indebted to the story in the *Golden Legend* of the Roman virgin martyr Agnes, Dominici conflated the phantasm of the new, yet unseen, bridegroom with that of a loving Jesus Christ, who sends his chaste bride a *forzerino* overflowing with "glowing seraphim, shining cherubim and resplendent thrones, domains like sapphires, green and virtuous emeralds, strong diamonds of power, red rubies of princedoms, the finest beryl of archangels, white pearls, big and round of the blessed angels. Of these companions you make together with Saint Agnes crowns, decorations, buckles, rings, and the richest belts."[50] These precious gifts signaled the bridegroom's fidelity and served to reward the chastity of his betrothed and to guarantee her future fidelity by garbing her in invincible virtue. For Dominici, marital love and fidelity were activated by the imagination of the seeing self. Sumptuous nuptial gifts would arouse in the mind of the young bride a phantasm of the bridegroom as the beloved: "Now as a bride receiving the rich *forzerino* from that husband whom she never saw, she feels much beloved when she is so richly rewarded, and she creates a noble image of him who so nobly sends, and not seeing, she loves and desires to see his figure. Much more does that love entering in you inflame you for God Almighty ... and in the bed of heavenly repose, naked by these gifts, make you your abode."[51] Here Dominici adeptly transformed the phantasm of the prospective husband into an intimate gift-giving lover pledging everlasting fidelity to his betrothed.

Undeniably, the desire for honor impelled Florentine husbands and their families to spend lavishly on nuptial gifts, while the desire for alliances initiated a sequence of exchanges between the families of the bridegroom and bride. Yet the forces of social competition counterbalanced by the forces of social equilibrium provide an incomplete context for understanding the role of nuptial gifts in inaugurating and fostering the interpersonal bonds between bride and bridegroom. Nuptial gifts announced the figure of the unknown husband before marriage, kindled marital love, intimacy, and fidelity, protected the new bride from maladies, assisted childbirth, and represented the authority of the husband over his deferential wife. The distinctive attributes and meanings of what was actually given by Florentine bridegrooms to their brides constitute the basis of my contention that nuptial gifts were principally an investment in auspiciousness.

Nuptial Expenses

Lacking a detailed study of nuptial expenses, it is not possible to answer definitively what proportion of the dowry was spent on gifts at the beginning of marriage. However, a reliable survey of *libri di famiglia* indicates that on average from the mid-fourteenth century through the early sixteenth century, Florentine husbands and their families spent on nuptial gifts and wedding festivities an amount representing from one-third to two-thirds of the promised dowry.[52] My own research, admittedly fragmentary, supports this finding. In 1356 Francesco di Iacopo Del Bene spent 647 florins on his wedding, dressing his bride, Dora di Domenico Guidalotti, and furnishing their bridal chamber. In return, he received a dowry of 950 florins paid in five installments between May 1356 and May 1357.[53] A century later it cost Bartolomeo di Filippo Valori more than 1,200 florins when he married Caterina di Piero Pazzi, who brought him a dowry of 2,000 florins.[54] Tribaldo d'Amerigo de' Rossi limited his expenditures to 324 florins, representing 26 percent of his wife's 1,250-florin dowry.[55] Rarely did nuptial expenses exceed the promised dowry. The lavish expenditures that sealed the marriage of Bernardo di Giovanni Rucellai to Nannina di Piero de' Medici and exceeded her dowry stand as a remarkable exception to the norm.[56] If we can say that nuptial expenses were inflated by the rhetorical virtuosity of their detractors, they nevertheless constituted a substantial drain on the husband's assets, especially from the mid-fifteenth century on, when the city's Dowry Fund (*Monte delle doti*) failed to pay husbands promised dowries as they came due.[57] For instance, new husbands like Tribaldo de' Rossi had to borrow money from their in-laws to cover nuptial expenses, while others, like Marco Parenti, arranged for advanced payment of their dowries.[58] Bartolomeo Valori's annoyance is noticeable when he recorded that his wife's Monte dowry had not yet come due and that he had received from his in-laws only 300 florins in cash, though he had forked out more than 1,200 florins for his bride's clothing and jewelry.[59] All these husbands were apprehensive about receiving the dowries promised them to compensate, in part, for their nuptial expenses. In recognition of their plight, the government in 1433 permitted husbands to deduct nuptial expenses from their dowries, which were treated as taxable assets.[60]

Husbands in Need

In his vividly perceptive family memoir, the merchant Giovanni di Paolo Morelli warned that the rampant craving for huge dowries predictably leads husbands to ruin: "For gluttony of money, do not drown yourself in a dowry, because no good ever comes of dowries, and if you have to restore the dowry, you will be ruined. Be satisfied with this: to possess whatever your station and that of the woman you take [as a wife] requires."[61] In his *Della famiglia*, Leon Battista Alberti prudently cautioned new husbands that their pockets as well as their peace of mind would be better served by a dowry that was "modest, certain, and payable immediately [*presente*] than large, doubtful, and payable over a period of time [*in tempo*]."[62] These admonitions fell on deaf ears. The steady increase in the size of dowries in the fourteenth and early fifteenth centuries, in Florence and far beyond the city's walls, made it ever more difficult for dowries to be paid fully before a husband transferred his wife into his household. As the Perugian jurist Petrus Philippus Corneus observed, "In many places it is the custom that almost always the husband acknowledges receiving the dowry, and yet on the same day, in the same place, and with the same witnesses (notwithstanding the acknowledgment), he is promised the same amount for the said dowry."[63] In Florence and elsewhere it was not unusual for husbands to agree to payment of their dowries "sub spe future numerationis" and in installments that might drag on for years.[64] But what remedies were available to a husband who was reluctant, or who refused outright, to wait and demanded his dowry immediately? A husband was entitled to sue his delinquent in-laws, but that was not a socially viable option.[65] As Alberti observed, litigation was counterproductive on account of the expenses incurred and enmities aroused. The alternative was for a new husband to suffer in silence, which would probably happen once he began living with his bride:

> For the bride now lives in your house, and during the first year it seems impermissible to do other than strengthen the new bonds of kinship [*parentado*] through frequent visits and convivialities. Perhaps you will feel it impolite to bring up the question of payment during festivities, for new husbands generally try not to interfere with the still tender bonds of kinship ... And if you try to act with more force, the in-laws will start lamenting their infinite needs, their bad fortune, the hardships of the times ... Moreover, no matter how harsh you may be toward them, you will not be able to resist the sweet and prayerful requests made by your wife in your own house and bedchamber

> on behalf of her father and brothers. Accordingly, you are bound in the end to suffer financial damage and enmity … That is why the dowry should be certain, payable immediately, and not too great.[66]

Under civil law, husbands could lawfully refuse to support and live with spouses for whom a dowry was promised but not fully paid.[67] Paulus de Castro opined that "when a husband is promised a dowry, if it is not paid to him fully, he is not obligated to support the expenses of marriage [*onera matrimonii*]; on the contrary, he can drive his wife away and send her back to her father's house."[68] The Florentine jurist Antonius de Strozziis concurred: "A husband who is promised a dowry by his brother-in-law that is not paid can send his wife back to her brother's house and even deny her basic necessities."[69] But Alberti did not advise new husbands to avail themselves of this drastic, shame-producing remedy, which was seldom employed by husbands belonging to the highest levels of Florentine society.

The plight of the lay canon lawyer Francesco di ser Benedetto Marchi offers a telling example of the countless Florentine husbands who resided with their wives, even though he had not received full payment of the 650-florin dowry promised him. In his *catasto* declaration of 1427, Marchi reported that he was in financial hell. His father-in-law, Filippo di Tommaso Guidetti, owed him 500 florins for the remainder of his promised dowry, which, he declared, would be recoverable only after long delay and with great difficulty.[70] Marchi's financial woes were aggravated by a string of debts, among which were 84 florins he owed his brother-in-law, Berto di Milano Salvini, for his own sister's dowry and 25 florins owed to the commune for the tax on the full dowry of 650 florins publicly acknowledged in a *confessio dotis*. Debts arising from nuptial expenses forced him to borrow money at usury from a Pratese Jew, with whom he left in pawn two belts that he had given to his wife.[71] For debts incurred on behalf of his father-in-law, he was also compelled to place in pawn his wife's apparel with a used-clothes dealer. Worse, Marchi's law practice had come to a halt. Miserable and humiliated, he had not left his home (where he lived with his wife, Diana, and their three-month-old son, Marco), except on holidays, for more than ten months, and accordingly asked the *catasto* officials to take into consideration his financial troubles when assessing his tax.[72] It was a self-serving appeal, to be sure. Nonetheless, although Marchi had received only 150 florins of a promised 650-florin dowry, the remainder of which he had faint hope of collecting,[73] he, like the overwhelming majority of partially endowed husbands of his station, was residing with and maintaining his wife.[74]

On the other hand, there is the oft-cited case of *contractus interruptus* occasioning *matrimonium interruptum* in which Paolo Niccolini waited three years (1430–3) before he introduced his bride, Cosa di Bernardo Guasconi, into his household. "During this period," Paolo recorded sourly, "I received the dowry in many installments and at many times. On the day I took her [to my house] some of it was still owing to me. I was not satisfied with so many small sums, and this was the reason why I waited so long to take her, because I wished to have the dowry first, to avoid quarrels."[75] Paolo Niccolini's behavior, however, was not representative of his station but was more typical of less well-to-do husbands in Florence and in the *contado* and *distretto*.[76] The weaver Antonio di Bastiano, for example, was not willing to live with his wife, Agnoletta d'Andrea, until he received the entire dowry. In her *catasto* declaration of 1480, Nanna, Agnoletta's widowed mother, described her daughter as "married but not gone to her husband [*maritata et non ita a marito*]," with a Monte dowry worth ninety florins but not payable until 1481. Meanwhile, Nanna gave her son-in-law temporary possession of a small house as partial payment of his dowry and as an inducement to begin living with his bride. If after six years Antonio had not yet begun to live with his wife, the house would revert to Nanna. It would belong to Antonio, with no strings attached, only when he installed Agnoletta in his household.[77] For brides whose impoverishment prevented them from living with their husbands, assistance from religious foundations and benevolent relatives was necessary.[78]

Many husbands were unable to collect the entire Monte dowry immediately because they had entered marriage before the initial, or subsequent, deposits made on behalf of their wives were payable. The evidence I have been able to unearth suggests that, contrary to Alberti's dire forecasts, a husband eager to collect a Monte dowry, either before or after the date of maturity, did not have to suffer in silence. He could demand that his in-laws consign to him, for his own use, property that would be returned on receipt of the Monte dowry. Temporary consignments of property represented a favored expedient. In her *catasto* return of 1480, the widowed mother of Frescobalda di Piero of San Miniato al Tedesco explained that she had married her daughter to Giorgio di Simone of Prato. Since Frescobalda's Monte dowry of 230 florins was not due for at least another three years, she consigned 230 florins of her own properties, which her son-in-law promised to return when he received the Monte dowry.[79] If the husband's demands were resisted by his in-laws, he might have his claim settled by arbitration. When Giovencho de' Medici married Francesca di Giovanni di Niccolò Manelli in 1462, he was promised a Monte dowry of 1,500 florins, with 413 collectible in November 1463 and another 591 in February 1464. He had already received 496 florins at the beginning of marriage. According to the terms of an arbitrated settlement of August 1463, Francesca and her husband were given the use of a farm in Antella until her entire dowry was finally paid.[80]

Typically, any fruits appropriated by the husband from these arrangements would not count as payment of the dowry. At the time the dowry was fully paid, could the husband's in-laws, therefore, demand restoration of such fruits by claiming that they were usurious, an illegitimate addition to the dowry? No, the canonists and civilians replied. Fruits of property pledged to the husband, according to the decretal *Salubriter*, should not suffer the stigma of usury, since it often happens the fruits of the dowry itself are insufficient to meet the expenses of marriage. They should be sanctioned as a legitimate supplement to the dowry.[81] Commenting on *Salubriter*, the canonists added that such fruits served as a licit interim substitute for dotal fruits and as an incentive to the husband to begin living with his bride.[82] The canonists' position was affirmed both by Antoninus and by San Bernardino in a Lenten sermon treating the morality of *interesse* (licit compensation).[83] Civilian jurists, too, affirmed the husband's claim to *interesse* for suffering financial damages because of nonpayment of the dowry.[84]

Some husbands had no option but to accept interest instead of the dowry itself. Based on data from the *catasto* of 1427, Pampaloni has shown that the going rate on overdue dowries in nearby Prato was 10 percent. That corresponded to the going rate of 9–10 percent that husbands expected to receive on overdue dowries in fifteenth-century Florence and its environs. Carlo di Scolaio Salterelli reported in his *catasto* declaration of 1480 that he owed his son-in-law 150 florins for the remainder of the dowry he had promised. Without sufficient resources and incapacitated by age, Salterelli could pay his son-in-law only 13.5 florins in three installments – that is, an annual rate of 9 percent.[85] Earlier, Bernardo di Nofri Mellini had acknowledged in his *catasto* declaration of 1427 that he and his brothers owed 230 florins on the dowry promised his brother-in-law, Romolo di Lorenzo, a secondhand-clothes dealer. They were paying Romolo "fiorini 10 per 100" and anticipated paying him in full from the proceeds of the future sale of a farm that served as collateral for their dotal obligation.[86]

For the influential canonist Johannes Andreae and his immediate followers, such cash payments to husbands, despite the in-laws' failure to fulfill their contractual obligations, were strictly speaking in violation of the usury prohibition.[87] But by the fifteenth century the leading canonists and moral theologians had joined with civilian jurists in permitting "dower-less" husbands to accept cash, so long as they applied it to the expenses of marriage. They explicitly sanctioned cash payments to husbands reputed to be merchants, reasoning that delayed payment of the dowry would force them to shoulder the expenses of marriage with cash earmarked for their commercial undertakings. The arguments sanctioning cash payments were made by jurists and moralists who recognized that accommodations were necessary in a commercial society in which cash was the primary medium of funding dowries, but who were equally adamant in upholding the usury prohibition. Indeed, they gave notice that the fruits of property consigned to husbands could neither exceed the expenses of marriage nor derive from fraudulent arrangements, where the son-in-law willingly and intentionally forwent payment of the dowry with the purpose of collecting interest.

So far I have been dealing with husbands who sought compensation on overdue dowries. There were instances, as legal opinions (*consilia*) dating from the fourteenth and fifteenth centuries testify, where a husband was entitled, but failed, to demand *interesse* on a dowry that was promised but never paid. One question legal consultors tried to answer was whether a husband, after the death of the person who had promised the dowry, could sue that person's heirs for compensation. Another was whether, after a husband's death, his own heirs could sue those responsible for paying the dowry. In general, *consilia* lent support to these claims, though the circumstances of the cases varied.

One opinion, written in the mid-fifteenth century by Galeottus de Gualdis, an official of the Mercanzia in Florence, dealt with a suit brought by a certain Battista di Iacopo.[88] On the decease of his father, Battista claimed compensation on a dowry that was promised, but not paid, to his father, Iacopo, by his mother (Lucrezia), her brother, and her own mother. Galeottus followed the principle set forth by Battista's lawyer in an earlier opinion (which I have not been able to locate): that a husband who bears the expenses of marriage can demand usury from the promissor of a dowry who delays payment. But referring to Papinian's opinion in Dig. 24, 1, 54, *Vir usuras*, Galeottus raised the issue of whether Iacopo, by failing to demand compensation during the marriage and by giving his wife clothing and other items for her use, had thereby acquitted her from the obligation to compensate him for his marital expenses. Basing his own opinion on *Vir usuras*, Galeottus determined that Iacopo had so released his wife. In consequence, Battista could not act against his mother but only against his grandmother and uncle. Regrettably, we remain ignorant of whether Battista ultimately succeeded in his quest.

Another opinion was written in 1517 by Antonius de Strozziis, the most active lawyer in Florence around the end of the fifteenth century and the beginning of the sixteenth. These are the facts of the case: Giovanni promised to deliver to Nicola, his son-in-law, within a certain time one-half of a farm as payment of a 250-florin dowry. Nicola then inducted his wife into his household (*duxit uxorem*) yet never received the property. Instead he received many small payments of cash totaling 170 florins. At the time of Giovanni's death – twenty-six years after he had promised to consign the property – he owed 80 florins to his son-in-law, described as "creditor pro dote sibi promissa."[89] Now it was asked whether Nicola could legitimately demand compensation. Citing the decretal *Salubriter*, Strozzi contended that since Nicola had borne the burdens of marriage and thus fulfilled his part of the dotal contract, while his father-in-law had dishonored the contract, he was unquestionably entitled to compensation. There remained the question of whether Nicola had in effect forfeited his claim, because he had waited so long to exercise it. Referring to other *consilia* on this issue, Strozzi argued that for reasons of equity, one must not presume that Nicola had released his father-in-law from paying compensation. As for the amount of compensation, Strozzi reckoned that it should be commensurate with the estimated value of the fruits that would have been produced by the property over the course of the twenty-six years. Nicola was also entitled to receive income (*redditus*) for the outstanding portion of the dowry due him. The responsibility for satisfying Nicola's claim rested squarely on the shoulders of his father-in-law's heirs: "For such a debt should be paid by the heirs in equal shares, because it is their duty to pay the creditors of the inherited estate."[90]

More fortunate husbands like the jurist Francesco Guicciardini received an advance on the remainder of their Monte dowries, serving to alleviate the *onera matrimonii* and cement the ties between the spouses' families.[91] When the Monte dowry finally became collectible, it was not the husband but his father-in-law or brothers-in-law who would receive the payment as recompense for the advance. The transfer of the Monte dowry was typically effected through assignment of the husband's claims (*cessio iuris*) – that is, by appointing his in-laws as his legal agents for the purpose of collecting the Monte dowry.[92] Numerous examples of such assignments, employed by those with relatively small as well as large dowries, could be presented, but two should suffice. Luca da Panzano, acting with power of attorney from his son-in-law, Iacopo di Ducino Mancini, received 627 florins from the Dowry Fund in January 1452. He had advanced Mancini the Monte portion of his daughter's dowry in February 1447.[93] Simone di Domenico, who had already received a dowry at the time he married Caterina di Tedice Villani, appointed both his father-in-law and brother-in law as his legal agents in order to collect his wife's Monte dowry of 61 florins.[94]

Regardless of who actually received payment from the Dowry Fund, the husband remained obligated to make formal acknowledgment of its receipt. Rather inadvertently, this regulation gave rise to legal complications. In November 1459 Niccolò di messer Carlo Federighi married Tita di Stefano Segni and acknowledged full payment of a dowry totaling 2,000 florins from his father-in-law. The 2,000 florins had been paid in lieu of Tita's Monte dowry. Two deposits in the Dowry Fund, each worth 1,000 florins, had been made on her behalf. One had matured in November 1459, but payment was delayed. Another was to mature several years later.[95] After Stefano died, his sons in July 1460 entered into an agreement concerning the disposition of Tita's Monte dowry. A preface to the agreement underscores the mutual understandings that made prepayment of the Monte dowry both desirable and feasible:

> In truth it has been customary that the dowry be handed over especially so that the expenses of marriage can be more easily supported, which are great first and foremost in the city of Florence. For that reason Stefano handed over and paid the dowry in cash to Niccolò, not having waited for the day on which the dowry credits in the Monte fell due. Not, however, with the intention that afterward, when the Monte credits fell due, he would give yet another dowry or that he would assign the said credits to augment the dowry, but rather with the intention that the amount given in cash would be assigned in place and would stand in place of Tita's Monte dowry for the greater advantage of Niccolò, and with the intention of recovering from the Monte credits the amount in cash he had handed over and paid to Niccolò.[96]

In the presence of witnesses, Niccolò and Tita first confirmed the arrangement with Stefano and then consigned to Tita's brothers the 1,000 florins in her original dowry account, which was now collectible. Niccolò was still required to present the Dowry Fund's officials with a *confessio dotis* before they would disburse the 1,000 florins – an act that obligated him to restore that amount to Tita in the event of his predecease, even though it had been consigned as repayment for the advance. Accordingly, on their acceptance of the 1,000 florins, his brothers-in-law agreed not to hold Niccolò liable for restoration.

Starting in 1475, the Dowry Fund paid husbands only 20 percent of their dowries in cash and the remainder in Monte credits.[97] Even these payouts were delayed as long as three years. With the launching of the Seven Percent Fund in the autumn of 1478, partial and delayed payments had become permanently institutionalized.[98] These events decreased confidence in the ability of new husbands to repay from their Monte dowries the advances they had received from their in-laws. In 1494 Tribaldo d'Amerigo de' Rossi admitted that he was unable to repay at 8 percent 610 florins he borrowed from his father-in-law in 1481, since the "evil times" that had descended on the city prevented him from collecting the remainder of his Monte dowry.[99] In 1501 Niccolò d'Andrea degli Agli was promised a dowry of 1,600 florins, 960 of which was due from the Dowry Fund the following year, upon his marriage to Caterina di Piero Parenti. Piero agreed to advance Niccolò 250 florins when he consummated his marriage. Niccolò, in turn, agreed to repay this amount when he himself was paid by the Dowry Fund. Yet, in the event that Niccolò failed to receive payment from the fund, he would nonetheless remain obligated to repay his father-in-law from his own pocket.[100]

The Florentine husbands depicted in this chapter are intended to be contrasted with the stereotype of the overbearing *capofamiglia* evoked by historians of medieval and Renaissance Italy. Far from being fortune hunters devouring their wives' dowries, a considerable number of Florentine husbands were lucky to receive full payment of the dowries to which they were legally entitled. Husbands like Francesco Marchi were hapless creatures, who would have been much better off following Alberti's advice to seek a modest dowry that was payable rather than a large one that was unpayable. But where the economy of auspiciousness and honor override bare calculations of cash, and where the size of a dowry one family promises another reflects each family's worth in the eyes of society, large dowries are taken for granted. It was the desire to keep intact their honor as well as the bonds of *parentado*, I suggest, that moved husbands to seek remedies other than litigation to collect the dowries promised them. Private settlements regularly involved payment of compensation in lieu of the dowry and financial arrangements that appeared to be in violation of the usury prohibition. Yet, from the mid-fourteenth century onward, the interest paid to husbands on overdue dowries was sanctioned by virtually all jurists and moral theologians in recognition of *li emergenti bisogni matrimoniali.*

3 Materials for a Gilded Cage: Nondotal Assets in Florence, 1300–1500

Dowries customarily accompanied brides into marriage in late medieval Italy. In commercial and financial centers like Florence, husbands typically received dowries in the form of cash payments or their equivalents, such as credits in the city's public debt (*Monte comune*), which were easily converted into cash. Under the prevailing system of the *ius commune* – the common body of legal rules, regulations, and juristic doctrines developed primarily from Justinian's *Corpus iuris civilis* – ownership and management of a dowry temporarily passed to the husband during the marriage. He could invest, mortgage, and convert a dowry into other property as he saw fit, unless he forfeited his legal right to do so in a special dotal pact. As the expressed purpose of the dowry was to relieve the burdens of marriage, a husband was expected to apply income from dotal property to support his wife and their common household. Upon receipt of a dowry, it was customary for a husband, together with his father or other members of his family, to acknowledge joint liability for the dowry in a *confessio dotis* in the presence of witnesses and the notary redacting the document. A husband was legally obligated, and could even be compelled by judicial authorities, to return to his wife an amount equivalent to the dowry he had received should it be manifest that he was verging on insolvency (see chap. 6 below). Upon his predecease, property belonging to the husband, to those assuming joint liability with him, and to all their heirs was necessarily secured for restoration of the dowry. If the wife predeceased her husband and there were no surviving children from their marriage, her husband was entitled under local municipal statutes (*ius proprium*) to a part or even all of the dowry. The statutes of Pisa, Siena, Arezzo, and Pistoia awarded such husbands one-half the dowry, the statutes of Montepulciano and Lucca a generous two-thirds (on condition that the wife died at least one year after having been introduced into her husband's household), whereas the statutes of Florence were even more generous, granting husbands the whole dowry.[1]

Besides the dowry, a Florentine wife might come with, or acquire during the marriage by gift, bequest, or descent, assets classified as nondotal.[2] According to medieval jurists, nondotal assets were of two types. One type was called *parapherna*, or *paraphernalia*: items over and above the dowry (*res extra dotem*). More specifically, *parapherna* were defined in a mid-fourteenth-century legal opinion as "those movable goods which the wife brings to the husband's household especially for her own use and for her own and husband's joint use."[3] As found in Roman and medieval Italian jurisprudence, the term *parapherna* generally designated a trousseau, the personal accouterments accompanying the bride into the husband's household, although any real and personal property she inherited or acquired by other means in an ongoing marriage might also be designated as *parapherna*. The other type, *bona non dotalia*, generally consisted of real property and movable goods belonging to the wife that she did not bring into her husband's household.

In Florence, however, in stark contrast to both Roman law and the *ius commune*, the successive statutory compilations (1325, 1355, and 1415) omitted specific reference to *parapherna*.[4] Nondotal assets were encompassed by the single category of *bona non dotalia*. These local statutes mirrored practice: the Florentine *confessiones dotium* and *libri di famiglia* (books containing an informal record of accounts and notable family events, with discrete entries arranged by date) that I have examined for this period fail to provide a single example of movable goods (*res mobiles*) that accompanied the Florentine bride to her husband's house at the beginning of marriage being designated as *parapherna*.[5] In Florence as in other Tuscan cities, Roman *parapherna* had been largely supplanted by its functional counterpart, *corredo*, *doni*, or *donora*,[6] comprising the bride's personal belongings, lingerie, and ceremonial dress and amounting to roughly 11 percent of a typical dowry accompanying well-to-do Florentine brides in the fourteenth and fifteenth centuries.[7] But unlike Roman *parapherna*, it cannot be emphasized too strongly, the Florentine bride's *donora* were given, received, and treated by notaries, jurists, and legislators as dotal property rather than nondotal assets. The bride might also receive from her family on the day she was sent to her husband's household supplementary personal items and pocket money designated as nondotal gifts, or *sopradonora*. Although these gifts were never called *parapherna* by their donors, they were regarded as such by medieval jurists.[8]

It is reasonably certain that nondotal assets did not play the instrumental role that dowries did in shaping the matrimonial and patrimonial strategies of Florentine families; nor did nondotal assets share with dowries the dubious distinction of becoming the focus of the myriad disputes that pitted many family members against one another. True, some abstract significance has been attributed by historians of medieval jurisprudence to nondotal assets, reflecting the attention such assets have been accorded by jurists and legislators.[9] The role of nondotal assets in the domestic economy and in the devolution of patrimony in late medieval Italy, however, has yet to be studied by social and legal historians, for fairly obvious reasons. Foremost is that we are much less informed about nondotal assets than we are about dowries, for which we have abundant archival information. At the same time, historians of law have assumed that once women were dowered they were legally excluded from succession to the paternal estate under both the *ius commune* and *ius proprium*.[10] Thus they have embraced the comfortable simplicity that what assets, if any, wives might receive beyond the dowry must have been incidental and inconsequential. For their part, social historians are quick to point out that there was no shortage of Italian women in medieval Italy who received testamentary bequests, but they fail to note the practical consequences arising from the legal distinction between dotal and nondotal assets and the ways in which such distinctions may have affected patrimonial strategies.[11]

To be fair, dotal assets are easier to identify than nondotal assets, not least because the former were customarily classified as such. The technical classifications, *paraphernalia* (and its variant *paraphrenalia*) and *bona non dotalia*, which were second nature to professional jurists, were almost never used as labels by the parties conveying nondotal assets and, apart from exceptional instances, by notaries drafting donations and last wills.[12] The terminological problem facing historians in deciding whether the wife's goods should be considered dotal or nondotal has also bedeviled anthropological investigations of property accompanying Mediterranean women into marriage.[13] The problem is compounded by the vagaries of scribal habits. Notaries were inconsistent in providing the marital status of women mentioned in the documents they drew up, thus leaving to us the necessary sleuthing to establish whether a woman acquiring or conveying assets should be classified as unmarried, married, or widowed. The operative reality of the wife's property was less tidy, and therefore more problematic, than our historiography has hitherto led us to believe.

Far from intending to remedy past omissions by presenting a comprehensive account of nondotal assets in Florence, the scope of this chapter is modest. It presents preliminary research findings that suggest the legal, material, and symbolic significance of nondotal assets and their fruits in fourteenth- and fifteenth-century Florence. It considers first the legal regulations governing their disposition both in an ongoing marriage and on termination of marriage; second, the actual arrangements by which nondotal assets were created, acquired, and encumbered; and third, their disposition on the husband's predecease. The ascendancy of the husband's legal capacity to control nondotal assets and the corresponding attenuation of the wife's capacity to hold separate property are placed in the foreground throughout. In the end, my aim is to raise methodological questions and to stimulate discussion rather than to reach firm conclusions about a subject whose content remains to be clarified and whose boundaries remain to be demarcated.

Under the *ius commune*, a cardinal distinction between dotal and paraphernal assets was that ownership of the latter was vested in the wife during the marriage. If, as the jurists observed, it was customary for the wife to place paraphernal goods in the husband's custody,[14] was she constrained to do so as a matter of law? The Florentine jurist, Franciscus de Albergottis of Arezzo, insisted, in what became a *locus classicus*, that the wife was under no such legal compulsion: "Sometimes the wife gives over the management of these paraphernal goods to the husband, and then she is seen to have conceded tacit administration and use of them; and sometimes she reserves management to herself, and then the husband has no claim to them."[15] In a related opinion on the same case, Baldus de Ubaldis affirmed that the husband managed *parapherna* but did not establish whether the wife's consent, tacit or express, was necessary;[16] yet his commentary on the *Codex* clearly indicated that her consent was indeed required. He stated unequivocally that the husband could not manage *parapherna* against his wife's wishes and that she, as *domina*, could reclaim *parapherna* during the marriage.[17] As far as can be discerned, every jurist from the thirteenth century on affirmed that should his wife expressly forbid him the right of administration, the husband could not meddle with her administration of *parapherna*.[18] Unlike dotal assets, then, the husband's use of *parapherna* depended on his wife's consent.[19]

With his wife's consent, her husband could exploit the fruits and revenues accruing from *bona immobilia* treated as *parapherna* so long as they benefited them jointly. His obligation to return such fruits or their equivalent to the wife or her heirs upon her predecease was conditional. If the wife or her heirs established that the husband had received these fruits with his wife's consent, it became a question of what portion of them had been expended and what portion was extant. All extant fruits had to be returned to the wife. If the fruits had been consumed, it then became a question of whether they were produced by *industria* or *natura*. Fruits produced by *industria* were characterized as those derived from the husband's diligent efforts, that is, his own labor and management. Included under this classification were the fruits of olive groves, vineyards, and arable fields. In remuneration for the risks attending his management, the husband was granted a portion of the fruits produced by his own labor. He was thus under no obligation to compensate his wife for any such fruits consumed in an ongoing marriage. Nor was he obligated to compensate her for the consumption of a moderate (*modicum*) amount of "natural" fruits. If the amount of natural fruits consumed was characterized as large, then compensation was mandatory. A husband seizing paraphernal fruits against his wife's wishes, or employing them solely for his own benefit or self-enrichment, was required to indemnify his wife or her heirs.[20]

In theory, the wife who allowed her husband to administer *parapherna* could demand, and even sue for, their return at any time during the marriage. In the same breath, the jurists took for granted that the husband, as legitimate and actual head of the family, would ordinarily take charge of any movables his wife brought into his household; if she knowingly and without objecting allowed him to receive and manage paraphernal fruits, her consent was to be presumed.[21] That is why the wife was admonished to possess valid legal instruments itemizing her personal belongings that were not included in the dowry as well as attesting that she had received consent from her husband to bring them into his household. Otherwise, to prove that they did not belong to her husband would be difficult, and they would be unrecoverable by the wife or her heirs at the termination of the marriage.[22]

The husband, under the *ius commune*, exercised control at his own risk. If *parapherna* were dissipated or declined in value as the result of a husband's profligacy or mismanagement, his wife or her heirs could demand compensation from his estate. On the other hand, the husband or his heirs were legally permitted to deduct from the *parapherna* restored to his widow or her heirs an amount equivalent to the value of any material improvements (*melioramenta*) the husband made to paraphernal property, typically a house or land. That did not prevent widows or their heirs from raising doubts over the extent and value of such improvements in suits involving the restoration of paraphernal property.[23]

Bona non dotalia, to which the wife retained the dual right of ownership and administration, generally consisted of assets the wife did not bring into her husband's household. In principle, they were for the wife's own use but could be enjoyed by the husband with his wife's express consent. Although the rules established by jurists for the disposition and restoration of paraphernal fruits and revenues were extended to *bona non dotalia*,[24] there is evidence (see below) that Florentine husbands were able to exercise control over all nondotal assets and fruits in an ongoing marriage, with or without their wives' consent, in disregard of legal niceties. Since the average age of Florentine husbands entering a first marriage was roughly thirty years, whereas the average age of their brides was around eighteen,[25] it is hardly surprising that senior husbands sought control of all nondotal assets and fruits, and younger brides had little choice but to entrust them to their spouses or their fathers-in-law, when spouses were not yet legally emancipated. Here it is worth making a comparative observation about the behavior of wealthy Roman matrons, who could always divorce their overbearing husbands and Florentine wives, who could not. According to Saller, "the women's property often gave Roman husbands an incentive to be attentive to their wives' wishes."[26] Arguably, some Florentine husbands chronically in debt may have found it necessary to placate their wives, who for reasons suggested below maintained independent control over nondotal assets. Yet there is scant evidence that Florentine wives from upper-echelon families enjoyed the same leverage attributed to affluent Roman wives by virtue of the dowry that accompanied them into marriage or the nondotal assets at their discretion.

Ascertaining whether a wife had in fact given her husband consent to administer or even to alienate nondotal assets was a recurrent issue facing medieval jurists. Speaking broadly, the attitude they brought to such disputes was paternalistic, and they were inclined to be as protective of women as they were of minors, or of anyone who suffered legal disabilities because of her or his presumed "essential fragility" or wayward judgment. As a wife was regarded as a gullible and submissive creature to be kept in a perpetual state of trembling and fear (*in tremore e in paura*),[27] in all things a legal dependent of her husband, it was easy for jurists to demonstrate a priori that she was incapable of freely giving consent to her husband. On the issue of the husband's administration of nondotal goods, it should be presumed that he acted against the wife's wishes (*contra voluntatem uxoris*), Franciscus de Albergottis alleged, unless there were positive proof to the contrary. His allegation takes its force from universal gender-centric presumptions on the nature of women and the mutual obligations between phallocratic husbands and submissive wives:

> The second presumption proceeds from the very nature of women, because a woman is the most covetous of the species ... It is unnatural to suppose that she would want to bestow the nondotal goods on her husband, for as a general rule human beings act according to their own nature and their accustomed and common habits ... The third presumption proceeds from the proper relationship of persons, for while it is fitting for husbands to support their wives from their own goods and from the fruits of dotal goods, it is not fitting for husbands to be fed and supported by wives ... The fourth reason proceeds from the joining together of persons and its defining quality – namely, that between husband and wife there is a joining together that is linked to deference on the wife's part, and there arises as a consequence of that docility the presumption of dissent or forced assent.[28]

Paternalism aside, the statutes of Florence granted the husband direct control over all nondotal assets, with one glaring exception (discussed below). What accounts for this divergence between the *ius commune* and Florentine law? It was not a consequence of that all-purpose causal agent of late medieval history, the Black Death, which first struck Florence in the spring of 1348; the Florentine statutes granting husbands control had been promulgated twenty-three years earlier, in 1325. Unquestionably the calamities wrought by the Black Death and subsequent plagues had a sweeping effect on the general devolution of patrimonial property and the restoration of dotal and nondotal assets in Florence;[29] nevertheless, apart from minor verbal modifications, the anteplague statutes regulating dotal assets were repeated in the postplague redaction of 1355. Although the statutes gave no clue for the rationale justifying divergence from the *ius commune*, it is conceivable that they were designed to make fully lawful husbands' de facto control of nondotal assets. If so, the period before 1325 should not be viewed as a golden age during which wives had unfettered authority over their own property and acted as autonomous agents. Even if this surmise is correct, the question is invited: beyond the issue of direct control, what stirred Florentine lawmakers to respond favorably to the husband's demand to administer nondotal assets? The statutory schemes were primarily aimed, I believe, at placing nondotal revenues at his disposal in order to alleviate mounting financial burdens owing to expenses attending marriage and the bruising struggle to maintain and enhance the status of the husband's family in a world of social and political competition (see chap. 2 above).[30] What was happening in Florence conformed to a wider pattern in which legislators across northern and central Italy were granting husbands broad control over all the wife's assets, nondotal as well as dotal.[31] A noticeable exception to this pattern was Venice.[32]

Paradoxically, the Florentine statutes of 1325 and 1355 regulating the disposition of nondotal assets in an ongoing marriage were flawed by a contradiction. At variance with the *ius commune*, by permitting the husband use and administration of property acquired by his wife in an ongoing marriage, even against her wishes, they yet upheld the *ius commune* in that they did not encompass all nondotal assets. The statutes reserved to the wife use and administration of property bequeathed by her parents and her maternal and paternal kin, except where her husband was expressly conceded the right of usufruct in the bequest. As the bulk of nondotal assets acquired by Florentine wives derived from testamentary bequests made by parents and other kin, the proviso sharply blunted the general thrust of the statute to enhance the husband's claim to nondotal assets. It would be a gross misreading of the statutes, however, to interpret the proviso as an attempt to empower wives by granting them control over their own patrimonies. And it is unlikely that the proviso could have been, or even was meant to be, strictly enforced against husbands who seized control of their wives' nondotal assets, whatever their source. Its ostensible purpose was precautionary: to safeguard the wife's patrimonial property from seizure by creditors for debts incurred by her husband. Under the statutes suit could be brought by anyone acting on behalf of the wife, and in any place, for the purpose of protecting such nondotal assets against all the husband's creditors (*contra omnes creditores viri*). In principle, at least, the husband's creditors, rather than the husband himself, stood to lose most from the statutes.

The responsibility for reconciling a statute at odds with itself fell to the jurists. The muddle that threatened to render the statutes inoperable was addressed by the Perugian jurist Angelus de Ubaldis (Baldus's brother), who sought to demonstrate that the statutes were intended to benefit the husband.[33] He presented a hypothetical case in which the rent from two houses that had been bequeathed to a woman by her mother was appropriated by her husband, who was now defunct. Two questions arose from this state of affairs. Did the husband have a right to acquire and enjoy the rent? Could his heirs be compelled to restore the rent to his widow? In spite of the contradictory nature of the statutes, Angelus insisted that the overarching intent of the legislators was to place nondotal assets and their fruits at the disposition of the husband. At the same time he admitted that in reserving to the wife control over bequests of nondotal assets, the legislators had prudently avoided adding insult to the injury already inflicted by the death of her kin. His solution – granting the husband usufruct regarding bequests received by the wife from the paternal side, while granting usufruct over maternal bequests to the wife – amounted to an arbitrary, if expedient, compromise. Since in the case at hand the rent derived from houses bequeathed by the wife's mother, her husband was not entitled to use them, and consequently his heirs could be compelled to make restoration to the wife.

Angelus's attempt to make the statutes internally consistent and operable was feeble, however. It failed both to eradicate the fundamental contradiction that made legislatorial intent difficult to determine and to answer the arguments from the *ius commune* that could be called forth to support the wife's claims. That the jurists in charge of revising the statutes in 1415 settled the matter once and for all by deleting the provision reserving to the wife control of paternal and maternal bequests was no accident. They also tightened the husband's grip on nondotal assets by prohibiting a wife from alienating such assets without her husband's consent. From 1415 on, a husband could confidently claim that communal law gave him an unqualified usufruct of all the assets acquired by his wife during the marriage. The husband's exclusive control over his wife's nondotal goods under the Florentine statutes of 1415 was reaffirmed in an opinion delivered by Angelus de Niccolinis in the second half of the fifteenth century. The wife, Lucrezia, had acquired interest-bearing credits in the *Monte comune* during the marriage. While the credits were registered in a Monte account under her name, it was her husband, Bastiano, who collected the interest (*paghe*). Among the issues the jurist was asked to settle was whether the husband's heirs were required to repay such interest on the *ius commune* grounds that the credits and fruits acquired in an ongoing marriage were nondotal goods that belonged to the wife. The heirs could not be compelled to repay the interest, Angelus held, for the husband's claim to the interest was wholly authorized by Florence's statutes.[34]

The husband's victory on the terrain of statutory law did not mean that he invariably gained control of nondotal assets in practice, however. Room was left for donors and testators to deny the husband control of nondotal property by attaching a condition to their gifts and bequests that would reserve usufruct to the wife exclusively. Numerous instances of such encumbrances between 1300 and 1500 testify to their enduring popularity and their perceived efficacy in safeguarding nondotal assets. According to the jurist Alexander Salvii de Bencivennis, moreover, who wrote a commentary on the Florentine statutes of 1415, a wife required her husband's consent to alienate nondotal assets only if they came to her during the marriage and if her husband enjoyed usufruct. When nondotal assets were acquired before marriage or a husband had no right of usufruct, his wife had a presumptive right under the *ius commune* to dispose of them as she wished.[35] A husband could also be denied usufruct if he had driven his wife from his household, subjected her to physical abuse, or squandered his own assets. In addition, his wife retained the remedy of having a lawsuit brought against any of her husband's creditors, to avert seizure of nondotal assets or to demand restoration of assets already seized.

At the husband's predecease, his wife could demand return of not only her nondotal assets but also the fruits from those assets not consumed during the marriage. At the wife's predecease, remaining fruits were recoverable by her heirs. The husband's claim to nondotal assets at his wife's predecease was defined for the first time in the statutes of 1325, carried forward in the redaction of 1355, and fortified in the redaction of 1415. If she died having made and left a last will, her husband succeeded to at least one-third of the nondotal assets, in the absence of surviving children or "other descendants."[36] Alternatively, if she died intestate, his succession to the one-third was automatic, with or without surviving children or other descendants. In both cases, the remaining two-thirds went to her nearest living kin.[37] These statutes were diametrically opposed to the *ius commune*, which had made the wife's property-owning capacity the salient feature of nondotal assets. They ran afoul of the teachings of canonists and theologians who approved and encouraged wives, even when their husbands refused to grant consent, to employ *paraphernalia* for the soul-saving acts of giving alms to the poor and making testamentary bequests *ad pias causas*.[38] The Florentine statutes were also at variance with the statutes of cities like Venice and Lucca, where "a wife may make a last will respecting *paraphernalia* which she may dispose as she pleases, even without the consent of her husband."[39] Although no rationale accompanied the innovation that made the Florentine husband part successor to his wife's nondotal assets, it should be understood as a calculated extension of the legislation that had permitted husbands to enjoy usufruct of nondotal fruits in an ongoing marriage.

Legal commentaries, opinions, and statutes leave the impression that nondotal assets formed a substantial part of the patrimony of Florentine wives (*bona mulieris*). Our ability to test the validity of this impression is, however, handicapped by skewed sources. The sparse number of *libri di famiglia* kept by Florentine women unfortunately furnish only limited details on the administration and destiny of the gifts and bequests they may have received.[40] Married women, unlike widows who acted as the heads of fiscal households, were legally incapable of submitting separate tax declarations (*catasti*), thus impeding us from taking full account of their own assets and debts. True, husbands were bound by communal law to report in their own tax declarations real estate, goods, money, and, most often, holdings in the *Monte comune* acquired by their wives in ongoing marriages (*constante matrimonio*), but these declarations unquestionably underreported their wives' nondotal assets.[41] Nondotal assets acquired by widows who later remarried were exempt from taxation and forced loans and therefore were not reportable to the officials of the *catasto*.[42] In addition, married couples sought to evade taxes by not reporting inheritances that wives accepted after having moved into their husbands' households. This tactic was censured in an enactment of 1456, which ordered that estates inherited by married women must be included in their husbands' tax declarations.[43] Finally, in marked contrast to the husband's vocal acknowledgment in thousands of *confessiones dotium* of the receipt of the dowry and the terms applying to its management, his silence concerning nondotal assets was compelled by the civil law prohibition against interspousal gifts,[44] which prevented him from formally acknowledging the receipt of any assets from his wife during the marriage. That said, what follows is intended to lay out some of the ways in which nondotal assets were created and conveyed and the sorts of conditions attached to them. Information on nondotal assets is largely gleaned from last wills, instruments conveying gifts (*donationes*), and the registers of Florence's *Monte comune*.

A husband created nondotal assets when he made a gift to his wife in contemplation of his death (*donatio mortis causa*). Unlike a gift between spouses made *inter vivos*, a gift *mortis causa* was permitted under the *ius commune*. Since it was revocable and became fully effective only on the donor's death, a *donatio mortis causa* closely resembled a legacy.[45] The *donatio mortis causa* was an attractive option in situations where donors wished to avoid subjecting property to the constraints of testate succession and potential litigation attendant on nontestate succession. Arrangements that reserved to the donor continued use and enjoyment of the assets donated (*donatio reservato usufructu*) were especially favored. Cristoforo di Francesco Buongiovanni of Gagliano, a citizen of Florence, donated farmland with a house to his wife, but he reserved usufruct to himself during his lifetime.[46] So did the widow Lippa di Puccio, who with the consent of her guardian in 1371 gave usufruct to half of a house with all its appurtenances to her married granddaughter, Agnese. Two conditions were attached to the donation. First, the property was for Agnese's sole and separate possession; her husband was not to acquire any rights to the donation. Second, Lippa prohibited her granddaughter from alienating the property, which on Agnese's death would pass to the hospital of Santa Maria Nuova.[47] Sometimes nondotal assets were created by children who donated property to their nonwidowed mothers. This was a practicable tactic for making property available to one's father, while at the same time shielding the property from his creditors.[48]

More common were premortem gifts (*donationes inter vivos*) conveyed to married daughters, granddaughters, and sisters before the donor's death.[49] A large percentage of premortem gifts were intended to supplement dowries. There are numerous examples of this practice in the registers of the *Monte comune*. In 1457 Luca di Giovanni Carnesecchi provided his married daughter Ginevra with a life annuity by transferring to her his right to collect interest on Monte credits with a face value of 350 florins.[50] In the same year, Orlando di Cuccio de' Medici conferred on each of his married daughters – Cilia, wife of Francesco di Giovanni Guicciardini, and Caterina, wife of Antonio di Francesco Boscoli – the right to collect interest on Monte credits with a face value of 300 florins for the duration of their lives.[51] The credits were actually worth much less; their market value in this period fluctuated between 15 and 30 percent of par value.[52] The promised rate of interest, which was 3.375 percent in 1457, fell to 3 percent in 1478, and the real rate of interest was in fact lower, if one takes into account the frequent and lengthy delays of interest payments on Monte credits. In spite of such uncertainties, which made Monte credits a speculative investment at best, there were several advantages that made them attractive to potential investors. Because of their broad availability, Monte credits were utilized as collateral in myriad credit transactions.[53] They were also used to pay premiums for the funding of dowries in the city's Dowry Fund (*Monte delle doti*). Claims to both overdue and future interest payable on Monte credits had value, as they could be discounted or applied by citizens to the payment of their taxes.[54] Regrettably, the Monte registers seldom divulge the nature of the transaction (sale, payment of a debt, premium for credit, and so on) or the exigencies triggering the transfer to third parties of claims to *paghe* held by wives.[55]

Under the Florentine statutes women, even if they were legally emancipated, could not enter into legal acts without formal authorization of a guardian (*cum consensu mundualdi*), whom, it must be stressed, they were free to appoint. As Kuehn has shown, Florentine wives tended to designate as guardians their own husbands, a finding equally applicable to wives transferring nondotal assets to third parties.[56] Margherita di Albertaccio Ricasoli, for instance, received authorization from her husband-guardian Saladino di Matteo Adimari to divide into separate shares thirty-five rental properties that she possessed jointly (*in simul*) with Niccolaio di Lorenzo Soderini.[57] When a wife transferred her Monte credits to third parties, she often did so with her husband's active involvement as well as his authorization. Giovanna, wife of Bernardo di Guccio Adimari, on receiving authorization (*licenza*) from her husband to transfer her credits, appointed him her legal representative (*procurator*) to carry out the transaction.[58] When a wife transferred credits with the permission and legal representation of someone other than her husband, she usually relied on her husband's kinsmen, a notary, or even her parish priest.[59] Procurators were most evident in transfers of relatively large blocks of nondotal credits. Occasionally a wife's credits were transferred without any notation of her having received permission from either her husband or anyone else.[60] Can we conclude in the absence of such permission that she was acting in violation of formal rules and independently of her husband's wishes, or of any man's wishes? It is possible that she had acquired the credits under terms that gave her the right to dispose of them as she wished, which would explain why her husband's permission was not required. But other, equally plausible reasons may help to explain the apparent absence of male authorization. For one thing, the wife may have acted with her husband's tacit consent; for another, permission to transfer credits, at least in the ledgers of the Monte, was recorded inconsistently. Furthermore, in accordance with Florentine legal practice, a guardian's authorization could legitimately be granted *after* a transaction was executed. Although the guardian's belated permission, as far as I can discern, was usually not recorded in the Monte's ledgers, it was subsequently added to the separate instrument effecting the transfer. This was neither mere surplusage nor an empty formality. Without the solemnity of the guardian's authorization the transfer would remain legally invalid, making the party to whom the credits were transferred liable for their return. In sum, the evidence is too porous to support the assertion that Florentine women acting without a guardian supply "a graphic illustration of female self-determination."[61]

The evidence is in fact overwhelming that Florentine wives customarily designated their husbands as recipients of interest payable on nondotal Monte credits they had acquired during the marriage. Next to the credits registered under the name of Giovanna di Giovencho di Giuliano de' Medici, for example, the scribe noted that "Matteo di Aghostino, a doublet maker and her husband, takes the interest during the marriage."[62] Wives could also assign their husbands the right of temporary possession, use, and enjoyment of real properties they received as gifts.[63] Occasionally, wife and husband shared a right to the credits or to the interest, or to both together.[64] Joint ownership or joint usufructuary rights were primarily, though not exclusively, limited to Monte credits. Sandro di Benedetto of Prato, a citizen of Florence, gave all his real property and Monte credits to both his sister Maria and her husband.[65] The instances of nondotal assets possessed jointly by husband and wife only faintly resemble community-property arrangements found elsewhere in medieval Italy and Europe.[66] There is no indication whether these assets were treated as true common marital property (*bona provenienda communiter de bonis viri et mulieris*) over which the wife had as much control as the husband. The procedural disabilities circumscribing Florentine wives meant that in most instances such joint assets would be subject to the husband's administration. Whether they were subject to the testamentary disposition of the first-dying spouse or to the testamentary power of the wife, since the assets came from her kin, is not certain. What remains beyond doubt is the rarity of the phenomenon of assets held jointly by spouses, which confirms that, in harmony with Roman law, the patrimonies of wife and husband continued to be reckoned as distinct legal entities.

Premortem gifts to married women were conveyed under varying circumstances. A father ritually provided a gift (*praemium emancipationis*) on the occasion of his married daughter's legal emancipation. For complex reasons, this practice was less common in Florence after 1430.[67] He might also convey to a married daughter title to properties that he wished to shield from creditors and tax officials. Above all, in exchange for their future care, elderly widows and widowers would bestow gifts on their sons, but lacking sons or male heirs, they would turn to their closest female kin. At the age of seventy-nine, the widow Agnola del maestro Ficino gave all her possessions (worth about 660 florins) to her niece Lessandra di Daniello Ficino, the wife of Biagio Buonaccorsi, with whose family Agnola was living.[68] The gift represented a financial contribution to the household in which Agnola would spend her last days in peace and comfort. Such gifts regularly came with stipulations spelling out the recipient's obligations. On condition that they provide her 20 florins a year, the widow Bartolomea di Francesco Lottini conveyed to her married daughter, to her son, and to another person dotal rights and properties she had received as a legacy from her husband, Giovanni di Piero Foresi.[69] The link between care and nursing in old age and intergenerational settlements and premortem gifts was common in late medieval society and remains so in Mediterranean society.[70] If storytellers like Giovanni Sercambi of Lucca can be believed, however, encumbered gifts did not guarantee the recipient's attentive care. Sercambi devoted a novella to a rich Venetian merchant, Piero Sovranzo, who divided 30,000 ducats among his three married daughters, in return for which he would live with each daughter and her husband for a month at a time. His daughters and sons-in-law turned out to be ingrates, treating him with disdain, but through cunning he was able to take advantage of their malignant greed to teach them (and Sercambi's audience) a harsh lesson in parental retribution.[71]

The principal means for the conveyance of nondotal assets, whether large or small, to married women were testamentary bequests,[72] many of which reserved to the wife usufruct during the marriage. Ser Bartolo di ser Chermontieri, a resident of the parish of San Felice in Piazza, left his married daughter Chiara a vineyard of undisclosed value, the right to which she could "hold, sell, exchange, and do with whatever she wished." The bequest expressly denied her husband any right (*ius*) to claim or appropriate the property.[73] Niccolò da Uzzano left his married daughter Bonda 1,500 florins beyond her dowry, to be paid within one year after his death. In addition, he bequeathed to her all his Monte credits and movable property, providing an estimated yearly income of 50 florins that would terminate with her death, after which these assets would be transmitted to the infirmary of Santa Croce.[74] In his last will of 13 July 1479, Giovanni Amici left his daughter Brigida a dowry of 1,000 florins – 938 florins payable by the Dowry Fund and 62 florins in cash – and a trousseau whose value was to be determined by her mother. He also bequeathed a farm with all its appurtenances in the Upper Valdarno, stipulating that the property was solely intended for Brigida's use during her lifetime and that it was not to be included in her dowry. Immediately after having consummated her marriage, Brigida was enjoined under the terms of the second bequest to pay the friars at the Convent of Santa Maria Novella 20 lire annually to support a service in memory of her father.[75]

The conditional bequests of Giovanni di Francesco Tornabuoni, uncle of Lorenzo de' Medici, manager of the Rome branch of the the Medici Bank, and art patron, were exceptionally generous yet conventional. Under the terms of his last will (26 March 1490), Ludovica, his sole daughter and at the time fourteen years old, would receive a 3,000-florin dowry payable by the Dowry Fund, but only after the consummation of her marriage and after her husband had duly acknowledged liability for the return of the dowry upon his predecease in a notarized *confessio dotis*. In addition, he left Ludovica nondotal movables in the form of rubies, pearls, and diamonds worth around 500 florins, with the proviso that they were to be treated as her property, over which she had complete authority during her lifetime ("ut sua bona propria et ad eam pleno iure pertineant et spectent tempore vite sue"). Upon Ludovica's death the jewels would pass to her children, who were entitled to the bequest after reaching the age of twelve years. Should Ludovica die childless, the jewels would pass to Giovanni's universal heir and Ludovica's older brother, Lorenzo, who, it happened, was executed in 1497 when he plotted to restore the Medici to power. Next, Giovanni provided a bequest of up to 500 florins in cash, which Ludovica could use for her own needs and expenses as they arose, and, once more, he specifically barred her future husband from claiming and appropriating the bequest. Finally, he left Ludovica an annual sum of 50 florins that she would receive for as long as she lived.[76]

Married as well as unmarried women received nondotal assets when the heads of disintegrating conjugal households with no available male heirs named them universal heirs.[77] If E.A. Wrigley's calculations on the fertility patterns of stationary preindustrial populations are applied to Florence, about 20 percent of all Florentine couples would have produced only daughters.[78] The naming of daughters, sisters, and other married female kin as universal heirs at all social levels, not only in Florence but throughout northern and central Italy, represented a last-ditch effort to find a haven for patrimonial property.[79] In this connection, did women in Florence show a stronger inclination than men to make bequests to their married female kin, as has been asserted for patrician women in Renaissance Venice and women in Siena?[80] This question cannot at present be answered satisfactorily.[81] My impression is that Florentine women bequeathing as well as donating money and property to married women were preponderantly widows without surviving male heirs or with sons who were clergy. As heads of fiscal households, they were more likely to distribute their assets among their female kin than wives, who remained subordinate to their husbands. The widow Antonia di Antonio of Panzano, a citizen of Florence, divided her estate, including a shop in the city, real property in the *contado*, and Monte credits with a face value of 3,350 florins, among her three married granddaughters.[82] The widow Maddalena di Salvestro Serristori provided legacies, ranging from 25 to 50 florins, to her four married sisters-in-law.[83] Giovanna di Michele of Terranuova left two houses to her married daughter, Antonia, with this conventional proviso: if Antonia died without legitimate heirs, the legacy would then revert to her mother's brothers.[84] Finally, the right to collect interest on 25 florins of Monte credits belonging to the widow Alessandra di Nanni of Ponte a Grignano would pass after her death to her daughter, Agnola, and after Agnola's death the credits would revert to the commune.[85] As Cohn forcefully reminds us, fathers, too, named daughters universal heirs, especially in Siena, where this practice was routine.[86]

Admittedly, last wills may tell us more about the intention to convey assets than about their actual conveyance; beneficiaries obviously would not receive anything if they were removed from subsequent codicils and last wills or if they predeceased testators.[87] Breathing a sigh of relief, Tribaldo di Amerigo de' Rossi recorded how his mother's legacy intended for his married sister Alessandra was short-circuited by her death: "I record how monna Piera, on 6 July 1492, left and gave her daughter Alessandra, and wife of Piero Repetti, 100 florins from her own dowry should Alessandra have children with Piero, and Piera concealed her bequest from me. Alessandra died without heirs, and had she died with heirs we would have been ruined."[88] Beneficiaries might also be denied bequests due to insufficient assets in the estates of testators, the result of large business debts, tax arrears, or the prior distribution of assets through premortem gifts.[89] Such were probably the circumstances that prompted Francesco Guicciardini to take the precaution of demanding collateral to secure a purchase of several farms from two married sisters who had inherited them, "because," he explained, "in fact the sisters possessed only the name of heir."[90] Caution, therefore, was well advised in transactions whose fulfillment was contingent on a future inheritance, and it must still be exercised by historians charting the devolution of property from generation to generation largely on the basis of last wills.

Having registered that caveat, I would point out that last wills, notably those of Florentine husbands, constitute a valuable and hitherto untapped source of information for the critical issue of who controlled nondotal assets in an ongoing marriage.[91] A husband's last will manifested his intention to restore to his wife the nondotal assets that she had received, but that he had controlled, during the marriage. In his will Sandro di Giovanni Biliotti restored to his wife, Ginevra di Zanobi Fei, her dowry and "117 florins which, he acknowledged, passed into the testator's own hands from Ginevra's goods, namely Monte credits with a face value of 200 florins, which he sold."[92] Beyond restoring her dowry of 1,200 florins, Bernardo di Giovanni Portinari left his wife, Gita di Iacopo Ardinghelli, 200 florins as compensation for the goods, things, and property rights that belonged to her, but that, as he had previously acknowledged in a private obligation (*scritta*) and now again in his last will, passed into his hands.[93] Filippo di Giovanni dell'Antella provided his wife, Maria di Stefano Bartolini, the following bequests: 20 large florins that he owed her for reasons not disclosed here, 100 large florins that she had inherited from her mother, but that were now in his possession (*in mano dello testatore*), and 200 large florins, the sale price he received for Monte credits with a face value of 458 florins and paying 7 percent interest, which had belonged to Maria. Each bequest (*legatum creditoris*, in legal jargon) was made in recognition of an obligation that Filippo had duly recorded in his account books.[94]

Not infrequently, husband-testators acknowledged that they had acquired nondotal assets by accepting legacies on their wives' behalf; they also acknowledged appropriating such assets to their own use and beneficial enjoyment (*in suam utilitatem convertit*). Barna di Luca Alberti, in his will of 4 May 1390, acknowledged that he had collected and appropriated to his own use the fruits, money, and rents from the properties that his wife, Agostina, had inherited *ex successione paterna vel materna*. The total amount of such proceeds was to be restored to his wife, less 100 florins he had provided to round out the dowry of her niece. On 16 October 1392, several years after Barna's death, Agostina received from her husband's estate 600 florins for the nondotal proceeds Barna had consumed.[95] In accordance with the wishes of Nanni di Manetto of San Miniato, his wife, Fiora, was to receive her dowry of 40 florins, plus 20 florins that he had formally acknowledged receiving on her behalf directly from the heirs of her first husband. Nanni had spent this sum, which he characterized as his wife's own money (*propria pecunia*), to purchase properties that provided him with revenue.[96]

Clauses containing an acknowledgment of the receipt and appropriation of nondotal assets protected a wife by recognizing her as a legitimate creditor. In effect, they were the functional equivalent of a *confessio dotium*, which, under the *ius commune*, the husband was constrained from executing in an ongoing marriage. Admitting that one should be on the lookout for fraud as the motivation for such testamentary confessions, Raphael de Raymundis went on to advise that they be construed as valid so long as the husband was reputed to be honest and his wife swore that his confession was true factually.[97] Should the husband's heirs refuse to restore nondotal assets by claiming that they belonged to the husband, or refuse to restore the revenues they produced by claiming that the husband had applied them to the common benefit of his family, the wife or her heirs, acting as creditors of the deceased, could introduce the last will to prove otherwise. By the same token, in fixing the amount of his debt the husband sought to shield his estate and his heirs against exaggerated or even fraudulent claims.[98]

To sum up, *bona non dotalia* was a legal construct that served to unify diverse types of property belonging to married women into a single conceptually cohesive phenomenon. Although a minority of adept Florentines may have understood the formalistic distinctions between dotal and nondotal assets, it doubtless perplexed, or eluded entirely, the large majority. If we could ask them to characterize in their own words *bona non dotalia* – what I have redescribed as nondotal assets – how would they have responded? I doubt that they would have qualified the *bona* they conveyed or promised to convey with the addition of *non dotalia*. The documents I have examined suggest that they thought of themselves as simply providing gifts and bequests to married women for any number of socially prescribed reasons, among which were to supplement the dowries of their married daughters, granddaughters, nieces, or sisters; to supply them with a stream of income so they might live honorably during the course of their widowhood; to compensate family members for the care of aged parents; to ensure that patrimonial assets would be transmitted to the last surviving kin; and to protect assets from creditors and the city's treasury. For the large majority of Florentines with wealth, the provision of such gifts and legacies was a "self-evident activity" marking and affirming the emotional bonds between married women and their original families.[99]

How widespread was this self-evident activity in fourteenth- and fifteenth-century Florence and other comparable cities? Systematic archival research should permit us to detail the sources and makeup of nondotal assets and to estimate what proportion of wives in Florence and elsewhere in northern and central Italy were likely to receive them. It should also furnish data to analyze the extent to which kinship, gender, number of surviving children, stage in the developmental cycle, and, not least, level of wealth impinged on the decision to donate and bequeath nondotal assets to married women. Other issues that demand investigation are the relative contribution of income earned from nondotal assets to the financial support of the wife's family and the husband's utilization of these assets as collateral in business transactions. Finally, the records of religious societies, monasteries, convents, and churches should yield data on the transformation of nondotal assets into pious gifts and bequests.

As legal historians have repeatedly observed and as feminist historians have lamented, the wife's formal loss of authority over nondotal assets was a victory for patriarchy that attenuated the proprietary capacity of women in central and northern Italy during the late Middle Ages and the Renaissance.[100] Unlike their counterparts in northwestern Portugal, for example, where wives could retain rights over their own property and dispose of it without marital authorization, wives in Italy would not regain the right to dispose of nondotal assets freely and without first obtaining their husband's consent until 1919.[101] After recognizing Italian women's *deterior conditio*, we should remember that Florentine legislators and jurists made a resolute effort to protect the wife's patrimony from husbands who were incompetent, improvident, or scoundrels; that the regulations and remedies they instituted to safeguard the wife's claim to her dowry and nondotal assets, though perhaps ineffective in curbing husbands hell-bent on consuming her property and defrauding her heirs, were enforced by the court of the *podestà*;[102] that nondotal assets were encumbered to deter husbands from exhausting them in payment of their own debts, in the hope that female beneficiaries would thereby be saved from the disgrace of destitution; that husbands themselves, through testamentary confessions, sought to ensure on their predecease restoration of the nondotal assets they had enjoyed during marriage. Patriarchy's victory was thus undeniably tempered by paternalism. Nevertheless, circumscribed by both patriarchy and paternalism, nondotal assets were just more materials for the construction of the Florentine wife's gilded cage.

4 The Morning After: Collecting Monte Dowries in Renaissance Florence

Mining the data-rich records of the government-sponsored Dowry Fund (*Monte delle doti*) of Florence, in operation from 1425 until the mid-sixteenth century, Molho's *Marriage Alliance in Late Medieval Florence* (1994) has illuminated the fund's pivotal role in the city's public finances and the matrimonial strategies of its "affluent, powerful, and well-established families."[1] The fund was established with the following objectives: to raise monies to defray galloping war outlays and to alleviate the burden of providing nubile women with attractive cash dowries necessary for contracting honorable childbearing marriages and, by extension, for replenishing Florence's plague-depleted population. For the city's topmost families, the link between the availability of dowries and Florence's long-term welfare was an unignorable fact of life. Their Roman forebears, for whom it was "absolutely essential for women to have dowries so that they can produce offspring and replenish the state with their children," would have marveled at the Dowry Fund's ingenious instantiation of Roman patriarchal teleology.[2] In complement to Molho's study, my chapter examines the requirements and procedures attending the collection of the Monte dowry. The fund's requirements were not conceived in a vacuum; they were shaped by mutually reinforcing interactions between, on the one hand, Roman civil and canon law norms and doctrines, and, on the other, local customs and government policies.

In 1433, the year the fund started to catch on, a menu of investment options was offered to Florence's citizens and legal residents of its *contado* and *distretto*. A model deposit of 60 florins, under a five-year term, would mature into a dowry of 140 florins; the same deposit, under seven-and-a-half-, eleven-, or fifteen-year terms, would mature into dowries of 250, 365, and 500 florins, respectively.[3] A matured dowry was payable not to the wife directly, but to her husband – only after establishing that he was a taxpayer in good standing and had consummated his marriage, made formal acknowledgment of his legal liability and provided sureties for the dowry, and paid the contract tax (*gabella dei contratti*). The tax was paid on the whole dowry, including whatever cash and properties were given or promised to the husband beyond the Monte dowry, even when the dowry was paid in installments. Last, payment of the dowry required consent of the bride's father, or, in the event of his decease, that of her brothers or other male kinsmen responsible for her affairs. Demanding the collaboration of husbands and their relatives-in-law, procurators, and third-party attestators, as well as the commune represented by the Monte officials, Signoria (Florence's chief executive magistracy), and legislative councils, the collection of the Monte dowry was a sociolegal event leaving in its wake a voluminous paper trail, the chief source for my chapter.

Taxpayers in Good Standing

While the large majority of citizen husbands were able to demonstrate that they had filed their tax declarations with the officials of the periodic tax census known as the *catasto* and were taxpaying residents of Florence,[4] a minority of husbands for varying reasons failed to qualify as taxpayers in good standing. Without anything like a modern administrative court from which citizens and legal residents of the *contado* and *distretto* could seek affirmative relief, the recourse for husbands initially prevented by the Monte officials from collecting their dowries, but now able to show that they had satisfied the taxpayer requirement, was to petition the Signoria. After the petition was approved by the Signoria, it was presented to the legislative councils for their approval. In 1471, affirmative relief was thus granted to Raimondo d'Antonio, a scribe employed by the Signoria. From the time of his birth he had resided in Florence, but before 1458 he had not filed a *catasto* declaration because, he explained, he was too poor to pay his taxes, and in consequence was denied his wife's Monte dowry. Relief was not a foregone conclusion. Fortunately, he was able to establish that his declaration was included in the *catasto* of 1458 and to show that he was presently a taxpaying resident of Florence.[5] Piero d'Alamanno de' Pezzi, a citizen of Florence residing in Avignon, could not collect his 1,000-florin dowry in 1476 because his declaration was omitted from the latest *catasto*. This was an inadvertent oversight, his petition stated, for he had been enrolled in all previous *catasti* and wished to be enrolled in the present one. He was eligible to collect the dowry after his petition won approval in 1477.[6] Exile was the excuse proffered by Giovanni di Oddo Franceschi to justify the omission of his *catasto* declarations. As the sentence of exile had recently been lifted, Franceschi was declared eligible to collect his wife's Monte dowry.[7]

Since Monte dowries were restricted to citizens and legal residents of Florence's *contado* and *distretto*, foreign husbands were required to request an exemption from the government permitting them to collect their dowries.[8] To assure that payments went to taxpayers in good standing, the government, in 1463, declared that only foreign husbands residing in Florence or its *contado* for ten years continuously, and who during that period had been enrolled in the registers of forced loans (*libri prestantiarum*) and had filed *catasto* declarations, were eligible to receive a Monte dowry.[9] Florentine lawmakers complained that although a number of resident foreigners had complied with the provision of 1463, they rarely paid taxes. Singled out were husbands of Polish and Germanic origins who had recently settled in Florence. In order to collect their Monte dowries, foreign husbands were required to pay a supplementary tax of 5 percent in addition to all other gabelles.[10] Despite challenges to their eligibility on the basis of their taxpayer status, resident foreign husbands, after satisfying all requirements, were eventually able to collect the Monte dowry.[11]

Consummation of Marriage

The Monte dowry would be paid, in the words of the enactment establishing the fund, "after the husband had consummated marriage and not before" (postquam vir consumaverit matrimonium et non ante).[12] Attestation of the married couple's first act of sexual intercourse was made through oral declarations furnished by the husband and the bride's father and brothers to the Monte officials.[13] The bride herself was not asked to attest the consummation. Typically in her late teens, with slight experience outside her family of origin, she was treated as a gullible minor easily manipulated to act against her own best interests, whose welfare in legal matters and in property transactions was ideally and in practice entrusted to her closest male kinsmen.[14] Under Roman civil law – keep in mind – the bride remained under the authority of her father (*patria potestas*), who was legally and morally responsible for his unemancipated married daughter's welfare.[15]

While communal legislators were reticent about the rationale behind the consummation requirement, it meshed with the government's natalist campaign, launched in the early fifteenth century, to enlarge the ranks of legitimately born citizens.[16] Needless to say, the requirement was in harmony with the conventional wisdom that a nonconsummated marriage may have been fine for the extraordinary couple Mary and Joseph, but ordinary married couples were positively enjoined to engage in procreative sex.[17] According to canon law norms, by freely consenting to contract marriage in words of the present tense (*per verba de presenti*), the bride had thereby given her implied consent to subsequent sexual intercourse with her husband, and, if averse to following through, she could be compelled by ecclesiastical authority to comply with her husband's unquestioned right to consummate the marriage. Consummation, in turn, established a "conjugal debt," the reciprocal rights of husband and wife, as spiritual and sexual partners, to enjoy power over each other's bodies.[18] Representing the union of Christ and his church and making the married couple's bond indissoluble, consummation was considered an integral element of marriage.[19] Church courts could, and did, dissolve unconsummated *de presenti* marriages on grounds of permanent sexual incapacity.[20]

For a visible number of laypersons, a nonconsummated *de presenti* marriage was incomplete, prompting doubts about whether the couple deserved to be called husband and wife (*maritus et uxor*).[21] The recording in the Monte registers of both the husband's acknowledgment of sexual intercourse with his wife and the corroboration of his relatives-in-law fortified the marriage bond in the eyes of the law and wider community. Public acknowledgment of the marriage's consummation also served to deter either spouse from attempting to exit the marriage by claiming that only a promise to contract marriage at some future date (*per verba de futuro*) was given, or that consent to marry was defective – to give but two reasons – because it was coerced or because one of the parties harbored mental reservations.[22]

Yet the question lingers: Why was there a requirement whose fulfillment hardly ever admitted direct verification, even if by chance eyewitnesses were available to swear that they had witnessed the newlyweds together lying naked in bed (*solus cum sola et nudus cum nuda in eodem lecto*)?[23] As the Florentine jurist Lapus de Castiglionchio Senior (d. 1381) observed, "by the nature of things sexual intercourse cannot be really proven."[24] Instead of fixating on consummation, the government could have directed husbands to present copies of their notarized marriage contracts (*instrumenta matrimonii*) to the Monte officials.[25] After all, there was juristic unanimity that a couple's vows exchanged in words of the present tense to accept each other in matrimony alone established a valid marriage.[26] Plus, Bartolus de Saxoferrato, late medieval Italy's leading jurist, famously held that the husband was entitled in whole or in part to the dowry (*lucrum dotis*) of his predeceased wife, even if he had never lived with her, so long as he had contracted legitimate marriage *per verba de presenti*. The entitlement, Bartolus and Angelus de Ubaldis insisted, encompassed both paid dowries and dowries promised but not fully paid.[27] Although these pronouncements had considerable valence, they nevertheless lent support to only one side of a debate conducted among jurists in late-fourteenth- and early-fifteenth-century Florence on the husband's entitlement to retain the entire dowry upon the wife's predecease.[28] For opponents, the husband's entitlement was contingent on his having consummated his marriage. For still others, the surviving husband's entitlement to *lucrum dotis* rested on his having assumed the burdens and expenses of marriage, evidenced by having publicly removed and transported his bride from her household into his own (*ductio uxoris in viri domum*; *menare*, in the vernacular).[29]

From the perspective of legal doctrine, these dueling views appear to be irreconcilable; from the perspective of practice, they were actually compatible. First, Florentines did not treat consummation of marriage as a primal act disconnected from the husband's installation of the wife into his own household. Rather, they assumed that the *ductio/menare* entailed consummation of marriage.[30] Second, evidence gathered from *libri di famiglia* (family journal-cum-account books)[31] suggests that the interval between the exchange of *de presenti* vows and the *ductio* – and presumably consummation of marriage – was usually, if not always, brief. Likewise, the husband's acknowledgment of having received the promised dowry (wholly or as a first installment) customarily occurred a day or two before as well as after the consummation of marriage in the period preceding the creation of the Dowry Fund.[32] Taking measure of both legal doctrine and practice, the committee of citizens, jurists, and notaries entrusted with drafting the Florentine statutes of 1415 established firm preconditions for the surviving husband's retention of the dowry. Henceforth the husband had a statutory right to retain the entire dowry of his predeceased wife, without surviving children, insofar as he had installed her in his own household. The performance of the *ductio*, which effected the legal removal of the wife from the father-in-law's household, exempted her from paternal debts.[33] If the husband had not yet performed the *ductio*, he still retained the dowry, without surviving children, when he had both contracted lawful marriage, evidenced by an *instrumentum matrimonii*, and had subsequently consummated the union.[34] This circumstance occurred when, before the *ductio*, the couple had consummated the marriage in the bride's family home.

Although the new statutory preconditions went a long way toward mitigating the uncertainties attending the husband's retention of the dowry, they did not eliminate the financial disquiet resulting from the wife's death at the outset of marriage, whether before or within a few months after its consummation. In such instances, the wife's original family felt that the imperatives compelling them to supply a dowry – as a contribution toward the couple's marital expenses and support for the wife in widowhood – ceased to exist. Worse, payment of a sizable dowry, they felt, resulted in an unjust "windfall" to the husband. Worries that the wife would predecease her husband during the first year of the marriage induced Florentine fathers and their surrogates to pay dowries in installments. This tactic is more noticeable before the creation of the Dowry Fund. Another tactic was the agreement by which the husband would return a portion of the dowry to his father-in-law or his heirs should his wife predecease him during the first year of marriage (see appendix 4 below). Outside Florence, Tuscan communities addressed these concerns by pegging the amount of dowry the husband could retain to the point in time of the wife's decease. In Montepulciano (1337) and Lucca (1362), the husband could retain two-thirds of the dowry, provided his wife died at least one year after the *ductio*.[35] Elsewhere, the longer the marriage, the more the husband could retain. The statutes of Barga (1360) provided that, in the absence of surviving children, the husband had the right to retain one-third of the dowry should the wife die within a year after the *ductio*; a year after the *ductio*, he retained one-half; and after ten years, two-thirds.[36] Uzzano (1389) permitted the husband to retain one-third of the dowry upon the wife's predecease anytime within the first three years of the marriage (*matrimonium*). After three years, the husband retained one-half.[37] In Massa e Cozzile (1420), the surviving husband could claim one-third of the dowry so long as he lived with his wife for at least one month. After ten years of marriage, the amount was increased to one-half.[38]

For their part, new husbands claimed that they earned retention of the dowry as compensation for the hefty costs of getting married. In the words of the Florentine jurist Philippus de Corsinis, "even before sexual intercourse, it is necessary for the husband to shoulder the expenses for the wife's clothing and other accessories, as well as expenses relating to the wedding."[39] Philippus's view was reinforced by the eminent jurists Paulus de Castro and Alexander Tartagnus, who presupposed that even if the wife died before the consummation of her marriage, her husband deserved to be compensated for the many expenses and burdens incurred at the outset of marriage (*in recompensationem expensarum et onerum que plerumque per maritos supportantur*).[40]

Nuptial expenses of Florentine husbands and their families conventionally ranged between one-third and two-thirds of the dowry but rarely equaled the whole dowry. Yet the overriding perception that the husband's nuptial expenses, especially ceremonial fineries embroidered with gold and silver threads and jewelry with which husbands customarily adorned their brides, were consuming whole dowries – a perception only episodically reflective of reality – took hold.[41] Leonardo Bruni, Florence's future chancellor, groused in a letter to his friend Poggio Bracciolini that he had practically exhausted his patrimony on his own wedding, celebrated in 1412.[42] Prone to teleological moralism, San Bernardino of Siena sermonized "that there are thousands of young men who could take wives if it were not for the fact that they have to spend the entire dowry they receive, and sometimes more, in dressing the wife fittingly!"[43] By protecting the husband's claim to the promised yet unpaid dowry should his wife die at the marriage's outset, the statute of 1415 reassured bachelors contemplating marriage that they would be appropriately compensated for their nuptial expenses.

The fund's consummation requirement, in my view, was less an innovation than a refinement of the 1415 statute. The requirement at once fostered honorable childbearing marriages, while it protected the husband's claim to the matured Monte dowry, even if the wife died before the *ductio* or afterward but before the husband collected the dowry.[44] The same logic informed the statutes of a number of Italian towns in northern and central Italy, which made the husband's claim to the dowry of his predeceased wife contingent on either having consummated his marriage or having performed the *ductio*.[45] The fund's consummation requirement, as Klapisch-Zuber insightfully proposed, spurred Florentine husbands to perform their conjugal duty pronto in order to collect the Monte dowry, as it were, the "morning after" consummation, while it simultaneously deemphasized the ritual significance of the *ductio*. On the other hand, I find Klapisch-Zuber's influential observation that the consummation requirement resulted in a reversal of Florentine practice, in that before the Dowry Fund consummation occurred only after payment of the dowry, whereas from the 1430s onward the dowry was paid only after consummation, somewhat overstated.[46] As I argued above, well before the creation of the Dowry Fund the interval between payment of the dowry and consummation was generally minimal, with payments occurring both immediately before and after consummation of marriage.

The Monte officials relied on the wife's father, brothers, or their legal representatives to corroborate the husband's declaration that he had consummated the marriage. If called upon, the husband's relatives-in-law could attest to the time and place of consummation, details memorialized in *libri di famiglia*.[47] Bartolomeo Valori recorded the successive dates when three of his daughters (Isabella, Ginevra, and Lucrezia) consummated their marriages at his house in Maiano. On 6 February 1476, Lucrezia and her husband Piero d'Antonio di Taddeo exchanged rings "and the same evening the marriage was consummated" (e la medesima sera consumi il matrimonio).[48] Lucrezia's dowry totaled 1,250 florins, including 1,000 florins payable by the Dowry Fund. The jurist Virgilio Adriani married his daughter Alessandra to Giovanni di Roberto Gianfigliazzi on 8 January 1488. One month later, he recorded, "The wedding was celebrated in my house, where the marriage was consummated, all at my expense."[49] Roberto was promised a dowry of 1,200 florins, 1,000 of which was payable by the Dowry Fund. On 20 April 1499, Giovanni di Girolamo Buongirolami recorded "I led my wife Gostanza and with her I consummated the marriage in the house of Antonio, my father-in-law."[50] These and other examples indicate that in the late fifteenth and early sixteenth centuries it was common for the marriage to be consummated in the bride's house.[51] Admittedly, there were exceptions. The daughters of Marco Parenti, Gostanza and Marietta, were sent by their father to their husbands' homes, where, he recorded, each "consummated the marriage and accordingly the dowry lodged in the Monte was earned."[52] In recognition of the social, legal, and financial consequences resulting from the act of consummation, it is not surprising that both the husband and father of the bride took care to record its occurrence.

For families resident in the city, the procedure for attesting consummation of marriage worked smoothly. Only a handful of urban husbands, in collusion with their fathers-in law, were accused of making false declarations. Vannuccio di Arriguccio, the husband of Niccolosa di ser Manno di Antonio, collected her dowry of 500 florins in July and August 1459. In the following November the Monte officials received attestation (*fede*) that Vanuccio could not have consummated his marriage, since Niccolosa had died before he claimed it took place. Ser Manno, her father, was hauled before the officials of the Monte, where he confessed the swindle and was fined 500 florins, an amount equal to his daughter's dowry.[53] When officials had reason to doubt whether a husband had actually consummated his marriage, he, his male relatives, or his father-in-law were required to submit a statement sworn in the presence of a notary attesting that consummation had occurred. In May 1452, for example, the Monte officials decreed that Baldo di Niccolò della Tosa could have his dowry after having provided a sworn statement attesting the consummation of his marriage.[54]

Husbands residing in the *contado* and *distretto* or outside the territory of Florence were required to submit written attestation of the consummation of their marriages. The earliest reference to this practice dates from February 1454, when two brothers, Moldano and Soldano of Poppi, swore that Niccolò Celfi went to the home of his new wife, Papera, and with her consummated their marriage.[55] These attestations usually included both the date and place of consummation. With his hands on the Bible, Calvacante di Ottaviano of the Val di Cecina affirmed in the presence of a notary and witnesses that on 10 May 1484 he had led (*duxit*) his wife, Dianora di Guaspare of Pisa, to her father's house and with her had consummated their marriage.[56] Clerics were occasionally called upon to furnish attestation of consummation of marriage as well as its solemnization. Francesco di Piero, chaplain of San Pier Forelli of Prato, wrote: "I solemnly attest to you, lord officials of the Monte, that Lady Tommasa, daughter of Giovanni di Paolo d'Iacopo, has received the sacraments in San Pier Forelli and consummated marriage with Martino di Zelone of the Porta Lione of Prato, and on that account I have made this attestation in my own hand on this day of 10 August 1482."[57] Martino collected a Monte dowry of 100 florins the following year.

Confessio Dotis

A consensus existed among medieval legal authorities, grounded in the opinion of the Roman jurist, Paulus, that securing dowries benefited the state by enabling women to marry.[58] To that end, the husband's properties by operation of civil law were pledged (*hypotheca tacita*) for the security and restoration of the dowry. Neither Roman civil nor Florentine law, however, required a husband to expressly acknowledge receipt of the dowry and to restore it to the wife in the event of his impending insolvency or predecease in a legal instrument (*confessio dotis*) prepared by a public notary.[59] Notwithstanding the lack of a formal legal requirement, it became an article of faith among dowry givers and receivers, as well as legal professionals, that the execution of a *confessio* was indispensable for minimizing risk and safeguarding the dowry. In addition to conclusive proof, the *confessio* provided another, though less consequential, benefit. Presentation of the *confessio* established a legal presumption, in the absence of a notarized marriage contract, that the party on whose behalf the dowry was given and the party receiving it were legitimately married.[60]

Since at least the early thirteenth century, it had been customary in Florence at the time of betrothal for the wife's father and brothers to demand from future husbands and their fathers a promise to acknowledge receipt of the dowry and assume contractual obligations to restore it in a *confessio dotis*.[61] In their *libri di famiglia*, the *patresfamilias* of Florence have left a beguiling impression that the execution of the *confessio dotis* was predicated on the father's consent and express assumption of joint liability (*in solidum*) with his legally unemancipated son.[62] On 3 September 1465, Paolo Niccolini wrote, "I and my son Lodovico acknowledged to have had and received for the dowry of the aforesaid Checca 2,006 florins and 10 soldi in gold, from the commune of Florence [specifically from the Monte officials], which I guaranteed, as is customary."[63] When Filippo di Niccolò Valori acknowledged a Monte dowry of 958 florins payable on behalf of his wife Bartolomea di Raffaello Antinori, he recorded that his father guaranteed (*sodo*) his dowry "secondo gli antichi costumi."[64] Earlier, Valori's grandfather, Filippo di Bartolomeo, had mourned that his father had died before he could formally acknowledge the second installment of his Monte dowry.[65]

Even emancipated sons occasionally received paternal consent before they executed a *confessio dotis*, marking the gravity with which fathers viewed their own accountability for their sons' dowries. When Filippo di Lorenzo Buondelmonti acknowledged a dowry of 1,400 florins (1,200 due from the Dowry Fund, plus 200 in cash) on behalf of his wife Gostanza di Marco Parenti, he obligated his own properties for the restoration of the dowry and bound his heirs to carry it out. As extra security, Buondelmonti's father accepted partial liability for the dowry, as did his brothers, Antonio and Simone. "And the sons obligated themselves," Marco Parenti (Buondelmonti's father-in-law) remarked, "with the permission of their father Lorenzo, even though all were emancipated."[66]

The force of this behavior-shaping custom was captured in a petition presented, in April 1442, by Giovanni della Casa to the consuls of the Guild of Lawyers and Notaries, who were charged with adjudicating civil law suits against its members. Giovanni alleged that it had been more than two years since he had married off his daughter, with a dowry of 525 florins, to messer Francesco Pucetti, a jurist and member of the guild. Francesco, it seems, had not been legally emancipated by his father, ser Piero, also a member of the guild.[67] Ser Piero had promised at the time of betrothal that both he and his son would formally guarantee the dowry upon its receipt "according to the practice and custom of the city of Florence." He had failed to observe his promise, however. Giovanni stressed that ser Piero's nonobservance was deliberate, for he had personally and repeatedly asked him to guarantee the dowry, but to no avail, jeopardizing his daughter's dotal rights and welfare. Ser Piero's nonobservance may have been willful, but it was not wayward; it was probably motivated by a desire to avoid payment of the contract tax on dowries, which was calculated on the basis of the *confessio dotis* (discussed below). After having verified Giovanni's allegations, the consuls approved his petition requesting that the guild order ser Piero to observe the agreement to execute the promised *confessio dotis* in conformity with the customs and statutes of Florence.[68]

Contrary to the impression left by extant *libri di famiglia*, table 4.1shows that the overwhelming majority of husbands (70 percent), either because they were legally emancipated by their fathers or because of their father's predecease, acknowledged and guaranteed the Monte dowry alone.[69] A husband acting alone, with his father still alive, was characteristically identified as emancipated (*emancipatus*), in effect, legally capable of executing a valid *confessio*. The adverbs "olim" and "quondam" preceding a father's name signaled his decease and the consequence that his son was a legally independent actor (for a pertinent example, see appendix 4, below). Of the 291 husbands from the city of Florence in table 4.1 who received paternal consent and guaranteed their Monte dowries jointly with their fathers, 271, or 93 percent, were unemanicipated.[70]

By definition, an unemancipated son (*filiusfamilias*) lacked legal capacity to undertake contracts in his own right (*sui iuris*) with third parties,[71] requiring the consent of his father (*paterfamilias*) to receive and guarantee the dowry. Fathers had a moral duty under Roman civil law to give their sons permission to receive the dowry and execute a *confessio* – otherwise they would be unable to marry. Bartolus de Saxoferrato held that the mere act of granting such permission made the father himself liable, so that by operation of law his own properties were pledged for the restoration of his daughter-in-law's dowry.[72] Husbands who had not yet reached the age of majority (eighteen years of age in Florence) and whose fathers had died before they could give consent were permitted to acknowledge and accept liability for the Monte dowry after having first secured the Monte officials' approval.[73] This seldom occurred, since the age at first marriage for Florentine husbands was around thirty.[74]

Roman civil law, which regulated the disposition of dotal properties, invested the *paterfamilias* with a fiduciary responsibility to administer the

Table 4.1. Monte Dowry Acknowledgments (*Confessiones*), 1475–81

	Total Acknowledgments		Acknowledgments by Type of Residence			
			City		Contado/Distretto	
Party	Number	Percent	Number	Percent	Number	Percent
Husbands alone	363	19.05	270	20.2	93	16.7
Husbands alone/ fathers dead	979	51.49	740	54.9	239	42.9
Husbands with fathers	483	25.35	291	21.6	192	34.5
Husbands with brother(s)	62	3.25	34	2.5	28	5.0
Husbands, fathers, and brother(s)	9	0.47	34	2.5	1	0.2
Husbands, fathers, and brother(s)	9	0.47	34	2.5	4	0.7
Total	1,905	100	1,348	100	557	100

Source: NA 15037 (15 Jul. 1475–14 Feb. 1480/1), 1r–444r.
Note: Numbers are rounded up at the first decimal place. I have rounded off all percentages. I selected for analysis the *confessiones* reported by Monte scribes in NA, 15037, 1r–444r (14 July 1475–15 Feb. 1480/1), in order to correlate my findings with the data contained in the *catasto* of 1480, which applied to legal residents of the city of Florence. For a methodological discussion of the 1480 *catasto*, see Molho, *Marriage Alliance*, 361–3.

dowry on behalf of his unemancipated son. To fulfill his responsibility, the *paterfamilias* acquired a qualified usufruct – not ownership – over the son's dowry, and he and his heirs were ultimately answerable for its proper administration and restoration to the son's wife or her heirs.[75] In these circumstances, it is hardly surprising that the wife's family regularly took the extra precaution of demanding that the *paterfamilias* also assume express liability jointly with his unemancipated son for the restoration of the dowry. Paternal consent and assumption of joint liability were recorded in the *confessiones* of the Monte dowry.[76] The wife's family's disinclination to transfer a dowry to an unemancipated husband, absent his father's consent and assumption of joint liability, was underscored by the Florentine jurist Angelus Octonis de Niccolinis. Without the father's assumption of joint liability, as was customary in Florence, unemancipated sons in Florence would have difficulty finding wives.[77] Here we have a graphic illustration of "collateralized social relations," of how "knowledgeable actors construct economic strategies in which they employ cultural and structural imperatives that help to manage the riskiness of transactions. Just as material assets can function as collateral to assure economic outcomes, collateralized social relations can also serve as a presumptive guarantee."[78]

Florentine husbands acknowledging Monte dowries jointly with their fathers tended to reside in the paternal household, even after they were emancipated.[79] Among the 291 Florentine husbands in table 4.1 acknowledging Monte dowries jointly with their fathers, 84 possessed surnames.[80] Within this group, 59, or 70 percent, were listed in the *catasto* of 1480 as coresident, with their own families, in the paternal household.[81] Some, like Lodovico di Paolo Niccolini, were emancipated soon after they acknowledged the dowry.[82] Others, like Giovanni di Staggio Barducci, were emancipated after a lengthy interval, as much as sixteen years after the *confessio dotis.*[83] Presumably, the preponderance of unemancipated husbands had to wait until their fathers died before being released from paternal authority. Twenty of the 291 Florentine husbands had been legally emancipated – on average five years, two months – before the *confessio dotis*. Of these, 13 were recorded in the *catasto* of 1480 as residing in their father's household.[84] Several, like Francesco di Guido Bonciani, had already been emancipated more than a decade before the *confessio dotis*. Bonciani was emancipated in April 1463 at the age of twenty-two. Thirteen years later, in June 1476, he acknowledged, with his father's consent, receipt of a dowry of 1,300 florins, including 928 from the Dowry Fund, from Margherita di Francesco Alessandri. In 1480, at the age of thirty-nine years, he, his wife, and their two children were residing in Guido Bonciani's household.[85]

The behavior of husbands and fathers resident in the *contado* and *distretto* was comparable to the pattern observed in the city of Florence, though some specific differences are noticeable. Most important, a greater proportion of husbands and fathers residing outside Florence (34 percent) acknowledged the dowry together. Two factors were behind this pattern. First and foremost, legal emancipation occurred less frequently outside the capital city,[86] resulting in the direct participation of non-Florentine fathers in guaranteeing the dowry. Second, since the age at first marriage was lower (26½ years) for men in the *contado* and *distretto*, a larger proportion of their fathers, in comparison to Florentine fathers, would have been alive when the *confessio dotis* was executed.[87] Table 4.1 also shows that the proportion of brothers acting jointly was greater outside Florence, which may reflect a relatively larger number of joint-family households composed of married brothers in the *contado* and *distretto*.[88]

When the husband's father and brothers assumed joint liability (*in solidum*), they became principal debtors with the husband for the restoration of the dowry. Even though the husband alone may have received and enjoyed the dowry, their liability was equal to the husband's, and they could be sued jointly or severally as principal debtors by the wife or her heirs. Less regularly, though no less important in point of law, the husband's kinsmen and sometimes outsiders also undertook to guarantee the dowry. Broadly speaking, under Roman civil law, the liability of guarantors (*fideiussores*) was secondary, so that they could not be sued before the principal debtor for performance of the dowry contract. But in Florence the secondary character of the guarantors' liability was removed by a compulsory waiver which made them directly and immediately liable for restoration of the dowry, having relinquished the defense that the creditor (the widow) must initially demand satisfaction from the principal debtor(s) before bringing action against his guarantors.[89] Having discharged their obligations, guarantors, in turn, could sue to recover their expenses from the principal debtor or his heirs. Like the risk of joint liability, the risks attending personal guaranties were so great that they were generally avoided by persons unrelated to the husband.[90] Risks were customarily borne by the husband's closest kin, by widowed mothers with the permission of their guardians[91] and brothers,[92] and less often by paternal uncles, male cousins, and emancipated sons.[93]

Guarantees were performed anywhere from several days to several years after the *confessio dotis*. Guarantors could minimize their risk by restricting their obligation to only a portion of the dowry. Carlo di Niccolò Strozzi recorded that his widowed mother guaranteed (*sodò*) 830 florins of a 1,550-florin dowry that he had acknowledged receiving from Lucrezia di Marchione Dazi.[94] On 14 February 1477 Cecca, the widowed mother of Tommaso di Francesco Alberti, guaranteed the entire dowry of 1,400 florins which he had acknowledged receiving on behalf of Maria di Marco Parenti, almost two years earlier. Perhaps in consideration of the size of the dowry, Cecca's guarantee, though necessary, was not sufficient in the eyes of the father-in-law, Marco Parenti. On the same day Tommaso's brothers, Antonio, Filippo, and Daniello, guaranteed the dowry as well, with the liability of each limited to 466⅗ florins.[95] Guarantors at times insisted that the husband convert the dowry into assets carrying slight risk. That is what Matteo di Luca Da Panzano did by agreeing to guarantee up to 150 florins of his brother's dowry on condition that the latter convert the cash payment into real estate. Matteo sought to disavow the guarantee when his brother, Totto, failed to comply with his request.[96]

Taxing Dowries

Requiring husbands to produce a *confessio dotis* before they received payment from the Dowry Fund, together with the ubiquity of cash and Monte credits in dowry settlements, diminished their ability to conceal or underreport the dowries they acknowledged receiving. The *Statuta* of 1415 had censured notaries operating in and around the city for colluding with husbands to conceal dotal transactions, in particular those involving real property, from the officials in charge of collecting the contract tax on dowries.[97] Beginning in the early 1440s, a summary of the information contained in the *confessio* was recorded in special books by the fund's scribes.[98] This information became regularized around mid-century when a new standard clause that specifically referred to the payment the husband acknowledged receiving from the Dowry Fund was introduced into *confessiones* redacted in Florence.[99] When questions arose about the name and number of the parties involved, the size and composition of the dowry (the amount paid in cash, Monte credits and properties, in addition to the amount paid by the Dowry Fund), and the scope of the husband's obligations, a permanent record, on which officials could depend for purposes of verification and taxation, now existed.

Relying on the *confessiones*, the Monte officials were able to carry out with considerable efficiency the policy, inaugurated in the 1460s, of deducting directly from the first payment of the Monte portion of the dowry an amount equal to 7 percent of the total dowry.[100] This policy applied to citizens and inhabitants of communities within Florence's territorial state.[101] The 7 percent represented a charge of 4 percent and the 3 percent contract tax. These charges and taxes stoked resentment among husbands who were required to pay the full 7 percent in advance on portions of the dowry that had not yet matured. This happened when the total dowry was generated by multiple deposits with differing dates of maturity – a predicament ensnaring 50 percent of the husbands who collected Monte dowries. They also bore the additional transaction costs of having a *confessio* drafted each time they received payment from the fund. Predictably, a number of these aggrieved husbands failed to appear at the fund's office with *confessiones* in hand within the required forty-five days after having acknowledged their dowries. Adding insult to injury, they were fined 8 percent of the total dowry for violating the requirement. In recognition that its policy was counterproductive, the government changed course in 1462, limiting the 4 percent tax to only the portion of the dowry reaching maturity, while it continued to collect the 3 percent contract tax on the whole dowry. Two further concessions were enacted into law: one, in 1470, which reduced the 8 percent fine, the other, in 1486, which conceded that the 3 percent contract tax would no longer apply to the whole dowry but only to matured portions of the Monte dowry, as well as the portion of the dowry the husband acknowledged to be payable directly by the wife and her family.[102]

For husbands facing delays in collecting their Monte dowries, there remained the dilemma of whether to acknowledge advances they received from their relatives-in-law in a *confessio*. If they did, they would be taxed twice, once for the advance and again for the Monte dowry, which, after it was collected by the husband, would be handed over to his relatives-in-law. Francesco di Piero Guicciardini disclosed in his *ricordi* how he was able to resolve this dilemma. In December 1508, he and his father confessed to having received 1,040 florins as part payment of the 2,000-florin dowry of his wife, Maria di Alamanno Salviati, whom he had married in November. Piero Guicciardini, on his son's behalf, had already received 1,000 florins in cash, while Francesco had acknowledged "receipt" of his wife's personal accessories and household items (*donora*), appraised at 200 florins, but which, he tells us, were worth much more.[103] According to the terms of a private arrangement, Alamanno Salviati would grant Francesco use of a house in Florence for three years, along with a sum of money, which would equal Maria's Monte dowry of 960 florins, due three years later, in 1511. In return, Alamanno would eventually receive his daughter's Monte dowry. To avoid paying taxes on the Monte dowry before it came due as well as on the advanced payment, neither sum would be acknowledged in the *confessio dotis* of 1508. "And this was done, Francesco rationalized, not to defraud the commune [*non per fare frode al commune*], but to avoid paying the tax on 2,960 florins, whereas in truth the dowry did not run to more than 2000 florins." The plan suffered a momentary setback on 8 February 1509, when the officials of the *gabella dei contratti* accused Francesco of failing to pay the tax on a dowry alleged to be more than 2,010 large florins. Presumably, he was neither penalized nor asked to pay additional taxes at that time, for three weeks later he was granted a pardon.[104]

Filippo di Bartolomeo Valori deliberately defrauded the commune by concealing from the tax officials the cash and properties that his father-in-law paid him directly. On 28 November 1476 he had acknowledged receiving 1,000 florins from the Dowry Fund, guaranteed restoration of the dowry, and paid the requisite taxes. Then, on 12 August 1478, his father-in-law, Averardo Salviati, paid him the remainder of the dowry, 800 florins in cash and a trousseau (*donora*) valued at 200 florins. He consulted with his father-in-law on ways to avoid paying the 7 percent tax, and they connived to forgo the *confessio dotis*, thus concealing the second payment from the tax officials. But Valori was apprehensive that his decision not to guarantee the additional 1,000 florins in a *confessio dotis* would save him 70 florins in the present but might not save his wife, Alessandra, from costly litigation whose outcome would be unpredictable when she sought restoration of her dowry in the future. After consulting with their closest relatives and several jurists, he and Salviati decided that

> I [Filippo] should obligate myself in a private agreement [*ischritta privata*], noting the obligation in my purple account book, section A, page 54, where Alessandra appears as creditor of the dowry that I received from the Monte and from Averardo for her. And on the above mentioned day [12 August 1478] I executed a private agreement in which I acknowledged having received the said 1,000 florins for Alessandra's dowry, and I obligated myself and my heirs to restore the said 1,000 florins, with witnesses and acknowledgment that the agreement was in my handwriting, and with all the other solemnities usually required for such an act. This was all drawn up by ser Piero di ser Filippo of Volterra, public notary, on the same day, so that the truth may appear for all time and that Alessandra can ask for her dowry back without litigation or contestation, because such is right and proper and this is what I want. And I have made this notation to be the light of truth to those who remain after me, that Alessandra is to have the 2,000 florins of dowry without restriction [*assolutamente*].[105]

With only sparse evidence, it is hazardous to guess whether Valori's solicitude was characteristic of Florentine husbands in this period.[106] It is certain that for husbands scheming to evade taxation on their dowries the cooperation of their relatives-in-law was indispensable. Doffo Spini noted that soon after he married off his daughter Nanna to Francesco di Pagolo Falconieri, his son-in-law acknowledged having received 400 florins for the dowry. He was to receive another 200 florins, but because of the *catasto* and the contract tax, Francesco refused to acknowledge publicly anything in addition to the 400. In lieu of the *confessio dotis*, Francesco promised to give Doffo a receipt for payment (*chiarezza*) at Avignon.[107]

After acknowledging a dowry of 650 florins conveyed with his wife, Sandra di Antonio Gori, Manno di Cambio Petrucci recorded that he had an agreement with his brother-in-law "not to guarantee the said dowry. And I neither guaranteed it nor did I want to guarantee it."[108]

The Signoria and legislative councils routinely provided affirmative relief, after examination of the contract tax records, to widows and their heirs who experienced difficulties retrieving dowries because they could not produce a *confessio dotis* executed years earlier.[109] A petition of 23 October 1460 presented by Piero di Sante di Domenico, a wine merchant from Montevarchi, was generic. Piero explained that his mother Bartola had contracted marriage with his father Sante in January 1433 *per verba de presenti*, after which Sante had acknowledged and guaranteed a 125-florin dowry in a *confessio dotis* executed by ser Vincenzo di Francesco, also of Montevarchi. Sante had died in 1442, Bartola in 1446. Although he had been appointed heir in his mother's last will, Piero had accepted the inheritance only in September 1460, probably owing to legal and financial troubles with her estate. Better late than never, he now wanted to lay claim to his mother's dowry, but the notary's copybooks were lost. Instead of the *confessio*, executed twenty-seven years earlier, he furnished attestation from a Florentine notary who had discovered the record "in the book of the contract taxes of the commune of Florence" (in libro gabelle contractum communis Florentie, signato B39, ad cartam 36), referencing Sante's *confessio dotis* and the amount of tax he paid. As they had resolved in many similar cases, the government approved the petition, authorizing Piero to demand from Sante's heirs properties, which had been in his father's possession during his lifetime, equal in value to his mother's dowry.[110]

Consent of the Bride's Father and Brothers

Finally, before the Monte officials authorized payment to the husband, they required consent (*licentia*, *licenza*) from the wife's father, or, if he had died, her brothers.[111] Their permission was usually recorded in *libri di famiglia*[112] and in the wife's Dowry Fund account.[113] There are indications that the wife's father and brothers or their representatives were sometimes present at the moment the fund's cashier disbursed the dowry.[114] More often, the wife's father or brothers relied on public instruments for authorizing payment of the Monte dowry.[115] Acting "in luogho di padre" to safeguard the dotal rights of wives without a living father, or brother at least eighteen years old, the Monte officials regularly granted husbands permission to receive payment from the fund.[116] Before doing so they were required by a law of 1441 to assure that husbands had provided security sufficient to guarantee restoration of the dowry in the event of their insolvency in an ongoing marriage or predecease.[117] This was accomplished by asking husbands to provide security in Monte credits or real property equal in value to the Monte dowry.[118]

The *balìa* of September 1453 prohibited disbursement of Monte dowries and other dotal properties of female wards less than eighteen years old under guardianship of the Orphan's Office (*Ufficio de' pupilli*) without the approval of its officials or that of two close relatives.[119] Approval was forthcoming only after the husband and his kinsmen assumed full liability for the dowry. This enactment ratified a policy already put into practice. On 3 March 1453, for example, the officials assured that the Orphan's Office's ward, Brigida di Lorenzo Sassoli, would be fully protected before her dowry was paid to her husband, Andrea di Lorenzo Masini. First, he along with his brothers Niccolò and Otto acknowledged Brigida's dowry of 780 florins, 600 from the Dowry Fund, 125 in *donora* from her brother, and 55 from officials of the Orphan's Office. On 4 May Andrea's other two brothers, Benedetto and Paolo, guaranteed the dowry in a separate instrument. Satisfied with the arrangement, the officials gave their approval for the release of the dowry.[120]

Conclusion

The requirements and procedures for collecting the Monte dowry was a sociolegal event entailing an ensemble of interacting legal norms and doctrines, customary practices, and government policies. Before collecting their dowries, new husbands were called to certify that they were taxpayers in good standing, creditworthy, and legitimately married, and had consummated their marriages and started new childbearing families – all components of family-centric citizenship in Renaissance Florence. New husbands embarking on fatherhood tended themselves to be fatherless or legally emancipated. It is remarkable that 70 percent of the husbands (table 4.1) executed *confessiones* assuming liability for the Monte dowry as legally independent actors. This finding contradicts the captivating image projected by myriad legal texts and *libri di famiglia* of the centrality of *patria potestas* in Florentine family life. Yet the tenaciousness of *patria potestas* as a cornerstone of collateralized social relations in fifteenth-century Florence and Tuscany should not be underestimated. Nineteen percent of the husbands in table 4.1 were released from *patria potestas* because their fathers elected to exercise that very *potestas* to legally emancipate them. Tellingly, of the husbands collecting the Monte dowry whose fathers remained alive, the majority were unemancipated and continued to reside seemingly unindividuated, even after having been married, in the paternal household.

By law and immemorial custom, the bride's role in the collection of the Monte dowry was passive. She was treated as a voiceless minor, asked neither to affirm the consummation of her marriage nor to approve the dowry's payment to her husband. These acts were performed on her behalf by the men in her immediate family, in particular, the roughly 60 percent of fathers who survived to marry off their daughters. The void left by the wife's father's death was normally filled by her de facto emancipated brothers. In verifying that the husband's guarantees were properly documented and legally enforceable and that the wife's father and brothers had approved the payment of the dowry, the Monte officials performed a valuable fiduciary responsibility welcomed by all parties. The intricate paper trail documenting the collection of the Monte dowry made possible a sophisticated secondary market in which husbands were able to sell and trade their claims to overdue Monte dowries.[121] And last but not least, the same paper trail served, after the husband's decease, as the primary means for confirming the dotal rights of thousands widows and their heirs.[122]

5 The Seven Percent Fund of Renaissance Florence

Previous studies of the ownership of government debt in fifteenth-century Florence and early modern cities have concentrated on the role of the public debt in fiscal policy and the distribution of wealth.[1] Taking a different tack, this chapter investigates the accepted legal practice of encumbering claims to government debt, and its role in securing credit transactions and in shaping the decisions of a heterogeneous group of investors holding government debt in Florence. Although scholars have often noted the existence of such encumbrances, their function has never been examined systematically. The encumbrances chosen for investigation here were attached to credits lodged in the so-called Seven Percent Fund of Florence. Since this fund was a direct offshoot of the *Monte delle doti* or Dowry Fund of Florence and was inextricably entwined with the *Monte comune*, the chief fiscal institution of Florence, it will be best to begin by presenting a brief sketch of the fiscal and institutional setting from which the Seven Percent Fund emerged.

After the creation of the *Monte comune* in 1345, citizens who lent money to the government were issued a negotiable claim known as Monte credits.[2] But citizens were not issued individual certificates of debt; instead, their names and the dates, amounts, and yields of their loans were recorded by government scribes in central account books. A distinctive feature of these credits was their transferabilty and encumberability.[3] When credits were traded, the scribes were authorized to reregister them in the name of the purchaser; when credits served as collateral, scribes duly noted the encumbrance in the creditor's account. Future transactions violating the terms of such encumbrances could not be executed. A local network of brokers developed to facilitate transactions on the secondary market. Initially (1345), an annual rate of 5 percent interest was authorized. Over the fifteenth century the government gradually lowered this rate, which stood at 2.25 percent in 1493. Nearly from the start, interest payments were late and sometimes skipped entirely. Irregular payments caused secondary market sales to take place at hefty discounts, periodically falling well below 25 percent of par value.[4]

Among the measures taken by the government in the 1420s to alleviate Florence's worsening fiscal crisis was the creation of the Dowry Fund.[5] In 1425 fathers were invited to provide dowries for their daughters by making cash deposits in the new fund which would mature as larger sums after terms of 7½ or 15 years. When the term of investment expired, if a marriage had been consummated, the dowry would be paid to the daughter's husband. Legal residents of the countryside (*contado*) and smaller towns (*distretto*) under Florentine jurisdiction as well as citizens of Florence were eligible to invest in the fund. By the 1440s, funds were insufficient to pay the dowries as they came due. The government announced that henceforth dowries due husbands would be paid in installments.[6] Worse yet, in 1475 husbands learned that they would be paid only one-fifth of their dowries in cash and the remainder in Monte credits.[7] This arrangement imposed a significant loss on husbands, as the fund's officials employed an artificially low discount rate in establishing the value of these credits.[8] Even these payouts were delayed as much as three years.[9] Meanwhile, interest paid on Monte credits became less and less regular, causing their market value to slump.[10] By autumn 1478 it had become imperative for the government to take vigorous action to placate these husbands.

In November the government decreed that it would continue its policy of paying only 20 percent of matured dowries in cash. The remaining 80 percent would now be inscribed in the newly authorized Seven Percent Fund, so called because it would pay interest in cash on credits at the rate of 7 percent annually.[11] Nominally, 7 percent credits were equivalent to agricultural property in the Florentine tax surveys (*catasti*) of 1427 and 1480, the rents and returns of which were assumed to represent 7 percent of capital value. In reality, the yield on 7 percent credits was somewhat higher than current yields on property and more than twice the official rate of interest paid on Monte credits in circulation.[12] In addition to offering a higher expected value of return, 7 percent credits were explicitly given a prior claim to the same sources of city revenues that had traditionally been used to pay the interest on Monte credits.[13] Like Monte credits, credits in the new fund could be freely transferred from one party to another and could serve as collateral in securing transactions. The same terms of transferability applied to future payments of interest.[14] To further enhance the attractiveness of the new fund to investors, the government declared that 7 percent credits as well as interest payable on these credits would be exempt from all taxes, including the contract tax (*gabella dei contratti*).[15] It was a boon to those husbands who, if they no longer expected to receive the full dowry as originally promised, were at least in possession of an asset that was valuable, easily transferable, and in demand.[16]

The scribes responsible for recording information in the ledgers of the Seven Percent Fund were exacting.[17] The accounts opened for each husband enrolled in the fund and for each subsequent owner of his credits were maintained in a nearly standard format throughout its operation. Each account includes the Christian names of the husband, his father, and his grandfather, and, when it existed, the name of his family. Legal residents of the *contado* and *distretto* were identified by their locality. Initially, the same information was included for wives, but after the first several hundred accounts only the Christian names of the wife and her father were recorded by the scribe. However, the name of the wife's family can be supplied from the registers of the Dowry Fund. Each account also provides the amount owed to the husband and two key dates: that on which the husband earned his dowry and, second, the date when the 7 percent account was opened.

The scribes also recorded a number of details regarding the legal claims of third parties to the principal and future payments of interest: the dates on which claims and encumbrances actually came into being and when they were recorded, the amounts and periods to which the encumbrances applied, the names of the secured parties, whether they were acting as legal representatives (procurators) for someone else, and if and when such encumbrances were relinquished. In a number of cases the precise relationship of the encumbrancer (*conditionario*, *condizionario*) or representative of the husband or wife is spelled out. Each account includes details on transfers – for example, the date on which a specified sum of credits was transferred to someone else's account and the name of the party to whom the credits were transferred. For our purpose, transfers also encompass cases in which the credits were redeemed by the fund – that is, when the husband or his legal representative was paid the remainder of the dowry in cash, retiring his credits in the fund. When either husband or wife died before the credits were traded or redeemed, dates of death were recorded, as was the disposition of the credits. All this was complemented by a complete record of interest payments and transactions that did not pertain to the dowry. These data permit us to follow the movement of credits from the husband to third parties or until they were redeemed by the fund.[18]

Encumbrances

The following analysis is based on abstracts of 1,180 accounts opened in the fund between 1479 and 1486. Eight hundred and fifty-two accounts, representing 72 percent of the total number of accounts analyzed, were subject to one or more encumbrances. Encumbrances on the accounts were subsequently relinquished by claimants in 142 cases. They can be conveniently grouped into three types, according to their function (table 5.1).

The primary function of type A encumbrances, accounting for 31 percent of the cases, was to effect the *future* transfer of credits to another party. Transfer was achieved by stipulating either that the credits belonged to someone other than the husband or, more frequently, that they should be paid to that party.[19]

Mention must be made of a particular characteristic of the type A encumbrances placed on the first group of accounts, opened in May 1479. In later groups of accounts, many encumbrances are recorded as having been attached to the credits before the accounts themselves were opened.[20] In contrast, the accounts of May 1479 contain no encumbrances placed before that date. In this group of accounts all type A encumbrances were placed on the date of the opening of the accounts. We assume that some husbands, having consummated their marriages, thus satisfying the original condition for the collection of the dowry, had chosen to sell the rights to whatever additional payments the fund would make at some unknown future date.[21] All such deals struck between individuals before the opening date were recorded en masse as encumbrances on the opening date.

The exact function of many type A transactions is not always apparent. In 285 (77 percent) of the cases the purchasing party was identified in our records simply as the husband's legal agent or representative (*procurator*).[22] In some instances, procurators were actually acting on behalf of the husband's in-laws who had advanced him the dowry.[23] In others, it is fairly certain, they were deploying or trading credits in the husband's interest – that is, they may well have been acting as middlemen authorized to trade and encumber Monte credits (*ad permutandum, finiendum et conditiandum credita montis*).[24] This appears to have been the function of the used-clothes dealer, Lionardo di Tommaso di Pagolo, who acquired diverse parcels of credits and then proceeded to transfer them to third parties in the name of the husband.[25] Payees who eventually returned the credits to the husband also appear to have been acting on the latter's behalf. In May 1479, for example, credits worth 481 florins in the account of Buonaccorso di Giovanni were assigned to the banking firm of Bartolomeo di Lionardo

Table 5.1. Numbers and Types of Encumbrances

	N	% of Total
No encumbrance	328	27.8
Type A	371	31.4
Type B	131	11.1
Type C	350	29.7
Total	1,180	100

Note: Type A: transfer of husband's credits to a third party; type B: husband's credits encumbered by a third party; type C: husband's credits encumbered by wife's family.

Bartolini and Company. The firm was designated as Buonaccorso's authorized agent. In the following August these credits were transferred to the Bartolini account. Subsequently, credits worth 281 florins were retransferred to Buonaccorso, 87 florins in 1480 and 194 florins in 1486, The remaining credits, worth 200 florins, as well as the interest paid on all the credits were retained by the bank.[26] Conceivably the bank retained the credits to offset payments made to Buonaccorso's creditors and kept the interest to offset its own expenses.[27] It is also conceivable that the credits were assigned as collateral for loans advanced by the bank to Buonaccorso himself. Later, two parcels of credits would have been returned to the borrower when he paid off some loans, while one parcel would have been retained by the bank in repayment of another loan.[28]

In other instances, it can be argued that the husband had assigned and ceded to the procurator all his legal rights (*cessio iuris*) to the credits. Here, the cessionary was presumably *procurator in rem suam* (a representative on his own behalf), independent of the cedent and thus legally empowered to trade the assigned credits as his own and in his own interest. The appointment of a procurator *in rem suam*, though not spelled out in our records, was nevertheless a constituent element of a *cessio iuris*, and, along with the contracts of novation and delegation, a conventional means of transferring rights to credits in Florence, Venice, Genoa, and elsewhere in this period.[29] In May 1479, for example, Iacopo di Filippo di Onofrio Gai of Pistoia assigned 100 florins of credits to his procurator, Chiaro di Francesco da Casavecchia. Seven months later the credits were transferred to Chiaro's account, and in turn they were encumbered by another party,

Francesco di Buoninsegna. On 28 November 1481, with the authorization of his encumbrancer, Chiaro transferred the credits to Bindaccio di Michele de' Cerchi, a Florentine banker. From the moment the husband transferred the credits to the procurator, the husband's name ceased to be recorded by the scribes in subsequent transactions regarding these credits.[30] Cerchi's private account book furnishes even more compelling testimony that a number of these transactions must have been unqualified sales. On 17 April 1483 Cerchi purchased from Pietro di Iacopo di Compagno of Pisa 267 florins of dowry credits – the dotal capital owed to husbands entitled to receive payment from the Dowry Fund and not yet inscribed in the Seven Percent Fund. The price was 112 florins or 42 percent of par value. Pietro had been the procurator of Giovanni di messer Michele, his brother-in-law, to whom the credits originally belonged. Now, Cerchi became Pietro's procurator, a position that he described as irrevocable (*suo prochuratore irrevochabile*). Cerchi's claim to proprietorship, his ability to dispose of the credits in his own interest, surely rested on his status as procurator *in rem suam*.[31]

In still other instances the relationship between husbands and procurators is difficult to discern in the absence of private documents. Periodically, the husband's credits were transferred to the procurator's account, becoming indistinguishable from other blocks of credits there.[32] At the time of redemption, the procurator, not the husband, received payment for the credits. In this manner Lorenzo de' Medici, Florence's leading citizen, who became the procurator of Count Gherardo di Bernabò della Gherardesca, received 606 florins from the fund in 1482.[33] In other cases, the credits remained registered in the husband's account, but at the time of redemption it was the procurator, not the husband, who received payment from the fund. For example, the credits of Antonio di Manetto da Brozzi were assigned, but not transferred, to his brother in May 1479. Antonio's brother received payment from the fund when the credits were redeemed in February 1484.[34] The ledgers also contain cases in which the credits were actually acquired by someone other than the procurator mentioned in the encumbrance.[35] In effect, there remain cases where it is not possible to determine conclusively the function of some transactions – whether ownership of dotal claims was actually transferred to third parties or whether the right to trade or hold these claims and collect interest had been bestowed upon legal representatives acting on behalf of the husband. Having noted these ambiguities, we will treat type A encumbrances as sales.

Broadly speaking, encumbrances of type B served to grant someone who was a member of neither the husband's nor the wife's family a security interest in the husband's credits. It is probable that in transactions where future payment was promised, the husband granted a security interest in an equivalent amount of 7 percent credits. When payment was received, this security interest was released.[36] On the other hand, if payment was not received, the credits could then be transferred from the husband to the third party. Two complementary formulas were employed to record such transactions, which together account for 11 percent of the cases. According to the first, the credits could not be transferred unless the husband received authorization from the encumbrancer.[37] The second expressly stipulated that the other party was entitled to trade the credits at any time, or within or after a prescribed period (typically a year), during which time the husband could not trade them.[38] The formulaic wordings of such encumbrances are tantalizingly elliptical. Fortunately, *libri di famiglia* shed light on the usage of the formulas found in the ledgers of the Seven Percent Fund. On 4 January 1506, for example, Piero di Marco Parenti agreed to grant Antonio di Lorenzo Niccolini the right to trade Piero's 7 percent credits, with a face value of 300 florins. This encumbrance, which took effect on 24 February, as Piero related in his account book, would furnish security for 1,250 pounds of wax that he had purchased on credit from Antonio on behalf of Tomaso di Gino Capponi. The price of the wax was 112 florins, and Piero agreed to pay this sum one year later. The agreement was actually registered under the name of the wool merchants Giuliano di Zanobi Cambi and Company, of which Antonio was a partner. A subsequent agreement concluded on 7 March 1507 now placed Piero's 7 percent credits at the disposal of the silk merchants Battista Dini and Company, who had paid 112 florins to Antonio in satisfaction of Piero's debt. On 15 March 1507 Piero paid back Battista Dini and Company the loan plus 12 percent interest.[39]

Happily, the wording of the encumbrances comprising type C was explicit: the husband's credits were to serve as security for his wife's dowry, an arrangement necessitated by the risks and uncertainties associated with transfers of dotal capital. Upon the husband's predecease, his heirs were legally obligated to restore to the wife assets equal in value to her dowry. In practice wives did not always receive the promised assets. Even though the statutes of Florence in conformity with civil law granted the wife a privileged *hypothec*, or mortgage, over her husband's estate, his heirs often delayed or failed altogether to make full restitution.[40] A husband was not legally required to restore the specific cash payments, movable goods, or real properties he actually received, but only their appraised value, called *dos estimata*, as recorded in the dotal contract.[41] By custom a husband was permitted to transfer these properties to third parties, a practice that increased the risk that his estate might lack the resources necessary to restore the dowry at his predecease. The specter of insolvency also threatened the ability of a husband to fulfill his dotal obligations.[42] Prudently fearing these eventualities, a large number of families relied on type C encumbrances to limit the ability of their sons-in-law to dispose of dotal goods and properties unilaterally.[43]

The most popular type C encumbrance stipulated that the credits must be held for the security of the dowry (*stia per sicurità di dota*), but they could be traded and encumbered by third parties if the encumbrance was formally waived or if the husband received authorization from a designated member of the wife's family, usually the father-in-law.[44] This type accounts for 38 percent of all first encumbrances. A variant of this type, though less popular, is worthy of mention: here the wife's relatives stipulated that the husband's credits were to be transferred to a third party, customarily a charitable institution such as the hospital of Santa Maria Nuova, for the purpose of converting them into real property as security for the dowry.[45] Type C encumbrances were occasionally used to repay the husband's in-laws an advance he had received on the dowry. Simone di Bernardo Niccolini, for example, was promised a Monte dowry of 1,000 florins on behalf of his wife Caterina di Bartolomeo Gherardi. By 1484, he had received 333 florins from the Dowry Fund, and in September of that year he was assigned 667 florins of credits in a 7 percent account opened in his name. Half the credits were encumbered by Iacopo di Gherardo Gherardi as security for part of his niece's dowry; the other half were Simone's to do with as he wished. Three months later, in December 1484, the credits encumbered for the dowry were transferred to Iacopo Gherardi's account.[46]

Holding Patterns

A varied group of husbands who had expected dowries in cash found themselves holding credits. Some husbands retained the credits, others sold, and still other investors chose to buy the credits from them. Which husbands sold? Which husbands did not? Did the behavior of husbands from the city differ from that of husbands from the *contado* and *distretto*? Above all, how did encumbrances impinge on the holding patterns? The accounts opened in the years 1480 and 1484 were chosen for analysis because of the relatively large number of cases they yield. Individual years must be analyzed separately, since the expected and actual redemption of credits varied according to the date the account was opened. The initial accounts opened in May 1479 also yield a large number of cases, but the delay in setting up these accounts and the uncertainty regarding the imposition of the encumbrances distorts the timing of holding patterns, and for that reason they have been excluded from the analysis. We can identify eight holding patterns based on the placement and removal of the first encumbrance and on the first transfer of the credits.[47]

Pattern I (*no encumbrances*; *credits held to redemption*): The simplest pattern occurred when husbands held on to their unencumbered credits until they were redeemed by the fund. The fund began redeeming credits held by the 1480 group after a period of ten years and eleven months. All husbands had been paid off by the end of the twelfth year (1492). The redemption of credits held by the 1484 group began after eight years, and all but three accounts were paid off by the end of the ninth year (1493). For example, the account of Buonaccorso di Niccolò Buti, with credits worth 83 florins, was opened in September 1484. The credits remained unencumbered and were redeemed in February 1493.[48]

Pattern II (*wife's family encumbers*): Husbands were constrained by their wives' fathers or brothers to hold on to their credits until redemption. This pattern was implemented by type C formulas, which stipulated that the credits must be held as security for the dowry, and could not be traded without authorization of the wife's father and brothers. Typically, this encumbrance was attached to the credits on or before the account was opened. For example, the account of Andrea di Bartolomeo, with credits worth 154 florins, opened in September 1480. Although the encumbrance attached to these credits required that they be held as security for the dowry of his wife, Piera di Antonio di Giuliano, it permitted the credits to be traded by the husband with the authorization of Piera's brother. As this did not happen, the credits remained in the account until they were redeemed almost twelve years later, in July 1492.[49]

Pattern III (*wife's family encumbers*; *credits transferred before redemption*): As in pattern II the wife's relatives employed type C encumbrances, but here the husband eventually traded his credits after first securing authorization from his wife's relatives. It is difficult to tell whether authorization was given for the simple transfer of credits to a third party or for the conversion of credits into another specific form of collateral. For example, the account of Duccino di Iacopo Mancini, with credits worth 667 florins, opened in September 1484. They were encumbered for the dowry of his wife, Francesca di Filippo Rinieri. After receiving authorization from

Francesca's brother, Duccino transferred his credits in four separate transactions, the first occurring in January 1491.[50]

Pattern IV (credits transferred immediately): Husbands desiring cash traded credits immediately (within two months) after the opening of the account. Sometimes they employed type A encumbrances, which normally preceded the opening of the account. For example, the account of Giovanni di Antonio, with credits worth 76 florins, opened in September 1484. One month later, these credits were transferred to a third party. Giovanni had actually traded his claim against the Dowry Fund four years earlier, in September 1480.[51]

Pattern V (credits transferred before redemption): Even though their credits were free from encumbrances, a number of husbands did not trade them immediately after the account opened. They held on to the credits for a relatively long time, eventually trading them to third parties and frequently employing type A encumbrances. For example, the account of Iacopo di Giovanni Bracci, with credits worth 67 florins, opened in September 1484. Never encumbered, these credits were traded to a third party in March 1491, shortly before they were redeemed by the fund.[52]

Pattern VI (third party encumbers; credits transferred before redemption): Husbands were constrained to hold on to their credits because they had granted a security interest to a third party using type B encumbrances. In a number of cases, after the secured party relinquished its interest in the credits, the credits were eventually traded to a different party. For example, the account of Domenico di Giorgio di Domenico, with credits worth 51 florins, opened in September 1480. By virtue of an agreement concluded in February 1484, Domenico granted the banker Bindaccio di Michele Cerchi a security interest in his credits. Domenico's right to trade his credits was suspended for one year, commencing on the date the security interest took effect. During that same period Bindaccio was entitled to trade the credits at his own discretion. But Bindaccio formally waived his interest eight months later, in October 1484. Liberated from all constraints, Domenico nevertheless waited sixteen months before he liquidated his holdings.[53]

Pattern VII (third party encumbers; credits held to redemption): The same scenario as in pattern VI was followed, except that instead of trading their credits husbands held them until they were redeemed by the fund. For example, the account of ser Giovanni di ser Matteo da Falgano, a citizen of Florence and an active notary, with credits worth 200 florins, was opened in September 1484. A type B encumbrance attached to his credits in

August 1485 was subsequently relinquished in September 1486. Although the interest paid on these credits was subject to six separate encumbrances, the credits themselves remained unencumbered in his account until February 1493, when they were redeemed.[54]

Pattern VIII (credits transferred to wife's family): Husbands transferred their credits to the wife's relatives, conceivably as repayment for cash advanced before the opening of their accounts in the Seven Percent Fund.[55] For example, the account of Bartolomeo di Giovanni di Luca Riccardi, with credits worth 667 florins, was opened in September 1484. At the same time, using a type C encumbrance, Bartolomeo granted a security interest in these credits to his brother-in-law, Iacopo di Scolaio di Tommaso. In October 1485, credits amounting to 200 florins were transferred to Iacopo's account.[56]

What role did residence play in determining the husband's decision to retain his credits? To answer this question, the accounts are divided into two categories, Florentine and non-Florentine. Husbands without toponymics are treated here as legal residents of Florence and therefore designated as Florentine. The rest, including all those domiciled in the *contado* as well as in the smaller urban centers such as Pisa, Pistoia, Arezzo, and so on, have been classified as non-Florentine. Admittedly, this classification is approximate. The division employed here reflects the form of the husband's name recorded in the ledgers of the fund. Those husbands with toponyms such as "d'Incisa," "da Montelupo," "da Volterra," and the like we classify as non-Florentine.[57] However, some of these husbands with toponyms actually lived permanently or seasonally in the city.[58] In contrast, the phenomenon of Florentine husbands – that is, citizens of Florence – residing permanently in the *contado* or *distretto* was rare. Thus, statistics computed for the non-Florentine group are weighted averages of the true values of the Florentine and non-Florentine groups. Any distinctions found between the two groups would be even starker if we could separate the husbands by actual residence.

A substantial number of non-Florentines held their credits until redemption (pattern I), even though it appears that they were not required to do so. As is evident in table 5.3, 20 percent of these husbands in 1480 and 18 percent in 1484 followed this pattern. By contrast, such passive behavior was less common among the Florentines: only 8 percent of them fell into this category in 1480 and even fewer, 4 percent, in 1484. There are several possible explanations for this difference. On the one hand, residents of the capital city learned the workings of the market in Monte credits and the possible advantages of holding or transferring their credits in the normal course of their lives. Residents of the *contado* and *distretto* did not

Table 5.2. Florentine and Non-Florentine Accounts

	1480	1484	Total
Full sample:			
Florentine	210	163	
Non-Florentine	119	155	
Total	329	318	647
Usable subset:			
Florentine	184	145	
Non-Florentine	115	141	
Total	299	286	585

Table 5.3. Holding Patterns

Pattern	1480, Florentine (%)	1484, Florentine (%)	1480, Non-Florentine (%)	1484, Non-Florentine (%)
I	11 (6)	6 (4)	23 (20)	28 (18)
II	37 (20)	24 (16)	18 (18)	15 (10)
III	38 (21)	2 (1.5)	6 (5)	6 (4)
IV	40 (22)	53 (36)	15 (13)	44 (28)
V	18 (10)	12 (8.5)	23 (20)	37 (24)
VI	12 (6)	6 (4)	8 (7)	5 (3)
VII	2 (1)	2 (1)	7 (6)	3 (2)
VIII	10 (5)	3 (2)	6 (5)	5 (3)
No. explained	168 (91)	108 (74)	106 (92)	143 (92)
Total	184 (100)	145 (100)	115 (100)	155 (100)

Note: I, no encumbrances, credits held to redemption; II, wife's family encumbers; III, wife's family encumbers, credits transferred before redemption; IV, credits transferred immediately; V, credits transferred before redemption; VI, third party encumbers, credits transferred before redemption; VII, third party encumbers, credits held to redemption; VIII, credits transferred to wife's family.

easily acquire this information, and traveling to the capital city or appointing procurators to execute trades would have been more costly to them.[59] These costs may have made participation in the market less attractive. On the other hand, many more husbands hailed from localities within easy access to Florence than from the distant corners of Florence's territorial state. There is no reason to believe that transaction costs would have deterred them from unloading 7 percent credits in the market. These credits represented an attractive investment for non-Florentine husbands, who chose to hold them until redemption rather than transfer them. Given the relatively limited range of local investment opportunities in comparison to those found in the capital city, there was an advantage in retaining an investment that was at once stable and profitable.

The relatively stable asset value and the availability of 7 percent credits also made them an excellent vehicle for the wife's family to ensure the preservation of her dowry. In the capital city, it was quite common for the wife's family to curtail the husband's ability to transfer 7 percent credits with encumbrances. Holding patterns II and III include 41 percent of Florentine accounts in 1480 and 17.5 percent in 1484. Conversely, in non-Florentine accounts such encumbrances constituted 21 percent of the cases in 1480 and 14 percent in 1484. If the difference between the two groups was slight in 1484, it is clear nevertheless that overall encumbrances were more popular among Florentine than non-Florentine husbands.

Obviously, a strong correlation exists between the presence or absence of explicit restrictions placed by the wife's family on the ways in which the husband could invest the dowry and the retention of capital in the fund. Among Florentine husbands 49 percent of the accounts opened in 1480 and encumbered by the wife's family were held to redemption, while only 14 percent of the unencumbered accounts were so held. Likewise, 94 percent of the accounts opened in 1484 and encumbered by the wife's family were held to redemption, while this happened in only 10 percent of the unencumbered accounts.[60] The accounts opened in 1480 began to be redeemed only in 1491, and the 1484 group in 1493. At first glance, the finding that encumbered credits were considerably less likely to be transferred appears trivial. Yet these percentages reveal only part of a complex operation. While the encumbrance remained in force, it was fairly common for the husband's in-laws to authorize him to use the credits as collateral in other transactions or to transfer them. Occasionally encumbrances were explicitly waived by the wife's family, permitting husbands to transfer their credits, yet while some husbands chose to sell immediately, others kept the credits for months and sometimes years, even though they were now perfectly free to transfer them. The following examples illustrate the variety and complexity of these practices.

Antonio di Niccolò Da Filicaia's 7 percent account was opened in September 1480 with 667 florins of credits that were encumbered by his father-in-law, Tommaso di Giovanni Lapi. From March 1483 until April 1492 the credits served as collateral, with Lapi's authorization, in a transaction that Da Filicaia had concluded with a third party. He was also permitted to transfer credits worth 100 florins in January 1491. In July 1492, one month after his father-in-law relinquished the encumbrance securing the dowry, Lapi's remaining credits were redeemed by the fund.[61] The credits (333 florins) lodged in the 7 percent account of Francesco di Giuliano di Iacopo Benitendi at the time of its opening in September 1480 were encumbered by Vittorio di Lorenzo Ghiberti, his father-in-law and son of the famous sculptor.[62] Ghiberti waived his encumbrance in November 1481, permitting Benitendi to use the credits as collateral in a transaction six months later, in April 1482. After this encumbrance lapsed in October of the same year, Benitendi transferred his credits in four separate lots.[63] The account of Roberto di Giovanni Venturi was opened in September 1484 with 634 florins in credits encumbered by his brother-in-law, Niccolò di Alessandro Machiavelli (cousin of Niccolò di Bernardo Machiavelli, author of *The Prince*). He relinquished the encumbrance in July 1486, permitting his brother-in-law to transfer a small parcel of credits (34 florins). Venturi held on to the remaining credits until they were redeemed in February 1493.[64] Finally, the account of Bartolomeo di Giovanni Riccardi, which was opened in September 1484 with a balance of 667 florins, was encumbered by his brother-in-law, Iacopo di Scolaio Ciacchi. In May 1485 the Monte officials encumbered a block of Riccardi's credits for one year. The purpose of the encumbrance is not entirely clear. Riccardi's father was in tax arrears, and under the terms of the encumbrance the Monte officials could claim the credits to satisfy the arrears. However, they permitted the encumbrance to lapse, thus leaving the credits in place. Six months later, in October 1485, credits worth 200 florins were transferred to Iacopo Ciacchi, perhaps as repayment for an advance on Riccardi's dowry. The credits left over were transferred in three separate transactions in 1488.[65]

Encumbrances placed by the wife's family on the husband's credits thus were not as inflexible as the percentages in table 5.4 might lead us to suppose at first glance. In consultation with their in-laws, husbands employed encumbered credits to secure nondotal transactions. There was joint recognition that the credits should be used productively, so long as the dowry was not put in jeopardy. This goal could be achieved because the wife's family had to approve any security transaction and sale contemplated by the husband. Yet why, it must be asked, if safeguarding the dowry was a paramount consideration, would the wife's family allow the husband to transfer credits dedicated to that purpose, and why would it sometimes relinquish the original encumbrance altogether? The decisions to remove

Table 5.4. Percentage of Credits Held to Redemption

	Florentine		Non-Florentine	
	1480	1484	1480	1484
Unencumbered	16	8	38	26
Dotal encumbrances	49	92	75	71
Nondotal encumbrances	14	24	45	31

the original encumbrance and to permit husbands to transfer credits, we assume, emerged in the course of negotiations between a husband and members of his own family and his in-laws. Despite the absence of evidence illuminating the decision-making process, it is probable that the decision to disencumber credits was made when the husband was able to provide alternative security – either other assets or guarantors.[66]

Husbands wishing to dispose of their 7 percent credits in the secondary market attracted a large pool of potential buyers. First and foremost were bankers and businessmen, professional traders in all types of Monte credits.[67] A second pool comprised investors who purchased the credits for income. The banker Bindaccio di Michele Cerchi recorded two purchases of 7 percent credits at 73 and 84 percent of par value on 7 May 1483 and 31 August 1484, respectively. If we view the credits as perpetuities (assuming that they would pay 7 percent forever but would never be redeemed by the government), these values correspond to approximately 9.6 and 8.3 percent annual returns.[68] Seven percent credits were a good option for investors preferring peace of mind to higher-yielding, but riskier, short-term commercial loans. Interest on 7 percent credits was paid with only minor delays from 1479 until at least 1496 (see appendix 5). Regular payment of promised interest (which resulted in relative price stability) and tax advantages, needless to say, combined to make 7 percent credits highly marketable "securities."

A third pool of investors included individuals wishing to enter into security transactions without paying the contract tax. In fact, a considerable number of individuals acquired 7 percent credits for the purpose of guaranteeing title to real property that they had sold. For example, Piera, identified as the wife of Tommaso di Neri d'Antonio de' Siri, acquired in December 1482 credits worth 67 florins. The encumbrance attached to these credits tells us that they could not be transferred without the authorization of the dyer Ugolino di Miniato (or his heirs), to whom in 1477 Piera and Tommaso had sold the rights to half a farm located in the *contado.* Should another party come forward asserting superior title to the farm property, Ugolino could lawfully claim the credits as indemnification for legal expenses undertaken in defense of his own title as well as for the loss incurred should he have to vacate the farm. At the same time Piera and Tommaso were entitled to retain rights to all interest payable on these credits. The identical encumbrance was attached to three other parcels of property that Piera acquired soon after.[69]

Fathers wishing to supplement the portion of their daughters' dowries paid by the Dowry Fund constituted a fourth pool of purchasers of credits in the secondary market. Typically, the father placed an encumbrance on the credits he purchased, stipulating that they remain in the fund (in trust, as it were) until the consummation of his daughter's marriage, when they would be transferred to her husband. Meanwhile, the father or someone he designated, usually his sons, would collect the 7 percent interest.[70] He also designated younger daughters or relatives who would succeed to the credits should the elder daughter die before marrying.

Conclusion

Building on our understanding of the practice of encumbrances, we have implicitly sketched a model of the market in 7 percent credits, in which at market clearing prices some husbands chose to retain their credits, while others chose to sell them. Both Florentine and non-Florentine husbands whose in-laws had encumbered their credits tended to hold them to redemption. Florentine husbands holding unencumbered credits almost always traded them before redemption. We have also implicitly raised a number of questions concerning what husbands did with the proceeds they received from the sale of 7 percent credits. What percentage of our sample chose to place funds in business and financial opportunities with potentially higher yields than those offered by the Seven Percent Fund? Likewise, what percentage speculated in Monte credits, or invested in real property, or applied such funds to support the husband's household? Unfortunately, the destination of funds realized by husbands from the sale of credits was seldom recorded, either in the husband's private accounts or in the ledgers of the fund. Arguably, trading credits in the secondary market and placing realized funds in higher-yielding but speculative investments would have been more common among wealthier husbands. By definition, they controlled more assets, which could satisfy dotal obligations even if their investments went sour. A wide variety of evidence from contemporary economies suggests that wealthier individuals place a larger share of their wealth in risky assets.[71] Because of the lack of reliable empirical evidence with which to test this hypothesis, our understanding of the behavior of husbands who sold their credits must for now remain conjectural.

6 Wives' Claims against Insolvent Husbands in Late Medieval Italy

Transfers of property between husband and wife in late medieval Italy have been the subject of numerous monographs since the 1970s. These studies have drawn upon, but also depart from, the standard accounts of legal historians, notably Brandileone, Ercole, Pertile, and Bellomo.[1] Where previous scholarship was preoccupied with the survival and revival of Roman law, later scholarship has been busy charting the demographic, social, and ideological history of the medieval family and the role women played within and between families.[2] Although their perspectives and aims differ, there is broad agreement that a momentous shift was underway in the twelfth century: the reemergence of the Roman dowry (*dos*) – the goods, monies, or estates a wife brought to her husband in marriage – and the concomitant decline of the Germanic *Morgengabe*, a gift the groom gave his bride on the consummation of marriage. The victory of the Roman dowry over the *Morgengabe*, it is also agreed, had enormous consequences for social relations and economic activities as well as for the disposition and devolution of property.[3]

Accompanying the victory of the Roman dowry was the development of the norms, rules, and procedures regulating the dowry's constitution, administration, and disposition. This chapter investigates a single, remarkable medieval legal development which has received negligible attention: the reaffirmation and enforcement of the remedy that Roman law made available to wives whose husbands were approaching or verging on insolvency (*vir vergens ad inopiam*). To prevent the dissipation and loss of the wife's dowry and patrimony, she was granted official permission to reclaim her dowry or to lay claim to an equivalent amount of her husband's property during the course of an ongoing marriage (*constante matrimonio*).

And she was permitted to perform a fistful of the legal actions necessary to defend her claim against her husband's creditors.

The chapter begins with an outline of Roman legal prescriptions governing the disposition of the dowry in an ongoing marriage. Next, it considers Manlio Bellomo's celebrated thesis on the radical transformation of these and related prescriptions in the twelfth and thirteenth centuries. The heart of the chapter is an investigation of civil law doctrine and jurisprudence which not only warranted the wife's action against a husband approaching insolvency but extended the remedy to other situations not envisioned by the compilers of Justinian's *Corpus iuris civilis*.

Under the rules set forth in the *Corpus iuris civilis*, the husband was vested with ownership of the dowry during marriage.[4] He was also vested with responsibility for administering dotal property and for applying its fruits to support the burdens of marriage. And he was entitled to receive compensation for the risks and necessary expenses incurred while discharging his moral and legal obligations. The husband's ownership and administration of dotal property was both ambiguous and restricted. The statement of the Roman jurist Tryphoninus is worth recalling: "Although the dowry is counted as the husband's property, it nevertheless belongs to the wife" (Dig. 23. 3. 75, *Quamvis in bonis*). Should he choose to alienate dotal property consisting of land, he was prohibited under the *lex Julia* from acting without first seeking his wife's consent. His ability to alienate movable goods, whose cash value had been appraised and thus fixed by agreement (*dos aestimata*),[5] was unrestricted. By operation of law, the husband's properties were pledged (*hypotheca tacita*) to the wife as security for the restoration of the dowry (*restitutione dotis*). This pledge took precedence over other liens on the husband's property.[6]

The husband's ownership of the dowry ceased upon termination of the marriage. He or his heirs were compelled to restore dotal properties or their equivalent value if that had been fixed, except in the case where the wife divorced her husband without justifiable cause. Restoration of the dowry, upon the husband's predecease, to the wife's *paterfamilias* or to anyone else was prohibited without her consent. Upon the wife's predecease, her husband was obligated to restore the dowry to her *paterfamilias* if he had been its donor. An *extraneus*, someone outside the wife's family, including both her paternal and maternal relatives, who provided the dowry could claim it upon the wife's death, if there had been an express agreement for its return. In the absence of an express agreement, the husband was obligated to return the dowry to his wife's heirs. When circumstances were such that the husband was under no obligation to return the dowry to his father-in-law or to anyone else, and when there were surviving children, the husband received a conditional right to use the dowry and enjoy its fruits, while formal ownership was vested in the children.

This helix of legal niceties would have been futile unless there remained dotal properties or their equivalent to be restored. The Roman jurists recognized the necessity of protecting the wife's property in an ongoing marriage against loss owing to her husband's insolvency. In an opinion of Ulpian, cited in *lex Si constante* (Dig. 24. 3. 24), a wife was permitted in an ongoing marriage to sue for the recovery of her dowry when her husband was reduced to poverty (*propter inopiam mariti*). At what point during the marriage could she sue? Before she could proceed, Ulpian answered, it had to be established that his resources were clearly insufficient to restore the dowry, presumably, as it were, upon termination of marriage (*soluto matrimonio*).[7] In other words, while the wife would be unable to recover the whole dowry, she was at least given the opportunity to lay claim to the remainder of her husband's properties.

The imperial constitution, *Ubi adhuc* (Cod. 5. 12. 29), promulgated by Justinian in 528, expressly established that where the husband had fallen into poverty in an ongoing marriage, his wife could provide for herself by taking physical control of her husband's properties that had been pledged to her for the dowry, as well as of the prenuptial gift (*donatio ante nuptias*) and other nondotal properties which belonged to her (*res extra dotales*). She was to be treated as a preferred creditor when defending her claim against her husband's subsequent creditors. This rule referred to the situation in which her husband's creditors held properties that had already been pledged as security for the dowry as well as the situation in which the wife herself held these properties. Where *Si constante* implicitly rejected the standard counterclaim by her husband's creditors that the wife might legally recover her dowry only after the termination of marriage, *Ubi adhuc* explicitly rejected it – indeed, encouraged the wife to take control over her husband's properties during the marriage.

Two legal actions were available to the wife. She could exercise her claim through an *actio rei vindicatio*, which enabled an owner to reclaim property held by someone else; or an *actio hypothecaria*, which enabled the wife to take possession of property in which she had a security interest. In principle, a wife who was legally emancipated (*sui iuris*) was free to exercise these remedies. Otherwise, if she was under the paternal power (*patria potestas*), it was her father who, with the wife's consent, instituted the action as coplaintiff. The rights and claims of creditors against the husband for any property he subsequently acquired were unimpaired.

Whatever separate agreement the wife and husband had concluded about the disposition of the dowry upon termination of marriage remained unaffected and continued to be in force.[8]

Since, by definition, the dowry's purpose was to support the burdens of marriage, the wife was prohibited from alienating properties restored for the dowry in an ongoing marriage. Like her husband, she was charged with the duty to use dotal fruits and income to support herself, her husband, and her children. Another Justinianic constitution (Nov. 97. 6, *Illud quoque sancire*) of 539 admonished the wife whose husband was mismanaging his affairs and squandering his own properties to act independently or in concert with a paternal ascendant (if under the paternal power) to recover the dowry and to administer it competently and prudently. Otherwise she would be held to blame and legally liable, if when threatened with the loss of her dowry, she failed to act while she still had the opportunity.[9]

The prescriptions set forth in the *Corpus iuris civilis* regarding ownership, administration, and restoration of dowries were vigorously debated, modified, and even reversed by medieval jurists.[10] By the fourteenth century, they unanimously affirmed that ownership of all dotal properties in an ongoing marriage was without qualification vested in the husband (*maritus est dominus rei dotalis*), though the wife retained a residual ownership rooted in natural law of dotal properties whose value had not been appraised and fixed (*dos inestimata*).[11] No longer could a wife act during an ongoing marriage to recover dotal properties alienated to third parties. This prerogative was vested in the husband as *dominus*. Alienation of dotal properties became infinitely easier through loopholes given juristic approval and the near universal custom of giving dowries a monetary valuation (*dos aestimata*). Not only was the wife's claim to her dowry attenuated; the rule compelling a husband to restore the dowry to his father-in-law upon his wife's predecease was also overturned. The husband, with surviving children, was now permitted to retain at least a portion of the dowry. Preference for the husband's claim to dotal property was strengthened and even expanded by the statutes of Siena, Pisa, Pistoia, and Florence, among others, which established that, upon the wife's predecease, husbands with or without surviving children could retain from one-third to the whole dowry.[12]

A number of explanations have been advanced to explain the conspicuous reversal of Roman rules which had favored wives and their kinsmen. Manlio Bellomo, in his classic study of marital property published over fifty years ago, pivots his explanation on the political sociology and psychology of the medieval Italian commune. Survival of families in the political struggles which characterized communal life made it incumbent upon the *capo di famiglia* to control his wife's property without interference from her kinsmen. As a son he expected to receive a share of his mother's dowry; as a father he was expected to transmit this bundle of dotal rights to heirs within his patrilineage (a group of kinsmen tracing its origins from a commonly regarded male ancestor on the father's side). The interdependence of patrimony and political rank, the obsession with continuity of the patrilineage, and the identification of family fortune with the fortune of its patrimony were defining features of the Italian commune of the twelfth and thirteenth centuries, the historical setting in which the rights of widows and their heirs were curtailed. As the Lombard jurist Albericus de Rosate put it, wealth (*substantia)* was the lifeblood of this male-dominated universe, destitution (*inopia*) its ruin.[13]

The *capi di famiglia*, morover, not only enacted legislation to avoid restoration of the dowry, but also resorted to other tactics: refusing outright or delaying restoration, alienating dotal goods and properties through fictitious sales, constraining wives to renounce their hypothecary rights, and insisting that widows receive means of support (*alimenta*) only if they forgo remarriage and remain with the surviving children in the husband's household and the orbit of his patrilineage. Just as daughters were excluded from inheritance once they were dowered, widows and their legitimate heirs were denied the recovery of dowries. Viewed from the vantage point of men in authority, women were seemingly little more than compliant figures in a social drama scripted, directed, and produced by men.

Bellomo's thesis, forcefully argued and presented with technical finesse and formidable erudition, has justifiably attracted adherents.[14] That Roman legal rules were radically transformed in the context of medieval political, social, and economic developments is an intransigent fact that cannot be denied. Nor can one deny the difficulties with which widows and their heirs had to contend in recovering their dowries or other goods to which they were entitled. The financial plight of this group in fifteenth-century Florence (where one in every four adult women was a widow) has been put into bold relief by Herlihy and Klapisch-Zuber.[15] Petition after petition was presented to the Signoria in Florence in which widows, their heirs, and descendants solicited governmental intervention in resolving disputes over the disposition of dotal properties. The ability of husbands, moreover, to alienate dotal property in an ongoing marriage, which served the requirements of liquidity in the nascent market economy, clearly jeopardized the wife's chances of recovering a dowry threatened by impending insolvency. And bankruptcy itself became an endemic feature of urban life, not only because of the constant volatility of the market economy, but also because of oppressive tax burdens.[16]

Despite its obvious merits, Bellomo's thesis postulating a general deterioration of women's legal capacities remains unidimensional and must be modified. It places excessive emphasis upon the husband's and his kinsmen's dominance over the wife and her patrimony, while neglecting to take seriously the enduring emotional and material bonds between a married woman and her own kinsmen.[17] It overemphasizes the inevitable conflicts between the wife's and husband's kinsmen, while giving short shrift to the bonds forged among relatives-in-law. It places too much weight upon the *capofamiglia* as a domestic predator of both his wife's and his mother's dowry, while failing to take seriously the "husband-father" who dutifully provided for the well-being of his wife in widowhood and his daughters in marriage.[18] It gives undue emphasis to formal prescriptions and androcentric texts, ignoring the productive domestic and economic roles that women surely played. It lends too much importance to the curtailment of the wife's dotal rights by statutory prescriptions, while ignoring statutory and legislative remedies consciously designed to safeguard her patrimony. Florentine petitions cited above bear witness not only to the afflictions of widows, but also to the willingness of the Florentine government to alleviate their plight. Above all, Bellomo's thesis places too much emphasis upon legal mechanisms which may have weakened the wife's dotal privileges, such as renunciation of hypothecary rights to her husband's property, while ignoring the enforcement of guarantees and remedies set forth in dotal contracts for the restoration of the dowry and marital donation (*donatio propter nuptias*) to the wife or her heirs.[19]

Another shortcoming of Bellomo's thesis is his failure to come to terms with the disparities between legal doctrine and municipal statutes and customs. How did jurists resolve disputes over the disposition and devolution of the wife's property when the common law (*ius commune*) – the Roman and canon law and the teachings and opinions of civilian and canon lawyers – and municipal statutes collided? Were legal doctrine and prescriptions disregarded, were they devoid of all practical significance? Such questions are not addressed by Bellomo, for he assumes that, with few exceptions, both the *ius commune* and municipal statutes were aligned in favoring the claims of the husband and his kinsmen. He also believes that by the mid-fourteenth century the contributions of jurists to these issues had become passive regurgitations of traditional doctrine and opinion. However, the intellectual energies of jurists such as Bartolus and Baldus and their disciples were, as we shall see, far from spent.[20] Their exegesis of the constitution, disposition, and devolution of the wife's property (*bona mulieris*) constitutes a veritable stockpile of model cases and solutions drawn from experience and deductive argument, which were employed by jurists who without hesitation defended the patrimonial interests of wives and their relatives.[21] Given the problems arising from statutory ambiguities and lacunae and from conflicts between statutes, jurists had ample opportunity to practice their technical expertise on the triangular relationship among the *ius commune*, municipal statutes, and dotal agreements, as witnessed by several thousand extant legal opinions (*consilia*) addressing disputes over dowries.

These jurists were, in fact, rendering their *consilia* in a setting starkly removed from the robust commune of the twelfth and thirteenth centuries depicted by Bellomo. "Unquestionably," Chabot observes, "the magnitude and recurrence of mortality crises in the fourteenth and fifteenth centuries, causing the rapid disappearance of heirs, appreciably disrupted patterns of succession."[22] Repeated visitations of the plague directly threatened the very continuity and biological existence of patrilineages. In this new socioecological setting, the disposition and devolution of the wife's property upon termination of marriage was not only determined by municipal legislators, the mediations of jurists, and the strategies and counterstrategies of wives, widows, surviving husbands, and their kinsmen and heirs, but also by chance. The devolution of the wife's property was neither entirely predictable nor unidirectional; its movement must be tracked on multiple roads and byways. Those who undertake the journey are advised to leave behind stereotypical verities about the subordination and oppression of women, about the squalid indignity of their lives (we know little about what motivated women, what they experienced and thought across the social and economic spectrum of late medieval Italy) and instead explore the terrain of partial and complementary truths.

Let us now turn our attention to the wife's legal recourse when her husband was approaching insolvency. For Bellomo, her legal recourse was limited to the realm of theory, representing little more than a reassuring fantasy. He acknowledges that the prescriptions enunciated in *Si constante* and *Ubi adhuc* were reaffirmed in the twelfth century by the *Summa trecensis* (*ca.* 1140), Rogerius, and Azo.[23] This reaffirmation, in his view, was not intended to encourage wives to exercise their legal recourse. Rather, it should be understood as pledge of allegiance to the dowry system's fundamental objective: to support the burdens of marriage.[24] Whatever the intentions we may attribute to these twelfth-century jurists, it is no less remarkable that the privilege enabling a wife to act against her husband in the event of impending insolvency was neither questioned nor reversed by medieval jurists, as were other Roman rules and privileges. During the century spanning the compilation of the *Glossa ordinaria* by Accursius and the foundational analysis of *Si constante* by Bartolus de Saxoferrato, the leading doctors of civil law – Odofredus, Jacobus de Arena, Jacobus de Ravanis, Dinus Mugellanus, Jacobus de Belvisio, Cinus de Pistorio, Jacobus Butrigarius, and Albericus de Rosate – unqualifiedly and unhesitatingly sustained the privilege enabling the wife to take legal action in an ongoing marriage against a husband teetering on the edge of insolvency to recover not only her dowry but also her nondotal properties and her husband's marital donation.[25] This fundamental legal privilege was also sustained by the preeminent canonists, Hostiensis, Gulielmus Durandus, Johannes Andreae, Antonius de Butrio, Petrus Ancharanus, Franciscus de Zabarellis, and Panormitanus (Niccolò de' Tedeschi).[26] The legal remedy against these unfortunate husbands was also endorsed by leading religious authorities in their *summae* or manuals of conscience, which had enormous influence upon penitential practice.[27] And it was enshrined in Rolandinus de Passageriis's *Summa totius artis notarie* (1255–73), the principal manual for notaries during the late Middle Ages.[28]

At the same time, jurists, especially civilians, vigorously debated the various meanings of *inopia* and associated expressions and established juridical tests and procedures to identify and verify the circumstances considered responsible for producing insolvency. They also debated which persons other than the husband and the wife could sue to recover her dowry (for example, the husband's father and creditors), which persons other than a wife could reclaim the dowry in an ongoing marriage (for example, her father and her children), which properties besides the dowry were subject to restoration, and which legal actions could be instituted. They also paid considerable attention to the legal effects arising from restoration with respect to the husband, his heirs, and, especially, his creditors. Their teachings provided the repertoire of authoritative guidelines and strategies for litigants, notaries, lawyers, and judges from the late-thirteenth century onward.

Si constante made the wife's actions for restoration of the dowry contingent upon the husband's insolvency (*propter inopiam mariti*) and its obvious and predictable result: that his resources would be insufficient to satisfy his wife's claims (*facultas ad dotis exactionem non sufficere*). It was obvious to jurists of the thirteenth century that a wife's chances of actually recovering her dowry under this law were minimal. It was fully recognized that *Si constante* could serve, against its intent, as a means for delaying and frustrating the wife's legitimate claim. To avoid this harmful consequence, *Si constante* was reformulated, and the grounding text of its reformulation was a model case presented by the *Glossa ordinaria*.[29] Titia gave a dowry to her husband Seius, who began to mismanage his assets (*maritus inchoat male uti substantia sua*), and it was asked whether during marriage she could bring a suit against her husband to recover the dowry. Yes, the *Glossa* replied, if the wife witnessed her husband's mismanagement of his assets, the consequence of which would be that if he satisfied his other creditors, he would not be able to satisfy his wife's claims. The husband, therefore, was no longer required to be factually insolvent, as he had been in *Si constante*, before his wife could take legal action. The formula, *maritus inchoat male uti substantia sua*, was not original but intertextual, that is, imported from *Illud quoque sancire* in the *Authentica* (the medieval designation of the *Novellae*). As Odofredus reminded his audience, "Today by virtue of the law of the *Authentica*, where the husband begins to mismanage his assets, a wife can demand her dowry or institute a hypothecary action."[30]

The differences among *Si constante*, *Ubi adhuc*, and *Illud quoque sancire* became a source of contention and may have been exploited by creditors or other parties opposing wives who sought to recover their dowries. Bartolus denied that these laws contradicted or detracted from each other; they were, he insisted, complementary, and a wife was fully entitled to reap the privileges and benefits provided by each law.[31] *Si constante* fully (*plene*) permitted a wife to act when her husband's condition was so lamentable that, after having deducted his debts, his properties no longer sufficed for the recovery of the dowry. The wife, however, could not bring suit unless her husband sank into "extreme poverty" (*extrema miseria*).[32] *Ubi adhuc* provided fuller (*plenius*) latitude to the wife. Even though the husband's properties might be sufficient to satisfy his wife's claim, still, if he was approaching insolvency (*vergens ad inopiam*), she could demand the return of her dowry. For example, a nobleman might have enough goods to satisfy his creditors as well as his wife yet find it necessary to spend everything he had in order to live honorably. This set of circumstances was considered tantamount to someone's inclining toward insolvency. Excessive expenditures for the maintenance of honor were incurred, ironically, by husbands of well-to-do and socially prominent families who lavished gifts of jewels, ornaments, and fine clothing upon their new brides. In former times, Bartolus related, a wife was unable to reclaim her dowry when her husband's resources were sufficient, but today she could in accordance with *Ubi adhuc*.[33]

Illud quoque sancire provided the fullest (*plenissime*) latitude to the wife. Under this law, the wife was permitted to take legal action to recover her dowry, even if the husband's resources were sufficient to satisfy his creditors, his wife, and his desire to live well. She could act when there was reason to believe that the husband, although wealthy, was approaching insolvency because he was mismanaging his assets.[34]

Although *Si constante*, *Ubi adhuc*, and *Illud quoque sancire* gave life to the normative metaphors which would mark the insolvent husband from the late twelfth century onward, they were silent on the procedural mechanisms by which the husband's financial condition would be ascertained. Roman jurists typically focused their attention on the circumstances giving rise to particular actions and lacked interest in developing procedures for the resolution of disputes. To discover the extent of her husband's assets or alleged insolvency in a contemporary divorce suit, a wife would have to resort to a variety of time-consuming and expensive procedures, involving lawyers, accountants, property appraisers, pension experts, and court stenographers. Our jurists, with few exceptions, taught that the husband's public reputation (*vulgi opinio*) should be the cardinal test in ascertaining his financial condition.[35] This would be achieved by making inquiries among his neighbors, who presumably know his affairs best. "If there are men under the sun who know their neighbor's secrets," Odofredus quipped, "they are neighbors."[36] A notable exception to the common doctrine was the teaching of Jacobus Butrigarius. He stressed that the husband's mismanagement of his assets was not proved by public reputation, but by witnesses who testified that he was a gambler, a swindler, or negligent in the handling of his properties. He did admit that the teaching of the *Glossa ordinaria* was valid with respect to *Ubi adhuc*, where *vulgi opinio* constituted sufficient proof of the husband's inability to pay his legal debts.[37]

This issue, as Bartolus observed, did not admit a straightforward solution. He denied that the circumstances triggering the wife's action – the husband's insufficient assets, his destitution, and mismanagement of his assets – are interchangeable just because the *Glossa ordinaria*, Dinus Mugellanus, and other jurists held that each circumstance can be proved in the same manner – namely, by common opinion.[38] Arguing dialectically (*pro et contra*), he first put forward the thesis that the husband's worth must be fully authenticated by documents and witnesses; it must be fully proved that his assets remain insufficient to pay off his debts; and the husband must be given the opportunity to prove that in fact he has sufficient resources.[39] The principle behind Bartolus's thesis is that cases whose outcome might result in great damage (*magnum preiudicium*) require full proof (*plena probatio*) and formal proceedings.[40] Swiftly reversing direction, Bartolus acknowledged that only partial proof (*semiplena probatio*) based on *vulgi opinio* and summary proceedings are required, because any damages suffered by the husband will be moderate or little. The rationale animating his counterthesis is that the husband will suffer only minor damage, because his wife is required to use income earned from the dowry now in her control for their mutual support.[41] Partial proof based on the husband's public reputation and summary procedure are also valid, Bartolus instructed, in ascertaining and establishing the husband's mismanagement of his assets and the extent of his insolvency.[42] Should the wife decide to bring suit against a third party holding the husband's goods, full proof of the husband's financial condition was required.[43] Bartolus urged judges presiding over cases of insolvency to be aware that its determination is contingent upon social rank and material circumstances. A knight or nobleman worth 1,000 (pounds) is considered poor, while a rustic worth less is considered rich.[44] After recommending to his audience Bartolus's theses, Baldus proffered this advice :

> I say that the discerning judge should not only make inquiries about the husband's reputation but also about the reasons for his reputation. Let us assume that he is reputed to be a spendthrift [*prodigus*]. The judge should examine the reasons which prompted those asserting that he is a spendthrift, and they should set forth their reasons: for example, they witness him daily behaving wastefully and spending far beyond what his resources can bear.[45]

The wife can also act against her husband, Bartolus instructed, when his reputation as a prosperous merchant is belied by the fact that he is actually verging on insolvency. He has in mind a wealthy husband who becomes a merchant, travels overseas, performs his profession with skill, but begins to suffer heavy losses resulting in impoverishment. His neighbors and acquaintances back home remain ignorant of his plight, believing that his properties are sufficient to satisfy both his creditors and his wife. Technically, under these conditions, the wife is barred from enlisting *Si constante* to advance her claim. Likewise, she is barred from enlisting *Ubi adhuc*, because even though the husband is in fact verging on insolvency, he is widely reputed to be wealthy. Finally, she is barred from enlisting *Illud quoque sancire*, because even though the husband has suffered business losses, his business career commenced profitably. Thus, the requirement that the husband began to mismanage his assets would not, literally speaking, be met. Rejecting a literal and strict interpretation of these laws, Bartolus asserted that the wife is able to act in this case in order to prevent the loss of her dowry.[46] It does not matter when a husband verges on insolvency, whether at the time he commences his business or at a later date; he still remains subject to his wife's preemptive action.[47]

Opinion was divided over whether a wife could act to recover her dowry in an ongoing marriage, if from the beginning of marriage her husband was already insolvent. Dinus, Albericus de Rosate, and Baldus were flatly opposed to the wife's action.[48] Both Jacobus de Ravanis and Cinus opined that if a wife knew that her husband was insolvent at the beginning of marriage, she was prohibited from acting; if she was ignorant, on the other hand, she was permitted to act.[49] Bartolus believed that a wife was always entitled to her dotal benefits and privileges in an ongoing marriage. *De iure*, a wife who gave a dowry to an insolvent husband did not enter into an implied agreement to forfeit her future right to take legal action. Even if she so desired, she was not entitled to renounce these benefits and privileges by an antenuptial agreement, either tacit or express.[50] The contrary opinion, Bartolus stressed, produces noxious results. "It would impede marriage for someone who is destitute and has mismanaged his affairs, since he would not find a wife with a dowry, and for that reason women would witness themselves, with the aid of these laws, abandoned. This our opinion is beneficial to marriages and therefore is to be upheld and accepted."[51] Baldus did not clarify the issue by espousing contradictory opinions. He advised his audience (to *Ubi adhuc*) that Dinus's negative opinion was preferable. His reasoning: an agreement in which a wife renounces her right to act in an ongoing marriage does not nullify the functional purpose of the dowry, and is in all respects valid. Yet, in his commentary on § *Quod locum* (Auth. 7. 8), he upheld Bartolus's teaching.[52]

Although these competing opinions were frequently cited by fifteenth-century jurists, I have not yet found actual disputes involving wives who were prevented from bringing suit on the grounds that their husbands were insolvent at the start of their marriages. Less academic and certainly more eye-catching were cases in which wives sought to recover their dowries from husbands placed under a ban for committing a civil wrong or a crime and from husbands who were actually exiled.[53] The plight of Florentine wives whose famous husbands were placed under the ban – Gemma di Manetto Donati (Dante's wife), Lisa di Monte (Matteo Villani's wife), Margherita di Bernardo (Lapus de Castiglionchio's wife), and the redoubtable Alessandra Macinghi Strozzi – was a source of domestic tension, as revealed in private letters and family memoirs. According to Bartolus, if all the properties of a *bannitus* are confiscated by a public authority, no doubt exists that his wife can take legal action to recover her dowry, for the husband is now considered to be completely insolvent. She can also take legal action if only part of his properties is confiscated, even though, in theory, he would appear to have sufficient resources to cover the claims of both his wife and creditors. Yet the realities of banishment and exile were otherwise. Exiles customarily suffered a host of legal disabilities: they were forbidden from communicating with their family, relatives, neighbors, and business associates and were barred from doing business within the territorial jurisdiction of their cities. The life of an exile was thus fraught with a series of hardships, often leading to insolvency. It was this reality which lay behind Bartolus's determination that the wife of an exile, whose properties were not yet confiscated, could nonetheless sue to recover her dowry on the grounds that her husband had begun to mismanage his assets.[54] Bartolus's determination quickly became the *communis opinio*.[55]

The ability of wives to lay claim to the properties of husbands placed under the ban was a political as well as recurring legal challenge. Governments were as obsessed with confiscating the goods of *banniti* as were wives with recovering their dowries. Where the *ius commune* favored the interests of the wife, statutory law favored the interests of governments. This friction is illustrated in the following dispute which occurred in late-fourteenth-century Florence during its war with Milan, a period of heavy taxation. In 1397 Tommaso di Rosso de' Ricci was condemned to death for refusing to satisfy his forced loan assessments (*prestanze*), a sentence that would be carried out if Tommaso did not pay up within a specified period. Both communal and neighborhood (*gonfalone*) officials responsible for levying these assessments were planning to confiscate Tommaso's properties, when his wife Francesca claimed that they were secured for her dowry of 1,500 florins. She produced two instruments in which her husband acknowledged receiving cash payments amounting to 1,500 florins and promised to restore the dowry to his wife or her heirs in every event in which he was legally bound to perform restoration. He also pledged his present and future properties as security. As Francesca underscored in her petition, she sought to recover her dowry so that she could support herself (*se alere possit*) on the technical grounds that her husband was mismanaging his assets and approaching insolvency.[56] Four local jurists, Rosellus de Rosellis, Rossus Andreozzi de Orlandis, Riccardus Francisci del Bene, and Johannes de Riccis, were commissioned in 1399, most likely by the city, to decide whether superior rights to Tommaso's goods were vested in the communal fisc and *gonfalone* or in his wife.

If the case were decided solely on the basis of Florentine statutes, Rosellus pronounced in the lead opinion, it was certain that Francesca's claim would have to be rejected outright. First, the claims of the communal fisc, as a rule, take precedence over the claims of prior creditors. Second, her action appeared to be blocked by two statutes, one prohibiting a wife's laying claim to the properties of her husband, so long as he is alive, against his creditors; another prohibiting restoration of the dowry except when the husband's death resulted from natural causes. Since Tommaso was not yet dead, and since his future fate, if the sentence were carried out, would be civil death, the statutes were said to trump Francesca's claim. Reversing his position, Rosellus now argued that the statutory prohibitions were outweighed by reasons grounded in the *ius commune*. The dowry was given and Tommaso's properties were expressly secured for its return in 1390 and 1392, respectively, that is, five to seven years *before* he was assessed for forced loans. Consequently, on the basis of the rule for intercreditor equity, *prior tempore*, *potior in iure*, the wife's rights were preferred to those of the fisc (*iura fisci*). In addition, the security interest in Tommaso's properties for the purpose of furnishing Francesca support (*alimenta*) remained untouched and operable. This reason rendered ineffective the two Florentine statutes cited above. They could not and did not prevail, because neither statute expressly prohibited the wife from demanding support from her husband's properties. "A great injustice" would result if creditors, with weaker legal privileges than the wife, were permitted to seize her husband's as well as her own goods.[57] For these reasons, Rosellus concluded, the wife could demand and secure support from her husband's properties consistent with the amount of her dowry.[58]

Rosellus's opinion was roundly approved by Rossus de Orlandis. Citing *Ubi adhuc*, *Illud quoque sancire*, and Bartolus's commentary on *Si constante*, he argued that Francesca had an unquestionable claim to be assigned an amount not exceeding her dowry from her husband's properties, and that in this case the *ius commune* prevailed over the *ius municipale civitatis Florentie*.[59] Francesca was assigned properties roughly equal to the value her dowry on 17 August 1401.[60] Her victory was not an isolated incident. Between 1375 and 1431, communal officials recognized the claims of ninety Florentine wives, including Margherita di Bernardo, wife of the canonist and redoubtable Guelf partisan Lapus de Castiglionchio, whose husbands had been condemned and exiled as rebels.[61] They received amounts equivalent to their dowries from the properties which had been confiscated and from the proceeds of confiscated property which had been sold.[62]

Husbands who become insolvent through no fault of their own (owing to an accident such as a shipwreck), Cinus, Baldus, and others taught, were not open to legal suit. Wives were admonished to share their husband's losses and stand firmly by them in times of adversity and misfortune.[63] Bartolus was pointedly silent on this particular issue, but it is difficult to believe that he would have agreed with either his mentor, Cinus, or his disciple, Baldus. For Bartolus, whatever the cause, the husband's evident insufficiency of assets to satisfy his wife's demand for the restoration of her dowry was sufficient grounds for instituting a legal action. Only in the exceptional case where the wife was considered mentally incapable (*furiosa*) of administering her own affairs in a responsible manner did Bartolus permit the dowry to be sequestered on her behalf. He advised that a judge acting on her behalf in the name of equity should sequester what remained of the dowry that her husband was squandering. The dowry was not to be restored to the wife, but to a third party enjoined to manage it in the mutual interest of husband and wife.[64] Civilian jurists tended to follow Bartolus's doctrine, teaching that with few exceptions the dowry should be directly restored to the wife.[65]

If canonists respectfully acknowledged the authority of civil law in cases of insolvency, they adhered to Pope Innocent III's influential decretal *Per vestras* (X 4. 20. 7) of 1206.[66] They taught that the husband can furnish his wife security for the dowry rather than the dowry itself; and that the dowry can be safeguarded by placing the insolvent husband's remaining assets in trust with a merchant. The practical significance of *Per vestras* is difficult to gauge, since wives' suits against insolvent husbands were, as far as we know, resolved in accordance with civil law. However, civilian jurists alleged *Per vestras* when they doubted the wife's ability to administer her dowry, or conversely, when they sought to justify the placement of cash, which the wife received from her husband in lieu of her dowry or from the husband's creditors in lieu of his property, with a reputable merchant.[67] The potential conflict between canon and civil law must not obscure the collective desire of all jurists, many of whom were doctors of civil and canon law, to keep both dowry and family intact.

A father-in-law who received the dowry, an altogether conventional occurrence when his son was not yet legally emancipated, was liable to be sued for its return if he himself was approaching insolvency. The *Glossa ordinaria* admitted that the daughter-in-law's action was not permitted by the *Digest*, and it filled the lacuna with a doctrine that won rapid approval in subsequent jurisprudence. The dowry could be recovered from the father-in-law when he was approaching insolvency on the grounds that equity, which furnishes the rationale for instituting an action against an insolvent husband, furnishes the same rationale for instituting an action against an insolvent father-in-law.[68] Bartolus, in another oft-cited text, laid down a series of distinctions and guidelines for determining the father-in-law's legal responsibilities for his son's dowry. When he received the dowry in his name only, the father, not the son, was obligated to restore it. However, when he received the dowry in the name of his son and with his son's consent, the obligation to make the restoration fell on the son's shoulders, not the father's. When the father received the dowry in his own name but with his son's consent, both were obligated to make the restoration. A son who received the dowry without his father's consent undertook full responsibility for restoration. If a father was alive at the time of his son's marriage, which accounted for around 30 percent of marriages in fifteenth-century Florence, the son customarily received the dowry with his father's approval, an act that obligated both to restore it.[69]

That both father and son were obligated to restore the dowry was beneficial for the wife, but could she undertake legal action if only one of them was verging on insolvency? Under *Si constante*, she was without legal recourse, since, in principle, there remained sufficient assets to secure her dowry. The *Glossa ordinaria* disagreed, explaining that legal action was justified because her dowry was undeniably in danger as a result of being managed irresponsibly.[70] Although this doctrine, too, rapidly gained a foothold in subsequent jurisprudence,[71] there was opposition from the French jurists Jacobus de Ravanis and Petrus de Bellapertica, who contended that the dowry remained secure so long as one codebtor possessed sufficient resources.[72] While Cinus reproved the reasoning of the *Glossa*, he taught that the wife was authorized by *Si constante* and *Ubi adhuc* to act against the solvent codebtor because, he contended, "it is in our interest to have many debtors."[73] Bartolus harbored deep reservations about the logic and propriety of permitting actions against the party not approaching insolvency. The doctrine of the *Glossa* and the opinion advanced by Cinus, he believed, were pernicious and against all laws where husband and father-in-law were not implicitly or expressly obligated as codebtors (*duo rei*).[74] In the end, however, he accepted the fundamental teaching of the *Glossa* that the solvent codebtor, whether husband or father-in-law, could be sued by the wife, with this qualification: that it could be shown that the father and son originally agreed to undertake a joint obligation to restore the dowry to the wife.[75]

The position of the *Glossa ordinaria* and Bartolus on determining the liability of codebtors for restoration of the dowry in cases of insolvency remained authoritative into the sixteenth century. This is amply illustrated by a *consilium* of the Florentine jurist Antonius de Stroziis drafted in 1504 on behalf of Vaggia di Giovanni Vernacci.[76] These are the bare facts of the dispute: Vaggia's husband Marco de' Tempi, together with his father Alberto, formally acknowledged receipt of Vaggia's 1,050-florin dowry in a *confessio dotis* and undertook the customary obligation to restore it; that is, any one of them would be liable in the event of restoration for an amount equivalent to the whole dowry (*in solidum et in totum*). Marco became insolvent and destitute, while his father remained both solvent and sufficiently wealthy to fulfill his obligation to restore the dowry. Apprehensive about losing her dowry and thus without the means to support herself and her family, Vaggia took legal action to recover her dowry from her husband and father-in-law, described here as codebtors (*duo rei*). The issue to be resolved was whether Vaggia's action was valid, when one codebtor was insolvent while the other's wealth sufficed to meet the wife's claim.[77]

Although Antonius's *consilium* is devoid of doctrinal originality, it does contain a valuable compendium of references on this specific issue and furnishes an opportunity to view the state of the question in the early sixteenth century. After setting forth the opinions of the *Glossa*, Bartolus, and later jurists in favor of the wife's claim, Antonius went on to cite opposing opinions. He cited the opinions of French jurists who opposed the wife's claims, where the resources of one codebtor make up for another codebtor's insolvency.[78] He cited the brothers Baldus and Angelus de Ubaldis, who limited the wife's action to only the insolvent codebtor, an opinion seconded by Raphael de Raymundis.[79] He cited the opinion of Alexander Tartagnus, who affirmed that the opinion of Baldus had more validity than Bartolus's and was therefore preferable, though he reluctantly conceded that the wife could act against both husband and father-in-law if they had undertaken a common obligation as business partners (*socii*).[80] He cited the opinion of Paulus de Castro, who validated the wife's action against a codebtor on condition that he not only be approaching insolvency, but also be the party responsible for her support (*alimenta*), usually but not always the husband.[81] And, finally, he cited the opinion of Ludovicus Pontanus, who contended against Bartolus that the wife had no legal action where one codebtor was solvent.[82]

For Antonius, the path leading out of this thicket of contrasting and conflicting opinions was paved by the *Glossa* and its adherents:

> From the above citations it is apparent that on this difficult question the doctors have declared in various ways and have issued opposing opinions. Nevertheless, the opinion of the *Glossa* is more common and is supported by many greater authorities. For as was stated above, Cinus, Riccardus Malumbra, Odofredus, Albericus, Bartolus, Jacobus de Belvisio, Johannes Andreae, Jacobus Butrigarius, and [Johannes] de Imola share the opinion of the *Glossa*. There are thus nine doctors who follow the *Glossa*, and their collective opinion is more than common, since others [in opposition] have few opinions with less authority, and especially since we have the *Glossa* sustained everywhere by this command: that we must not depart from its opinion in matters of legal deliberation and judgment, according to Baldus.[83]

Strozzi's quantitative argument and his deft manipulation of Baldus's texts carried the day: it was on the basis of his *consilium* that Vaggia's claim was vindicated.[84]

What role did the wife's father play in the case of insolvency? Was paternal consent required before the wife could undertake legal action? In theory, it would seem that paternal consent was necessary if the father furnished the dowry (*dos profecticia*) and if his daughter remained legally unemancipated. In practice, it was in the interest of the wife to act in concert with her father to prevent the loss of her patrimony. However, under *Illud quoque sancire* the wife alone was permitted to recover her dowry when it represented a large sum and her action thus prevents serious loss, and when her father was himself unwilling to lay claim to the dowry or refused to permit his daughter to do so. The wife could also act without paternal consent, Bartolus added, when her dowry was small and her father was destitute, since, should the dowry be lost, he would not be able to supply another one.[85] When she was unable to obtain paternal consent owing to her father's absence, there was a doctrinal consensus that the wife alone had the right to take legal action. Conversely, the father was permitted to recover the dowry when it was imperiled by the husband's impending insolvency and when the wife herself was unwilling or legally incapable of acting. His action was permitted, the *Glossa ordinaria* reasoned, because he bore the risk and responsibility of endowing his daughter a second time if her dowry was irretrievably lost.[86] For the very same reason, according to Albericus de Rosate, he could seek to recover the dowry, even without her consent, if the wife failed to act out of negligence when her husband was approaching insolvency.[87] A father who successfully recovered the dowry was forbidden to use if for self-enrichment and was legally bound to employ dotal income for the benefit of his daughter and son-in-law's common household.

Under no circumstances could a third party (*extraneus*) – someone other than the wife or her father – act to recover the dowry in an ongoing marriage. This doctrine applied to the circumstance in which a third party gave the dowry on behalf of the wife and stipulated that the dowry be returned to him. The *Glossa ordinaria*, followed by a legion of jurists, ruled that such stipulations were valid only upon termination of marriage. The third party's action was denied on the grounds that it would divert funds intended and necessary for the wife, husband, and their children and thus violate the dowry's raison d'être, and that in point of law "true" restoration of the dowry was triggered by the termination of marriage, not the husband's impending insolvency.[88] For the same reason, the wife was prohibited from ceding her claim against her husband's properties in the case of insolvency to a third party. There was no question, however, that a third party who received the dowry in lieu of the husband or his father was liable to be sued for its return if he himself was approaching insolvency.[89] Only the wife or her father could institute suits against third parties.

Bartolus extended the remedies furnished by *Si constante* to children whose mother had died and whose father's incipient insolvency endangered their mother's dowry. Permitting children to take legal action against their father to recover their mother's dowry was in clear violation of *Si constante* and related laws. Under Roman law, as Bartolus himself taught, an administrator must be appointed to manage the assets of a spendthrift or father approaching insolvency (*curator prodigi*, *curator bonorum*). But where the father had squandered or lost his deceased wife's dowry and his acts had resulted in the dissipation of his own patrimony, Bartolus advised that judicial intervention was necessary to preserve the dowry for the children.[90] Instructive here is an arbitrated agreement concluded in Florence between Francesco di Arnaldo Manelli and his daughters Papera and Tita. In May 1413 Manelli formally acknowledged receipt of a dowry of 880 florins on behalf of his wife, Ginevra di Lorenzo Gualterotti. As was customary, he promised to restore or consign the dowry to Ginevra or her heirs in those cases in which he was legally required to do so. About 1423, Francesco was sent by the Florentine government to Alexandria, Egypt, where he served as consul. Owing to circumstances beyond his control, he was forced to remain in the east. Meanwhile, his wife had died, Papera had reached marriageable age, and as a result of his prolonged absence from Florence his assets were imperiled. In the words of the agreement of 3 September 1429, reached between the father's procurator and the administrator of the daughters' affairs, Francesco Manelli "incepit male uti substantia sua et ad inopiam versit et vergit." To protect their marriage prospects as well as their welfare, his daughters requested their mother's dowry plus 20 florins they had already expended for their support (*alimenta*). As Manelli's estate was bereft of cash, ownership of properties in the city and in the surrounding countryside, estimated to be worth 900 florins, was transferred to Papera and Tita. If, when the properties were sold, the price recovered was below 900 florins, Manelli remained obligated to pay the difference.[91]

By the mid-fourteenth century, a consensus had been reached on the series of legal actions a wife could institute against a husband squandering the dowry and simultaneously approaching insolvency.[92] She could institute a personal action (*actio personalis de dote*), which applied to situations in which the husband squandered the actual dowry he received. She could institute an action to recover properties not identical with the actual dowry (*actio utilis in rem* and *rei vindicatio utilis*). This action especially applied to properties purchased by the husband with dotal monies. These actions also applied to a dowry or a component of the dowry whose cash value had been appraised at the time the husband had acknowledged its receipt. If the cash value of the dowry was not fixed (*dos inestimata*), Bartolus opined, the wife could petition legal officials to sequester her dowry and hold it in safekeeping, presumably until the husband could show that he was now solvent and well able to take care of his family. The wife could also employ the *rei vindicatio*, laying claim to dotal properties that belonged to her as owner but were in her husband's or another's possession. These overlapping actions, though important, may have had limited application in practice. The major component of dowries in urban centers like Florence, Siena, Pisa, and Bologna was cash. Dowries were liquid and thus immediately disposable. The likelihood that a wife would recover the actual dowry which had been given at the time of marriage was more apparent than real.

The most effective weapon in the wife's arsenal was the hypothecary action (*actio hypothecaria*). Here the wife had an implied (*tacita*) and privileged claim over her husband's personal goods and real properties commensurate with the amount of her dowry, trousseau, and her husband's marital donation. Her hypothec extended to rights (*iura*) and claims the husband held, for example, to rental income, annuities, and credits or shares in interest-bearing government loan funds, such as the *Monte comune* of Florence and *Monte vecchio* of Venice. One category of property exempt from the hypothecary action was merchandise that a businessman had previously sold. Merchandise remaining in his possession was considered to be obligated for the dowry.[93] This distinction was clearly a practical necessity to protect merchants who had purchased merchandise in good faith and who were ignorant of the husband's financial condition. The wife was required to institute the hypothecary action against her husband before acting against a third party in actual possession of the dowry.[94] Her claim, the jurists unanimously argued, was superior to the general hypothecs of all her husband's creditors, even if theirs had come into existence at an earlier date. The suspension of the venerable Roman rule, "one who is first in time has superior right" (*prior tempore, potior iure*), was part of the bundle of privileges which, it was envisioned, would enable the wife to recover and preserve her dowry.[95]

There was considerable controversy over the wife's claim to those of the husband's properties which had been specifically pledged (*hypotheca expressa*) to his creditors before her own implied hypothec took effect, that is, *before* the husband received the dowry. One opinion, associated with Martinus, was that goods formerly and expressly pledged to a third party were not exempt from the wife's claim. This opinion was shared by Jacobus de Arena, Cinus, and Jacobus Butrigarius.[96] Jacobus de Ravanis and Petrus de Bellapertica opined that the wife's implied hypothec was valid except against creditors whose claims to her husband's goods were even more preferable and privileged than hers.[97] Finally, there was the opinion associated with Bulgarus, which flatly prohibited the wife from laying claim to goods formerly and expressly pledged to her husband's creditors. It was Bulgarus's opinion, reincarnated in the teachings of the *Glossa*, Odofredus, Dinus Mugellanus, Albericus de Rosate, Bartolus, Baldus, Paulus de Castro and others, which eventually triumphed.[98] This triumph, in turn, most likely stimulated countermeasures by which the wife and her family demanded that the husband pledge specific assets as security for the dowry.[99]

There were times when the husband's hypothecary creditors were unwilling to restore to the wife the goods and properties of her husband in their possession. Restoration might result in financial loss – for example, when the hypothecary creditors had increased the value of her property through improvements or when they would be prevented from enjoying rental property for which they had paid in advance. In these situations junior hypothecary creditors could exercise the *ius offerende pecunie*, the right to pay the prior or senior hypothecary creditor (the wife) the amount owed by the common *debitor* (the husband) and thus retain the property. Although this legal option was permitted by the *ius commune*, it was declared inoperable in the *casus inopie* by the *Glossa*, Cinus, and Bartolus.[100] The wife's dependence upon a stable income base for support, it was reasoned, would be endangered if the husband's creditors were permitted the *ius offerende pecunie*. Baldus, in a key text, dissented. He limited the teachings of the *Glossa* and Bartolus to those cases in which the wife sought the return of her dowry (including dotal properties that had in some way been altered) that were in the hypothecary creditor's possession. When the wife instituted a simple hypothecary action to reclaim her husband's properties, there was no question in Baldus's mind that the *ius offerende pecunie* was operable, especially in cases where the hypothecary creditors actually possessed the husband's goods.[101] Paulus de Castro, Raphael de Raymundis, Johannes de Imola, and Alexander Tartagnus took Baldus's opinion one step further. Citing the model case established by *Per vestras*, they maintained that it was entirely legitimate for the hypothecary creditor to exercise the *ius offerende pecunie*. It was left to a judge to arrange for the cash payment to be placed with a merchant, thereby providing a secure haven for the cash as well as a source of income.[102] This doctrine, which was intended to afford security to the husband's hypothecary creditors, prevailed over the teachings of the *Glossa* and Bartolus.

Did a wife inadvertently renounce her right to act in an ongoing marriage if, when the dowry was transferred to the husband, it was specified that its restoration to her and her heirs would occur only upon termination of the marriage (*soluto matrimonio*)? This was not a pseudoproblem, since dotal instruments invariably included such clauses in accordance with notarial formularies. Did the omission of reference to restoration of the dowry in an ongoing marriage (*constante matrimonio*), therefore, constitute proof that the wife had renounced her claim in the event that her husband became insolvent? The *Glossa ordinaria* did not tackle this issue, while Dinus left it unresolved. Jacobus de Ravanis and Jacobus de Arena argued that the wife had forfeited her rights in an ongoing marriage, but they were opposed by Cinus, who permitted the wife to act because her demand that the dowry be returned in an ongoing marriage in the case of impending insolvency did not constitute genuine restoration. Cinus's opinion was reaffirmed by a legion of jurists, including Bartolus, who reiterated that by law the wife could not renounce the benefits and remedies granted her by the *Digest*, *Code*, and *Authentica*.[103]

Similarly, was the wife banned from acting in an ongoing marriage if the statutes of the community made restoration of the dowry contingent upon termination of marriage, a condition appearing in almost all of the *Statuta* I have examined for northern and central Italy? That condition does not appear to have been an important doctrinal issue, as jurists, judges, and legislators were unanimous that restoration of the dowry in cases of insolvency did not count as true restoration and that in the event of conflict the *ius commune* would prevail over local statutes. Bartolus's dictum, *casus inopie remanet in iure communi*, most likely accounts for the omission of the *casus inopie* from so many compilations and editions of municipal statutes in Italy dating from the late Middle Ages.[104] Notable exceptions are Arezzo, Ravenna, Vicenza, and the university towns of Pisa and Bologna, whose statutes expressly authorized a wife to sue her insolvent spouse and lay claim to his properties.[105]

One city which did witness disputes over the statutes regulating restoration of the dowry was Florence, where restoration under the *Statuta* of 1325 was conditional upon termination of marriage due to the husband's natural death.[106] Jacobus Butrigarius was asked to resolve a dispute pitting a certain Caterina against her insolvent husband's solvent codebtors (*correi*), who claimed that they were not open to suit because of the wording of the *Statuta*. The dotal contract, they also claimed, specified that their obligation to perform restoration took effect only upon termination of marriage. Butrigarius, in his opinion, admitted that Caterina had no legal claim against her husband's codebtors under the wording of the statutes.[107] In a full and perfected restoration, the wife would be free to use and alienate the dowry as she saw fit. In this case, the dowry was inalienable and was required to serve the common benefit of her family. Nonetheless, Butrigarius continued, her action was permitted by the *ius commune* – namely, *Ubi adhuc*, *Si constante*, and *Illud quoque sancire*.[108] It was also permitted by equity, which limits the application of the statutory prohibition and which "regulates the meaning of statutory words, as it is neither appropriate for, nor will equity permit, a wife to be without a dowry and for the same reason, her husband and children."[109] Finally, by virtue of the *ius commune* the *casus inopie* was exempt from dotal pacts involving third parties making restoration conditional upon termination of marriage. For these reasons, Butrigarius concluded, the dowry could be restored to the wife during an ongoing marriage, notwithstanding Florence's statutes.[110] Butrigarius's opinion was well known and cited approvingly by Baldus.[111]

In Florence as elsewhere, husbands and their sureties promised to restore and repay the dowry and marital donation in every instance in which they were required to do so. The question arose in Florence whether this contractual obligation to perform restoration could serve to obstruct the wife's suit against a husband facing insolvency. Put in another way, did the formulaic guarantee "restituere, solvere, et pagare in omnem eventum restituende dotis et solvende dotis" encompass restoration in an ongoing marriage? Ludovicus Pontanus counseled that it did, while he conceded that the dowry was intended to relieve the burdens of marriage and therefore remained inalienable.[112] But these burdens, he contended, continued after the husband's death, making it imperative that the wife's dowry was restored in expectation of her second marriage. Ingenious and unorthodox, Pontanus's argument at least recognized two significant facts of Florentine life: Florentine husbands tended to predecease their wives, and young widows with dowries could and did remarry.[113] Pontanus also denied the conventional argument that full and perfected restoration of the dowry could not occur in an ongoing marriage. Restoration, he explained, was defined as the transfer of possession of a thing and its fruits. This was exactly what happened when the dowry was recovered by the wife from a husband approaching insolvency. As for the supposition that the words "solvende" and "reddende" were excluded from the definition of "restituere," Pontanus replied that these words, which were customarily employed in dotal instruments, were understood to include the return of the dowry "constante matrimonio."

In the absence of a statutory provision permitting a wife to recover her dowry in an ongoing marriage, the wifes's father and brother took legal precautions to strengthen her dotal rights. Numerous dotal contracts stipulated that the husband and all other parties would be obligated to restore the dowry during marriage as well as upon its termination.[114] This issue was eventually put to rest in the revised corpus of Florentine statutes promulgated in 1415, which formally recognized the right of wives to recover their dowries from husbands approaching insolvency in an ongoing marriage.[115]

Jurists also argued that a husband could not forestall his wife's action by merely acknowledging his obligation in a written document (*carta*) that would serve as evidence in litigation. Nor could he forestall her action by providing sureties, that is, guarantees issued by third parties that they would perform the husband's obligation in the event he was incapable. Such sureties were common and considered operable, but only upon termination of marriage. Given the imminent danger to the dowry and to the well-being of the family, jurists plugged what they believed was a loophole through which the husband would be able to frustrate the wife's legitimate claims. They reasoned that a written promise, no matter how solemn, is easily broken and that it is safer to have something in hand rather than a written guarantee.[116] Canonists, as we have seen, permitted the husband to offer his wife solemn promises and guarantees to serve in lieu of restoration. Their collective opinion may have carried weight in ecclesiastical courts, but not in the civil law arena, where the *casus inopie* was customarily played out.

The inherent incapacity of the wife to alienate the properties of a husband approaching insolvency as well as her own dowry raised serious doubts about her ownership (*dominium*) during marriage. Yet, by permitting the wife to undertake the *actio rei vindicatio*, jurists were, in theory, acknowledging her capacity to act as *domina* of her dowry.[117] An especially vexing issue was whether she became *domina* of the husband's properties assigned to her by a judge.[118] Looking backward from the perspective of the fifteenth century, it is clear that the teachings of Bartolus, quickly buttressed by Baldus, formed the core doctrine on this contested issue. For Bartolus, the incidence of ownership was not predicated on the freedom of alienation but dependent on the specific type of legal action undertaken by the wife.[119] When her suit was based on the husband's wrongdoing (*actio in personam*), she acquired ownership of properties paid to her instead of the actual dowry. When she sued to recover specific properties in her husband's possession – claiming, for example, that she was their lawful owner (*actio in rem, rei vindicatio*), she was obviously not *domina* by means of a transfer of ownership (*traditio*), but by reason of civil law. However, when she instituted a hypothecary action, it was certain that under *Ubi adhuc* she did not acquire ownership of the assigned properties, but only a real security (*pignus*).[120] Here, transfer of possession, not ownership, took place. The meaning of the word "to assign" (*assignare*), Bartolus observed, was equivocal, signifying both the transfer of possession and ownership.[121] Under ordinary circumstances, *assignare* was presumed to signify transfer of possession. But in the exceptional case of insolvency, he hesitantly concluded, *assignare* was presumed to signify transfer of ownership.[122]

For the husband approaching insolvency, there was an obvious advantage in transferring ownership as well as possession of the properties assigned to his wife. As owner, it was the wife, not the husband, who would bear the responsibility and risks of managing the assigned properties. Should their value decrease during her administration, the loss was entirely hers. She, not the husband, was now liable for taxes imposed on the assigned properties. Florentine tax records reveal that the properties assigned in lieu of the dowry to the wives whose husbands were exiled were assessed for forced loans (*prestanze*). Some wives protested, claiming statutory protection – specifically, that under the Florentine statutes they were exempt from paying taxes while their husbands were still living. True enough, but the jurists tasked by the city with settling this conflict appropriately countered that the moment ownership and possession of the properties were transferred to the wife she became fully liable for the tax assessments that would have been payable by the husband before the assignment.[123]

The husband's voluntary transfer of ownership was also recognized as a stratagem for protecting property from his creditors. As a privileged creditor, the wife had a claim to the assigned properties that was preferred to the claims of all other creditors. Fearing collusion between husband and wife, jurists opposed not only voluntary transfers, but also voluntary confessions of impending insolvency made by husband and wife together or by the husband alone.[124] Both Dinus and Cinus presumed voluntary confessions of impending insolvency to be fraudulent and the ensuing assignment of properties to the wife indistinguishable from an unlawful gift damaging creditors.[125] Cinus conceded the validity of such confessions when made in a legal forum where evidence and testimony attested to the husband's insolvency. To win their claim against the husband, his creditors would have to prove not only that they suffered damages, but equally that the husband alone or husband and wife in concert acted with demonstrable intent to defraud the husband's creditors. Couples intent on defrauding creditors would probably have made their confession quietly, in the presence of a judge-notary (*judex ordinarius*) or extrajudicially in a document, beyond the glaring notoriety of public legal proceedings. Dinus and Cinus ruled that in this case the husband's creditors could lay claim to his properties by merely showing that they had suffered damages. Their opinion, which eliminated the requirement to provide proof of fraudulent intent, was clearly advantageous to creditors seeking to assert their claims against the husband's assets.

Bartolus, on the other hand, favored the wife and husband.[126] The voluntary confession was valid, he contended, in so far as it was truthful: that the husband was in fact approaching insolvency. The assignment of properties to the wife effected by a voluntary confession made by a genuinely insolvent husband before a judge-notary, or even extrajudicially, was not revocable. Bartolus's teaching rested on the premise that any contract made between husband and wife which served to safeguard and benefit the dowry, and concurrently did not impoverish the husband, was valid. Creditors wishing to contest the voluntary confession and the assignment had to go to court and prove both that the confession had been made with fraudulent intent and that they in fact had suffered damages. Bartolus agreed that any amount assigned to the wife exceeding the value of the dowry which the husband originally acknowledged receiving in a *confessio dotis* (another common stratagem to defraud creditors) constituted an unlawful and revocable gift.

Whatever their doctrinal differences, all jurists, as well as notaries and legislators, recognized that the remedy provided by the *ius commune* to safeguard the wife's dowry and patrimony unleashed the baleful consequence of providing husbands and wives with a golden opportunity to defraud creditors. The line dividing a fraudulent from a lawful assignment of properties to the wife, either owing to her petition and suit or to the husband's voluntary confession, was often barely perceptible. In practice, it was relatively easy for the husband, with his wife's collusion, to conceal assets. Even when the wife petitioned for the restoration of her dowry and the assignment of her husband's properties before a judge-notary, there was no certainty, given the delays in the redactions of documents and the loss of notarial documents during periods of plague, that this act would inevitably become public knowledge.[127] Lack of transparency damaged the husband's creditors at the time of the assignment, as well as unfortunate potential creditors who remained ignorant of the husband's insolvency. Not only was the smooth functioning of the marketplace at stake, but also the integrity of the communal fisc whose tax revenues were jeopardized by fictitious insolvencies.

It was left to local governments to deter the abuse of this legal remedy by bringing insolvency to the attention of the public. Public notification would alert creditors, and, by heaping shame upon the insolvent husband and his kin, might serve as a deterrence. In Pisa, assignments of monies and properties to the wife were required to be registered in a special cartulary conserved in the chancery. In Vicenza, a wife was forbidden to receive the assignment of her husband's properties, unless a formal announcement of her husband's insolvency and the impending assignment was made in the Great Council and by heralds in customary public places. In fifteenth-century Florence, cases of insolvency were enmeshed in a web of red tape, and petitions for the assignment of the insolvent husband's goods to the wife required prior approval of the Signoria with the legislative councils, and later the Otto di Guardia, the magistracy in charge of internal security.[128]

By making governmental approval mandatory before assignment of the husband's properties could take place, Florence violated the spirit and the letter of the *ius commune*. It must be stressed, however, that regulations and procedures crafted on the local level were not designed to eliminate the wife's legal remedy, but only its abuse. Although it is impossible at present to discern whether these measures mitigated the incidence of fraud, public registration and notification of insolvency have furnished the modern historian with evidence that recourse to this legal remedy was common. In Florence, 460 cases are recorded between 1435 and 1535 in which women instituting actions against husbands said to be approaching insolvency were awarded properties roughly equivalent to their dowries.[129] One such case, occurring at the end of the Florentine republic, centered on Piero di Niccolò Da Filicaia, a member of an old, distinguished family and the author of a treatise on recreational mathematics (*Libro di giuochi mathematici*). He married Lena di Antonio Albizzi in 1516 and the following year acknowledged receipt of a dowry of 1,500 florins, 900 payable by Florence's Dowry Fund and 600 in cash. Piero's paltry financial resources did not match his elevated social status. He inherited few properties when his father died in 1510, did not accumulate wealth from his business dealings, and since 1520 had experienced financial troubles. Acting to safeguard her dowry, Lena petitioned the Otto di Guardia on 2 November 1528 to authorize its restoration for the reason that "Pierus eius vir vergit ad inopiam." Lena's petition was approved on the twenty-first and it appears that Piero died immediately after in the plague engulfing Florence. Lena was able to recover a substantial portion of her dowry, which provided a measure of support during the long years of widowhood until her death in 1568.[130]

Insolvency was not necessarily a permanent condition, leading jurists to consider the matter of temporary insolvency and its ramifications in the following model case. A husband approaching insolvency returns the dowry or assigned properties to his wife in accordance with the law. Later, either by inheritance or some other means, he becomes wealthy, and now wishes to recover what he returned or assigned to his wife. Does the husband have a legal action to take back the assigned properties or payment made to the wife? Since the *Corpus iuris civilis* did not give any guidance on this issue, it was left to the *Glossa ordinaria* to fill the void. The *Glossa* categorically opposed the husband's action, as the payment made to the wife was lawful and merited.[131] By logical extension, the wife recovered her dowry or acquired her husband's property in good faith and has just title to them. Odofredus and Jacobus de Ravanis seconded the *Glossa*'s defense of the wife,[132] while Dinus held that the dowry should remain with the wife as it would if the marriage had terminated.[133] Dissenting, Riccardus Malumbra and Oldradus de Ponte sided with the husband.

Malumbra reasoned that, owing to the husband's change in fortune, the cause (*inopia*) precipitating restoration to the wife ceases to exist. In consequence, the dowry can be returned to its former condition, that is, to the husband. Similarly, Oldradus opined that the husband's newly acquired wealth removes the impediment to the husband's action.[134] Jacobus de Arena asked whether the properties recovered by the wife resulted from a hypothecary action or from a payment for her dowry. In the first instance, the husband can lay claim to his properties, because they are not considered to be in the wife's permanent possession; they remain with her only as long as the husband remains insolvent. In the second instance, the husband cannot act to recover what he paid to the wife because it belongs to her. The husband, Jacobus de Arena observed, has no cause to complain, since by law his wife must use the dowry for their common benefit.[135]

In the fourteenth century, the *Glossa*'s position was championed by Cinus, Bartolus, and Baldus, whose teachings were accepted as the *communis opinio*. After reviewing earlier opinions, Cinus advised taking the path that is safer and more beneficial for the dowry. And Cinus was inclined to believe that the dowry is safer in the wife's possession, because any goods acquired by the husband after having made restoration to his wife were subject to the lawful claims of his creditors.[136] Bartolus, too, placed a premium on the dowry's security. The husband's supervening wealth, he contended, does not erase the cause for restoration: to provide security for the wife. Looking forward, restoration and the husband's new wealth are not contradictory but complementary, because both produce the optimum result of furnishing security for the wife's dowry. For this reason, the restoration cannot be overturned.[137] Baldus held the opinion of the *Glossa ordinaria* to be "truer" than the opinion of Malumbra and Oldradus. He reasoned that once the dowry is restored to the wife, she becomes its permanent owner, which prevents her husband's action. At the same time, her right to act against her husband is in every respect extinguished (*consummatus*). Should the dowry revert to her husband, the wife would have no legal recourse either upon termination of marriage or if he became insolvent once again. It is implicit in Baldus's logic that the certain injury the wife would suffer from the dowry's reversion to the husband must be avoided.[138] Multiple insolvencies and reclamations, for our jurists, were a nightmare they chose not to contemplate.

To conclude briefly, the Roman law remedy empowering wives to sue for the recovery of the dowry from husbands approaching insolvency in an ongoing marriage was emphatically reaffirmed and extensively amplified by medieval jurists. The remedy was designed to promote the welfare of the married couple and their children; to safeguard the wife's property so that upon her husband's predecease she could live honorably in widowhood; and, after her own death, to assure the transmission of the dowry to her children and other family members. The paramount challenge facing these jurists was to make the remedy operable in a world crisscrossed by local jurisdictions with their volatile commercial market economies – a world radically different from the late Roman imperial civilization that gave birth to the *Corpus iuris civilis*. The challenge was met; conceptual and practical obstacles were overcome. The chief contribution of medieval jurists lay in the domain of procedure,[139] in fashioning institutional measures for the vigorous enforcement of the remedy, not only in Italy but also across the western Mediterranean.[140] There was a pervasive belief, corroborated by professional experience, that delay would blunt the remedy's effectiveness. Drawn-out court proceedings were discouraged in favor of preemptive measures and summary procedure. As we have seen, the enforcement of the wife's remedy was so overwhelming successful that couples unburdened by scruples seized it as an opportunity to defraud their creditors.

The fact that the wives parading through the glosses, commentaries, opinions, and statutes examined in this chapter were recognized as full-fledged legal persons endowed with the capacity of acting to defend and preserve what rightfully belonged to them should not be equated with a conscious concern for female rights and control over the dowry. Such an equation would be egregiously anachronistic. The dominant focus of all these texts was the secure management of the dowry in an ongoing marriage and its orderly transmission after the marriage's termination.

7 Women Married Elsewhere: Gender and Citizenship in Medieval Italy

Grounds

"In many sections of our law," the early-third-century Roman jurist Papinian declared, "the position of females is inferior to that of males."[1] It is unnecessary to rehearse the gender-specific rules that disabled Roman women, unmarried and married, in the spheres of private and public law; these have been amply documented and examined. It is also well known that three centuries later the *Corpus iuris civilis* of the emperor Justinian eliminated various disabilities limiting women's capacity to contract, to make a last will, and to inherit. In the public sphere, Roman women were excluded from offices and honors, from performing the truth-telling function of the jurist, and from representing others in court.[2] In the fateful words of the Roman jurist Ulpian, recorded in the *Digest* (50. 17. 2, *Feminae*), "women are barred from all civil and public functions and therefore cannot be judges or hold a magistracy or bring a lawsuit or intervene on behalf of anyone else or act as procurators." In Robinson's summation, "public law remained a closed field, and social and economic realities kept women practically subordinate in Justinian's law, but the theoretical equality of the sexes before the private law was largely achieved."[3]

In the patrilineal setting of medieval Italian communities, the legal capacities of women were again circumscribed, even more tightly than in Papinian's day. The social reproduction of patrilineal regimes depended on sons succeeding their fathers as heads of the household and as masters of the family's patrimonial properties.[4] Under the *Corpus iuris*, daughters and sons at least theoretically inherited equally, but under medieval patrilineal regimes, daughters were ordinarily excluded from inheritance by law. They were endlessly advised to be content with their dowries, which by custom and law were supposed to be commensurate with the resources of the bride's father (*secundum facultatem patris*).[5] Absent surviving brothers, a minority of daughters would inherit the father's estate as if by default.[6] Yet, even though the dowry, together with extradotal properties or *paraphernalia*,[7] often represented a sizable amount, the bulk of the father's estate was generally destined for sons and other male relatives on the father's side. In the public sphere, Guerra Medici reminds us that in medieval Italy "urban women did not take oaths, did not participate in the assemblies, and did not take part in public life. They had no access to public places where decisions were made on the life of the community."[8]

Although debarred from active citizenship, a free Roman woman born legitimately in the late Roman Empire was regarded a citizen of Rome (*civitas romana*), the common fatherland (*communis patria*).[9] She also enjoyed citizenship (*ius civitatis*) in the city of her origin (*origo*). The *ius civitatis* derived from paternal descent rather than from one's actual place of birth or domicile. Legitimate children acquired their father's *origo*, or place of origin, illegitimate children, their mother's place of origin. A betrothed woman did not change her domicile before contracting marriage.[10] In contrast, unless she remarried, a widow retained her husband's domicile.[11] The married woman's assumption of her husband's domicile, it cannot be emphasized too strongly, did not entail the loss of her own place of origin. The immutable attachment to one's place of origin was a hallowed Roman law principle enshrined in *l. Adsumptio originis* (Dig. 50. 1. 6) and *l. Origine propria* (Cod. 10 39 [38]. 4): "It is evident that persons, by their own will, cannot be released from their place of origin."[12] Although she was discharged from undertaking public duties in her own place of origin, the Roman wife remained accountable for charges on real property located there that she inherited from her father (*munera patrimonii*).[13]

Justinians's *Corpus iuris* was the product of a vast empire, in which the status of a Roman citizen signified attachment to a common fatherland, not to a particular territorial community. Since the married couple shared a common Roman citizenship, intercity marriage did not alter the wife's status as a *civis romana*. Dual citizenship, strictly speaking, was not envisioned, for Roman citizenship superseded local citizenship.[14] In stark contrast, medieval jurists operated in a world of intense localism, of politically independent lawmaking communities with their campanilistic ethos. No wonder that citizenship terminology and practices in medieval Italy were neither monolithic nor systematic. They differed from town to town, were highly variable and even contradictory within an individual community, and emerged in relation to specific political and socioeconomic conditions.[15] That said, original citizenship signified attachment to a local community with jurisdiction over a particular territory.[16]

The immigration policies of medieval Italian towns also allowed for dual citizenship: original citizenship (*civilitas originaria*) and citizenship acquired by municipal statute (*civilitas ex statuto/privilegio*). For example, one could be concurrently a citizen of Florence by origin and Pisa by municipal enactment. In the population-depleted fourteenth and fifteenth centuries, towns everywhere granted citizenship to foreign men who married native women and established residence in the wife's hometown.[17] Notable but rare were peace agreements in which men from several towns were designated to marry women from each other's towns. In consequence of the reciprocal exchange, the new husbands were awarded citizenship in the wives' hometowns.[18] Grants of statutory citizenship were basically restricted to men. Town registers of newly made citizens reveal that only a minuscule number of unmarried adult women and widows were granted citizenship via statute or decree.[19] Northern cities, in contrast, including Bremen, Coesfeld, and Speyer, welcomed independent women, to whom they frequently granted citizenship.[20]

On the mapping of married women's citizenship, the disparity between the *Corpus iuris* and medieval jurists is striking. Although it is difficult to pinpoint the initial departure from the Roman model of a married woman's civil status, the seeds of departure were planted by the close of the twelfth century in *Summae* devoted to explicating and supplementing the last three books of the *Codex* (10–12), or *Tres Libri*, as they were called in the Middle Ages.[21] Of interest are the opinions of Pillius de Medicina, a venerated professor at the University of Bologna and then Modena, who continued the *Summa Codicis* of his teacher, Piacentinus; and Pillius's contemporary, Rolandus de Lucca, a jurist and public official whose experience in fiscal administration informed his architectonic *Summa Trium Librorum*, the last version of which appeared at the beginning of the thirteenth century. Large extracts of Pillius's *Summa*, including the passage on women's civil status that I discuss below, were incorporated by Rolandus into his own *Summa*, and later by Azo Portius into his *Summa Codicis*.[22]

At the end of a passage elucidating Roman law norms and rules on the civil status of women, Pillius asserts that "to the extent that a wife follows the domicile of the husband, she turns away from her own place of origin ("propriam declinat originem"), as, for example, § *Item rescripserunt mulierum* [Dig. 50. 1. 38. 3]."[23] What is the import of this passage? Is the husband's place of origin different from the wife's, and is he therefore a foreigner? Considering that it was common for women married to foreigners to move to the husband's place of origin (and vice versa), the inference that he is a foreigner is reasonable. Does the passage mean that the wife turns away from, and therefore forsakes, her own place of origin with respect to citizenship? Such a reading is doubtful, for it runs afoul of the entrenched Roman law prohibition, which Pillius endorses repeatedly, against voluntary renunciation of one's place of origin.[24] Assuming for argument's sake that "declinat propriam originem" refers to citizenship, it is probable that, for Pillius, the change occurred by the impersonal operation of law rather than her own free will. Yet § *Item rescripserunt mulierum*, authorizing the change in the wife's civil status, is silent about loss of citizenship. Rather, it states "that a woman as long as she is married is regarded as a resident (*incola*) of the community to which her husband belongs." The expression "declinat propriam originem" almost certainly alludes to the wife's original domicile. To avoid ambiguity and misconstruals, jurists in the later Middle Ages employed the expression "domicilium originis," which was foreign to Roman thinking and did not exist in the *Corpus iuris*, to indicate that original domicile, rather than original citizenship, was the referent. In sum, for Pillius, the wife residing with her husband in his town forsakes her place of origin *only* to the extent that she is released from performing public duties.[25] In all other matters the wife's umbilical connection to her place of origin remains unbroken, the import of which is that the passage from Pillius is consistent with the Roman laws that he is elucidating.

As Menzinger shows, Rolandus stressed the territorial character of taxation so that women were obligated to pay taxes on real or patrimonial property in the jurisdiction in which it was located. In support of the needs of communal treasuries, he advocated that special privileges exempting women, knights, and clergy from taxes and public duties should be eliminated and that taxes should be levied proportionate to the taxpayer's assessed wealth.[26] As for the civil status of a woman married elsewhere, Rolandus carefully adheres to the *Digest* and *Codex*, citing the rule that the wife concurrently assumes the husband's domicile and relinquishes hers in her place of origin, where she is no longer compelled to perform public duties. Furthermore, this rule is warranted by Paul's Letter to the Ephesians (5:23 and 31), in which women are subject to their husbands as to the Lord. In Paul's imagery, "the husband is the head of the wife," with whom "she becomes one flesh with her husband."[27] This is the first instance that I have come across of what will become an oft-cited justificatory linkage between the Bible and the alteration of the wife's civil status. There is no indication in Rolandus's disquisition that the wife becomes a citizen in her husband's town or ceases being a citizen of her own hometown.

For reasons that remain cloudy, the Roman model of married women's citizenship was openly and decisively modified in the early thirteenth century with the appearance of Accursius's massive *Glossa ordinaria* to the *Corpus iuris*, which "was universally accepted as an essential and standard accompaniment to the texts of Justinian."[28] After reiterating the principle that residence depends exclusively on the intentional choice of the person acquiring domicile, the *Glossa* holds that the principle does not apply to a married woman who unavoidably becomes a domiciliary resident of her husband's town. Mindful of that principle, the *Glossa* continues, "the term resident (*incola)* is improperly applied to the wife, for she becomes a citizen (*civis*) [of her husband's town]." By analogy, she becomes a citizen involuntarily, just as the freed slave adopts his master's place of origin and the adopted person that of his adoptive father.[29] More radically, the *Glossa* breaks with the Roman model by asserting that *lex Adsumptio originis* does not extend to the case of marriage ("fallit propter matrimonium").[30] Though not spelled out, the corollary is that the wife married elsewhere ceases to be a citizen of her own place of origin.

The *Glossa*'s model of married women's civil status validated political and economic conventions. Fearing the loss of taxable property, nearly all communities in northern and central Italy introduced statutes prohibiting foreigners from acquiring real property subject to a community's jurisdiction.[31] Foreign husbands of native women, who acquired valuable properties through the wife's dowry, were the primary targets of these laws. In order to prevent these men from controlling such properties, communities enacted laws imposing penalties on native women with substantial dowries and inheritances who married foreigners and resided in the husbands' towns. Penalties included monetary fines, forfeiture of property, and the inability to inherit from family members remaining in the wives' hometowns. These penalties were not imposed on foreign husbands who established domicile in the wives' hometowns.

For medieval jurists, the transfiguration of the woman married elsewhere into a citizen of her husband's town was linked to the unipersonality of the married couple, a sacramental union in which the wife, joined to the husband's flesh, was the subordinate partner.[32] As the couple through the sacrament of marriage is joined in one flesh, so are they joined in one citizenship and in one domicile, where the wife willingly submits to her husband's authority and leadership. Divine, natural, and civil law were thus harmonized in one body and one citizenship. The primacy given to the juridical unity of the family enhanced the dominance of the husband

and his heirs over the wife and her property. As a citizen of her husband's town she would be fully subject to its laws. Any benefits the husband might accumulate from this change were offset by his wife's corresponding loss of original citizenship, which disqualified her from acquiring the legal benefits and protections (*beneficia statutorum*) reserved for citizens of her hometown.[33] Specifically, in her hometown, the woman-married-elsewhere's capacity as a citizen to enter into contracts, to receive a dowry, together with gifts and legacies of extradotal properties, and to seek relief in the courts was abridged.

Enter Bartolus

Bartolus de Saxoferrato, the preeminent jurist of the first half of the fourteenth century, was respectfully critical of the *Glossa*'s authority. He was as committed as any jurist to the unipersonality of the married couple, to the husband's supremacy, to gender-based distinctions, and to updating the *Corpus iuris* to complement contemporaneous practices. Yet he was an independent-minded jurist, who viewed the woman-married-elsewhere's compulsory loss of citizenship and legal benefits as inequitable and materially harmful. And he was remarkably adept at crafting remedies for the disabilities, intentional and unintentional, inflicted upon women by ill-advised statutes.

His remedy for a woman married elsewhere was presented in his commentary on the paragraph § *Item rescripserunt mulierum* (Dig. 50. 1. 38. 3), where he asked whether a wife loses her original citizenship, notwithstanding the force of *lex Adsumptio*.[34]

> I ask whether a wife becomes a citizen of the city to which her husband belongs, or simply a resident? The text of the law seems to say that she is a resident, and I do not know of any law saying that she becomes a citizen. The *Glossa* says, however, that she becomes a citizen, and that here the term resident [*incola*] is used improperly, which I think is true enough, by analogy to the case of an adopted child, and because a wife becomes one flesh with her husband. Further, I ask if a wife who married elsewhere ceases to be a citizen of that city which is her place of origin? It seems that this is not the case, for place of origin cannot be changed, according to *lex Adsumptio*. The *Glossa* says the opposite. If she cannot be called to perform public services, shoulder personal burdens, and appear in court [in her place of origin], it seems that she is no longer a citizen of that city. It does not matter if one alleges *lex Adsumptio,* because according to the *Glossa* this is a special case.[35]

Bartolus had recently addressed this question, he reported, in a dispute over a city statute that prohibited foreigners from purchasing immovable property in its territory. The prohibition was premised on the rule that statutory benefits enjoyed by citizens are not applicable to foreigners.

Does the statute, he asked, apply to a woman married elsewhere who wishes to buy immovable property in her place of origin? He answered memorably:

> Suppose that a woman originating from that city who marries elsewhere wants to buy immovable property there, what should we say? Briefly, we can say that she changes her place of origin in regard to everything by which the person of the wife can be drawn away and separated from the services of her husband, and therefore she cannot be called and forced in that city to shoulder personal burdens, perform public services, or be summoned to court, and this is what the laws cited above say. In regard to other things, she does not change her place of origin, as we say in the case of a freedwoman, married with the consent of her master, who remains a freed person, although not with respect to the duties a freeborn owes to the patron, and consequently she can buy immovable property, which, in my opinion, is equitable. And if someone should kill her, that person should be punished just as if a citizen had been killed. And I believe that she also enjoys other privileges granted to citizens.[36]

Bartolus's solution served to reconcile the conflict between the *Corpus iuris* and the *Glossa*. First, citing *lex Adsumptio* and the authoritative analogy of the freedwoman, he repatriated the woman married elsewhere, who once again had recourse to the *beneficia statutorum* of her original city, and he repaired the wife's legal ties to the family she left behind. Nevertheless, a return to the status quo before the *Glossa* was unthinkable. Accordingly, Bartolus concurred that the wife acquired her foreign husband's citizenship, thus assuring her respectful compliance, though he acknowledged that this change was not authorized by *Corpus iuris*. Bartolus did not explicitly elaborate on the temporality of the wife's new civic status – namely, when she actually became a citizen of her husband's place of origin and whether she remained a citizen upon termination of marriage. Discussing the rule *mulier sequitur forum viri* at the beginning of his commentary on § *Item rescripserunt mulierum*, Bartolus asserted that the change in the wife's domicile was predicated on a valid marriage contracted through words of present consent (*verba de presenti*). A betrothal contracted through vows of future consent (*verba de futuro*) did not alter a fiancée's civic status.[37] The formulaic "one flesh" signified consummation of marriage, but a valid marriage with the ensuing change in the wife's civic status was not dependent on consummation or public installation (*transducta*) of the bride in the husband's residence.[38] The wife, upon her husband's predecease, even before moving to his place of origin, was deemed a legal resident there, so long as she remained a widow. Bartolus's position on the wife's domicile, understood within the unfolding logic of his commentary, was surely meant to apply as well to the citizenship of a woman married elsewhere.

Along with the *Corpus iuris* and the *Glossa*, Bartolus's commentary on § *Item rescripserunt mulierum* became a controlling text for jurists occupied with the issue of intercity marriages. His solution was fair, for it maximized the wife's and husband's benefits, while it minimized their disadvantages. It pleased the majority of his successors, who intuitively believed that original citizenship derived from nature and was therefore immutable. But his solution was never treated as a universal panacea for the range of largely unforeseeable problems arising from intercity marriages. Intercity marriage and dual citizenship generated inevitable jurisdictional conflicts, as we can see in the following examination of three oft-cited *consilia* (legal opinions) written by Baldus de Ubaldis of Perugia.

Baldus de Ubaldis

As Bartolus's postmortem reputation swelled in the second half of the fourteenth century, so did, contemporaneously, the reputation of his most brilliant and productive disciple, Baldus de Ubaldis, who soon became the leading Italian jurist and consultor.[39] The range of Baldus's work is impressive: commentaries on the *Corpus iuris* and on canon and feudal law, treatises, and roughly three thousand *consilia*, most of which were occasioned by actual cases.[40] Manuscript copies of his *consilia* are found throughout Europe and even across the Atlantic, at the University of Chicago. His *consilia* were printed and reprinted – for instance, in Brescia (1490–1), Milan (1491–3), Venice (1575 and 1599), and Frankfurt am Main (1589). Touching on virtually every area of private and public law, his opinions were instantly consequential and remained influential into the eighteenth century. They illustrate that local law was not self-evident, self-enforcing, or self-rectifying, but required the continual intervention of cosmopolitan jurists applying the *ius commune* and their interpretative skills to local cases. For the historian, they furnish invaluable detailed snapshots of critical moments in the lives of fourteenth-century women, from the cradle to the grave. Hundreds of his *consilia* are dedicated to married women's property (*bona mulieris*), especially the constitution, disposition, and devolution of dowries.[41]

In working with Baldus's *consilia* and those of other jurists, one must be alert to multiple methodological challenges. First and foremost, the printed editions are marred by grammatical errors, falsifications, lacunae, and interpolations. It is absolutely necessary to return to manuscript copies (which also contain errors) for the purpose of establishing reliable and intelligible texts. Fortunately, the Barberini manuscripts in the Biblioteca Apostolica Vaticana contain an excellent collection of Baldus's *consilia*, autographs as well as copies, with additions and corrections made by Baldus himself or by his scribe.[42]

Second, *consilia* were integral to the formal process of dispute resolution, but it is exceptional that readers are afforded more than a glimpse of the concrete contingent facts of the dispute (*punctus*) moving public officials (*podestà*, *capitano del popolo*, *vicario*), judges, or litigants to request Baldus's opinion. In addition, the outcome of a case and the presiding judge's sentence are rarely reported. With luck and laborious sleuthing, one can occasionally find supplementary materials providing answers to extratextual questions conventionally posed by historians.

Third, the applicability of local statutes was almost always a central issue. Normally, consultors like Baldus included in a *consilium* an abstract or brief citation of the relevant statutes, copies of which were surely on their desks at the moment of composition. To grasp the legal issues at stake in a case, it is necessary to consult the redactions of the statutes cited by Baldus – but many of them, let it be stressed, are no longer extant or remain in manuscript awaiting critical editions.

Fourth, the identity of the party commissioning a *consilium*, crucial to interpreting the direction of the jurist's arguments, is often difficult to discern. This is especially true regarding Baldus's *consilia*, for which there are only scant references throwing light on the source of his commissions. Undoubtedly, some of his opinions were *consilia sapientis* produced at the request of officials, judges, and both parties (one party with the consent of the other, or the two parties together).[43] A *consilium sapientis* was designed to be impartial and by convention almost always determined the judge's sentence. However, the overwhelming majority of Baldus's *consilia* were probably *pro parte*, commissioned by individual litigants.[44] Presiding judges were not strictly bound to follow an opinion rendered on behalf of a client. But beyond an instant case, a *consilium pro parte*, particularly when rendered by a distinguished consultor like Baldus, carried the same doctrinal authority for the consultocrats as a *consilium sapientis*.

Domina Agnes

Lady Agnes was the protagonist of a case in the town of Castiglion Aretino, situated in the Valdichiana between Arezzo and Cortona. The case and Baldus's *consilium* perhaps date between 1379, when he returned from Padua to teach in Perugia, and December 1384, when Castiglion Aretino, having been forced to submit to Florence's rule, became Castiglion Fiorentino forever after.[45] The reference in the opening line of the *consilium* to "dicta domina Agnes" may allude to a preceding summary of the factual and legal issues the jurist was asked to address. This summary, unfortunately, was not included in the Barberini manuscript and printed editions. Internal evidence indicates that the case involved a homicide and that Agnes was alive at the time of the crime.[46] Since a defendant in a criminal case could not request a *consilium*, Baldus's opinion must have been a *consilium sapientis*, probably commissioned by the *podestà*.

Originally from neighboring Montecchio Vesponi, Agnes married a citizen of Castiglion Aretino. Baldus first considered the question of whether Agnes, by virtue of her marriage, was a citizen of her husband's place of origin (*origo*):

> Granted that the said lady Agnes was and is the wife of a true, natural, and original citizen of Castiglion, she also – seeing that insofar [*tanquam*] as she is joined to her husband's place of origin by virtue of marriage and insofar [*tanquam*] as she is made a part of her husband's body – is said to be and is of Castiglion Aretino for the duration of the marriage. For marriage is of such capacity and nature that it transfers the wife's place of origin to that of her husband. This is also established by virtue of the union in which that which is stronger draws to itself that which is less worthy. But there is no greater union than the conjugal union by which husband and wife are made one flesh, even, as it were [*quasi*], one substance in two persons. For that reason, the lady Agnes should be reckoned as [*tanquam*] a true and original citizen of the land of Castiglion. Since by divine law there is one flesh and divine law stands as truth and not fiction, it follows that the wife is properly made a fellow citizen of her husband, and this is what the *Glossa* holds as does Bartolus.[47]

Baldus's opinion harbors subtleties meriting attention. Bartolus is cited as an authority on a par with the *Corpus iuris* and the *Glossa*. But unlike Bartolus, Baldus was a doctor of canon as well as civil law (*utriusque iuris*), who reflexively cited canon law to explain why the wife involuntarily assumes her husband's place of origin and domicile. In addition, Baldus's penchant for medieval Aristotelian doctrines is noticeable in the image of a submissive and less worthy wife pulled away from her place of origin by her noble and stronger husband.[48] Baldus also subscribed to the conventional Aristotelian view that the male sex is characterized by an active generative force, the female sex by a passive generative force. Thomas Aquinas and his adherents, following Aristotle, contrasted females, who passively assist in the economy of procreation, with men, "who are ordained to a more noble vital activity, namely intellectual knowledge."[49]

Transfer of the wife's place of origin to that of the husband's is said to be authorized by divine, civil, and canon law, the *Glossa*, and Bartolus. But no mention is made of an authorizing statute. Drafted by learned jurists under the guidance of a committee of notable citizens, the statutory compilations of Italian communities omitted express declarations that a foreign woman married to a native man would be treated as a citizen, or conversely that a native woman married to a foreign man could look forward to an alteration or even loss of her citizenship. Pragmatic citizen-lawmakers of the fourteenth century had no incentive – fiscal, legal, or political – to expressly renounce jurisdiction over a group of citizens and their property. The conviction that the attribute of original citizenship was a permanent feature of one's legal persona, and therefore could not be eradicated, impeded the translation of the *Glossa*'s and Bartolus's doctrine into statutory law. Instead, citizens in violation of a community's statutes would be punished with fines and banishment, including confiscation of property. In this politico-legal setting, monetary penalties, rather than actual loss of citizenship, would suffice to inhibit native women from marrying elsewhere. Overall, it was best to tread softly, leaving the determination of the married woman's civic status, complicated by the theory that her status was transformed by divine and civil law, to jurists who would be asked to deal with individual cases as they arose.

What Bartolus left implicit, Baldus makes explicit. Agnes is not merely a citizen of her husband's place of origin, but is made a "true and original citizen." That Agnes "is of Castiglion Aretino" signifies, technically, that she is a true and legally valid citizen, whether or not she has domicile in Castiglion Aretino.[50] Significantly, she retains her new citizenship as long as she is married. By the same token, does Agnes cease being a citizen of

Montecchio Vesponi during the marriage? Baldus's language implies that she loses her original citizenship, since her place of origin is transferred to her husband's. And a few lines later, he refers to Agnes's status in the past tense (*erat Monticchiensis*). In light of the Roman law rule that one cannot claim multiple places of origin, the inference that Agnes ceases to be a native of Montecchio Vesponi on becoming an original citizen of Castiglion Aretino is tenable. That inference, as we shall see, runs directly counter to Baldus's repeated insistence that marriage does not – indeed, cannot – abolish the wife's natural filiation to her own fatherland (*patria*) or city (*civitas*).[51]

Like Bartolus, Baldus understood that making the wife a citizen and more radically an original citizen of her husband's *origo* had no basis in Roman law. That is why he relied on biblical and Aristotelian imagery, which had the effect of sowing confusion and contradiction. Baldus's argument that Agnes's newly minted status as a "true and original citizen" of Castiglion Aretino is not founded on legal fiction, because it procedes from divine law, is belied by the very language he employs. In the Latin text for the passage translated above he purposely uses the conjunction *tanquam* three times as a signpost to signal that what follows is not to be construed as fact, something that in reality happens, but "as if" or so to speak happens in this manner. Tellingly, he uses the adverb "quasi" to signal that the concept of one substance in two persons to express the union of husband and wife is an artificial construct proceeding from jurisprudential interpretation.[52]

For Baldus, legal fiction is a truth-giving artifact of the jurist's imagination. "Legal fiction," he explains, "is a falsehood accepted as truth on behalf of a most special just cause expressed in law."[53] Typically, the "most special just cause" served to adapt established law to new social facts and institutional arrangements – in our case, creating and granting original citizenship by statute to a heterogeneous group of individuals. Time and again he affirmed a city's capacity to create new citizens with roughly the same benefits and privileges enjoyed by original citizens. Baldus had firsthand knowledge of this procedure. In the words of Florentine enactment of October 1359 Baldus and his direct male descendants were to be regarded forever as "veri, originarii et antiqui cives populares" of Florence.[54] But he was emphatic that such statutory grants of original citizenship to non-original citizens, though unequivocally valid, were predicated on legal fiction – analogous to the legal fiction of adoption and the legitimation of children born out of wedlock. At first glance, the marriage bond, an institution confirmed by divine law, seemed to preclude the element of legal fiction. Not so, according to the canonists, including Baldus, who had no hesitation in describing the marriage bond as a *fictio iuris*. As Mayali observes: "On a conceptual level, the expression 'duo erunt in carne una' was also very early understood as the expression of a juridical fiction."[55] In the case of the wife married elsewhere, the joining of husband and wife into one flesh, engendering the transformation of her civic status, exemplified what Baldus called a unitive legal fiction (*fictio unitiva*).[56]

Turning to other questions, Baldus asks whether Agnes, granted that she was formerly of Montecchio, could be regarded under the statutes of Castiglion Aretino as a *Castiglionensis* in civil and criminal cases.[57] The answer was negative, because of an anomaly that rendered the statute inoperable. The statutes of Castiglion Aretino prescribe that while in its jurisdiction a *Monticchienis* should be regarded as a *Castiglionensis*, and the reverse, while in Montecchio a *Castiglionensis* should be regarded as a *Monticchiensis*. This applies to any legal situation or case (*in quocunque casu*). The statute of Montecchio carries an equal-treatment provision but is limited to three cases: civil, criminal, and damage caused by negligence, accident, or design (*damnum datum*). Because true reciprocity is lacking between the two statutes, Baldus argued, neither one applies in this case.[58]

From the above, it is certain that Castiglion Aretino was the place of prosecution. It remains uncertain whether Agnes was the victim or the offender, and whether the homicide was committed in Castiglion Aretino or Montecchio. Plausibly, this was a case of spousal homicide.[59] Agnes may have been killed by her husband in Castiglion Aretino, where he would have been subject to the penalty imposed for the crime of homicide. But suppose that he killed Agnes in Montecchio or another place outside the jurisdiction of Castiglion Aretino; that would prompt the question of whether she should be treated as a citizen or a foreigner. If she were treated as a foreigner, her husband would then be immune from prosecution in his own place of origin, because the crime had been committed beyond its jurisdiction. Recall that Bartolus dealt with a similar case involving the murder of a woman married elsewhere and famously insisted that her murderer should be prosecuted for having killed a fellow citizen. His opinion was cited in another case in which a husband hailing from Montepulciano killed his wife in her place of origin, Siena's *contado*, or countryside. He fled to nearby Montepulciano, where he was captured. The penalty facing the husband depended on whether his wife was considered a foreigner or a citizen of Montepulciano. In his *consilium sapientis*, Jacobus Thome de Firmio determined that, even though his foreign-born wife was killed in Siena's countryside and thus beyond the city's jurisdiction, the husband was prosecutable for homicide in Montepulciano for killing a fellow citizen, for which the penalty was death.[60]

It is remotely conceivable that Agnes killed her husband or another citizen of Castiglion Aretino. In that event, it was in her interest to be considered a citizen, not a foreigner. Again, at stake was the severity of punishment, which typically doubled when a foreigner offended a citizen.[61] The inapplicability of the equal-treatment provisions would have been welcome news to Agnes, if indeed she had committed the crime. At any rate, the *ius commune*, which Baldus determined to be the operative law in this case, dictated that Agnes be regarded as an original (*originaria*) of Castiglion Aretino. Under the *ius commune*, the penalty for homicide was capital punishment. But Baldus recommended a penalty of 500 pounds, intimating that the statutory penalty for the crime in question was monetary rather than capital punishment.[62] Without the statutes of Castiglion Aretino and knowledge of what events actually took place, any attempt to reconstruct the basis for the outcome of *Domina Agnes* is obviously hazardous.

La Perugina

No married woman of the city or countryside of Assisi (*Nulla mulier civitatis Assisii vel comitatus*), of whatever legal position or rank, may enter into contracts or make a last will without the presence of her husband. So declared the Trecento statutes of Assisi. It happens that a woman who is an original citizen of Perugia marries a citizen of Assisi, where she lives for a long time and where she makes a last will in the presence of her husband. Later, she returns to Perugia and in her husband's absence and without his consent she unilaterally annuls the last will. She proceeds to make a second will in Perugia, where, Baldus observes, the *ius commune* remains in force. The validity of the second last will hinges on the resolution of two questions. First, does the wife, through her marriage to an Assisian, necessarily become a citizen of Assisi? Second, is a woman married to an Assisian who later returns to her own natural fatherland (*patria*) legally capable of making a last will in accordance with Perugia's laws, or is her will-making capacity restricted by the laws of her husband's hometown?[63]

Assisi's Trecento statute (*Nulla mulier*) cited by Baldus is apparently no longer extant but probably survived with modifications in the redaction of 1469, published in Perugia between 1534 and 1543, which is cited here.[64] His *consilium*, though undated, may have been composed around 1374, when Baldus served as a legal adviser to the commune of Assisi. He also authored several other *consilia* involving cases in Assisi, including another dealing with *Nulla mulier*.[65] Without concrete evidence, it is impossible to determine conclusively whether Baldus's opinion was written as a *consilium sapientis* or *pro parte*. However, the tenor of its conclusion suggests to me that it was more likely to have been commissioned by the husband.

Nulla mulier's preamble announced the necessity of restricting the testamentary freedom (*ius testandi, licentia testandi*) and patrimonial capacities of Assisian women to promote civic harmony and to safeguard the proprietary rights of Assisian men.[66] The restriction was consistent with the statute's ideological subtext that women, because of their inherent mental incompetence and physical weakness (*imbecillitas sexus*), required close supervision in the performance of legal acts.[67] It was feared that if left to their own devices, untethered women would impoverish their husbands and their families through excessive almsgiving. The preamble offered what jurists considered a legally effective defense against charges that *Nulla mulier* violated the *ius commune* and canon law, which granted all citizens the right to make last wills without obstruction and, moreover, granted legally independent women (*sui iuris*) the capacity to dispose of their property as they deemed best, though always subject to the natural right of their children.[68] As a matter of strict law these charges were compelling, but the drafters of *Nulla mulier* rejected them on the paternalistic grounds that in protecting women and promoting the city's welfare the statute performed a greater good. That would be accomplished by securing the rights of a woman's husband and their mutual children to her dowry and other properties and in their absence the rights of the wife's paternal relatives to her estate.

According to the 1469 redaction of *Nulla mulier*, in addition to last wills and codicils, all forms of alienation of a woman's property and obligations (contracts of sale, gifts, and exchanges) were prohibited unless they were concluded in the presence and with the consent of both her husband and her father (if he was alive).[69] Before a husband could exercise his own *potestas*, he had to have legitimately contracted and consummated the marriage, and as a matter of public knowledge cohabited with his wife in the same house for at least two months.[70] Whether the father's consent had been similarly required in the Trecento redaction is likely but not known. In any event, under the civil law the father's consent was deemed necessary because his married daughter, even though she had left his *origo*, did not escape the reach of his *potestas*. Without paternal consent, she could not make a last will, alienate property, or choose a burial place.[71] In the absence of her husband and father, presumably because of their predecease, the presence and consent of her adult sons were required; in their absence, those of her grandsons. Next in line were her brothers born of the same parents (*fratres carnales*), and so forth.[72] All had to be at least twenty-five years old and, to avoid delays, resident within Assisi or no more than thirty miles from the city.

How did the drafters of *Nulla mulier* confront the ability and universal desire of women, whether married, unmarried, or widowed, to give alms? Canonists defended the right of a married woman, even when her husband was opposed, to employ nondotal properties for giving alms.[73] Thomas Aquinas agreed, so long as the wife's almsgiving was moderate and did not impoverish her husband.[74] And women could imitate the betrothed Saint Lucy, popularized in Jacobus de Voragine's *Golden Legend*, whose holiness was exemplified by the pious distribution of her nondotal property to the poor.[75] The imperative of securing one's own spiritual safety (*pro amima sua*) through almsgiving was not lost on *Nulla mulier's* drafters, who were forced to modify their hardline stance and make an important concession. The statute permitted women to expend up to 20 percent of their properties, nondotal as well as dotal, on testamentary bequests and necessities for themselves – and without having to do so in the husband's and father's presence and without first procuring their consent.[76] The husband's *potestas* did not extend to the earnings of a wife for work performed outside the home – for example, as an artisan, innkeeper, merchant, or midwife. Such earnings belonged to the wife, not to her husband, so long as her work was not connected to her domestic duties.[77] Statutes like Assisi's *Nulla mulier*, popular across northern and central Italy (save Venice),[78] were a mainstay of the political-legal structure restricting the capacity of women to dispose of their properties freely or without statutory authorization.

The Assisian husband's vested right in his Perugian wife's dowry upon her predecease was the core issue of *La Perugina*.[79] A few jurists pronounced that a husband's claim fell under the statutes of the locale where the dowry contract was executed,[80] which in *La Perugina* was probably Perugia. Accordingly, the Assisian husband, upon his wife's predecease without children, would acquire one-third of the dowry under the statutes of Perugia of 1342.[81] But Bartolus's teaching that the husband's claim to the dowry was a special case falling under the statute of his domicile carried the day. By coincidence, a Perugian husband and his Assisian wife were the protagonists of the hypothetical case used by Bartolus to illustrate his doctrine.[82] In his hypothetical case, the husband would acquire one-half of his wife's dowry under the statutes of Assisi. In reality, however, the statutes of Assisi provided surviving husbands one-third of the dowry.[83] Consequently, Bartolus's doctrine would not have benefited the husband, since his vested right in the dowry was identical in Perugia and Assisi.

Bartolus's successors, including Baldus, objected to his doctrine that the husband was entitled to his statutory share of the dowry, regardless of whether he supported the burdens of matrimony, so long as he contracted marriage *de presenti*. They held instead that a husband was entitled to receive the statutory share as compensation for supporting his wife.[84] Their holding applies to the three cases examined in this chapter, in which the husband publicly introduces the wife into his own home, not to those in which he lives in his wife's hometown, which would place him under its jurisdiction.

Baldus, in his lengthy exegesis of *lex Cunctos populos* (Cod. 1. 1. 1), shared the position that the husband's domicile prevails in regard to his dotal claims.[85] But he focused on the conflict between local statutes and the *ius commune* rather than on the conflict between two local jurisdictions. In the hypothetical case presented by Baldus, the statute of the husband's place of domicile grants him one-half of his wife's dowry upon her predecease without children. He takes as his wife a woman of Assisi, where he accepted the dowry and where the *ius commune* is in force. It was not necessary for Baldus to spell out to his audience that under the *ius commune* a man who marries in Assisi is required to restore the whole dowry of his predeceased wife to her father or his heirs unless the parties expressly made different contractual arrangements. The *ius commune* here is synonymous with Justinian's *Corpus iuris* or Roman law,[86] not the revisionist opinions of medieval jurists who championed local customs and statutes awarding surviving husbands up to the entire dowry.[87]

In Baldus's hypothetical case the husband's domicile prevails, but not for Bartolus's reason that this is a special case favoring the husband. For Baldus, this reason was not so much wrong as dubious. Suppose the *ius commune* operates in the husband's domicile. Under Bartolus's doctrine, the husband must restore the whole dowry, an absurd and noxious result that Bartolus himself would have deplored. Baldus therefore took another approach. Whatever amount of dowry is due the husband on his wife's predecease is determined by the custom of the husband's region. Yet, alleging the *ius commune*, he reasoned that since payment of the dowry to the husband is assumed to have occurred in his domicile, the law there has precedence.[88] And if the law of his domicile is the *ius commune*, he must restore the whole dowry to her father or his heirs. This in fact was Baldus's approach in an actual case that occurred in Asti in the 1390s.[89]

Baldus's analysis is crucial to any conjectural reconstruction of the material stakes of the dispute to which he devoted the *consilium* analyzed here. The wife's first will, redacted in Assisi, served to guarantee her husband's claim to one-third of the dowry as prescribed by the city's statutes. In the second will, redacted in Perugia without the husband's consent, the wife, now near death, possibly instructed that the dowry must be restored to her father or his heirs as prescribed by the *ius commune*. In that event, the husband would be obligated to restore the whole dowry. Yet it was precisely this outcome that both the *Glossa* and Bartolus, despite their differences on the status of the woman married elsewhere, sought to prevent. Whatever circumstances moved the wife to make a second will that probably favored her kinsmen, her act threatened her husband's mastery and the legal and ideological foundations on which it rested.

Baldus's zigzagging opinion opened by acknowledging the doubts arising from an identification of the wife with *Nulla mulier civitatis Assisii*. "A woman of Perugia married to an Assisian retains her own natural origin, which may not be abolished, though by a certain legal fiction it can be concealed, which at times happens when marriage forcibly carries off the wife to the husband's city as if she were born there."[90] However, *Nulla mulier* does not apply to the wife for the following reasons. Legal fiction does not operate in statutes, as here, contravening the *ius gentium* and *ius commune*. Since the case of the woman married elsewhere is not specifically mentioned in *Nulla mulier*, the wife does not fall within the statute's scope. In addition, prohibitory statutes like *Nulla mulier*, which impose disadvantages, call for literal, not liberal and connotative, interpretation.[91]

Baldus then advanced the Aristotelian-biblical argument already encountered in *Domina Agnes* that a wife is drawn to her husband's *origo*, which replaces her own, a transformation effected by the power of the matrimonial union. "But certainly," he objected immediately, "this argument does not seem to be true." Natural law dictates that one's *origo* is quintessentially immutable, and this holds for one's name, which may not be extinguished. To be of Perugia means to be a Perugian citizen forever. That the wife in question is of Perugia stands as fact corresponding to "natural truth." "A married woman, therefore, loses neither her privileges nor the common laws of her natural fatherland, because natural laws may not be changed." Although a wife is transferred to her husband's domicile, she retains, as if she were a son, a natural filiation with her fatherland.[92] By way of analogy, Baldus cited *lex Cum in adoptivis*, in which the bonds between a natural father and his son are not dissolved by adoption. Though the son is legally a full member of his adoptive family, he does not cease being a kinsman of his natural family. For Baldus, adoption cannot sever a natural father from his son because their bond is divine (*nexum divinum*).[93]

Furthermore, the designation "de civitate vel de comitatu" corresponds to someone whose place of origin is truly Assisi. "For one is said to be truly and properly from someplace who is from that place according to natural truth and not according to fiction." Baldus, a virtuoso of legal fiction, opposed only its improper use. When used properly, legal fiction was perfectly acceptable, as in the interpretation of the utterance "de provincia." If the preposition "de" precedes the word "province" but not "city," then "whoever is from the province of Tuscia," although an indefinite expression, is understood to include inhabitants domiciled in the province.

Baldus interjected yet another consideration. The designation "de civitate" can refer to the domain of civil law and legal relations – that is, to those things of a city that are governed by civil law. *Ius civile* encompasses the laws made by cities (*ius civile civitatis*) as well as Justinian's *Corpus iuris*.[94] In the domain of civil law, a woman of Perugia married to an Assisian is a true and proper citizen of Assisi. Baldus's point reflected Bartolus's doctrine that civil law has generative power, via municipal legislation, to produce newly minted true citizens partaking of the same privileges and benefits of citizenship as those enjoyed by original citizens.[95] In short, the designation "de civitate," if understood civilly, applies to the Perugian wife, who, as a true citizen of Assisi, is subject to the provisos of *Nulla mulier*. Alternatively, if "de civitate" is understood materially, it refers to a specific city enclosed by walls, within which citizenship and civic filiation derive from the fact of natural and legitimate descent. Within this circumscribed domain, the foreign-born wife can acquire fictive, but not true, Assisian citizenship – a civic status that, in Baldus's analysis, exempts her from *Nulla mulier*, which extends to true citizens exclusively.[96]

The pretzeled syntax of citizenship, as manipulated by Baldus, failed to resolve the questions precipitating his *consilium*. But he did not leave *La Perugina*'s challenge unanswered. Baldus upheld Roman and Lombard law's golden rule of conjugal relations: a wife is always subject to her husband's power (*potestas viri*). As he explained in his lecture on *lex Si uxorem* (Cod. 6. 46. 5), she is in the *potestas* of her husband in three main respects: "namely, in residence, which she must take up with him;

in works, because she must work for her husband; and in jurisdiction, because she must obey the court and laws and statutes of the husband."[97] Consequently, even though the *ius commune* says the opposite, *La Perugina* must comply with Assisi's *Nulla mulier*, particularly regarding the disposition of her dowry[98] – an abrupt ending making Baldus's dialectics appear, retrospectively, as consummate shadowboxing prefatory to his foreordained defense of the prerogatives of husbandhood.

But let us forgo the self-righteous pleasure of impugning Baldus's motives, which is anachronistic and methodologically distracting. His opinion reads as a *consilium pro parte* rendered on behalf of the Assisian husband, making his ultimate determination forensically inevitable. The question of the legal effects of intercity marriage was equally inevitable in this type of case, and Baldus's arguments and verbal constructions were taken seriously by succeeding generations of jurists.[99] They were acutely aware, as Baldus was, that the husband's *potestas* was hardly invincible. Indeed, husbands were perceived as vulnerable souls deserving legal protection in their struggle with women like *La Perugina*, who had the potential to ruin their men if left free to do as they saw fit.[100] It should come as no surprise that the drafters of the next redaction of Assisi's statutes (1469) granted additional protection to surviving husbands. The statute awarding the surviving husband one-third of his wife's dowry, though now applied to all persons deemed "original citizens of the city of Assisi and to all other persons of Assisi's contado and district and *to foreign women whom the men of Assisi take or may have taken as wives*" (my italics).[101]

Domina Stefania

Lady Stefania, an original citizen of Viterbo, married Raniero di Bussi of Baschi sometime in the late fourteenth century. We do not know if the couple resided in Viterbo or in the husband's hometown, an Umbrian agricultural center on the road leading to Orvieto. She and Ranerio had at least two children: Francesco, who survived his mother, and Giovanna, who predeceased her. In her last will Stefania divided her estate among her son and three granddaughters. Francesco was instituted heir for one-third of her properties, while Giovanna's three daughters were instituted heirs for the remaining two-thirds.[102] After Stefania's death, her will was contested for violating Viterbo's *Nulla mulier* statute, probably by her son, for he had the most to lose.[103] I have no direct evidence indicating that Baldus's *consilium* was written on behalf of the granddaughters. Yet I am inclined to treat his *consilium* as *pro parte*, because of his capacious defense of Stefania's last will.

"No woman," Viterbo's statute declared, "having sons or daughters from a son may make a last will, codicil, or contract extending beyond the persons of her sons, and if she otherwise made such a last will, codicil, or contract they are *ipso iure* invalid." This passage, which Baldus cited, derived from the 1356 redaction of Viterbo's statutes, only a fraction of which is extant.[104] The statute was probably revised in the redaction of 1469,[105] in response, I believe, to the criticisms leveled by Baldus and like-minded jurists. The statute was designed to protect daughters as well as sons from a mother's acts serving to prejudice the children's claims to her dowry and properties. It was also designed to reserve the bulk of the maternal estate for descendants reckoned as kinsmen of the husband-father. In our case, Francesco and his direct male descendants were so reckoned, as was Giovanna, but, it must be emphasized, not her daughters, who were agnates of their own father.

Unlike *Domina Agnes* and *La Perugina*, where the central issue was whether the laws of the husband's place of origin were binding on his foreign-born wife, *Domina Stefania* focused on the obverse: whether the laws of the place of origin of a woman married to a foreigner continue to be binding on her. At first Baldus contended that under the laws of her hometown Stefania's last will, which violates Viterbo's statute, is invalid for by-now-familiar reasons. First, her attachment to Viterbo is permanent; it may not be voluntarily relinquished nor eliminated. Second, the reality of her binding attachment to Viterbo is anchored in natural truth that is not obscured by the image of marriage. Third, just as a married woman is not released from her father's *potestas*, she similarly remains yoked to the *potestas* of her fatherland. Fourth, the statute extends to all her property in Viterbo's territory. Fifth, no law exists by which a native woman is liberated, through marriage, from Viterbo's statute-making authority and jurisdiction.[106]

Reversing course, as the dialectical format of *consilia* required, Baldus argued that the place of origin and legal venue of a woman married elsewhere is changed by virtue of marriage. As a widow, she continues to be subject to the jurisdiction and laws of her husband's *origo*, where she can be summoned to court. This applies so long as she continues to reside in her husband's *origo*, suggesting that Stefania may have relocated to Baschi. Nor is Stefania subject to Viterbo's statute, since it pertains to persons, rather than to the properties they possess that are located within its jurisdiction.[107]

Even if one grants that as a woman married elsewhere Stefania is personally exempt from Viterbo's statute, jurists determined that such an exemption does not apply to her property situated in Viterbo's territory. Her last will, with respect to such properties, must be judged null and void. In order to defend Stefania's last will, and the claims of the granddaughters to Stefania's Viterbo property, Baldus had to show that the statute itself was invalid. He began with the observation that the statute is concurrently prohibitory and beneficial; it prohibited mothers from bequeathing property unless beneficial to their children. But to whom does "children" refer? It necessarily includes the granddaughters, for when property is bequeathed for the benefit of children, it is ordinarily understood that grandchildren are contemplated. This understanding operates in the statute as well, so that the words "extra personas filiorum" similarly include granddaughters. In order to prevent grandmothers from naming as heirs their granddaughters, the statute must expressly state "extra filios qui neptes." But a proviso excluding children from an inheritance due them under natural law is inconsistent with the beneficial purport of the statute and the *ius commune*. Just as a parent may not disinherit a child except for a compelling reason, so the city may not exclude granddaughters from the maternal inheritance to which they are entitled.[108] The proof text is *lex Cum ratio naturalis* (Cod. 48. 20. 7 pr), which declares that natural reason in the manner of an unspoken law awards children an inheritance from their parents, while it bars the removal of children from succession except for worthy reasons.

Nor is the statute's purposeful beneficence toward children determined by their sex. The words "habens filios et filias" show that the statute includes female children. But these words form part of a longer verbal construction, "habens filios et filias ex filio," which indicates that the statute wants to exclude from inheritance the mother's daughters and their children. The addition of "ex filio" was testimony to, and symbolic of, the driving force behind the statute: the masculinist desire to privilege and sustain agnate families. Yet the exclusionary thrust of the addition was exceptional, and Baldus admitted that he did not know whether the omission of the feminine gender from the addition was a case of faulty legal drafting. If taken literally, the statute can be said to exclude the granddaughters, since it is weighted clearly in favor of males. In the same breath, Baldus rejoined, a literal interpretation of the statute results in its invalidity. To be sure, the statute has much in common with the masculinist bias that had resulted in the inferior legal position of women in pre-Justinianic jurisprudence. But the jurisprudence of Papinian's day is no longer in force, Baldus declared, having been superseded by Justinian's *Corpus iuris*, which, in matters of inheritance, placed daughters and sons and grandsons and granddaughters on an equal footing. The statute, therefore, stands in violation of the *ius commune*.[109]

Viterbo's *Nulla mulier* statute also violates natural law and papal temporal jurisdiction in the lands of the church, in which the city was prominently situated. As Baldus reasoned:

> It seems wicked to say that a mother may not institute as heirs her daughter or granddaughter, and if it happens that a statute expressly wishes this, it may not do so, because it violates natural law. Take the case of a mother who has a son and a daughter with a father who dies destitute. The mother wants to make a last will because, as it happens, she wants to leave something for spiritual bequests and, as a matter of necessity, something for the safety of her own soul, and she wishes to leave something for her daughter, lest she go begging. If the statute is understood verbatim, it would force the girl to go begging. If we attend to the externals of the statute, the designation of the daughter as heir (*instituto*) is invalid. Wherefore I say that in the lands of the church, where such statutes are invalid, and inasmuch as they are altogether wicked and against all natural reason, and inasmuch as the pope would in no way ratify them, either such a statute is invalid, or it must be understood rightly and it must be supplemented by natural reason.[110]

In support of his position, Baldus turned to the venerable opinions of his predecessors Dinus Mugellanus and Cinus de Pistorio. Baldus attributed to these jurists the opinion that statutes prohibiting a father or grandfather from leaving daughters or granddaughters their legitimate share of the paternal estate (*legitima*) are null and void.[111] By analogy, for Baldus, their opinions can apply to mothers and grandmothers, too. Furthermore, the deficiencies making municipal ordinances invalid can be amended with the aid of the *ius commune*. This key principle licensed Baldus to refashion Viterbo's statute for the purpose of making it conform to the normal standards of the *ius commune* and natural law. Under the elementary rules of statutory interpretation, the masculine gender includes the feminine in statutes enacted with the intention of providing benefits. In such statutes the feminine "filiae" is normally understood to be included in the masculine "filii," which means children as well as sons. Since Viterbo's stature, enacted for the benefit of sons, makes no mention of daughters or granddaughters, the latter may not be excluded from inheritance. In the wake of Baldus's reasoning, either the statute is invalid or, through equitable interpretation, it must be comprehended that the words "extra filios" are supplemented with "vel filias" and other children – namely, Stefania's granddaughters. In both cases "the last will made by lady Stefania is equitable and in accord with the precept of natural reason and so must be observed."[112]

Whether Baldus's staunch defense of the granddaughters' claims determined the judge's sentence, or sparked an out-of-court settlement or even further litigation, is unknown. On the issue of papal ratification, Baldus may have misspoken. Without ratification by the pope, Viterbo's overlord, the city's statutes would lack validity, yet the redaction cited by Baldus must have received papal ratification.[113] Baldus's critique of Viterbo's statute was implicitly rejected in the 1469 redaction, which stated that the statute was enacted to benefit a mother's sons ("in favorem filiorum masculinorum mulieris"). To that end, inheritance of the maternal estate was restricted to daughters and sons and the children of the sons. Still excluded from the maternal grandmother's estate were the children of daughters. The revised statute, because it patently contradicted the *ius commune* and natural law, was an easy target for litigants and their legal advisers, who would not have missed an opportunity to invoke Baldus's authority.

Viterbo's city fathers enacted uncompromising statutes, but lacking true princely authority, they could not prevent citizens from mounting legal challenges to their laws, nor could they stop notaries from drawing last wills and contracts in violation of the city's statutes. Understandably, they enlisted the majesty of papal authority to affirm the statute's validity. An addendum to the statute, issued by Pope Innocent VIII (1484–92), would have disappointed Baldus. It first reprimanded the "many women" who conveyed their dowries and other properties to the detriment of their male descendants and kin, and second, the notaries who enabled these women to circumvent the statute. Innocent pronounced that the statute must be wholly observed for the sake of the republic and the preservation of its agnate families. Notaries were prohibited from drafting last wills and instruments making such violations possible.[114] It is noteworthy that among the family members who appear in the statute, the woman married elsewhere is made conspicuous by her absence. For surely widows like Stefania, who possessed an alternative legal base in their husband's hometown, acted as legally independent persons rather than as *nullae mulieres* and contributed to the undermining of the statute's viability, which eventually necessitated papal intervention.

Overcoming the Presence of the Past

The woman-married-elsewhere's citizenship in late medieval Italy was an arena of conflict, contradiction, and ambiguity. Her native and adoptive cities, her father and husband, her children and kinsmen all vied for control over her body, property, and personhood – that is, her ability to enter into contracts, undertake binding obligations, or commit any legal act. Bartolus's theory of dual citizenship served to mediate these conflicts by aligning municipal statutes with the *ius commune* and by providing remedies for women reduced to the status of *nullae mulieres*. While Baldus did not openly endorse Bartolus's theory, he did concur that women engaged in intercity marriage acquire dual citizenship. Pitting natural law against the *Glossa*, he insisted that marriage to a foreigner does not extinguish the wife's legal standing as an original citizen of her place of origin. The *Glossa*'s model of women-married-elsewhere's citizenship, though defanged and largely superseded by the theories of Bartolus and Baldus, persisted as a potential source for legal authorities and especially lawmakers intent on expatriating women married elsewhere. To understate the problem, a woman engaged in the practice of intercity marriage was placed in a precarious position; she was neither here nor there, penalized in her hometown for marrying out, while never accepted as a full-fledged citizen in her husband's hometown.

This was still the situation after the First World War, according to the American reformer Emma Wold, legislative secretary of the National Woman's Party. In her foreword to a 1928 compilation of nationality laws as affected by marriage, prepared for the House of Representatives Committee on Immigration and Naturalization, she explained: "In some countries the wife is now out, now in, one hour a national, the next upon her marriage, an alien, and not inconceivably, in a third upon her husband's death, a national again. The possible variations of nationality situations that may be imagined are no more dizzying than the actual situations resulting from the wedding of nationality and marriage."[115]

For Wold, the rule that upon marriage to a foreigner the wife ceases to be a national of her country and becomes a national of her husband's did not antedate the French Revolution.[116] The rule was firmly established in the French Civil Code of 1804 (Code Napoléon) and was imported into the civil codes of countries in central and southern Europe, including Italy.[117] Wold's history is shaky, but she is on target with her observation that the French Civil Code was a formative source of law for married women's citizenship and nationality.

With the unification of Italy in 1861 came the unification of citizenship. Unification did not at all eradicate the centrifugal forces of regionalism and localism, but medieval doctrines of citizenship as they specifically related to defunct city-states and regional states had become obsolete. Citizenship referred to *status civitatis* in the territory of the new Kingdom of Italy and the Liberal State. The acquisition and loss of state citizenship now monopolized the attention of the legal community. However, the guiding assumption of medieval women's citizenship – that an innately inferior wife must yield to her husband's *potestas* and follow him like a dumb animal for the sake of family solidarity – continued to animate the laws and treatises on married women's citizenship and the encyclical *Rerum novarum* (1891) of Pope Leo XIII.[118]

Meanwhile, the antiquated doctrine, originating not with Roman law (as most legal scholars believe) but with the *Glossa*, that a native woman married to a foreigner involuntarily loses her original citizenship while she simultaneously acquires her husband's citizenship found fertile soil in the new Italian State.[119] In addition to its appealing transparency, the doctrine was undeniably compatible with the notion in the French Civil Code of the juridical unipersonality of the married couple and with the subordinate position of the woman married elsewhere. It was no accident that the jurists responsible for Italian Civil Code of 1865, drawing on French and native sources, expatriated female citizens upon marriage to a foreigner on the condition that they become citizens under the laws of the husband's country.[120] Likewise, they expatriated female citizens married to Italian men who became foreigners, provided that they maintained a common residence with their husbands, and acquired their husband's foreign citizenship. The double standard was also alive and well. Marriage conferred the Italian husband's citizenship upon his foreign-born wife, without exception.[121] These regulations were carried forward in the new law on citizenship promulgated in June 1912.[122]

After the First World War Italian women attained substantial rights, with the repeal of the requirement that a wife's legal acts (for example, managing her personal property and opening a bank account) must have her husband's permission (*autorizzazione maritale*), and with the removal of the barriers that prevented women from entering the professions. Italian women marrying foreigners, however, did so with the apprehension that they would become strangers in their own country. After the Second World War, women won the franchise and exercised their right to vote for the first time in the elections of 1946 for the Constituent Assembly. A few years later, in 1948, the constitution of the postwar republic declared that all citizens, regardless of sex, were considered to have equal social dignity and husbands and wives were to be treated as equal partners. Yet the constitutional proclamation of conjugal equality had no impact on the 1912 law regulating married women's citizenship.

A pathbreaking agreement on married women's citizenship, developed at the United Nations and embodied in the Convention of New York of 1957, was ignored in Italy. Adopted by forty-six nations, the convention provided among other things that "each contracting state agrees that neither the celebration nor the dissolution of a marriage between one of its nationals and an alien, nor the change of nationality by the husband in an ongoing marriage, shall automatically affect the nationality of the wife."[123] Only in the 1970s did the gap between constitution-based conjugal equality (modernity) and the inferior status of married women (antimodernity) become a ripe topic for legal scholars of international private law, who called for reform of Italy's laws on citizenship.[124]

On 16 April 1975, the Constitutional Court declared that the citizenship law of 1912, as it pertained to a married woman's involuntary loss of citizenship, was unconstitutional. The law of 1912, which had become an intolerable anachronism, was said to be inconsistent with "the principles of the Constitution that attribute equal social dignity and equality before the law to all citizens without regard to sex and regulate marriage on the basis of the moral and juridical equality of husband and wife."[125] The Constitutional Court's decision became a "leading case" protecting once and for all the citizenship of Italian women with foreign husbands.[126] The decision was made in anticipation of impending legislative action on married women's citizenship.[127] On 22 April 1975, with thousands of women demonstrating in Rome for the modernization of Italy's antiquated family law and the legalization of abortion, parliament enacted a comprehensive family law reform that included partial repeal of the citizenship law of 1912. Henceforth, a native woman kept her Italian citizenship when she married a foreigner or when her husband acquired foreign citizenship, except when she expressly renounced it.[128]

With the emancipatory family law reform of 1975, the tenacious legacy of the *ius commune* was in great measure overcome, as Italian women achieved the status of autonomous citizens with civil capabilities equal to those of male citizens. In addition to the capacity to marry foreigners without penalty, the reform permitted women to retain their maiden names and to choose jointly with their husbands a place of domicile. The vestigial institution of the dowry, an archsymbol of women's subjugation, was summarily abolished.[129] Italian women achieved what had been unimaginable and appalling to previous generations of jurists and legislators committed to a patrilineal, patrimonial, and paternalistic society in which they comfortably lived and self-servingly reproduced.

The march toward gender equality, however, was incomplete. As Roberta Clerici remarks, the law conferred Italian citizenship on foreign wives of Italian men, yet failed to extend Italian citizenship to foreign husbands; thus, the decision of the Constitutional Court as well as the family reform law had maintained a double standard and created a constitutional anomaly.[130] This situation was eventually rectified in 1983, when parliament made it possible for a foreign husband of an Italian citizen to acquire his wife's citizenship if he satisfied a residence requirement. As a matter of parity, no longer did a foreign wife of an Italian citizen automatically acquire her husband's citizenship.[131] For the first time, she was given a choice about becoming an Italian citizen. At the same time, the Constitutional Court ruled that a woman transferred her nationality to her children born after 1948 (when the Italian Constitution came into force), thus affirming the principle that Italian nationality could be inherited by maternal descent. Subsequent rulings extended this principle to children born before 1948.[132]

Finally, the Citizenship Act enacted by parliament in 1992 made it easier for Italian women with foreign husbands to retain their original citizenship in cases where they were required to become citizens of their husband's country.[133] Above all, the act provided a fast-track procedure for the foreign spouse of an Italian citizen to acquire citizenship and nationality. After only six months of marriage, foreign spouses of couples resident in Italy could apply for citizenship. For couples residing outside Italy, the duration-of-marriage requirement was three years. As designed, the new law triggered a boom in citizenship acquisition via marriage, increasing to 31,609 in 2007 from 3,857 in 1992 and amounting to nearly 90 percent of naturalizations. The boom also entailed a disturbing number of sham marriages. In reaction, parliament enacted a law in 2009 that required foreign spouses of couples resident in Italy be married at least two years before applying for citizenship. The new requirement had the intended result of slowing the pace of naturalization through marriage.[134] This latest development does not alter the sober fact that the contested figure of the woman married elsewhere, which occupied citizens, legislators, jurists, and courts in Italy for centuries, has basically disappeared, while the role of marriage as a vehicle for the extension of citizenship and nationality has never been more visible.

8 Dowry, Domicile, and Citizenship in Late Medieval Florence

Countless *consilia*, or legal opinions, produced by Florentine jurists for both individual clients and municipal judges from the fourteenth through the sixteenth centuries concerned the disposition and devolution of dowries. Especially prominent were disputes regarding the wife's recovery of her dowry on the husband's predecease, and conversely the husband's retention of the dowry on his wife's predecease. In resolving these disputes, jurists considered the material facts, relevant municipal laws, and the *ius commune* – a vast body of Roman civil, canon, and feudal law, including glosses, commentaries, and *consilia* dealing with the rights and claims to dotal property. This chapter centers on a *consilium* written in February 1440 addressing a dispute over the dowry of a Florentine woman who predeceased her husband, an inhabitant and native of Pescia, a town located in the Valdinievole about thirty miles northwest of Florence.

The statutes of Pescia and Florence differed on the portion of dowry (*lucrum dotis*) the husband, without surviving children (*sine liberis*) from the marriage, was entitled to retain on his wife's predecease as compensation for nuptial expenses.[1] Florence's statutes allotted *lucrum* equal to the entire dowry, Pescia's equal to one-half, and the jurists were given the task of deciding which city's statutes were applicable. A sealed autograph of the *consilium*, submitted by Petrus de Exio (Piero di Jacopo Ambrosini), a jurist from Iesi in the region of the Marche who taught canon and civil law at the Studio of Florence, is preserved in the city's Archivio di Stato.[2] The *consilium* was submitted with sealed endorsements (*subscriptiones*) of four other jurists: Johannes Geronimi de Eugubio, a Florentine citizen originally from Gubbio, and Ambrosini's colleagues at the Florentine Studio, Benedictus de Barzis of Perugia, Tomas Jacobi de Salvettis of Pistoia, and Dominicus Nicolai de Martellis of Florence.

A brief description (*casus*) of the private acts and statutes relating to the dispute and a summary of the adversaries' arguments preceded the *consilium*.[3] Around February 1436, a certain Florentine citizen promised a Pesciatine man (referred to throughout as Pisciatinus) that his daughter, Albissina, would consent to take him as her lawful spouse and that she would accept from him a wedding ring. Pisciatinus then promised the father that he would consent to take the daughter as his lawful wife. Last, the father and Pisciatinus agreed that the amount and composition of the dowry would be determined by two Pesciatine arbitrators chosen by the parties. These mutual agreements were recorded by a Florentine notary in a betrothal contract (*contractum sponsalitium*).[4] A few days later, the couple's marriage was performed in the home of the bride's father and recorded in a *contractum matrimonii*. Shortly after, the couple consummated the marriage in the husband's home in Pescia, an act enabling him to lay claim to a 150-florin dowry paid on his wife's behalf by the *Monte delle doti*, Florence's Dowry Fund.[5] In a *confessio dotis*, yet another standard notarial instrument, also drawn up in Florence in conformity with the city's statutes, the husband acknowledged receipt of the Monte dowry and promised repayment of the dowry to the wife or her heirs in the event he verged on insolvency in an ongoing marriage or upon his predecease. In addition, it was specified that the *confessio* would be valid and enforceable in Florence, Pistoia, Pisa, Siena, Genoa, Venice, and Rome.

Albissina's total dowry was probably somewhat greater than 150 florins, for it was customary to supplement Monte dowries with additional cash and personal property. Albissina's family was far from poor, but the modest amount of her Monte dowry placed her family on the lower rungs of Florentine society. The average dowry paid by the Monte officials in the 1430s was 417 florins, while elite families paid roughly 1,000 florins to attract socially estimable husbands for their nubile daughters.[6] The wife's family's lack of surname also suggests modest status. All of this helps to explain why Albissina's father was constrained to arrange marriage with an inhabitant from the provinces.

Three statutes were in play:

1. A Florentine statute of 1415 on the acquisition rights by one party for another regarding property in Florence and places not subject to its jurisdiction.[7] The statute permitted the party to whom the rights were transferred to unilaterally reject or modify the terms of the transfer.
2. A Florentine statute of 1415 on succession to the wife's dowry and other goods upon her predecease.[8] The provision relevant to our case is the award to the husband of the whole dowry on the wife's

predecease on condition that the marriage was lawful, had been consummated, and had produced no surviving children.

3. A Pesciatine statute of the early fifteenth century on succession to the wife's dowry, which awarded the husband one-half the dowry upon the wife's predecease with no children surviving at the time of her death.[9] The husband's *lucrum* represented an increase above the one-third awarded in Pescia's statutes of 1339.[10]

Pesciatine practice was consistent with that of other towns in Tuscany, including Lucca, Pisa, Pistoia, Piombino, San Miniato al Tedesco, San Gimignano, and Siena, which also pegged the husband's *lucrum* at up to one-half the dowry.[11] From a Tuscan perspective, Florentine practice was exceptional, comparable to that of the Lombard towns of Bergamo, Lodi, Milan, Monza, and Pavia, where husbands were similarly awarded *lucrum* equivalent to the entire dowry on the wife's predecease.[12]

Albissina died childless, leaving her husband in possession of the entire dowry acknowledged in the *confessio dotis*. The wife's heirs, most likely her father and close kin, sued the husband for the return of one-half the dowry pursuant to the customs of Pescia and the town's statutes. They alleged, first, that as a matter of law (*de iure*) the husband's domicile – that is, his permanent residence, where he intended to remain and return – must be given preference over the wife's domicile; and second, that the notarial documents introduced and cited as evidence must be construed in light of Pescia's laws.[13] In the *ius commune*, the validity of a contract was ordinarily decided in accordance with the *lex loci contractus*, the laws of the locality in which it was concluded. Questions regarding payment and performance were decided in accordance with the *lex loci solutionis*, the laws of the place designated for payment and performance. The *contractus dotis*, in which the wife and legal representatives promised to pay the dowry to the husband, was designated by jurists as a special contract over which the laws of the husband's domicile (*lex domicilii*) were preferred to both the *lex loci contractus* and the *lex loci solutionis*. The classification of the *contractus dotis* as a special contract was intended to protect a husband who temporarily left his hometown, married elsewhere, and as a foreigner would suffer disadvantages under the laws of the wife's domicile. This special classification governed both the wife's claim to repayment of the dowry and the husband's claim to its retention upon his wife's predecease.[14]

Second, the wife's heirs underscored the centrality of the husband's domicile respecting the promise of the dowry to Pisciatinus, the determination of its amount and composition, and the consummation of the marriage.

In his defense, the husband asserted that since the betrothal and marriage contracts and the *confessio* had been drawn up in Florence in accordance with that city's laws, the husband's *lucrum* was determined by Florentine law.[15] He denied that *lex loci solutionis* referred to Pescia's laws on the grounds that although the *confessio* specified a number of places for repayment of the dowry, Pescia had been omitted. Furthermore, as the wife had not exercised her ability granted by the first Florentine statute cited above to object to the *confessio* when she had had the opportunity to do so, it had to be presumed that she had ratified its terms.[16]

In practice, the *contractus dotis* was usually drawn up where the bride and her family resided. As reported in the *casus*, however, the wife's heirs referred to a *promissio de dote* (which legally was equivalent to a *contractus dotis*) made in Pescia. This crucial detail was indirectly corroborated by the husband, who, in his defense, failed to claim that the *contractus dotis* was redacted in Florence, when doing so would have strengthened his case immeasurably. On the other hand, Ambrosini's *consilium* itself explicitly stated that the *contractus dotis* was made in Florence. It appears that there were two instruments: a *contractus dotis* made in Florence, carrying the father's promise to pay a dowry, and a *promissio de dote* made in Pescia, stipulating the amount and composition of the dowry.

Neither the *casus* nor the *consilium* indicates whether the wife's heirs as plaintiffs brought suit in Florence or Pescia. Similarly, we do not know who commissioned the *consilium*. To better understand the tenor of Ambrosini's arguments, it makes a difference if the *consilium* was commissioned by the court or one of the parties. In a *consilium* commissioned by the court, called a *consilium sapientis*, the jurist was charged with arriving at an impartial resolution of the dispute. By contrast, in a *consilium* commissioned by a party, the jurist was expected to argue zealously on his client's behalf. Another difference was that the *consilium sapientis* almost always determined the court's sentence, whereas a *consilium pro parte* was not binding on the judge.[17] Judges routinely requested a *consilium sapientis* in cases involving conflicts between statutes of different localities and between the *ius commune* and local statutes and customs. Our case exhibits these conflicts and was further confounding in that Pescia had submitted to Florence's rule in 1339 and then been annexed into its district.[18] Not only was Pisciatinus a native citizen and permanent inhabitant of Pescia; as a *districtualis*, he was also subject in certain cases to the jurisdiction of Florence's courts and statutes.[19] On the other hand, as Ambrosini's *consilium* was strongly supportive of the husband's claim, it is just as easy to infer that the husband had requested it. Over all, the strained reasoning and hodgepodge of arguments Ambrosini wielded to reach his conclusions inclines me to the view that the *consilium* was submitted on the husband's behalf.

Ambrosini's *consilium* was divided into two parts: the first provided a cursory justification of the claim brought by the wife's heirs; the second, a lengthy vindication of the husband's counterclaim. The principal authorities Ambrosini adduced were the *Digest* and *Codex* in Justinian's *Corpus iuris civilis* and its accompanying *Glossa ordinaria* compiled in the thirteenth century by Accursius. He also cited the commentaries of Cinus de Pistorio, Bartolus de Saxoferrato, and Bartolus's student Baldus de Ubaldis of Perugia. His principal canon law sources were the *Decretum* of Gratian and the *Liber extra* of Pope Gregory IX in the *Corpus iuris canonici* and the influential commentary of the canonist Johannes Andreae.

The *consilium* opened with the supposition that in assigning the *lucrum dotis* the laws and customs of the husband's domicile were preferred.[20] In support, *lex Contraxisse* (Dig. 44. 7. 21) was cited to show that the applicable law regarding the husband's *lucrum* was the *lex loci solutionis*: the law of the place where his heirs were legally bound to repay the wife's dowry upon his predecease – that is, his domicile. *Lex Exigere* (Dig. 5. 1. 65) was cited for the complementary rule that "a wife should demand her dowry in the place where her husband had his domicile, not where the dowry agreement was drawn up; for it is not the sort of contract in which the place where the dowry agreement was made has to be considered rather than the man to whose domicile the wife herself was due to return under the terms of marriage."[21] Bartolus supplied an oft-cited example to illustrate the way the law should be applied to the *lucrum dotis*. Here the wife was from Assisi and the husband from Perugia, where he had his domicile. The dowry contract was drawn up in Assisi, whose statutes awarded the husband one-third of the dowry on the wife's predecease without surviving children. Bartolus opined that the husband was instead entitled to demand one-half of the dowry as prescribed by Perugia's statutes.[22] Baldus agreed with Bartolus that laws of the husband's domicile were looked to, but he adamantly objected to his teacher's doctrine that the dowry contract was special, making it exempt from the *lex loci contractus*. For Baldus, the laws of the husband's domicile determined the *lucrum dotis*, because that was where the husband's heirs were obligated to repay the dowry.[23]

Although Pisciatinus had contracted marriage in the wife's domicile, he had done so as a foreigner (*advena et forensis*) and had subsequently returned with his new bride to Pescia, where he had consummated the marriage. Besides, the wife, by having married a foreigner living elsewhere, had necessarily relinquished her original domicile while she had simultaneously acquired domicile in her husband's town. The *ius commune*'s bias in favor of the husband's domicile had absolutely nothing to do with the amount of *lucrum dotis* he might be assigned under the statutes of his home town. Rather, the jurists took for granted that the wife must submit to her husband in all things, which included the assumption of citizenship and domicile in his town, making her directly subject to its laws.[24] In our case husbandly superiority was both symbolically and materially contradicted by the inferior *lucrum dotis* to which Pisciatinus was entitled under Pescia's statutes and the *ius commune*.

Undaunted by the uphill task of overcoming the accumulative weight of interpretation and argument making the laws of the husband's domicile the venue for determining the *lucrum dotis*, Ambrosini began with the argument that, on the contrary, the husband's *lucrum* was determined by the laws of the place where the marriage was contracted – Florence. The argument derived from Johannes Andreae, who in turn had adopted the opinion of an earlier canonist, Franciscus de Vercellis.[25] Yet this opinion was rejected by later canonists, including Antonius de Butrio, Petrus Ancharanus, and Abbas Panormitanus, who affirmed Bartolus's classification of the *contractus dotis* as a special contract that privileged the law of the husband's domicile.[26]

Next, Ambrosini denied that the *lex loci solutionis* was looked to in this case. When a contract was made in one place and another was designated for performance and payment, then the *lex loci contractus* was observed, even when one of the parties was a foreigner.[27] Dinus Mugellanus and Bartolus were enlisted as supporting authorities, but neither jurist expressed the views attributed to him. Dinus held that the *lex loci contractus* governed contracts involving land and buildings (*fundus*),[28] while Bartolus, citing *l. Exigere*, stated that the *lex loci contractus* did not apply to the dowry (*fallit in dote*).[29] Ambrosini now made a distinction between one's forum – the place where one could sue and be sued – and the customs of the place allotting the *lucrum dotis*. The *lex loci solutionis* and the laws of the husband's domicile prevailed with respect to the court (*forum*): thus "the husband may not be sued in the place of contracting for the dowry, but only in his place of domicile."[30] With respect to the custom for allotting the *lucrum dotis*, the *lex loci contractus* must be observed. In the case at hand, the *locus solutionis* actually facilitated Pisciatinus's claim, because his *confessio dotis* had expressly nominated Florence as a place for repayment of the dowry, while it omitted naming Pescia.[31]

Thus far Ambrosini's arguments were inconclusive. Taking a different tack, he asserted that "Pisciatinus was not a foreigner in the city of Florence, but rather a citizen." Since Pisciatinus neither was a citizen by origin (*civis originarius*) nor made a citizen by statute (*civis ex statuto*), how did he become a citizen of Florence? Ambrosini resorted to argument by analogy. The Roman jurist Ulpian declared, "Whoever is born in a village is regarded as a member of the *patria* to which the village in question belongs."[32] Like ancient Rome, Florence was the *communis patria* of all those born beyond its walls in communities, including Pescia, subject to its territorial jurisdiction. Just as any free man was a citizen of the *communis patria*, Rome, so was Pisciatinus a citizen of the *communis patria*, Florence. For the same reason, when Pisciatinus contracted marriage in Florence, he did so not as a foreigner but as a citizen. By operation of law, Pisciatinus was therefore a citizen of the *locus contractus* and subject to its laws.[33]

This was all well and good, but really what mattered was not the husband's reputed Florentine citizenship, but the laws of the husband's domicile, Pescia. Ready for this objection, Ambrosini countered that Pisciatinus was in fact an inhabitant of Florence, where he could be found every day and in whose law courts he could sue and be sued as an inhabitant.[34] The use of the present tense, "cotidie conversatur et habitat in civitate Florentie," suggests that Pisciatinus was living in Florence at the time of the lawsuit. Ambrosini stopped short of arguing that Pisciatinus had made Florence his domicile. The present case nevertheless stood in marked contrast, he pointed out, to the one contemplated by Bartolus and his followers. They had contemplated a case in which the husband and wife had different domiciles and were subject to entirely independent jurisdictions. As long as these circumstances obtained, lawsuits over the dowry must be adjudicated, as *l. Exigere* mandated, in the husband's domicile. They had not envisioned the supervening case where the husband's domicile had been subordinated to his wife's, subjecting him to Florence's courts and laws and thereby neutering the subject communities' customs and laws and rendering *l. Exigere* inapplicable.[35]

Whether Ambrosini's *consilium* helped Pisciatinus defeat his wife's heirs is unknown, as there is no indication of the case's resolution in the judicial sources I have examined. More positively, the *consilium* highlights the anomalies and tensions attending mixed marriages within Florence's multijurisdictional territorial state. The rule that a foreign wife assumed her husband's citizenship and domicile bolstered the theory of the unipersonality of the married couple and, in consequence, the husband's mastery over his wife. A logical extension of this theory was the doctrine developed in the Middle Ages that the customs and statutes of the husband's domicile determined the amount of *lucrum dotis*. Jurists were mindful that the *lucrum* allotted in the wife's domicile could be greater than that in the husband's, but the awareness of this gap is not visible in their commentaries on *l. Exigere*,[36] and there is no evidence that they attempted to provide a gap-filling rule.

Today, parties engaged in interstate and international transactions rely on a contractual clause specifying which state's or country's law and forum will apply in settling disputes arising from the contract. No doubt the explicit expression of the parties' intention in a choice-of-law clause works to reduce conflict-of-law disputes. Although the choice-of-law clause was used by late medieval Italian testators in their last wills, I have not found a single example of it regarding the husband's *lucrum dotis* in the Florentine dowry contracts and *confessiones dotium* I have examined. Still, lawsuits like the one pitting Pisciatinus against his wife's heirs were rare, probably for several reasons. For the purpose of avoiding conflict, it may have been that the husband and the wife's kin informally agreed in advance that should the wife predecease her husband, with no children surviving, he would retain the dowry. It is also conceivable that some husbands, finding themselves in the same predicament facing Pisciatinus, accepted the inferior *lucrum dotis* uncomplainingly.

The transfiguration of Florence's territorial subjects into citizens of the *communis patria* enabled Pisciatinus to enjoy the valuable benefits conferred by Florentine law exclusively on Florentine citizens. In theory, Pisciatinus was given the option of complying as he wished with the provisions of Florentine law, rather than with the customs and laws of his own community, in order to gain material benefits and procedural advantages. Had it come to pass, such indiscriminate "statute shopping" would have negated the premises of the intricate multijurisdictional configuration of the Florentine territorial state[37] and the sought-after predictability and certainty provided by the widely accepted rules designed to resolve multijurisdictional disputes. In reality, the Florentine territorial state in the fifteenth century, as Najemy reminds us, remained "a patchwork of separate and for many purposes still largely autonomous legislative entities."[38] No wonder Ambrosini's frontal assault on *l. Exigere* and Bartolus, save for his colleagues' perfunctory endorsements,[39] fell on deaf ears.

9 Pisa's "Long-Arm" *Gabella Dotis* (1420–1525): Issues, Cases, Legal Opinions

Husbands in late medieval and early modern Tuscany were obligated to pay a contract tax (*gabella dotis*) on the amount of dowry they acknowledged and legally guaranteed in a standard legal instrument called *confessio dotis*.[1] Questions arose when a citizen contracted marriage, concluded a *confessio dotis*, and paid the contract tax in a foreign city, usually where he maintained a separate legal domicile, situated beyond the territorial jurisdiction of his native city. "Jurisdiction" (*iurisdictio*), a treelike construct with many branches, is used in this chapter narrowly to refer to the robust political and judicial powers that towns, cities, or principalities could legitimately assert over persons and properties located within their territories.[2] In practice, these powers were asserted to compel citizens and subjects to perform acts, such as the payment of the *gabella dotis*, which they otherwise would not perform voluntarily. When citizens residing beyond the territorial jurisdiction of their native cities protested that they were not liable to pay the *gabella dotis*, claiming that the laws authorizing the *gabella* did not apply to them, the officials routinely turned to jurists for impartial expert advice and determinate solutions. This procedure was employed in multijurisdictional disputes that were not directly resolvable by administrative fiat or a preset application of local law (*ius proprium*).[3] In constructing their arguments, jurists relied on the transterritorial norms of the *ius commune*, a gargantuan body of learned Roman civil and canon law filtered through the varied interpretations of generations of jurists, many of whom were university professors.[4]

My study focuses on three multijurisdictional disputes over the *gabella dotis* that occurred in the orbit of Pisa under Florentine rule and the legal opinions (*consilia*) they engendered. The *consilia* that I discuss represent merely a fraction of the published and unpublished *consilia* that deserve to be studied for the valuable perspectives they furnish on the legal conundrums of individual Pisan citizens and the governance of their city during the long first century of Florence's domination.[5]

To avoid the facile impression that these cases and opinions marked the beginning of a natural and orderly progression toward modern institutional arrangements and concepts, I have avoided employing postmedieval terms such as "private international law," "comity," "conflict of laws," "extraterritoriality," "sovereignty," and the like. It is worth recalling that the mature "choice-of-law doctrine" – a fundamental feature of contemporary international law that gives parties the discretion to freely choose the law of a particular country to govern their contracts – was developed in the second half of the nineteenth century by the Risorgimento Italian jurist Pasquale Stanislao Mancini.[6] To be blunt, in premodern Italy party autonomy regarding the payment of contract taxes, including the *gabella dotis*, was contemplated neither by the drafters of local statutory compilations nor by *ius commune* jurists.

The approach I have taken meshes with Giorgio Chittolini's antiteleological view "that terms and concepts need to be historically contextualized within a specific political, juridical and institutional language."[7] That said, the payment of the contract tax in each case intersected with issues of dual citizenship, legal domicile, double taxation, and jurisdictional pluralism, raising a fundamental question of whether citizens of one locality who had domicile and executed contracts in another locality with independent jurisdiction could be compelled to pay contract taxes in their native cities. Today, disputes involving cross-border double taxation are adjudicated under the terms set forth in the European Community Treaty on direct taxation, as well as bilateral conventions for the avoidance of double taxation and fiscal evasion that Italy has concluded with other states: for instance, Australia (1977), the United States (1985), and Israel (1995).[8]

1

The protagonist-husband of the first case, Agapito di Matteo di ser Cegna dell'Agnello, was a merchant and citizen of Pisa. In 1407, he and his brother Iacopo were residing in hospitable Lucca, along with other Pisans forced to leave their native city in the wake of Florence's brutal and liberty-destroying conquest in 1406.[9] Condemned as rebels by Pisa's new masters, the brothers were exiled to Genoa, where they were still residing at the time of the dispute in 1423. Little is known about Agapito's activities after 1407, but evidence from the Corte de' Mercanti of Lucca reveals that he continued to have commercial dealings in Lucca.[10] Around 1411, he married Tommasa, a daughter of Giovanni di Piero Maggiolini, a silk merchant; Giovanni and his nephews, as indicated by the *catasto* of 1428–9, were Pisa's richest citizens. Their gross taxable wealth was estimated at 23,080 florins, quite impressive, as the Maggiolini were among the most heavily taxed Pisans under Florence's domination.[11] The Maggiolini belonged to the anti-Florentine Raspanti faction, so it is not surprising that Giovanni spent the years immediately after Florence's conquest of Pisa as a political exile in Lucca. In 1413, he was exonerated from charges of fomenting rebellion against Florence.[12] A leading member of the Pisan colony in Lucca, he counted among the forty-three Pisans who acquired Lucchese citizenship in this period.[13]

Agapito married Tommasa in Lucca, where he received and legally guaranteed Tommasa's dowry and consummated the marriage. The *confessio dotis* was drawn up by a Pisan notary, ser Eustachio di ser Angelo Montefoscoli, also a newly created citizen and resident of Lucca.[14] Ten years into the marriage Tommasa died in Genoa, where the couple was then residing. Soon after, Agapito took a second wife, Caterina, a daughter of Luca Spinola and member of one of Genoa's topmost families. The couple married in Genoa, where a local notary executed the *confessio* for Caterina's dowry. We are informed that the contract taxes on both Caterina's and Tommasa's dowries were paid in Genoa.

At this juncture, the Florentine officials (*provveditori*) in Pisa in charge of managing and collecting taxes on all contracts concluded by Pisan citizens demanded that Agapito pay the contract taxes on both dowries at the rate of 2 denarii for each lira.[15] Under Pisa's laws, citizens who concluded dowry contracts within fifty miles of the city proper were liable for the contract tax.[16] Since the distance between Pisa and Lucca was less than fifty miles (today, around eleven miles, or seventeen kilometers), Pisan citizens, like Agapito, who concluded contracts in Lucca were subject to the tax. He also owed the tax on the dowry conveyed in his second marriage, the *provveditori* claimed, solely by virtue of his status as a Pisan citizen. This claim was alleged to be valid, notwithstanding that the marriage was performed in Genoa (today, around eighty-seven miles, or one hundred thirty-nine kilometers, from Pisa) and that Agapito had already paid the contract tax in Genoa, his long-standing place of domicile.[17] In defense, Agapito countered that he was not liable for the contract tax on either dowry, because both his marriages had been performed outside Pisa's territorial jurisdiction, as had the contractual promises made by the brides' families to pay the dowries and the ensuing *confessiones dotium* in which he had guaranteed and assumed liability for the dowries he acknowledged having received.

The source of my summary description of the dispute is a manuscript in the Archivio di Stato of Florence, largely a collection of copies of the legal opinions of the jurist Nellus de Sancto Geminiano.[18] In early April 1423, Nellus, Urbanus de Cevoli, and a third, unidentified jurist were apparently asked by the Florentine *provveditori* in Pisa to submit impartial opinions called *consilia sapientis* on whether the Pisan laws applied to the dowries Agapito acknowledged in his *confessiones dotium*. At the time, Nello was serving in Florence as government lawyer (*sapiens communis*). After having earned his doctorate in civil law at Bologna in 1398, he spent his entire career in Florence, where he was a successful and productive practitioner. His many *consilia*, including a cluster dealing with Pisan legal disputes, are largely preserved in manuscripts found in Florence and await being properly described, edited, and studied. Nellus taught civil law at the city's Studio (1418–22), held diverse administrative positions, notable among them that of government lawyer, and served on diplomatic missions. *De bannitis*, which he completed in 1424 and later published in several printed editions, came to be admired as an astute treatment of political banishment.[19] Like other Florentine jurists at the time, Nellus was versed as much in the ways of wielding power as he was in the manipulation of the rules of law.

Urbanus de Cevoli was a minor Pisan jurist who received his doctorate in civil law at the University of Pisa between 1406 and 1411. At the time of the dispute he was serving as Pisa's official advocate (*advocatus Pisani communis*), and he was appointed a Pisan ambassador in 1427.[20] Few of the *consilia* that he undoubtedly penned in his capacity as a public and private advocate are extant.

Ordinarily, the public officials or representatives of the party requesting the opinions would have forwarded the consulting jurists a file of the *acta* – namely, copies of the relevant local laws, contracts of marriage, *confessiones dotium*, and attestation that Agapito had truly established legal domicile in Genoa. This file, which would have filled at least several folios offering precious details for clarifying significant ambiguities surrounding the dispute, was omitted from the manuscript containing copies of the three *consilia*. Despite a protracted search in Pisa and Florence, I have been unsuccessful in finding a copy of the "long-arm" law that made the contract tax applicable to Pisa's nonresident citizens within fifty miles of the city. Nor have I found the law that made the expansive contract tax specifically applicable to the dowries of Pisan citizens.[21] To my knowledge, these laws have not been cited by modern scholars. Our only sources for their existence are the *consilia* in which they were repeatedly cited.[22] In all likelihood, the laws were enacted under Florentine rule, figuring among a host of measures designed to extract maximum revenue from Pisa's citizens, wherever they resided.[23] Taxes harvested from Pisa were sent directly to Florence.[24] Lest we think Florentine fiscal policies were exceptional, recall that Pisan authorities increased the *gabelle* imposed on foodstuffs and wine in Lucca when Pisa ruled Lucca, from 1342–1369.[25]

At first glance the two Pisan laws appear to constitute an astounding assertion of the city's jurisdiction over cities such as Lucca that were completely independent of Pisa. Before Florence's conquest in 1406, Pisan territorial jurisdiction had never extended fifty miles beyond the city proper. After the conquest, the jurisdiction that Pisa had formerly exercised over its *contado* (the city's surrounding area extending seven miles outward) and other dependencies had passed to Florence. Even without knowing the full text of the laws, it is fantastical to believe that Pisan lawmakers under Florentine domination suddenly, willfully, and untenably asserted legal jurisdiction over all the communities and lands within fifty miles of their city. If that were the case, the jurists would have debated and rejected the assertion, which failed to happen.

Rather, the law asserted that any Pisan citizen who entered into contracts within fifty miles of the city would have to pay a contract tax. Even so, the question arises: on what legal grounds did lawmakers chose the fifty-mile territorial boundary, rather than, say, a hundred or hundred and fifty miles? My hunch is that the fifty-mile boundary was inspired by canon law rules concerning the calculation of legal distance (*dieta legalis*). In Roman and canon law, *dieta legalis* referred to the distance one could walk in a day, which was pegged at twenty miles (*vicena milia*).[26] The relevant rule was probably provided by the canon *Praesenti* in Boniface VIII's *Liber sextus* (VI 3. 4. 34), which established that the benefices of members of the Roman curia who happened to die in neighboring places (*in locis vicinis*) – understood as two *dietae*, or forty miles, from the place where the pope and his curia were residing at the time – would revert to the papacy.[27] If my hunch is correct, the fifty-mile boundary was intended to encompass neighboring places, including jurisdictionally independent Lucca, roughly within two days' walking distance of Pisa. Conceivably, a territorially expansive contract tax had long been a feature of Pisan and Florentine fiscal practice, but evidence to support a prior history is lacking.[28]

Comparatively speaking, the geographic extent of Pisa's contract tax on dowries was actually limited. Citizen-husbands of Siena and Pistoia, at various times, were obligated to pay a contract tax on their dowries, wherever they were received, not only beyond the territorial jurisdictions of the two cities but even outside Italy![29] Needless to say, the idea that Pisa, Siena, or Pistoia could effectively tax dowry or other contracts executed by their citizens *extra territorium* was wishful thinking. As is well known, the contract tax was based on information that the drafting notary was required to transmit to the officials in charge of collecting *gabelle*.[30] This procedure worked reasonably well when a city had leverage over the notary who was subject to its jurisdiction and licensed to work there. On the other hand, the records of Pisa's *gabelle dei contratti* that I have examined fail to confirm that the officials in Pisa regularly received information from foreign notaries or third parties on contracts concluded by Pisan citizens in independent jurisdictions.[31] The primary effect of Pisa's long-arm *gabella dotis* was to authorize its tax officials to collect the *gabella dotis* from citizens should they return to the city after having received a dowry within fifty miles of Pisa, even if in an independent jurisdiction.

The hypervigilant Florentine *provveditori* in charge of collecting *gabelle* were aware of the impediments to tracking dowry contracts made within Florence's own considerable territory, to say nothing of those made outside it.[32] They recognized that Pisan citizens like Agapito dell'Agnello, having already paid the contract tax in a foreign territorial jurisdiction, would have had zero incentive to comply with Pisan law. The lack of timely information about the dowries, plus Agapito's understandable aversion to paying the contract tax twice, helps explain the long delay in attempting to collect the tax. My guess is that a Pisan citizen living in Genoa, with ties to the Florentine regime in Pisa, informed the authorities of Agapito's dowries. Informants were usually rewarded with a portion of the fine imposed on the "tax evaders" whom they had denounced to the officials.

Another question that cannot be answered with certainty concerns the low-yielding statutory tax rate on dowries. At 2 denarii for each lira, the rate corresponded to 0.83 percent, yielding on a dowry of 1,000 florins a paltry 8 florins, 6 soldi. This rate was substantially less than the going rate of 3⅓ percent payable on dowries contracted in the city of Pisa itself, or the going rates of around 3 percent in Florence and 2½ percent in Lucca.[33] By way of illustration, in 1428, Battista di Bondo Lanfreducci, a wealthy Pisan citizen, paid a *gabella* of 15 florins, 16 soldi, that is, at a rate of 3⅖ percent, on a dowry valued at 450 florins that he acknowledged receiving in Pisa.[34] The standard rate paid on dowries recorded in the registers of the *gabelle dei contratti* was 3⅓ percent.[35] One is left to speculate on the reasons for the apparent gap between the statutory and going rates. Arguably, the statutory rate may have been introduced as a supplementary tax on top of the *gabella* husbands would have paid in the localities where they had contracted marriage and acknowledged receipt of the dowry. Yet future research on Pisa's contract tax in the fifteenth century may show that the reported gap is a mirage and that in fact there was minimal difference between the rates.

2

The first opinion, composed by an unidentified jurist, opened with a flat denial that Agapito's dowries were subject to the contract tax. The fundamental laws *Ut animarum* in the *Liber sextus* (1. 2. 2) and *Cunctos populos* in Justinian's *Codex* (1. 1. 1), were cited for the bright-line rule that a city's laws were binding on the acts performed by its subjects where it had jurisdiction, but not on acts they performed outside its territory (*extra territorium*).[36] Correspondingly, the Pisan laws were classified as offensive (*odiosum*) for contradicting *ius commune* rules and illegitimately imposing what amounted to a new tax, therefore making it unenforceable in a foreign jurisdiction. Implicit here was another rule: advantageous laws (awarding exemptions and privileges) might apply to citizens residing beyond the city's jurisdiction, while offensive laws (imposing taxes and burdens) were not applicable (*quod odiosa sunt restringenda, favores ampliandi*).[37] Forgoing more arguments that would only have belabored the obvious, the jurist succinctly resolved that Pisa's contract tax could not be imposed, first, because the promises, payments, and *confessiones* for the two dowries were made outside Pisan territory, and second, because Agapito lived with each wife in Genoa, where he had already paid the tax on their dowries.[38] He could also have pointed out that Agapito's actions were no different from those of the many foreign husbands residing ("ad presens habitans," "commorans"), marrying, and receiving dowries in Pisa, who routinely paid Pisa's *gabella dotis* in compliance with the city's laws.[39]

The second opinion, composed by Urbanus de Cevoli, also maintained that the Pisan law was unenforceable "in a foreign territory" (in alieno territorio). He argued that the very wording of the law militated against its application to Agapito's case. The law stated that whoever had taken a wife and led her into his household ("uxorem ceperit et eam duxerit") was required to pay the *commune* of Pisa a tax of 2 denarii for each lira of the wife's dowry and trousseau (*corredo*).[40] The wording was construed to mean, first, that the *gabella dotis* was triggered by the consummation of the marriage – that is, by "taking" and "leading" the wife, not by the promise of the dowry and the husband's assumption of liability ("promissio dotis et confessio"); and, second, that the "taking" and "leading" had to be performed in Pisan territory.[41] The interpretation was clever but seemingly arbitrary. No authority, reason, or indicia of legislative purpose were offered to support the interpretation that *gabella* was due only if the marriage was consummated in Pisan territory. At any rate, the upshot was that insofar as the "taking" and "leading" were performed outside Pisan territorial jurisdiction, Agapito was freed from payment of the *gabella*.

In the third and final opinion, Nellus de Sancto Geminiano, disagreeing with his colleagues, defended the enforceability of Pisa's laws. Agapito, he insisted, was at least liable for the *gabella* on Tommasa's dowry received and acknowledged in Lucca, for both acts occurred within fifty miles of Pisa. In support, he referred to instances in Justinian's *Corpus iuris* where citizens residing or traveling beyond the jurisdiction of their native cities were nevertheless bound by their laws.[42] In theory, the alignment between Pisan law and the *ius commune* applied equally to the second marriage. Nellus relented, however, conceding that only the *gabella* on the first dowry received in Lucca should be paid. While the second dowry, received in Genoa, was not subject to the contract tax, Nellus held that by virtue of his Pisan citizenship Agapito continued to be bound by Pisa's laws and jurisdiction wherever he chose to live, no matter how distant from his native city.[43] Nellus's emphasis on the perduring character of original citizenship was unobjectionable. After all, Agapito's decision to contest the matter with the tax officials affirmed his recognition of Pisa's original jurisdiction. Still, Nellus's opinion, in my view, was ill-founded. The forensic maneuver of silently passing over of the *ius commune* rule that the laws of the locality in which a contract is concluded (*lex loci contractus*) have priority was tantamount to an admission of the porous legal grounds on which the Florentine *provveditori*'s claim was staked.

3

The enforceability of Pisa's contract tax on the dowries of Pisan citizens residing in Genoa was also addressed by the Florentine jurist and humanist Benedictus Accoltus Aretinus (Benedetto Accolti of Arezzo). After receiving his degree in civil law from the University of Bologna at the age of seventeen, Accoltus taught at the University of Florence, and after matriculating in the city's Guild of Lawyers and Notaries in 1440, he enjoyed a thriving practice. He was elected first chancellor of the republic in 1458, a dignity he held until his death.[44] A manuscript copy of his *consilium* on the Pisan contract tax, written sometime after 1440, is found in the Archivio di Stato of Florence.[45] A marginal notation announced the *consilium*'s theme: "Whether the tax on dowries should be paid in the place where the contract is executed or in the husband's place of origin" (An gabella dotis solvatur in loco contractus celebrati vel in loco originis). Perhaps for political reasons, the jurist employed the pseudonym Sempronius to disguise the husband's real name.[46] Once more, we have to make do with a condensed summary of the case, because the file containing the relevant *acta* that undoubtedly rested on the jurist's desk when he composed his opinion was omitted from the manuscript in which the copy of the *consilium* has been preserved. Accoltus offers no hint of who commissioned his *consilium*.[47]

By origin Sempronius was considered a Pisan citizen, by residence and domicile a citizen of Genoa. Although there is no indication that Sempronius was a *civis ex privilegio* or *ex conventione*, that is, granted the privilege of Genoese citizenship by legislative enactment, Accoltus reiterated that under the *ius commune* he was a citizen of Genoa on the basis of his residence and payment of taxes there.[48] While residing in Genoa Sempronius married a Genoese woman, from whom he received a dowry. The question put to Accoltus was whether Sempronius could be compelled to pay the dowry contract tax in Pisa.[49] At first blush, it seemed that the tax was enforceable, since a city's laws bound its citizens even when they resided beyond its territorial jurisdiction. And following Roman law norms, buttressed by the *Glossa ordinaria* and the commentaries of Bartolus de Saxoferrato and Baldus de Ubaldis of Perugia, Accoltus maintained that the laws of Pisa had priority over those of Genoa, because one's place of origin (*locus originis*) was nobler than one's domicile.[50]

Invoking Bartolus's multifaceted authority once again, but performing a U-turn, Accoltus denied that the Pisan law applied to the dowry received by Sempronius or that it was enforceable beyond Pisa's territorial borders. It was an entrenched rule of the *ius commune* that contracts were subject to the laws of the locality in which they were concluded.[51] Similarly, with regard to the contracts of dowry and marriage, one looked to the law of the place in which the husband "led" his wife, established domicile, and was paid the dowry. Assuming that the marriage occurred in Genoa, where Sempronius resided and duly paid taxes on his contractual transactions and residence, it followed that his marriage was governed by Genoese laws and customs.[52] Indeed, Accoltus correctly avowed, "it is customary in all the parts of Italy that *gabelle* are paid even by foreigners for contracts and things brought to the city where they are found."[53]

It was also a rule that the imposition of *gabelle* was a matter of strict law (*stricti iuris*). Technically, this meant that because the Pisan officials' ability to impose *gabelle* derived from an authority inferior to the emperor's, the contract tax could not be imposed beyond the city's territorial jurisdiction. For being at odds with the *ius commune*, the Pisan statute was again classified as offensive (*odiosum*), making it unenforceable.[54] Simply put, Pisa's authority to impose *gabelle* was strictly limited to its own territory. Accoltus then cited Baldus for the argument that a newly enacted law (*ius*) may not apply beyond the lawmaker's jurisdiction.[55] The Pisan law was also unenforceable for failing to state expressly and positively that the contract tax should be binding on subjects found outside Pisa's territory.[56] Finally, if it were true that Sempronius could be required to pay the *gabella* in Pisa, the result would be doubly offensive in that he would be paying a *gabella* in Genoa and Pisa for the very same thing. Such an irrational outcome, Accoltus admonished, should be prevented because of the resulting harm to Sempronius.[57]

Accoltus now addressed the tax obligations of individuals possessing dual citizenship. His authority was Bartolus and the *Glossa ordinaria*, the starting points for the examination of the problems arising from dual citizenship. Bartolus held that if anyone was a citizen of two cities and had property in both, then each city was restricted to imposing taxes on the portion of his property located within its own jurisdiction.[58] Bartolus's doctrine enabled Accoltus to argue that because Sempronius was a citizen of both Pisa and Genoa but had received a dowry consisting of property located in Genoa, he was obligated to pay the contract tax in Genoa rather than Pisa. Accoltus conceded that all things being equal, that is, if one was called to pay taxes in one's *origo* and place of domicile simultaneously, the *ius commune* dictated that one's *origo* indubitably took priority. This normative scheme was irrelevant here, for the reason that Sempronius had already paid the contract tax in Genoa, defeating Pisa's claim to priority as *civitas originis*.[59] Last and obvious was Genoa's great distance from Pisa, more than fifty miles, placing Sempronius's dowry far beyond the reach of Pisa's contract tax.[60]

Accoltus's *consilium* was endorsed (*subscripserunt*) by three other Florentine practitioners, Sallustius Guilielmi of Perugia, Johannes Geronimi de Eugubio, and Benedictus de Barzis of Perugia, who taught civil law at the University of Florence between 1335 and 1442.[61] They unhesitatingly restated Baldus's position that where a statute required payment of a contract tax, the statute did not apply to a contract made by a subject outside the legislator's territory, "because statutes of this kind authorizing *gabelle* are against the *ius commune*."[62]

4

The primary source for our third case is a *consilium* of the Milanese jurist Philippus Decius. Numbered 457 in the printed editions of Decius's *consilia*, his *consilium* became a "leading opinion" and was cited in manuals for legal practitioners.[63] At issue was the contract tax regarding the dowry that "dominus Vitalis hebraeus et civis pisanus" had received in Venice, where he had also contracted and consummated his marriage. The case was adjudicated before the Sea Consuls of Florence (Consoli del Mare) stationed in Pisa. Although their jurisdictional authority over commercial and fiscal matters had shriveled over the course of the fifteenth century, the Sea Consuls continued to be responsible for the administration of individual Pisan *gabelle*.[64] Decius was asked to resolve a two-pronged question regarding Vitale's status as a citizen of both Pisa and Florence. First, was Vitale, by virtue of his status as a *civis pisanus*, required under *ius commune* rules or Pisan laws to pay the *gabella dotis* in his native city? Second, if he was not required to pay the Pisan *gabella*, was he then required to pay the contract tax as a reputed *civis florentinus* in accordance with certain *Capitoli*, or negotiated conventions, often renewable, establishing the terms by which Jewish bankers were granted an exclusive license to lend money at interest for a limited number of years in the city, *contado*, and *distretto* of Florence?[65]

An outstanding jurist and "remarkable personality with great appeal," who, in addition to his *consilia*, produced commentaries on the *Corpus iuris* and the *Liber extra* of Pope Gregory IX, Decius was still teaching at the Studio in Pisa in 1525 when he penned what would become "*consilium* 457."[66] The party asking Decius to submit his *consilium* remains a mystery. It is entirely conceivable that the Florentine tax officials in Pisa, tasked with the enforcement of Florence's fiscal policies, demanded that Vitale pay the contract tax on the dowry. Vitale, after obtaining legal advice, would have responded through his procurators that he was not obligated to pay the tax. Presumably, because of the doubts raised by Vitale's counterclaim and his prominence and connections, the matter eventually landed before the Sea Consuls, who decided civil law cases on the basis of Pisan law and the *ius commune*. Next, the office of Sea Consuls would have asked Decius to submit a *consilium sapientis* for a definitive and immediate resolution of the matter.[67] It is equally conceivable that Vitale commissioned Decius to submit a *consilium pro parte*,[68] so that his wholehearted defense of Vitale's counterclaim would have been undertaken for an eminent and wealthy client. This scenario is highly plausible in light of the da Pisa's history of requesting jurists, including Bartholomaeus Socinus of the University of Pisa, Johannes Crottus of the University of Bologna, and Francesco Guicciardini in Florence, for *consilia pro parte* in disputes between the family and government officials in Lucca, Pisa, and Florence.[69]

Decius offered no further clues about the identity of "Vitalis" beyond the six-word reference in the opening of his *consilium*. To my knowledge, there is only one candidate who matches the identification of "lord Vitalis, Jew and Pisan citizen." It is almost certain that the reference was to Vitale (Yehiel Nissim) di Simone da Pisa, a prominent banker, scholar, and philanthropist.[70] He was born into Pisa's legendary Jewish banking family,[71] with its headquarters in Florence and financial dealings in Lucca, Siena, Arezzo, Bologna, Ferrara, Verona, Padua, and Venice. Vitale's grandfather, Vitale di Isacco, was on close terms with Lorenzo de' Medici, to whom he lent money, and from the late fifteenth century onward the family's ties to Florence were exceptionally strong.[72] Resting on their religious and cultural patronage as well as their financial and commercial activities, "the fame of the da Pisa," Luzzati observes, "went beyond the Italian borders and reached southern France and the Iberian Peninsula."[73]

With the death of Vitale di Isacco in 1490, Isacco and Simone, his two sons, assumed leadership of the family bank and commercial interests. Loyal adherents of Florence, the brothers were expelled from Pisa and had their urban and rural properties confiscated when Pisa regained its independence in 1494 with the encouragement and protection of the French king, Charles VIII of France, who had invaded Italy and routed the Florentines. After the restoration of Florentine rule in Pisa in June 1509, Isacco and Simone were able to regain the majority of their properties, including the building in the heart of the city that housed the da Pisa bank and a synagogue, called *la casa dell'ebreo*.[74] Simone died in 1510; Isacco a few years after. In 1516 the da Pisa family was authorized to reopen and operate its bank in Pisa for ten years.[75]

In 1525 Vitale di Simone married Diamante, the daughter of Anselmo Del Banco (alias Asher Meschullam), a German-Jewish banker with lending operations in Padua and Venice.[76] Details on the amount of Diamante's dowry are lacking, but, judging from the dowries received by Vitale's relatives, the amount would have been substantial and commensurate with his elevated social and economic status.[77] After contracting and consummating his marriage in Venice, Vitale returned with his bride and dowry to the family's home in Pisa, where he attracted the attention of the Florentine tax officials intent on collecting the contract tax for his dowry. Vitale's return to Pisa is attested by the adventurer and pseudo-Messiah David Reubeni, who vividly recounted his visit in 1525 to Vitale's home, commending his host's learning, gracious hospitality, and aid to less fortunate coreligionists.[78]

Vitale's civic status as a *civis pisanus* derived from his family's long-established domicile in the city, dating back to the early Quattrocento. *Ius commune* jurists construed toponyms like "da Pisa" and "de Pisis" to signify one's place of origin (*origo*), where one was an original citizen (*civis originarius*), rather than the place where one had established permanent legal abode (*domicilium*).[79] When a person was designated by the appellative "pisanus," as was Vitale, it denoted that he was an original citizen of Pisa entitled to the core legal rights and protections enjoyed by all original Pisan citizens. The reason that these designations applied to Vitale lay in the venerable and operative rule that Jews were bound by the *ius commune* – more specifically, by the *lex Iudaei* (Cod. 1. 9. 8), which decreed that regarding venue, laws, and rights in civil litigation, Jews were subject to the common law of Rome. Commenting on the *lex Iudaei*, Bartolus affirmed that outside matters of their own religious practices and faith, "the Jews enjoy those things that pertain to Roman citizens."[80]

Meanwhile, Vitale was prohibited by another *ius commune* rule from public dignities, honors, and offices, which would have placed him in authority over Christians, violating an ancient taboo.[81] Yet the prohibition against Jews holding public offices reserved to Christians in no way attenuated the authenticity of Vitale's original citizenship, just as the restriction of holding public office to a subset of adult men and a host of other civic disabilities did not attenuate the core legal rights and protections to which original female citizens were entitled in accordance with the norms of the *ius commune* and dispositions of Pisa's statutes. It cannot be stressed enough that in this period neither the *ius commune* nor town statutes in central and northern Italy made citizenship contingent on baptism into the Christian faith.[82] Vitale's religion and status as a Jew, which were never at issue in this dispute, were treated by legal authorities as distinct from his status as a Pisan citizen. This consequential distinction is captured in Decius's words for designating Vitale's civic identity. Vitale was designated a "hebraeus et civis pisanus," not a composite "civis hebraeus pisanus."[83]

Enlisting the fifteenth-century authorities in company with Bartolus and Baldus, Decius argued that under *ius commune* rules Vitale was not required to pay the Pisan contract tax. "With regard to the first question, concerning the *ius commune*," he began, "it would seem clear cut that [Vitale] is not obligated, because the *gabella* is a burden that results from the contract and it follows that the *gabella* should be paid where the contract is concluded."[84] He cited the opinion of Alexander Tartagnus that if the *gabella* was paid where the contract was made, it did not have to be paid in another locality, because one should not be compelled to pay the *gabella* twice for the same thing.[85] Could the husband be compelled to pay, if, after having contracted and consummated his marriage and paid the *gabella* in a place located outside the territory of the taxing authority, he returned with his wife to live together in his place of domicile? On the authority of *consilia* by Petrus Philippus Corneus and Bartholomaeus Socinus in analogous cases, he was not compellable.[86] Similarly, Vitale could not be compelled under Pisa's laws to pay its contract tax, as the laws did not apply to husbands who contracted and consummated their marriages outside Pisan territory[87] – a *ius commune* rule that we already encountered in the opinions discussed above.

The claim that the *Capitoli* made Vitale liable for the Florentine contract tax presented a thornier challenge. Arguing *pro et contra*, Decius first defended the government's claim before demolishing it. The *Capitoli* were probably those issued in 1514 and extended for another five years in 1524 by the officials of Florence's public debt (*monte comune*), who authorized the banking operations of several Jewish families. Among them were the "heirs of Simone di Vitale da Pisa," that is, his only son, Vitale.[88] In these and earlier *Capitoli* issued in the fifteenth century, Jewish lenders and their associates were required to pay a hefty annual tax (*taxa pro fenerando*) for the monopoly of operating in the city, *contado*, and *distretto* of Florence. Otherwise, they were exempt from all ordinary and extraordinary taxes, with the exception of *gabelle*, which they were required to pay just as other Florentine citizens (*prout tenentur cives florentini*). Thus, for example, the Jewish lenders were required to pay the *gabella contractus* on the acquisition and purchase of real estate not to exceed a certain value, and on all other goods, save the account books, items, and gold transported between the city and *contado*, which were connected with their lending activities.

Another standard provision of the *Capitoli* was the privilege that for the duration of their license the "Jews [bankers, family members, employees, and associates] in respect to their rights and in civil and criminal causes and suits should be regarded and treated to the same extent as true citizens of Florence" (hebrei in eorum iuribus et in causis seu casibus in civilibus et criminalibus debeant reputari et tractari tamquam veri cives civitatis Florentie).[89] The juridico-technical meaning and ramifications of this and similar privileges in the *Capitoli* of towns and cities of central and northern Italy, which conferred temporary citizenship on Jewish bankers and their entourages, have been debated by modern scholars, as they had been previously by jurists in the late Trecento and Quattrocento.[90] I am persuaded by Toaff's argument, supported by ample evidence, that the terms of citizenship set forth in the *Capitoli* generally provided a temporally limited yet valuable and legally enforceable set of substantive immunities, privileges, and institutional protections which enabled Jewish bankers like Vitale da Pisa to conduct their lending and commercial operations in relative security.[91] In short, for the duration of the *Capitoli*, Vitale da Pisa would be – and was – treated in legal matters as a bona fide citizen of Florence, a status that carried potentially unwanted burdens as well as coveted benefits.

In fact, according to the tax officials, it was Vitale's very status as a citizen of Florence that made him liable for the *gabella dotis*, just as all Florentine citizens who married elsewhere and later return home were obligated. As Decius explained, "citizens of Florence who contract and consummate their marriages and receive a dowry outside Florence's territory, should they return afterwards with their wives to Florence, are compelled to pay the *gabella* there in accordance with custom or statute."[92] Civic equality meant that tax burdens had to be shared in equal measure by all citizens, with no exceptions. In support of this principle, Decius cited Baldus that if someone was granted the privileges and benefits (*favores*) of citizenship, he had to share the burdens (tolls and other personal and property imposts) as well as the benefits of citizenship equally with all other citizens, because civic burdens were necessarily intrinsic to citizenship itself.[93] For this stipulative reason, deference should be paid to Florentine custom and statutes.

Pivoting to Vitale's defense, Decius held that not all citizens were equally equal, a prime example of which was the status of foreign university professors and students during their academic tenures and period of studies.[94] To attract foreign scholars to their *studia*, city governments established that professors and students would be treated as citizens *in omnibus*, a vague legal construct that inadvertently made them vulnerable to civic burdens, jeopardizing the privileges and immunities they had traditionally enjoyed under the *ius commune* since the twelfth century. Following Bartolus's lead, his successors concurred that the purpose of this policy was to expressly favor scholars by enabling them to receive the benefits of citizenship while avoiding the legal disadvantages and obstacles faced by foreigners. Construing *in omnibus* to mean that scholars were liable for civic burdens was contrary to both the *ius commune* and benevolent governmental policies aimed at promoting scholarship and learning.

Decius applied the same interpretive logic to the *Capitoli.* Jewish bankers, just as university scholars, were said to enjoy the benefits of citizenship, while they were purposely released from its burdens.[95] He thus denied the allegation based on a narrowly literalistic interpretation of the *Capitoli* that the privileges and immunities conferred on the Jewish bankers made them coequal Florentine citizens. In no way were the privileges and immunities granted to the Jewish bankers identical and exclusively limited to those enjoyed by ordinary Florentine citizens. This narrow understanding of the *Capitoli* was considered offensive and "against the explicit intention of the parties" (contra manifestam intentionem partium). The intention of both parties, the Jewish bankers and the commune of Florence, was that the Jews would enjoy the immunities and benefits attached to Florentine citizenship but be exempt from things offensive and repugnant (*odia*), a category that included the *gabella dotis.* There is an implicit irony to Decius's rejection of literalism, for it was the Jews who were repeatedly called to task by theologians and jurists for their allegedly stubborn adherence to literal interpretation.[96]

Baldus's essentialist reasoning, Decius continued, was irrelevant, because it was keyed to someone who was truly made a *civis ex privilegio* and inducted into the citizenry, which compelled him to participate equally with other true citizens in the burdens of citizenship. Such compulsion was missing in the case of those whose citizenship was contingent on the meaning of the imperative expression, "they ought to be treated as citizens." Its operative meaning refers to the benefits of citizenship only, as in the example of scholars, which, Decius insisted, was exactly how the language of the Florentine *Capitoli* should be construed.[97] Echoing Bartolus, he closed the *consilium* with the pithy declaration that "one can be made a citizen without civic burdens."[98] All of this demonstrated to Decius's professional satisfaction why Vitale da Pisa was justly exempt from payment of the Florentine *gabella dotis.*

5

I have been unable to discover the final disposition in any of the three cases. Even though they were not procedurally required to accept a *consilium sapientis* as constituting the final judgment in the case, the presiding officials in garden-variety tax disputes usually accepted a *consilium sapientis* as binding, even more so when the consultor was of the stature of Phillipus Decius, then Italy's premier jurist. This approach would have been followed in cases like ours, in which the jurists were nearly unanimous in affirming *ius commune* rules against the extraterritorial reach of Pisa's laws and Florence's tax-demanding officials. Admittedly, the protagonist-husbands in two of the cases were hardly ordinary and unsurprisingly became inviting targets of the Florentine tax officials in Pisa. Agapito dell'Agnello was a high-profile Pisan exile who commanded large dowries. Vitale da Pisa's return to Pisa with his bride was a notable social event, while his lavish lifestyle visibly accentuated his megawealth. Yet, unless the officials had commissioned and received supplementary *consilia* supporting their original decision to impose the contract tax (and we have no indication that they did), it is hard to fathom the grounds on which the officials would have refused to accept the jurists' determinations.

Whatever the final disposition of our three cases, the *consilia* I have examined show, first of all, that the Florentine officials who administered Pisa sought to adhere to the rule of law, by relying on the expertise of jurists working in Florence and Pisa, rather than on mandating preferred outcomes, to resolve disputes posing a challenge to Florentine fiscal policies and entailing a potential loss of revenue. The concept of citizenship in late medieval and Renaissance Italy, the *consilia* reveal, was malleable and contestable.[99] The substantive and operative meanings legislators, public officials, and jurists attributed to the designation *civis* were context-dependent and often contradictory, as strikingly revealed in Vitale da Pisa's case. A sine qua non for negotiating these cross-cutting meanings is a firm grasp of *ius commune* interpretive methods and doctrines as well as the intricacies of local political and institutional contexts.

Finally, the *consilia* offer instructive insights into the multijurisdictional puzzles that resulted in the fifteenth and early sixteenth centuries when native citizens established legal domicile and acquired citizenship in foreign jurisdictions. Matters became further tangled, as in the case of Vitale da Pisa, who acquired citizenship in Florence which had superior jurisdiction over his native city. Wherever they traveled, citizens remained in principle subject to the jurisdiction of their hometowns, but not with respect to the *gabella dei contratti*, which in compliance with *ius commune* doctrines and rules was payable in the place where the contract was formalized and performed. That explains why the jurists were almost unanimously and straightforwardly opposed to "long-arm" laws imposing taxes on contracts executed by citizens in foreign jurisdictions.

Original Publication Information

1. Osvaldo Cavallar and Julius Kirshner. "Making and Breaking Betrothal Contracts (*Sponsalia*) in Late Medieval Florence." In *Panta rei: Studi dedicati a Manlio Bellomo*, edited by Orazio Condorelli, vol. 1, 395–452. Rome: Il Cigno, 2004. Reprinted with the kind permission of Il Cigno Edizioni.
2. Julius Kirshner. "*Li Emergenti Bisogni Matrimoniali* in Renaissance Florence." In *Society and Individual in Renaissance Florence,* edited by William J. Connell, 79–109. Berkeley, Los Angeles, London: University of California Press, 2002. © 2002 by the Regents of the University of California. Reprinted with the permission of the University of California Press.
3. Julius Kirshner. "Materials for a Gilded Cage: Non-dotal Assets in Florence (1300–1500)." In *The Family in Italy from Antiquity to the Present,* edited by David I. Kertzer and Richard P. Saller, 184–207. New Haven, CT: Yale University Press, 1991. © 1991 by Yale University. Reprinted with the permission of Yale University Press.
4. Julius Kirshner. "The Morning After: Collecting *Monte* Dowries in Renaissance Florence." In *From Florence to the Mediterranean and Beyond: Essays in Honour of Anthony Molho*, edited by Diogo Ramada Curto, Eric R. Dursteler, Julius Kirshner, and Francesca Trivellato, vol. 1, 29–61. Florence: Leo S. Olschki, 2009. Reprinted with the permission of Casa Editrice L. Olschki.
5. Julius Kirshner and Jacob Klerman. "The Seven Percent Fund of Renaissance Florence." In *Banchi pubblici, banchi privati e monti di pietà nell'Europa preindustriale: Amministrazione, tecniche operative e ruoli economici: Atti del convegno (Genova, 1–6 ottobre 1990)*, vol. 1, 369–98. Genoa: Società Ligure di Storia Patria, 1991. Reprinted with the permission of the Società Ligure di Storia Patria.

6. Julius Kirshner. "Wives' Claims against Insolvent Husbands in Late Medieval Italy." In *Women of the Medieval World: Essays in Honor of John H. Mundy*, edited by Julius Kirshner and Suzanne F. Wemple, 256–303. Oxford: Basil Blackwell, 1985. Reprinted with the permission of John Wiley and Sons Ltd.
7. Julius Kirshner. "Women Married Elsewhere: Gender and Citizenship in Italy." In *Time, Space, and Women's Lives in Early Modern Europe*. Sixteenth Century Essays and Studies, vol. 57, edited by Anne Jacobson Schutte, Thomas Kuehn, and Silvana Seidel Menchi, 117–49. Kirksville, MO: Truman State University Press, 2001. Reprinted with the permission of Truman State University Press.
8. Julius Kirshner. "Dowry, Domicile, and Citizenship in Late Medieval Florence." In *Florence and Beyond: Culture, Society and Politics in Renaissance Italy: Essays in Honour of John M. Najemy*, edited by David S. Peterson with Daniel E. Bornstein, 257–70. Toronto: Centre for Reformation and Renaissance Studies, 2008. Reprinted with the permission of the Centre for Reformation and Renaissance Studies.
9. Julius Kirshner. "Pisa's 'Long-Arm' *Gabella dotis* (1420–1525): Issues, Cases, and Legal Opinions." In *Europa e Italia: Studi in onore di Giorgio Chittolini / Europe and Italy: Studies in Honour of Giorgio Chittolini*, edited by Paola Guglielmotti, Isabella Lazzarini, and Gian Maria Varanini, 223–48. Florence: Firenze University Press, 2011. Reprinted with the permission of Firenze University Press.

Appendix 1

The betrothal of Lena di Bernardo Sassetti by her uncle Paolo d'Alessandro Sassetti to Lodovico di Filippo Fabrini Tolsini, in 1384, which took place in the church of the Cistercian Badia Fiorentina.

Ricordanze of Paolo d'Alessandro Sassetti
Source: ASF, CS, ser 2a, no. 4, 69v

MCCCLXXXIII[1]

Ricordanza che maritamo la Lena, figliuola che fu di Bernardo nostro fratello, per mezanità d'Andrea di messer Francieshco Salviati. Et Filippo del maestro Tedaldo ne fu il sensale.

Dì XX di marzo, anno 1383, inpalmamo e fermamo, col detto Andrea di messer Franciescho Salviati, in presenzia del detto Filippo del maestro Tedaldo, mezano e sensale, che la detta Lena sia, nel nome di Dio e di riposo di loro e di noi, donna di Lodovicho di Filippo Fabrini Tolsini, giovane d'anni XXXVI in XL, con dota di fiorini settecento d'oro, tra denari e donora; e così fermammo col detto Andrea di messer Franciescho.

Poi mercholedì XXX di marzo, anno MCCCLXXXIIII, nel nome di Dio e di pacie e consolazione di loro e di noi, la giurammo e compromettemo nella chiesa della Badia di Firenze. Carta per mano di ser Michele di ser Aldobrando; e mezani ala dota Andrea di messer Franciescho Salviati sopradetto e Ghino di Bernardo d'Anselmo.

Poi domenicha di III d'aprile, anno MCCCLXXXIIII, la venne a vedere il detto Lodovicho suo marito e dielle l'anello. Carta per le mani d'Ugho di Domenicho Vecchietti. Chontanti, per parte della dota che dare gli dobiamo, fiorini cinqueciento d'oro, sanza niuna comfessagione.

Poi dì XI maggio, anno MCCCLXXXIIII, gli demmo, per le mani del detto Ugho Vecchietti e compagni, per parte della dota che dare gli dobiamo, fiorini cientotrenta d'oro, sanza nuiuna comfesione.

Poi dì XII di maggio, anno MCCCLXXXIIII, gli mandamo due forzieri nuovi, entrovi le 'nfrascritte chose e la stima della valuta di ciò partitamente ...

Appendix 2

A model betrothal contract included in a Florentine manual for notaries compiled in 1391 by ser Iacopo di ser Francesco Toscanelli

Formulario di ser Iacopo di ser Francesco Toschanelli (1391)
Source: ASF, NA, Appendice 5, inserto 4, 57v

Arra sponsalitiarum

In Dei nomine, amen. Anno dominice incarnationis MCCCXXX, indictione et die, etc. Attum Florentie, etc. Presentibus testibus, etc. Antonius olim Lapi, populi S. Laurenti, promisit et convenit et pattum fecit Ricoverino Fey, dicti populi, dare eidem in uxorem dominam Tessam eius sororem, termino quo dixerit Giannes Lapi dicti populi; et dabit eidem pro dote et nomine dotis dicte sororis sue illam pecuniam quam predictus Giannes dixerit; et faciet et curabit ita et taliter quod dicta domina Tessa[1] consenti<e>t in dictum Ricoverinum tanquam in suum legiptimum virum; et ab eo recipiet anulum pro complemento matrimonii, et omnia et singula[2] faciet, que natura contractus matrimonii postulat et requirit. Et versa vice dictus Ricoverinus promisit et convenit dicto Antonio accipere dictam dominam Tessam in proximo termino quo dixerit dictus Giannes; et confite<bi>tur ab ipsa domina Tessa,[3] sive ab altero pro ea, illam dotem et quantitatem pecunie antecedente quod predictus Giannes dixerit; et quod faciet eidem domine Tesse[4] donationem de suis bonis presentibus et futuris, secundum usum et constitutiones Comunis Florentie; et in eam consentiet tamquam in suam legiptimam uxorem et eidem dare anulum pro effectu matrimimoni<i>; et omnia faciet, que natura contractus matrimonii postulat et requirit. Pro quibus omnibus et singulis observandis et firmis tenendis fuerunt inter se vicissim et invicem in veritate confessi se pro arris et nomine arrarum sponsalitiarum recepisse et habuisse libras CC florenorum parvorum, quas alter eorum, qui fallet et in fide non staret, servanti et in fide stanti dare et solvere et restituere promisit duplicatas, et damna omnia et expensas dicta de causa resarcire, et post nicchilominus firma tenere omnia et singula[5] suprascripta. Pro quibus omnibus et singulis observandis et adimplendis et firmis tenendis, et pro pena solvenda si comissa fuerit, obligaverunt inter se vicissim et ad invicem se et eorum heredes et bona presentia et futura, que constituerunt se pro eo precario possidere. Renuntiantes inter se vicissim et ad invicem exceptioni non celebrati contractus et non habitarum et non receptarum arrarum sponsalitiarum et pecunie quantitatis, fori privilegio et omni alii (sic) exceptioni et legum, iuris et constitutionum, eis vel alteri eorum pertinentibus vel confitentibus in predictis. Cui predicta volenti et confitenti precpi, ego Ugholinus notarius infrascrpitus, per guarentigiam, etc., quatenus observet et adimpleat omnia et singula[6] supradicta, ut supra continetur.[7]

Appendix 3

Two *consilia* of Angelus de Ubaldis on the enforcement of betrothal contracts in late fourteenth-century Florence and Tuscany

Consilium I

Source: *V* = BAV, Vat. lat. 2540, 209va–10va, cons. 25.
ed. = Angelus de Ubaldis, *Consilia* (Lyon, 1551), 125r–v, cons. 234.

Punctus.[1] Statuto comunis Florentie cavetur quod, super debito et quibuscumque contractibus guarentigiam continentibus, per viam actionis vel exceptionis nichil posset opponi, vel de simulatione,[2] vel contractu per vim, dolum vel metum extortum,[3] vel aliud dici,[4] obici vel opponi. Et non obstante petitione vel exceptione, que fieret de predictis, iudex vel officialis coram quo peteretur vel opponeretur precise teneatur et debeat executioni mandare tale debitum et contractum usque ad integram satisfationem, nisi obstenderet scripturam debiti sibi vel alteri pro eo redditam, cancellatam, vel instrumentum finis, solutionis, vel cassationis.[5]

Contingit quod adsendentes mares et femine vicisim promiserunt se facturos et curaturos quod filius unius filiam alterius recipiet in uxorem et econtra. Et quilibet ipsorum seorssum unus ab altero, licet in eodem instrumento, confessus fuit se ararum nomine recepisse florenos auri mille, quos promisit reddere duplicatos, si predicta omnia et singula non observaverit cum effectu. Deinde postea contingit successive quod unus eorum predicta non observat. Alter autem observare vult, et per eum non stat. Et petit, qui observare vult, dictas arras confessatas simplas et non duplas. Queritur utrum[6] instrumentum dicte[7] guarentigie executionem mereatur,[8] attenta forma dicti statuti.

In Dei nomine et sue matris virginis glorioxe, amen.[9] Visis statuto et contractu predictis, prima fatie videtur instrumentum predictum guarentigie nullam executionem mereri, pro eo quia dictus contractus bonis moribus contradicit, cum matrimonia tam[10] contracta quam etiam[11] contrahenda pene vinculo astringi non debeant, sive pena sit promissa hincinde per coniunges re vel spe, sive per parentum coniunges, ff. de verbo., ob., l. Titia [Dig. 45. 1. 134], ubi est casus. Cum igitur honestati bonisque moribus pactum repugnet, doli mali sine dubio obstat exceptio, ut ibidem. Quinymo et pacta omnia et conventiones bonis moribus et honestati contradictorie nullas vires habent, nullumque ius agendi, excipiendi, aut naturalem obligationem producunt, C. de pac., l. <Pacta> que contra [Cod. 2. 3. 6], ff. de pac., l. Iuris gentium, § Si ob[12] malefitium [Dig. 2. 14. 7. 3], et § Pretor ait [Dig. 2. 14. 7. 7]. Et ideo talia pacta iuramento non firmantur, de regulis, <c.> Non est obligatorium [VI 5. 13. 58], et ibi per Io. An. et Dy.[13]

Nec obstare videtur statutum predictum, quoniam in[14] principio loquitur de precepto guarentigie facte de debito vel de re contenta in talibus scripturis. Hoc autem constat non esse debitum.[15] Et licet statutum loquatur de re contractata[16] in talibus scripturis, tamen temperanda sunt verba et restringenda, ita et taliter quod nichil absurdum, nichil turpe aut moribus bonis et honest<at>i contradicens resultet,[17] ff. de bonis libertorum, l. Nam absurdum [Dig. 38. 2. 7]. Si[18] enim sic iudaice et[19] tenaciter verba statuti ampleteremur[20] sequeretur quod omnis pactio et omnis contractus, quantumcumque turpissimus <et> iniquus, redactus in mundum, si preceptum guarentigie contineret, deberet exequutioni mandari. Unde et[21] si quis ascendentem vel dessendentem[22] promisisset sibi in matrimonio copulare, aut transversalem in gradu prohibito, sub pena, aut quis promisisset sacrilegium, homicidium, aut[23] aliud detestabile perpetrare sub pena et recepisset preceptum guarentisie, eo[24] non obstante pena posset exigi. Hoc autem contradicit legi divine et humane, tam cano<n>ice quam civili, etiam si dicte policitationes vel pacta essent iuramento firmata, ut superius dictum est.

Pro hac parte facit multum quia ubi lex de dispositione aliqua inter vivos vel ultime voluntatis statuit, non prius ad dispositum in statuto recurritur quam constet dispositionem hominis inter vivos vel in ultima voluntate validam, l. iv, § Condennatum [Dig. 42. 1. 4. 6], de re iudi., et l. Divus [Dig. 29. 1. 24], ff. de testamento mili., que notabilis est ad hoc. Si autem vera sunt antecedentia, quod dicta pactio sit bonis moribus contradicens et honestatem inquinet, necessario sequitur conclusio ante dicta.

Contrarium puto verum. Pro cuius investigatione considero quod omnem adiectionem penarum super observantia matrimonii iam contracti vel etiam contrahendi improbat lex canonica et civilis[25] honestati et bonis moribus contrariam, ut dicta l. Titia [Dig. 45.1.134], in principio, et extra de spon., <c.> Gemma [X 4.1.29], sed non arras, ut ibi per Inno.[26] Unde et si arras penam dicere possumus, prout voluit[27] Bernardus in dicto c. Gemma,[28] non tamen effectum pene habent arre per omnia. Quia si per omnia sortientur eundem effectum, sicut[29] pene adiectio bonis moribus contradicit indifferenter et indistincte, sic[30] et arrarum interiectio duplicata vel triplicata esset similiter[31] interdicta, cum duplum, triplum et[32] quadruplum non sit dubium quod est pena respectu solventis, et etiam recipientis, ergo nec primordialis arra nec[33] eius multiplicatio bonos mores indifferenter[34] vel honestatem corrunpit vel aliqualiter inquinat. Si enim hoc esset neque[35] statutum iuris canonici vel civilis[36] teneret, quia esset legi evangeliorum et Dei directe oppositum et contrarium, quoniam esset inductivum et provocativum pecati. Statuit ergo sanctio iuris civilis quod cum in contrahendis nuptiis potestas libera esse debeat quod in arris datis ob matrimonium contrahendum, si matrimonium non contrahitur nulla iusta causa subsistente, arre duplicate per recipientem restituuntur, si eius culpa matrimonium non contrahitur et[37] date perduntur si culpa dantis matrimonium non contrahitur, vacante dispositione antique prudentie, que usque ad quadruplum ipsas arras assendere[38] permittebat. Unde tam per antiquam iuris prudentiam, quam per novam, matrimonia[39] non erant libera ab omni metu penarum. Quia non a pena, que incurritur per dationem arrarum, sed solum ab illa que a principio sub nudo nomine pene in dispositione intericitur,[40] ut patet aperte in l. <In> arris , coniuncta l. finali [Cod. 5. 1. 5], C. de spon., in qua ponitur et describitur nova iuris prudentia, quod si extra diffinitionem illius legis cautio penam in stipulatum[41] deductam contineat, ex nulla parte vires habebit, propter liberam potestatem, que in nuptiis contrahendis esse debet, ut superius est ostensum. Non igitur bonis moribus contradicit aut honestati repugnat mutua arrarum promissio, sed solum evacuatur virtus, ex[42] eo quod arre date non sunt. Et evacuatur virtus maxime eius in transensu[43] et excessu, cum olim usque ad quadruplum, hodie vero duplum non possint[44] transcendere.

Cum igitur arrarum confessio nullo iure naturali, canonico vel civili[45] sit interdicta, sed solo statuto iuris civilis, ut dicta l. finali, hoc modo valet,[46] quia evaquatur[47] virtus eius, non autem legis interdictum resistit potentie confitendi,[48] apparet plus quam evidenter quod actus confitendi arras non est legibus neque moribus interdictus, sed solum evacuata est virtus confessionis, actui vero[49] promittendi penam simplicem et primordialem sub pene nomine nuncupatam lex resistit et contradicit. Et ideo[50] illa nec[51] iuramento firmatur.[52]

Nunc ad propositum reducendo dico dictas confessiones arrarum nullas fore, quia extra diffinitionem dicte legis ultime emanarunt, non obstante quod dicte confessiones seorssum sint facte, ex quo facte sunt uno contextu, quia propter contextualitatis actum presumere debemus eas mutuas,[53] ut l. Si ventri, § In bonis [Dig. 42. 5. 24. 2], ff. de privil. credi, <de rebus auctoritate iudicis>, ff. si cer. pe., l. Lecta, § Dicebam [Dig. 12. 1. 40 in c.]. Sed licet sint[54] nulle, de nullitate obici non potest, ex quo preceptum guarentigie continetur in eis, contra quod non potest obici de vi, dolo, vel metu, vel aliquid aliud dici, obici vel opponi, ut patet in dicto statuto, super debito vero et quibuscumque contractibus. Nec mirum, quia multi sunt actus nulli funditus ipso iure, et tamen dici vel allegari non possunt nulli, eo quod statutum iuris civilis vel municipalis os claudit volenti allegare nullitatem, vel quia iudici adimit potestatem omnem et iurisdictionem allegandi talem nullitatem, C. de servo pig. da. manumisso, l. Si creditoribus [Cod. 7. 8. 5], et facit C. de leg., l. ii [Cod. 1. 14. 2], de minori., l. Ait pretor, § Permictitur [Dig. 4. 4. 7. 2 in c]. Valet enim statutum ut aliquis non audiatur, licet non valeat[55] sub hac forma, ut alicui iustitia denegetur, quia tunc disponeret directo contra ius Dei, secundum Innoc., de constitutionibus, <c.> Que in ecclesiarum[56] [X 1. 2. 7]. Facit ad predicta quod not. Io. An., de rescrip., c. Statutum [VI 1. 3. 11], lib. vi., in glo. in verbo, "nec audiantur."[57]

Per hoc apparet responssum ad omnia supradicta exempla de pacto de coniungendo sibi in matrimonio descendentem vel assendentem aut[58] transverssalem in gradu prohibito, vel etiam de comictendo maleficia,[59] quoniam illis rescistit lex divina et humana, ac etiam naturalis vel quasi. Unde nullum pactum et nullla convenctio in contrarium facta evacuatur ex post facto, ymo in initio resistitur potentialiter contrahendi. Pro hoc notabiliter aduco, quia quedam sunt, que moribus et honestati universali et universaliter contradicunt, ut est mecari, occidere, furari, incestas nuptias comittere, et similia. Et super istis nullum pactum, nulla conventio fieri potest. Et ita loquuntur exempla. Quedam sunt, que bonis moribus contradicunt solum statuto[60] iuris civilis, non tamen sunt eodem statuto inhiri prohibita velut bonis moribus contraria, sed solum evacuatur omnis virtus eorum, ut quod dolus in contractibus absit. Et tunc statutum iuris municipalis multum operari potest et contrarium disponere.

Exemplum: dolus dans causam contractui bone fidei reddit contractum nullum ipso iure, secundum veram opynionem, ff. de dolo, l. <Et> elleganter [Dig. 4. 3. 7]. Et hoc solum inductum est statuto iuris civilis contractum annullante. Cui ergo dubium erit quod contrario statuto in territorio statuentium contrarium observabitur, ut in statuto predicto non permictente opponi de simulatione, neque de dolo, neque de metu. Et tamen quodlibet predictorum bonis moribus contrarium reddere potest contractum nullum ipso iure. De simulatione constat C. plus valere quod agitur [Cod. 4. 22], per totum. De dolo similiter constat in dicta l. <Et> elleganter. De metu similiter constat in aliquibus casibus, ut l. Si mulier, § Si dos [Dig. 4. 2. 21. 3], ff. quod me. cau. Maxima ergo est differentia, an aliquid sit contra bonos mores solum secundum ymaginationem et dispositionem iuris civilis, quo casu disponi[61] potest oppositum per ius municipij,[62] ut in l. Omnes populi [Dig. 1. 1. 9], <de iusti. et iur.,> et l. iii., § Quid <tamen> si[63] lex [Dig. 47. 12. 3. 5 in c.], de sepul. viola., an aliquid sit contra bonos mores in genere secundum ius divinum vel gentium vel nature aut[64] quasi nature, ut[65] patet exemplum in l. ii [Cod. 2. 2. 2], C. de in ius vocan. Et hoc casu neque statutum neque pactum quiquam operari possunt, etiam si[66] utriusque esset par conditio et natura, secundum notata in l. una [Cod. 10. 47[46]. 1], C. de decre. decurionum.

Concludo igitur ex premissis, attenta dispositione dicti statuti in dicto §[67] super debito, dictum instrumentum exequtionem merreri in arris confexatis et earum <in> simplo. Hoc autem audacter dico, si comunis stilus et consuetudo notariorum civitatis Florentie rogatorum de similibus[68] instrumentis est pactiones dictarum arrarum in eadem forma reducere. Tunc enim constat notorie iuris civilis tantum mores per mores[69] contrarios locales alteratos. Et ideo dico mori locali standum esse, et illum fore precipuum[70] in decisione causarum, C. quemad. te. aperiantur, l. ii [Cod. 6. 32. 2], C. que sit long, consu. [Cod. 8. 52[53]], in rubro et nigro, per totum, ff. de evict., l. Si fundus [Dig. 21. 2. 6], C. de usuris, l. Eos [Cod. 4. 32. 26], cum symilibus.

Pro hoc adduco fortiter, quia licet et pene aut arre evictari possint[71] ante latam sententiam per exceptionis obiectum,[72] tamen lata sententia in volentem frustra volens conqueritur, C. de rebus ere., l. Generaliter [Cod. 4. 1. 12], post principium, C. de appel., l. Hii qui ad civilia [Cod. 7. 62. 7]. Sed preceptum guarentigie est sententia lata per iudicem cartularium in volentem et sponte recipientem ex iurisdictione prorogata, que prorogari potuit, ff. de iudic., l. i. [Dig. 5. 1. 1], in fine glo. magne. Et ita dico et consulo, Ego Angelus de Ubaldis, legum doctor.[73]

Consilium II

Source: *V* = BAV, Vat. lat. 2540, 222vb–23r, cons. 41.
ed. = Angelus de Ubaldis, *Consilia* (Lyon, 1551), 135rv, cons. 251.

Punctus.[74] Domina Massina cum consensu[75] sui legitimi mundualdi promisit et convenit Eusepio[76] presenti, etc., se ipsam facturam et curaturam, et facere et curare, ita et taliter, etc., quod Sera, filia dicte domine Massine, cum fuerit etatis xii. annorum complete,[77] quam etatem dixit quod habebit completam in anno Domini M III^{C} LXXXX, ab incarnatione,[78] de mense februarii, statim dicto mense completo, consentiret in Pelegrinum, filium dicti Eusepij,[79] tanquam in suum sponsum et virum legitimum, et ab eodem anullos maritales sive matrimoniales reciperet, et cum eo contrahet legitimum matrimonium, et seipsam dominam Masinam daturam et soluturam eidem Pelegrino in dotem, et pro dote, et dotis nomine, dicte Sere illam quantitatem florenorum auri et pecunie seu rerum illis[80] temporibus et modo et forma, et quod predicta fient per ipsas Seram et dominam Masinam illis temporibus et modo et forma, quando, prout, et sicut, et quemadmodum,[81] dicent et declarabunt prudentes et discreti viri, Anthonius et Laurentius.[82] Et econverso dictus Eusepius, pater dicti Pelegrini, promisit et convenit dicte domine Massine presenti, etc., pro dicta Sera filia sua se facturum et curaturum,[83] et facere et curare, ita et taliter, omni iure et facti exceptione remota, quod dictus Pelegrinus, eius filius, cum fuerit etatis complete[84] xiiii annorum, quam etatem dixit quod habebit in MCCCLXXXXI, ab incarnatione, de mense maii, statim completo dicto mense, consentiet[85] in dictam Seram, etc.

Adde hic prout consultum fuit supra[86] in consilio 25,[87] quod incipit, "Visis statuto et contractu predictis," etc. Prout igitur in puncto predicto consului, sic iterum et de novo omnia in predicto consilio contenta aprobo et affirmo tanquam iuridica et iuste consulta. Verum in facto de quo presentialiter sum consultus additur, quod arbitri nichil laudaverunt de tempore sponsaliorum et matrimonii contrahendi, nec laudare possunt ad presens, eo quod alter arbitrorum decessit, et sic dictum compromissum expiravit. Et quod ellapso mense februarij anni Domini MCCCLXXXX, dictus Pelegrinus non erat annorum xiiii, sed eos complere debebit inmediate post finitum et completum mensem maij, anni Domini MCCCLXXXXI, et sic recte calculo computato dictus Pelegrinus, post finitum dictum mensem februarij, invenit se esse xii. annorum et x mensium, quo tempore, nisi malitia suplesset etatem, non erat habilis ad matrimonium contrahendum, licet posset contrahere sponsalia, et per consequens ex parte sua non potuisset nec potuit contrahere matrimonium cum dicta puella, nisi malitia[88] suplesset etatem,[89] ut dixi, patet quod interpellatio facta per eum immediate post dictum mensem februarii non constituit dictam mulierem interpellatam in mora, quoniam, qui tenetur ad dandum vel faciendum ex contractu corelativo et ultro citroque obligatorio, non potest agere, neque conventum in mora constituere, nisi primo impleat ex parte sua, quod implere tenetur, de act. empt., l. Iullianus, § Offerri [Dig. 19.1.13.8], et l. Qui pendentem vendimiam [Dig. 19.1.25]. Sed dictus Pelegrinus, impediente etate atque natura, matrimonium contrahere non poterat cum puella, ergo oblatio[90] de implendo derisoria fuit. Nec obstat si dicatur saltim[91] poterat contrahere sponsalia. Unde, quia sponsalia non fuerunt contracta, saltim[92] ex hoc capite non contractorum sponsaliorum videtur mulier interpellata in mora constituta, et per consequens dicte arre reddi debent duplicate.

Nego enim hoc, cum conventio fuerit concepta in hac forma, videlicet, quod dicta puella consentiet in dictum Pelegrinum tanquam in suum sponsum et virum legitimum, et ab eodem anullos matrimoniales recipiet, et cum eo contrahet legitimum matrimonium. Unde verba illa "sponsum," "virum" pro eodem ponuntur, sicut moris est Tuschorum, mulieres subarantium per anullum in digitos anullares, quia tunc invicem et mutuo consentientes, et unus in alterum, et econverso, desponsans consentit in desponsatam, ut in suam sponsam et uxorem legitimam. Et ipsa[93] ut in sponsum et virum. Sicque per mediatores verba dicentes, ut moris est, interrogatur desponsanda si consentit in talem ut in suum sponsum et virum. Et vir similiter interrogatur si consentit in illam ut in suam sponsam et legitimam uxorem, et ambo respondent quod sic. Non igitur senserunt[94] dicti contrahentes ut seorsum fierent sponsalia et succesive matrimonium, sed quod uno contextu expedirentur omnia. Quia igitur[95] omnia expediri non poterant, non fuit mora contracta.

Pro hoc facit quia[96] dicta verba "sponsum" et "virum" idem significent[97] et inportent, quia prolata sunt per mulierem iuris ignaram, apud quam talis dicendi varietas non cadit, ff. de testa, tu., l. Quid si nepotes [Dig. 26.2.6], in glo. Et verba in dubio semper intelligenda et interpetranda sunt secundum communem usum loquendi, per quem[98] <non> alteratur significatum proprium nominum verborum et rerum, ut l. Labeo, versiculo, "nec mirum," de supel. lega. [D. 33. 10. 7. 1]. Pro hac parte fortissime facit, quia, si non fallor, non est verum quod per interpellationem factam incontinenti de dicto mense februarii pro parte dicti Pellegrini, vel per interpellationem, que fuisset facta pro parte dicte puelle immediate post mensem maij, fui<s>set mora contracta, nisi primitus laudum emanasset de matrimonio contrahendo, quoniam dicte partes tempus matrimonii contrahendi, et quantitatem dotis, et forma obligationis de restituendo[99] dotem, videntur[100] reposuisse in voluntate arbitratorum communiter electorum, de quibus utraque pars plenam confidentiam gerebat.[101] Et hoc ostenditur, ut omnis evitetur assurditas omnisque imposibilitas, que ex verbis dicti contractus resultat, si verba dicti contractus aliter intelligantur quam dixerim. Resultat enim impossibilitas de natura, nisi iuvetur a dicta[102] malitia, quod dictum matrimonium contraheretur inmediate post mensem februarij. Cum dictus Pelegrinus tunc esset impubes et a pubertate distans per tempus xiiii. mensium, resultat absurditas quia, si inmediate dicto mense completo matrimonium deberet contrahij saltim de facto, et postea successive post mensem maii de iure esset iterum contrahendum. Cum enim matrimonium sit nomen iuris, et de matrimonio partes convenerint, intelligendum est de valido et subsistente de iure, cum verba civilia sint intelligenda civiliter, non de facto, ut l. i.,[103] § Hec verba, quod quisque iuris [Dig. 2.2.1.2], C. si manci., ita fuerit alienatum, 1. Ea quidem [Cod. 4.57.5], cum concordantiis ibi allegatis. Impossibillia igitur et assurda cum de omni dispositione quantum possibile est debeant amoveri, de bonis libertorum, l. nam assurdum [Dig. 38.2.7], de regulis iuris, l. Semper in stipulationibus [Dig. 50.17.34], de verbo., ob., l. Quotiens [Dig. 45.1.59], ff. de rebus du., l. Quotiens [Dig. 34.5.11[12]], idem sermo non debemus sermones dicti contractus ita intelligere, quod primo contrahatur matrimonium de facto, secundo de iure, arg. pro hoc de verbo., signi., l. Boves, § Hoc sermone [Dig. 50.16.89.1]. Hoc etiam esse verum declarat series instrumenti, si recte[104] construatur. Et sermo semper construendus est ita quod salvetur ratio directa dicti sermonis, C. de fideicom., l. Eam quam [Cod. 6.41.14], et ff. de auro et ar. leg., l. Plautius [Dig. 34.2.8]. Rectus autem constructus verborum in dicto instrumento contentorum est hic, videlicet, punctetur post illa verba "de mense februarii, statim dicto mense completo," et verbum "habebit" quod est supra determinet illud "complete." Et est sensus, quod domina Sera erit xii. annorum completorum de mense februarii statim dicto[105] mense completo. Non autem illud participium "completo" determinet verbum "consentiet," quod inmediate sequitur; ymo illud verbum "consentiet" determinet[106] omnia subsequentia verba ad versiculum, "Et econverso dictus Eusepius." Sequentia autem plura sunt: primo, contrahere matrimonium; secundo, dare et solvere dotem, prout et sicut dicent et declarabunt dicti arbitri. Et quod fiat relatio ad matrimonium, apparet ex illis verbis, "Et quod predicta fient per ipsas Seram et dominam Massinam illis temporibus," etc., quod verbum "predicta" est indefinitum et pluralis numeri. Unde, nisi fiat relatio etiam ad matrimonium, non congrue poneretur. Importatur enim per illud verbum "predicta" clausula generalis, que in fine posita, reffertur ad omnia precedentia, cum est eadem causa relationis, ut l. iii, § Filius, de liberis et postu. [Dig. 28.2.3.2]. Si igitur tempus matrimonii contrahendi, et dotis solvende, et quantitatis dotis, et forma predictorum in simplici[107] voluntate arbitratorum collata sunt ante declarationem factam per arbitros de tempore et de forma, nulla mora[108] potest contrahi, vel incurri, rebus sic se habentibus, prout proponuntur.

Concludo, moram non esse contractam ex parte dicte puelle per interpellationem factam incontinenti post dictum mensem februarij. Moveor dictis duabus rationibus, videlicet, quia dictus Pelegrinus incontinenti matrimonium ex parte sua non poterat consummare, impediente natura,[109] nisi tunc a malitia iuvaretur, ut superius dixi. Secundo, quia tempus matrimonij contrahendi non fuit per arbitros declaratum, et,[110] prout dixi, participium illud "completo" non determinatur a verbo "contrahet," ut sic sit sensus, quod[111] ipsa contrahet matrimonium inmediate illo mense februarij completo; imo determinatur, ut dixi, a dicto verbo "erit." Et sic sit rectus verborum constructus modo predicto, videlicet, quod dicta domina erit completo dicto mense februarij etatis annorum xii, quasi dicat et non ante ipsum mensem completum. Et sic construendo et intellige<n>do, omnis cessat assurditas, per aliam vero constructionem in evidentem assurditatem incurrimus.

Et ita consulo ego, Angelus de Perusio, et cet.[112]

Appendix 4

Chirico di Giovanni, goldbeater, inhabitant of the parish of San Miniato fra le torre, and citizen of Florence, acknowledges receipt of and assumes liability for a dowry of 403 florins, 14 soldi, and 4 denarii, payable in two future installments by the Dowry Fund, from ser Giovanni di Zenobio, father of Chirico's wife, Lena. Chirico and ser Giovanni enter into a supplementary agreement that should Lena die before Chirico within a year of the date of the *confessio*, with no children surviving their marriage, Chirico is obligated to return one-third of the dowry to Lena's father or his heirs, notwithstanding the statutes of Florence under which a husband of a predeceased wife is entitled to retain the entire dowry.

Confessio dotis of Chirico di Giovanni of Florence (1 Feb. 1464/5)
Source: ASF, NA, 5345, 5rv.

Dos domine Lene filie ser Iohannes Zenobii ser Iohannis Gini

Item postea, dictis anno, indictione, et die primo mensis februarii. Actum Florentie, in domo seu palatio residentie consulum Artis Lane civitatis Florentie, presentibus testibus etc. Bartolomeo Niccholai Mosdini, populi S. Marie in Champo de Florentia, et Petro Bartolomei, aromatario al Chappello, et Thommasio Iohannis domini Tommasii de Altovitis, et aliis.

Chiricus filius olim magistri Ieronimi, battilaurus, civis florentinus et de populo S. Miniatis inter Turres de Florentia, fuit confessus etc. habuisse etc. in dotem et pro dote domine Magdalene, alias vocate Lene, filie ser Iohannis Zenobii ser Iohannis Gini, notarii et civis fiorentini, et uxoris dicti Chirici (ut de matrimonio constat manu mei notarii predicti) florenos auri quadringentos tres soldos XIIII. denarios IIII. ad aurum a dicto ser Iohanne, patre dicti Lene, et pro eo ab officialibus montis Communis Florentie, de quibus venit tempus restitutionis per totum mensem ianuarii proxime preteriti de florenis trecentis quinquaginta soldis duobus et denariis XI. ad aurum; et de florenis quinquaginta tribus s. XI. et d. IIII. ad aurum veniet tempus restitutionis per totum mensem augusti proxime futuri 1465, de denariis dotium montis puellarum. Et de quibus florenis CCCCIII. s. XIIII. d. IIII. dictus Chiricus vocavit se bene pagatum, tacitum et contentum etc. Et propterea fecit donationem propter nuptias dicte Lene, licet absenti, et dicto ser Iohannes[1] eius patri, presenti etc., de libris quinquaginta florenorum parvorum, secundum formam statutorum etc. Quas dotem et donationem etc. prefatus Chiricus promisit etc. restituere etc. in omnem casum et eventum dicte dotis restituende et donationis solvende et seu consignande constante matrimonio vel soluto. Cum pacto etc. quod eveniente casu etc. dicta domina etc. possit propria auctoritate etc. bona et de bonis etc., et dictus Chiricus hereditatem intrare etc. et ea vendere et non probare solutionem etc. Et cum aliis pactis etc. utilibus etc.

Et cum pacto solempni stipulatione vallato inter dictum ser Iohannem ex parte una, et dictum Chiricum ex parte alia, quod in casu (quod absit) quod evenerit casus mortis domine Lene infra annum ab hodie, sine filiis, quod tunc et eo casu dictus Chiricus teneatur restituere dicto ser Iohanni vel eius heredibus tertiam partem dicte dotis, non obstante statuto communis Florentie quod vir[2] lucretur dotem uxoris premortue etc. Que omnia etc. promisit etc. attendere etc., sub pena dupli etc., que etc. Obligavit etc. Renuntiavit etc. gurarantigia etc.

Appendix 5

Schedule of Interest Due and Paid on the 7 Percent Account of Lorenzo di Bonaccorso Pitti, 1479–96

Source: ASF, MG, 954, 40r, 508r; MG, 955, 315r, 816r; MG, 957, 427r, 836r

We claim in the body of chapter 5 that in contrast to *monte* credits, interest payments on 7 percent credits were made regularly and on time. By statute, interest of 7 percent of the face value of the credits was payable annually in three installments of 2 ⅓ percent on 1 January, 1 May, and 1 September. To support our claim, we reproduce the interest payment record of Lorenzo di Bonaccorso Pitti from 1479 to 1496. Pitti's account opened in May 1479 with 239 florins' worth of credits that he had purchased in the secondary market. The portion of his wife's dowry payable by the Dowry Fund, or credits worth 466 florins, was deposited in his account by September 1480. Over the years the amount of credits in Pitti's account fluctuated as a result of sales and additional purchases.

Since information concerning the government's decisions to disburse interest on 7 percent credits is extremely fragmentary, we cannot assume that the recorded date of payment was the first date payment could have been collected. A comparison of the record of interest paid on Pitti's account with the records of other contemporary accounts indicates that the date when creditors collected interest was variable.[1] It is likely that in some instances interest might have been paid to Pitti a few days earlier, if he had requested it. Given our inability to calculate with precision the difference between the first date interest was collectable and the date it was collected, we summarize the interest payment record for Pitti's account as follows. All the other payments were made on average thirty days later than the date on which interest was due.

Table A5 Schedule of Interest Due and Paid on the 7 Percent Account of Lorenzo di Bonaccorso Pitti, 1479–96

Credits (Face Value, in Florins)	Interest	Date on Which Interest Was Due	Date on Which Interest Was Paid	Delay (Days)
239	5	1 Sept. 1479	12 Oct. 1479	41
239	5	1 Jan. 1480	11 Jan. 1480	10
239	5	1 May 1480	10 May 1480	9
239	5	1 Sept. 1480	13 Sept. 1480	15
705	16	1 Jan. 1481	16 Jan. 1481	15
705	16	1 May 1481	14 May 1481	13
838	19	1 Sept. 1481	12 Sept. 1481	11
838	19	1 Jan. 1482	18 Jan. 1482	17
838	19	1 May 1482	21 May 1482	20
838	19	1 Sept. 1482	23 Sept. 1482	22
838	19	1 Jan. 1483	28 Feb. 1483	58
799	18	1 May 1483	28 May 1483	27
799	18	1 Sept. 1483	22 Sept. 1483	21
799	18	1 Jan. 1484	23 Jan. 1484	22
799	18	1 May 1484	1 June 1484	31
799	18	1 Sept. 1484	28 Sept. 1484	27
799	18	1 Jan. 1485	28 Jan. 1485	27
799	18	1 May 1485	28 May 1485	27
799	18	1 Sept. 1485	26 Sept. 1485	25
799	18	1 Jan. 1486	—	—
799	18	1 May 1486	6 June 1486	36
799	18	1 Sept. 1486	27 Sept. 1486	26
799	18	1 Jan. 1487	1 Feb. 1487	31
799	18	1 May 1487	6 June 1487	36

(*Continued*)

Table A5 *Continued*

Credits (Face Value, in Florins)	Interest	Date on Which Interest Was Due	Date on Which Interest Was Paid	Delay (Days)
799	18	1 Sept. 1487	15 Oct. 1487	44
799	18	1 Jan. 1488	6 Feb. 1488	36
799	18	1 May 1488	3 June 1488	33
799	18	1 Sept. 1488	23 Oct. 1488	52
799	18	1 Jan. 1489	14 Feb. 1489	44
1012	23	1 May 1489	2 June 1489	32
1012	23	1 Sept. 1489	26 Oct. 1489	55
1012	23	1 Jan. 1490	4 Feb. 1490	34
1012	23	1 May 1490	5 June 1490	35
812	19	1 Sept. 1490	27 Oct. 1490	56
812	19	1 Jan. 1491	31 Jan. 1491	30
812	19	1 May 1491	26 May 1491	25
346	8	1 Sept. 1491	10 Oct. 1491	39
900	21	1 Jan. 1492	24 Jan. 1492	23
766	18	1 May 1492	16 June 1492	46
766	18	1 Sept. 1492	1 Oct. 1492	30
1433	33	1 Jan. 1493	15 Jan 1493	14
1091	25	1 May 1493	4 June 1493	34
1032	24	1 Sept. 1493	2 Oct. 1493	32
1032	24	1 Jan. 1494	14 Jan 1494	13
1032	24	1 May 1494	24 May 1494	23
1032	24	1 Sept. 1494	19 Sept. 1494	18
1032	24	1 Jan. 1495	26 Jan. 1495	25
1032	24	1 May 1495	12 May 1495	11
1032	24	1 Sept. 1495	15 Sept. 1495	14
1032	24	1 Jan. 1496	19 Jan. 1496	18

Appendix 6

Selected Jurists and Theologians

Abbas Panormitanus/ Niccolò de' Tedeschi (d. 1445)
Accursius (d. 1260)
Albericus de Rosate (d. 1360)
Alexander Salvii de Bencivennis (d. 1423)
Alexander Tartagnus (d. 1477)
Angelus Carlettus de Clavasio (d. 1495)
Angelus Caroli de Niccolinis (1474–1509)
Angelus de Ubaldis (d. 1400)
Angelus Matthei de Niccolinis (1473–1542)
Angelus Othonis de Niccolinis (d. 1499)
Antoninus Florentinus/sant'Antonino di Firenze (d. 1459)
Antonius de Butrio (d. 1408)
Antonius de Rosellis (d. 1466)
Antonius Vanni de Stroziis (d. 1523)
Azo (d. ca. 1230)
Baldus de Ubaldis (d. 1400)
Bartholomaeus de Saliceto (d. 1412)
Bartholomaeus Fumus (d. ca. 1555)
Bartholomaeus Socinus (d. 1506)
Bartolus de Saxoferrato (d. 1357)
Benedictus Accoltus Aretinus (d. 1464)
Benedictus de Barzis Perusinus (d. 1459)
Bernardus de Parma (d. 1266)
Cinus de Pistorio (d. 1336)
Dinus Mugellanus (d. ca. 1303)

Dominicus de Sancto Geminiano (d. 1424)
Dominicus Nicolai de Martellis (1476)
Dominicus Tuschus (d. 1620)
Franciscus de Albergottis (d. 1376)
Franciscus de Vercellis (fl. 1275)
Franciscus de Zabarellis (d. 1417)
Guido de Baysio (d. 1313)
Gulielmus Durandus (d. 1296)
Honofrius de Bartolinis (d. ca. 1416)
Hostiensis (d. 1271)
Innocentius IV (1254)
Jacobus Butrigarius (d. 1347)
Jacobus de Arena (d. 1296)
Jacobus de Belvisio (d. 1335)
Jacobus de Ravanis (d. 1296)
Jason de Mayno (1519)
Johannes Andreae (d. 1348)
Johannes Crottus (d. 1516)
Johannes de Erfordia (d. ca. 1320)
Johannes de Imola (d. 1436)
Johannes de Riccis (d. 1402)
Johannes Geronimi de Eugubio (d. 1454)
Johannes Petruccius de Montesperello (1464)
Lapus de Castiglionchio Senior (d. 1381)
Laurentius de Ridolphis/Lorenzo d'Antonio Ridolfi (d. 1443)
Ludovicus Pontanus/Romanus (d. 1439)
Marianus Socinus (d. 1467)
Nellus de Sancto Geminiano (d. 1430)
Odofredus (d. 1265)
Oldradus de Ponte (d. ca. 1335)
Paulus de Castro (d. 1441)
Petrus Ancharanus (d. 1416)
Petrus de Bellapertica (d. 1308)
Petrus de Exio/Piero di Jacopo Ambrosini (d. 1472)
Petrus Philippus Corneus (d. 1492)
Philippus de Corsinis (d. 1421)
Philippus Decius (d. 1535)
Raphael de Raymundis Cumanus (d. 1427)
Riccardus Francisci del Bene (d. 1411)
Riccardus Malumbra (d. 1334)

Rolandinus de Passageriis (d. 1300)
Sallustius Gulielmi Perusinus (d. 1461)
San Bernardino da Siena (d. 1444)
Stephanus de Bonaccursiis (d. 1433)
Tomas Jacobi de Salvettis (d. 1472)

Abbreviations

AGN Arte dei Giudici e Notai, Florence
ASF Archivio di Stato, Florence
ASI Archivio storico italiano
ASLu Archivio di Stato, Lucca
ASPi Archivio di Stato, Pisa
Auth. *Authenticum*, constitution of Justinian
BAV Biblioteca Apostolica Vaticana, Vatican City
BNCF Biblioteca Nazionale Centrale, Florence
C. *causa* (in citations of *Decretum Gratiani*)
c. canon (in citations of *Decretum Gratiani*)
c. capitulum, *canon* (in the text)
Clem. *constitution clementina*, constitution of Clement V
Cod. *Codex Iustiniani*
Cod. Theod. *Codex Theodosianus*
coll. *collatio* (in citations of the *Authenticum*)
CRS Corporazioni Religiose Soppresse, Archivio di Stato, Florence
CS Carte Strozziane, Archivio di Stato, Florence
DBI Dizionario biografico degli Italiani
D. *distinctio* division in the first part of *Decretum Gratiani*
Decretum Grat. *Decretum Gratiani*
dictum Grat. *dictum Gratiani*, comment of Gratian before or after a fragment

Dig. *Digesta Iustiniani*
Extrav. comm. *Extravagantes communes*
ff. *Digesta Iustiniani* (in the text)
gl. ord. *glossa ordinaria*
Inst. *Institutiones Iustiniani*
l. lex, law in Justinian's *Corpus* (in the text)
Magl. Magliabechiano, Biblioteca Nazionale Centrale, Florence
MC Monte Comune, Archivio di Stato, Florence
MG Monte delle Graticole, Archivio di Stato, Florence
NA Notarile Antecosimiano, Archivio di Stato, Florence
NAE Notificazione di atti di emancipazione, Archivio di Stato, Florence
Nov. *Novella Iustiniani*
PR Provvisioni-Registri, Archivio di Stato, Florence
q. *quaestio*, division within a *causa* of *Decretum Gratiani*
RDC Revue de droit canonique
RDIPP Rivista di diritto internazionale privato e processuale
RHD Revue d'histoire de droit
RHDF Revue historique de droit français et étranger
RIDC Rivista internazionale di diritto comune
RISG Rivista italiana per le scienze giuridiche
RSDI Rivista di storia del diritto italiano
rubr. *rubrica*
s.f. *sine folio* (no foliation)
SMN Santa Maria Nuova, Archivio di Stato, Florence
s.v. *sub verbo*, gloss to a law or decretal
TUI Tractatus universi iuris
VI *Liber sextus decretalium Bonifacii VIII*
X *Decretales Gregorii IX* (*Liber extra*)
ZRG (*KA*) *Zeitschrift der Savigny-Stiftung für Rechtsgeschichte, Kanonistische Abteilung*
ZRG (*RA*) *Zeitschrift der Savigny-Stiftung für Rechtsgeschichte, Romanistische Abteilung*

Notes

Introduction

1 Bellomo, *The Common Legal Past*. On the sources of the *ius commune*, see Dondorp and Schrage, "The Sources"; Lange and Kriechbaum, *Römisches recht im Mittelalter*, 355–419.
2 Dondarini, ed., *La libertà di decidere*. On the production, use, and textual transmission of the statutes of Florence, see Biscione's comprehensive *Statuti*.
3 Edigati and Tanzini, *Ad Statutum Florentinum*.
4 Hajnal, "European Marriage Patterns in Perspective."
5 Herlihy and Klapisch-Zuber, *Tuscans and Their Families*, 202.
6 Goldthwaite, *Private Wealth*, 257
7 Kent, *Household and Lineage*, 293.
8 For example, Gavitt, *Gender, Honor, and Charity*, 120: "Certainly Goldthwaite's study, by focusing on the economic fortunes of Renaissance families, underemphasized the extended lineage ties that bound them together. Certainly Kent, by focusing on the social networks that bound Florentine families of high social standing, neglected some of the economic issues that often divided families within the same lineage. Furthermore, both historians, by defining the family in terms of the fortunes of its male actors in the public world, certainly missed the social and psychic toll that lineage solidarity took on members of the family who were juridically disadvantaged in the inheritance grid."
9 On this point, see Molho, "Visions of the Florentine Family." In a 1991 article addressing the scholarship that appeared after the publication of his book, Kent was forced to acknowledge the varied roles women played in Florentine patrician families. See his "La famiglia patrizia," esp. 88–91.
10 Herlihy and Klapisch-Zuber, *Tuscans and Their Families*, 342.

11 Goody, "The Evolution of the Family," 119.
12 Klapisch-Zuber, "State and Family," 21.
13 Klapisch-Zuber, *Women, Family, and Ritual.*
14 Klapisch-Zuber, "The Griselda Complex," 219.
15 See the review of the Italian version of Klapisch-Zuber's studies by Hughes, "La famiglia e le donne," 629–34.
16 Strocchia, "Death Rites," 138.
17 Crabb, *The Strozzi*, 18.
18 Tomas, *The Medici Women*, 4.
19 Our works are listed in the comprehensive bibliography.
20 Botticini and Siow, "Why Dowries?"; Botticini, "A Loveless Economy?"
21 Botticini and Siow, "Why Dowries?" 1386.
22 Kuehn, *Heirs*, 120ff.
23 Molho, *Marriage Alliance*, 38ff.
24 See Kirshner and Klerman, "The Seven Percent Fund of Renaissance Florence," chap. 5 in this volume.
25 Here are a few examples of references to investment of dowries in fourteenth- and fifteenth-century Florence: In 1336, the brothers Caroccio and Duccio Alberti invested their mothers' as well as wives' dowries in the family partnership (Passerini, *Gli Alberti*, vol. 1, 22–3, doc. 4). Pepo d'Antonio Albizzi invested his dowry to become a partner with his father in a woolen shop (Hoshino, *L'arte della lana*, 312–13). The economic fortune of the Riccardi family is said to have originated with the dowry that Anichini Riccardi received from a rich widow (Malanima, *I Riccardi*, 5ff.). Married four times, the silk merchant Goro Dati used the dowries he received to liquidate debts, restore stolen assets, and recapitalize and expand business operations (Pandimiglio, *I libri di famiglia*, 106, 108, 114, 136, 139). In 1434, Dietisalvi di Nerone di Nigi Dietisalvi placed his wife's dowry of 1,300 florins in a workshop (*bottegha*) (*Libro di famiglia di Dietisalvi di Nerone Dietisalvi*, Manoscritti, vol. 85, 101r [5 Feb. 1433/4]). Tognetti suggests that Piero Capelli used the 1,400-florin dowry from Costanza di Niccolò Cambini to start a business with her brothers (Tognetti, *Il Banco Cambini*, 83). Giuliano di Giovenco de' Medici began lending large sums of money at interest after receiving 800 florins of his wife's dowry in 1448 (Edler de Roover, "Restitution," 778). Tommaso di Tolsini de' Medici used part of his wife's dowry of 1,100 florins to invest in Florence's public debt (*monte comune*) and purchase properties and expressed a desire to invest in the silk business (NA, 14717, 15v [10 Nov. 1474]). Three generations of Guicciardini invested dotal capital in business (Goldthwaite, *Private Wealth*, 122–5). In his *catasto* return of 1480, the wool merchant Piero di Girolamo

Ciacchi reported that he had invested "a lot of the money" from the dowry he had received from his wife (1,200 florins of which came from the Dowry Fund) in a woolen shop, but the investment came to naught as expenses far exceeded profits (Catasto 46 [1480], 232r).

26 Zucca Micheletto, "À quoi sert la dot?" and the author's companion study, "Reconsidering the Southern Europe Model," 360–4.

27 For a helpful overview, see Lanaro and Varanini, "Funzioni."

28 My translation of the Italian title: see Bellomo, *Ricerche sui rapporti.* For a synopsis of his book, see his entry, "Dote (Diritto Intermedio)," in the *Enciclopedia del diritto.*

29 On the *Morgengabe*, see Kirshner, "*Li Emergent Bisogni Matrimoniali,*" chap. 2 in this volume, p. 58.

30 As recently as 2010, Bartoli Langeli remarked "il gran libro di Manlio Bellomo ... ormai più che cinquantenne ma tuttora valido." See his "Parole introduttive," 12.

31 Quote from Epstein, "The Family," 188, summarizing his findings of chap. 4, "Family: The Principal Heirs," in his *Wills and Wealth*, 67–97.

32 There is little evidence to back up Stuard's assertion, following Bellomo, that "the ready cash [via dowries] that fell into the hands of men when they married underwrote European commercial expansion." See Stuard, "Dowry and Other Marriage Gifts," 228.

33 Among the studies that could be cited, see Jehel, "Le rôle des femmes"; Pistarino, "La donna d'affari"; Epstein, "Labour"; Kamenaga Anzai, "Attitudes towards Public Debt"; Chabot, "La reconnaissance"; Cohn, "Women and Work"; Marshall, *The Local Merchants*, 40–1; Riemer, "Women, Dowries, and Capital Investment"; Rugolo, "Donna e lavoro"; Figliuolo, "Lo spazio economico," 766, 778; Molà, "Le donne"; Mainoni, "Il potere di decidere," 242–3; the papers in *Dare credito alle donne*, edited by Petti Balbi and Guglielmotti; and especially the papers of Sorelli, Guzzetti, and Clark published in *Donne, lavoro, economia a Venezia e in Terraferma*, edited by Bellavitis and Guzzetti.

34 See Kirshner and Klerman, "The Seven Percent Fund of Renaissance Florence," chap. 5 in this volume. For security arrangements in Venice, see Chojnacki, "Getting Back the Dowry," 89ff.

35 Chabot, "Lineage Strategies," 140–1; and her analysis in *La dette des familles*, 273ff.

36 Rinaldi, "Figure femminili"; and Guzzetti, "Dowries."

37 For a critique of this view, see my "Genere e cittadinanza." See also Menzinger, "La donna medievale."

38 See Tanzini, *Alle origini.*

1. Making and Breaking Betrothal Contracts (*Sponsalia*) in Late Trecento Florence

1 Onclin, "L'âge"; Metz, "L'enfant dans le droit," 23ff.; Orlando, *Sposarsi*, chap. 6: "Spose bambine," 143–72.

2 For a general overview of Christian marriage, with an excellent bibliography, see Gaudemet, *Le mariage*. On the legal issues and doctrines relating to *sponsalia*, see Esmein, *Le mariage*; Dauvillier, *Le mariage dans le droit*; Rasi, *La conclusione del matrimonio*, 32–76; Gaudemet, *Sociétés et mariage*, 379–91; idem, *Le mariage*, 169–71; Valsecchi, "'Causa matrimonialis,'" 463–72. On the glossators, see Rasi, "Il diritto matrimoniale"; Donahue, "The Case of the Man." For actual cases, see Lévy, "L'officialité de Paris," 1266–74; Meek, "Women, the Church," 82–5.

3 Cicchetti and Mordenti, *I libri di famiglia*; Klapisch-Zuber, *La maison et le nom*; Cherubini, "I *libri di ricordanze*," 269–87; Ciappelli, *Una famiglia*; Pandimiglio, *I libri di famiglia*.

4 We cite the English translation: Klapisch-Zuber, "Zacharias." See also Fabbri, *Alleanza matrimoniale*, 150–93; and Chabot, *La dettes des familles*, 195–222. On betrothal practices in the Roman world, see the engaging and informative discussion of Treggiari, *Roman Marriage*, 83–160; and Evans Grubbs, *Law and Family*, 140–82. See also Astolfi's detailed *Il fidanzamento*. For comparisons between Italian and Northern European betrothal and marriage rituals, see Seidel, *Jan Van Eyck's Arnolfini Portrait*; and Hall, *The Arnolfini Betrothal.*

5 The *Glossa* explained that the meaning of *pactum* derived from a striking of the palms. See the gloss *Percussit* to *l. Sciendum* (Dig. 50. 15. 1): "id est pactum fecit, nam dicitur a percussione palmarum"; and the gloss *Pactum* to *l. Huius edicti* (Dig. 2. 14. 1. 1); after Accursius has given Isidore of Seville's etymology of "pactum," he states: "Vel dicitur pactum a percussione palmarum." For an examination of this ritual depicted in medieval legal texts and in sculpture and wood carvings, see Leisching, "'Et teneat.'" See also Musson, "Images of Marriage," 127–32. On the motif of the handclasp (*dextarum iunctio*) in Roman funerary art, see Davies, "The Significance of the Handshake." The term *impalmare*, which is now a literary or facetious term, originally meant to promise a girl as a bride as well as to shake someone's hand as a sign of agreement.

6 In fourteenth-century Haute-Provence, a customary expression for betrothing a young woman was "ipsam domicellam firmavit," which Coulet suggests is semantically related to an agricultural lease (*fermage*) and rental service. See Coulet, *Affaires d'argent*, 66–7.

7 Sacchetti, *Il trecentonovelle*, novella 189, 638–41; Sercambi, *Novelle*, novella 8, 127–40, esp. 127–8. For a discussion of young adolescent girls who were pressured into hasty marriages in the literary context of Shakespeare's *Romeo and Juliet*, see Young, "Haste, Consent, and Age."

8 Cammelli, *I sonetti del Pistoia*, 53.

9 The verse "a tutti due in un punto il col scavezza" is typically – and wrongly – understood by both editors and commentators to mean that the broker had broken the necks of the betrothed with one blow. See, for example, Cammelli, *Rime edite ed inedite di Antonio Cammelli*, 271, n. 20. On this point, we appreciate the advice of our colleagues Elissa Weaver and Gabriella Zarri.

10 For Petrus de Ancharano's view, see Brundage, *Law, Sex, and Christian Society*, 497.

11 Bancarel, *Le mariage entre absents*. According to Grubb, "Veneto memoirs ... indicate that the girl's consent to a future union, if indeed it was even sought, was not regarded as worth recording." See Grubb, *Provincial Families*, 9.

12 Quotation from Brundage, *Law, Sex, and Christian Society*, 436–7, who suggests that premarital sex was common in rural France, England, and Corsica. See also Weigand, "Ehe- und Familienrecht in der mittelalterlichen Stadt," esp. 372–3; Le Roy Ladurie, *Montaillou*, 139–78; Goldberg, *Women in England*, 9: "The impression gleaned from church court records is that few young women would consent to sex until an agreement to marriage had been made." For Finch ("Sexual Relations," 252) premarital sex was "an integral part of the process by which marriages and other stable unions came to be formed." See also Finch, "Sexual Morality," 267ff.; Korpiola, *Between Betrothal*, 222ff., 249ff.; Salonen, "Marriage Disputes."

13 Lefebvre-Teillard, "Règle et réalité"; Zarri, "Il matrimonio tridentino," 243–8.

14 Quotation from Rocke, "Gender and Sexual Culture," 162. Ruggiero dubs Venetian antenuptial fornication as "fornication and then marriage." See his *The Boundaries of Eros*, 16–44; and Cazzetta's brilliant *"Praesumitur seducta,"* 51ff. For Aragon, see Falcón-Pérez, "Le mariage en Aragon," 159ff.

15 BNCF, Fondo Panciatichiano , vol. 147 (Zibaldone di Lorenzo Ridolfi), 2v: "Memoria insuper quod die II[a] aprilis 1388 Nicolaus germanus meus firmavit in uxorem pro me filiam Angeli de Barucciis de Florentia, Caterine nomine, et vocatam Pichinam, et die XX[a] eiusdem, idem Nicholaus per verba de futuro, nomine meo, desponsavit eamdem, et die III[a] maii anni predicti misit sibi forzerinum iuxta morem consuetum. Et ego eam vidi solum die

XII[a] julii anni predicti." Our transcription slightly differs from Martino, "Umanisti, giuristi, uomini," 186, n. 43.

16 On the origins of these rituals, see the superb study of Anné, *Les rites des fiançailles*. See also Astolfi, *Il fidanzamento*, 143ff. For the Middle Ages, Brandileone, "Contributo allo studio," 401ff.; Rasi, "La conclusione del matrimonio," 264ff.; Zanetti, "Sul valore giuridico"; Quaglioni, "Segni"; Cattaneo, "La celebrazione"; Stevenson, *Nuptial Blessing*; Niccoli, "Baci rubati."

17 Abbas Panormitanus (Niccolò de' Tedeschi), *Consilia* (Venice, 1578), 32r, cons. 48. Prenuptial gifts were also treated as valid evidence in breach-of-promise suits in Victorian England. See Frost, *Promises Broken*, 30.

18 Bellomo, *Ricerche sui rapporti*, 27–60 and 223–44.

19 Kreutz, "The Twilight of *Morgengabe*." See also Braccia, "*Uxor gaudet.*"

20 Izbicki, "*Ista questio*," 48–9; Guerra Medici, *L'aria di città*, 39ff.; Bestor, "The Groom's Prestations," 141ff.; and her "Marriage Transactions"; and, of course, Klapisch-Zuber's classic essay, "The Griselda Complex."

21 ASLu, Statuti del Comune di Lucca, 6, 144v, lib. 4, rubr. 132, *De anulo sponsalitio et de donamentis sponse a sponso factis.*

22 See the *consilium* of the lay canon lawyer Stephanus de Bonaccursiis, with *subscriptiones* by Philippus de Corsinis and Laurentius de Ridolphis, in BNCF, Fondo Principale, II, II, 370, 7r–v. The *consilium* was penned in March 1412/13. For rings as a material sign of marriage in Renaissance Florence, see Musacchio, *Art, Marriage*, 22–6. See also Demoulin-Auzary, *Les actions d'État*, 189–93.

23 Klapisch-Zuber, "Zacharias," 184–6. See also d'Avray, "Marriage Ceremonies."

24 Perugia attempted to prevent breaches of promise of future marriage by requiring the redaction of *sponsalia* by a public notary. See Severino Caprioli, ed., *Statuto*, 361, rubr. 386, *Qualiter fiat contractus de sponsalitiis: Statuimus quod quando aliquis desposaverit uxorem, de sponsalitiis fieri faciat publicum instrumentum, ut ab aliqua partium in posterum non valeat negari.* On the role of the notary in redacting *sponsalia* and marriage agreements, see Leisching, "Eheschliessungen"; Di Renzo Villata, "Il volto della famiglia," 384–96. A Bolognese *sponsalia* contract of 1210 is published by Tamba, *Una corporazione*, 127–30. The statutes of Perugia and Rolandinus de Passageriis's notarial manual leave the impression that *sponsalia* contracts redacted by notaries were common. Our research in the notarial records of Trecento Bologna and Perugia, necessarily restricted and preliminary, does not lend support to this impression. In our investigation of several dozen files of notarial documents in the Archivio di Stato of Perugia and Bologna we found countless contracts of marriage and

confessiones dotium but not a single betrothal contract. We wish to express our appreciation to Paola Monacchia, Director of the Archivio di Stato of Perugia, and Maria Rosaria Celli Giorgini, Director of the Archivio di Stato of Bologna, for generously facilitating our research.

25 Beginning in 1356, the statutes of Florence required that all *sponsalia* had to be contracted publically in a church. See Klapisch-Zuber, "Zacharias," 193.

26 Ibid., 184–5; Molho, *Marriage Alliance,* 256ff.; Brucker, "Ecclesiastical Courts," 320.

27 Princes, it seems, had little compunction about breaking betrothal agreements on grounds of political expediency. See Chareyon, "De l'histoire."

28 Cohn, *The Laboring Classes*, 19–23.

29 Polonio, "'Consentirono l'un l'altro,'" 7–8; Seidel Menchi, "Percorsi variegati," 35ff.; Zarri, "Il matrimonio tridentino," 204ff. For the case of a law student who, while attending the university of Bologna, was married *per verba de futuro* to his Palermitan bride (Violante Belingerio), see Garufi, *Il matrimonio*, 62–72, 161–73, 200–4. The instrument was drafted in Palermo in 1349. The breach between popular attitudes toward marriage and canonical theory is highlighted by Helmholz, *Marriage Litigation*, 31–3, 72–3; and Sheehan, "The Formation," 5–7. Pederson, "Did the Medieval Laity," argues unconvincingly that lay litigants in the archdiocese of York showed "a very sophisticated understanding of the law" (115), and "displayed a surprisingly informed knowledge of the canon law rules of marriage" (150). What surprises us is Pederson's disregard of the methodological and contextual challenges facing historians attempting to assess the litigants' familiarity with, let alone "very sophisticated understanding of," legal rules and procedures from the records of court proceedings. These challenges and others have been amply met by Donahue, *Law, Marriage*, a richly detailed, painstaking, and ever-questioning analysis of marriage cases litigated in the church courts of York, Ely, Paris, Cambrai, and Brussels.

30 NA, 9039. Alphabetical lists of the betrothal and marriage contracts are found at the beginning of the volume.

31 See above, n. 7.

32 NA, 9039, 33r, 430r.

33 Ibid., 69r, 430r.

34 Bender, *Negotiating Marriage*, 199ff. We are grateful to the author for granting us permission to cite her doctoral dissertation.

35 NA, 19768, 1v (27 Jan. 1353/4), 3r (4 Feb. 1353/4), 6r–v (16 Feb. 1353/4), 23r (20 Sept. 1353), 30v (18 Jan. 1354/5), 31r (1 Feb. 1354/5); NA, 210, 36v (28 Nov. 1367); NA, 218, 96r (5 June 1398); NA, 1208, 56v (29 Jan. 1395/6), NA, 1209, 53v (23 Jan. 1398/9), 105v (19 Apr. 1400), 160v (17 Feb 1400/1), 161r

(20 Feb. 1400/1), 174v (29 May 1401); NA, 1216, 903r (22 Apr. 1425); NA, 1213, doc. IV (22 Apr. 1425); NA, 382, 47v–48v (28 June 1428). The same practice is found in Arezzo and Perugia. For Arezzo, see NA, 1921 (ser Bartolomeo di Taviano), 5v (31 Mar. 1392), 8r–v (28 Apr. 1392), 22r–v (8 June 1393), 24v–25r (12 Oct. 1393), 29v–30r (4 Mar. 1394/5), 30r–v (4 Mar. 1394/5), 34r–35r (12 Aug. 1394), 40r–v (3 June 1394). For Perugia, see Archivio di Stato, Perugia, Notarile 49 (ser Niccolò di Lucolo), 29r–v (16 May 1401), 33v–34v (30 June 1401), 73r (23 Apr. 1403). Our analysis has subsequently been confirmed by Kuehn, "Contracting Marriage," 393–8.

36 The occurrence of betrothal and marriage on the same day was not so strange as it may seem. For other examples, see *Libro di famiglia* of Niccolò del Buono Busini (1400–13), CS, ser. 4, vol. 564, 30v (22 Dec. 1404); *Libro di famiglia* of Antonio di Leonardo Rustichi (1412–36), CS, ser. 2a, vol. 11, 13v (21 Jan. 1417); Foster, *The Ties That Bind*, 400.

37 Interestingly, the short intervals in Florence are similar to the intervals separating betrothals and marriages in the early Roman Empire. See Treggiari, *Roman Marriage*, 153–5.

38 NA, 9039, 97v, 250r.

39 Helmholz, *Marriage Litigation*, 35. On the enforceabilty of sworn promises to marry, see Innocent III's decretal, *Praeterea hi* (X 4. 1. 2). According to Seidel, *Jan Van Eyck's Arnolfini Portrait*, 70, betrothals in Ghent and Bruges had the binding force of contracts. Like so many historians, Hall, *The Arnolfini Betrothal*, 61, minimizes the binding force of *sponsalia* contracts by accenting the legal reasons for breaking them. This approach creates the misleading impression that *sponsalia* are analogous to contemporary engagements to marry.

40 Though compulsion may seem to be a flagrant violation of the principle of freedom of marriage, excommunication in this case was deemed legitimate because the parties made their promises under oath.

41 As Di Simplicio points out, the expression *sponsalia de futuro* "is not similar to the word engagement, as it is understood in the twentieth century." Furthermore, *fidanzamento* and its cognates, *fidanzato* and *fidanzata,* were not used in the Trecento and Quattrocento. See his *Peccato, penitenza*, 250.

42 On the issue of parental consent and coercion, see O'Donnell, *The Marriage of Minors*; Tocci, "Il *consensus parentum*"; Korpiola, "An Uneasy Harmony"; Cozzi, "Padri, figli"; Aznar Gil, "El consentimiento paterno"; Hacke, "*Non lo volevo*"; Kirshner, "Children."

43 The discussion of the Pisa case is adopted from Kirshner, "Children," 127–8.

44 Evans Grubbs, *Law and Family*, 155.

45 Parties who secretly married (*per verba de presenti*) a person other than the betrothed frequently appeared in the records of church courts. See Lefebvre-Teillard, "Règle et réalité," 210–17; Vleeschouwers-Van Melebeek, "Aspects du lien." For the dissolution of *sponsalia de futuro* by the officality of Paris, because of attempted bigamy (*bina sponsalia*), see Donahue, "*Ex Officio* Cases," 406ff.

46 For a list of cases in which the *sponsalia* could be dissolved, see Johannes Andreae, *De sponsalibus et matrimoniis*, in *TUI* (Venice, 1584), vol. 9, 2r–v. For the absence of the *sponsus* for a protracted period, see *l. Si is qui puellam* (Cod. 5. 1. 2).

47 Lefebvre-Teillard, "*Ad matrimonium.*"

48 Pommeray, *L'officialité archidiaconale*, 346–8; Weigand, "Zur mittelalterlichen kirchlichen Ehegerichtsbarkeit," 312–13. On Regensburg, see now Deutsch, *Ehegerichtsbarkeit*, 267–8. The evidence on the frequency of disputes over the enforcement of betrothals in late medieval rural England is mixed: see Ingram, "Spousal Litigation," 41ff.; Donahue, "Female Plaintiffs." See now Donahue's *Law, Marriage.*

49 Dolezalek, *Das Imbreviaturbuch*; Polonio, "'Consentirono l'un l'altro,'" 8ff.; Meek, "Women, the Church" 82–5; idem, "Un'unione incerta."

50 Brucker, "Ecclesiastical Courts," 244–5; idem, *Giovanni and Lusanna*, 129. Several examples of broken betrothal contracts in Florence are discussed by Chabot, *La dettes des familles*, 198–9. For post-Tridentine Florence, see Lombardi, "Il matrimonio"; idem, "Fidanzamenti"; and idem "Intervention by Church." On trials concerning breach of promise to marry adjudicated in the archiepiscopal court in pre-Tridentine Bologna (1544–63), see Ferrante, "Marriage and Women's Subjectivity"; and her "Gli sposi contesi." On pre-Tridentine Venice, see Cristellon, *La carità*, 256. In truth, even after the Council of Trent, the number of cases adjudicated in Italian church courts remained small. For the figures, see Ciappelli, "I processi." According to Stow, among Jews in the Roman Jewish ghetto "there were at least twenty-three broken engagements out of about 560 matches registered by Jewish notaries during the fifty years 1536–85, or 4.1%." See his "Marriages Are Made," 473. North of the Alps: Korpiola, *Between Betrothal*, 183ff.; and her "Marriage Causes," 222–35; Salonen, "Marriage Disputes," 206–8; Deutsch, *Ehegerichtsbarkeit*, 311. Between 1592 and 1651, 191 women brought suit over broken marriage promises, defloration, and nonmarital pregnancies in Munich's highest civil court. See Strasser, *State of Virginity*, 92–117.

51 Dean, "Fathers and Daughters," 91–2; Del Gratta, *Giovan Battista*, 60, 259.

52 The Florentine merchant Giovanni di Pagolo Morelli recounted in his *ricordi* that before he married Caterina d'Alberto Alberti in 1395, he originally

wanted to marry another woman, and hoping to win her, he had forgone opportunities to marry into other prominent families. The woman's father, whose name was not divulged, promised that he would marry his daughter to Morelli, and the alliance was affirmed by the ritual handclasp in Santa Croce. But before the *sponsalia* took place, the father withdrew his promise. Still feeling rage at having been deceived and betrayed (*tradimento*), Morelli related that "I have seen, and I still see," revenge (*vendetta*) inflicted on both the father and his family. Revealingly, the inflicted revenge was metaphorical: the "grandissima grazia" (greatest blessing) of having married Caterina and his prosperous financial position were his revenge. See Morelli, *Ricordi*, 342–3.

53 Compagni, *Cronica*, I, cap. 2, 7–8; Villani, *Nuova cronica*, I, lib. 6, cap. 38, 267–9; Bruni, *History*, I, Book 2, 106–7; Machiavelli, *Florentine Histories,* 55–6, bk. 2, chap. 3. See also the discussion of this dramatic episode by Faini, "*Il convito del 1216.*"

54 Sercambi, *Novelle*, novella 8, 129: "La donna contentissima disse a messer Lanfranco che trovasse uno notaio che venga con messer Renaldo acciò che il matrimonio si fermi, pensando che messer Renaldo non si pentisse."

55 Needless to say, the father of the *sponsus* also could give *arrhae* on behalf of his son. Though Roman legislation considered various possibilities – for instance, whether the *sponsa* was *sui iuris* and whether she had reached puberty – for our purpose, this part of the legislation is irrelevant, since, especially in the Middle Ages, it was the parents of the *sponsus* or *sponsa* who gave or promised *arrhae*.

56 On Roman *arrhae sponsaliciae*, see Cod. 5. 1. 5, *Mulier iuris sui*; Anné, *Les rites des fiançailles*, 122–5, 425–6; Evans Grubbs, *Law and Family*, 163–4; 174–82; and her *Woman and the Law*. 113–22. See also Zimmermann, *The Law of Obligations*, 230–4.

57 Scalfati, ed., *Un formulario notarile,* 83–4: *De promissione et iuramento dandi aliquam in futurum in sponsam uxorem sub arris sponsalitiis*. For later examples, see De Angelis et al., eds., *I notai fiorentini*, vol. 1, fasc. 3 (novembre 1305–maggio 1309), 1–2 (doc. 480); 49–50 (doc. 531); 62 (doc. 545); 63 (doc. 546); 125 (doc. 609); 132–3 (doc. 618). In Pisa and its *contado* the breaching party was required to pay double the *arrhae* and all litigation expenses. The injured party was also authorized to have the breacher's property seized in satisfaction of the claim. See the *sponsalia* contracts in NA (ser Meo Buonfigliolo), 3r–v (20 June 1402); 5r–v (2 June 1402); 25v–26v (8 Nov. 1403); 28v (9 Nov. 1403); 35r–36r (26 April 1404). For Siena, see a *consilium* of the Perugian jurist Honofrius de Bartolinis, on a dispute over the nonperformance of a betrothal contract that occurred

in Siena around 1408. Its *punctus* refers to the mutual exchange of 1,000 florins of *arrhae* money, which was acknowledged by the parties in the *sponsalia* contract. See BNCF, Magl. XXIX, 165, 39v–41r, 39v: "Insuper dictus Deus [the father of the *sponsa*] ex una parte et dictus Antonius [the *sponsus*] ex alia, videlicet una pars ab alia et econtra, confessi fuerunt habuisse et recepisse et eis datum et numeratum fuisse et cetera nomine arrarum sponsalitiarum florenos auri mille." The party failing to observe the terms of the contract was obligated "reddere duplichatus" that amount to the aggrieved party.

58 Since the acknowledgment of *arrhae* was a fictitious transaction, we have chosen not to translate *arrhae* in this context as earnest money, for this last term conveys the idea of an actual cash transfer from one party to the other, which did not happen.

59 For Laurentius's affirmation, see his endorsement of a *consilium* written by Agabitus Matthei of Perugia. In addition to Laurentius's endorsement, substantial endorsements were provided by Franciscus Mansueti of Perugia, Salustius Gulielmi of Perugia, Stephanus Iohanni de Bonaccursiis of Florence, and Philippus Tommasii de Corsinis of Florence: see Ziletti, ed., *Matrimonialium consiliorum ... primum volumen*, 6v–17r. Laurentius wrote, "apud nos," meaning in Florence and the surrounding territory, "arrhae communiter ad summam conventae dotis dantur" and "si arrhae in veritate datae non sunt, ut communiter non dantur." Further, in his contained endorsement he referred the judicial authority to a *consilium* he had submitted in 1392 and to an earlier *consilium* of Angelus de Ubaldis of Perugia – probably the *consilium* of Angelus we have edited below, in appendix 3.

60 Martines, *The Social World*, 37–9; Molho, *Marriage Alliance*, 324ff.; Fabbri, *Alleanza matrimoniale*, 71ff.

61 NA, 9039, 255r–v (17 Feb. 1419/20), 395r–v (22 Nov. 1421). The observation that *arrhae* and dowry tended to be roughly equivalent has been made by Hughes in connection with the Zaccaria family of Genoa between 1271 and 1282. It is not clear from Hughes's incomplete description whether the stipulation of *arrhae* was mutually binding and whether it was fictional or involved a real transfer of cash. See Hughes, "Il matrimonio nell'Italia," 26–7. For the rough equivalence between dowry and *arrhae*, see Brucker, *The Society of Renaissance Florence*, 32–7, esp. 36. In a marriage negotiation involving the Del Bene family, Lemmo Balducci, whose daughter was betrothed to Amerigo del Bene, objected to setting the penalty for breaking the *sponsalia* at 2,000 florins. Among other reasons, the bride's father alleged that a penalty of 2,000 florins would spread the rumor that he had given

a corresponding dowry ("ogni persona sprerà ch'io dia di dota fiorini II^{M} d'oro"). For the transcription of the original documents, see Brucker, *Firenze nel Rinascimento*, 253–7; for the citation, 256. For another example of the parity between *arrhae* and dowry, see the *consilium* of the fourteenth-century consultor Andreas de Monte Ubbiano (= Monte Vibiano, a *castello* on a hilltop south of Perugia). Here, Corrado, father of the *sponsa*, promises to pay the *sponsus* a dowry worth 300 florins upon consummation of the marriage. In addition, Corrado acknowledges receipt of 300 florins in *arrhae* from the guardians of the *sponsus*, and in turn promises to pay the *sponsus* 600 florins (*reddere duplicitas*) if and when the *sponsa* does not fulfill the terms of the betrothal contract. The jurist determined that the guardians had not actually paid the *arrhae* (*numeratio non probatur*) and therefore had no claim against the *sponsa*. The *consilium* is located in the Biblioteca Nazionale Universitaria of Turin, Cod. H. I. 13, 73r–v.

62 NA, 9039, 201r (30 May 1419), 239v–40r (22 Dec. 1419).

63 *Formularium diversorum contractuum*, 49v–50r (*instrumentum sponsalitii*). The copy we consulted is found in ASF. In fifteenth-century Ragusa, the standard penalty for breaking the betrothal was a hefty 1,000 gold ducats. See Rheubottom, *Age, Marriage*, 84.

64 Brandileone, "Contributo"; Koschaker, "Zur Geschichte"; Volterra, "Studio sull'*arrha sponsalicia*"; idem, "Sponsalia"; Cornil, "Die *Arrha,*" 51–87; Astolfi, *Il fidanzamento*, 181–208.

65 Anné, *Les rites des fiançialles*, 87–135.

66 On the content of this fragment, see Astolfi, *Il fidanzamento*, 190–7.

67 For the *arrhae* in the early Middle Ages, especially in Germanic law, see Reynolds, *Marriage in the Western Church*, 67–100, 113–14.

68 The prohibition of penalties should not be taken to mean that they were not attached de facto to betrothal contracts. At the end of the ninth century, Emperor Leo the Philosopher recognized the lawfulness of inserting a penal stipulation in a marriage contract. On his legislation on *sponsalia*, see Ferrari, "Diritto matrimoniale."

69 The term *extorsio* aptly conveys the strong condemnation of the practice of exacting a penalty from the party in default. In 1517, the Florentine Synod reiterated the prohibition to attach any penalty to marriages and, in the same context, the bishops forbade people from acknowledging and promising *arrhae*. Moreover, in order that everybody would fully understand the content of the norms, the decrees related to marriage and *sponsalia* were published in vernacular. For the text, see Mansi, *Sacrorum conciliorum*, vol. 35, col. 252, cap. IX: "Et il medesimo dichiarò haver luogo nelle arre promesse o confessate in fraude di detta pena."

70 Dig. 45. 1. 134: "Ex stipulatione, quae proponeretur, cum non secundum bonos mores interposita sit, agenti exceptionem doli mali obstaturam, quia inhonestum visum est vinculo poenae matrimonia obstringi sive futura sive iam contracta."

71 See, for instance, Hostiensis (Henricus de Segusio) to *c. Gemma* (X 4. 1. 29), in *Commentaria* (Venice, 1581), 9r, no. 1. For this canonist, the major issue (*principale*) is the *sponsalia*, which were invalid because of the age of the two partners, and the *accessorium* is the penal stipulation, which violated the principle of freedom of marriage. If the main element is invalid, then a subsidiary one – the penal stipulation – is all the more so. Though medieval canonists gave various reasons for invalidating the penal stipulation, they concurred that the pope grounded his decision in the sacred principle of freedom of marriage and suggested that in this case age was not a contentious issue.

72 Later canonists, for instance, Johannes Andreae and Abbas Panormitanus, attempted to defend Bernardus's method, saying that he did not intend to give a solution (*resolvere*) to the case, but only to present the legal arguments (*allegare*) that jurists may use in such a case.

73 For the principle "ubi eadem ratio ibi idem ius" that Bernardus applied to a penal stipulation and *arrhae*, see Cortese, *La norma giuridica*, vol. 1, 297–338.

74 Gloss *Stipulatio* to *c. Gemma*, in *Decretales* (Venice, 1572), 849.

75 Odofredus to *l. Alii desponsata* (Cod. 5. 1. 1), in *Commentaria* (Lyon, 1550), 262v, no. 3: "Sed canoniste per suum textum dicunt et glossant ... quod idem est in arris quod in pena, quia sicut debent esse libera matrimonia a vinculis penarum, sic etiam et arrarum, quia non videmus differentiam inter penam et arram." Cinus de Pistoria to *l. Mulier* (Cod. 5. 1. 5), in *Commentaria* (Frankfurt am Main, 1578), 287v, no. 15: "Dicunt canoniste quod nulla reperitur ratio diversitatis, et ideo dicunt, idem iuris in arris quod est in pena, et ideo non servant istam legem. Sed ipsi non intelligunt nos." Baldus to *l. Titia* (Dig. 45. 1. 134), in *Commentaria* (Lyon, 1498), s.f. : "Bernardus ... videtur dicere quod nulla est diversitas. Ideo idem ius, secundum canones, licet secus secundum leges." Angelus de Ubaldis to *l. Mulier*, in *Commentaria* (Venice, 1579), 109r, no. 6: "Canoniste tamen in cap. Gemma ... dicunt quod non est differentia inter arram et penam."

76 Hostiensis (Henricus de Segusio) to *c. Gemma*, in *Commentaria* (Venice, 1581), 9r; and Archidiaconus (Guido de Baysio) to *c. Ubi* (C. 30 q.2 c.1), in *Commentaria* (Venice, 1601), 436r. That Hostiensis's comment – namely, that no decretal or canon prevents the aggrieved party from asking for the

return of the *arrhae* – was a reprimand of the *Glossa* is asserted by Johannes Andreae; see his commentary to *c. Gemma*, in *Commentaria* (Venice, 1581), 13v, no. 7: "et sic esset reprehensio." For a defense of Bernardus's position, see Antonius de Butrio to *c. Gemma*, in *Commentaria* (Venice, 1575–8), 13r, no. 6.

77 The dense construction of Innocentius's commentary to *c. Gemma* poses several questions to which we cannot give satisfactory answers. Was his silence on the gloss a disavowal of Bernardus's position? Or was he working with a *repertorium* from which he abstracted only the relevant sections on Roman law? Or did he think that *arrhae* pertained to civil law and were therefore of little concern to the canonists?

78 Cod. 5. 2. 1. The printed text has "C. de re. pig., l. i." – a scribal error for "C. si rector provinciae vel ad eum pertinentes sponsalia dederint" (Cod. 5. 2). Hostiensis had doubts about the correctness of the allegation (C. de remissione pignorum) and indicated "de dona. inter vir. et uxo." as a more pertinent citation; see Hostiensis (Henricus de Segusio) to *c. Gemma*, 9r, no. 1.

79 Cod. 5. 1. 2; Dig. 23. 1. 17.

80 Note that the text of the printed edition uses the expression *pena arrarum*.

81 Cod. 5. 1. 3. The edition has "ff, de sponsa<libus>, <l.> arre," which is inappropriate.

82 Cod. 5. 1. 5. 3–4.

83 Innocentius IV to *c. Gemma*, in *Commentaria* (Frankfurt am Main, 1570), 466r–v.

84 Bartolus to *l. Titia*, in *Commentaria* (Venice, 1526–9), 56r: "Ego autem ab opinione gl. nostrarum et Inno. non recedo, scilicet quod est differentia inter penam et arras."

85 Petrus de Bellapertica to *l. Titia*, in *Commentaria* (Frankfurt am Main, 1571), 353r, no. 4: "Doctores satagunt rationem reddere."

86 Odofredus to *l. Alii desponsata* (Cod. 5. 1. 1), in *Commentaria* (Lyon, 1552), 262v; and to *l. Titia*, in *Commentaria* (Lyon, 1552), 136v, no. 3. See also Cinus to *l. Mulier*, 207v, no. 15.

87 Jacobus de Arena to *l. Mulier*, in *Commentaria* (Lyon, 1541), 32r. Jacobus's commentary is followed by an addition attributed to Oldradus (de Ponte). The addition is significant, for it lists a series of further differences between *arrhae* and penalty.

88 Petrus de Bellapertica to *l. Titia*, 353r, no. 4. The ramifications of this exception can be seen in Cinus and, more explicitly, in Johannes Andreae, for whom the *arrhae* and their amount were set in accordance with the social status of a person.

89 The colorful expression "facto bursali" comes from Odofredus. On the difference, see also Albericus de Rosate to *l. Titia*, in *Commentaria* (Venice, 1585–6), 94r, nos. 4–6.
90 For other canonists who accepted that a difference existed between *arrhae* and a penalty, see Gulielmus Durandus, *Speculum iudicale* (Basel, 1574), II, 440, lib. III, part. IV, De sponsalibus et matrimoniis, § Primo, no. 4; Goffredus de Trani, *Summa super titulis Decretalium* (Lyon, 1519), 170v, De sponsalibus, no. 1; Antonius de Butrio to *c. Gemma*, 13r, no. 7.
91 For the principle that, with respect to delivery, whatever has been agreed upon is undoubtedly valid, see *l. In traditionibus* (Dig. 2. 14. 48).
92 Hostiensis (Henricus de Segusio) to *c. Gemma*, 9r, no. 2.
93 Probably Cinus de Pistorio. Antonius de Butrio and Abbas Panormitanus, when reporting Johannes Andreae's argument, cited Cinus, too.
94 Johannes Andreae to *c. Gemma*, 13v, no. 9. Johannes's suggestion presupposes the knowledge of the exemption Petrus de Bellapertica granted to kings – that is, upon contracting marriage they may promise a big penalty instead of *arrhae*.
95 Abbas Panormitanus (Niccolò de' Tedeschi) to *c. Gemma*, in *Commentaria* (Venice, 1617), 12r, no. 8: "Multum mihi placet opini<onem> Io. An., ut consideretur qualitas et quantitas personarum, maxime respectu recipientis."
96 Jason de Mayno to *l. Titia*, in *Commentaria* (Turin, 1573), 186v–89v: "nulla concludens ratio diversitatis sed tantum persuasiva potest assignari," citation at 197v, no. 22.
97 Petrus Aldobrandinus, *Summa totius artis notarie* (Venice, 1546), 81v (a marginal addition to Rolandinus, *Summa* [Venice, 1546], 81v).
98 On the difference between "persuading" and "convincing," see Perelman and Olbrechts-Tyteca, *The New Rhetoric*, 26–31.
99 Baldus to *l. Mulier*, in *Commentaria* (Lyon, 1498), s.f.: "Et primo circa arras [quero] utrum requiratur vera traditio? Et dicunt doctores quod sic, ut patet hic in litera in verbo 'accepit,' quod verbum est repetitum in multis partibus huius legis. Nam hoc veritatem significat."
100 Bartolus to *l. Titia*, 56r; and, for a *consilium* in which he reiterated the same position, see *Consilia* (Venice, 1585), 15r, cons. 45. The case involved the daughter of a prominent family, the Petrucci (probably of Siena). In presenting Bartolus's doctrine, Abbas Panormitanus noted "et maxime hoc procedit hodiernis temporibus, in quibus contrahentes confitentur recepisse alter ab altero magnam quantitatem arrharum, que in veritate nunquam fuerunt numerate, sed est nuda et simplex confessio"; see Abbas Panormitanus (Niccolò de' Tedeschi) to *c. Gemma*, 12r, no. 8.

101 For a discerning analysis of the issues involved in a unilateral acknowledgment of *arrhae*, see Jason de Mayno to *l. Titia*, 188v, no. 26–7.

102 Bartolus to *l. Titia*, 56r: "Quid si in veritate ego numeravi tibi pecuniam nomine arrarum, et tu mihi eandem vel aliam eiusdem quantitatis? Respondeo: fraus est, et data non videntur."

103 Perugia, Archivio di Stato, Ospedale di S. Maria della Misericordia, perg. no. 650. This document, which was apparently unknown and therefore not cited in the earlier version of our study, was recently discovered by Osvaldo Cavallar.

104 Baldus to *l. Mulier*, s.f.: "Nam in dubio standum est confessioni si est renunciatum exceptioni non numerate pecunie."

105 Angelus de Ubaldis to *l. Titia*, in *Commentaria* (Venice, 1579), 88r, no. 1, citing the gloss *Data* to *l. Assiduis* (Cod. 8. 18. 12).

106 His judgment was rendered on the case cited in no. 57 above: "quod non valet talis confessio quoniam aparet quod fui confessus habere a te, quia fuisti confessus habere a me, non autem intervenit vera numeratio;" BNCF, Magl. XXIX, 165, 41r. For other *consilia* taking the same line, see Federicus de Senis, *Consilia* (Rouen, 1513), s.f., cons. 184: "Tamen quia hodie in fraudem pene stipulantis arras in maxima quantitate et promittit quis restituere duplicatas, et tamen nihil recepit, crederem de iuris rigore et mente iuris talem stipulationem arrarum fraudulentam fore, et sic alias consului, et in hac opinione erat bone memorie dominus Ugelius, episcopus Perusinus decretorum doctor;" Antonius de Butrio, *Consilia* (Venice, 1575–8), 243r–44r, cons. 71; and Marianus Socinus, *Consilia* (Venice, 1579), vol. 1, 3r–4r, cons. 3.

107 Paulus de Castro to *l. Titia*, in *Commentaria* (Venice, 1582), 43v–44r.

108 Abbas Panormitanus (Niccolò de' Tedeschi) to *c. Gemma*, 12r, no. 8.

109 On grounds of *l. Qui sic solvit* (Dig. 46. 3. 55): "Qui sic solvit ut reciperet, non liberatur."

110 On how jurists used the term *causa*, see Cortese, *La norma giuridica*, vol. 1, 183–255. Following Roman law, medieval jurists tended to uphold the validity of both transactions (*mutuum* and *depositum*), though the former was taken in vew of the latter. See Baldus, *Consilia* (Venice, 1575), vol. 3, 88v–89r, cons. 317. For the typical case, see *l. Si tibi* (Dig. 12. 1. 20), and the *Glossa*.

111 Baldus to *l. Mulier*, s.f.

112 Baldus to *l. Perfectam* (Cod. 4. 45. 2), in *Commentaria* (Lyon, 1498), s.f. Perhaps aware that Baldus had delved too far into speculation, Jason de Mayno wrote "de quo scribentes non faciunt mentionem" – meaning that on purpose jurists ignored Baldus's view when dicussing *arrhae*. See his commentary to *l. Titia*, 188v, no. 24.

113 See, for instance, the lengthy examination of this issue Jason de Mayno made in his commentary to *l. Titia*, 189r, no. 29–30; and Paulus de Castro to *l. Titia*, 44r, no. 4, who also did not view favorably the idea of a double penalty as proposed by Baldus.

114 Bartolus to *l. Titia*, 56r, no. 5.

115 Angelus de Ubaldis to *l. Titia*, 88r: "Quia l. ultima <l. Mulier> concedit simpliciter potestatem tradendi arras quascumque et vult eas reddi duplicatas. Unde non est restringenda ad certam summam, quia hoc non reperitur l. cautum." See also Baldus to *l. Titia*, where Bartolus's position is dismissed without giving a reason.

116 The question whether instead of cash a pledge may be given, which was of paramount importance in a society with limited availability of cash, was addressed by Accursius in his gloss *Matrimonia* to *l. Titia*. He admitted that a pledge may be given instead of the *arrhae*, but not as a penalty.

117 As Albericus de Rosate pointed out, the use of the term *pignus* itself is not without problems. Since a *pignus* was given so that it would remain with the receiver, except where marriage was not contracted, calling it *pignus* contradicts the definition given in the title *De pignoribus et hypothecis* (Dig. 20. 1). See Albericus de Rosate to *l. Titia*, 94r, no. 4. Admittedly, this term was improperly used.

118 For model notarial instruments containing such a clause, see Moschetti, *Il cartularium veronese*, 6–8, rubr. *Carta nuptiarum futurarum cum dote arrarum*, and rubr. *De sponsalibus. Quot modis contrahantur*; Zaccaria di Martino, *Summa artis notarie*, 261, rubr. *Carta arrarum sponsalium*; and Rolandinus, *Summa*, 80v–83r, where the parties respectively pledge a house and a piece of land. The legal device Rolandinus employed for this transaction was the so-called *constitutum possessorium*, by which a party transfers possession of an immovable to another but continues to hold it under another title. While the party who receives the immovable as *arrhae* enjoys possessory protection, the giving party remains therein as a tenant. For a *quaestio* by the jurist Oldradus de Ponte on a piece of land given as *arrhae*, see Bellomo, "Tracce di *lectura*," 255–7, where the *quaestio* has been partially edited.

119 Bartolus to *l. Titia*, 56r, no. 10. And Dig. 31. 1. 88. 7, *Lucius Titius*, § *Impuberem*, which was employed by medieval jurists for establishing the rule that a bequest may be doubled only when it is a quantity, not a thing (*species*). And also the gloss *Casus* to *l. Plane*, § *Si eadem res* (Dig. 30. 1. 34. 1), for the difference between *species* and *quantitas*. A *species* is an individual thing, analytically distinguishable from a *genus*, which consists of kinds of things possessing common qualities. *Genus* indicates fungibles, where one

thing may be replaced by another of the same quality, since all the objects included in this category exercise the same economic function.

120 On the symbolic value of land in medieval culture, see Grossi, *L'ordine giuridico*, 74–5.

121 In Roman law, *certum* means a fixed sum or quantity of things constituting the object of a transaction, obligation, or claim.

122 For a pledge as an identifiable object (*res certa*), see the gloss *Quod magis est* to *l. Pignus* (Dig. 13. 7. 1).

123 Baldus to *l. Mulier*, s.f.

124 See, for instance, Angelus de Ubaldis to *l. Titia*, 109r, no. 6.

125 Paulus de Castro to *l. Titia*, 44r, no. 4.

126 Abbas Panormitanus (Niccolò de' Tedeschi) to *c. Gemma*, 13v, no. 10, where he lists the major jurists who supported the pledge and their reasons.

127 Odofredus to *l. Titia*, 136v, no. 3: "Sed pignora, ut fit in civitate ista, trado amico communi, ut si stet per me vel ex parte mea, pignus perdatur; vel si per te mulierem vel ex parte tua pignus tuus perdatur." Note that Odofredus speaks of returning the pledge; there is no discussion of returning double its value.

128 Abrahams, *Jewish Life*, 177; Goitein and Sanders, *A Mediterranean Society*, 65ff. For examples of broken promises of future marriage among Jewish families, see Toaff, *Love, Work, and Death*, 27–8.

129 Odofredus to *l. Alii desponsata*, 262v, no. 3: "sed dicunt quod debent dari pignora ad invicem, sicut fit tota die in civitate ista."

130 Rainerius de Forlivio to *l. Titia*, in *Lectura* (Lyon, 1523), 86v.

131 Baldus to *l. Perfectam* (Cod. 4. 45. 2), s.f.

132 Rolandinus, *Summa*, 83r.

133 Emperor Theodosius granted an action (*ex bono et aequo*) for withdrawing from the *sponsalia*. This action was granted to a *sponsa* who had reached puberty and was *sui iuris*, against the person who contracted the *sponsalia* for her. On this, see Cod. Theod. 3. 5. 11. 4.

134 Azo to tit. *De sponsalibus* (Cod. 5. 1), *Summa Azonis* (Venice, 1581), coll. 771–4.

135 Gloss *Matrimonia* to *l. Titia*: "forte valet interesse." See also the gloss *Si sororem* to *l. Si stipulor* (Dig. 45. 1. 35), for the assertion that a stipulation violating the accepted ethical standards of a community (*boni mores*) is not binding. Since the reiteration of this principle occurred in relation to marriage, Accursius's view seemed inconsistent to other jurists.

136 Odofredus to *l. Alii desponsata*, 262v, no. 2.

137 Petrus de Bellapertica to *l. Titia*, 354, no. 5.

138 On these two concepts, which were also widely employed in the debate on usury, see Spicciani, *Capitale e interesse*, 17–48; see also Wieling, *Interesse und Privatstrafe*, 26ff.

139 Cinus to *l. Alii desponsata*, in *Commentaria* (Frankfurt am Main, 1578), 286v, no. 5.

140 The distinction was accepted also by Albericus de Rosate, who included the fee for the mediators among the losses a party may suffer; see his commentary to *l. Alii desponsata*, in *Commentaria* (Venice, 1585–6), 245r, no. 4; and to *l. Mulier*, 245v, no. 6.

141 Johannes Andreae to *c. Gemma*, 13v, no. 7; Antonius de Butrio to *c. Gemma*, 23r, no. 7; idem, *Consilia* (Venice, 1575), 243–4, cons. 70; Franciscus de Zabarellis to *c. Gemma*, in *Commentaria* (Venice, 1502), 6v, no. 6; Abbas Panormitanus (Niccolò de' Tedeschi) to *c. Gemma*, 12v, no. 11.

142 Baldus to *l. Mulier*, s.f.

143 Briegleb, *Geschichte des Executiv-Prozesses*, 35–83; Campitelli, *Precetto di guarentigia*; and the same author's "Una raccolta di *quaestiones*." For many examples of disputes over contracts carrying the *preceptum guarentigie*, see Chiantini, *Il consilium sapientis*.

144 Odofredus to *l. Alii desponsata*, 262v, no. 2.

145 Adding an oath to the *sponsalia* was more problematic; see Odofredus to *l. Titia*, 136v, no. 4; and to *l. Alii desponsata*, 262v, no. 2. Bartolus also agreed that an oath could not be introduced to validate the will of the parties, when the betrothal contract could not be redacted within the parameters of law. See his commentary to *l. Titia*, 56r, no.11: "Quero an in predictis casibus, ubi de iure non valet, potest firmari iuramento? Respondeo: non." On the oath, see Prodi, *Il sacramento del potere*, 63–160.

146 Baldus to *l. Mulier*, s.f.: "Et ideo consuetudo generalis approbat istam confessionem et istam dationem arrarum, et maxime statuta Italie ubi intervenit guarentigia, id est preceptum."

147 On the jurist, see Chiappelli, "Un *consilium* inedito"; Scalvanti, "Notizie e documenti"; Cuturi, "Angelo degli Ubaldi"; Denifle, *Die Entstehung*, 564–5; Colliva, "Angelo degli Ubaldi"; Spagnesi, *Utiliter edoceri*, 52–4, 105–7, 109; Valentini, "L'ordine degli apparati"; and Cuturi, "Angelo degli Ubaldi," 219–20, for the date of Angelus's death.

148 Some examples: Kirshner, "A Question of Trust"; idem, "Materials for a Gilded Cage," chap. 3, in this volume; idem, "Citizen Cain of Florence"; idem, "Privileged Risk"; and Cavallar and Kirshner, "*Licentia navigandi.*"

149 For the sake of brevity and operating on the assumption that his fellow jurists, the judge, and the court would be familiar with earlier doctrines and

opinions, Angelus reduced the extensive debate over the permissibility of *arrhae* to the opinions of Bernardus of Parma and Innocent IV.

150 For the actionability of a natural obligation under the *ius commune*, see Gordley, *The Philosophical Origins*, 40–67.

151 On illegality and immorality in Roman law contracts, see Zimmermann, *The Law of Obligations*, 697–715.

152 For the argument based on absurdity as used by the jurists, see Sbriccoli, *L'interpretazione dello statuto*, 356–66.

153 Angelus's statement is true if one surmises that the double is the ordinary penalty for the breaching party. For the fourfold payment, a specific stipulation must be inserted in the contract of betrothal.

154 For the legislation against the magnates, see the classic study of Salvemini, *Magnati*; and now Klapisch-Zuber's valuable study *Retour*. For the legislation on contumacy prohibiting a person in contempt of the court from presenting defenses, see Caggese, ed., *Statuti della Repubblica fiorentina*, vol. 2, *Statuto del Podestà dell'anno 1325*, 80–1, lib. 2, rubr. 2, *Qualiter procedatur contra contumacem*, and 181, lib. 3, rubr. 2, *De officio trium iudicum maleficiorum*; ASF, Statuti di Firenze, Podestà [1355], no. 18, 9r, lib. 3, rubr. 5; *Statuta populi et communis Florentiae* (Freiburg [Florence], 1778–83), vol., 1, 234, lib. 3, rubr. 2, *De officio iudicum maleficiorum et de modo procedendi in criminalibus*.

155 Angelus's *consilium* did not go unnoticed, and his passing note on the invalidity of reciprocal acknowledgment of *arrhae* was cited, for instance, by Jason de Mayno to *l. Titia*, 189, no. 29.

156 On guardianship of women in Florence, see Kuehn, "*Cum consensu mundualdi.*"

157 The betrothal of prepubscent children in Florence and the Tuscan countryside was hardly common but not invisible either. See Klapisch-Zuber, "Childhood in Tuscany," 109–11; some Florentine examples: NA, 316 (19 April 1445), 6v: *sponsalia* between Gherarda "infant daughter" of Ugo d'Albizzo Ughi and Lorenzo, the orphaned son of di Piero di Lorenzo Borsi; Fabbri, *Alleanza matrimoniale*, 26; Jacks and Caffero, *The Spinelli*, 246 (involving betrothal of the minor children of Tommaso Spinelli and Jacopo Pitti). For another Florentine betrothal contract closely resembling that between Massina and Eusepio, see Marianus Socinus, *Consilia*, vol. 1, 3r, cons. 3. In the case on which the Sienese jurist was asked to give his opinion, both the *sponsus* and *sponsa* were younger than the required minimum of seven years, the dowry was set at 800 florins and the *arrhae* at 500, both parties reciprocally acknowledged the receipt of the *arrhae*, and the standard *preceptum guarentigie* was added to the contract. Socinus advised that,

despite the insertion of the *preceptum guarentigie*, the breaching party was not obligated to return double the amount of the *arrhae*, because the contract was utterly invalid owing to the ages of the *sponsus* and *sponsa*.

158 The expression *ab incarnatione* was inserted in the edition printed in Lyon in 1551.

159 A similar argument was made by Florentine jurists in another case of March 1412/13 cited in no. 22 above. This case involved a *sponsa* of ten years of age who exchanged *verba de presenti* with her *sponsus* and on whose behalf a dowry was promised. Was the marriage valid? If not, was the *sponsa*'s father released from his promise to pay the dowry? The jurist Stephanus de Bonaccursiis, with endorsements from Philippus de Corsinis and Laurentius de Ridolphis, concluded that neither the marriage *de presenti* nor the promise of the dowry was valid: "Et primo quod matrimonium per verba de presenti contractum inter impuberes vel quorum unus pubes et alius impubes, qui non sunt proximi pubertati, vel in quibus malitia non supplet etatem, non est matrimonium sed iuris interpetratione sunt tamen sponsalia de futuro, licet verba haberent consensum exprimentia de presenti." See BNCF, Fondo Principale, II, II, 370, 7r. Meek, "Un'unione incerta," 111, mistakenly translates the technical expression "in eam aetatem malitia non suppleret" as "difettava di quella 'malitia' che in qualche modo avrebbe potuto compensare la sua minore età." In view of canons *c. De illis* (X 4. 2. 9) and *c. Tuae nobis* (X 4. 2. 14), and the glosses *Nubilis* and *Prudentia*, the term *malitia* may be understood as *vigor naturalis* and *potentia coeundi* – in short, physical capacity to have sexual intercourse. For this meaning, see Johannes Andreae to *c. De illis* (X 4. 2. 9), 18v, no. 3. How the term *militia* – which in postclassical Latin also means unfruitfulness or barrenness, as in the expression *terrae malitia* or *malitia arboris* – came to be used in this way requires further investigation. For the maxim in Roman law, see *l. Si alterius circumveniendi* (Cod. 2, 42 (43). 3).

160 For reasons prompting families to enter into a betrothal contract, see Salatiele, *Ars notarie*, 178–9. In gloss *Servare* added to the model instrument of *sponsalia*, Salatiele wrote: "nota quod hec promissio fieri consuevit quando parentes viri et mulieris volunt inter se facere parentelam ob aliquam inimicitiam mitigandam."

161 Grossi, *L'ordine giuridico*, 223–35.

162 Timoteo, "Family Law," 268.

163 Cazzetta, "*Praesumitur seducta*"; and Subotnik's entertaining "Sue Me, Sue Me." The lyric is from Frank Loesser, *Guys and Dolls* (Frank Music Corp., 1949).

164 Frost, *Promises Broken*; and Craig, *Promising Language*. For nineteenth-century Germany and Switzerland, see Bors, *Bescholtene Frauen.* Bors deals with the question of women who became pregnant during the engagement and were then abandoned by their fiancés. He discusses the provision in the Prussian *Allgemeine Landrecht* of 1794 that pregnant women could not sue for breach of promise of future marriage, but could sue to acquire the legal status of divorced women in order to obtain the social rank and the name of the child's father and, more important, support for the child. In the cases he analyses, the men invariably counterclaimed that the mothers had slept with other men and therefore the children were not theirs. Our gratitude to Susanne Lepsius for signaling this book to us.

165 Coombs, "Agency and Partnership," 3.

166 Tushnett, "Rules of Engagement," 2584. For the nineteenth century, see Grossberg, *Governing the Hearth*, 33–63.

167 In Germany, however, there is an exception: engaged persons may not be forced to testify in court against each other.

168 Oberto, *La promessa.*

169 Aquino and Tallarita, "La promessa di matrimonio." A subsidiary issue, one that also arose in the Middle Ages (see above, n. 140), is whether marriage brokers are entitled to their fees if, after an engagement has been brokered, the marriage itself is not celebrated.

170 Tushnett, "Rules of Engagement," 2591. For the reasons behind the invention and adoption of the groom's wedding band and the double ring ceremony, which became popular in the 1940s and 1950s in the United States, see Howard, "A 'Real Man's Ring.'"

171 While we were revising this paragraph, a story appeared in the *New York Times* regarding a Pennsylvania Supreme Court ruling on whether a lie about the value of an engagement ring voided a prenuptial agreement. Mr. Porreco told his teen-age fiancée, who was thirty years younger than the groom, "that the ring was worth $21,000, about half of her net worth at the time of marriage." After they married and separated, "she discovered that the stone in her engagement ring was a fake." The majority of the court ruled *caveat sponsa*: that the groom's "misstatement did not amount to fraud because she (the bride) should not have trusted her fiancé." The witty dissenting opinion was written in verse by Justice J. Michael Eakin, whose penchant for judicial poetry has been criticized. For this Sacchetti-like tale, see Adam Liptak, "Justices Call on Bench's Bard to Limit His Lyricism," *New York Times*, 15 December 2002, National Section. As Susanne Lepsius reminds us (private communication), in contrast to the United states, expensive engagement rings are not customarily given in Germany,

Scandinavia, and Eastern Europe. Rather, the engagement ring is typically a gold band that is worn on the left hand before marriage and then transferred to the right hand after marriage. A valuable ring, often set with diamonds, is customarily given by the husband to his wife to celebrate the birth of their first child.

172 Cited by Iglar, "The Rules of Engagement."

2. *Li Emergenti Bisogni Matrimoniali* in Renaissance Florence

1 The pungent expression *li emergenti bisogni matrimoniali* was used by Piero di Marco Parenti in his *Libro di famiglia* (CS, ser. 2[a], vol. 17 bis, 127v).

2 I have edited the *consilium* in Kirshner, "*Maritus lucretur dotem*," 138: "quia etiam ante carnalem copulam opportet maritum subire expensas propter vestes et alia ornamenta uxoris et alia preparatoria nuptiarum."

3 Paulus de Castro, *Consilia* (Venice, 1581), vol. 1, 76va, cons. 154: "Et per experientiam videmus tam Florentiae quam Bononiae, ubi non pervenitur ad verba de presenti et annuli dationem, nisi ea die qua ducitur vel praecedenti, et tamen omnia praeparamenta sunt facta et expensae vestium et iocalium, ut tota dos sit consumpta." Paulus de Castro's opinion concerned the rights of a husband to the dowry of his predeceased wife. Dealing with the identical issue, the Florentine jurist Rosellus de Rosellis noted that "maritus facit magnas expensas in nuptiis pro indumentis et aliis honeribus matrimonii, que valde transcedunt fructus dotis, et tunc communiter matrimonium carnali copula consumatur." Rosellus's *consilium* is edited in Kirshner, "*Maritus lucretur dotem*," 145.

4 Upon the husband's predecease, ownership of precious nuptial items passed to his heirs, not to his wife. But the husband's heirs, according to the jurists, could not reclaim precious vestments and jewelry that a testator-husband had specifically bequeathed to his wife. See Izbicki, "*Ista questio*"; Bartolus de Saxoferrato to *l. In hiis*, § *Servis uxoris* (Dig. 24. 3. 66. 1), in *Commentaria* (Venice, 1570–1), 30v–31r; and his *Consilia* (Venice, 1585), 14va, cons. 50: "Veritas est quod vestes festive et pretiose non sunt uxoris, nec eidem a viro donate videntur, et sic non potest morte confirmari rerum datio, cum ei tradere videntur ad usum tantum, ut tamen magis sint apud virum quam quesita uxoris." This regulation conformed to the legal presumption, derived from *l. Quintus Mucius* (Dig. 24. 1. 51), that whatever a wife received, she received from her husband, unless she could prove otherwise. On this legal issue, see also Guerra Medici, *L'aria di città*, 39ff.; and Bestor, "The Groom's Prestations." Bestor's study enlarges our understanding of the jurisprudential context in which the nuptial items the bridegroom sent to his

bride came to be treated as gratuitous loans of things that the borrower (the wife) or her heirs were required by law to return to the lender (the husband) or his heirs.

5 Macinghi Strozzi, *Lettere*, 548–9; trans. in Cochrane and Kirshner, eds., *The Renaissance*, 116.

6 San Bernardino, *Prediche volgari sul Campo*, vol. 2, 1075, sermon 37. See also Izbicki, "Pyres of Vanities," 211–34; Nico Ottaviani, "*De vanitate mulierum.*" For an overview of San Bernardino's views on marriage, see Rusconi, "St. Bernardino of Siena."

7 San Bernardino, *Prediche volgari sul Campo*, vol. 2, 1017–19, sermon 35.

8 San Bernardino, *Le prediche volgari*, 2:92, sermon 28; trans. in Cochrane and Kirshner, eds., *The Renaissance*, 119–28.

9 I cite the edition in *Prose di Giovanni della Casa*, 126–7.

10 Niccolò Machiavelli, *Belfagor*, in his *Opere*, 1035–44, quotation on 1038; trans. in *The Portable Machiavelli*, 423.

11 Plautus, *Aulularia*, vol. 1 of *Plautus*, 499.

12 The deep-seated belief that the vanity of women discouraged men from marriage, resulting in the inability of Italians to increase their numbers in the years after 1348, was recycled in the twentieth century by Gentile, "Le leggi suntuarie," vol. 4, 210; and Pierro, "Le leggi suntuarie."

13 Herlihy, "Family and Property"; Goldthwaite, *Wealth and Demand*, 13–71 – but see Martines's critical review of Goldthwaite's book: "The Renaissance and the Birth of a Consumer Society."

14 See Levi Pisetzky, *Il costume e la moda*, 17–30; Stuard, "Gravitas and Consumption," who relates the extravagant dress of Florentine and Venetian merchants to their untold wealth and desire to comport themselves as European nobility. For Florence, see now Frick's highly informative *Dressing Renaissance Florence*. See also the essays in O'Malley and Welch, eds., *The Material Renaissance*. For an exceptionally informed and panoramic study of medieval clothing, see Muzzarelli, *Guardaroba medievale*.

15 Veblen, *The Theory of the Leisure Class*, esp. 126–7; Simmel, "Fashion (1904)," in *On Individuality and Social Forms*, 294–323; Bourdieu, *Distinction: A Social Critique*. In the economy of symbolic violence, according to Bourdieu, women contribute to their own domination by reflexively performing the roles assigned to them by a male-dominated society. See his *La domination masculine*.

16 "Vestimenta vero pretiosa et alia ornamenta, que uxori traduntur, ut magis con<ten>ta et magis honorifice incedat, illa sunt viri." This view was shared by virtually all the jurists who treated the issue of nuptial vestments and ornaments. Angelus's *consilium* is found in BAV, Vat. lat. 8069, 189r–v.

Since the *consilium* was imperfectly edited by Izbicki (n. 4 above), Osvaldo Cavallar and I have prepared a new edition. A translation of Angelus's *consilium* will appear in our forthcoming volume *Medieval Italian Jurisprudence: A Selection of Texts in Translation.*

17 Barbaro, *De re uxoria*, 65; trans. in Kohl, Witt, and Welles, eds., *The Earthly Republic*, 206. See also Allerston, "Wedding Finery"; Chojnacki, "From Trousseau to Groomgift."

18 On Florentine sumptuary laws from the fourteenth into the sixteenth century, see Rainey, *Sumptuary Legislation* – an exhausting as well as exhaustive study. For analytical discussions, see Hughes, "Sumptuary Law"; Brundage, "Sumptuary Laws and Prostitution"; Muzzarelli, "La disciplina delle apparenze"; idem, *Gli inganni*; Berti, "I capitoli *De vestibus mulierum*"; Ceppari Ridolfi and Turrini, *Il mulino della vanità*; Nico Ottaviani, "De glie ariede"; idem, "*Res sit magni*"; Bowd, *Venice's Most Loyal City*, 117–26.

19 Kovesi Killerby, "Practical Problems"; Rainey, "Dressing Down"; Cavallar and Kirshner, "*Licentia navigandi.*" Lax and sporadic enforcement punctuated by bouts of moral rigorism was also the experience beyond the Alps; see Bulst, "Kleidung als sozialer Konfliktstoff."

20 Klapisch-Zuber, "Le complexe de Griselda." For the English and Italian translations, see Klapisch-Zuber, "The Griselda Complex" and "Il complesso di Griselda." Klapisch-Zuber discusses her methodological approach in "Écriture de famille, écriture de l'histoire," the introduction to her *La maison et le nom*, 5–15. Her study of nuptial prestations is also critically discussed by Bestor (n. 4 above). See also Bestor, "Marriage Transactions." For an interpretation of gifts of "bridal jewellery," inspired by Klapsich-Zuber and Mauss, and by Judith Butler's formative concept of gender as performance, see Randolph, "Performing the Bridal Body."

21 The *Morgengabe* was a substantial gift (equivalent to one-third of the dowry in Salic law, one-fourth in Lombard law) given to the bride on the morning after the consummation of marriage. See Feller, "Morgengabe." In late Roman law, the *donatio propter nuptias* comprised the gifts given by the husband's family to the wife before or during the marriage. In general, the *donatio propter nuptias* had to be equal to the dowry (Cod. 5. 14. 9–10). See Anné, *Les rites des fiançailles*, 318ff. On the general decline of the *donatio propter nuptias* in medieval Italy, see Bellomo, *Ricerche sui rapporti*, 27–60, 223–44. Likewise, on the decline of the *Morgengabe*, see Kreutz, "The Twilight of *Morgengabe*." For the function and relevance of the *donatio propter nuptias* in late medieval and early modern Genoa and its *dominio*, see Braccia, "*Uxor gaudet.*"

22 Klapisch-Zuber, "The Griselda Complex," 224.

23 On the symbolism of rings, see the critical discussion of Anné, *Les rites des fiançiailles*, 11–62.

24 For Florence, see Castelli, "Le virtù delle gemme"; Kieckhefer, "Erotic Magic." On the medical value of pearls, see Donkin, *Beyond Price*. On the medicinal qualities of coral, see Alexandre-Bidon, "La dent et le corail." For an example of the apotropaic use of coral in Florence, see Musacchio, *The Art and Ritual of Childbirth*, 132.

25 Altieri, *Li nuptiali*, 53. *Balasci*, or balas-rubies of rose red or orange, are found near Samarkand in modern Uzbekistan and were treated as precious gemstones in late medieval and Renaissance Italy. Battaglia, ed., *Grande dizionario*, vol. 1, 950, s.v. *balascio*. There are myriad references to *balasci* in Florentine *libri di famiglia* or *ricordanze*. For example, Martelli, *Ricordanze*, 104; Castellani, *Ricordanze A*, vol. 1, 132, 165; Randolph, "Performing the Bridal Body," 187.

26 *Libro di famiglia* of Niccolò del Buono di Bese Busini (CS, ser. 4a , vol. 564, 2r): "1 ghirlanda di perle a fruscholi"; *Libro di famiglia* of Giovanni Buongirolami (CS, ser. 2a, vol. 23, 129r–130r); Macinghi Strozzi, *Lettere*, 17–20 (pearls given by Marco Parenti to his future wife, Caterina Strozzi); Perosa, ed., *Giovanni Rucellai*, 29; Biagi, *Due corredi nuziali*, 13. See also the last will (26 Mar. 1490) of Giovanni di Francesco Tornabuoni, who provided that in addition to her 3,000-florin dowry, his daughter Ludovica would receive various pieces of jewlery of pearls, rubies, and diamonds valued at around 500 florins. His will is edited by Cadogan, *Domenico Ghirlandaio*, 370–1.

27 Landucci, *Diario fiorentino*, 6–8. In her *L'arte della seta*, Florence Edler de Roover provides information on the rings, belts, gems, silk fabrics, and accessories weavers purchased for their wives. Carlo Carnesecchi has published a marvelous document (1452) regarding a professional garland maker who made expensive garlands decorated with pearls for Florentine brides but acquired the pearls by stealing them from wives who already possessed such garlands. Some of these pearls he gave to his lover, some as payment to a prostitute. See Carnesecchi, "Niccolò *delle Grillande*."

28 Mazzi and Raveggi, *Gli uomini e le cose*, 107–9; Piccinni, "Le donne nella mezzadria," 172–3.

29 In general, see Fingerlin, *Gürtel*; Levi Pisetsky, *Il costume e la moda*, 148–51; Viale, "Cinture nuziali." In Andreas Capellanus's *De amore* (II, 21), a *cingulum* is included among the legitimate gifts a lover may accept from her partner (thanks to Paolo Cherchi for this reference). For references to marriage girdles and belts in Florence, see Musacchio, *Art, Marriage*,

168–74; Hoshino, "Francesco di Iacopo"; Petrucci, ed., *Il libro di ricordanze dei Corsini*, 66; Macinghi-Strozzi, *Lettere*, 20; Rinuccini, *Ricordi storici*, 251, where Cino Rinuccini in 1461 commissioned Antonio del Pollaiuolo to make a *cintola d'ariento* for his sister-in-law. For another commission, see Beck, "Desiderio da Settignano," 213, doc. 3. Landucci, *Diario fiorentino*, 6, presented his bride with "una fetta per la cintola e arienti e doratura." The damask weaver Giovanni di Luca gave his wife a girdle (*cinto*) made of crimson damask with a fringe of gold metallic, cited in Edler de Roover's *L'arte della seta*, 81. For the sumptuary legislation regulating the wearing of belts by men as well as women, see Rainey, *Sumptuary Legislation*.

30 Hind, *Nielli*, 34, nos 87–8.

31 Boccaccio, *Genealogie deorum gentilium libri*, vol. 1, 142, chap. 22: "Dicunt insuper huic cingulum esse quod ceston nominant, quo cinctam eam asserunt legitimis intervenire nuptiis." On Boccaccio's treatment of dress, see Weaver, "Dietro il vestito"; on dress as a class marker in the visual representation of Boccaccio's women, see Buettner, *Boccaccio's "Des cleres,"* 60ff.

32 Altieri, *Li nuptiali*, 52: "Ma appresso anche de molti la Arraglia medesmamente se exequisce col cegnere la sposa, in memoria de cesto cioè vinculo se dunassi per Vulgano alla sua Venere; del qual senne hebbe sì meravigliosa opinione, che quando vese defecti presentarlo, se tenga essere incesto, et non legitimo et vero matrimonio." By virtue of giving his bride a nuptial belt before the exchange of marriage vows, the bridegroom had legally pledged to fulfill the promise he made to marry her. See Bizzarri, "Per la storia dei riti nuziali in Italia," in her *Studi di storia*, 619, 628. Relevant here is a matrimonial case brought before the Curia Patriarcale of Udine. The relatives of a certain Lucrezia found her together with her lover, Leonardo. They threatened to injure Leonardo on the spot if he did not marry Lucrezia. He refused, claiming that he could not marry her because he had neither a ring with him nor a marriage girdle to give Lucrezia. This excuse became the basis for his contention that he had no intention to marry: "Ego non attuli mecum neque anulum neque cingulum quia non erat facturus nuptias et accepturus uxorem"; cited by Rasi in "La conclusione del matrimonio," 255. See also Cavallar and Kirshner, "Making and Breaking Betrothal Contracts," chap. 1 in this volume, 24 and n. 22.

33 Brundage, *Law, Sex, and Christian Society*, 504ff; see also Kirshner, "The Morning After," chap. 4 in this volume, 97.

34 Festus was the epitomizer of the *De significatu verborum* of Verrius Flaccus. His epitome was in turn epitomized in the eighth century by Paul the Deacon: Festus, *De verborum significatu*, 63: "*Cingillo* nova nupta praecingebatur, quod vir in lecto solvebat ... *Cinxiae Iunonis* nomen

sanctum habebatur in nuptiis, quod initio coniugii solutio erat cinguli, quo nova nupta erat cincta." On Festus and other Roman authors (Catullus and Ovid) who mention the untying of the nuptial belt, see Hersch, *The Roman Wedding*, 109–12. On the custom of the Spartan husband removing his bride's ceremonial belt before consummating marriage, see Lapus de Castiglionchio the Younger's (d. 1438) Latin translation of Plutarch's *Lycurgus*: Lapus, *Vitae illustrium virorum*, 15: "ac sponsae cingulum solvens, eam sublatam in lectum transferebat." For the ancient Greek customs of young maidens dedicating their belts to Athena Apatouria and the loosing of the bride's belt preparatory to sexual intercourse, see Schmitt, "Athéna Apatouria."

35 Andreas Capellanus, *De amore*, I, 1; for the fourteenth-century Tuscan translations, see Andreas Capellanus, *Trattato d'amore*. See also Cline, "Heart and Eyes"; Donaldson-Evans, *Love's Fatal Glance*, 9–49; Couliano, *Eros and Magic.*

36 Freud, *On Sexuality*, 7:69.

37 Bolmont, et al., "Love is in the Gaze," 2.

38 San Bernardino, *Prediche volgari sul Campo*, vol. 2, 1092, sermon 37: "sì ben ch'io voglio che tu stia ornata e dilicata, ma con discrezione ogni cosa, e con modo onesto." The Franciscan moralist Angelus Carlettus de Clavasio agreed with Bernardino but also extended exculpation to husbands who deck themselves out to please their wives: *Summa angelica* (Lyon, 1520), 258, s.v. *ornatus*, no. 1: "Nam vir ornans se vel mulier ut non appareat in contemptum honestis personis vel ut placeat vir uxori sue et uxor viro et huiusmodi ex tali intentione licitus est quilibet ornatus."

39 Bernardino's chilling condemnation of passionate marital love derived from mainstream canon law and moral theology and ultimately Seneca's *De matrimonio*, frag. XIII. 84. On the sins of the "too ardent lover of his own wife," see Sastre Santos, "Sobre el aforismo"; Weigand, "Liebe und Ehe bei den Dekretisten"; Payer, *The Bridling of Desire*, 118–31; Gordley, "*Ardor quaerens intellectum.*" For Bernardino's views on the spiritual reasons permitting wives to refuse sex with their husbands, see Elliot, "Bernardino of Siena."

40 San Bernardino, *Prediche volgari sul Campo*, vol. 2, 1241, sermon 42.

41 San Bernardino, *Le prediche volgari*, vol. 2, 86, sermon, 28; trans, in Cochrane and Kirshner, *The Renaissance*, 119–28.

42 Alberti, *Dinner Pieces*, 141. Alberti anticipated John Berger's famous formulation that "men look at women. Women watch themselves being looked at" (Berger, *Ways of Seeing*, 46). Alberti's stance on women is discussed by Freccero, "Economy, Woman, and Renaissance Discourse."

43 Wyke, "Woman in the Mirror," 147.

44 Bartholomaeus Fumus, *Summa Armilla*, 364v, s.v. *ornatus*, no. 1: "Si non habet malam intentionem, neque propter hoc ornat se vel hoc facit, ut proprio marito placeat, vel propter alium respectum, qui non est peccatum mortale, non mortaliter agit, etiam quod multi peccent eam personam appetendo, et ipsa sciat se appeti, hoc enim scandulum tantum passivum in ea secundum Caietanum [Thomas de Vio] ibi in Summa."

45 Denholm-Young and Kantorowicz, "*De ornatu mulierum*": 25 no. 3; 37–8 nos 25–6 (I cite an offprint with different pagination from that of the article that appeared in the journal); repr. in Kantorowicz's *Rechtshistorische Schriften*, 341–76. The *consilium* was written in 1447 at Padua in response to an episcopal decree, the author and place of which have not been determined. Antonius de Rosellis's views were shared by Johannes Petruccius de Montesperello – namely, "quod uxor teneatur obedire marito, non obstante statuto episcopali in talibus ornamentis." It is possible that Petruccius may have addressed his opinion to the same episcopal ordinance; see his *Consilia* (Venice, 1590), vol. 1, 219r–21r, cons. 104. Earlier, Baldus de Ubaldis had defended the behavior of married women, who, at the insistence of their husbands, wore dresses with low-cut necklines revealing their breasts in violation of an episcopal ordinance. Although Baldus affirmed that women could be excommunicated for wearing seductive dresses to church or on holy days, he rejected the bishop's claim to interfere with sartorial behavior sanctioned by lay customs. For the text, see Lally, *Baldus de Ubaldis*, vol. 2, 304–5.

46 Antoninus (sant'Antonino of Florence), *Summa theologica* (Venice, 1581–2), 190r, pt. 2, tit. 4, cap. 5 (*De praesumptione, in quo agitur de ornatu mulierum inordinato, utrum sit mortalis*), § 6. On this and related texts, see also Izbicki, "Pyres of Vanities." For Archbishop Antoninus's strictures on the painting of naked women, see Gilbert, "The Archbishop." The argument that women deserved qualified exemption from sumptuary regulations to attract husbands and please them was a standard defense: see Kovesi Killerby, "*Heralds of a Well-Instructed Mind*," 257–8.

47 Denholm-Young and Kantorowicz, "*De ornatu mulierum*," 25, no. 4: "Set voluntates mulierum in istis non habent regulare nisi mariti, quibus deus voluit feminas subesse."

48 Although modern writers use the term *cassoni* to refer to Florentine wedding chests, they were customarily called *forzieri* in the fourteenth and fifteenth centuries. By custom the bridegroom gave the bride two *forzieri*. See Callmann, *Apollonio di Giovanni*, esp. 40ff.; Watson, *The Garden of Love*; Baskins, "*La Festa di Susanna*"; idem, *Cassone Painting*; Klapisch-Zuber,

"Les noces feintes"; Witthoft, "Riti nuziali"; Chabot, *La dettes des familles*, 201–17; Jacqueline M. Musacchio suggests that the image of the rape of the Sabine women was meant to encourage a new bride to produce children for the sake of her husband's lineage. See "The Rape of the Sabine Women"; and her *The Art and Ritual of Childbirth*, 132–4.

49 Bornstein, "Le donne di Giovanni Dominici."

50 Dominici, *Il libro d'amore*, 432 (thanks to Lydia G. Cochrane and Osvaldo Cavallar for sharpening my translation of Dominici's text). Agnes's martyrdom was set in motion when she rejected the offer of marriage and gifts of jewels from the son of a Roman prefect who had fallen madly in love with the winsome twelve-year-old girl *at first sight*. For remaining faithful to her true lover and spouse, Christ, Agnes was richly rewarded. Jacobus de Voragine, *The Golden Legend*, vol. 1, 102: "'He [Christ] has placed a wedding ring on my right hand,' she [Agnes] said, 'and a necklace of precious stones around my neck, gowned me with a robe woven with gold and jewels, placed a mark on my forehead to keep me from taking any lover but himself, and his blood has tinted my cheeks. Already his chaste embraces hold me close, he has united his body to mine, and has shown me incomparable treasures, and promised to give them to me if I remain true to him.'" For the ideological context in which Agnes was transformed from *virago* into *virgo*, see Burrus, "Reading Agnes."

51 Dominici, *Il libro d'amore*, 433: "Or come sposa ricevente il ricco forzerino da quel marito, lo quale mai non vidde, si sente molto amata, quando è così altamente presentata, si fa concetto nobil sia chi nobilmente manda, non vedendo ama e desidera l'aspetto. Molto più tu del sommo Dio t'infiamma, lasciando lo 'ntelletto per questo specchio scuro fuori della divina essenzia, l' amor dentro entrando, dove nel letto del divin riposo, da' doni nominati ignuda, faccia tua residenzia."

52 Klapisch-Zuber, "The Griselda Complex."

53 Carte Del Bene, 48, filza 50. See also Hoshino, "Francesco di Iacopo," 35–6, who gives a partial transcription of the text listing del Bene's wedding expenditures.

54 *Libro di famiglia* of Bartolomeo di Filippo Valori, BNCF, Fondo Panciatichiano , vol. 134, 5r, now edited in Polizzotto and Kovesi, eds., *Memorie*, 67–8.

55 *Libro di famiglia* of Tribaldo d'Amerigo de' Rossi (1481–1501), BNCF, Fondo Principale, II. II. 357, 2r–6v. In 1510 Primerano di Piero Primerani spent 478 lire, 19 soldi, and 4 denari to outfit his wife, Fiametta di Soldo Cegia. His expenditure represented a mere 17 percent of the 700-florin

dowry he was promised. See *Libro di famiglia* of Primerano di Piero Primerani, CRS (S. Ambrogio), vol. 348, 7r.

56 Perosa, ed., *Giovanni Rucellai*, 28–34.

57 On the *Monte delle doti*, see Molho, *Marriage Alliance.*

58 For Tribaldo, see n. 99 below; for Parenti, see Macinghi Strozzi, *Lettere*, 3–9.

59 *Libro di famiglia* of Bartolomeo di Filippo Valori, 5r; Polizzotto and Kovesi, eds. *Memorie*, 67.

60 Conti, *L'imposta diretta,* 171–2.

61 Morelli, *Ricordi*, 211: "Della dote non volere per ingordigia del danaio afforgarti, però che di dota mai si fece bene niuno; e se l'hai a rendere, ti disfanno. Sia contento a questo: avere quello ti si richiede secondo te e secondo la donna togli." On this theme, see Fabbri, *Alleanza matrimoniale*, 65–6.

62 Alberti, *I libri della Famiglia*, 135; trans. in Cochrane and Kirshner, *The Renaissance*, 87.

63 Petrus Philippus Corneus, *Consilia* (Venice, 1572), vol. 1, 60ra, cons. 62: "nam in multis locis est de more quod quasi semper maritus fatetur se recepisse dotem et eodem die, loco, et testibus (non obstante confessione) promittitur eadem quantitas pro dicta dote"; Angelus de Ubaldis, *Consilia* (Lyon, 1551), 74r, cons. 145: "Gener a socero confessus fuit se habuisse dotem et non obstante dicta confessione dictus socer promisit dicto genero mille nomine dotis."

64 When Vieri di Francesco del Bene married Salvaggia di Giovanni Aldobrandini in 1405, he received 400 florins of the 700-florin dowry promised him. He was paid another 100 florins in 1406, while the remainder was paid in installments over the next five years; NA, 13528 (16 May 1428). Numerous references to overdue dowries can be found in the *catasto*. See, for instance, Catasto of 1427, 61, 606v (Cardinale di Neri); 608r (Ciaro di Pagolo, notaio); 859r (Guglielmo di Piero Adimari); ibid., 34, 14v (Niccolò del Buono Busini); 304r (Baldassare di Cione della Testa da Panzano); Catasto of 1433, 33, 34r (Giovanni di Antonio di Gini); 290v (Ser Nuto di Feo Nuti); 300v (Nigri di Lippo da Montelungo); Catasto of 1480, 992, 162r (Bernardo di Marco); 337v (Francesco di Domenico).

65 For a rare exception, see the lawsuit brought by Ser Giuliano di Giovanni Lanfredini against his father-in-law, Filippo de' Ricci, for the remainder of his overdue dowry; Podestà, 4823, s.f. (29 Nov. 1447).

66 Alberti, *I libri della famiglia*, 135–6; partial translation in Cochrane and Kirshner, *The Renaissance*, 87. It is conceivable that in addition to voicing conventional wisdom, Alberti was expressing the fears of Xenophon (*Oeconomicus* 13) and Aristotle (*Nicomachean Ethics* 1161 A3), who believed that a wealthy wife would threaten the husband's superiority.

67 For the civilian position: Bartholomaeus de Saliceto to *l. Pro oneribus* (Cod. 5. 12. 20), in *Commentaria* (Lyon, 1515), 18v; Angelus de Ubaldis to *l. In insulam*, § *Usuras* (Dig. 24. 3. 42. 2), in *Lectura* (Lyon, 1548), 12v; Ludovicus Pontanus (Romanus) to *l. De divisione* (Dig. 24. 3. 5), in *Commentaria* (Venice, 1580), 14r, no. 16; Franciscus Accoltus de Aretio to *l. Rei iudicatae exceptio* (Dig. 44. 2. 4), in *Commentaria* (Venice, 1589), 31v, no. 7; and Alexander Tartagnus to Dig. 24. 3. 42. 2, in *Commentaria* (Venice, 1570), 58v, nos. 1–2. However, the canonists insisted, and the majority of civilian jurists concurred, that since husband and wife were partners in spiritual life and two in one flesh, a husband was thereby obliged to provide her basic support and necessities (*alimenta*: food, clothing, and shelter), even if she was dowerless. Even without his wife's dowry, a husband is said to benefit (*utitur*) from her body and service. See Pene Vidari, *Ricerche sul diritto*, 449ff; idem, "Il trattato," 100–2.

68 Paulus de Castro to Dig. 24. 3. 42. 2, in *Commentaria super Infortiato* (Lyon, 1553), 32v, no. 2: "quia quando maritus promittitur dos, si sibi non solvitur integraliter, non tenetur onera matrimonii subire, imo potest uxorem repellere et ad domum patris remittere."

69 Antonius de Stroziis, *Repertorium*, in CS, ser. 3a, 41, vol. 18, 177r: "Vir propter dotem promissam a fratre et non solutam potest uxorem remittere ad domum fratris et denegare alimenta ei necessaria."

70 Catasto of 1427, 61, 727r: "Filippo di Tommaso Guidetti mio suocero mi resta a dare per resto di dota fiorini cinquecento o circa, cioè f. 500. Non ne posso ritrarre danaro, benchè pure gli credo ritrarre, ma chon lunghezza e faticha."

71 Ibid.: "Il giudeo da Prato dee avere di chapitale lire 24 piccoli e l'usura mesi otto o circa; àe in pegno due cintole della donna mia." Interestingly, Niccoletto Tartagni of Imola (apparently the grandfather of the celebrated jurist Alexander Tartagnus) also deposited with a Jewish pawnbroker precious vestments that he had given his wife on the occasion of their marriage. These vestments were subsequently sold. After Nicoletto's death a dispute arose over his widow's claim to be compensated by her husband's heirs for the loss of the nuptial gifts she once possessed; see Angelus de Ubaldis, *Consilia* (Lyon, 1551), 189r–v, cons. 339, who denied the widow's claim on the grounds that ownership of the vestments was transmitted by the husband to his heirs. Klapisch-Zuber, "The Griselda Complex," 244, cites Tivoli's sumptuary law (1308), which gave as a primary justification for limiting nuptial expenses the new husband's financial straits, which compelled him to borrow at usury from the city's Jews and as security place in pawn the very vestments he had sent his bride.

72 Catasto of 1427, 61, 727v: "Et per dette chagioni, e anche per detti miei debiti per non avere avuta la dota, non sono uscito di chasa se non i dì feriati già sono mesi dieci e più, e no' ò potuto exercitare l'arte mia, benchè pocho si faccia. Et pertanto vi priegho consideriate lo stato mio per modo io vi sia rachamandato." Cited also by Brucker, "Florentine Voices," 23. A remarkably similar lament was made in 1452 by the Sienese canonist Marianus Socinus to Siena's tax officials. Saddled with debts, including a loan from a Jewish moneylender, Marianus urged the officials in charge of determining his tax assessment to take into consideration that he was earning next to nothing from his practice of law, either in Siena or elsewhere, and that in two or three years he faced the burden of marrying off a daughter: "Ne la città non ghuadagnio quasi niente perché non accetto avochationi e di fuore per la ghuerra el ghuadagno è mancato ed ò una fanciulla che da qui a düe o tre anni se a Dio piacerà bisognia maritalla." His tax declaration is published by Nardi, *Mariano Sozzini*, 136–9.

73 According to Marchi's tax declaration of 1433, Filippo Guidetti still owed his son-in-law 500 florins for the dowry; Catasto of 1433, 482, 515r–v.

74 Not surprisingly, whether or not fathers received a promised dowry, they were bound to support their children and, as a practical matter, their wives, too. Niccolò Adimari was living with his wife, Maria, the daughter of the jurist Francesco di Iacopo da Empoli, even though he had received only 275 florins of his 800-florin dowry (Catasto of 1427, 81, 96r).

75 Quoted from Niccolini da Camugliano, *The Chronicles*, 114. In another example, Remigio di Lanfredino Lanfredini expressed fears that his sister Lippa might be returned to her family, even after she had been inducted into her husband's household, because her dowry had not been fully paid. See Kuehn, "Honor and Conflict," 307.

76 Fifteenth-century *catasti* are the main source of evidence for husbands who refused to cohabit with their wives because they had not yet received their dowries; see Herlihy and Klapisch-Zuber, *Les Toscans*, 592; Mazzi and Raveggi, *Gli uomini e le cose*, 109; Gregory, "Daughters, Dowries and Family," 221; Balestracci, "Il testamento di Giacomo Galganetti," 165–6 (on brides *nuptae et non traductae* hailing from Lucca's countryside).

77 Catasto of 1480 (Campione del Monte), 40, 217r; MC, 3735, 10r; MC, 3742, 137r.

78 Henderson, *Piety and Charity*, 316–21. However, Henderson mistakenly states (317) that as a rule a husband would consummate his marriage only after he received the dowry due him. On dotal assistance, see also Chabot and Fornasari, *L'economia della carità*; Chabot, "La beneficenza dotale"; Fubini Leuzzi, "*Condurre a onore*"; Balestracci, "Il testamento di Giacomo Galganetti."

79 Catasto of 1480 (Campione del Monte), 39, 308r–v (Francesca di ser Piero di Michele). The first installment of Frescobalda's dowry was paid in 1484 (MC, 3742, 256r).

80 MC, 3734, 201r, 208r. The first payment was made on 5 December 1463; the second on 15 March 1464.

81 X 5. 19. 16, *Salubriter* – a fragment of a letter of Pope Innocent III incorporated by Raymond of Peñafort into the *Decretals* of Pope Gregory IX.

82 See McLaughlin, "The Teaching of the Canonists," 131–4; Noonan, *The Scholastic Analysis*, 103–4; Blomeyer, "Aus der Consilienpraxis," 327–30; Quaglioni, "*Standum Canonistis?*"

83 Antoninus, *Summa theologica* (Venice, 1581–2), 31r–v, pt. 2, tit. 1, cap. 7 (*De usura ...*) § 27; San Bernardino, *Quadregesimale de evanglio aeterno*, sermon 42, art. 1, cap. 2, in *Opera omnia*, 4:352–4. Their views were shared by the Franciscan moralist Angelus Carlettus de Clavasio, *Summa angelica* (Venice, 1581), s.v. *usura*, no. 25, 350r–v; and by Battista Trovamala de Salis, *Summa casuum conscientiae* (Venice, 1499), s.v. *usura*, no. 21, 259.

84 For the civilians, see Bartolus to *l. Cum quidam*, § *Praeterea sancimus* (Cod. 5. 12. 31. 5), in *Commentaria* (Venice, 1570–1), 175r; to *l. In insulam*, § *Usuras* (Dig. 24. 3. 42. 2), 27b; Baldus to Dig. 24. 3. 42. 2, in *Commentaria* (Lyon, 1498), s.f.; Raphael de Raymundis (Cumanus) to Dig. 24. 3. 42. 2, in *Commentaria* (Lyon, 1554),18va; Ludovicus Pontanus (Romanus) to Dig. 24. 3. 42. 2, 77rb; Paulus de Castro to Dig. 24. 3. 42. 2, 32va; Johannes de Imola to Dig. 24. 3. 42. 2, in *Commentaria* (Lyon, 1547–9), 20vb; Alexander Tartagnus to Dig. 24. 3. 42. 2, in *Commentaria* (Venice, 1570), 58vb; Petrus Philippus Corneus, *Consilia* (Venice, 1572), vol. 2, 171ra–173ra, cons. 145.

85 Catasto of 1480 (Campione del Monte), 34, 117v: "Io Carlo Salteregli non fo nulla; sono vecchio d'età d'anni 65 e ò debito con mio genero Tomaso di Bernardo di mona Biagia, fiorini 150 di resto di dota ... e con altri più di fiorini 50 e a mio genero pagho 9 per cento l'anno in 3 paghe; sono fiorini 13½ di sugiello." Based on data from the *catasto* of 1427, Pampaloni has calculated that the going rate on overdue dowries in Prato was 10 percent; Pampaloni, "Prato nella Repubblica," vol. 2, 44.

86 Catasto of 1427, 34, 395r.

87 For what follows, see McLaughlin, "The Teaching of the Canonists," and the texts cited in nn. 82 and 83.

88 CS, ser. 3a, 41, vol. 10, 250r–51v.

89 CS, ser.3a, 41, vol. 5, 332r: "Consideratis his que in facto presuponuntur. Iohannes promisit consignare infra certum tempus Nichole eius genero quedam bona immobilia, scilicet dimidiam unius poderis [MS: immobilia – poderis *supr.*] pro florenis 250 in quibus restabat [MS: Nichole *post* restabat

del.] creditor pro dote sibi promissa. Quod Nichola duxit uxorem et Iohannes nunquam consignavit dictum predium [MS: et non solum lapsum fuit tempus illius sed etiam plures anni et *post* predium *del.*], mortuus est dictus Iohannes et lapsi sunt anni XXVI vel circa a die quo erat consignanda dicto Nichole dicta bona. Interim tamen dictus Nichola recepit in pecunia numerata in pluribus vicibus de summa predicta florenorum 250, florenis 170, adeo quod hodie restat creditor in florenis 80 tantum."

90 Ibid., 333r: "Unde puto dictum generum posse petere interesse [MS: suum *post* interesse *del.*] quod passus fuit propter non solutam integram dotem tempore statuto, quod interesse debet attendi et comensurari secundum fructum illorum bonorum que promiserit sibi consignare hoc modo, estimando quantum valebat dimidia illius predii. Item quantum fructabat dicta dimidia, quia si socer servasset promissa, gener debebat habere [habere *ex* habuisset *corr.* MS] dicta bona pro quantitate extimata et habuisset fructus illorum bonorum quibus caruit propter non servata promissa, et plus [*sic*] tales redditus dari debet tantum pro centenario dicto genero, eius in quo remanet creditor. Et tale debitum solvi per heredes pro equali portione [MS: pro – portione *supr.*], quia est honus hereditarium solvere creditoribus iuxta l. 1, C. si cer. pe. [Cod. 4. 2. 1], et l. Pro hereditariis, C. de heredit. act. [Cod. 4. 16. 2]. Ita respondit. Ego Antonius de Strozzis."

91 Guicciardini, *Ricordi*, 86; MC, 3746, 123r (the account of Guicciardini's wife, Maria Salviati).

92 On the assignment of Monte credits and Monte dowries, see Kirshner, "Encumbering Private Claims."

93 See Luca da Panzano's *ricordanze* in CS, ser. 2a, vol. 9, 126v; now edited in Molho and Sznura, eds., "*Brighe, Affanni*"; and MC, 3734, 11r. For additional examples, see ibid., 34r (account of Angelica di Antonio di Piero); MC, 3727, 77r (Caterina di Morello Morelli); MC, 3738, 160r (Oretta di Caterina di Buonafidanza Gherardini); MC, 3739, 12v (Agnola di Luigi di Tommaso da Panzano); MC, 3743, 60r (Ginevra di Giorgio Aldobrandini); MC, 3744, 155r (Lucrezia di Giovanni Migliorelli).

94 MC 3744, 1r.

95 Owing to gaps in the record of the registers of the Dowry Fund, I have information only for Tita's original account, opened in 1444 and scheduled to mature fifteen years later (MC, 3734, 18r).

96 NA, 10183, 46r–49v (19 July 1460), 46v–47r: "Verum quia dos dari consuevit maxime ut onera matrimonii, que presertim in civitate Florentie magna sunt, facilius supportari possint. Idcirco dictus Stephanus ut supra dedit et solvit de contanti dicto Niccholao dictam dotem non expectato die dicti crediti dotis super dicto monte descripto. Non tamen animo et intentione ut

postmodum eveniente dicto tempore dicti crediti montis aliam etiam dotem daret et seu in augumentum dotis cederet dictum creditum, sed animo et intentione ut dicta quantitas data de contanti cederet in locum et esset loco dicte dotis super monte predicto descripto predicta Tita pro maiori utilitate dicti Nicholai, et animo et intentione rehabendi ex dicto credito montis illud quod de contanti dederat et solverat dicto Niccholao."

97 Molho, *Marriage Alliance*, 66ff.

98 Kirshner and Klerman, "The Seven Percent Fund of Renaissance Florence," chap. 5 in this volume.

99 *Libro di famiglia* of Tribaldo d'Amerigo de' Rossi (1481–1501), BNCF, Fondo Principale, II. II. 357, 8r: "non avendo el modo a dargli perchè la dota non si poteva ritrarre per li temporali chativi."

100 CS, ser. 2a, vol. 17 bis, 10v.

3. Materials for a Gilded Cage

1 Kirshner, "*Maritus lucretur dotem*," 112; Niccolai, *La formazione*, 170 ff.; ASLu, Statuti del Comune di Lucca (1362), no. 6, 143r–v, lib. 4, rubr. 120, *De muliere defuncta in matrimonio et de modo restituende dotis.*

2 On nondotal assets in late Roman law, see Gerner, *Beiträge zum Recht*, and the review essay of the book by Wolff, "Zur Geschichte," as well as García Garrido, *El patrimonio*, 28–40, 146–9. The key Roman legal sources relating to *parapherna* are translated in Evans Grubbs, *Women and the Law*; in the *ius commune* before 1300, see Bellomo, *Ricerche sui rapporti*, 131–42; for seventeenth-century Rome, Ago, "Oltre le dote," an informative study on a neglected subject, yet which itself neglects research on the bundle of Roman and medieval *ius commune* norms and rules that continued to direct the formation, disposition, and devolution of nondotal assets in the seventeenth century. For late medieval France, see, inter alia, Hilare, *Le régime*, 102ff.; Lafon, *Les époux bordelais*, 77ff.; Landés-Mallet, *La famille*, 106–8. For English common law, see Donahue, "Lyndwood's Gloss propriarum uxorum"; Biancalana, "Testamentary Cases in Fifteenth-Century Chancery," 289ff.

3 "Bona parafernalia, et hec sunt bona mobilia que uxor defert in domum mariti maxime ratione sui proprii usus vel causa communis sui et viri." My translation, from an opinion rendered by Franciscus de Albergottis of Arezzo on a dispute that occurred in the *distretto* of Florence sometime after 1350. For an edition of Albergotti's opinion and a related opinion by Baldus de Ubaldis, see Kirshner and Pluss, "Two Fourteenth-Century Opinions" (quotation on 74). For another manuscript copy of Albergotti's opinion,

see Bologna, Collegio di Spagna, MS 70, no. 50, 113r–v. Albergotti became a citizen of Florence, where he taught and practiced law until his death in 1376. On Albergotti, see my "Messer Francesco," and "Baldo degli Ubaldi's Contribution," 328–9.

4 Caggese, ed., *Statuti della Repubblica fiorentina*, vol. 2, *Statuto del podestà dell'anno 1325*, 111, lib. 2, rubr. 35, *De eo quod uxor alicuius acquisverit*; ASF, Statuti di Firenze, Podestà [1355], no. 18, 152v, lib. 2, rubr. 39; *Statuta populi et communis Florentiae* (1415), vol. 1, 161–2, lib. 2, rubr. 65.

5 Nor is the term *parapherna* found in Genoese notarial records: Epstein, *Wills and Wealth*, 250, n. 11. In Milan, on the other hand, *parapherna* was used to designate personal effects brought by wives to their husbands at the beginning of marriage: Caso, "Per la storia."

6 *Corredo* was commonly used in *confessiones dotium* drafted in Florence before the mid-fourteenth century. In *confessiones dotium* of the fifteenth century *donora* had all but replaced *corredo* as the designation for the bride's personal articles.

7 Klapisch-Zuber, "Le zane della sposa."

8 Lena di Bernardo Sassetti brought her husband a 700-florin dowry, 630 in cash and 70 in *donora*. When she arrived in his household on 12 May 1384, she came with additional personal items worth approximately 60 florins; see the *ricordi* of Paolo di Alessandro Sassetti, CS, ser. 2a, vol. 4, 70r, 74v, 143r: "Cose date ala Lena in donora e in sopradonora quando <a> dì xii magio, anno mccclxxxiiii, n'andò a marito nel nome di dio e di buona ventura."

9 Bellomo, *Ricerche sui rapporti*, 131–42.

10 Mayali, *Droit savant et coutumes*; Donahue, "Lyndwood's Gloss propriarum uxorum," 24: "Succession of the *dos* and to the *donatio propter nuptias* were governed by fixed rules; the paraphernalia were not important enough to warrant separate treatment of testamentary power over them; a married women was unlikely to have a patrimony, since custom, if not the *ius commune*, would have excluded her from inheritance from her father once she was endowed, and the *ius commune* did not entitle her to a forced share of her husband's patrimony."

11 Cohn, "Donne e Controriforma"; Goldthwaite, *L'economia della Firenze rinascimentale*, 755–9.

12 This observation was made by Lafon in his excellent study, *Les époux bordelais*, 98: "le notaires bordelais manient largement la notion d'extra-dotalité, sans d'ailleurs lui appliquer un substantif technique précis, mais en se servent de périphrases." A proverbial exception that proves the rule is a *confessio dotis* (10 Jan. 1456) of the Sienese jurist Bartholomaeus Socinus who, together with his father, the canonist Marianus, acknowledged receiving

1,000 florins for the dowry of Bartholomaeus's wife, Lodovica Orlandini, and 2,000 florins in "bona, iura et res tamquam bona parafrenalia dicte Lodovice." Listed as paraphernal property were five farms and a villa in picturesque Borgo Scopeto located in the Sienese Chianti. The *confessio dotis* is published by Bargagli, "Documenti senesi," 274–5.

13 J. Davis, *The People of the Mediterranean,* 181–4.

14 Note, however, Antonius de Stroziis's elliptical comment: "Et licet dicat quod in bonis parafernalibus que comuniter traduntur viro, forte dicendum totum contrarium" (CS, ser. 3a, 41, vol. 6, 183r).

15 Kirshner and Pluss, "Two Fourteenth-Century Opinions," 74: "Et istorum parafernaliorum quoniam uxor tradit viro custodiam et tunc videtur ei concedere tacitam eorum administrationem et usus ut dictis iuribus et quoniam sibi reservat custodiam et tunc vir nullum ius pretendit in illis."

16 Ibid., 76.

17 Baldus to *l. Hac lege* (Cod. 5. 14. 8); and to *l. Ubi ad huc* (Cod. 5. 12. 29), in *Commentaria* (Lyon, 1498), s.f.

18 Accursius to *l. Hac lege* (Venice, 1569), 723rab; Odofredus to *l. Hac lege*, in *Commentaria* (Lyon, 1552), 280ra, no. 1: "Et in lege ista dicitur quod maritus in rebus paraphernalibus mulieris sue nullam habet communionem uxore prohibente: licet de rigore iuris videretur, quod ex quo mulier committit personam suam viro, quod res suas deberet committere. Tamen de equitate dicendum est, licet uxor committit personam suam, res paraphernales non committit. Unde in rebus paraphernalibus maritus nihil habet facere uxore prohibente"; Bartholomaeus de Saliceto to *l. Hac lege*, in *Commentaria* (Lyon, 1515), 25va.

19 Antonius de Stroziis, CS, ser. 3a, 41, vol. 6, 183r: "Unde requiratur consensus uxoris, prout est quando uxor tradit viro bona parafernalia."

20 In addition to the references cited in n. 3, see Bartolus to *l. Si mulier* (Cod. 5. 14. 11), in *Commentaria* (Venice, 1570–1), 176rb; idem to *l. Si heres* (Dig. 35. 2. 90), 138va; Albericus de Rosate to *l. Si mulier*, in *Commentaria* (Venice, n.p.: 1585–6), 261vb–62ra; Baldus de Ubaldis to *l. Si mulier*, in *Commentaria* (Venice, 1599), 197ra; Paulus de Castro, *Consilia* (Frankfurt am Main, 1584), vol. 2, 92r–v, cons. 199; Franciscus Accoltus de Aretio, *Consilia* (Venice, 1572), 42r–43v, cons. 31.

21 See the *consilium* of Raphael de Raymundis with concurring opinions by Prosdocimus de Comitibus, Johannes Franciscus de Capitibus Listae, Johannes de Imola, and Paulus de Castro: Raphael de Raymundis (Cumanus), *Consilia* (Venice, 1576), 53v–54r, cons. 105; Alexander Tartagnus, *Consilia* (Lyon, 1547–9), vol. 1, 39v–41r, cons. 42, no. 3. The same logic underlay the Bolognese statutes of 1335 and 1357. See Trombetti

Budriesi, ed., *Lo Statuto del Comune di Bologna dell'anno 1335*, vol. 2, 574, lib. 7, rubr. 31, *De dotibus restituendis et ipsarum parte lucranda et de fructibus rerum parafrenalium*; Archivio di Stato of Bologna, Statuti (1357), no. 12, 114r–v, lib. 5, rubr. 30, *De dotibus restituendis et ipsarum parte lucranda et de fructibus rerum parafrenalium*: "Preterea statuimus quod si quis receperit fructus vel redditus quoscunque ex bonis parafrenalibus uxoris sue, voluntate uxoris non possit ipsa, vel eius heres, ipsos fructus vel redditus petere vel extimationem ipsorum. Que voluntas semper presumatur, nisi voluntas contraria legiptime probaretur." Bergamo also translated this presumption into communal law: see Storti Storchi, ed., *Lo statuto di Bergamo*, 192, collatio X, rubr. 3, *De eo quod habuerit uxor, que presumantur de bonis viris*: "Item quod si aliqua mulier, maritum habens, habeat aliquas possessiones vel bona cuiuscumque condictionis presumantur et intelligantur esse mariti, nisi probetur vel hostendatur ad eam pervenisse ex successione, donatione vel legato."

22 Baldus to *l. Si ego Seiae*, § *Dotis autem causa* (Dig. 23. 3. 9. 2), in *Commentaria* (Lyon, 1498), s.f.; Franciscus Accoltus de Aretio, *Consilia* (Venice, 1572), 43r, cons. 31, no. 6. This was also the practice among Roman noble families; Modigliani, *I Porcari*, 154ff.

23 See, for example, Podestà, 2740, 95r–96r (12 Feb. 1374/5); 2741, 29v–30v (22 Jan. 1374/5); ibid., 108r–9r (14 Feb. 1374/5).

24 As Albergotti opined: "Quedam sunt bona mulieris neque dotalia neque parafernalia, veluti ea que sunt extra dotem et extra ea que uxor in viri domum inducit. Et ista differunt ab utraque specie predictorum, quia vir in istis non habet dominium ut in dotalibus habet neque administrationem ex tacita seu presumpta voluntate uxoris" (Kirshner and Pluss, "Two Fourteenth-Century Opinions," 74). Paraphrasing Albergotti's opinion, Antonius de Stroziis made clear that *bona non dotalia*, unlike parapherna, did not accompany the wife into the husband's household. Regarding *parapherna*, "ista consistunt in bonis mobilibus que uxor portat secum in domum viri, ratione sui vel comunis usus"; and *bona non dotalia*, "quedam alia bona <que> habet mulier, que non sunt inducta in domum, sed sunt propria ipsius uxoris et in illis maritus nullam habet administrationem" (CS, ser. 3a, 41, vol. 6, 182r).

25 Herlihy and Klapisch-Zuber, *Les Toscans*, 205–7; Kirshner and Molho, "The Dowry Fund," 431–3.

26 Saller, "*Pietas*, Obligation and Authority," 408–9.

27 Paolo da Certaldo, *Libro di buoni costumi*, 105, no. 126. There is an echo in this passage of Eph. 5:33, where Saint Paul admonishes a husband to love

his wife as he would himself, but also that a wife should live in fear of her husband ("uxor autem timeat virum suum").

28 Kirshner and Pluss, "Two Fourteenth-Century Opinions," 75: "Secunda presumptione sumpta ex propria natura mulierum, quia genus avarissimum est ... Mo<n>strum est ipsas velle largiri, non presumendum, quia regulariter entia agunt secundum propriam naturam et solitum et communem eorum morem ... Tertia presumptione presumpta ex congruenti personarum portione, quia decet viros substentare uxores de propriis vel de fructibus bonorum dotalium, non viros nutriri et substentari ab uxoribus ... Quarta ratione presumpta ex personarum coniunctione et eius qualitate, videlicet quod inter virum et uxorem coniunctio habens annessam reverentiam ex parte uxoris, propter quam ex pacientia resultat presumptio discensus seu voluntatis coacte."

29 Falsini, "Firenze dopo il 1348," 437–82.

30 Hughes, "Sumptuary Law"; Klapisch-Zuber, "The Griselda Complex."

31 Bellomo, *Ricerche sui rapporti*, 139–42; Ercole, "La dote romana"; E. Rinaldi, "La donna negli statuti," 192; Storti Storchi, "La tradizione longobarda," 118. Savona: Balletto, ed., *Statuta antiquissima Saone (1345)*, vol. 2, 183–4, lib. 6, rubr. 8, *Quod aliquis non possit petere ultra sortem pro extradotibus*, which makes no distinction between *parapherna* and *bona extra dotalia*. For a Trevisan statute of 1385, Betto, ed., *Gli statuti del comune di Treviso*, vol. 2, 381–2, rubr. 3, *De dotibus mulierum et fructibus rerum parafernalium earum*: "Et quod de omnibus bonis, quecunque et undecunque habuerit uxor, fructus habere debeat et lucrari maritus constante matrimonio sicut fructus rei dotalis, et huic statuto per pactum aliquod vel modo aliquo renunciari non possit." Feltre: *Statutorum magnificae civitatis et communis Feltriae* (1439), 200, lib. 3, rubr. 75, *Qualiter maritus lucretur fructus bonorum uxoris quomodo* [?] *sibi spectantium*. Ferrara: Superbi, "*In dotem pro dote*," 110–11. Forlì: *Statuta civitatis Forolivii* (1504), 215, lib. 2, rubr. 43, *Quod fructus bonorum uxoris sint mariti*. Likewise, this was the dotal regime in the Tuscan town of Buggiano: ASF, Statuti delle comunità autonome e soggette, Statuti di Buggiano (1366), rubr. *Que bona intelligantur dotalia*, 31r: "Intelligantur etiam dotalia bona iocalia <et> donamenta, seu bona parafernalia, que uxor portaret seu deferret ad domum viri."

32 Guzzetti, "Women's Inheritance and Testamentary Practices," 83. In the fourteenth century, Venetian law was extended to Treviso, then under Venice's control and superior jurisdiction. In 1346, Mariabella, the wife of Morando da Fossata, wanted to know whether she had a right to dispose of nondotal assets (*bona sua extra dotem*), which under

Treviso's statutes was restricted (see preceding note). The question was put to Doge Andrea Dandolo and his legal advisors. In his reply sent to Treviso's Venetian *podestà*, Andrea Corner, the doge made a cardinal distinction. The wife may not dispose of her nondotal assets in the husband's possession and direct control. On the other hand, she may sell, transfer, or pledge any nondotal assets in her possession and direct control – notwithstanding Treviso's statutes to the contrary. See Cagnin, *Cittadini e forestieri*, 352–3.

33 Angelus de Ubaldis, *Consilia* (Lyon, 1551), 31vb–32ra, cons. 42.

34 BNCF, Magl. XXIX, 173, 129r–31r, 129r: "Primum dubium in hac causa vertitur nunquid page percepte ex creditis montium consignatis domine Lucretie per commune Florentie constante matrimonio cedant lucro ipsius viri, an vero ad ipsam dominam Lucretiam pertineant, in quo verissimum et indubitatum fore censeo tales pagas mariti lucro cedere ex dispositione statuti, quo cavetur quod si uxor alicuius aliquid acquisiverit vel ad ipsam aliquod pervenerit constante matrimonio, quocunque iure, fructus et redditus et proventus ad maritum pertineant etc. Que verba statuti hunc casum comprehendunt, ergo et ipsius statuti dispositio in eo locum habet." Angelus was paraphrasing the statutes. See *Statuta populi et communis Florentiae* (1415), vol. 1, 161, lib. 2, rubr. 65, *De acquisitis per uxorem vivente viro*: "Si uxor alicuius acquisiverit aliquid (Ed: aliquod), vel ad ipsam devenerit quocumque iure vivente viro suo legitimo, ipse talis vir, ea uxore volente vel invita, possit, et valeat una cum tali uxore toto tempore vitae ipsius uxoris, uti et frui praefatis bonis acquisitis et fructus, redditus et proventus percipere, nisi bona sic acquisita devenisse<n>t ad talem mulierem sub conditione."

35 BNCF, Fondo Principale, II, IV, 435, 49r, gl. *et mulier in ipsa talia bona*: "Si qua fuissent acquisita uxori constante matrimonio et in quibus vir habet usumfructum; alioquin remanet libera facultas mulieri prout de iure communi conceditur." Note that neither the statute of 1415 itself nor Bencivenni's gloss indicates the source of the nondotal assets. Note further that Alexander states that the assets "were acquired for the wife (*uxori*) during marriage," not by the wife (*uxore*) herself.

36 See the petition on behalf of Domenico di Bartolo of Castro Fiorentino, now a resident of Florence, to take possession of one-third of the *bona non dotalia* belonging to his deceased wife, Lorenza. Her heirs objected that Domenico's petition should be denied on the grounds that he was never Lorenza's lawful husband (*non fuit legitimus vir*). Domenico, in turn, claimed that he indeed had lawfully contracted and consummated his marriage with Lorenza. The dispute can be followed in Podestà, 2742,

63r (31 Jan. 1374/5); ibid., 65v (1 Feb. 1374/5); Podestà, 2743, 14r–v (12 Jan.1374/5); ibid., 38v–40v (22 Jan. 1374/5).

37 ASF, Statuti di Firenze, Podestà (1355), no. 18, 168v, lib. 2, rubr. 74, *Qualiter succedat in dote et in aliis bonis uxoris premortue*; *Statuta populi et communis Florentiae* (1415), 223, vol, 1, lib. 2, rubr. 129, *Qualiter succedatur in dotem uxoris premortue*: "In aliis vero bonis uxoris predictae non dotalibus si testata decesserit, vir succedat saltem in tertia parte bonorum non extante aliquo filio, vel filia, vel aliis descendentibus ex eis. Si vero intestata decesserit succedat vir in tertia parte bonorum non dotalium. Et in residuo ipsorum bonorum succedat proximior in gradu ipsi uxori." According to Alexander de Bencivennis, her surviving children had no remedy if their mother had donated paraphernal assets to the church but reserved their fruits to herself and then bequeathed to her husband the right to collect up to one-third of the fruits after her death (BNCF, Fondo Principale, II, IV, 435, 70r–v, gl. *in uxore predicta*). On this rubric, see Lepsius, "Paolo di Castro," 82–97; and Edigati and Tanzini, *Ad Statutum Florentinum*, 151–82.

38 Hostiensis (Henricus de Segusio), *Summa aurea* (Venice, 1574), 5. 38. *De poenitentiis et remissionibus*, *Quid de facientibus eleemosynam de alieno,* col. 1861, no. 62 c: "Si habet res paraphernales, id est, proprias praeter dotem, potest et debet inde facere eleemosynam, etiam viro invito"; Antoninus (sant' Antonino of Florence), *Summa theologica* (Venice, 1581–2), 71r, pt. 2, tit. 1, cap. 15 (*De furto* ...) § 1. See also Donahue, "Lyndwood's Gloss propriarum uxorum," 27.

39 For Venice, see Guzzetti, "Women's Inheritance and Testamentary Practices," 83. In Lucca, the successors of a woman who died intestate possessed a presumptive claim to one-fourth of her paraphernal goods: ASLu, Statuti del Comune di Lucca (1362), no. 6, 143r–v lib. 4, rubr. 120, *De muliere defuncta in matrimonio et de modo restituende dotis*: "Et similiter testari possit de bonis parafrenalibus in quibus possit disponere eciam sine consensu mariti prout voluerit; dum tamen nulla mulier nupta vel vidua in sua ultima voluntate vel eciam in infirmitate sua possit de suis bonis alienare seu iudicare, quin heredes eius ab intestato succedentes eciam pater, ascendentes et descendentes habeant quartam partem bonorum eius."

40 Notable exceptions are the *ricordi* of the wily widow Alessandra Macinghi Strozzi, CS, ser. 5a, vol. 15 (Libro di debitori e creditori e ricordi di Alessandra Macinghi vedova Strozzi, segnato A, 1453–73); those of Selvaggia di Bartolomeo Gianfigliazzi, the commanding widow of Filippo Strozzi: CS, ser. 5a, vols. 55, 56, 60, and 61; on whom see Goldthwaite, *Private Wealth*, 77–81; and the *ricordi* of Caterina d'Antonio de' Bardi, the widow of Giorgio di Baliano Flatro, a Cypriot physician who became a citizen of

Florence: see Contessa, "La costruzione," 151ff. A few more examples are noted by Chabot, *La dette des familles*, 181–2.

41 ASF, Castato 17 (1427), 150r: the husband Aghostino d'Iacopo, *legatore* (master packer) declares his wife's house in Piazza Santo Spirito, which rents for 12 lire annually, and two parcels of land that she owns jointly with her sister; ibid., 34 (1427), 285r: Bindaccio di Granello declares the properties belonging to his daughter-in-law, Caterina, who resides with her husband, Andrea, in Bindaccio's household. Listed are ten properties outside Florence that she owns jointly with her sisters, generating 40 florins annually in rental income. Also listed are Caterina's holdings in the *Monte Comune* and 30 florins owed her by Berto di Ridolfo Peruzzi; Catasto 60 (1427), 369r–v: Ser Baptista di Giovanni Becciante of Pisa, now a Florentine notary, reports the possessions and goods belonging to his wife, Tora, but which he controls and enjoys. For declarations of married women's Monte holdings, see Catasto, 33 (1433), 899r: joint household of three brothers (Riccho, Rinieri, and Francesco) declaring the Monte credits with overdue interest (*paghe sostenute*) of Rinieri's wife, Lorenza di Giunta Guidotti; ibid., 956v: Rinieri di Niccolò Peruzzi declares "la rendita a sua vita" that his wife, Tomasa, receives from a parcel of Monte credits; Catasto 60 (1427), 367r–68r: declaration of the Florentine jurist Nello di Giuliano da San Gimignano that he inherited from his deceased wife, Nencia, her claim to collect the interest from 650 florins of Monte credits, which she had received during her life. He also reports a debt of 43 florins owed to his second wife, Albiera; Catasto 61 (1427), 706v: declaration of maestro Domenico del maestro Giovanni reporting his wife's Monte credits; and ibid., 730r: declaration of Francesco di Taddeo Gherardini reporting his wife's Monte credits.

42 *Statuta populi et communis Florentiae* (1415), vol. 2, 342–3, lib. 4, *De extimis*, rubr. 23, *Quod uxor non cogatur solvere libram, praestantiam vel aliquod onus vivente viro*: "Et si qua mulier tempore quo esset vidua vel nondum nupta, prestantiata vel allibrata esset, seu in oneribus communis Florentiae descripta, seu vel haereditario nomine alicuius, seu efficeretur haeres alicuius praestantiati vel allibrati, seu aliter in oneribus communis Florentiae descripti, statim cum nupserit et viro tradita fuerit, intelligatur et sit finita dicta praestantiato, allibratio, incameratio et descriptio, nec possit amplius praetextu illius, et super illa distributione gravari, praestantiari vel molestari, nisi ratione praestantie vel gravaminis iam indictae et bannitae seu indicti et banniti antequam nuberet, sed ex tunc intelligitur et sic in perpetuo absoluta a dicta allibratione, praestantiamento vel descriptione." Interestingly, this statute was reproduced in the tax declaration of the jurist Giovanni di messer Buonaccorso da Montemagno of Pistoia. His wife, Lena, widow of

Giulio Giraldi, had received from her deceased husband's estate a farm and additional pieces of land in Borgo a San Lorenzo providing a rental income of 75 lire. According to Giovanni, "come marito e procuratore della decta mona Lena," these properties are exempt under the statutes of Florence from past and future taxes and forced loans, because, as Lena states, she acquired them while a widow and therefore before her marriage to Giovanni: "Item dice la decta mona Lena, la decta heredità et beni esserle pervenuti a llei quando ella era vedova, et secondo la forma dello Statuto del Comune di Firenze non esser prestantiata ne gravata per adrieto per dichiariagione de' Regolatori et così non devere essere acatastata ne gravata per l'avenire. Et produce lo statuto del comune di Firenze, De extimis, rubrica XXIII, cuius tenor est in alia facie posteriori, in fine." See Catasto, 61, 988r–89r (1427). In May 1456, the Sienese jurists Bartholomaeus and his father Marianus Socinus were granted a tax exemption on the substantial paraphernal properties that they had acknowledged receiving in January of that year in the name of Bartholomaeus's wife, Lodovica Orlandini, on the grounds that neither ownership nor possession was transferred to them ("non transit dominium neque possessio"). See n. 12 above, and Bargagli, "Documenti senesi," 275.

43 PR, 147, 44v–45r (29 Apr. 1456).

44 For the Roman prohibition: Dumont, *Les donations*; Misera, "Die Zeugnisse"; Cherry, "Gifts between Husband and Wife"; Hamza, "Les motifs de la prohibition de la donation"; for the medieval *ius commune*: Bestor, "The Groom's Prestations"; Laurent-Bonne, "Why Prohibit Donations?"

45 Vismara, "I patti successori," 761ff.; Abouçaya, "Les différents conceptions," 378–431.

46 NA, 6207, 280r–81r (28 Nov. 1460). Further examples are found in NA, 195, 77v–78r (8 July 1341), 210v (18 June 1348).

47 NA, 205, 51r–v (9 Mar. 1371/2); Kuehn, "*Cum consensu mundualdi*," 138.

48 See the donation of the widow Filippa di Ruggeri, whose mother would receive on the daughter's predecease Filippa's dowry worth 420 florins (NA, 205, 12v–13r [8 June 1353]), and the donation of Giovanni di Antonio, whose stepmother would receive on the donor's predecease his claim for the balance due on the sale of several properties (NA, 7046, s.f. [1 Oct. 1432]).

49 For premortem gifts made in the fourteenth century, see NA, 7414, 88r–v (29 July 1316); NA, 195, 25v–28r (30 May 1339), 68v (7 Aug. 1349); NA, 7417, 11r (8 June 1344), 55r–v (7 Feb. 1345/6), 65r (1 May 1347), 70v (23 Aug. 1347); NA, 1200, 68r (21 Jan. 1370/1); for the fifteenth century, NA, 9035, 35r (2 Sept. 1401); NA, 9036, 37r (7 Mar. 1406/7); NA, 9037, 212r (2 May 1410); NA, 13288, s.f. (6 Aug. 1445); NA, 6252, 169r (17 Mar. 1454/5);

NA, 14713, 99v–100r (30 Dec. 1465); NA, 14722, 70v–71r (17 Oct. 1485); NA, 14723, 10v (4 July 1487).

50 MC, 2599, 143r: "Che monna Ginevra, donna d'Antonio di Filippo Nicholi, pigli le paghe durante la sua vita."

51 MC, 2599, 194v. Orlando also made identical donations to his two unmarried daughters, Lena and Alessandra.

52 Conti, *L'imposta diretta*, 34.

53 See Kirshner, "Encumbering Private Claims"; Kirshner and Klerman, "The Seven Percent Fund of Renaissance Florence," chap. 5 in this volume.

54 On these practices, which stimulated much of the speculative activity in Monte credits at the end of the fifteenth century, see Molho, "L' amministrazione del debito pubblico."

55 Bartolomea, wife of Giuliano di Matteo Pezzati, for example, held 594 florins in Monte credits; she transferred her claim to collect *paghe* on a parcel of credits (300 florins) between 1 September 1454 and August 1458 (MC, 2599, 34r). Lorenza di Bernardo di Miniato, wife of Giovanni di Francesco di ser Andrea, who held 2,018 florins in Monte credits, transferred to Simone d'Antonio Canigiani her claim to *paghe* on 200 florins in credits, from 1 Sept. 1456 forward (ibid., 152v).

56 Kuehn, "*Cum consensu mundualdi.*"

57 NA, 1843, 89r–90v (23 Feb. 1464).

58 MC, 1802, 115v (19 Mar. 1366). Similarly, Mattea received consent from her husband, Girigoro di Lorenzo, to trade 355 florins in credits and appointed him procurator to carry out the transaction (MC, 1319, 62r [8 Feb. 1372/3]).

59 MC, 1802, 23r (17 Dec. 1365): "Monna Margherita, moglie di messer Lapo da Chastiglionchio, quartiere Santa Croce, a Guido di Tribaldo da Chastiglionchio, detto quartiere, fiorini 380 del'uno tre, per licenza del piovano Antonio de' Chavalcanti suo procuratore"; MC, 1319, 173r (21 May 1376): "Monna Dianora, moglie di Niccholò di ser Franciesco e figlia di Nastagio Buccelli, quartiere Santo Spirito, a monna Piera ... di licenza di Lorenzo di ser Francesco suo procuratore."

60 Lisabetta, wife of Giovanni di messer Iacopo, transferred credits without her husband's consent (MC, 1802, 67v, 10 June 1366): "Monna Lisabetta, figliuola fu di Gherardo Corbizzi e moglie di Giovanni di messer Iacopo, quartiere Santa Croce, a messer Donato Gherucci Barbadoro, quartiere Santo Spirito, fiorini 150 di monte vecchio."

61 Rosenthal, "The Position of Women," 377.

62 MC, 2601 (year: 1456), 120r: "Che Matteo di Aghostino farsettaio suo marito pigli le paghe durante il matrimonio." Giovanna's credits had a face value of 410 florins. Other examples: MG, 956, 275r (7 Oct. 1484): account

of Giana di Giuliano, wife of Jacopo di Matteo; ibid., 302r (7 Jan. 1484/5): account of Margherita, wife of Lorenzo di Bernardo Ridolfi; ibid., 497r (5 Mar. 1487/8): account of Ginevra di Matteo Mazzuoli, wife of Francesco di Stefano; MG, 960, 704r (23 Nov. 1481): account of Maddalena di Filippo, wife of Iacopo di Tedescho.

63 NA, 5346, 300r–v (5 June 1473). Here Pasqua di Giovanni assigned her husband, Bartolomeo di Paolo di Meo, a life usufruct to properties in and around Florence that she had received as gifts. She accomplished this by appointing him her legal representative.

64 Poltrone di messer Luigi Cavalcanti and his wife, Margherita, were listed as joint owners of credits (MC, 2559, 199v); Nanna di Filippo Arrigucci was listed as the sole owner of Monte credits with a face value of 703 florins, but she and her husband, Bencivenni di Parente di Michele, shared in the right to collect interest: "Che la detta e Bencivenni suo marito e ognuno intero pigli le paghe" (ibid., 188r); Lapo di Giovanni and his wife, Alessandra, were listed as joint owners of credits with a face value of 250 florins, but it was stipulated "che Lapo detto durante il matrimonio pigli le paghe" (ibid, 140r).

65 NA, 10188, 17r–v (8 May 1473). See also the testament of Gello di Maso Gelli, who left several rural properties to be possessed jointly by his nephew, his nephew's wife, and his own wife (SMN, 70, 4r [19 Apr. 1409/10]), and the testament of India di Marco Salviati, widow of Giovanni di Piero Baroncelli, who left seven-twelfths of a farm worth 300 florins to Mariotto, an illegitimate son of her father-in-law, and his wife (NA, 10185, 64v [19 Dec. 1463]).

66 Zordan, "I vari aspetti"; Romano, *Famiglia, successioni*, 100ff.; Mineo, *Nobiltà di stato*, 119ff.; Novarese, "Un *consilium* maltese"; Hilaire, "Vie en commun"; Howell, *The Marriage Exchange*, 208ff.; Donahue, "What Causes Fundamental Legal Ideas?"

67 Kuehn, *Emancipation*.

68 Buonaccorsi, *Libro di ricordi*, 176.

69 NA, 10185, 81v–82v (23 Dec. 1463). Bartolomea's daughter Tita, married to Piero di Tommaso Deti, was one of the recipients. In another case, Andrea di Piero of Pontassieve donated half his movable goods and his share of real properties held in common with his brother to his two daughters, one of whom was married; NA,10181, 78r–v (18 Feb. 1457/8).

70 Signori, "Family Traditions: Moral Economy," 291ff.; J. Davis, *The People of the Mediterranean*, 187; Brettel, "Property, Kinship, and Gender."

71 Sercambi, *Novelle*, 1: 326–33, nov. 57

72 I exclude from my discussion very small testamentary legacies of a few florins, including cash, personal effects, household items, and ritual objects

such as rosary beads made by women to other women (never married, married, widows) – a ubiquitous customary practice marking and affirming the relationships among kinswomen and female relatives-in-law. For a striking analysis of such bequests, and the "ways testamentary practices in Douai shaped the rituals of gift-giving," see Howell, "Fixing Movables" (quotation on 91).

73 NA, 7414, 26r (18 July 1313). For additional examples of bequests that denied the husband's appropriation of nondotal bequests, see Sapori, "Il libro," 102; SMN, 67, 106v (5 Oct. 1383), 142v (30 June 1383), 168v (5 Aug. 1384); NA, 16841, 39r–41r (4 May 1477), 6752, 55r–v (3 Apr. 1493). According to the terms of Angelo di Tommaso Corbinelli's last will (27 Apr. 1419), his daughters, Bartolomea and Giulia, after having married, would receive in addition to their dowries a life usufruct to the 5 percent interest payable on Monte credits valued at 300 florins. Corbinelli stipulated that the bequest was intended solely for the use of his daughters ("sed sit proprium dictarum eius filiarum"). For the legacy, see the meticulous edition of Corbinelli's multifaceted last will in Armstrong, "Usury," 226, no. 24. For testamentary bequests of nondotal assets to married women in Venice, see Chojnacki, "Patrician Women," 190; now in his *Women and Men in Renaissance Venice*, 123.

74 NA, 9041, 168r–75r (27 Dec. 1430, with codicils of 4 Mar. and 7 Apr. 1430/1). It was customary for a wife to receive a life usufruct of income-producing properties that reverted to a religious institution upon her death. See Orlandi, "Il convento," 147–8; and MC, 2601, 234r, where the right to collect interest payable on Monte credits with a face value of 200 florins, registered under the name of Spedale di Santa Maria Nuova di Firenze, belonged to Chosa di Iacopo Cafferelli and her husband, Zanobi di Cristoforo Maggiolini, during their lifetimes; the same terms applied to Tancia di Giovanni di Pagolo and her husband, Bernardo di Iachopo Canacci (ibid., 235r).

75 SMN, 70, 385v. For a similar bequest, see the testament of Francesco di ser Filippo of San Miniato, which named his sister, the wife of a Florentine citizen, universal heir and enjoined her to fund a mass and an annual service "pro anima testatoris" (NA, 16841, insert 4, 74r–75v [28 Aug. 1503]).

76 Tornabuoni's will is edited by Cadogan, *Domenico Ghirlandaio*, 369–71.

77 Examples: NA, 205, 80r (23 Sept. 1378): testament of Giovanni di Neri, who named his married daughter Antonia universal heir; SMN, 67, 132v (17 July 1383): testament of Nicholosa, widow of ser Iachopo of Fucecchio, a Florentine citizen, who named her married daughters Bartolomea and Andrea universal heirs; ASF, Archivio della Gherardesca, no. 55 (19

Apr. 1420/1): testament of the widow Margherita di Benedetto Peruzzi, who named her married sister Taddea universal heir; NA, 9042, 133v (9 May 1427): testament of Francesco di Agnolo Ricoveri, who named his married sister, Sandra; ibid., 155r–58v (9 July 1430): testament of Bamba di Zanobi de' Bardi, widow of Agnolo di Giovanni da Uzzano, who named her daughter Alessandra universal heir; NA, 3373, 195v (17 Oct. 1431): testament of Ricciardo di Domenico Cambini, who named his married daughter universal heir; NA, 16795, s.f. (10 Apr. 1475/6): testament of Vermiglio di Sandro di Giovanni, who named his married niece universal heir; NA, 14718, 146v (27 Jan. 1476/7): testament of the widow Francesca di Matteo di Stefano Scolari, who named her daughter Alessandra, wife of Andrea di Francesca Zati, universal heir; NA, 10194, 228r–29r (10 July 1486): testament of the widow Caterina di Giovanni Marrazani, who named her married daughter Iacoba universal heir; NA, 14724, 128v (23 Apr. 1490/1): testament of the widow Lorenza di Poggio Bracciolini, who named her daughter Vaggia, wife of Giovanni Cavalcanti, universal heir. Instructive here is the last will of the silk merchant Andrea Banchi, one of the wealthiest men in Florence, with an estimated fortune of around 18,000 florins, not including family houses and properties, at the time of his death in 1462. When he made his will (14 Mar. 1459/60), his sole surviving child was Caterina, the wife of Domenico Ginori. Two sons and another daughter, Bice, had died earlier. Banchi named the Spedale degli Innocenti as his universal heir, to which he bequeathed two-thirds of his fortune, excluding the family properties. The remaining one-third, or around 6,000 florins, was left to Caterina and his granddaughter, Alessandra, Bice's only child. See Edler de Roover, "Andrea Banchi," 276–7.

78 Wrigley, 'Fertility Strategy.'

79 Mazzi and Raveggi, *Gli uomini e le cose*, 329–31, 339–40; Vallaro, "*Considerans fragilitatem*," 193–4; S. Ricci, "*De hac vita transire*," 71ff.; Emigh, *The Undevelopment*, 74–5; Cohn, *The Cult of Remembrance*, 180, 187, 197; Lumia, "Morire a Siena," 146–51; Lumia-Ostinelli, "'Ut Cippus,'" 39–41; Kent, *Household and Lineage*, 74; Crabb, *The Strozzi of Florence*, 36–40, and 266 (table B.1, "Universal Heirs"); Tripoldi, *Gli Spini*, 108–9; Wray, *Communities*, 250–1; Barbero, *Un'oligarchia*, 297–300; Smith, "Locating Power," 441; Stuard, *A State of Deference*, 83–7; Nico Ottaviani, "La practica testamentaria," 363–70; Lombardo and Morelli, "Donne e testamenti," 100–2; Mainoni, "Il potere di decidere," 254–8. For Marseille, see Smail, "'Démanteler le patrimoine," 350–4.

80 Riemer, *Women in the Medieval City*, 138ff.; Chojnacki, "Patrician Women," 190; now in his *Women and Men in Renaissance Venice*, 123.

See also the informative study of Guzzetti, *Venezianische Vermächtnisse*, 146, who shows that in fourteenth-century Venice women testators tended to favor daughters and other female beneficiaries over sons, in contrast to women testators in Florence, who generally preferred sons and male relatives; idem, "Dowries," where the author emphasizes that Venetian women left substantial parts of their dowries to daughters and other women, thereby disadvantaging their sons. Similarly, for noblewomen in Zadar on the eastern Adriatic coast: Grbavac, "Testamentary Bequests," 70. For a critique of Chojnacki's and Guzzetti's views, see Chabot, "*A proposito* di 'Men and Women.'"

81 Based on a small nonrandom sample of Florentine wills, Crabb (*The Strozzi*, 37) observes that "when bequests are taken into account as well as universal heirs, women were less likely to mention daughters in their wills than were men." See also Chabot, *La dette des familles*, 87–9.

82 NA, 682, 67r–68r (11 Jan. 1425/6). Her granddaughter Bartolomea was married to Matteo di Domenico Corsi; Francesca to Alamanno di Silvestro de' Medici; Ginevra to Piero di Maffeo Tedaldi. The widow Bartolmea di Iacopo di Lippo left her married sister, Piera, 20 florins (NA, 12523, 46v [15 June 1416]). Likewise, the widow Zanobia di Marco left her married relative Domenica di Olivia "usufructum et redditum" of "plures petias terrarium" (ibid., 53v [21 May 1416]).

83 NA, 14719, 166r (11 Sept. 1480).

84 NA, 683, 143r–44v (13 June 1429). Similarly, Giovanni di Pagolo Morelli in his testament of 1430 left his daughter Mea, the wife of Antonio di Luca da Filicaia, usufructuary rights to the income of Monte credits with a face value of 500 florins. Should Mea die without legitimate and natural heirs, the credits would then revert to Giovanni's own heirs: Pandimiglio, "Giovanni di Pagolo Morelli," 175; reprinted in his *Famiglia e memoria*, 247–8.

85 MC, 2599, 1v.

86 Cohn, *The Cult of Remembrance*, 197.

87 One of the *consilia* of the Florentine jurist Riccardus del Bene concerned the revocation of a legacy of an olive press to a married woman in the town of Buggiano in the Val di Nievole. See ASF, Carte Del Bene, no. 54 115r–16r (27 Apr. 1411): "Domina Contessa etc. codicillando cassavit et revocavit legatum factum domine Tomaxie suprascripte, uxori Lemmi Pacini, de una pila ad oleum tenendum, et omnia alia in supracripto testamento contenta confirmavit."

88 *Libro di famiglia* di Tribaldo d'Amerigo de' Rossi (1481–1501), BNCF, Fondo Principale, II. II. 357, 74v: "Richordo chome monna Piera sopradetta, a dì 6 di luglio 1492, lasciò e donò al'Alesandra sua figliuola, dona di Piero

Repetti, fiorini 100 de la dote sua s'ela aveva figliuoli di detto Piero, e lasciogliela di naschoso a me; morì la detta Alesandra sanza 'rede, che se moriva chon 'rede stavamo disfatti." It is not entirely clear from the wording of the passage whether the bequest was made by a codicil or a *donatio mortis causa*.

89 Herlihy, "The Florentine Merchant Family." See now Kuehn, *Heirs*, a superb sociolegal study of inheritance in Renaissance Florence. On the various methodological challenges presented by the use of testaments from medieval Italy for historical research, see Bertram, "Mittelalterliche Testamente."

90 Guicciardini, *Ricordi*, 111. Suits over the fulfillment of testamentary legacies are found in the records of the court of the *podestà*. See, for instance, Podestà, 2742, 35r–v (22 Jan. 1374/5), where Giovanna, wife of Orlando di Gherardo, laid claim to 100 florins bequeathed to her by her widowed mother, Marietta de' Bardi. The court ordered that she could take possession of goods worth 100 florins from her mother's estate, but only after she swore on a Bible that her mother was truly deceased. Similar case in Podestà, 2744, 6r–v (11 Oct. 1374). See also Chabot, "Widowhood and Poverty."

91 According to Hilaire, *Le régime*, 106, husbands in fifteenth-century Montpellier regularly acknowledged the rights of wives to the nondotal goods (furnishings and household items) that accompanied them at the time marriage was contracted.

92 NA, 14661, 258r–v (16 May 1424): "Item eidem legavit florenos auri centum decemseptem quos dixit sibi testatori pervenisse de bonis dicte domine Ginevre, videlicet de florenis auri ducentis scriptis super monte et quos vendidit." In his last will (24 May 1445), ser Niccolò di Antonio Cardi first provided for the return of his wife's dowry of 190 florins. Next, he provided for the return of Santa's nondotal goods in the following manner: "Et ultra dictas suas dotes relinquo eidem de bonis meis florenos viginti auri, quos tam ab ea quam etiam ab altera persona pro ea confiteor habuisse et recepisse tam in pecunia quam in aliis diversis rebus ultra dictas suas dotes" (BNCF, Magl., XXIX, 193, 72v).

93 SMN, 70, 186r (29 July 1436): "Et ultra dictos florenos mille ducentos dicte domine legavit et sibi dari et restitui voluit florenos ducentos auri, quos dixit ipsum habuisse et ad eius manus pervenisse de bonis, rebus et iuribus ad ipsam dominam pertinentibus et expectantibus, de quibus florenis ducentis dixit ipsum fecisse quamdam scriptam privatam sua manu."

94 NA, 15852, 103r–4r (25 Oct. 1513). Maria's Monte dowry, which her husband began collecting in 1471, amounted to 1,200 florins (MC, 3737, 13r). On the superior value of the *fiorino largo*, see Edler, *Glossary*, 124.

95 Agostina's dowry of 678 florins had been restored on 13 June 1390, almost immediately after Barna's death (SMN, 67, 310r–v). Similarly, Francesco di Lorenzo Manelli of San Iacopo sopra Arno, in his will of 31 Jan. 1455, acknowledged that he had collected and appropriated to his own use the interest due on Monte credits with a face value of 100 florins, which his father-in-law had bequeathed to his wife. In consideration, the total amount of interest he had collected was to be restored to his wife, Margherita di Alberto di Zanobi (NA, 19075, 307r–8r).

96 NA, 13497, 109r (12 Feb. 1436/7): "Et ultra dictos florenos auri quadraginta ab ea nomine dicte dotis receptos et confessatos eidem uxori sue legavit et reliquit et sibi restitui voluit, iuxit et mandavit florenos auri viginti quos a dicta domina Fiore uxore sua fuit confessus in alia parte habuisse et recepisse de ipsius propria pecunia sibi domine Fiori restituita ab heredibus quondam Pieri Cambii olim primi eius mariti et pro eisdem heredibus ab Antonio olim ser Donati de Sancto Miniato predicto, quos florenos auri viginti receptos ab ea et pro ea et a quibus supra dixit et confessus fuit expendisse et de eis emisse quasdam possessiones et petias terrarum et ipsos et dictarum terrarum ususfructum et redditus in sui testatoris utilitatem convertisse."

97 Raphael de Raymundis (Cumanus), *Consilia* (Venice, 1576), 20r, cons. 2, no. 1.

98 Such concerns were behind the legacy intended for Selvaggia, the wife of Francesco di Geri. In addition to her 250-florin dowry, Francesco left her 300 florins and a bed with an estimated value of 50 florins (*secundum bonam et pinguem extimationem*) as full compensation for the monies and goods that had been left to Selvaggia by her grandmother and other relatives, but which Francesco had appropriated to his own use. Under the terms of the legacy, Selvaggia would be obligated to release her husband's heirs from, and to agree not to bring suit for (*pactum de ulterius aliquid non petendo*), any further payment regarding the said monies and goods: SMN, 67, 16r (9 Nov. 1378).

99 This practice applies to the countryside as well as cities. See the evidence for fourteenth- and fifteenth-century Stroncone, in Umbria: Ciccarelli, ed., *Donne e testamenti*, 37, no. 57, 62, no. 118, 64, no. 122, 69, no. 130, 70, no. 133, 71, no. 136; for Siena and its countryside: Brizio, "In the Shadow," 125.

100 Guerra Medici, *I diritti delle donne*.

101 Leicht, *Storia del diritto italiano*, 219–22.

102 Kirshner, "Wives' Claims against Insolvent Husbands," chap. 6 in this volume.

4. The Morning After

1 Molho, *Marriage Alliance*, 125.
2 Dig. 24. 3. 1, *Dotis causa*.
3 Kirshner and Molho, "The Dowry Fund," 412ff.
4 Husbands who headed households were responsible for filing *catasto* declarations; where the husband with his own family remained in his father's household, it was the father's responsibility to file the declaration.
5 PR, 162, 35r (4 Apr. 1471).
6 PR, 168, 49v (26 Apr. 1477). For the Monte account of Piero's wife, Elisabetta di Francesco di Berto Peruzzi, see MC, 3738, 319r.
7 PR, 178, 151v (24 Dec. 1487).
8 For exemptions granted husbands from Siena, Ancona, Provence, and Ferrara, see PR, 152, 138v–39r (25 Aug. 1461); PR, 154, 123v–24r (2 Aug. 1463), 124v–25r (2 Aug. 1463), 139r–40r (19 Aug. 1463).
9 PR, 154, 285r–86r (21 Dec. 1463). For approvals under the new dispensation granted to husbands from Avignon, Arles, Ragusa, Padua, Milan, Pisa, Spain, Marseilles, and Orvieto, see PR, 157, 85v–88r (19 June 1466); PR, 158, 199v (30 June 1468), 201r–v (7 Nov. 1468); PR, 165, 12v–13r (21 Apr. 1474), 225v–26r (25 Feb. 1474/5); PR, 169, 48v (6 June 1478); PR, 171, 50r–v (22 Aug. 1480).
10 PR, 171, 120r–21v (24 Jan. 1480/1). On German husbands in the Dowry Fund who failed to pay taxes, see Böninger, *Die deutsche Einwanderung*, 95–6.
11 Foreign husbands were sometimes compelled to wait years before the Monte officials released their dowries. Married to Ermellina di Zanobi Della Fonte in 1489, Lellio di Giovanni Leazani of Bologna finally received payment eighteen years later, in 1507 (PR, 197, 59v [21 Feb. 1506/7]).
12 PR, 114, 143r–44v (23 Feb. 1424/5), edited in Kirshner, *Pursuing Honor*, 62.
13 For references to the "fideiussio consummationis matrimonii," see MC, 1116, 65v (28 June 1438).
14 For a rare example of a wife acknowledging (*confessio*) consummation of her marriage, see Bartholomaeus Socinus, *Consilia* (Venice 1571), vol. 2, 80v, cons. 223, no. 3.
15 Kuehn, "Women, Marriage, and *Patria Potestas*."
16 Molho, *Marriage Alliance*, 28. Rocke, *Forbidden Friendships*, 28ff., links the campaign waged against sodomy to public policies supporting marriage. According to Rainey, *Sumptuary Legislation*, vol. 2, 479–80, increasing the population of Florence was the ultimate objective of the sumptuary legislation of 1433 aimed at women's extravagant dress, which was supposed

to make married life more affordable and therefore more attractive to marriage-averse bachelors. Similar concerns were expressed in the preambles of sumptuary legislation enacted across central and northern Italy. See Kovesi Killerby, *Sumptuary Law*, 51–60. Another governmental measure in Florence designed to increase the birth rate was a 200-florin deduction for every family member from the total assets reported to the *catasto* officials. See Herlihy and Klapisch-Zuber, *Tuscans and Their Families*, 10.

17 Haas, *The Renaissance Man*, 17–36. On this theme, see d'Avray, *Medieval Marriage*, 171ff.

18 Brundage, "Implied Consent"; Reid, *Power over the Body*, 110–15; Marchetto, *Il divorzio imperfetto*, 279–86.

19 Toxé maintains that for theologians and canonists, consummation (*copulatio*) had "a symbolic, spiritual, and sacramental dimension, and that is why it is not just one element among other obligations of marriage": Toxé, "La *copula carnalis*." See also d'Avray, *Medieval Marriage*, 168–99; Brundage, *Law, Sex, and Christian Society*, 505.

20 Brundage, *Law, Sex, and Christian Society*, 456–8; d'Avray, *Medieval Marriage*, 189ff. For a discussion of several court cases, see Ferraro, *Marriage Wars*, 69–103. For a comprehensive treatment, see Molina Meliá, *La disolución*, 27–80.

21 Valsecchi, "'*Causa matrimonialis*,'" 407–513; Marchetto, *Il divorzio imperfetto*, 197–206; Trexler, *Synodal Law*, 125. Donahue, *Law, Marriage*, 629, suggests that "it is possible that we are looking at a change in marriage practice that is informed, if not motivated, by the fact that by the fifteenth century, Italians became aware that unconsummated *de presenti* marriages were no longer indissoluble."

22 For the canon and civil law on this point, see Rasi, *La conclusione del matrimonio*; Valsecchi, "'*Causa matrimonialis*'"; Marchetto, "Matrimoni incerti."

23 On canonistic discussions of the standards of proof for the consummation of marriage, see Kelly, *The Matrimonial Trials*, 225–6; Brundage, *Law, Sex, and Christian Society*, 456, 504–5. For a live case in mid-fifteenth-century Florence, in which proof of consummation of marriage was a core issue, see Brucker, *Giovanni and Lusanna*, 55. For another relevant case brought into the archiepsiscopal court of York, see Donahue, *Law, Marriage*, 116–17. See also Charageat, "*Cópula carnal*."

24 Lapus de Castiglionchio Senior, *Allegationes* (Venice, 1571), 30r, alleg. 54, 30r: "Nam per rerum naturam non posset vere probari copula carnalis." On Lapus's career, see Spagnesi, "Dominus Lapus." Lapus's opinion, which dealt with a case of disputed paternity, was frequently cited. See, for

example, Tuschus, *Practicarum conclusionum* (Lyon, 1634–70), vol. 1, 380–1, concl. 105 (*Carnalis copula ex quibus probetur*). See also Philippus Decius's confirming observation made in his *Consilia* (Venice, 1580–1), vol. 2, 226v, cons. 577, no. 2: "quod mulier fuerit carnaliter cognita difficilis probationis: quia concludenter probari non potest, sicut de filatione." None of the jurists made mention of the inspection and display of the nuptial bed sheets for signs (blood and semen) that the marriage had been consummated.

25 As Brundage reminds us, consent always involved intention, so that proving exchange of consent was not easier than proving consummation, since the parties "could always deny that the[ir] words signified interior consent, and in fact they often did so": *Law, Sex, and Christian Society*, 269, n. 59. More broadly, on evaluating the intention of the consenting parties, see Rosier-Catach, *La parole efficace*, 324–51. On lay and customary conceptions of consent, see Cristellon, "Marriage and Consent."

26 Cecchi, "Il matrimonio-contratto"; Werckmeister, "L'apparition de la doctrine."

27 On *lucrum dotis*, see my "Dowry, Domicile, and Citizenship," chap. 8 in this volume. For what follows, see Kirshner, "*Maritus Lucretur Dotem*"; Lepsius, "Die Ehe, die Mitgift," and her "Paolo di Castro," 82–7. See also Bartolus de Saxoferrato's *consilium* on the husband's entitlement to the promised dowry in Gubbio: *Commentaria* (Venice, 1526–9), vol. 9. 42r, cons. 133. However, I have modified my earlier views, having benefited from Donahue's thoughtful critique of my paper ("*Maritus Lucretur Dotem*"), particularly his reasoned rejection of my assertion that a *communis opinio* of jurists that the husband's claim to the dowry was dependent on having consummated his marriage emerged in the late fifteenth century. See Donahue, "Was There a Change in Marriage Law?"

28 I refrain from using "widower," as neither the term nor the concept existed in this period.

29 These issues were addressed in an unsigned *consilium*, dating from the late fourteenth century, that was included among Baldus de Ubaldis's *consilia*. The case, which occurred in Sarteano, addressed the question of whether under the commune's statutes a husband was entitled to one-third of his predeceased wife's dowry, which he had been promised but had never received, even though he (1) had not consummated the marriage, (2) had not introduced her into his household, and (3) had not undertaken the burdens and expenses of marriage ("Queritur utrum vir, qui uxorem non duxit nec cognovit carnaliter nec honera matrimonii supportavit, debeat habere lucrum, de quo loquitur dictum statutum quod incipit 'Si mulier nupta'"). In denying the husband's claim, the jurist pointed out that the statute referred

to a marriage in which the husband and wife were *in fact* living together as a married couple, referred to a dowry that had been received by the husband and not a dowry that had been merely promised, and required the husband to have transferred his wife into his own home before he could claim the one-third. I cite the manuscript in BAV, Barb. lat. 1402, 25r–v; for the printed edition, see Baldus, *Consilia* (Venice, 1575), vol. 4, 107r–v, cons. 467.

30 On "menare" as a signifier of the consummation of marriage, see Klapisch-Zuber, "Zacharie," 160; English translation in "Zacharias," 189–90; Fabbri, *Aleanza matrimoniale*, 182ff. While Donahue ("Was There a Change in Marriage Law," 58) is, of course, correct that medieval jurists distinguished between *ductio ad domum mariti* and *matrimonio consummato carnali copula*, it is also true that civilian jurists, including Baldus de Ubaldis, acknowledged the legal presumption of consummation of marriage arising from the introduction of the bride into the husband's household: see Kirshner, "*Maritus Lucretur Dotem*," 135; Marchetto, *Il divorzio imperfetto*, 199–203; and Philippus Decius, *Consilia* (Venice, 1580–1), vol. 2, 226v, cons. 577, no. 5: "quia si mulier desponsata per verba de presenti accessit ad domum mariti, ita quod fuerit in potestate illam cognoscere, habetur pro cognita, et maritus lucretur dotem."

31 For an overview of this source, see Mordenti, "Les livres"; Cherubini, "I *libri di ricordanze*."

32 See Kirshner, "*Maritus Lucretur Dotem*," 120–3; Fabbri, *Alleanza matrimoniale*, 188; and Cohn, *The Laboring Classes*, 19, who, on the basis of examination of a large sample of notarial records from the fourteenth and fifteenth centuries, indicates that the act of marriage *per verba de presenti* and the husband's act of acknowledging receipt of the dowry "were redacted on the same day or were separated only by several days; they are seldom found separated by more than a month." For similar patterns in Arezzo and Perugia, see Cavallar and Kirshner, "Making and Breaking Betrothal Contracts," chap. 1 in this volume. For Lucca, Meek, "Il matrimonio," 363–6. d'Avray's view (*Medieval Marriage*, 183) that in Italy a considerable time lag existed between marriage *per verba de presenti* and its consummation and that couples commonly had to wait until the dowry had been paid before sleeping with each other is, at least with respect to Florence in the fourteenth and fifteenth centuries, untenable.

33 Kuehn, "Contracting Marriage," 401.

34 See Kirshner, "*Maritus Lucretur Dotem*," 133–6.

35 See Kirshner, "Materials for a Gilded Cage," chap. 3 in this volume, n. 1. For similar regulations in Lombard cities, see Bellomo, *Ricerche sui rapporti*, 202, n. 58.

36 Angelini, ed., *Lo Statuto di Barga*, 52, lib. 1, rubr. 12, *De dote mulieris defuncte marito lucranda vel restituenda.* This scheme is similar to the dotal pacts employed in fourteenth-century Friuli, where the dowry was paid by the bride's family one year after the day on which she was introduced into her husband's household ("infra annum et diem postquam eam matrimonialiter conduxerit domum"). In the event that she predeceased her husband within the first year of marriage, the bride's family obligated itself to pay the husband two-fifths of the promised dowry. See Davide, *Lombardi in Friuli*, 280, 389.

37 Vannucchi, and Lo Conte, eds., *Lo statuto di Uzzano*, 61, lib. 2, rubr. 16, *De dotibus et dotium restitutione et lucro.*

38 Lo Conte and Vannucchi, eds., *Lo statuto di Massa e Cozzile*, 50, lib. 2, rubr. 12, *De eo qui remanet marito de dotibus uxoris premorientis.*

39 For the Latin text, see my "*Li Emergenti Bisogni Matrimoniali*," chap. 2 in this volume, n. 2.

40 See Paulus de Castro, *Consilia* (Frankfurt am Main, 1584), vol. 1, 227–28v, cons. 434; Alexander Tartagnus, *Consilia* (Lyon, 1547–9), vol. 7, 82r–v (quote on 82v), cons. 129.

41 Although husbands retained ownership of these ceremonial items and, as Klapisch-Zuber shows, customarily repossessed them soon after the couple began living together, moralists, jurists, and legislators generally agreed that husbands were nonetheless entitled to compensation for wedding expenses. See Klapisch-Zuber, "Le complexe de Griselda," 200–8; English translation, "The Griselda Complex," 231–41.

42 D'Elia, "Marriage, Sexual Pleasure," 382. Bruni received a dowry of 1,100 florins from his wife, Tommasa di Simone della Fioraia. See Martines, *The Social World*, 199; Giustiniani, "Il testamento," 261.

43 San Bernardino, *Le prediche volgari*, vol. 1, 246 (sermon delivered in 1424 in Florence): "Troverebbonsi migliai di giovani che piglierebbono moglie se non fusse che in vestire la donna conviene si spenda tutta la dota che n'anno e talvolta più!" Cf. Rainey, *Sumptuary Legislation*, 470.

44 The husband's claim to the Monte dowry on his wife's predecease was not expressly affirmed by the legislation establishing the fund or in subsequent enactments. In practice, the officials of the Dowry Fund approved the husband's claim to his predeceased wife's Monte dowry so long as the period applicable to her deposit had elapsed and so long as the couple had consummated the marriage.

45 Among the examples: Menichetti, ed., *Lo statuto vecchio del comune di Gubbio* (1338), 86–7, lib. 2, rubr. 39, *De parte dotis applicanda maritis et de alimentis uxori prestandis* (addition of 1376); Milan, Biblioteca Ambrosiana,

M107 suss., *Statutorum communis Mantuae, liber secundus* (1404), 473r, rubr. *De dote per maritum lucranda uxore defuncta matrimonio sine liberis*; *Liber statutorum Civitatis Castelli* (1376), 26r, lib. 2, cap. 49, *Maritus lucretur dimidiam dotis uxore praemoriente matrimonio sine liberis*; Regni, ed., Bevagna, 66, lib. 2, rubr. *Quando mulier moritur maritata sine filiis tertia pars dotium remaneat penes virum*; *Statuta civitatis Pisauri noviter impressa* (1412), 38r–v, lib. 2, rubr. 95, *Maritus lucretur dimidiam dotis uxore praedefuncta sine liberis matrimonio iam consumato; ante vero matrimonium consumatum quartum partem*; *Statutorum et reformationum magnifice civitatis Senogallie, volumen*, 25v, rubr. 60, *De lucro dotis faciendo per virum muliere praedecedente in matrimonio et de rebus eidem mulieri transmissis in matrimonio nondum per carnalem copulam consummato*; *Ius municipale Vincentinum* (1425), 153v, lib. 4, rubr. *De dotibus mulierum*; Buzzi, ed., *Lo statuto del comune di Viterbo*, 142–3, lib. 2, rubr. 83, *De lucro dotis*; Magi, ed., *Radicofani* (1441), 110, lib. 2, rubr. *In quanta parte succeda l'uomo alla donna*; Ascheri and Mancuso, eds., *Abbadia San Salvatore*, 178, dist. II, rubr. 47, *Del guadagno della dote e parte d'essa da acquistarsi dal marito per la morte della moglie*: "E le cose che son dette di sopra di guadagno, habbino luogo in matrimonio perfetto e consumato per copula carnale o per condur la moglie in casa del marito doppo che haveranno cominciato ad abitare insieme matrimonialmente e non altrimenti"; for Busseto's statutes (1429), *Statuta Pallavicinia*, 54, lib. 1, rubr. 44, *De dote per maritum lucranda sine filiis praemorientis*: "Statutum et ordinamentum est, quod si aliquis subditus vel suppositus praefati Domini nostri acceperit aliquam in uxorem, eam que in domum suam duxerit et matrimonium perfecerint, vel communi opinione vicinorum habeatur pro perfecto, et pro marito et uxore reputentur, et contingat ipsam mulierum praemori sine filiis, maritus lucretur totam dotem datam vel promissam." For Carpi, Modena, and Mirandola, see Kirshner, "*Maritus Lucretur Dotem*," 113.

46 Klapisch-Zuber, "Zacharie"; English translation in "Zacharias."

47 None of the forty or so *libri di famiglia* or *ricordanze* that I have examined mentioned bloodstained linens as a sign of the marriage's consummation, suggesting that confirmation of the bride's virginity did not come into play in Florentine nuptial practice. For a fascinating exploration of the bride's corporal topography, with early modern examples of the revirgination of women before marriage, see Finucci, "The Virgin's Body."

48 *Libro di famiglia* of Bartolomeo di Filippo Valori, BNCF, Fondo Panciatichiano, vol. 134, 7r, 8r; now edited in Polizzotto and Kovesi, eds., *Memorie*, 72, 73, 76. Beyond Florence, the interconnection of consummation of marriage and the husband's receipt of the dowry was

memorialized in the *libro di ricordi* of Bartolomeo Morone, a Milanese Jurist. See Covini, ed., *Il libro di ricordi*, 71, no. 15 (year:1416).

49 *Libro di famiglia* of Virgilio d'Andrea Adriani, CS, ser. 2a, vol. 21, 66v: "Questo dì di gennaio 1488, chol nome di dDio e della Vergine Maria e di tutti e Sancti del Paradiso, io Virgilio doctore sopradecto maritai la decta Alexandra al nobile e generoso giovane Ruberto di Piero di Ruberto Gianfilgliazzi. E oltre decti fiorini 1000, gli decti fiorini dugento d'oro contanti e chosì gli promessi tra danari e donora. E di poi a dì otto di febraio 1488 detto, n'andò a marito col nome di dDio. E fecionsi le nozze in chasa mia, che quivi si consumò il matrimonio, a ogni mia spesa."

50 *Libro di famiglia* of Giovanni di Girolamo Buongirolami, CS, ser. 2a, vol. 23, 30r: "Ricordo come questo dì d'aprile 1499 come colla gratia di Dio io menai la Gostanza mia donna et seco consumai il matrimonio in casa d'Antonio mio suocero, il che ad (MS: al) laudem Dei." See also *libro di famiglia* of Bindacci de' Cerchi, Archivio Cerchi, vol. 319, 26v, where he recorded that on 26 April 1498 his son-in-law consummated the marriage with his daughter Marietta in his home – "la [Marietta] a menò e chonsumò il matrimonio in chasa mia a mia spesa" – and that on 27 April he executed a *confessio* for Marietta's Monte dowry.

51 Klapisch-Zuber, "Zacharie"; Witthoft, "Marriage Rituals," 45–6.

52 *Libro di famiglia* of Marco di Parente, CS, ser. 2a, vol. 17 bis, 72r, 79r. His daughter Gostanza and Filippo di Lorenzo Buondelmonti consummated their marriage on 1 June 1472. Her father sent Gostanza "a casa di detto Filippo e consumorono il matrimonio e allora fu guadagnata la dota fatta in sul Monte." His daughter Marietta and Francesco di Giannozzo degli Alberti consummated their marriage on 13 April 1475.

53 MC, 3734, 64v. Similar cases are found in MC, 3735, 3v (account of Lisabetta di Matteo di Bartolomeo da Nipozzano): "non aveva consumato il matrimonio quando ebe detta dote per cui il padre fu condemnato in fiorini 500"; MC, 3746, 42v (account of Maria di Lorenzo di Luca Naccetti).

54 NA, 6136, 30r: "deliberaverunt quod Baldus supradictus habeat dotem suam, recepta fide quod dictus Baldus consumavit dictum matrimonium."

55 NA, 6138, s.f. (1 Feb. 1453/4).

56 NA, 4820, 79r: "Calvacante antedictus coram me notario et testibus infrascriptis dixit, asseruit et ad sancta Dei Evangelia iuravit super animam suam tactis corporaliter scripturis, quod ipse Calvacante die XXVI mensis aprilis proxime preteriti ducit dictam dominam Dianoram uxorem suam in domum dicti Guasparis Corbini positam in capella Sancti Simonis Porte Maris, et cum ipsa matrimonium consumavit dicta die carnali copula inter eos subsecuta et omnia et singula fecisse et perfecisse que ad consumationem

dicti matrimonii requiruntur." Additional examples are found in NA 4819, 23r (1 June 1481), 36r (29 Jan. 1482/3), 39r (1 Mar. 1482/3); NA, 4820, 25v (5 Apr. 1483), 54r (23 Apr. 1483), 72r (10 June 1483), 113r (6 Oct. 1483), 177r (23 Nov. 1483), 178r (30 Nov. 1483), 187r (24 Dec. 1483), 246r (8 Feb. 1483/4).

57 NA, 4820, 68r: "Io ser Francesco di Piero prete et cappellano nella pieve da Prato et cappellano della chiesa di Sancto Piero Foralli da Prato. Fo fede a voi signori uficiali dell' Monte chome mona Thomasa figliuola di Giovanni di Pavolo d'Iachopo ò rimessa in sancto in decta chiesa di Sancto Piero Foralli et consumato matrimonio chon Martino di Zelone di Porta Lione da Prato, et però ò facta questa fede di mia propria mano, oggi questo dì 10 d'ochosto [d'agosto] 1482." Other examples are found in NA, 4820, 101r (20 July 1483), 154r (16 Nov. 1483); NA 4819, 60r (17 Apr. 1483).

58 Dig. 23. 3. 2, *Rei publicae interest.*

59 The *confessio dotis* was omitted from the notarized contracts listed by Ranerius de Perusio and Salatiele, major notarial theorists of the thirteenth century. See Rainerius de Perusio, *Die Ars Notariae*, III/2, 68; Salatiele, *Ars Notarie*, 15–17. As far as I can tell from the wording of the relevant Florentine statutes redacted in 1415, there was no requirement that the *confessio dotis* be prepared by a public notary. *Statuta populi et communis Florentiae*, 1:156–9, lib. 2, rubr. 61, *De dote et donatione restituendis, et exigendi modo*; ibid., 160, rubr. 63, *De tacita hypotheca bonorum viri pro dote ...*

60 Baldus to *c. Ex parte vestra* (X 1. 4. 10), in *Commentaria* (Venice, 1595), 59r, no. 10. Under Roman civil law, the transformation of a concubine into a wife was evidenced by the drawing up of dotal instruments: Castello, "Lo strumento dotale."

61 Scalfati, ed., *Un formulario notarile*, 83–4, *De promissione et iuramento dandi aliquam in futurum in sponsam uxorem sub arris sponsalitiis*, and 51–3; De Angelis et al., eds., *I notai fiorentini*, vol. 3, 49–50, 62, 125, 132–3. See also Zdekauer, "La confessione," and his "Le doti." For early examples of the Florentine *confessio dotis*, see Mosiici and Sznura, eds., *Palmerio di Corbizo*, 244; Scalfati, ed., *Un formulario notarile*, 51–3. In Pisa, the writing requirement for dowry contracts was established early, in 1146. See Storti Storchi, *Intorno ai Costituti*, 74. For Lucca, see Meyer, ed., *Ser Ciabattus*, 195, 197, 347.

62 The earliest references to the *confessio dotis* that I have found in Florentine *libri di famiglia* are in Vitale, ed., *Il quaderno*, 19, 35, 40, 57. For a nuanced analysis of references to dotal guarantees in Florentine *libri fi famiglia*, see now Chabot, *La dettes des familles*, 135–86.

63 *Libro di famiglia* of Paolo di Lapo Niccolini, Florence, Archivio Niccolini da Camugliano, Registri antichi, no. 4, 142r: "A dì 3 di settenbre 1465, io Paolo Nicholini e il sopradetto Lodovicho, mio figluolo, chonfessammo avere avuto e ricevuto dal Comune di Firenze over<o> dagli'ufìcali del monte, per dota della detta Checha [di Stefano Segni], fiorini dumilasei s. 10 a oro, i quali sodai chome s'usa." The passage was misread by Niccolini di Camugliano in her still informative book *The Chronicles*, 153. Paolo had consummated his marriage on 1 September in the house of his brother-in-law, Bernardo Segni.

64 BNCF, Fondo Panciatichiano, vol. 134, 2r (year: 1519); Polizzotto and Kovesi, eds., *Memorie*, 125; MC, 3750, 92r.

65 BNCF Fondo Panciatichiano, vol. 134, 9r (year: 1478); Polizzotto and Kovesi, eds., *Memorie*, 79.

66 CS, ser. 2, vol. 17a bis, 68v–69r (4 June 1472): "Filippo confessò la dota di f. 1166 ⅔ larghi per f. 1400 di sugello e obligò se' e sue herede per beni in tutto et sodorono detta dota Lorenzo suo padre per f. 500 larghi per valuta di f. 600 di sugello e Antonio e Simone frategli di detto Filippo e figliuoli di detto Lorenzo sodorono detta dota chiaschuno, et obbligaronsi di licenza di Lorenzo loro padre, benché fussino tutti mancepati."

67 Messer Francesco's name does not appear in the city's registers of emancipation, on which see n. 70 below.

68 AGN, 129, 37r: "Dinanzi a voi, messer proconsulo e signori consoli dell'arte de' Giudici e Notai della città di Firenze, reverentemente expone e dice Giovanni di Licho della Chasa, cittadino fiorentino, che già sono anni due et più il detto Giovanni maritò una sua figliuola a messer Francesco di ser Piero Pucetti, cittadino et advocato fiorentino, et dettegli per dotta della decta fanciulla fiorini cinquecentoventicinque d'oro. La quale dota il decto ser Piero promise al decto Giovanni confexare, sodare, promettere et sodare insieme col decto messer Francesco in ogni caso s'avesse a restituere, rendere o consegnare, et secondo l'usanza et chostume della città di Firenze. Et più volte richiesto il decto ser Piero che gli debba confexarla, promettere et sodarla, chome promise e rimasene d'acordo, sempre à cessato e cessa volero fare, contro la voluntà del decto Giovanni et preiuditio della decta sua figliuola, donna del decto messer Francesco. Et però adomanda che per voi, messer lo proconsulo et consoli et vostra sententia, si dichiari, pronuntii tutte le predette chose essere state et essere vere, et condempniate il decto ser Piero a confexare, promettere et sodare la decta dota secondo la consuetudine, forma et statuti della città di Firenze, observando intorno acciò tutte le solempnità et cautele che in simili contracti si costuma et richiede." Ser Piero was

then cited to appear before the consuls of the guild. This case was first brought to light by Martines, *Lawyers and Statecraft*, 19.

69 Comparable percentages are found in Lovere, a small country town near Bergamo, where 77 percent of new husbands acknowledged and guaranteed dowries without their fathers between 1453 and 1518. See Silini, "Famiglia, società e patrimonio," 76.

70 This calculation is based on matching the names of the 291 husbands who acknowledged the dowry with their fathers against the names and dates of emancipation recorded in the registers of emancipation maintained by the city and preserved in Notificazioni di atti di emancipazione, nos. 1–17. By law, all acts of emancipation in fifteenth-century Florence were required to be registered with the Signoria. As Kuehn has shown in *Emancipation*, 77ff., apart from occasional omissions, the emancipations recorded in the city'sregisters capture their actual occurrence in Florence. A computer-generated list of these data contained in the registers was generously furnished to me by David Herlihy and Thomas Kuehn. I was able to match only thirty-nine names, and of these only twenty husbands had been emancipated before they acknowledged the dowry jointly with their fathers. Accordingly, I have inferred that 271 husbands, at the time they acknowledged their Monte dowries with their fathers, were unemancipated.

71 Under Florentine law, unemancipated sons matriculated in a guild were permitted to engage in business and credit transactions without their father's express consent. This exemption did not extend to the execution of the *confessio dotis* and related guarantees. See Kuehn, *Emancipation*, 42–8, 127–8.

72 Bartolus to *l. Si cum dotem*, § *Transgrediamur* (Dig. 24. 3. 22. 12), in *Commentaria* (Venice, 1526–9), 17r–v: "Respondeo et dico quod sufficit quod pater simpliciter consentiat et per hoc obligatur ipse et bona. Pro hoc do regulam quod ubicunque cogitur pater consentire, et se obligare simpliciter, consentiendo se obligat."

73 For an example, see the *approbatio confessionis dotis* given by Monte officials to Bartolomeo di Filippo Valori (NA, 6138, s.f., 18 Sept. 1453). Born on 31 August 1436, Bartolomeo was seventeen at the time of his *confessio*. His father had died in 1438.

74 Herlihy, "Deaths, Marriages, Births," 143.

75 Cod. 6. 61. 1, *Cum venerandae*; *Glossa ordinaria* to Cod. 6. 61. 1 (*casus*) (Venice, 1591), 1049a: "Lex ista hoc addit quod quicquid lucratur filius in potestate constitutus ab uxore vel filia a marito, totum acquitatur patri quantum ad usumfructum."

76 For example, NA, 5345, 401r–v (18 Aug. 1451): "Carolus olim Angeli Filippi ser Iohannis Pandolfini, civis florentinus, et Filippus eius filius et cum consensu, verbo, licentia etc. dicti Caroli sui patris presentis etc., et quilibet eorum se in solidum et in totum obligando, fuerunt confessi etc. in dotem etc. a Simone olim Francisci ser Gini de Ginoris, cive florentino, dante et solvente pro dote etc. domine Smeralde filie Simonis et uxoris Deo dante dicte Filippi, florenos auri mille quadringentos unum, soldos duos et denarios decem ad aurum hoc modo, videlicet: pro dicto Simone ab officialibus montis Comunis Florentie, dantibus et solventibus de denariis montis puellarum et pro parte dotis dicte domine Smeralde, florenos mille unum auri, soldos duos et denarios decem ad aurum; et pro dicto Simone a Bernardo Uguccionis et sotiis, in pecunia numerata, florenos ducentos auri, et a dicto Simone in rebus mobilibus et donamentis inter ipsos comuni concordia extimatis, florenos ducentos auri: et sic in totum florenos mille quadringentos unum, soldos duos et denarios decem ad aurum."

77 Niccolini's opinion is in BNCF, Magl., XXIX, 173, 125r–26v, 125v: "Cui fundamento responderi potest: primo, quod in casu proposito, non cessat hec ratio (MS: ratior), nisi pater obligaretur pro dote, ut probatum est, filius non inveniret commode uxorem in civitate ista ... Unde in proposito dico quod ideo filius invenit uxorem quia pater consensit, per quem consensum videtur etiam consentire ad ea que erant per patres consueta fieri in civitate Florentie, et sic ad se obligandum, et quod alias non repperisset ipse Pierantonius uxorem."

78 Biggart and Castanias, "Collateralized Social Relations," quote on 473–4.

79 The finding supports Bellomo's and Kuehn's observations that emancipation did not dissolve the bonds uniting father and son: Bellomo, *Problemi di diritto*, 207; Kuehn, *Emancipation*, 47–8. Note, too, the confirming observations of Herlihy, "The Florentine Merchant Family," 199–200. Gardner, *Family and "Familia,"* 12–13, stresses that legal emancipation provided new opportunities "for mutual benefaction" between *emancipati* and their former *patresfamilias* in the early Roman Empire. Legally emancipated adult sons in the first centuries of the Roman Empire, in contrast to those in Renaissance Florence, tended to establish separate households (ibid., 67–74). The same pattern of filial independence is found in early modern Turin by Cavallo, "O padre."

80 Given the notorious difficulties in accurately matching names from different sources, I have limited my analysis to husbands with surnames in order to reduce false matches.

81 Monte Comune o delle Graticole, copie del catasto (1480) dell'Archivio del Monte. For her expert assistance in identifying *Monte delle doti* husbands in the *catasto* of 1480, I am grateful to dottoressa Gabriella Battista.
82 *Libro di famiglia* of Paolo di Lapo Niccolini, 142r (25 Sept. 1465): "A dì 25 di novembre 1465 [MS: 1466] io Paolo Nicholini manceppai e dalla mia paterna potestà liberai Lodovicho, mio figluolo legittimo e naturale"; Niccolini di Camugliano, *The Chronicles*, 154–5; Kuehn, *Emancipation*, 72–3.
83 NAE, 12, 39v (10 Jan. 1488/9).
84 The reasons why emancipated sons tended to remain in their fathers' households are discussed by Kuehn, *Emancipation*, 49ff.
85 See NAE, 7, 211r (6 Apr. 1463); NA, 15037, 124r (22 June 1476); Catasto (1480), 54, 253r.
86 Kuehn, *Emancipation*, 80, 95, 164.
87 Herlihy, "Deaths, Marriages, Births," 143. The age at first marriage, computed from the *catasto* of 1427, was 27.4 in the secondary cities of Pisa, Pistoia, Arezzo, Prato, Cortona, and Volterra; 26.4 in the smaller towns; and 25.6 in the Florentine *contado*. Using the same data from the 1427 *catasto*, Rebecca Emigh has computed that "more than half of fathers were dead when their offspring reached age twenty-five. By the time their offspring reached the age of thirty, more than 60 percent of fathers had died." See her "Property Devolution," 400.
88 Herlihy and Klapisch-Zuber, *Tuscans and Their Families*, 331ff.
89 Kirshner, "A Question of Trust."
90 For exhortations to steer clear of damage-producing risks borne by guarantors, see Paolo da Certaldo, *Libro di buoni costumi*, 89, 135; Morelli, *Ricordi*, 238; Petrarca, *Remedies for Fortune*, III, bk. II, *Remedies for Adversity*, no. 14 (*Surety Bonds*), 55–7.
91 Examples: NA, 5345, 261v (11 Sept. 1448): guarantee given by Chosa, widowed mother of Filippo di Bastiano Lippi, to Smerelda di Cristoforo, for part of her daughter-in-law's dowry; NA 6149, s.f. (8 July 1474): guarantee given by Dianora, widowed mother of Agostino di Giovanni, and Tancia, his maternal aunt, to Francesca di Sassolino Sassolini; NA, 5347, 155r (2 Aug. 1482): guarantee given by Lena, widowed mother of Mariano di Francesco Masini; NA, 9139, 105rv (21 Apr. 1494): guarantee given by Lena, widowed mother of Francesco di Stefano, to Bartolomea di Domenico. Lena's suretyship and the *confessio dotis* performed by Francesco and his brother Domenico occurred on the same day.
92 Examples: NA, 6136, 36v (24 Oct. 1452): guarantee given by Niccolò di Bartolomeo Gualterotti, on behalf of his brother Lorenzo, to Clara di

Tommaso Alberti; NA 7910, 177v (3 and 6 Oct. 1453): guarantees given by Benedetto and Battista di Francesco Strozzi, on behalf of their brother Vanni, to Dora di Gianozzo Pandolfini; NA 5346, 176r–77v (25 Aug. 1467): guarantees given by Bindaccio di Francesco Boninsegni, on behalf of his brother Ridolfo, to Gostanza Ginori; ibid., 129v (4 May 1481): guarantees given by Tommaso di Giovanni Franceschi, on behalf of his brother Luca, to Gostanza di Cecco Altoviti; NA 9140, 186r (13 June 1506): guarantee given by Giovanni di Lodovico Bacherelli, on behalf of his brother Prospero, to Piera di Giovanni Bartoli.

93 For paternal uncles, see NA, 6132, 43v (1 Dec. 1444); NA 5345, 312v–16r (12 May 1450); for cousins, see NA 7910, 184r (12 Feb. 1453/4).

94 *Libro di famiglia* of Carlo di Niccolò Strozzi, CS, ser. 4a, vol. 74, 48v. Carlo acknowledged his dowry, 1,100 florins of which came from the Dowry Fund, on 18 January 1496; his mother, Francesca, guaranteed his dowry on 5 February of the same year.

95 CS, ser. 2a, vol. 17 bis, 72r, 74r. Maria's dowry consisted of 1,200 florins from the Dowry Fund, plus 200 in cash and *donora* from her father. In another example, Antonio di ser Battista Bartolomei recorded "chome a dì 11 ovvero 12 luglio 1455 sodai a Bartolomeo mio fratello per parte di sua dota" (*Libro di famiglia* of Antonio di ser Battista d'Antonio Bartolomei, Acquisti e Doni, vol. 11, 4r).

96 CS, ser. 3a, 41, vol. 5, 462r–v (a draft of an opinion written by Antonius de Stroziis in 1518).

97 *Statuta populi et communis Florentiae*, vol. 2, 114, lib. 4, rubr. 11, *Tenens bona de dote, vel alia, licet non appareat instrumentum solvat gabella*. The contract tax on dowries in Florence and Siena was introduced at the end of the thirteenth century. See Rainey, *Sumptuary Legislation*, vol. 1, 45; Bowsky, *The Finance*, 154. For its application, see Nardi, *Mariano Sozzini*, 118, doc. 9.

98 See also NA, 6132–50 (Dini, Niccolò di Michele, 1444–75); NA, 15038 (Niccolò di Antonio di Benedetto, 1475–80); NA, 7780 (Fortini, Bartolomeo, 1493–9); NA, 5283 (Ciardi, Lorenzo, 1522–5); NA, 13386 (Matteo di Giovanni da Falgano, 1538–41).

99 The new version of the *confessio dotis* was codified in the most celebrated of Florentine formularies, *Formularium diversorum contractuum secundum stilum et modum Florentinum*, 51v–53r, "Confessio data in pecunia." The *Formularium* was compiled by Lorenzo Vanelli and originally published in Florence ca. 1487. The copy of the *Formularium* cited here, which was published in Venice in 1506, is in ASF.

100 Regarding the inevitability of the contract tax on the Monte dowry, Paolo Niccolini remarked that "si usa oggi paghare [la ghabella] per tutti delle dote che sono in sul monte." See *Libro di famiglia* of Paolo di Lapo Niccolini, 142r (3 Sept. 1465).

101 The Monte dowries of husbands who were legal residents of communities located in the *contado* and *distretto* were exempt from local taxes. Tanzini, *Alle origini*, 133.

102 Molho, *Marriage Alliance*, 57–8.

103 The appraisal of *donora* at less than their real value was a standard tactic to avoid violating the monetary limits placed on *donora* by sumptuary laws as well as to reduce the husband's contract tax payable on the dowry. On *donora*, see Klapisch-Zuber, "Le complexe de Griselda," 185–213; English translation, "The Griselda Complex"; Musacchio, "The Bride and Her *Donora*."

104 Guicciardini, *Ricordi*, 86. For Maria Salviati's partially illegible Monte account, see MC, 3746, 123r.

105 BNCF, Fondo Panciatichiano , vol. 134, 9r. The passage is transcribed by Molho, *Marriage Alliance*, 309, n. 29, and now in Polizzotto and Kovesi, eds., *Memorie*, 79–80.

106 Another instance of husbandly oversolicitousness is found in the accounts of Matteo di Simone Strozzi, where he recorded the receipt and *confessio* of the dowry brought by his wife, Alessandra Macinghi, who was around fourteen years old at the time of their marriage on 10 June 1422. For the date of Alessandra's marriage, see the introduction to Gregory, *Selected Letters*, 3. In addition, Matteo recorded that he expressly made Alessandra his creditor for the dowry. Presciently anticipating that he would predecease her, he wanted to assure that upon his death his heirs would restore the dowry to his widow. CS, ser. 5a, 11 (Debitori e creditori A. di Matteo di Simone Strozzi, 1424–34), 94r: "La Lexandra mia donna e figluola di Filippo di Nicholò Macigni de' avere f. milleseciento d'oro per altrettanti posto io Matheo abbia ad dare [MS: avere] in questo c. 14: sono per la dota di lei, ricievetti in questo modo, cioè f. 1400 da Giovachino e Andrea e Charlo di Nicholò Macigni, tutori della heredità di Filipo suo padre e a lloro fratello, e f. 200 in aredio di donora, e chosì chonfessai adì 4 di giugno 1422, charta fatta per mano di ser Stefano di [lacuna] notaio all' arte del chambio. Soderanno detta dotta Lionardo e Piero di Filippo e Simone mio padre. Fonnela creditricie perché quando a dDio piaciessi chiamare prima l'anima mia che la sua, gli' à avere dove le piaccia adomandare – f. 1600." These guarantees served their purpose, for in 1440, after Matteo's death, his heirs

transferred to Alessandra properties equivalent to her full dowry. See Crabb, *The Strozzi*, 49.

107 *Libro di famiglia* of Doffo di Nepo Spini, CS, ser. 2a, vol. 13, 64v: "A dì 14 aprile anno detto [1428] in casa sua confessò di dota f. quattrocento d'oro ... E promisemi il detto Francescho che f. dugento che fa dota alla detta Nanna, farmene chiarezza quando fosse a Vingnone. E per cagione del catasto e della ghabella non volle confessare più." On Doffo di Nepo Spini, see Tripoldi, *Gli Spini*, 57–85. For a tax-evading scheme involving Dietisalvi Dietisalvi's acknowledgment of Margherita Ginori's dowry in 1429, see Kent, *Household and Lineage*, 92–3.

108 *Libro di famiglia* of Manno di Cambio Petrucci, CS, ser. 2a, vol. 17, 32r: "E rimanemo d'achordo non sodare detta dota. E no' l'ò sodato, e no' l'ò a sodare." In an earlier example, Paolo Sassetti recorded that when he arranged the marriage of his niece, Lena, to Lodovicho di Filippo Tolosini, in 1384, the dowry was paid to her husband without any *confessio* (*senza niuna confessagione*), presumably for the purpose of evading the contract tax. See *Libro di famiglia* of Paolo di Alessandro Sassetti, CS, ser. 2a, vol. 4, 69v; transcribed by Cavallar and Kirshner, "Making and Breaking Betrothal Contracts," chap. 1 in this volume.

109 On the probative value of Florence's fiscal records, see Kirshner, "Custom, Customary Law," 170ff.

110 PR, 151, 271r–72r. For other examples, see PR, 129, 113r–14r (28 Aug. 1438); PR 138, 31v–32v (22 Apr. 1447), 67r–68r (2 June 1447), 129r–30r (30 Aug. 1447), 223r–24r (26 Feb. 1447/8); PR 154, 52r–53v (27 Apr. 1463); PR 160, 151v–52r (28 Sept. 1469), 169v–70v (20 Oct. 1469); PR 161, 260v–61v (16 Feb. 1470/1). Asserting that the *confessiones* guaranteeing restoration of their dowries were lost, numerous widows petitioned the Arte dei Giudici e Notai to verify that their *confessiones* had in fact been redacted. See, for example, AGN, 94, 6v (5 Sept. 1390), 36r–v (12 Oct. 1390), 40r–41r (25 Oct. 1390), 49v–50r (12 Nov. 1390); AGN, 96, 16v–17r (1 June 1394), 18v–19r (3 June 1394), 31r–33v (29 June 1394); AGN, 12 (21 Mar. 1442/3).

111 For example, the officials authorized payment of 400 florins on behalf of Gostanza di Luigi da Castiglionchio to her husband, Torello di Piero Torelli, "in quantum fuerit consummatum matrimonium et dos confessata et soluta ghabella. Loysius pater dicte Costantie consensit"; MC, 1124, 4v. Further examples are found in ibid., 10v.

112 *Libro di famiglia* of Francesco di Tommaso Giovanni, CS, ser. 2a, vol. 16bis, 4r: "La Nanna [di Francesco] andò a marito martedì a dì 8 di febraio 1445. Di poi a dì di detto esso Giovanni [di Filippo Arrigucci] confessò aver ricevuto fiorini mille d'oro, cioè fiorini 504 in sul Monte e quali diceva in lei

et io detti licentia se gli dessino e fiorini 500 tra contanti e donora"; *Libro di famiglia* of Bernardo di Stoldo di Luca Rinieri, Conventi Soppressi, 95 (San Francesco), vol. 212, 169r: "E detto dì 9 di dicenbre [1483] fo ricordo chome fino sabato a dì VIIII di novenbre prossimo passato detti licenza al monte che fussino dati a detto Gentile [Bernardo's son-in-law] la sua dota di fiorini mille di sugello v'aveva su e detto dì quivi al monte la sodò e insieme cho' llui Bartolomeo di Tomaso Sassetti, suo padre"; 170r: "E di poi a dì 28 di novenbre detto 1485 detti licenza al Monte che dessino al detto messer Nicchołò [Bernardo's son-in-law, and son of Simone di Giovanni Altoviti] e fiorini mille di monte e tanto chonfessò"; *Libro di famiglia* of Giovanni di Girolami Buongirolami, CS, ser. 2a, vol. 23, 130v: "Et detto dì [28 June 1499] Antonio [di Bernardo Ridolfi] mio suocero licentiò fiorini 800 larghi di Monte di dote guadagniate in nome di detta Gostanza"; *Libro di famiglia* of Carlo di Lorenzo Strozzi, CS, ser. 3a, vol. 138, 3v: "Richordo come a dì XIII di giungnio 1494 Simone d'Antonio Chanigiani [Carlo's brother-in-law], cho' licentia d'Antonio suo padre, chonfessò avere ricevuto fiorini di sugello"; *Libro di famiglia* of Carlo di Niccolò Strozzi, CS, ser. 3a, vol. 44, 49v: "Marchione mio suocero mi dette overo mi fece dare licenza al Monte [5 Feb. 1495/6]."

113 For fathers, see MC, 3746, 32r (account of Santa di Bartolomeo Setterelli), 34v (Lucrezia di Priore), 191r (Ginevra di Bastiano Albertinelli), 192r (Agata d'Antonio di Francesco), 192v (Piera di Mariotto Dello Steccuto), 251r (Lucrezia di Bernardo de' Medici); MC, 3751, 112v (Faustina di ser Piero); MC, 3754, 51r (Bartolomea di Girolamo Anselmi). For fathers and brothers together, see 3746, 3r (Bartolomea di Zanobi di Michele), 194r (Spinetta di Macallo Macalli). For brothers alone, see MC, 3739,117r (Castora di Giovanni di Lando da Cascina); MC, 3746, 35r (Diamante di Domenico d'Orlando), 37v (Pippa di Francesco Pasquini); MC, 3747, 183r (Lucrezia d'Antonio Acciaiuoli); MC, 3751, 41r (Bartolomea di Luigi Velluti), 112r (Dianora di Giorgio Rinieri), 113r (Maddalena di Bastiano Marraffi), 193r (Nanna di Gabriello di Marco); MC, 3753, 10r (Lorenza di Piero Pitti); MC, 3754, 114r (Maria di Bartolomeo Pedoni). Occasionally, the wife's paternal uncle provided consent: for example, MC, 3756, 193r (Cristofana d'Antonio di Ciucante da Gambassi); MC, 3747, 65r (Dianora di Cristofano Bracci).

114 MC, 3746, 35v (account of Dianora di Domenico di Latino Palmieri): "presente detto Domenico di Latino, suocero di detto Giovanni"; 37v (Pippa di Francesco Pasquini): "presente Pagholo e Zanobi di Francesco di Pagholo."

115 As did the artist Benozzo Gozzoli during the period he was working on the frescoes for the Campo Santo in Pisa; NA, 4819, 178rv (25 Nov.

1483): "Et viso qualiter dictus Petrus dictam dominam Bartholomeam [Gozzoli's daughter] in eius uxorem legiptimam desponsavit, ut patet per cartam rogatam et strictam a me Karolo notario ... et sciens et cognoscens dictus mihi Benozius qualiter dictus Petrus eius gener et vir et maritus legiptimus dicte domine Bartholomee fuit et est fide et facultatibus ydoneus ad habendum et recipiendum dictam infrascriptam dotem et cognoscens et sciens dictam dominam Bartholomeam fuisse et esse bene cautam et securam de dote et iuribus dotalibus suis supra notatis in omni casu et eventu ipsius dotis et antefacti restituende ... Id circo per hoc presens publicum instrumentum dedit et concessit plenam licentiam et liberam potestatem et auctoritatem dominis officialibus montis civitatis Florentie ... dandi, solvendi ac numerandi dicto Petro viro ... seu ipsius procuratori." Other examples: NA 4820, 89r (24 June 1483), 93r (17 June 1483), 98r (8 Aug. 1483), 113r (6 Oct. 1483), 147r–v (18 Oct. 1483), 175r (3 Dec. 1483), 202r (27 Jan. 1483/4). In another example, Corso di Matteo Corsini, the paternal uncle of Marietta Corsini, Niccolò Machiavelli's wife, on 22 August 1501, gave permission through his procurators for the release of his niece's Monte dowry. See Kirshner and Molho, "Niccolò Machiavelli's Marriage."

116 MC, 3746, 33r (account of Lena di Romolo Cafaggi da Rovezzano); MC, 3747, 67r (Caterina di Damiano d'Antonio); MC, 3753, 162r (Maria di Giovanbattista Pintelli); MC, 3754, 115r (Argentina di Giovanni Ansaldi); MG, 10, 48v (Taddea di Lorenzo di ser Pagolo Dietaiuti). Many more examples from the mid-sixteenth century in MG, 22, 46v, 50r–76v, 178r, 160r–74v; MG, 24, 50r–55r; MG, 25, 35r–39v, 112r; MG, 26, 40r–43v, 59r, 150r–64r; MG, 954, 50r; MG, 957, 379r. Over 40 percent of the wives' fathers would have been dead before the husband appeared at the office of the Monte to collect his dowry. See Emigh, "Property Devolution."

117 PR, 132, 6v–9r (24 Mar. 1441/2).

118 MC, 1121, 1r (13 Sept. 1446), 78r (29 Oct. 1446); NA, 6139, 34v (9 May 1454); MG, 954, 517r (Sept. 1480); MG, 957, 379r (May 1484).

119 Balìe, 27, 147rv. This measure was incorporated into the statutes of the *Ufficiali de' pupilli*: Morandini, "Statuti e ordinamenti," 544. The first example I have found of an *approbatio* granted by the *Ufficio de' pupilli* is in NA, 6140, s.f. (24 Oct. 1454).

120 NA, 7910, 172v–73r.

121 On the secondary market in claims to overdue Monte dowries, see Kirshner and Klerman, "The Seven Percent Fund of Renaissance Florence," chap. 5, in this volume.

122 Though unusally extensive, the paper trail in Florence was not unique. Restoration of dowries in Venice was also based on highly probative

documents, in particular, *securitatis carte* and *instrumenta dotis*, which were functional equivalents of the *confessio dotis*. See Linda Guzzetti's informative and instructive "Dowries," 430–73.

5. The Seven Percent Fund of Renaissance Florence

1 See the references in the following note and the studies of Tracy, *A Financial Revolution*; Lorenzen-Schmidt, "Umfang und Dynamik"; Baum, "Annuities"; and Lane, "Public Debt."

2 See Molho, *Florentine Public Finances*; and his "L'amministrazione del debito pubblico"; Conti, *L'imposta diretta.*

3 See now Kirshner, "Encumbering Private Claims."

4 According to the accounts kept by Bindaccio di Michele de' Cerchi, prices of Monte credits fluctuated between 12 and 16 percent of face value in 1481 and remained in the range of 10 to 12 percent from 1483 through 1485. Many of these transactions involved claims to future as well as to overdue payments of interest, and options to buy credits for a set price at a future date. See Archivio Cerchi, 315 and 317. For a description of Cerchi's banking activities, see Goldthwaite, "Local Banking."

5 Kirshner and Molho, "The Dowry Fund"; Molho, "Investimenti nel Monte"; and now his magisterial *Marriage Alliance*.

6 PR, 142, 171v–72r (18 July 1451).

7 PR, 166, 1r–7r (21 Mar. 1473/5).

8 PR, 169, 73v–74r (14 Oct. 1478).

9 Ibid., 57r–v (14 Aug. 1478).

10 Ibid., 73v–74r (14 Oct. 1478), referring to a slump in prices in the spring of 1478.

11 The enactment establishing the Seven Percent Fund is found in ibid., 84v–86v (14 Oct. 1478). It applied to all dowries that would come to maturity through February 1479. The first accounts were opened in May 1479. Approximately once in each following year a new group of husbands whose Monte dowries had come due was enrolled in the fund.

12 Goldthwaite, *Private Wealth*, 60–1, suggests that from 1479 to 1483 the annual return on land for Filippo Strozzi came to slightly more than 3 percent. The landholdings of Giuliano Capponi appear to have returned about 2 percent annually (ibid., 222–3, 231). For additional details, see ibid., 151, 177–8, 246–50. See also the critical discussion of the problems attendant upon calculating rents from rural properties by Pinto, "Forme di conduzione."

13 Marks, "The Financial Oligarchy," 141.

14 PR, 169, 85r: "Possa ciascuno et il credito et la provisione vendere, permutare, conditionare, oblighare, o in altro trasferire in tutto o in parte et libero et a tempo come volessi, et mai non sia in alcuno atto alcuna spesa, ma gli stantiamenti e tutte le scripture si faccino gratis."

15 Ibid.: "Non s'abbia detto credito a rapportare ad alcuna gravezza, et non si possa porre gravezza ordinaria o extraordinaria per via recta o indirecta su detto credito o provisione."

16 Many husbands holding claims to Monte dowries that came to maturity in the 1480s, however, faced long delays before they were finally admitted to the Seven Percent Fund. The government sought to mollify these husbands by establishing two new funds, the Four Percent Fund and the Three Percent Fund. All portions of matured dowries which since 1483 had not been paid out in cash or been registered in the Seven Percent Fund were to be inscribed in these funds: the older ones in the Four Percent Fund, the more recent ones in the Three Percent Fund. As accounts in the Seven Percent Fund were redeemed by the government, equivalent accounts in the Four Percent Fund would be reopened in the Seven Percent Fund, and similarly from the Three Percent Fund to the Four Percent Fund: Consiglio del Cento, 3, pt. 2, 72r–73r (23 Mar. 1490/1), edited by Kirshner, *Pursuing Honor*, 68–71.

17 The ledgers of the Seven Percent Fund are found in the archive of the *Monte delle Graticole*. Our analysis is based on information contained in the following volumes: MG, 954 (Libro Giallo segnato A); MG, 955 (Libro Rosso segnato B); MG, 956 (Libro Bianco segnato C); MG, 957 (Libro Azzurro segnato D); MG, 958 (Libro Verde 2° segnato E); MG, 959 (Libro Nero segnato F); MG, 960 (Libro Rosso 2° segnato G); MG, 961 (Libro Bianco 2° segnato H). These ledgers also contain accounts of those individuals who had acquired legal title to the deposits of girls who had died. In lieu of restoring them, as it had promised, the government was paying 7 percent on such deposits. The same regulations governing the accounts of husbands applied to the holders of these deposits. We have not abstracted information regarding the secondary market in these deposits.

18 Computer files of these records were created at the University of Chicago in 1980 and then verified by Kirshner in Florence where they were compared with the original documents. The sheer quantity of data made unfeasible our intention to capture all the information included in each account. The following data were accordingly excluded from the abstract: information beyond the first two encumbrances, transfers of credits, payments of interest, and all other transactions in which the husband engaged. We also excluded those cases where we have not been able to supply the names of

the wife's father and grandfather because the corresponding Dowry Fund records could not be located. The handful of multiple accounts opened several years apart for the same husband, occurring when portions of the wife's dowry came to maturity at different intervals, have been collated. For the first three hundred cases in our sample, the opening amount of the account was not 80 percent of the Monte dowry, as prescribed by the legislation of 1478, but that portion of the dowry – always less than 80 percent – which had not yet been paid to the husband. These accounts are found in MG, 954, 3r–85r, 462r–86r. Example: Having consummated his marriage with Lisa di Manno d'Uberto Adimari in 1477, Bartolomeo di Domenico Giugni was entitled to receive 766 florins. His account in the Seven Percent Fund had an opening balance of only 172 florins, as Bartolomeo had already received 594 florins from the Dowry Fund; MC, 3747, 101r; MG, 954, 14r.

19 The following formulaic expressions were used in type A encumbrances: *appartengono*, *attengono*, *appartiene*; *pagate*, *annosi a pagare*, *sì paghino*; and *assene a dare* and *dassi la decta dota*.

20 For example, the credits in the account of Michele di Bernardo Fei, which opened in September 1484, were encumbered in March of the same year (MG, 956, 220r). By the same token, the credits in the account of Maso di Paolo di Iacopo, which opened in September 1484, were encumbered in December 1480. In both cases the encumbrances were of type A (ibid., 224r).

21 These alienations were recorded in private documents, not in the ledgers of the Dowry Fund. This created opportunities for fraud, for both prospective buyers and encumbrancers had no way of knowing whether the husband's dotal rights had already been sold or encumbered. An enactment of 18 April 1488 lamented that such fraud was actually being perpetrated. It also lamented that husbands were jeopardizing the dotal claims of wives and their relatives by dumping their claims at bargain prices or without having observed the customary solemnities that served to safeguard the rights of the wife and her family to the dowry. As a result of these baleful consequences, the government ordered the officials of the *Monte comune* to open a special register in which they could keep track of the transactions pertaining to the dotal claims of those husbands who were waiting to have accounts opened in the Seven Percent Fund (Consiglio di Cento, 2, 128r–29r).

22 This was essentially the only way in which procurators could enter into transactions involving encumbrances (94 percent of all cases involving procurators were type A). In the absence of a systematic study of procurations and procurators, see the crisp remarks of Lopez, "Familiari, procuratori e dipendenti," 334ff.; and his "Proxy in Medieval Trade."

See also Reyerson, *The Art of the Deal*, 125–37. For procuration and procurators in Roman law, see Behrends, "Die Prokurator"; Angelini, *Il "procurator."*

23 MG, 954, 4r; MG, 955, 55r; MG, 957, 134r (account of Antonio di Salvestro di Giovanni); MG, 954, 5r (Antonio di Altomanno Chavicculi), 12r (Bartolomeo di Pino), 35r, 271r, 407r; MG, 955, 426r, 830r (Giovanni di Caterino Pilliccini da Colle); MG, 954, 49r; MG, 955, 8r (Niccolò di Piero di Tommaso); MG 954, 567r; MG 955, 166r (Luca di Papino Dandi); MG, 956, 257r (Santi di Antonio da Bruciano da Valdelsa).

24 This was the language used in procurations; see NA, 15038, s.f. (23 Nov. 1484). Many such procurations are found in NA, 9139 (1491–9). For earlier examples, see NA, 5345, 18r (2 Dec. 1463), 217r (1 July 1468), 355v (30 April 1473). A good example of this practice is also found in the *Libro di famiglia* of Francesco di Tommaso Giovanni: CS, ser. 2a, vol. 16 bis, 14v (7 Nov. 1436), 22v (18 Aug. 1441).

25 MG, 954, 79r: "Ànne avuto a dì marzo 1480, fiorini centocinquanta per lui [Lionardo di Tommaso di Pagolo] a Andreuolo di Ridolfo di Francesco di Domenico, i quali sono fiorini 60 per Zanobi di Piero di Michele, et fiorini 30 per Simone di Lando di Francesco, et fiorini 44, soldi 8, denari 9 per Guglielmo di Niccholaio, sarto."

26 MG, 954, 80r, 253r; MG, 955, 150r. There are other examples of this practice in the account of Lionardo Bartolini and Company as well as in the account of Lionardo di Tommaso di Pagolo (MG, 954, 79r).

27 On the practice of using offsets in lieu of specie in Florence, see Spallanzani, "A Note"; Melis, "Sulla non-astrattezza"; Goldthwaite, *The Building*, 306–13. For England, see Postan, "Private Financial Instruments," 41: "The usual purpose for which debts were assigned was the settlement of other debts. A merchant contracting an obligation to somebody else would 'set over' to him his own debts, and thus effect a payment without the actual employment of coin. How general this practice was is demonstrated by nearly all the contemporary records relating to the activities of medieval merchants."

28 This scenario is suggested by the use of Monte credits as collateral to secure loans made by the banker Giuliano de' Medici in 1448–52. See Edler de Roover, "Restitution," 779–85.

29 On *cessio iuris*, see Kaser, *Das römische Privatrecht*, vol. 1, 647–55; Astuti, "Cessio (premessa storica)"; Luig, *Zur Geschichte*; Harke, "Zum römischen Recht." Similarly, English Common Law permitted the assignment of debts by the creation of attorneys: see Postan, "Private Financial Instruments," 40ff.

30 MG, 954, 39r, 350r.
31 Archivio Cerchi, 317, 2v. In the same manner Cerchi purchased "dowry credits" from twenty husbands in 1480 and 1481. Prices ranged from 46 to 68 percent of par value (MG, 954, 315r; MG, 956, 86r, 98r; MG, 957, 113r, 394r, 501r, 651r).
32 See, for example, the account of Lionardo Bartolini and Company (MG, 954, 67r; MG, 955, 150r).
33 MG, 954, 91r–92r; MG, 955, 86r. For another example, see the accounts of Giuliano di Pollonio di Niccolò and his procurator ser Francesco di ser Antonio Pugi (MG, 954, 80r, 196r; MG 955, 402r).
34 MG, 954, 83r, 484r; MG, 955, 236r.
35 See the account of Barone di Agnolo, whose credits were assigned to his brother but were in fact transferred to the banker Piero di Francesco Mellini and Company (MG, 954, 462r).
36 Thirty-seven percent of such encumbrances were relinquished, as opposed to only 14 percent of type A encumbrances and 11 percent of type C encumbrances.
37 Some examples: the encumbrance attached to the credits of messer Baptista di Bartolomeo Nelli stipulated that his credits "non s'anno a pagare senza licenza di Francesco messer Carlo Federighi" (MG, 954, 17r); the encumbrance attached to the credits of Giovanni di Carlo Bilotti stipulated that his credits "non si paghino senza licenza di Piero di Zanobi di Piero da Marignolle" (ibid., 29r).
38 For example, the encumbrance attached to the credits of Baldassare di Iacopo Foresi, a shoemaker from San Gimignano, reads: "A dì 18 di magio 1485, pose conditione a fiorini centotrentacinque, soldi 8, denari 4 a' oro larghi che per dì qui a uno anno non se ne possa fare alchuno contratto senza licenza di Iachopo di Bartolomeo del Zaccheria, ma passato il detto tempo il detto Iachopo ne possa fare la sua volontà, et possa et debba in detto anno pigliare le paghe di licenza di Michele di Bernardo de' Marzi da San Gimignano suo procuratore, charta di prochura per ser Filippo di ser Giovanni de' Gamucci da San Gimignano sotto dì 15 di maggio 1485" (MG, 956, 12r). Del Zaccheria relinquished his encumbrance on 6 July 1486.
39 *Libro di famiglia* of Marco di Parente, CS, ser. 2a, vol. 17 bis, 100v: "posi chondizione di fiorini ccc. larghi di dote di 7 per cento, che da dì 24 di febraio 1505 in là Antonio di Lorenzo Niccholini ne possi fare la sua volontà, la qual chosa feci per sua sichurità di libre 1250 di cera gialla ebbi da lui per pregio di fiorini centododici larghi d'oro in oro, d'achordo, per pagharglile a dì 24 di febraio 1505, chome appare per la 1a scripta chantante in nome di Giuliano di Zanobi Chambi e compagni, lanaioli, in cui diceva

allora la chompagnia di detto Antonio Nicholini, alla quale scripta mi sono soscripto io di mia mano, e più v'è soscripto Tomaso di Gino Chapponi, a stanza di cui e per cui io Piero ho facto el sopradecto merchato ... A dì 7 di marzo di licentia del sopradetto Antonio Nicholini si ripose la conditione a detti 300 d'oro di grossi a stanza di Batista Dini e compagni, setaiuoli, per fiorini 112 larghi d'oro in oro, paghorono a detto Antonio, a ragione per 1° anno di 12 per cento, montorono in tutto fiorini 125½ d'oro in oro, per tutto dì 7 di marzo 1506, e di chosì n'e scripta tra detto Batista e compagni e me, soscripta di mia mano. Paghoronsi a dì 15 marzo 1506 di contanti e riebbi la scripta."

40 Chabot, "Widowhood and Poverty."

41 On a dispute over the restoration of *dos estimata*, see Kirshner, "A *Consilium* of Torello."

42 On this issue, see Kirshner, "Wives' Claims against Insolvent Husbands," chap. 6 in this volume.

43 Note that type B encumbrances were occasionally used to secure dowries. On 12 January 1434/5, for instance, Matteo Palmieri agreed not to trade 400 florins worth of Monte credits in his possession without the authorization of Bartolomeo di Francesco Puccini. The agreement was valid for a year, during which Bartolomeo was granted the right to trade these credits as he wished. Palmieri explained that he had entered this agreement as a favor to Simone di Filippo del Nero. The last named had just married Bartolomeo's daughter, Lionarda, and needed the 400 florins in Monte credits as security for part of the dowry he received from her father. Simone agreed to reimburse Palmieri for all damages he might suffer from this transaction. Palmieri, *Ricordi fiscali*, 223. As far as we can tell, the encumbrance lapsed after a year. For additional examples of this practice, see ibid., 192, 199, 218, 221, 232, and 243; and Edler de Roover, "Restitution," 779ff.

44 For example, the credits of Puccio di Bartolomeo di Puccio, with a face value of 400 large florins, were encumbered in this way: "Che detto credito stia per sicurità di dota in forma consueta, ma possasi promutare et conditionare di licenza di Giovanni, padre della detta Ginevra (Puccio's wife) o di sue herede" (MG, 956, 244r).

45 MG, 954, 10r (account of Alberto di Bartolomeo di Alberto), 58r (Salvatore di Bartolomeo di Michele), 517r (Andrea di Francesco di Michele); MG, 955, 310r (Giuliano di Iacopo Totti); MG, 956, 5r (Andrea di Sandro di Tano): "Che decti crediti [7 percent] si ponghino allo Spedale di Sancta Maria Nuova per comperare beni immobili per sicurità di dota della decta Antonia [Andrea's wife] ad dichiaratione di Giovanni di Salvadore di Domenico di Biancho, fratello di decta Antonia o di sue herede."

46 MG, 956, 259r, 486r; MC, 3738, 324r. For further examples of husbands transferring 7 percent credits to in-laws, presumably to repay an advance on the dowry, see MG, 954, 546r; MG, 955, 259r, 562r; MG, 951, 213r, 623r (account of Iacopo di Cristofano); MG, 954, 538r; MG, 955, 477r, 858r; MG, 951, 450r (Bartolomeo di Leonardo di Cenni); MG, 956, 133r, 699r (Bartolomeo di Giovanni Riccardi).

47 From abstracts of 1,180 accounts we have selected for analysis only those accounts opened in August 1480 and August 1484. The numbers of cases are indicated in table 5.2. We have coded the exact dates on which each of the transactions occurred. The analysis reported here considers only the frequency of events in completed records. Since the events take place through time, some decisions regarding the selection of data induce nonrandom censoring. We have conducted our analysis ignoring this censoring. This introduces biases into the estimation of hazard functions (the probability of selling credits in this period conditional on their still being held) and summary statistics from such data. The major source of such difficulties in this analysis, resulting in the "usable subset" group, is due to the exclusion of those cases in which either the husband or wife died before the credits were transferred or redeemed. Owing to the complexity and variability of the legal rules governing the disposition and devolution of credits upon death of either spouse, exclusion seems the easiest way to deal with cases involving inheritance and restoration of the dowry to the wife upon the husband's predecease. The longer a husband waited before he traded his credits or before they were redeemed for cash by the fund, the more likely it became that he would die before these events occurred. The result is that trading in credits will appear to be somewhat more common than computations based on the true hazards would indicate. Since deaths occur in only 10 percent of the cases, we consider the bias to be minor and make no attempt to correct for it.

48 MG, 956, 125r, 753r.

49 MG, 954, 521r; MG, 955, 251r, 658r; MG, 957, 307r, 690r.

50 MG, 956, 155r, 266r; MG, 958, 657r.

51 MG, 956, 174r.

52 MG, 956, 197r.

53 MG, 954, 476r; MG, 955, 233r, 809r.

54 MG, 956, 178r, 390r; MG, 958, 734r.

55 This scheme is suggested by the agreement between Niccolò d'Andrea degli Agli and his father-in-law, Piero di Marco Parenti. In January 1501, Niccolò was promised a dowry of 1,600 florins, 960 of which was due from the Dowry Fund the following year, upon his marriage to Piero's daughter,

Caterina. Piero agreed to provide an advance payment of 250 florins to Niccolò when he consummated his marriage, while Niccolò agreed to repay this amount when he himself was paid by the Dowry Fund. Even if Niccolò did not receive payment from the fund, he would remain obligated to repay his father-in-law from his own pocket (*Libro di famiglia* of Marco di Parente, CS, ser. 2a, vol.17 bis, 10v).

56 MG, 956, 133r, 699r. On this practice, see Kirshner, "*Li Emergenti Bisogni Matrimoniali*," chap. 2 in this volume, 73–5.

57 In law as well as common usage such toponyms signified place of origin rather than permanent abode or residence. See Kirshner, "A *Consilium* of Rosello."

58 This presumption is grounded in the knowledge that Florentine tax censuses of citizens of the city include individuals with toponymics who were actually residing in Florence at the time the censuses were redacted. For example, in the *catasto* of Florence of 1480 there were thirteen individuals with the toponymic "da Volterra" listed as heads of fiscal households. Likewise, there were household heads with the toponymics "da Terranuova" (eleven), "da Borgo San Lorenzo" (nine), and "da Romena" (eight), and so on.

59 Pertinent here is an enactment of 6 April 1473, which extended the deadline for the redemption of Monte credits received by husbands from the Dowry Fund, because of some poor farmers who had been unaware of the deadline (PR, 164,17v–18r).

60 Encumbrances placed by third parties have been excluded from the statistics reported in table 5.4. The holding patterns for these cases are similar to those for the unencumbered cases. Among Florentine husbands whose accounts were encumbered by third parties, only 14 percent in 1480 and 25 percent in 1484 held their credits to redemption.

61 MG, 954, 259r.

62 Vittorio worked as his father's assistant on the Renaissance masterpiece the *Gates of Paradise* for the Baptistery of the Cathedral of Florence, where the portrait bust of Vittorio can be viewed next to Lorenzo's even more renowned self-portrait bust. On which, see Radke, ed., *The Gates of Paradise*.

63 MG, 954, 478r; MG, 955, 292r, 461r.

64 MG, 956, 253r, 466r, 747r; MG, 958, 75r.

65 MG, 956, 133r, 699r. Bernardino di Pagno Albizzi, whose 7 percent credits (548 florins) were encumbered by his father-in-law, actually transferred credits (30 florins) to the Monte officials, in payment of his own father's taxes (MG, 954, 530r; MG, 955, 255r, 812r).

66 The encumbrance attached to the 7 percent credits of Palamidese d'Alberto Panciatichi stipulated that he could trade or reencumber his credits, either when his brother Giovanni personally guaranteed the dowry or when he received authorization from his father-in-law, Simone di Andrea Capponi (MG, 956, 62r).

67 Their speculative activities and role as financial intermediaries call for detailed analysis. See the accounts of Bartolomeo di Leonardo Bartolini and Company (MG, 954, 57r); Pagolo di Giovanni di Ippolito Della Casa (MG 954, 63r); Bindaccio di Michele Cerchi (MG, 956, 86r, 98r; MG, 957, 113r, 394r, 501r, 651r); Leonardo di Bernardo Dei (MG, 956, 424r; MG, 958, 125r, 418r; MG, 957, 772r); Francesco di Giuliano de' Medici (MG, 956, 100r); Piero di Francesco Mellini, Guido di ser Giovanni Guiducci and Benedetto di ser Francesco Guardi (MG, 954, 396r; MG, 956, 269r); Micho di Niccolò Capponi (MG, 956, 279r); Angiolino di Lorenzo Capponi (MG, 958, 114r); Rinieri di Francesco Sertini (MG, 958, 279r); Francesco di Bonavere di Piero and Francesco di Bese Ardinghelli (MG 956, 89r).

68 Archivio Cerchi, 317, 5v, 22v.

69 MG, 954, 87r, 356r. For other examples, see MG, 955, 788r, 960r; MG, 957, 93r, 211r, 282r, 289r, 397r, 456r, 619r, 622r, 644r, 646r, 724r, 768r; MG, 960, 697r, 699r, 701r, 713r, 721r, 775r.

70 MG, 956, 449r; MG, 961, 660r, 699r; MG, 962, 120r, 415r, 694r; MG, 963, 25r, 40r, 103r, 276r.

71 See Arrow, *Essays*, 96, and 104; Hicks, "Liquidity"; Pratt, "Risk Aversion," 122–36.

6. Wives' Claims against Insolvent Husbands in Late Medieval Italy

1 Pertile, *Storia del diritto*, vol. 3; Brandileone, *Scritti di storia*; Ercole, "L'istituto dotale"; idem, "Vicende storiche"; Bellomo, *Ricerche sui rapporti*. For an overview of the literature, see Vismara, "I rapporti patrimoniali."

2 Hughes, "From Brideprice to Dowry," and the bibliography cited therein; Herlihy, "The Medieval Marriage"; Schmid, "Heirat, Familienfolge"; Fossier, "Les structures de la famille"; and the more recent studies of Klapisch-Zuber, Kuehn, Chojnacki, Guzzetti, Chabot, and others cited in the bibliography of this volume.

3 The victory, however, was far from universal. Lombard law and custom persisted in Apulia into the sixteenth century and in Lombardy and the Friuli into the fourteenth century: Amati Canta, *Meffium, morgincap, mundium*; De Stefano, *Romani, longobardi*; Storti Storchi, "La tradizione longobarda"; Davide, "La permanenza degli assegni nuziali." Christiane

Klapisch-Zuber, in a provocative study, has argued that the gifts lavished upon Florentine brides by grooms and their families perpetuated the role that the *Morgengabe* had played; "Le complexe de Griselda." For discussion sparked by Klapisch-Zuber's thesis, see Kirshner, "*Li Emergenti Bisogni Matrimoniali*," chap. 2 in this volume.

4 On the Roman law regarding marital property, see Girard, *Manuel élémentaire*, 1007–24; Corbett, *The Roman Law*, 147–210; Cannata, "Dote"; Treggiari, *Roman Marriage*, 323–64; on private agreements (*pacta*) concerning the management and disposition of the dowry during marriage and upon its termination, see Magagna, *I patti dotali*.

5 On *dos aestimata*, see Kirshner, "A *Consilium* of Torello."

6 A hypothec was a form of real security carrying no obligation to transfer to the creditor either money or possession.

7 For the translation of *lex Si constante*, see Watson, ed., *The Digest*, 722–3.

8 For a translation of lex *Ubi adhuc*, see Fred H. Blume, trans., and Timothy Kearley, ed., *Annotated Justinian Code*, George William Hopper Law Library, University of Wyoming (http://www.uwyo.edu/lawlib/blume-justinian/ajc-edition-2/index.html).

9 For a translation of *Illud quoque sancire*, see *Annotated Justinian Code* in the preceding note. The larger context of Justinian's constitution concerns the dowry's contribution (*collatio*) in the division of the paternal and maternal inheritances.

10 For what follows, see Bellomo, *Ricerche sui rapporti*, 61ff.; and his *La condizione giuridica*. The advantiging of the husband's claims to the dowry must be seen in a broader European context, in which the tracing of descent and the transmission of property by inheritance in the eleventh century became exclusively determined by the ideology of patriliny, whereas in the early Middle Ages patriliny and matriliny coexisted in practice as well as in theory; Duby, "Structures de parenté."

Herlihy has offered a coherent summary of the historical conditions which made this transformation possible: "The Church's now effective insistence on monogamous marriage was a precondition, but surely not the principal cause of this realignment of elite families around patrilineal lines. The crucial factor seems to have been diminishing opportunities and resources available for the support of elite households. The establishment of more stable feudal principalities, the partial pacification of European life, reduced the profits of pillage, save along the distant frontiers. The chief remaining resource was the landed patrimony. Elite families struggled to preserve the extent and integrity of their holdings. They forced their younger sons to delay or eschew marriage, or sent them forth to make their fortunes. Daughters did not enjoy even this option. Their fathers or brothers gave these girls – some girls – the dowries they now needed for marriage, but this represented the extent of their claim upon the family patrimony. The position of women, central in the cognatic system of the early Middle Ages, clearly deteriorated as the lineage took on a pronounced agnatic cast." See Herlihy, "The Making of the Medieval Family," 124.

11 On this doctrine, see also Pluss, "Baldus de Ubaldis"; and Fugazza, *Diritto*, 30–6. On ownership in Roman law, see Birks, "The Roman Law Concept of Dominium." On *dominium* in medieval legal thought, see Grossi, "*Dominia e Servitutes.*"

12 See Niccolai, *La formazione*, 201–5; and my "*Maritus Lucretur Dotem*," 13–17.

13 Bellomo, *Problemi di diritto*, 40–2. See also Storti Storchi, "La condizione giuridica delle donne," 56.

14 Izbicki, "*Ista questio*"; Larner, *Italy in the Age*, 68–9; Violante, "Alcune caratteristiche," 46ff.; Cammarosano, "Aspetti delle strutture"; Pene Vidari, "Dote"; Garlati, "La famiglia." According to Bartoli Langeli ("Après la 'Morgengabe,'" 123), Bellomo's *Ricerche sui rapporti patrimoniali tra coniugi* remains the best legal history work dedicated to this subject.

15 Herlihy and Klapisch-Zuber, *Les Toscans*, 610–11; Klapisch-Zuber, "The 'Cruel Mother.'" In the same vein, see the older study of Zdekauer, "Le donne."

16 On bankruptcy and insolvency, see Santarelli, *Per la storia*; Cassandro, *Le rappresaglie*; Mueller, *The Venetian Money Market*, 121–251; Piergiovanni, "Banchieri e falliti"; Kuehn, "*Multorum Fraudibus Occurrere*"; idem, *Heirs*; on taxation, see Bowsky, *The Finance*; Luzzatto, *Il debito pubblico*; Violante, "Imposte dirette"; Molho, *Florentine Public Finances*.

17 For what follows, see Klapisch-Zuber, "'Parenti, amici e vicini'"; Kent, *Household and Lineage*; Chojnacki, "Patrician Women"; idem, "Dowries and Kinsmen"; Forcheri, "I rapporti patrimoniali"; Hughes, "Domestic Ideals"; Riemer, *Women in the Medieval City*, 60ff.; Brizio, "La dote"; Kuehn, "Women, Marriage, and *Patria Potestas*"; Mainoni, "Il potere di decidere"; Lanaro and Varanini, "Funzione"; and Kirshner, "Materials for a Gilded Cage"; and Kirshner and Klerman, "The Seven Percent Fund," chaps 3 and 5, respectively, in this volume.

18 This point is underscored by Storti Storchi, "La condizione giuridica delle donne."

19 Concrete evidence for the restoration of dowries in thirteenth-century Bologna and fourteenth-century Venice is especially striking; see R. Rinaldi, "Figure femminili"; and Guzzetti, "Dowries."

20 See Kirshner, "Women Married Elsewhere," chap. 7 in this volume; Kuehn, "Social Processes."

21 Pluss, *Baldus de Ubaldis*.

22 Chabot, *La dette des familles*, 106. For the contrary position, see Kent, *Household and Lineage*, 63–163. For the effects of the Black Death on dotal and testamentary practices in Marseilles, Smail, "Démanteler le patrimoine."

23 Fitting, ed., *Summa trecensis* [*Summa Codicis des Irnerius*], 145. Authorhip of the *Summa trecensis* is now attributed by André Gouron to the Provençal jurist *mâitre* Géraud. For the debate over the *Summa*'s authorship, see Lange, *Römisches Recht*, vol. 1, 402–7. Azo to Cod. 5. 12 (*De iure dotium*), *Summa aurea* (Lyon, 1557), 127rb: "Et dicetur deduci ad inopiam vel vergere ad inopiam, cum erit evidentissimum mariti facultates sufficere non posse ad exactionem dotis et aliorum onerum quae imminent viro, ut ff. soluto matrimonio, l. Si constante [Dig. 24. 3. 24]. Hodie tamen videtur quod fiat exactio statim ex quo maritus inchoat sua substantia male uti, ut in authen. de aequalitate dotis, § Aliud quoque [Auth. 7. 8]. Et puto hoc exaudiendum secundum opinionem, vel famam communem, quia dicunt homines eum male agere factum suum, argum. ff. de fundo instructo lega., l. Cum de lanionis, § Asinam. [Dig. 33. 7. 18. 2]. Sed licet dixerim exigi posse dotem, et soluto matrimonio et quandoque eo constante, aliter tamen et aliter fit exactio: nam soluto matrimonio ita fit exactio ut mulier de dote exacta faciat quicquid velit, eo constante, si exigat, non habet licentiam alienandi eas res vivente marito, sed fructibus earum verum potest uti ad sustentationem sui et mariti et filiorum communium, ut infra eodem, l. Ubi [Cod. 5. 12. 29]." A similar view was expounded in the Provençal paraphrase of the *Codex Justinianus* of the twelfth century known as *Lo codi*: Fitting, ed., *Lo Codi*, 163–4: Cod. 5. 11. 2, Cod. 5. 14. 1–3; and Derrer, ed., *Lo Codi*, 119, 121.

24 Bellomo, *Ricerche sui rapporti*, 147–9. Bellomo stresses the wife's incapacity to alienate the restored dowry and the requirement that it must be used to support the burdens of marriage, while he ignores the *mens legis* of *Si constante*, *Ubi adhuc*, and *Illud quoque sancire*, one that was endorsed by all jurists to prevent the total loss of her dowry and patrimony.

25 *Glossa ordinaria* to *l. Si constante* (Dig. 24. 3. 24) (Venice, 1591), 22b; to *l. Ubi adhuc* (Cod. 5. 12. 29), 708rab ; to *Illud quoque sancire*, *v. inchoante* (Nov. 97. 6 = Auth. 7. 8), 263rab; Odofredus to *l. Si constante*, in *Commentaria* (Lyon, 1552), 10rb–va; Jacobus de Ravanis to *l. Ubi adhuc*, in *Lectura* (formerly attributed to Petrus de Bellapertica) (Paris, 1519), 230v–31r; Dinus Mugellanus to *l. Si constante*, in *Apostillae super infortiato*, BAV, Urb. lat. 156, 68vab; Borgh. lat. 274, 22rb–va; Vat. lat. 1416, 4rab; Vat. lat. 1420, 4rb; Vat. lat. 2514, 6rb; Jacobus de Belvisio to Coll. VII,

tit. 8, *De equilitate dotis et propter nuptias donationis, v. Illud quoque*, in *Commentarii* (Lyon, 1511), 54vb; Cinus de Pistorio to *l. Ubi adhuc*, in *Commentaria* (Frankfurt am Main, 1578), 307ra–8vb; Jacobus Butrigarius to *l. Ubi adhuc*, in *Commentaria* (Paris, 1516), 152rb–va; Albericus de Rosate to *l. Ubi adhuc*, in *Commentarii* (Venice, 1585–6), 256vb–58rb; Bartolus to *l. Ubi adhuc*, in *Commentaria* (Venice, 1570–1), 174v; idem to *l. Si constante*, 16ra–20ra. The opinions of Jacobus de Arena are reported by Albericus and Bartolus. There are several of Jacobus de Arena's glosses to *l. Ubi adhuc* in Vat. lat. 1428, 133vab. For subsequent treatments, see Baldus to *l. Si constante*; and to *l. Ubi adhuc*, in *Commentaria* (Lyon, 1498), s.f. (I cite a copy of this edition found in the Old Library, Queens College, Cambridge); Angelus de Ubaldis to *l. Si constante*, in *Lectura* (Lyon, 1548), 8vb–9ra; Bartholomaeus de Saliceto to *l. Ubi adhuc*, in *Commentaria* (Lyon, 1515), 19v–20v; Ludovicus Pontanus (Romanus), *Consilia* (Lyon, 1565), 205r, cons. 462; idem to *l. Si constante*, in *Commentaria* (Lyon, 1547), 44v–49ra; Paulus de Castro to *l. Si constante*, in *Commentaria super Infortiato* (Lyon, 1553), 22ra–23rb; Alexander Tartagnus to *l. Si constante*, in *Commentaria* (Venice, 1595), 41rb–44ra; Johannes de Imola to *l. Si constante*, in *Commentaria* (Lyon, 1547–9), 13va–15ra; Raphael de Raymundis (Cumanus) to *l. Si constante*, in *Commentaria* (Lyon, 1554), 12rb–13ra; Petrus Philippus Corneus to *l. Dotis quidem* (Cod. 6. 20. 5 = Auth. 7. 8, *Quod locum*), in *Commentarius* (Lyon, 1553).

26 Hostiensis (Henricus de Segusio) to *c. Per vestras* (X 4. 20. 7), in *Commentaria* (Venice, 1581), 47ra; Gulielmus Durandus, *Speculum iudicale* (Frankfurt am Main, 1592), 4. 4 tit. *De dote post divortium restituenda*, 464–5, nos. 18–24, with additions by Johannes Andreae; Antonius de Butrio to *c. Per vestras*, in *Commentaria* (Venice, 1575–8), 62r; Petrus Ancharanus to *c. Per vestras*, in *Commentaria* (Bologna, 1580–1), 159r–65v; Franciscus de Zabarellis to *c. Per vestras*, in *Commentaria* (Venice, 1502), 27b; Abbas Panormitanus (Niccolò de' Tedeschi) to *c. Per vestras*, in *Commentaria* (Lyon, 1520–1), 50r–v.

27 Johannes de Erfordia, *Summa confessorum*, *De dote*, vol. 2, 337; Bartholomaeus de Sancto Concordio, *Summa Pisanella, s.v. dos* (Venice, 1479); Antoninus (sant'Antonino of Florence), *Summa theologica* (Venice, 1581–2), 32r, pt. 3, tit. 1, cap. 23 (*De dotibus et donationibus propter nuptias*), § 7; Angelus Carletus de Clavasio, *Summa angelica* (Venice, 1569), *s.v. dos*, no. 14; Bartholomaeus Fumus, *Summa Armillia* (Venice, 1554), 144v, *s.v. dos*, no. 23.

28 Rolandinus, *Summa totius artis notarie* (Venice, 1546), I, II, *De dotibus*, 78 ra: "Sed tunc de necessitate restituitur quando maritus ad inopiam vergit, ut C. de iure do., l. Nisi [*sic*], scilicet cum incipit dilapidare bona sua et

substantia propria male uti, ut authen., de aequalitate do., § Illud quoque [Auth. 7. 8; Nov. 97. 6], et hoc forte, quia ideo vir suspectus est, quod dissipaturus dotem sit"; cf. Salatiele (d. 1280), *Ars notarie*, vol. 2 (lib. IV), p. 267, rubr. *Instrumentum receptionis dotis.*

29 *Glossa ordinaria* to *l. Si constante* (*casus*), 22b: "Titia dedit dotem Seio marito suo; maritus inchoat male uti substantia sua, quaeritur utrum constante etiam matrimonio mulier contra eum posset agere ad dotem? Et dicitur, quod sic, si mulier viderit eum ita male uti et ita male usum circa substantiam suam; quod si satisfaciat aliis creditoribus non possit satisfieri mulieri"; see also *Glossa ordinaria* to *l. Ubi adhuc*, *vv. Ad inopiam* (ibid., 708a).

30 Odofredus to *l. Ubi adhuc* in *Commentaria* (Lyon, 1552), 277r, no. 4: "sed hodie iure Authenticorum ex quo maritus incipit uti male substantia sua, potest exigere dotem vel agere hypothecaria; ut infra, de coll. l. Dotis in authen. Quod locum [Cod. 6. 20. 5, *Dotis quidem* = Auth. 7. 8]."

31 Bartolus to *l. Si constante*, 16ra, no. 1: "Mihi autem videtur quod circa hoc sunt tria iura, scilicet ius Digestorum, et hoc providet mulieri plene. Ius Codicis, et hoc providet plenius. Et ius Authenticorum, et hoc providet plenissime, et nullum alteri derogat, immo diversis casibus loquuntur."

32 Ibid., no. 2: "Nam secundum haec iura Digestorum mulier tunc poterat agere, cum vir erat in illa extrema miseria, quod bona sua non sufficiebant ad exactionem dotis deducto aere alieno, nec ante poterat agere, et istud est solum in dote."

33 Ibid., no. 3: "Sed per ius Codicis provisum est plenius, quod licet bona mariti sufficiant ad exactionem dotis, tamen si maritus laborat inopia: puta, quod sit nobilis homo et habet in bonis parum, tamen habet in bonis tantum quod sufficit creditoribus et doti; tamen quia oportet eum vivere honorifice, omnia expendit, et mulier peteret necessitatem, secundum ista tempora mulier non poterat agere, sed hodie potest per dictam legem Ubi [Cod. 5. 12. 29] et in l. In rebus, § Omnis, eodem titulo [Cod. 5. 12. 30. 2]." On the "gifts" presented to the wife, which by law reverted to the husband and his heirs, see Bartolus to *l. In hiis*, § *Servis uxoris* [Dig. 24. 3. 66. 1], 30vb–31ra. See also Klapisch-Zuber, "Le complexe de Griselda"; and Kirshner, "*Li Emergenti Bisogni Matrimoniali*," chap. 2 in this volume.

34 Bartolus to *l. Si Constante,* 16r, no. 4: "Item per ius Authenticorum est provisum plenissime. Ecce, vir habet tantum, quod sufficit creditoribus et doti, et est dives et habet tantum quod potest bene vivere; tamen est dubium quod vergat ad inopiam, male utitur substantia sua et secundum ista iura mulier non poterat agere, sed hodie est sibi provisum plenius, ut etiam tunc possit agere. Unum ergo ius non corrigit aliud, sed addit alteri iuri plenius providendo."

35 *Glossa ordinaria* to *l. Ubi adhuc*, *vv. Ad inopiam*, 708a: "Hodie autem constat prius et post posse agi, scilicet quando vir cepit male uti sua substantia, ut Authen., de aequa, dot., § Illud, collat. VII [Auth. 7. 8], quod inspiciam secundum opinionem vulgi, argum. ff. de fun. instruc., 1. Cum de lanionis, § Asinam [Dig. 33. 7. 18. 2]." Rolandinus, *Summa*, 78rb : "Sed sufficit ad hoc ut mulier possit agere, et sibi de dote providere, maritum inchoasse male uti sua substantia, ut praeallegato § Illud quoque [Auth. 7. 8], quod inspicitur secundum opinionem vulgi seu famam communem, ut quia dicunt homines eum incepisse male agere factum suum vel dicunt talis incepit navigare, et poterit mulier in praedicto casu agere personali actione contra maritum, et accipere de bonis suis in solutum si non satisfacit sibi"; Jacobus de Ravanis to *l. Ubi adhuc*, 230va: "Dico quod nos recurremus ad vulgi opinionem: unde quando erit opinio in civitate de seipso quod ipse male administrat res suas et male facit que habet facere, tunc dicemus cum male uti re sua, ut ff. de questionibus, l. De minore [Dig. 48. 18. 10] et ff. de fundo instruc., l Cum de lanionis, § Asinam [Dig. 33. 7. 18. 2]." Jacobus de Ravanis's opinion is reported by Cinus de Pistorio to *l. Ubi adhuc*, 307a, no. 3. Dinus's opinion is reported by Bartolus to *l. Si constante*, 16rb, no. 6: "Dynus dicit quod probabitur secundum vulgi opinionem"; his opinion is found in glosses to *Si constante*, *vv. evidentissime apparuent*: "per oppinionem vulgi, ut infra, de questionibus, l. De minore, <pen>ult. [Dig. 48. 18. 10. 5] et de fundo instruc., l Cum de lanionis, § Asinam [Dig. 33. 7. 18. 2], dy. [Vat. lat. 1416, 4ra]."

36 Odofredus to *l. Ubi adhuc*, 277bv, no. 4: "Sed quero, quando maritus dicitur inchoare male uti substantia sua, et certe non eo ipso quod propter solitum ordinem duos denarios expendit. Sed ex quo vulgi opinio est, quod mittit in navem vel male faciat facta sua: nam si sunt homines sub sole qui sciunt secreta vicinorum suorum, sciunt vicini et in talibus vulgi opinio spectatur, ut ff. de questionibus, l. De minore, penul. [Dig. 48. 18. 10. 5], et de fundo instruc., l. Cum de lanionis [Dig. 33. 7. 18]." An early example of *vulgi opinio* at work occurred at Siena on 2 April 1253, when Benvenuta di Ildebrandi was assigned and took possession of real estate and personal property from her insolvent husband's (Maestro Domenico's) estate: "Omnibus pateat evidenter quod, cum adhuc matrimonio constituto inter dominam Benvenutam, uxorem magistri Dominichi quondam Dietaiuti, iidem Magister Domenicus male uti sua substantia incohasset et ad inopiam deveniret, sicut vulgi sui populi ecclesie Sancti Gilii oppinio publice testabatur, quia se multis creditoribus pro se et aliis obligavit, ita ut si eis primitus solveretur, facultates ejusdem non sufficerent ad dotes easdem expendiedas, et inanes plerosque alios sumptus fecit, volens eadem mulier uti

legis consilio et forma conventionis inite inter se et magistrum Dominicum supradictum, ne dotibus suis et lucro donationis propter nuptias sibi facte a dicto viro suo indebite fraudaretur"; edited by Zdekauer, *La vita privata*, 96–7.

37 Butrigarius's opinion is reported by Albericus de Rosate to to *l. Ubi adhuc*, 257r, no. 2: "Contrarium tamen tenet Iacobus Butrigarius et dicit quod maritus male utatur substantia sua non <potest> probari per vulgi opinionem, set opus sit probari per testes, qui deponent, quod sit lusor, baratator, vel negligens in administratione rerum suarum. Opinionem tamen glossa dicit veram quoad legem Codicis, quia tunc opus erat probare, maritum ad inopiam vergere, quia cum ista probatio sit mere negativa, scilicet probare aliquem non esse solvendo, sufficiat probari per vulgi opinionem."

38 Bartolus to *l. Si constante*, 16r, no. 6: "Ista verba videntur invenere, idem esse, bona ad dotis quantitatem non sufficere, et virum esse inopem et male uti substantia sua, cum eodem modo videantur probari. Sed ego praedicta posui supra ut diversa, ideo singulariter examinemus."

39 Ibid., no. 7.

40 On Bartolus's treatment of proof, see Fraher, "Conviction," 51–4; Lepsius, *Von Zweifeln zur Überzeugung*, 33ff. On public reputation (*fama*), see Gauvard, "La *fama*"; Kuehn, "*Fama* as a Legal Status."

41 Bartolus to *l. Si constante*, 16v, nos. 9–10: "Cum ergo ex hac sententia que fertur in hoc iudicio ipso marito fiat modicum praeiudicium, ideo dotem esse tantam mulier probat plene: quia si de hoc dubitaretur fieret plenum preiudicium aliis creditoribus, sed non esse tot bona que sufficiant debitis computatis ad exactionem dotis, probatur per vulgi opinionem, quia summaria et semiplena probatio per famam videtur haberi ... Nam haec sententia parum praeiudicat viro, cum fructus deserviant oneribus matrimonii, ut dicta lex Ubi, et infra dica. Quod puto verum quando agitur contra ipsum virum."

42 Ibid., nos. 13–16. Bartolus's thesis was sustained by Baldus to *l. Ubi adhuc* and to *l. Si constante*; Petrus Ancharanus to *c. Per vestras*, 161v–62r, nos. 23–5; Raphael de Raymundis (Cumanus) to *l. Si constante*, 12vb; and Bartholomaeus de Saliceto to *l. Ubi adhuc*, 19v, no. 4: "Opinatur enim vulgus iuxta proverbium antiquum quo dicitur in vulgari nostro: 'Richezza maldisposta a povertà se acosta' [Wealth used badly brings one to the brink of impoverishment]. In latino: 'Divitie male disposite paupertati sunt proxime.' Cum enim hoc non posset bene et necessario concludenter probari, sufficit probari verisimiliter et secundum opinionem vulgi, quia non in duorum vel trium testium iudicio hoc consistit, sed in opinione et iudicio vulgi."

43 Bartolus to *l. Si constante*, 16v, no. 10: "Sed si ageretur contra extraneum, tunc credo que deberet probari plene secundum glossam, dicta lex Cum de lege [Dig. 22. 3. 17], et infra dicam."

44 Ibid., no. 14: "Arbitrabitur autem hic iudex diversimode secundum diversitatem personarum et factorum, unde miles vel nobilis homo habens mille in bonis est pauper; unus rusticus habens minus est dives."

45 Baldus to *l. Ubi adhuc* (see n. 25 above): "Ego dico quod discretus iudex non solum debet interrogare de fama sed de ratione fame. Pone enim quod fama est quod aliquis est prodigus, debet interrogare iudex qua ratione moveantur isti dicentes quod iste est prodigus et tunc debent assignare rationem: verbi gratia, quia vident eum quotidie dilapidare et valde ultra expendere quam portent sue facultates."

46 Bartolus to *l. Si constante*, 16v, no. 17: "In proposito ergo favore dotis ne mulier possit perdere dotem, si vir pervenerit ad perfectam paupertatem, utroque modo intelligam, ut sive vir male inchoaret respectu initii sive male exitum habeat, consuletur mulieri."

47 An example of such preemptive action in early-fifteenth-century Florence is presented by Kuehn, "Inheritance and Identity," 148–9.

48 Dinus to *l. Si constante* (Urb. lat. 156, 68va): "In principio huius legis. Constante matrimonio exigitur dos, id est, si evidenter appareant facultates viri non sufficere ad quantitatem dotis et hoc dicit. Quid si ab initio non erat solvendo? Dic non habere locum remedium huius legis, ar. infra, ut [MS: si] in pos., l. Si is, a quo, § finali [Dig. 36. 4. 3. 3]"; Albericus de Rosate to *l. Ubi adhuc*, 257r, no. 5; Baldus to *l. Ubi adhuc.*

49 Jacobus de Ravanis to *l. Ubi adhuc*, 230vb: "Ego concedo quod si mulier dedisset dotem marito inopi quod non allegaret ignorantiam. Ipsa non haberet constante matrimonio dotis repetitionem. Sed si contraxit cum eo <qui> credebat eum divitem et solvendo, tunc ego dico quod perinde [ED: pro] est ac si postea esset factus non solvendo"; Cinus de Pistorio to *l. Ubi adhuc*, 307v, no. 9: "Pone, quod mulier accepit maritum inopem et dedit sibi dotem, nunquid habebit tunc remedium huius legis? Dico distinguendum, aut mulier scivit talem et accepit eum, quia forte placuit sibi persona propter formam; tunc imputet sibi, ut ff. ut in possess, leg., l. Si is, a quo, § ultimo [Dig. 36. 4. 3. 3]. Aut ignoravit et tunc perinde est, ac si de novo fieret egenus." This question had been debated in the early thirteenth century by Albertus Papiensis: see Bellomo, *Quaestiones*, 391 no. [427].

50 Bartolus to *l. Si constante*, 17r, no. 23: "Ego credo quod semper mulier habeat tale beneficium. Primo, quia ante contractas nuptias mulier non potest aliquod pactum facere expresse, per quod longiori die repetatur dos, ne conditio eius fiat deterior."

51 Ibid.: "Praeterea sententia praedicta esset nuptiis impedimento, nam pauper et qui male facit facta sua non invenerit uxorem cum dote, eo quod mulieres viderent se auxilio istarum legum destitutas. Ista autem nostra sententia nuptiis est favorabilis et ideo est tenenda et admittenda."

52 Baldus to *l. Ubi adhuc* and to *l. Si constante* (see n. 25 above): "Sed quid si ab initio vir non erat solvendo, utrum mulier habebit beneficium istius legis, et dicit Dynus quod non ... Bartolus dicit contrarium, quia si mulier velit expresse renunciare beneficio huius legis non posset ... Tu tene opinionem Dyni et Petri [= Jacobi de Ravanis], quia istud pactum est secundum naturam dotis quod non agatur constante matrimonio et omnino valet pactum"; Baldus to *l. Dotis quidem*, § *Quod locum* (Cod. 6. 20. 5 = Auth. 7. 8), in *Commentaria* (Lyon, 1498). Bartholomaeus de Saliceto (to *l. Ubi adhuc*, 20r, no. 11) adhered to Bartolus's teaching, while Ludovicus Pontanus (Romanus) (to *l. Si constante*, 46v, nos. 26–7) returned to the teaching of Dinus.

53 On banishment and exile, see Cavalca, *Il bando*; Pazzaglini, *The Criminal Ban*; Starn, *Contrary Commonwealth*; Milani, *L'esclusione dal comune*; Shaw, *The Politics of Exile*.

54 Bartolus to *l. Si constante*, 16v–17r, nos. 18–20. Relevant to this theme is a *questio disputata* that dates from the late thirteenth century and circulated under the name of the Bolognese jurist Tommaso della Fossa. Titius is exiled in perpetuity for having committed homicide or another grave crime. His wife now demands restoration of her dowry, though not on the grounds that Titius is approaching insolvency. In fact, Titius is ready and willing to support his wife in the place to which he is exiled. The wife counters that she is not obligated to follow her husband into exile and therefore demands restoration of her dowry – a position that the jurist supports. See Bellomo, *Quaestiones*, 28, no. [66].

55 Ludovicus Pontanus to *l. Si constante*, 46v, no. 25; Johannes de Imola to *l. Si constante*, 13va; Nellus de Sancto Geminiano, *De bannitis*, 369v: "Titius satis dives sumpsit uxorem et ab ea recepit dotem cum promissionibus consuetis, deinde bannitus est. Queritur, an uxor possit petere sibi dotem consignari per legem Si constante vel per legem Ubi adhuc ... Bartolus in lege Si constante, in quarta questione primae questionis, concludit quod si omnia bona publicantur, nulla est dubitatio. Potest enim tunc petere per remedium legis Si constante. Item, etiam dicit si pars bonorum est publicata, l. Si marito, eodem tituli [Dig. 24. 3. 31]. Si vero retinet omnia bona sed exulare cogitur, tunc quia cepit uti male substantia sua, potest petere consignationem per dictum § Illud." However, Nellus added this qualification: "Sed hoc ultimum intelligo in bannito

personaliter vel in tanta quantitate, quod dici possit eum male cepisse ... Si vero sit bannitus in parva quantitate, puta in 200 libris, et habet magnam substantiam, tunc licet non solvat vel quia non vult vel quia absens ignorat, non puto tale quid considerandum."

56 BNCF, Magl. XXIX, 117, 100r–3v, 100r: "In anno Domini mccclxxxx et mense novembris dicti anni, Tomasus olim domini Rossi de Riccis de Florentia fuit confessus habuisse in dotem, una cum quibusdam aliis, a domina Brianda Iohannis de Portinariis, dante in dotem domine Francische, uxoris ditci Tommasii, florenos mille trecentos recti ponderi et conii florentini, quam quantitatem dictus Tommasus, una cum aliis, promiserunt reddere, solvere et restituere dicte domine Francische vel eius heredibus in omni casu et eventu dotis restituende ex forma et secundum formam statutorum et ordinamentorum et consuetudinis civitatis Florentie. Et pro predictis et aliis in instrumento dicte dotis contentis, observandis obligavit se et eius heredes et bona tunc presentia et futura. Et quod postea, in anno Domini mccclxxxxii et mense novembris dicti anni, dictus Tomasus fuit confessus habuisse a dicta domina Brianda, dante pro complimento dotis dicte domine Francische, florenos cc auri, quos similiter reddere et restituere promisit dicte domine Francische in omni casu dotis reddende et restituende. Et pro predictis et in aliis in instrumento dicti augmenti dotis observandis obligavit se et sua bona presentia et futura. Et quod postea, de anno Domini mccclxxxxvii et mense octobris dicti anni, dictus Thomasus in generali distributione prestantiarum civitatis Florentie apprestantiatus et reductus fuit in dictis prestantiis in florenis auri quinque cum dimidio, quos non solvit et recusavit huc usque. Et quod post dictam distributionem, in anno Domini mccclxxxxvii per regimina civitatis Florentie condepnatus fuit dictus Tomasus quod si quo tempore pervenerit in fortiam dicti communis, quod ducatur ad lochum iustitie et ibidem caput a spatulis amputetur ita et taliter quod penitus moriatur ... Et quod postea dicta domina Francischa seu eius procurator pro ea auctoritate curie communis Florentie voluit habere et habuit vigorem et pro executione dicte dotis et augmenti dotis et pro eo quia propositum fuit dictum Tomasum extitisse condemnatum ut supra fit mentio, et vergere ad inopiam et male uti substantiam ipsius Tommasii et pro consignatione dicte dotis et augmenti dicte dotis tenutam in certis bonis dictis Tommasii."

57 Ibid., 100r: "Iniquitas magna esset quod alii creditores qui non sunt tam privilegati possint capere bona viri et uxoris."

58 Ibid.: "Concludo igitur quod dicta domina Francischa usque ad quantitatem alimentorum sibi debitorum secundum quantitatem sue dotis et qualitatem personarum dicti Tommasii et ipsius domine Francische secundum que

considerantur alimenta ... debet preferri comuni Florentie in predictis prestantiis et hominibus dicti gonfalonis habentibus iura a dicto comuni Florentie."

59 Ibid., 102r: "In proposito ergo potest indubitanter dicta domina Francischa petere sibi de bonis dicti Tomasi assignari usque ad quantitatem dicte dotis ex predicta causa ut dictis iuribus, et in eis habet prima et potiora iura quam comune Florentie vel vexillum predictum, ut in rationibus et iuribus per prefatum patrem et dominum meum supra allegatis. Et hoc sine dubio verum est de iure comuni. Nempe vero predictis obstare videtur ius municipale civitatis Florentie."

60 The list of properties (*bona assignata pro dote domine Francisce uxoris Tommasii de Riccis*) is found in *Capitani di Parte Guelfa* (numeri rossi), 50 (1375–1431), 121r.

61 On the consignment of Lapo's properties "a monna Margherita per la dota" in 1383, see Manoscritti, vol. 79 (Ricordanze di figluoli furono di Messer Lapo da Chastiglionchio di Firenze), 83v. For the restoration of Alessandra Macinghi Strozzi's dowry, see Crabb, *The Strozzi*, 49.

62 Starn, *Contrary Commonwealth*, 114. For further instances of the assignment of properties and income to wives of Florentine husbands condemned as rebels, who were either executed or banished from the city, see Baxendale, "Exile in Practice," 730–3; Ganz, "Paying the Price," 40–5.

63 Cinus de Pistorio to *l. Ubi adhuc*, 308ra, no. 15; Albericus de Rosate to *l. Ubi adhuc*, 257vb, no. 13; Baldus to *l. Ubi adhuc*: "Tertio vero casu principali quando mulier est solicita quia adverso casu maritus laborat inopia, ut quia flumen portavit podere suum vel naufragium est passus, tunc non habet locum quod mulier possit conqueri constante matrimonio, quia [ED: que] debet esse particeps infortunii mariti, ut ff. so. ma., l. Si, cum dotem, § Sin autem in sevissimo [Dig. 24. 3. 22. 8]"; Bartholomaeus de Saliceto to *l. In rebus dotalibus*, § *Omnis autem* (Cod. 5. 12. 30. 2), 21v, no. 2.

64 Bartolus to *l. Si constante*, 16rab, no. 5, and to *l. Si cum dotem*, § *Sin autem in saevissimo* (Dig. 24. 3. 22. 8), 14va. Albericus de Rosate shared Bartolus's position; to *l. Ubi adhuc*, 257v, no. 13: "Sed salva pace tantorum virorum contrarium communiter in iudicio vidi servari, ut si maritus vergat ad inopiam culpa sua, vel sine culpa, locus sit exactioni dotis, secundum formam huius legis. Nam praellegato § Illud [Auth. 8. 7] favore mulierum inductus est, ut non expectetur inopia viri, sed sufficiat eum male uti substantia sua, ergo in mulierum lesionem non debet retorqueri, et quia legum coerctio vitanda est, maxime dotium favore, et hoc satis innuit textus, in dicto § Illud."

65 Paulus de Castro to *l. Si constante*, 22rb, no. 7; Alexander Tartagnus to *l. Si constante*, 42rb, no. 6. One exception was the wife who herself contributed to the dissipation and mismanagement of the dowry. Albericus de Rosate to *l. Ubi adhuc*, 257rb, no. 6: "Sed quid si maritus et uxor sunt ambo dissipatores et male utentes substantia sua, nunquid habebit locum hec lex? Vidi terminari quod non, quia tunc cessant rationes et mens huius legis, quia dos non esset in tuto et dissipari posset, et ideo deponenda est dos in aliquo tuto loco." Johannes de Imola held that when both husband and wife were suspected of dissipating the dowry or the husband's properties, the dowry and the properties should be sequestered and invested with a merchant for the purpose of producing legitimate profit; to *l. Si constante*, 14rb.

66 See references in n. 26 above. The decretal *Per vestras*, sent to the archbishop of Genoa in 1206, addressed a case involving an insolvent husband, his wife, and a third party, Master R, with whom she had invested her dowry. The pope ordered the husband to furnish security that would serve to safeguard the dowry or invest the dowry with some merchant, "so that from legitimate gain the husband can bear the burdens of marriage." For a discussion of the contribution of *Per vestras* to the debate over the usury prohibition, see Noonan, *The Scholastic Analysis*, 136–7; Baldwin, *Masters, Princes, and Merchants*, vol. 1, 280–1; Pryor, "The Origins of the Commenda Contract," 17–18.

67 See Angelus de Ubaldis to *l. Si constante*, 99r.

68 *Glossa ordinaria* to *l. Si constante*, v. *mariti*, 22b: "Quid in socero, si ipse vergat ad inopiam et receperit dotem? Hic quidem vel alibi non exprimitur, nisi de marito vergente ad inopiam, et alias generaliter et prohibetur agi constante matrimonio, ut C. de praesci. 30 an., l. Cum notissimi, § Illud [Cod. 7. 39. 7. 4]; puto tamen idem in socero quod in marito servari, quia eadem ratio equitatis intervenit, scilicet ut mulieri consulatur, ut C. ad leg. Fal., l. finali [Cod. 6. 50. 19]"; Rolandinus, *Summa*, 78rb; Odofredus to *l. Ubi adhuc*, 277vb, no. 5; Jacobus de Ravanis to *l. Ubi adhuc*, 230vb; Cinus de Pistorio to *l. Ubi adhuc*, 307vb, no. 6; Jacobus de Belvisio to Auth. 8. 7, *Illud quoque sancire*, in *Commentarii* (Lyon, 1511), 54vb; Johannes Andreae, *additiones* to Gulielmus Durandus, *Speculum iudicale* (Frankfurt am Main, 1592), 4. 4. tit. *De dote*, 464; Bartolus to *l. Si constante*, 17r, no. 25; Baldus to *l. Si constante*.

69 Bartolus to *Si cum dotem*, § *Transgrediamur* (Dig. 24. 3. 22. 12), 15r, no. 2. On the father's coliability for the dowry in fifteenth-century Florence, see Kirshner, "The Morning After," chap. 4 in this volume.

70 *Glossa ordinaria* to *l. Si constante*, v. *mariti*, 22b: "Item quid si maritus et socer tenentur, et alter tantum ad inopiam vergat? Respondeo secundum has

leges non posse agi constante matrimonio, quia utriusque vel alterius bona sufficiunt, et ideo non agitur, ut hic, sed hodie agetur, quia negari non potest coepisse male geri res pro dote adstricta."

71 Rolandinus, *Summa*, 78rb; Odofredus, to *l. Ubi adhuc*, 277rb; Jacobus de Arena to *l. Si constante*, in *Commentaria* (Lyon, 1541), 90rb; Jacobus de Belvisio to Auth. 8. 7, *Illud quoque sancire*, 54vb.

72 Jacobus de Ravanis to *l. Ubi adhuc*, 230vb. I have not had an opportunity to examine the manuscripts containing Petrus de Bellapertica's treatment of the issues relating to *inopia*, but his influence is recorded by Alexander Tartagnus to *l. Si constante*, 41v, no. 3: "Sed ultramontani post Petrum tenent contrarium etiam si sint duo rei debendi, videlicet quod non possit agi contra vergentem ad inopiam, nec etiam contra alium, quia divitie unius supplere debent pro inopia alterius."

73 Cinus de Pistorio to *l. Ubi adhuc*, 307v, no. 7: "Pone, quod socer et maritus ambo receperunt dotem et obligaverunt se. Modo incipiat alter ad inopiam vergere, nunquid tunc erit locus huic legi? Glossa breviter dicit quod de iure isto non, sed per ius novissimum sic, quo iure statim, cum male incipit uti substantia sua, locus est auxilio, sicut hoc est in uno male utente, sic est in duobus ex quo alter male utitur eodem ratione adversitatis. Glossa salva reverentia sua male sentit et male loquitur. Dico enim quod de iure isto locum habet huius legis auxilium, ex quo unus ex obligatis incipit esse non solvendo, quia interest nostra, plures debitores habere, ut ff. de lib. le., l. 3 [ED: 4] in fine [Dig. 34. 3. 3. 5]."

74 Bartolus to *l. Si constante*, 17r, no. 33: "Aut sunt obligati ambo, non tamquam duo rei, ut in casu nostro, et supra eodem l. Si cum dotem, § Transgrediamur [Dig. 24. 3. 22. 12]: puta, quando mulier dedit uni dotem contemplatione utriusque, vel ubi obligati sunt ambo, non tamen tamquam duo rei, quia unus cogitavit de obligatione alterius, et sic non est actum tacite vel expresse quod sint duo rei, et tunc non credo quod propter inopiam alterius possit agi contra alium, quia est contra omnia iura."

75 Ibid.: "Ratio diversitatis est quando sunt duo rei et quando non sunt, quia primo casu debet imputari sibi quod alterius obligationem participavit, unde eius inopia sibi noceat. Secundo casu nihil potest sibi imputari, unde alterius inopia nihil debet nocere, ut no. Dy. in cap. mora in fine, extra, de regu. iur. lib. VI. [VI 5. 13. 25]." Cf. Dinus Mugellanus *Commentarius in regulas iuris pontifici* (Cologne, 1578), 251.

76 CS, ser. 3a, 41, vol. 14, 574r–76r (hereafter cited as Antonius de Stroziis).

77 Antonius de Stroziis: "Viso instrumento dotis in quo Marchus filius Alberti et Albertus pater dicti Marci, et quilibet dictorum Marci et Alberti in solidum et in totum se obligando fuerunt contenti habuisse et recepisse

in dotem domine Vaggie uxoris dicti Marci florenos 1050 modis et formis de quibus in dicto instrumento continetur. Et viso qualiter dictus Marcus maritus deductus est ad inopiam et paupertatem ita quod domina Vaggia non potest alere se et suos ex dote sua; et attentis dictis testium pro utraque parte examinatorum, est videndum an sit locus repetitioni dicte dotis ex eo quod probetur Marcum maritum vergere ad inopiam, non obstante quod facultates soceri ad dotem obligati sufficiant, et non obstante quod non asseratur Albertus socer vergere ad inopiam: et sic an sola paupertas mariti – dato quod socer sit facultatibus [*sic*] ideoneus, faciat locum repetitioni."

78 See n. 72 above.

79 Antonius de Stroziis: "Baldus autem et Angelus in d. l. Si constante, volunt quod possit agi contra illum tantum qui sit factus inops, non contra alterum, quia non est inconveniens quod ex post facto surgat inequalitas in duobus reis, l. Eandem, § <Sed> si quis, ff. de duobus reis [Dig. 45. 2. 9. 1]." Cf. Baldus to *l. Si constante*; Angelus de Ubaldis to *l. Si constante*, 9ra, no. 1. I have not been able to locate Raphael de Raymundis's text.

80 Alexander Tartagnus to *l. Si constante*, 41v, no. 3.

81 Paulus de Castro to *l. Si constante*, 22v, no. 8.

82 Ludovicus Pontanus, *Consilia*, 205r–v, cons. 462; to Dig. *l. Si constante*, 45rab.

83 Antonius de Stroziis, 575v: "Ex predictis apparet quod in hac difficultate doctores vario modo locuti sunt et sunt in diversis opinionibus. Tamen opinio glose est magis communis et pluribus et maioribus auctoritatibus fulcita. Nam ut dictum est supra, illam tenuit Cy., Richar. Mal., Odofr., Alberi., Bar., Iaco. de Bel., Io. An., Iaco. Butr. et Imol., et sic sunt novem doctores post glo., et ista opinio est plusquam communis, cum alie opiniones habeant paucos et minoris auctoritatis, maxime cum habemus glosam ubique hoc tenore, a cuius opinione in consulendo et iudicando non est recedendum secundum Bal., in l. Precibus, C. de impub. et ali. sub. [Cod. 6. 26. 8], quia in dubiis non possumus adherere meliori opinioni, Bal., in l. II, C. de sen., que si. cer. qua. [Cod. 7. 46. 2], et cum glosa non potest errari secundum Bal., in l. finali, § Necessitatem, C. de bo. que lib. [Cod. 6. 61. 8. 1a], cuius auctoritas ceteris antecellit secundum Bal., in l. Cum hereditas, C. deposit. [Cod. 4. 34. 9]." Johannes de Imola (to *l. Si constante*, 13vb) adhered to the opinion staked out by the *Glossa*. I have not been able to track down the opinions of Ricardus Malumbra and Jacobus Butrigarius, whose works were unavailable to me.

84 Antonius de Stroziis, 575v–76r: "Et secundum istam opinionem ego consilui. Et fuerunt late omnes sententie in favorem domine Vaggie, pro consilio meo." On the technique of *communis opinio* and the authority of the *Glossa*,

see Engelmann, *Die Wiedergeburt der Rechtskultur*, 189–227; Cavina, "Carlo Ruini consulente"; Di Renzo Villata and Massetto, "La facoltà legale," 433–4.

85 Bartolus to *l. Si constante*, 17v, no. 47.

86 *Glossa ordinaria* to *l. Si constante*, *v. mariti*, 22b: "Item quid si non mulier, sed pater eius velit agere? Respondeo idem, cum ipse teneatur eam denuo dotare." Note Bartolus's qualification (to *l. Si constante*, 17v, no. 50): "Adverte, hoc dictum intelligo si filia sibi consentit, vel causam condicendi non habet." See also the comments of Paulus de Castro to *l. Si constante*, 22va, nos. 9–10; and Alexander Tartagnus to *l. Si constante*, 41va, no. 4. For an insolvent husband who returned the dowry to his father-in-law, see NA, 10038 (19 Sept. 1420), s.f. Here, Angelo di Balducci Angelli of Cortona had received a dowry of 75 florins paid on behalf of his wife Margherita by her father Matteo Santucci. Angelo returned the dowry to his father-in-law because "videmus et cognoscens quod dictus Angelus se vergere ad inopiam, paupertatem, calamitatem et miseriam et quasi omnia sua bona consumpsisse et se incepisse male uti rebus."

87 Albericus de Rosate, to *l. Ubi adhuc*, 257r, no. 13: "Quid si mulier est negligens in utendo beneficio huius legis, nunquid pater eius uti poterit? Dic quod sic, ut d. l. Si constante, in principio, ff. so. ma. et ibi no."

88 *Glossa ordinaria* to *l. Si constante*, *v. mariti*, 22b: "Item quid si extraneus dedit pro muliere et est sibi pactus? Videtur pactus in casum soluti matrimonii tantum ... Item iam non esset unde alerentur ipsa et vir et filii, quod est quando ei redditur"; Rolandinus, *Summa*, 78va; Odofredus to *l. Ubi adhuc*, 277rb, no. 5; Jacobus de Ravanis to *l. Ubi adhuc*, 230vb; Jacobus de Belvisio to Auth. 8. 7, *Illud quoque sancire*, 54v; Cinus de Pistorio to *l. Ubi adhuc*, 308ra, no. 12; Bartolus to *l. Si constante*, 18r, no. 55; Baldus to *l. Ubi adhuc*.

89 *Glossa ordinaria* to *l. Si constante*, v. *mariti*, 22b: "Item quid si alius recepit dotem et se obligavit, quod fieri potest, ut de do. cau., l. finali [Cod. 5. 15. 3]? ... Respondeo idem, quia eadem aequitas"; Rolandinus, *Summa*, 78va; Odofredus to *l. Ubi adhuc*, 277rb, no. 5; Cinus de Pistorio to *l. Ubi adhuc*, 308r, no. 13; Bartolus to *l. Si constante*, 18ra, no. 60.

90 Bartolus to *l. Si constante*, 18rb, nos. 62–3; Baldus to *l. Ubi adhuc*; Johannes de Imola to *l. Si constante*, 14rb.

91 NA, 9040, 431r–32v. For another case of *inopia* around this time, NA 9039, 260r–63v (14 Mar. 1418/9).

92 Cinus de Pistorio to *l. Ubi adhuc*, 308ra, nos. 14–15; Bartolus to *l. Si constante*, 18va, nos. 70–3; Baldus to *l. Ubi adhuc*; Alexander Tartagnus to *l.*

Si constante, 41rb, no. 1; Gulielmus Durandus, *Speculum iudicale* (Frankfurt am Main, 1592), 4. 4. tit. *De dote*., 464–5.

93 Cinus de Pistorio to *l. Ubi adhuc*, 308va, no. 22; Bartolus to *l. Si constante*, 18va, no. 73; Baldus to *l. Ubi adhuc*; Albericus de Rosate to *l. Ubi adhuc*, 257rb, no. 13; Bartholomaeus de Saliceto to *l. Ubi adhuc*, 20va; Ludovicus Pontanus (Romanus) to *l. Si constante*, 47rb–47va, no. 33; Alexander Tartagnus to *l. Si constante*, 43va, no. 27.

94 On competing liens of hypothecary creditors in Roman law, see Schanbacher, *Die Konvaleszenz von Pfandrechten*; Wacke, "Die Konvaleszenz von Pfandrecht."

95 This was the *communis opinio*: *Glossa ordinaria* to *l. Ubi adhuc*, 708a (*casus*): "An constante matrimonio, vir ad inopiam vergat, mulier dotem repetere possit, quaeritur? Dicitur quod sic et si tenet res mariti, adversus creditores mariti agentes habebit exceptionem. Si non tenet, aget adversus creditores qui tenent res viri. Si ipsa sit prior tempore seu posterior, modo priores non sint privilegio aliquo muniti, et hoc in prima." The classic exception to this rule was the fisc, or imperial treasury, whose claims took precedence over the claims of prior creditors: see *l. Si is qui mihi* (Dig. 49. 14. 28).

96 Jacobus de Arena to *l. Assiduis* (Cod. 8. 17 [18]. 12), in *Commentaria* (Lyon, 1541), 55b, no. 3; Cinus de Pistorio to *l. Ubi adhuc*, 308v, no. 26, and to *l. Assiduis*, 495r–v, no. 8; Jacobus Butrigarius to *l. Assiduis*, 73va.

97 Jacobus de Ravanis to *l. Ubi adhuc*, 230v–31r. Petrus de Bellapertica's opinion is cited, inter alia, by Cinus.

98 *Glossa ordinaria* to *l. Assiduis*, *vv. hypotheca* and *licet anterioris sint*, 1283–4; Odofredus, to *l. Ubi adhuc*, 277r, no. 4: "et ideo vos dicetis mulier prefertur posterioribus, ut infra qui po. in pig. ha. [Cod. 8. 17(18). 12. 1. and 2]; anterioribus habentibus expressas hypothecas non prefertur, ut ibi; anterioribus habentibus tacitas, sic." Bulgarus's opinion is cited by Albericus de Rosate to *l. Assiduis*, in *Commentarii* (Venice, 1585–6), 151r, nos. 4 and 5: "In iudiciis communiter vidi servari opinionem Bulgari"; Bartolus to *l. Assiduis*, in *Commentaria* (Venice, 1570–1), 106v, nos. 3 and 7; Baldus to *l. Assiduis*, in *Commentaria* (Lyon, 1498); Paulus de Castro to *l. Si constante*, 21v, no. 2.

99 See, for example, Kishner and Klerman, "The Seven Percent Fund of Renaissance Florence," chap. 5 in this volume, and Kirshner, "Encumbering Private Claims."

100 *Glossa ordinaria* to *l. Cum tibi* (*casus*) (Cod. 8. 17 (18). 10), 1281; Jacobus de Arena to *l. Cum tibi*, in *Commentaria* (Lyon, 1541), 55r, no. 1; Cinus de Pistorio to *l. Cum tibi*, in *Commentaria* (Frankfurt am Main, 1578), 494r,

no. 3; Bartolus to *l. Si constante*, 19r, no. 88; Albericus de Rosate to *l. Cum tibi*, in *Commentarii* (Venice, 1585–6), 150v, no. 1.

101 Baldus to *l. Si constante*; to *l. Dotis quidem*, § *Quod locum*. See also the opinion of Angelus de Ubaldis, who is said by Quattrocento jurists to have shared his brother's view on this issue, but whose opinion, as far as I can tell, is inconclusive; Angelus de Ubaldis to *l. Si constante*, 9ra.

102 Paulus de Castro to *l. Si constante*, 20rb; Raphael de Raymundis (Cumanus) to *l. Si constante*, 12va; Johannes de Imola to *l. Si constante*, 14vb; Alexander Tartagnus to *l. Si constante*, 44rb, no. 31. The opinions of these jurists were cited in a *consilium* of the Florentine jurist Lucas de Corsinis (d. 1511), who defended the right of the husband's hypothecary creditor to pay the wife cash in lieu of the husband's properties in his possession (CS, ser. 3a, 41, vol. 11, 223r).

103 Jacobus de Ravanis to *l. Ubi adhuc*, 230vb; Cinus de Pistorio to *l. Ubi adhuc*, 307vb, no. 10. The opinions of Dinus and Jacobus de Arena are reported by Bartolus to *l. Si constante*, 18v, no. 53: "Teneo cum Cino: quia si mulier ab initio voluisset expresse huic repetitioni renunciare non potuisset, ut iam dixi"; Baldus to *l. Ubi adhuc*; Albericus de Rosate to *l. Ubi adhuc*, 257r, no. 8.

104 Bartolus to *l. Si constante*, 18ra, no. 55. Towns whose statutes apparently omitted the *casus inopie*, but where wives were nonetheless laying claim on the basis of the *ius commune* to their insolvent husbands' properties, were the following: Siena: see n. 36 above (but by 1545, and most likely earlier, Siena provided this remedy: Ascheri, ed., *L'ultimo statuto della Repubblica di Siena (1545)*, 245–6, dist. 2, rubr. 140, (*De causis in quibus constante matrimonio, fieri debeat restitutio seu consignatio dotis*); Lucca: Meek, "Women between the Law and Social Reality"; Florence: Santini, ed., *Documenti dell'antica*, 303–4, document of 1244; Volterra: NA, 10054, s.f. (3 Dec. 1439); Verona: University of Chicago, Regenstein Library, Department of Special Collections, Rosenthal MS 310; and Varanini, "Società cristiana," 6, discussing the tribulations of Jewish inhabitants in late-fifteenth-century Verona ("sono relativamente frequenti le procedure giudiziarie a salvaguardia dei beni dotali, da parte di ebree i cui mariti si dubita possano *vergere ad inopiam*"); and Venice: Martelozzo Forin, "Note sulla famiglia del giurista pisano Benedetto da Piombino," 54–5. It was not until 1553 that Venice enacted a law enabling wives to retrieve their properties from husbands teetering on insolvency. See Ferraro, *Marriage Wars*, 185, n. 10.

105 Arezzo: Marri Camerani, ed., *Statuto di Arezzo, 1327*, 173, rubr. 63, *De dotium et donationum propter nuptias restitutione, qualiter ius reddatur*; Pisa: Bonaini, ed., *Statuti inediti*, vol. 1, 237, lib. I, rubr. 130, *De vergente*;

Ravenna: Tarlazzi, *Appendice ai monumenti*, II, 82–4, no. 64 (1271). For Bologna (1352), see Torelli, *Lezioni di storia*, 130; Vicenza: Vicenza, Biblioteca Bertoliana, MS Gonzati 566, *Liber statutorum communis Vincentie* (1311), lib. II, rubr. 5 (I owe this reference to Professor James Grubb); Rieti: M. Caprioli, ed., *Lo statuto della città di Rieti*, 139, lib. II, rubr.18, *De iure dotium* (second half of the fourteenth century); Bacchetti, ed., *Statuti di Belluno del 1392*, 204 (I), lib. II, rubr. *De iudiciis*; Como: Mangini, ed., *Statuta civitatis et episcopatus Cumarum (1458)*, 204, rubr. 54 and 55. Less explicit but no less effective were statutes, like that of Piacenza (1323), in which the wife was permitted to institute an action during marriage for the restoration of her dowry in cases such as *inopia* permitted by the *ius commune* ("in casibus concessis a iure petat dotem in bonis mariti"). See Fugazza, ed., *Lo statuto di Piacenza*, 56, lib. 3, rubr. 19, *De dote exigenda in bonis viri viventis.*

106 Caggese, ed., *Statuti della Repubblica fiorentina* (*Podestà*), vol. 2, 99, lib. II, rubr. 17, *De dote et donatione restituenda*: "nec ad restitutionem teneatur aut compelli vel cogi possit ratione mortis alterutriusque coniugum vel aliqua alia ratione vel causa, nisi ratione mortis naturalis tantum."

107 BAV, Vat. lat. 8067, 294r: "Questio proponitur ex facto. Quidam Fence per se vel per procuratorem constituit dotem domine Caterine sue filie, et eius constitutionem confessi fuerunt, scilicet maritus et quidam cum eo, habuisse dictam dotem et ad eius restitutionem se in solidum obligaverunt. Modo marito ad inopiam vergente aliis correis existentibus solvendo. Queruntur duo: Primo de restitutione dotis, an possit advocari ab ipsis qui solvendo sunt? Aliud dubium sive questio: cessante restitutione dotis, an possit agi ad alimenta? Et circa primam questionem insurgit dubium ex forma statuti quo restitutio et repetitio dotis denegatur, nisi in casu mortis naturalis, et in hoc ponderandum est quod statutum sic conceptum de restitutione deneganda et repetitione in casu mortis vel alia ratione, nisi in casum [*sic*] mortis naturalis."

108 Ibid.: "Sed hec non est plenaria restitutio que fit per casum inopie, cum adhuc vir cum uxore habeat in promiscuo usu et res est facta quasi dotalis et inalienabilis et sic deserviens matrimonio tam marito quam uxori et liberis eius, et per hoc impropria est restitutio eius, et sic non comprehenditur forma statuti communis Florentie et eius prohibitione, sed remanebit sub iure communi quo restitutio fieri debet in casu inopie, et habet locum l. Ubi adhuc, C. de iure dotium [Cod. 5. 12. 29], l. Si constante, ff. solu. ma. [Dig. 24. 3. 24]."

109 Ibid., 294v: "Probat equitas, que modificat verba statuti, non est conveniens et equitas non patietur quod mulier careat dote et ideo ipse et liberi eius."

110 Ibid.: "Et per hoc concluditur ad premissa quod dos de qua queritur veniat mulieri reddenda et restituenda, non obstante stipulatione vel pacto tertii. Et per consequens non obstante statuto communi Florentie eadem ratione assistente; et hoc quantum ad restitutionem dotis."

111 Baldus to *l. Ubi adhuc*: "non tamen ista est vera restitutio dotis sed magis in tuto posita secundum Ia[cobum] Buttrigarii qui consuluit quod si statutum dicit quod mulier non possit petere restitutionem dotis constante matrimonio, quod hec verba non extenduntur ad hanc in tuto positam, quia non est propria restitutio. Et sic statutum intelligeretur solum secundum ius commune."

112 For what follows, see Ludovicus Pontanus (Romanus) to *l. Si constante*, 45r–v, no. 12.

113 Klapisch-Zuber, "The 'Cruel Mother.'"

114 Examples: NA, 862, s.f. (Sept. 1343): "predictus Laurentius fuit confessus habuisse in dotem a dicta domina Katerina uxore sua libras centum XXV ... promisit eidem domine etc. dictas dotes et donationes ... restituere et solvere et pagare in omnem eventum restituende dotis et solvende donationis, constante matrimonio vel soluto, in civitate Florentie, Pistorii, etc."; ibid. (5 Nov. 1343): "dictus Pierus fuit confessus habuisse in dotem a predicta domina Bartola uxore ... libras quinquaginta ... promictens dictas dotes et donationes ... reddere, solvere et pagare in omnem eventum dicte dotis restituende et donationis solvende, constante matrimonio vel soluto, in civitate Florentie, etc."; NA, 206, s.f. (3 May 1353): "quam dotem et donationem prenominatus Tendi promisit ... reddere, solvere, pagare et restituere in omnem casum et eventum dotis reddende et donationis solvende, constante matrimonio vel soluto"; NA, 1202, s.f. (31 July 1394): "predicti ... promiserunt et solempni stipulatione convenerunt ... eidem domine Tommase et suis heredibus dictam dotem reddere, dare, solvere et restituere in omni casu et eventu dicte dotis restituende constante matrimonio vel soluto"; ibid. (23 April 1409): "quas dotes et donationes predicti Gherardinus et Stefanus ... in totum et in solidum promiserunt dicto Zenobio ... reddere, dare, solvere et restituere in omni casu et eventu dicte dotis restituende et donationis solvende, constante matrimonio vel soluto, in civitate Florentie, Pisarum, Bononie, Ianue, Venetiarum etc." Such guarantees are found in dotal pacts after 1415 as well.

115 *Statuta populi et communis Florentiae*, vol. 1, 161, lib. II, rubr. 64, *Quod nulla mulier vivente viro possit defendere bona viri, nisi in certis casibus*: "Viro vero vergente ad inopiam, mulier agere possit in bonis viri, et ea petere secundum formam iuris communis usque ad quantitatem et ratham suae dotis et donationis et augmenti, et ea defendere contra quoslibet creditores,

facta prius extimatione secundum formam statuti." In his gloss on the phrase "secundum formam iuris communis," the Florentine jurist Alexander Salvi de Bencivennis refers to *l. Ubi adhuc* and Bartolus's commentary on *l. Si constante*. For Alexander's gloss, see BNCF, Fondo Principale II IV 435, 45r.

116 *Glossa ordinaria* to *l. Ubi adhuc*, *vv. Ad inopiam*, 708ab: "Sed pone in nostro casu virum velle dare fideiussorem de dote restituenda uxori soluto matrimonio, nunquid evitabit exactionem dotis ad praesens? ... Sed dico contra, quia infra dicit quod retinere debet ad sustentationem sui et uxoris"; Rolandinus, *Summa*, 69vb; Odofredus to *l. Ubi adhuc*, 277rb, no. 5; Cinus de Pistorio to *l. Ubi adhuc*, 307vb, no. 8: "Praeterea cum maritus vergit ad inopiam, est obligatus ad dotis restitutionem, nec potest dando fideiussores liberari. Praeterea cautio fragilis est, et tutius est habere rem quam fideiussores"; Albericus de Rosate to *l. Ubi adhuc*, 257ra, no. 4; Baldus to *l. Ubi adhuc*; Alexander Tartagnus to *l. Si constante*, 43rb, no. 19: "Teneo communem opinionem, maxime per rationes allegantur per Cynum in d. l. Ubi, quia non est equum mulierem se committere fragilitati cautionis."

117 Cinus de Pistorio to *l. Ubi adhuc*, 308ra, no. 15: "Hodie vero, ubi maritus dissipat, fit mulier de subdita domina." Cf. *Glossa ordinaria* to *l. Ubi adhuc*, *vv. Eas res*, 708b.

118 Bartolus to *l. Si constante*, 18rb, no. 92: "Secundo quaero, an mulier hoc casu consequatur dominium rerum assignatarum pro dote? Quidam quod sic, quando agitur personali, nam tunc res dantur in solutum, et mulier consequitur dominium. Ita videtur Glossa in d. l. Ubi ... Alii, ut Ubertus de Bobio, tenet contrarium, quod probant ex dicta l. Ubi, nam ibi prohibetur alienari, dicit ipse, ergo non dantur sibi in solutum; ergo nec transfertur dominium ... Credo glossa bene dicere, et videtur casus in Authen. de aequal. do., § Illud ibi, sic eius habitura erat in collationis ratione proprias res, et cetera."

119 On the myriad ways an owner's freedom of alienation can be restricted by law, see Birks, "The Roman Law Concept of Dominium," 20–3. A standard example is the husband who is owner of a dowry consisting of land, but which he may not alienate under the *lex Julia* without the consent of his wife. Restrictions on the freedom of owners to dispose and convey property as they saw fit are a core feature of communal statutes in this period.

120 Bartolus to *l. Si constante*, 18r, no. 2: "Aut mulier agit hypothecaria, et tunc certum est quod non consequatur dominium, sed pignus tantum, <ut> dicta l. Ubi. Aut actione in rem, et tunc dominium non consequitur per traditionem, sed suum esse ex legis ratione declaratur, <ut> dicta l. In rebus, C. de iure do. [Cod. 5. 12. 30]. Aut agitur in personali, et dantur sibi res in solutum, et consequitur dominium, ut dictum est."

121 Ibid., nos. 92–3: "Aut dubitatur, verbi gratia: mulier petit de rebus viri sibi assignari usque ad dotis quantitatem, et iudex in sententia assignavit. Modo istud verbum "assignare" est dubium, potest nam intelligi per translationem dominii ... Item poterit se habere loco pignoris, ut loco custodie."

122 Ibid., no. 93: "Solutio ibi non procedit aliqua causa, unde in dubio non praesumitur causa donationis, sed causa custodie: hic secus"; Baldus to *l. Ubi adhuc*: "Extra quero, pone quod constante matrimonio: quia vir male utebatur substantia sua, hoc liquidato, et viro legitime citato. Iudex dixit ita tibi mulieri assigno tale predium viri tui pro dote tua. Numquid per ista verba significat translationem dominii in mulierem, an vero possideat solummodo iure pignoris? Dicit Bartolus in l. Si constante, quod verbum 'assigno'quandoque significat iuris translationem quandoque non, secundum quod ratio iuris patitur, et hec doctrina est vera, ex qua infert quod in casu dotis restituende, ista assignatio intelligatur facta loco restitutionis et sic cum translatione dominii." After citing Baldus's opinion, Ludovicus Pontanus (Romanus) to *l. Si constante* (48r, no. 41) stated: "que probat quod verbum, 'assigno' actioni adiectum a iudice prolatum, denotat ipsius actionis translationem. Dum autem circa hoc vult quod per hec verba, 'assigno tibi dotem,' a iudice prolata: in dubio intelligitur in mulierem translatum dotis dominium." In an opinion of uncertain authorship preserved in a collection of *consilia* of Marianus and Bartholomaeus Socinus, we read: "nam ista communis conclusio doctorum quod ubicumque agitur ad dotis consignationem actione personali, tunc consignatio operatur dominii translationem, ut concludit Bartolus in d. l. Si constante"; Marianus Socinus and Bartholomaeus Socinus, *Consilia* (Venice, 1579), vol. 1, 113va–15va, cons. 61. See also the critical discussion of these texts by Alexander Tartagnus to *l. Si constante*, 43v, nos. 32–3.

123 Kuehn, "Family Solidarity in Exile," 431–7.

124 These questions were raised in a *questio* by the thirteenth-century jurist Martinus de Fano. See Bellomo, *Quaestiones*, 306, no. [214].

125 For what follows, see Cinus de Pistorio to *l. Ubi adhuc*, 308r–v, no. 19, who followed the opinion of Dinus, while rejecting "quidam moderniores dicunt, quod est casus quod confessio non praeiudicat." See also Albericus de Rosate to *l. Ubi adhuc*, 258v, no. 18.

126 Bartolus to *l. Si constante*, 19v, nos. 95–100.

127 Herlihy has pointed out that, in Pisa from 1100 onward, "increasing demands for the notary's services were causing extensive delays in redaction. Sometimes notaries might die before they had formally redacted all their rough drafts"; *Pisa in the Early Renaissance*, 4 and chap. 1: "The Notarial Chartulary." See also Meyer, "Hereditary Laws"; Gaulin, "Affaires Privées."

128 For Pisa and Vicenza, see references in n. 105 above. For Florence, see PR, 126 (9 Mar. 1434/5), 430rff; PR, 128 (23 Dec. 1437), 215rff. This legislation was part of a sweeping campaign against the fraudulent abuse of emancipation, repudiations of inheritance, and the like: see Kuehn, "*Multorum Fraudibus Occurrere*"; and his *Heirs*. On fraudelent use of the wife's legal remedy in late medieval Perpignan, see Winer, *Women*, 32.

129 Notificazioni di atti di emancipazione, vols. 3–17 (years: 1435–1535). The cases are recorded at the end of each volume. I am extremely grateful to Thomas Kuehn for alerting me to these cases.

130 Ulivi, "Su Pietro Di Niccolò Da Filicaia," 1–7. For a profusely documented case of 1545, in which Camilla de' Bardi sued to recover her dowry from her husband, Jacopo di Piero Guicciardini, a merchant whose commercial dealings unraveled, see Archivio Guicciardini, Processi 12 ("Sei pezzi di scritture dell'inopia d. monna Camilla de' Bardi, moglie di Jacopo di Piero Guicciardini"). I owe this reference to my friend the late Gino Corti. On Jacopo, see the bio-bibliographical profile by Moreno, "Guicciardini, Jacopo," in *DBI*, 118–21. Earlier, Jacopo's brother, Francesco Guicciardini – a jurist as well as a writer and statesman – had counseled several wives whose husbands were approaching insolvency. See Cavallar, *Francesco Guicciardini, giurista*, 340, 344, 348.

131 *Glossa ordinaria* to *l. Ubi adhuc*, *v.* abutatur, 708b: "Quid autem si maritus efficiatur dives, an recipiet dotem? Respondeo non, secundum H <ugolinum>, ex causa iusta est soluta." On the citation of Hugolinus's glosses by Accursius, see Bellomo, "La scienza del diritto," 173ff., 189ff.

132 Odofredus to *l. Ubi adhuc*, 277r, no. 2, and Jacobus de Ravanis to *l. Ubi adhuc*, 231ra: "Sed queritur ponamus maritus vergit ad inopiam et sic mulier dotem exegit constante matrimonio, deinde maritus factus est dives et solvendo, nunquid ergo recuperabit dotem a muliere? Videtur quod sic, quia cessante causa cessat effectus. Videtur contra, nam ex quo dos iusta de causa reddita est; videtur quod non debeat de cetero reddi marito, ut ff. qui satisda., cog., l. Sciendum, in finali [Dig. 2. 8. 15] quod dicit, vult quod quilibet habet salva sua pacta in casum suum."

133 Dinus to *l. Si constante* (Urb. lat., 156, 68va): "Sed quid si restituta dote maritus factus est dives postea, an dos redibit in pristinum statum? Videtur quod non, ut l. Sciendum, § ultimo, supra, qui satisdare co. [Dig. 2. 8. 15] et l. Ubi adhuc, circa fi. [Cod. 5. 12. 29]; ar. contra, infra, de operis novi nuntiatione, l. Praetor [MS: Plane] ait [Dig. 39. 1. 20] cum lege equivalente et de inoff. te., l. Eum qui [Cod. 3. 28. 14] et l. Contra maiores [Cod. 3. 28. 16], supra, qui satis co., dy. Videtur non audiendus maritus postea, quia perinde habetur ac si matrimonium esset solutum, ut l. Ubi; sed dic favore dotis conservandum non subeuntem, dy."

134 The opinions of Ricardus Malumbra and Oldradus are reported by Baldus to *l. Ubi adhuc*: "Sed contra glossam facit ff. ut in pos. le., l. Si pecunie, § fi. [Dig. 36. 4. 6] et l. Hoc amplius, de dam. infe. [Dig. 39. 2. 9], ubi dicitur quod id tollit rem iam factam ex post facto superveniens quod impedit ab invito interveniens secundum Old[radum]. Idem tenet Ri[cardus] Mal[umbra], quia cessat causa restitutionis: ergo in primum statum debet dos reponi, ff. de condi. sine cause, l. Si fullo [Dig. 12. 7. 2]."

135 Jacobus de Arena's opinion is reported by Albericus de Rosate to *l. Ubi adhuc*, 268r, no. 17.

136 Cinus de Pistorio to *l. Ubi adhuc*, 308va, no. 24.

137 Bartolus to *l. Si constante*, 19vb–20ra, nos. 107–8: "Ego sustineo gl[ossam] et sic probo ... haec restitutio facta est ad securitatem mulieris et divitie supervenientes tendunt ad eundem effectum, scilicet ad securitatem mulieris, ergo non tollit restitutio iam facta."

138 Baldus to *l. Ubi adhuc*. For the *communis opinio*, see Angelus de Ubaldis to *l. Si constante*, 9r, no. 5; Alexander Tartagnus to *l. Si constante*, 44ra, no. 39; Johannes de Imola to *l. Si constante* 15ra; Petrus Ancharanus to *c. Per vestras*, 166a, no. 66; Antonius de Butrio to *Per vestras*, 62r, no. 8.

139 Their contribution is unsurprising, given the creation and development of the science of procedure in the Middle Ages; Van Caenegem, "History of European Civil Procedure"; Vallerani, *Medieval Public Justice*; Nörr, *Romanisch-kanonisches Prozessrecht.*

140 Hilaire, *Le régime*, 186–9; Courtemanche, *La richesses de femmes*, 121–6; Michaud, *Un signe*, 125–9; Smail, "Démanteler le patrimoine," 364–8; Winer, *Women*, 32–3; Kelleher, *The Measure of Woman*, 55–7; Lightfoot, "Family Interests?"

7. Women Married Elsewhere

1 Dig. 1. 5. 9: "In multis iuris nostri articulis deterior est condicio feminarum quam masculorum."

2 Feldner, "Der Ausschluss der Frau vom römischen *officium*."

3 Robinson, "The Historical Background," 56. On the proprietary and contractual capacities of Roman women, see idem, "The Status of Women"; Gardner, *Women in Roman Law*, 5–29; Guerra Medici, *I diritti delle donne*, 51–64; Arjava, *Women and Law*, esp. 230ff. For English translations of the fundamental Roman law texts on the status of women, see Evans Grubbs, *Women and the Law*, 16–80.

4 Romano, *Famiglia, successioni.*

5 Bellomo, *Ricerche sui rapporti*, 163–85; Mayali, *Droit savant*; Guerra Medici, "L'esclusione delle donne"; Lumia, "Morire a Siena"; Kuehn, "Person and Gender," 93–7.

6 See Kirshner, "Materials for a Gilded Cage," chap. 3 in this volume, which also considers daughters named universal heirs of their mother's estates.

7 Ibid.

8 Guerra Medici, *L'aria di città*, 19. Beyond the issue of women barred from public office and wielding public authority and power are the vexed questions of distinguishing public and private spaces and the extent to which women actively occupied public spaces in Italian urban communities. On which see Tomas, "Did Women Have a Space?"; R. Davis, "The Geography of Gender," and the bibliography cited therein; Muir, "In Some Neighbours"; Guzzetti, "Le donne"; and for medieval Flanders, Kittell's methodlogically astute study, "Women, Audience, and Public Acts."

9 Thomas, "*Origine*" *et* "*commune patrie*"; Goria, "*Romani*, cittadinanza ed estensione"; Garnsey, "Roman Citizenship."

10 Dig. 50. 1. 32, *Ea quae desponsa.*

11 Dig. 50. 1. 22. 1, *Filii libertorum*, § *Vidua mulier amissi.*

12 Cod. 10 39 (38). 4: "Origine propria neminem posse voluntate sua eximi manifestum est."

13 Dig. 50. 1. 38. 3, *Imperatores,* § *Item rescripserunt mulierum.*

14 Nörr, "Origo." A rule-validating exception, which relates to children of parents of different communities, was reported by Ulpian in *l. Municipes aut nativitas* (Dig. 50. 1. 1. 2). By special privilege, the children of mothers hailing from Troy, Delphi, and the southern coast of the Black Sea (Pontus), who were *municipes* (citizens) in their father's *origo*, were additionally to be treated as *municipes* in the mother's *origo*. Another exception relates to freed slaves (*libertini*), who adopted the place of origin of their master or multiple places of origin when they had several masters (Dig. 50. 1. 7, *Si quis*). On which see Gardner, *Being a Roman Citizen*, 7ff.

15 Davide, "La cittadinanza (secoli XIII–XV)." At Udine, until the end of the fourteenth century, the term *vicinus* identified an inhabitant with the rights and duties pertaining to citizenship; from the beginning of the fifteenth century, the same inhabitant was identified by the term *civis*.

16 See Kirshner, "*Civitas sibi faciat civem*"; Quaglioni, "Le radici," 127–44; Waley, *The Italian City-Republics*, 64–8; Costa, *Civitas*, 13ff.; Oldfield, "Citizenhip and Community"; Mueller, *Immigrazione e cittadinanza.* On the the variabilty of citizenship terminolgy and practices in northern Europe in the late Middle Ages, see Dilcher, "Zum Bürgerbegriff"; and Howell, "Citizenship and Gender"; and the contributions in Schwinges, ed., *Neubürger.*

17 Kirshner, "*Mulier Alibi Nupta*," 154–60.

18 Lett, "Genre e paix."

19 Kirshner, "*Mulier Alibi Nupta*," 151–4; Cagnin, *Cittadini e forestieri*, 228–31. A colorful example is Donina de Porris (or Porro), daughter of a noble Milanese jurist, intrepid lover of Bernabò Visconti, and shrewd businesswoman, who was granted Venetian citizenship in 1381. See Barbieri, "Donne ed affari." For other women granted Venetian citizenship, see the online data base *Cives* (http://www:civesveneciarum.net).

20 Studer, "Frauen im Bürgerrecht." On citizenship granted women who arrived in Avignon between 1367 and 1370 and who were also registered as household heads, see Rollo-Koster, "The Woman of Papal Avignon," 41ff.

21 Conte, *Tres Libri Codicis*.

22 On Pillius's life and writings, see Lange, *Römisches Recht*, vol. 1, 226–36. On the inclusion of Pillius's text into Rolandus's *Summa*, see Conte and Menzinger, *La Summa*, LVII–LVIII, LXXXVIff. On Azo, ibid., XXff.

23 The passage from Pillius is cited in Rolandus's *Summa* critically edited by Conte and Menzinger, ibid., 135–6, Cod. 10. 40, § 25–8, quote at § 28: "quod adeo uxor mariti domicilium sequitur quod propriam declinat originem, ut ff. ad municipal. l. ult. § Item rescriptum mulieris [Dig. 50. 1. 38. 3], quod non contingit in aliis qui domicilium mutant, ut superiori titutlo estensum est."

24 Ibid., 120, Cod. 10. 39, § 2; 121, Cod. 10, 39, § 11: "Nullus enim, ut dictum est, voluntate sua propriam potest declinare originem, etiam si rescriptum imperiale impetravit ... nisi forte publica necessitas hoc exigerit"; Cod. 10. 39, § 85.

25 Dig. 50. 1. 38. 3: "Item rescripserunt mulierem, quamdiu nupta est, incolam eiusdem civitatis videri, cuius maritus eius est, et ibi, unde originem trahit, non cogi muneribus fungi."

26 Menzinger, "La donna medievale," 127ff.

27 Conte and Menzinger, *La Summa*, 229–30, Cod. 10. 64, § 5: "In personalibus autem muneribus, si mulier sit nupta quia efficitur una caro cum viro, testante Dominio, et 'erunt duo in carne una ... et vir caput muleris sit' [Eph. 5. 31 and 23], sequitur domicilium viri et relinquit originarium; mulieres enim honore maritorum erigimus et gerere nobilitamus, et forum ex eorum persona statuimus." Rolandus probably had 1 Cor. 11:3 in mind as well: "caput autem mulieris, vir." Scholars now date the epistles to the Colossians and Ephesians after Paul's death.

28 Bellomo, *The Common Legal Past*, 172.

29 *Glossa ordinaria* to *l. Cives quidem*, v. *adlectio* (Cod. 10. 40 [39]. 7) (Venice, 1569), 53b: "Et nota quod incola fit solo animo facto eius qui acquirit domicilium, at civis fit alterius facto tantum, vel suo, vel alterius, ut in predictis exemplis in principio huius [that is, by manumssion, adoption,

and co-optation]. Et secundum hoc ratione patrie communis fit civis, non incola, ut ff. ad. mun., l. Roma [Dig. 50. 1. 33]; sed in muliere videtur contra, quia incola fit, ut ff. ad. mun., l. finalis, § 3 [Dig. 50. 1. 38. 3], et domicilium dicitur sortiri, ut infra, eadem l. finali. Et tamen ex alterius etiam facto pendet matrimonium, sed improprie dicitur ibi incola, nam civis fit." On the acquisition of citizenship through manumission, see Masi Doria, *Civitas*, 1–14; through adoption, Thomas, "*Origine*" *et* "*commune patrie*," 76ff.; Roumy, *L'adoption*, 230ff.

30 *Glossa ordinaria* to *l. Origine* (Cod. 10. 39 [38]. 4), v. *Origine* (Venice, 1569), 52va.

31 Kirshner, "*Mulier Alibi Nupta*," 154–8; Cecchi, "Disposizioni statutarie"; Della Misericordia, *Divenire comunità*, 383–8; Lett, "Genre e paix," 150–1.

32 Müller, "*Vir caput mulieris*." Note that recent scholarship has moved away from the theme of wifely subordination, exploring instead how the *unitas carnis* of the married couple engenders spousal equality: see the studies of Mayali, "*Due erunt in carne una*"; and Signori, "Similitude, égalité et réciprocité." Beginning with locus classicus Eph. 5:23, and then drawing on letters of remission, Hoareau-Dodineau ("*Vir est caput mulieris*?") analyzes how local community norms and customs defined and circumscribed the roles of both husband and wife in fourteenth-century France.

33 For the theoretical basis of the rule *forenses non gaudent beneficiis statutorum*, see Storti Storchi, *Ricerche sulla condizione*, 67–93; idem, "The Legal Status of Foreigners," 103ff.

34 My discussion of Bartolus's theory in this chapter amplifies my analysis in "*Mulier Alibi Nupta*," 161–6, where I also provide a working edition of his commentary to *l. Imperatores*, § *Item rescripserunt mulierum* [Dig. 50. 1. 38. 3], 173–5, which Osvaldo Cavallar and I have translated for our forthcoming *Medieval Italian Jurisprudence*, an anthology of medieval legal texts in English translation. The passage that I quote from Bartolus's commentary is based on our translation. Note that for the sake of readability I have omitted several citations of the *Codex* and *Digest* in Bartolus's text.

35 Ibid., 173–4.

36 Ibid., 174: On conceiving the relationship between husband and wife as that between *patronus* and *liberta*, see Kuehn, "Women, Marriage, and *Patria Potestas*," 202–3.

37 Kirshner, "*Mulier Alibi Nupta*," 173.

38 Bartolus to *l. Sancimus* (Cod. 5. 4. 24), in *Commentaria* (Venice, 1570–1), 170va, no. 1.

39 On Baldus's career and works, see Lange and Kriechbaum, *Römisches Recht im Mittelalter*, vol. 2, 749–95. A wealth of new material is found in two

collections of studies from 2000 celebrating the sixth centenarary of Baldus's death. One collection, inspired and guided by Vincenzo Colli, is published in *Ius Commune: Zeitschrift für europäische Rechtsgeschichte* (2000); the other in Frova et al., eds., *VI centenario della morte di Baldo degli Ubaldi, 1400–2000*.

40 For the figure three thousand, which includes unpublished as well as published *consilia*, I relied on the research of Vincenzo Colli of the Max-Planck-Institut für europäische Rechtsgeschichte, who is currently preparing an indexed census of Baldus's *consilia*. First fruits of his project are found in his "Il Cod. 351." See also Pennington, "Allegationes." For more research on *consilia*, including a bibliography, see Baumgärtner, ed., *Consilia im späten Mittelalter*, and a companion volume, Baumgärtner et al., eds., *Legal Consulting*. The essays by Padoa-Schioppa, Storti Storchi, Massetto, Di Renzo Villata, and Zorzoli in *Ius Mediolani* contain valuable materials on *consilia* in Milan and Lombardy. See also Vallerani's incisive study, "*Consilia iudicialia*."

41 See Kirshner and Pluss, "Two Fourteenth-Century Opinions"; Pluss, "Reading Case Law"; idem, "Baldus of Perugia"; Massetto, "Il lucro dotale."

42 Vallone, "La raccolta Barberini."

43 For example, a *consilium* dealing with nondotal properties opens: "Puncta super quibus petitur consilium sapientis sunt infrascripta" (MS 6, Regenstein Library, University of Chicago, 29vb–30va; hereafter cited as MS 6). Note that this incipit is missing in the Venetian edition of Baldus's *consilia* printed in 1575, vol. 3, 118va, cons. 418.

44 For payment to Baldus in 1372 for having written a *consilium* for a client, see Cenci, ed., *Documentazione di vita assisana*, vol. 1, 165.

45 Taddei, *Castiglion Fiorentino*, 136ff.

46 My search for this specific case in the Trecento records of the *podestà*, preserved in the Archivio Storico Comunale of Castiglion Fiorentino, proved fruitless.

47 The text cited here is based on my collation of MS BAV, Barb. lat. 1401, 71r–v, cons. 108, with the Venetian edition of 1575, vol. 5, 26r, cons. 100 (hereafter cited as Cons. 100): "In Christi nomine, amen. Considerato, quod dicta domina Agnes fuit et est uxor veri, naturalis et originarii Castellionensis, etiam ipsa tanquam eidem origini unita per virtutem matrimonii et tanquam pars corporis viri effecta dicitur esse et est de Castellione Aretino durante matrimonio. Nam matrimonium est istius virtutis ac nature, quod transfundit originem uxoris in originem viri, ut legitur et notatur in l. Origine, de mu. et origi., li. X° [Cod. 10. 39 (38). 4]. Hoc etiam probatur ex virtute unionis, in qua id quod potentius est trahit

ad se id quod est minus dignum, ut plene legitur et notatur extra, Ne sede vacante, c. i [X 3. 9. 1]. Sed nulla est maior unio, quam unio coniugalis, per quam vir et uxor efficiuntur una caro; etiam est quasi una substantia in duabus personis, ut l. 1, ff. rerum admotarum [Dig. 25. 2. 1], et ff. ad Sillaniano, l. 1, § Si vir aut uxor [Dig. 29. 5. 1. 15], et extra, de bigamis, c. Debitum [X 1. 21. 5]. Et ideo dicta domina Agnes tanquam vera et originaria civis dicte terre Castellionis debet reputari, cum iure divino sit una caro, et ius divinum consistat in veritate et non in fictione, sequitur quod proprie uxor est effecta concivis viri, et ita tenet glossa in l. Cives, Cod. de incolis [Cod. 10. 40 (39) 7], et Bartolus, ff. ad municipalem, l. fi., § Item rescripserunt." This *consilium* and others by Baldus on women married elsewhere are cited and briefly discussed by Canning, *The Political Thought*, 182–3; and Wells, *Law and Citizenship*, 8. Both authors ignore the juridical and factual questions specifically addressed by Baldus in his opinions, the methodological and textual challenges his opinions present to modern scholars, and the broader historical context attending the construction of women's juridical personality.

48 Baldus's predilection for philosophizing is discussed by Horn, "Philosophie in der Jurisprudenz," and Kriechbaum, "Philosophie und Jurisprudenz."

49 Børreson, *Subordination and Equivalence*, 158, citing S. Th. I, 92, 1, c; Bullough, "Medieval Medical"; Cadden, *Meanings of Sex*, 24ff., 169ff.

50 On the theory behind this point, see Kirshner, "A *Consilium* of Rosello." According Baldus, moreover, the wife's *forum*, the jurisdiction where one can sue and be sued as a legal resident, follows that of her husband, even if they are living together in the wife's hometown. See Baldus to *l. Cum quaedam puella* (Dig. 2. 1. 19), in *Commentaria* (Venice, 1599), 77v, no.1a.

51 Note that Trecento jurists used *patria* and *civitas* interchangeably.

52 Baldus employs similar language in an oft-cited *consilium* dealing with a woman identified as a native of Mantova who marries a man identified as a native of Parma ("Seya origine paterna Mantuana nupsit Titio originario civitatis Parme"). Does Seya, by virtue of marriage, become an original citizen of Parma? No doubt, she does, according to Baldus: "Si ergo probata est origo, non est dubitandum, quod ista Seya et Parmensis origine propria, et ab eventu dicitur originaria et tamquam originaria subicitur legibus municipalibus et econverso gaudet benefitio legum municipalium, qui sicut quis oritur civitati." The text cited is based on my collation of MS BAV, Barb. lat. 1406, 65r–66r, cons. 461, with the Venetian edition of 1575, vol.1, 146r–v, cons. 456.

53 Baldus to *l. Ea quidem* (Cod. 9. 2. 7), in *Commentaria* (Venice, 1599), 208ra, no. 7: "Fictio est falsitas pro veritate accepta ex specialissima et

iustissima causa in iure expressa." See also Barassi, "Le *fictiones juris*"; Todescan, *Diritto e realità*, 105ff.; Thomas, "*Fictio legis*." For Baldus's use of legal fiction in regard to statutory citizenship, see the contrasting views of Kirshner, "*Ars imitatur naturam*"; and Canning, *The Political Thought*, 174ff.

54 Cuturi, "Baldo degli Ubaldi in Firenze," 3.

55 Mayali, "*Due erunt in carne una*," 173.

56 Baldus to *l. Qui in provincia* (Dig. 23. 2. 57), in *Commentaria* (Venice, 1599), 187rb, no. 7 (addition to his *lectura antiqua*): "quae virum et uxorem fingit unam carnem." Other examples of *fictio unitiva*: two days forming one day and father and son one body.

57 The statutes of Castiglion Aretino and Montecchio Vesponi are no longer extant.

58 Cons. 100: "Secundo, est considerandum de dicto statuto in libro secundo, nunquid sit pena de eo tanquam de persona, que debeat haberi et tractari in civilibus et criminalibus causis in communi Castillionis tanquam Castillionensis, considerato quod erat Monticchiensis. Et dicendum est, quod non. Nam verba statuti sub rubrica 'quod Monticchienses tractentur ut Castillionenses,' habent istam modificationem et conditionem, videlicet dummodo versa vice Castillionenses et districtuales tractentur in castro Monticchi ut Monticchienses in quocunque casu. Et nota hoc verbum 'in quocunque casu.' Nam, aut nos consideramus modum tractandi ex dispositione legis, aut ex contingentia factorum. Siquidem ex legum dispositione apparet quod statutum, quod Castellionenses tractantur ut Monticchienses in tribus causis, scilicet: civilibus, criminalibus et in dampnis datis. Et de aliis nichil est statutum, puta in datiis, collectis et similibus. Ergo illa verba 'in quocumque casu' non sunt verificata, quia sunt verba universalia, et sic conditio, que requirit dictum statutum sub rubrica 'quod Monticchienses, etc.' non est impleta. Ergo dispositio illius statuti est nulla, ut ff. de pigno. ac., l. Si necessarias, § Si annua [Dig. 13. 7. 8. 3]. Item, quia apparet statutum Monticchiensium cassum, nec ad mulierem pertinet de iuris apicibus disputare." Such reciprocal pacts were standard, especially between neighboring communities. A reciprocal citizenship pact was concluded in 1337 between Arezzo and Castiglion, which was edited by Ghizzi, *Storia della terra*, pt. 3, 203: "Item quod cives et comitatini civitatis Arretii tractentur, et tractare debeant Castilionenses in civilibus, et criminalibus quaestionibus tamquam Castilionenses; et eodem modo tractentur, et tractare debeant Castilionenses et eorum districtuales, Arretii in omnibus questionibus tamquam cives." For a reciprocal citizienship pact between Parma and Reggio at the beginning of the fifteenth century, see Albini, "Una reciproca."

59 On spousal homicides in this period, see Lansing, "Poisoned Relations."
60 BAV, Vat. lat. 8068, 88v–89r: "Sed adhuc remanet maius dubium. Nam ista mulier fuit occisa in comitatu Senarum, ergo homicida illuc remictendus. Et sic per potestatem Montispoliciani puniri non potest, ut l. Si cui, § finali, ff. de accusationibus [Dig. 48. 2. 7. 5], C. ubi de criminibus agi oportet, aut. Qua in provincia [Cod. 3. 15. 2]. Dico, quod hiis non obstantibus, potestas predictus potest inquire et punire. Nam, cum uterque sit civis illa ratione originis, ut l. Origine, C. de municipibus et originariis, libro X [Cod. 10. 39 [38]. 4], illa ratione sequele et coniunctionis, ut notat glossa in dicta l. Cives [Cod. 10. 40 [39]. 7], et l. Imperatores, § Item rescripxerunt [Dig. 50. 1. 38. 3], uterque subiacet eius iurisdictioni." The English translation of Jacobus's *consilium* based on my edition will appear in *Medieval Italian Jurisprudence* (n. 34 above). For the relevant statute of Montepulciano, see Morandi, ed., *Statuto del comune*, 170–1, lib. 3, rubr. 12, *De pena homicidii.*
61 For example, in Marri Camerani, ed., *Statuto di Arezzo, 1327*, 209, lib. 4, rubr. 22, *De pena homicidii*; 213, rubr. 32, *De pena forensis offendentis civem et e contra*): The fine for homicide imposed by the statutes of Arezzo was 2,000 pounds. Foreigners who committed crimes against citizens had to pay double the fine citizens would pay for the same crimes. Castiglion Fiorentino, Archivio Comunale, *Statuti* (1384), 130r, lib. 3, cap. 8, *De pena forensis offendentis Castilionensis*: "Si quis forensis quomodocumque offenderet Castilionensem vel eius districtualem, condemnetur et condemnari debeat in duplo illius pene qua condemnaretur Castilionensis, si offendisset talium Castilionensem" (my transcription). A complete transcription of these statutes, prepared by Ornella Catani and Daniela Serafini, is preserved in the Archivio Comunale.
62 Cons. 100: "Satis est enim, quod originaria dici potuit, ut ff. de adulteriis, l. Si ex lege [Dig. 48. 5. 44]. Si vero nos consideramus facti contingentiam, <et> tunc si actendamus probationem, videtur probatum de non tractatu. Si vero consideramus iuris dispositionem, debuit et debet probari de dicto tractatu, de quo disponit statutum. Nam cum facti sit, non praesumitur, et quod in facto consistat, est textus, ff. de verb, obli., l. Quidam cum filium [Dig. 45. 1. 132]. Et ideo pro dicto homicidio debet imponi pena pecuniaria v[c] librarum denariorum et non pena capitis." Under the statutes of Castiglion Fiorentino, capital punishment was the penalty for the premeditated murder of a citizen, 500 pounds for the murder of a foreigner, and 200 pounds for inflicting accidental death: *Statuti* (1384), 128r, lib. 3, cap. 3, *De pena occidentis et veneno tossicantis*. According to Baldus, when penalties (for example, monetary) are lighter than those imposed by the *ius commune* (for

example, capital punishment), they are enforceable, save when the monetary fine is ridiculously low. See his *Tractatus duo de vi*, 22.

63 The text cited here is based on my collation of BAV, Vat. lat. 1401, 103r–v with the Venetian edition of 1575, vol. 5, 35v–36r, cons. 139 (hereafter cited as Cons. 139): "Statuto communis Assisii cavetur, quod nulla mulier civitatis Assisii vel comitatus eiusdem cuiuscumque conditionis et status existat, possit contrahere vel testari sine presentia sui viri, si nupta fuit. Modo quedam mulier paterna et propria origine et vere Perusina nupta fuit Assisii et ibidem cum viro longo tempore moram traxit et tandem fecit testamentum cum presentia sui viri. Demum ista mulier Perusina est reversa, et absente dicto suo viro et non consentiente, dictum primum testamentum mutavit et revocavit; quod secundum testamentum factum fuit in civitate Perusii ubi viget ius commune. Queritur, nunquid dictum secundum testamentum valeat necne? Ex isto temate dua oriuntur dubia. Primo, an mulier Perusina nupta Assisinati dicatur esse mulier civitatis vel comitatus Assisii. Secundo, an dicta mulier reversa ad propriam patriam naturalem possit facere testamentum secundum leges proprie patrie quocumque loco valuerint, an non ligetur legibus fori mariti."

64 *Statuta Magnificae Civitatis Asisii*, 8v, lib. 2, rubr. 23, *Quod mulier non possit testari, contrahere, alienare nisi prout infra capitulum*. I cite the copy in the Biblioteca del Senato, Rome (Statuti 1209).

65 On Baldus as an *advocatus* of the commune of Assisi in 1374, see Cenci, ed., *Documentazione di vita assisana*, vol. 1, 167; for Baldus's other Assisian *consilia*, see ibid., 165 (year: 1372); MS 6, 15rb–vb (= Venetian edition of 1575, vol. 3, 117rb–va, cons. 412); 45ra–vb (= Venetian edition of 1575, vol. 3, 6rab, cons. 14); 82rb–va (=Venetian edition of 1575, vol. 3, 113ra, cons. 399): "Statuto civitatis Assisi cavetur nulla mulier posset testari seu aliam ultimam voluntatem condere." For the full contents of MS 6, see Izbicki and Kirshner, "*Consilia* of Baldus."

66 *Statuta Magnificae Civitatis Asisii*, 8v: "Pro tranquillo et pacifico statu hominum civitatis Asisii et comitatus eiusdem et ad conservationem iurium ipsorum."

67 So alleged Baldus's brother, Angelus de Ubaldis in a *consilium* involving the application of Todi's *Nulla mulier* statute. See his *Consilia* (Lyon, 1551), 184vb, cons. 333: "Quia dictum statutum emanavit in favorem mulieris propter imbecillitatem sexus." On the Roman and Byzantine sources for this (in)famous construct, see Beaucamp, "Le vocabulaire"; Crook, "Feminine Inadequacy"; Dixon, "*Infirmitas sexus*"; Saradi-Mendelovici, "A Contribution"; for early modern Italy, see Feci, *Pesci*, 46–9.

68 For a sixteenth-century overview of these statutes, see Tuschus, *Practicarum conclusionum*, vol. 7, 456–7, concl. 677 (*Statutum circa successionem mulierum nuptarum extra territorium excludens eas, quando habeat locum vel secus, et an valeat, vel non*). A crisp discussion of the constraints on medieval Italian testators is found in Romano, *Famiglia, successioni*, 49ff. On testamentary freedom and its limitations in canon law, see Sheehan, "The Influence of Canon Law"; and Reid, *Power over the Body*, 153–210.

69 *Statuta Magnificae Civitatis Asisii*, 8v: "Statuterunt et ordinaverunt, quod nulla mulier civitatis Asisii vel comitatus eiusdem cuiuscumque conditionis et status existat possi, nec debeat modo aliquo testari, codicillari, donare seu aliquam ultimam voluntatem facere vel disponere, seu venditionem, permutationem, donationem, concessio[n]em, transactionem vel aliquam alienationem seu obligationem cuiuscumque generis et conditionis existat facere sine presentia et consensu sui viri et patris, si virum et patrem habeat; et si patrem tantum haberet et non virum, sine presentia et consensu patris; et si virum habeat et non patrem, sine presentia et consensu viri." For Baldus's analysis of "presentia et consensu sui viri et patris," see his commentary to *l. Soluto matrimonio*, § *Voluntatem* (Dig. 24. 3. 2. 3), in *Commentaria* (Venice, 1599), 4vb–5rb.

70 *Statuta Magnificae Civitatis Asisii*, 9r: "Et vir intelligatur ille ad prestandum presentiam et consensum modo predicto, qui cum muliere contraxerit matrimonium et consumaverit, vel cum ea steterit publice tamquam viri in una et eadem domo saltim per duos menses. Et ad probandum consummationem matrimonii sufficiat iuramentum viri et uxoris."

71 Kuehn, "Women, Marriage, and *Patria Potestas*."

72 *Statuta Magnificae Civitatis Asisii*, 8v.

73 See the opinion of Hostiensis cited in Kirshner, "Materials for a Gilded Cage," chap. 3 in this volume, p. 282, n. 38.

74 Thomas Aquinas's much-cited view is in *Summa Theologiae*, 2a2ae. Q 32, A 8 ad 2.

75 Jacobus de Voragine, *The Golden Legend*, vol. 1, 28.

76 *Statuta Magnificae Civitatis Asisii*, 8v–9r: "Liceat tamen dictis mulieribus sine presentia et consensu dictarum personarum testari, codicillari et ultimam voluntatem disponere et facere de bonis ipsorum et dotibus eorundem usque in quantitatem viginti librarum denariorum pro qualibet centenario dotis ipsius mulieris et bonorum omnium que habent; et etiam pro necessitatibus suis inter vivos alienare usque in dictam quantitatem supradictam prohibitione aliqua non obstante."

77 For example, Baldus to *l. Si uxorem tuam* (Cod. 6. 46. 5), in *Commentaria* (Venice, 1599),165ra, no. 7: "Ceterum si uxor faceret aliquam artem, vel

mercantiam, vel esset chyrugica vel obstetrix, que quidem non sunt opere domestice et familiares, id quod acquirit ex istis operis, non acquireret viro, quia nec ad preceptum viri tenetur negociari."

78 Schupfer, "L'autorizzazione maritale"; Niccolai, *La formazione*, 291–3; Vernelli, "Note sulla condizione"; Feci, *Pesci*, 25ff.; Chabot, *La dette des familles*, 52ff. Not surprisingly, like all things in decentralized Italy, *Nulla mulier* statutes were marked by local differences. For example, in Spoleto women were given the right to dispose of one-fourth of their properties, including their earnings, in contrast to one-fifth in Assisi. See *Statutorum Magnificae Civitatis Spoleti*, 53v, lib. 3, cap. 25. See also Chiodi, "Scelte normative," 254–5. For Siena, Brizio, "La dote," 13. For Venice, Guzzetti, *Venezianische Vermächtnisse*, 45–6; idem, "Women's and Testamentary Practices," 83.

79 A husband pronounced guilty of killing his wife thereby forfeited his claim to her dowry.

80 Bartolus to *l. De quibus* (Dig. 1. 3. 32) in *Commentaria* (Venice, 1526–9) 21vb, no. 27; to *l. Exigere* (Dig. 3. 1. 65), 165vb; for a sixteenth-century overview, see Rolandus a Valle, *Questiones de lucro dotis*, in 356va, *Quaestio* XIII. For a solid analysis, though limited to printed sources, Lorenz, *Das Dotalstatut.*

81 Briganti, *La donna*, 30–1; for Perugia's statute, Salem Elsheikh, ed., *Statuto del Comune e del Popolo di Perugia*, 360, lib. 2. cap. 3, *Degle stromente dotaglie e ke agiano força de confessione.*

82 Bartolus to *l. Cunctos populos* (Cod. 1. 1. 1), in *Commentaria* (Venice, 1570–1), 4ra, nos. 18–19: "Statutum est Assisii, ubi est celebratus contractus dotis et matrimonii, quod vir lucretur tertiam partem dotis, uxore moriente sine liberis. In hac vero civitate Perusii, unde est vir, statutum est quod vir lucretur dimidiam; quid spectabitur? Certe statutum terrae viri, ut d. l. Exigere." See also Kirshner, "Dowry, Domicile, and Citizenship," chap. 8 in this volume.

83 *Statuta Magnificae Civitatis Asisii*, 12v, lib. 2, rubr. 43, *Quod in adventu dotis restituende tertia pars remaneat viro.*

84 Rolandus a Valle, *Quaestiones de lucro dotis*, 352r–53r, *Quaestio* IV. Despite inconsistencies, Baldus generally held that the husband's statutory share of the dowry should be treated as compensation for having supported his wife.

85 Baldus, *Tractatus duo de vi*, 33–4, and for what follows.

86 The *ius commune* as Roman law is not unique to this passage; it is generally assumed throughout Baldus's civil law commentaries and *consilia.*

87 On the Roman husband's obligation, upon his wife's predecease, to return the dowry (*dos profectitia*) to his father-in-law, see Gardner, "The Recovery

of the Dowry." For the medieval revisions of Roman dowry law, see Bellomo, *Ricerche sui rapporti*, 187–205. See also Kirshner, "The Morning After," chap. 4 in this volume, p. 99.

88 These general points are discussed by Lorenz, *Das Dotalstatut*.

89 In the Venetian edition of 1575, vol. 3, 9va, cons. 31. My dating of the *consilium* is based on the assumption that Baldus wrote it while a professor at the University of Pavia (1390–1400).

90 Cons. 139: "Iste passus est michi satis dubius propter verba statuti dicentis 'quod nulla mulier civitatis Assisii' etc. Nam Perusina nupta Assisinati propriam et naturalem originem retinet que non potest extingui, licet possit velari quadam iuris fictione, que est, quoniam matrimonium rapit nuptam ad civitatem viri ac si ibi nata esset." By choosing the verb "rapit," Baldus was signaling that the force uprooting and seizing the wife and propelling her to the husband's city was so strong that it was tantamount to abduction (*raptus*). On abduction marriages in Roman law, see Evans Grubbs's close-grained study "Abduction Marriages."

91 Cons. 139: "Tamen ibi est fictio, que non videtur habere locum in statutis aliquid disponentibus contra ius gentium et contra ius commune, ut fi. so. ma., l. Si vero, § De viro [Dig. 24. 3. 64. 9]. Unde statutum non videtur loqui in hac muliere, de qua queritur, ut ff. ad municip., l. 1 [Dig. 50. 1. 1]. Ad hoc facit glo. vulgaris in l. iiia, § Hec autem, ff. de neg. ge. [Dig. 3. 5. 3. 7], ubi glo. notat quod de casibus fictis necesse est specialem legem fieri. Alias non comprehendentur sub lege generaliter loquente etiam sub iure communi, nedum sub iure municipali quod est stricte interpretationis." On literal and liberal interpretation, see Sbriccoli, *L'interpretazione dello statuto*, 214–30, 422–9; Horn, *Aequitas*, 30–2.

92 Cons. 139: "Nam matrimonium sua natura novat originem mulieris et ad originem viri transfundit propter potentiam eiusdem unionis. Nam cum vir er uxor efficiantur unum corpus et una caro, id, quod est potentius, rapit id, quod minus potest, et in se totaliter transfert, ut not. Cod. de mu. et ori., l. Origine. Ad hoc facit quod not. in c. i. Ne sede va. [X 3. 9. 1]. Sed certe ista ratio non videtur vera. Nam sicut substantia originis non potest mutari, ita nec nomen potest perimi et ideo etiam de origine nupte mulieris iura tractant et disponunt de origine secundum originem suam, ut legitur et notatur in l. 1, Cod. de mulieribus et in quo loco, libro x°. Unde mulier nupta non perdit privilegia nec iura communia patrie sue naturalis, quia naturalia mutari non possunt, ut ff. de cap. min., <l.> Tutelas [Dig. 4. 5. 7] et l. Legatum [Dig. 4. 5. 10], et ff. ad muni., l. Assumptio. Nam origo facti est, et in facto consistit et facta cause quoad naturalem veritatem pro infectis haberi non possunt ... Et licet uxor transeat ad domicilium viri, ut ff. de iur. om. iu., l. Cum

quedam puella [Dig. 2. 1. 19] et ff. de iudiciis, l. Exigere dotem [Dig. 5. 1. 65] et ff. ad municip., l. De iuri. [Dig. 50. 1. 37] et l. Lucius [Dig. 50. 1. 21], tamen patriam et cognationem naturalem retinet, que inseparabilis est, ut arg. Cod. de adoptio, l. Cum in adoptivis, in penultima columpna [Cod. 8. 47[48]. 10. 1f]." For another *consilium* in which Baldus opined that civil law or a municipal statute "non potest tollere naturalem affectionem," see the Venetian edition of 1575, vol. 5, 16v, cons. 54.

93 Baldus to *l. Cum in adoptivis* (Cod. 8. 47[48]. 10. 1f). On this and related texts, see Roumy, *L'adoption*, 135, 145ff., 223ff.

94 For Baldus, Justinian's *Corpus iuris* is synonymous with both the *ius civile* and *ius commune*. See Horn, *Aequitas*, 54.

95 See Kirshner, "*Civitas sibi faciat civem*." On the requirements for acquiring Assisian citizenship, see *Statuta Magnificae Civitatis Asisii*, 19r, lib. 1, rubr. 21, *De novis civibus recipiendis*. This statute does not apply to foreign women married to Assisians, because the citizenship of these women is governed by the provisions of the *ius commune*.

96 Cons 139: "Et ista nomina 'de civitate vel communitate' significant originem, ut not. ff. de excu. tuto., l. Sed et reprobari, in verbo 'Cumanenses' [Dig. 27. 1. 6. 6]. Nam de aliquo loco proprie et vere dicitur ille, qui est de illo loco secundum originem et naturalem veritatem et non secundum fictionem, arg. Cod. de hiis qui veniam et., l. finalis [Cod. 2. 44(45). 4]; secus, si ista dictio 'de' apponeretur provincie sed non civitati, ut si verba dicerent 'quicumque de provincie Tuscie' et cetera. Nam nomen 'provincie' generalissimum est et etiam incolas comprehendit propter suam latitudinem in modo significandi ei attributo a iure, ut legitur et not. ff. de verborum signi., l. Provinciales [Dig. 50. 16. 190]. Solo hic considerandum est primo, numquid, quando fictio sive interpretatio iuris communis disponit super interpretatione alicuius vocabuli, talis interpretatio habeat locum in statutis utentibus illo vocabulo, et dico, quod sic, ut ff. ad l. Falc, l. 1, § 1 [Dig. 35. 2. 1. 1]. Secundo est considerandum, quid est dictum 'de civitate,' utrum sit dictum, id est de hiis, qui reguntur iure civili illius civitatis, an sit dictum et de loco sic confinato <et> muris cincto. Nam si verba accipiuntur civiliter, id est primo modo, ista mulier nupta Assisi est vere et proprie de civitate Assisii et de civilitate, id est, sub iure civili illius civitatis. Est enim vere civis, quia vera civilitas potest induci per dispositionem legalem et non solum per ius commune, sed etiam per ius municipale, ut not. Bartolus, ff. de usucap. l. Si is qui pro emptore [Dig. 41. 3. 15]. Sed si ista verba intelliguntur materialiter 'pro loco muris cincto,' tunc vera sine fictione dici non potest." The restriction of true citizenship to those originating and residing within the city walls was designed to prevent *contadini* and rustics from claiming

citizenship status. See Bartolus, *Consilia* (Venice, 1585), 46ra, cons. 196, no. 6. On this theme, Chiodi, "Tra la *civitas* e il *comitatus*," esp. 275ff.

97 Kuehn's translation, "Woman, Marriage, and *Patria Potestas*," 203.

98 Cons. 139: "Finaliter videtur dicendum, quod ius commune trahatur ad municipale et e contrario, et quod ista mulier debeat sequi statuta originis viri, per que statuta est quodam modo quoad hec in potestate viri, sicut etiam de iure longobardo, et ideo maxime de dote sua obstante statuto disponere non possit, licet de iure communi esset contrarium." On the husband's *potestas* in Lombard law, see Cortese, "Per la storia," esp. 378–9; Storti Storchi, "La tradizione longobarda," 79ff.

99 Tuschus, *Practicarum conclusionum*, 8: 735, concl. 387, *Uxor sortitur domicilium et forum mariti*, nos. 14–16, where Baldus's opinion on Assisi is cited.

100 On the topos of women who refuse to be submissive to men, thereby challenging sexual hierarchies, see S. Smith, *The Power of Women*.

101 *Statuta Magnificae Civitatis Asisii*, 12v, lib. 2, rubr. 43: "Et hoc locum habeat et intelligatur in originalibus civibus Asisii et in omnibus aliis eiusdem comitatus et districtus et in mulieribus forensibus quas homines de Asisio habent et haberent pro uxore. Et intelligatur et locum habeat in preteritiis, pendentibus et futuris et in aliis quorum matrimonium non est solutum."

102 The text cited here is based on my collation of BAV, Barb, lat 1401, 45v–46r with the Venetian edition of 1575, vol. 5, 58rab, cons. 226 (hereafter cited as Cons. 226): "Premissis verbis statutis Viterbiensis disponentis sub hac forma: 'Nulla mulier habens filios vel filias ex filio possit testari, codicillari vel aliquem contractum facere extra personas filiorum, et si secus fecerit testamentum, codicillarii et contractus sint nulli ipso iure.' Accidit quod domina Stefania origine Viterbiensis nupta Baschiensis, quia uxor Ranerii Busse, dicto Ranerio mortuo, condidit testamentum, in quo inter cetera Franciscum eius filium etiam dicti quondam domini Ranerii in tertia parte hereditatis et bonorum suorum sibi heredem instituit et tres eius neptes ex Johanna, quondam ipsius domine Stefanie filia, in reliquis duabus partibus heredes instituit atque fecit. Mortua est dicta domina Stefania." For another *consilium* of Baldus on a case in Viterbo, see MS 6, 35vab, and the Venetian edition of 1575, vol. 3. 2vab, cons. 3.

103 None of these characters appears, for Viterbo, in Pinzi, *Storia della città*; or Dilonardo Buccolini, "Note sul popolazionismo"; or, for Baschi, in A. Ricci, "Storia di un comune"; Celata, "La condizione contadina"; or Rossi Caponeri, "Nota su alcuni testamenti."

104 The statute cited by Baldus is found neither in the redaction of 1251–2 nor in the extract of the 1356 redaction, which is limited to criminal law. It is

likely, however, that the statute was originally included in the 1356 redaction of Viterbo's statutes, in the section dealing with civil matters. See Egidi, ed., *Statuti della provincia romana*, 93–269 (1251–2); 271–82 (1356). Signorelli's *Leggi e costumi*, an old study on marriage and family in late medieval Viterbo, is inadequate and needs to be updated. On the legal position of women in Lazio, see D'Alatri's summary, "Donne di ieri"; and the analysis of Lombardo and Morelli, "Donne e testamenti."

105 I used the manuscript in the Biblioteca degli Ardenti in Viterbo: II, A, 7, 8, 175v–78r, lib. 2, rubr. 74, *Qualiter mulier habens filios vel filias non possit testari, codicillari nec aliquem contractum facere extra personas filiorum.* I also consulted a seventeenth-century copy of the 1469 statutes in the Biblioteca del Senato: *Statuti* 765, 101v–2r, lib. 2, rubr. 74. The 1469 statutes are now edited in Buzzi, *Lo statuto del comune di Viterbo*, 145–7, lib. 2, rubr. 85.

106 Cons. 226: "Queritur, nunquid dictum valeat testamentum et videtur quod non, quia vidua lege sue originis potest prohiberi testari, quia veritas nature matrimonii imagine non obumbravit<ur>. Est enim inseparabile quicquid origine coheret, ut ff. ad municipales, l. Adsumptio, et ff. de captivis, l. In bello, § Facte [Dig. 49. 15. 12. 2]. Adeo ut naturalis veritas nec auctoritate senatus mutari possit, ut l. i et secunda, ff. de usufructu earum rerum, que usu consumuntur [Dig. 7. 5. 1 and 2]. Cum enim sit subiecta ratione originis, ergo statutum valet in ipsius persona. Preterea ipsa adhuc remanet subiecta quoad bona, que habet in originis territorio, ut l. i, Cod. de mulieribus et in quo loco, libro x°. Ergo respectu talium bonorum valet statutum. Nam si testamentum militis potest valere respectu certorum bonorum, ergo et legis dispositio, ut notant doctores in l. Cunctos populos [Cod. 1. 1. 1]. Preterea ista mulier prius fuit subiecta statuto quam nupta, et ideo nuptie non liberant eam a vinculo statuti, arg. ff. ad municip., l. Incola et hiis [Dig. 50. 1. 29]. Preterea nupta non liberatur a potestate patris, ergo nec a potestate patrie, ut not. Cod. de condi. insertis, l. Si uxor [Cod. 6. 46. 5]. Licet enim nupserit, tamen iura sue patrie non remictit, sicut nec patronus, qui non consensit nuptiis liberte, ymo et si consensit, ut Cod. de operis libertorum, l. Quod ex liberta [Cod. 6. 3. 11]. Preterea facere statuta non est iurisdictionis contentiose, sed est quedam iurisdictio per se, ut ff. de adil. ed., l. Sciendum [Dig. 21. 1. 63], et nulla lege cavetur, quod a tali iurisdictione per matrimonium sit exemptus: ergo remanet sub statuto."

107 Ibid.: "In contrarium videtur. Nam per matrimonium ius originis mutatur, ut Cod. de municipibus et originariis, l. Origine. Et fit quedam novatio et transumptio, ut ff. de iuri. omnium iudicum, l. Cum quedam puella [Dig. 2. 1. 19]. Preterea non tenetur parere foro originis, ut ff. ad municipales, l. De

iure [Dig. 50. 1. 37]. Preterea istud statutum disponit respectu persone, sed hoc respectu non subiacet sue origini, ut not. in dicta l., de mulieribus et in quo loco, et idem in vidua, quod in nupta, ut ff. de senatoribus, l. Femine [Dig. 1. 9. 8 pr]."

108 Ibid.: "Solutio, in hoc puncto dicendum est, quod statutum duo disponere videtur: unum prohibendo et aliud tacite conferendo bona filiis in quorum favore disponit, ut ff. ad Trebel., l. Qui filium, in principio [Dig. 36. 1. 1. 76]. Unde hoc respectu valet statutum quoad bona, que sunt in suo territorio, ut Cod. non licere habitatoribus metrocomie, l. 1., libro xi° [Cod. 11. 56. 1]. Sed esto quod ita sit, tamen in casu nostro statutum non prohibet testari in neptis, quia non dicitur extra filios qui neptes instituit, ut Cod. de condi. insertis, l. 1 [Cod. 6. 46. 1], et quod not. ff. solu. ma., l. Si dotali [Dig. 24. 3. 48]. Cum enim debeatur ei hereditas iure nature, absonum esset dicere quod non posset eis relinqui, ut l. Cum ratio, de bonis dampnatorum [Dig. 48. 20. 7 pr]."

109 Ibid.: "Statutum enim non videtur ponderasse sexum secundum naturalem, erga liberos habendam caritatem, cum dicat 'habens filios vel filias.' Ecce femininum genus. Nescio tamen si scriptura statuti sit corrupta, quia si diceretur 'habens filios vel filias ex filio,' tunc statutum magis precise loqueretur ad excludendum, quia ponderaret sexum masculinum, sicut in multis ponderatur, ut ff. de statu hominum, l. In multis [Dig. 1. 5. 9]. Et de media iurisprudentia olim hoc erat, ut patet in l. Maximum vitium [Cod. 6. 28. 4], et institi., de hereditatibus, § Item vetustas [Inst. 3. 1. 15]."

110 Ibid.: "Sed iniquum videtur dicere quod mater non possit instituere filiam vel neptem, et forte si statutum hoc vellet expresse, non posset: quia esset quid contra ius naturale. Et pone: mater habet filium et filiam, et pater decessit inops. Mater vult tacere testamentum, quia forte vult relinquere aliqua ad pias causas et pro necessitate salutis anime sue, et vult filie aliquid relinquere, ne mendicent. Si intelligatur statutum ut verbum sonat, cogetur filia femina ire mendicando. Nam non valet institutio, si actendamus corticem statuti. Quapropter dico, quod in terris ecclesie, in quibus terris non valent statuta, qua sunt omnino iniqua et contra omnem naturalem rationem, et qua papa nullo modo confirmaret, aut tale statutum non valet, aut est intelligendum sane et supplendum mediante naturali ratione."

111 Ibid.: "Et dominus Dynus tenet c. Indultum [VI 5. 13. 7], quod non valet statutum quod pater vel avus non possit relinquere legitimam filie vel nepote. Ymo plus, quod non valet si diceret, quod non teneatur relinquere, et idem tenet Cynus Cod. de nuptiis, l. Sancimus [Cod. 5. 4. 27]." Dinus's opinion, in fact, referred to the obligation of a father toward his children. He also allowed fathers to disinherit their children for the reasons expressly

stated in the *ius commune* – for instance, if the children maltreated the father. See his discussion of *c. Indultum* in Dinus Mugellanus, *De regulis iuris pontificis commentaria* (Lyon, 1577), 115, no. 5. Cinus's opinion is more nuanced than one is led to believe from Baldus's citation, and Cinus also restricts his discussion to fathers and their children. See his commentary to Cod. 5. 4. 27 in Cinus de Pistorio, *Commentaria* (Frankfurt am Main, 1578), 294va, no. 10.

112 Cons. 226: "Preterea masculinum concipit feminum in actu favorabili, unde statutum factum favore filiorum non facta mentione de filiabus vel neptibus, nec pro nec contra. In suo favore includit feminas, sed non in hodio, ut ff. de ventre in possessionem mictendo, l. 1, § Quare [Dig. 37. 9. 1. 3]. Ex quibus concluditur, quod aut statutum non valet in casu isto, aut iusta interpretatione debet intelligi, quod sub illo nomine 'extra filios' intelligatur conceptive 'extra filios vel filias' et idem de ceteris liberis. Et hoc probatur ex coniunctione duarum legum, C. familie hercis., l. finalis [Cod. 3. 36. 26], et C. de testamentis, l. Hac consultissima, § Ex imperfecto [Cod. 6. 23. 21. 3]. Nam natura favorabilis est et ex lege nature communis est, ut in Auth. de testamentis imperfectis, circa principium [Auth. 8. 3 = Nov. 107]. Ex quibus concludo testamentum iustum, et secundum dictamen naturalis rationis factum a dicta domina Stefania servandum."

113 On the pope's temporal authority over Viterbo and the rest of the papal state, see Waley, "Viterbo nello Stato"; Prodi, *Il sovrano pontifice*, 15–40; Canning, "A State like Any Other?" For a different approach that stresses relative local autonomy instead of papal sovereignty, see Lanconelli, "Autonomie comunali."

114 Biblioteca degli Ardenti, *Statuti* (1469), 177r–78r, lib. 2, rubr. 74; Biblioteca del Senato, *Statuti* 765, 101v–2r, lib. 2, rubr. 74. On Innocent VIII's relations with Viterbo, see Pinzi, *Storia della città*, vol. 4, 291–326.

115 Statement of Emma Wold, "Effects of Marriage upon Nationality," *Hearings before the House Committee on Immigration and Naturalization*, 70th Cong., 1st sess. (1928), 3. See also Sapiro, "Women, Citizenship, and Nationality"; Rupp, *Worlds of Women*, 146–50. On the repercussions of the Expatriation Act of 1907, see Bredbenner, *A Nationality of Her Own*; and Cott, "Marriage and Women's Citizenship."

116 Note that the *parlement* of Paris in 1668 deprived of citizenship any French woman who remained abroad after the death of her foreign husband. Vanel, *Histoire de la nationalité*, 79.

117 Under the French Civil Code, a French woman married to a foreigner follows the condition of her husband and is deprived of her civil rights and the quality of a French woman. If she becomes a widow and resides

in France, she can apply for repatriation (bk. 1, tit. 1, chap. 2, sect. 1, art. 19). On the influence exercised by the French Civil Code on the norms concerning citizenship in the codes of other countries, including the preunification codes of Italy, see Sechi, "Cittadinanza"; Astuti, "Il Code Napoléon." According to Waltz, *The Nationality*, 65, as of May 1936 there were about twenty-five states in the world where, upon marriage to a foreigner and the acquisition of her husband's nationality, the wife lost her own nationality.

118 Manfredi and Mangano, *Alle origini*; Vincenzi Amato, "La famiglia," 629ff.; Saraceno, "Women, Family, and the Law."

119 Storti Storchi, *Ricerche sulla condizione*, 201–4.

120 *Codice Civile*, lib. 1, tit. 1, art. 14: "La donna cittadina che si marita a uno straniero, diviene straniera, sempreché col fatto del matrimonio acquisti la cittadinanza del marito." The distinguished jurist Pasquale Mancini was responsible for the insertion of the proviso that loss of citizenship is contingent upon the wife's acquisition of her foreign husband's citizenship. Without this proviso, Mancini and his allies rightly feared, a number of Italian women who married foreigners would become stateless. See Sechi, "Cittadinanza," 283.

121 Fiore, *Della cittadinanza*, 58–9, 73–5, 99–106, 133–4.

122 Quadri, "Cittadinanza." For two illuminating studies on court cases and doctrinal issues relating to the citizenship law of 1912, see Clerici, "Problemi in tema"; idem, "Nuove prospettive," esp. 678–86.

123 For the text of the Convention of New York, see *Yearbook on Human Rights for 1957* (New York: Secretariat of the United Nations, 1957), 301–2. For a richly informative collaborative study of recent trends on the acquisition and loss of citizenship and nationality in fifteen European countries, see Bauböck et al., eds., *Acquisition and Loss.*

124 Giardina, "L'egualianza dei coniugi." According to Clerici, *La cittadinanza*, 110, "Dal canto suo, il regime italiano sulla cittadinanza si dimostra sino all metà degli anni settanta impermeabile a quei valori, malgrado essi siano nel frattempo penetrati nell'ordinamento in virtù della Costituzione repubblicana."

125 For the text of the decision, see "Corte Costituzionale, sentenza 16 aprile 1975, n. 87," *Giurisprudenza italiana* 20 (1975): 515–21. The court also recognized that involuntary loss of citizenship harmed women by barring them from public-sector jobs reserved for Italian citizens.

126 Clerici, "La nuova legge," 747ff.

127 I am not suggesting that there was official contact between the independent judges of the Corte Costituzionale and the senators, only the intersection of parallel developments.

128 Finocchiaro and Finocchiaro, *Riforma del diritto*, vol. 1, 266–9. Art. 143-ter. 25 reads: "(Cittadinanza della moglie) – La moglie conserva la cittadinanza italiana, salvo sua espressa rinunzia, anche se per effetto del matrimonio o del mutamento di cittadinanza da parte del marito assume una cittadinanza straniera." An early draft of this text was introduced on 25 May 1972 – that is, roughly three years before the decision of the Corte Costituzionale. A penultimate draft of this text was finalized by a commission of the Senate on 23 January 1975. The family reform law was signed into law on 19 May 1975 by the president of the republic, and went into effect on 20 September.
129 Clerici, "Gleichheit im Familienrecht," esp. 108–11.
130 Clerici, "Nuove prospettive."
131 For the text of the law (21 April 1983), see *RDIPP* 19 (1983): 675–6.
132 On the twists and turns of laws relating to Italian citizenship and nationality, especially from 1992 onward, I have relied on Arena et al., "Italy"; Zincone, "Citizenship Policy Making"; Zincone and Basili, "Report on Italy."
133 *RDIPP* 28 (1992), 655ff. For an analysis of the law, see Clerici, "La nuova legge," 741–76; Bariatti, *La disciplina*, esp. 29–34.
134 Tintori, "Naturalization Procedures," 3.

8. Dowry, Domicile, and Citizenship in Late Medieval Florence

1 On nuptial expenses in Florence, see Kirshner, "*Li Emergenti Bisogni Matrimoniali*," chap. 2 in this volume.
2 CRS, 98, vol. 263 (*Consigli e decisioni legali*), 293r–98r (henceforth cited as *Consilium*). On Petrus de Exio (also known as Ambrosini), see Abbondanza, "Ambrosini, Pietro"; Martines, *Lawyers and Statecraft*, 503; Kirshner, "Encumbering Private Claims," 73–4; Kuehn, "Social Processes"; idem, "Some Ambiguities," 249, 250; idem, *Illegitimacy*, 233–4, 237, 250–3; Park, "The Readers," 295–302; Davies, *Florence*, 30, 33, 41, 160, 168, 195–6.
3 *Consilium*, 293r–v.
4 On *sponsalia* contracts in Florence, see Cavallar and Kirshner, "Making and Breaking Betrothal Contracts," chap. 1 in this volume.
5 On the *Monte delle doti*, see Molho, *Marriage Alliance*. Before a husband could collect the Monte dowry, he had to attest that he had consummated the marriage: see Kirshner, "The Morning After," chap. 4 in this volume.
6 Kirshner and Molho, "The Dowry Fund," 422, table 5; Herlihy and Klapisch-Zuber, *Les Toscans*, 414–19.
7 *Statuta populi et communis Florentiae* (1415), vol. 1, 140, lib. 2, rubr. 39, *Qualiter alteri per alterum acquiratur*).

8 Ibid., 222–3, lib. 2, rubr. 129, *Qualiter succedatur in dotem uxoris premortue.* For discussions of this statute, see Kirshner, "*Maritus Lucretur Dotem*," 132–6; Chabot, "La loi." For a comparative analysis with respect to Jewish customs in early modern Tuscany, see Siegmund, "Division of the Dowry."

9 ASF, Statuti delle comunità autonome e soggetti, no. 566 (Pescia, 1417–85), 4v, rubr. 49, *De muliere decedente infra quinquennium.*

10 Onori, ed., *Lo statuto di Pescia del 1339*, lib. 1, 75, rubr. 53, *Quod vir lucretur tertiam partem dotis mortua uxore.*

11 The Tuscan practice of awarding the husband one-half the dowry upon his wife's predecease, without surviving children, endured into the nineteenth century. See Paoli, *Del matriminio*, 57, n. 1.

12 The information on the husband's *lucrum dotis* is based on my examination of the corpus of printed editions of Tuscan and Lombard statutes preserved in the Biblioteca del Senato in Rome, and on Niccolai, *La formazione*, 170–218; and Massetto, "Il lucro dotale."

13 *Consilium*, 293v: "Dicitur pro parte heredum dicte mulieris quod ipsi tenentur rehabere a dicto viro virtute dicti statuti Piscie et virtute dicti matrimon<i>i consumationis facte in dicta terra Piscie per copulam carnalem, et etiam vigore promissionis de dote predicta et eius declarationis facte in Pisciatinos. Et quia de iure inspicitur locus mariti, et quod secundum consuetudinem terre viri dos debet reddi, et sic per consequens secundum ordinamenta Piscie: ex quibus sequitur quod potius instrumenta supra narrata videantur facta, ymmo facta sint, secundum eos, prout et secundum quod disponitur per ordinamenta Piscie predicte."

14 Lorenz, *Das Dotalstatut*, 18–43.

15 *Consilium*, 293v: "Pro parte viri respondetur quod primus contractus sponsalitii fuit celebratus in civitate Florentie, cui initio est standum, et etiam ipsius primi contractus sponsalitii occasione et occasione matrimonii contracti per verba de presenti et occasione confessionis dotis, omnia facta in civitate Florentie et secundum ordinamenta comunis Florentie, ipse vir lucratus fuit totam dotem, stantibus statutis supra allegatis in dicta civitate Florentie, que statuta omnino sunt servanda, secundum eum, in dicto casu, et quod dictum statutum de dote et eius successione habet locum in casu suprascripto, et non statutum Piscie supra allegatum quod probari dicitur et ostendi pluribus de causis."

16 *Consilium*, 293v: "Et quia ius dicte stipulationis, facte per dictum notarium rogatum de dote pro dicta muliere secundum ordinamenta Florentie, dicte mulieri quesitum fuit taliter quod postquam ipsa mulier, que habuit notitiam de dote predicta et eius confessione facta secundum dicta ordinamenta Florentie, ipsi confessioni consensit, aquievit et ei non contradixit, propter

quam secuta eius morte, eius heredes minime contradicere possunt, et quod melius, ille vir promisit mulieri facere solutionem de dicta dote in pluribus locis nominatis in instrumento, non tamen in terra Piscie."

17 Kirshner, "*Consilia* as Authority," 107–16.

18 Brown, *In the Shadow of Florence*, 16–17.

19 Most important, Florentine laws came into play when gaps existed in the subject community's statutes. As Jane Black ("Constitutional Ambitions") shows, the assertion that Florentine law supplanted the *ius commune* as the gap-filling law was contested by jurists throughout the fifteenth century. See also Lepsius, "Paolo di Castro," 97–100.

20 *Consilium*, 294r: "Christi nomine invocato [MS: invocato *suprascr.*]. Viso suprascripto punto et dubio, eoque diligenter inspecto, primo videtur dicendum attendi debere consuetudinem loci viri. Nam cum vir contrahit in loco domicilii uxoris, videtur contrahere tanquam advena et forensis, et cito inde recessurus et secum ad domicilium suum uxorem ducturus, ut l. Exigere, ff. de iudic. [Dig. 5. 1. 65], facit l. Heres absens, § 1, ff. eo. ti. [Dig. 5. 1. 19. 1]; et tanquam solutionem restitutionis dotis fiendam et destinate in domicilio viri, ut dicta l. Exigere, facit l. Contraxisse , ff. de actio. et obli. [Dig. 44. 7. 21], et per consequens ac si sibi contraxisset, locus ille destinate solutionis debet attendi, ut d. l. Contraxisse. Nam in decisione et quoad decisiva inspicitur locus contractus, et locus destinate solutionis videtur locus contractus, ut dicta l. Contraxisse, et l. Si fundus, ff. de evict. [Dig. 21. 2. 6], et l. i, in principio, ff. de usuris [Dig. 22. 1. 1pr], et l. iii, in fine, ff. de testi. [Dig. 22. 5. 3. 6], et plene not. per doctores in l. i, C. de summa Trinitate et fide captolica [Cod. 1. 1], et in l. ii, C. quemadmodum testa. aperi. [Cod. 6. 32. 2], et maxime cum uxor per matrimonium mutet domicilium suum et transferatur in domicilium viri, ut l. Imperatores, § Item rescriperunt [MS: Idem responderunt], ff. ad munici. [Dig. 50. 1. 38. 4], facit l. Cum quedam, ff. de iuris. omnium iud. [Dig. 2. 1. 19]. Vel secundum alios est spetiale in dote, ut non locus contractus sed domicilii viri inspiciatur, per dictam l. Exigere. Ibi 'nec enim quid genus' etc. et secundum illius consuetudinem dictum lucrum dotis ex statuto proveniens divideretur, ut l. dicta l. Exigere, licet in aliis contractibus locus contractus inspiciatur, ut dixi in dicta l. Si fundus, cum aliis supra allegatis. Unde utroque predictorum modorum concluditur consuetudinem loci domicilii viri, et sic Pescie, et non uxoris, et sic Florentie, debet attendi in dicto lucro fiendo, quod expresse sequitur Bar. et Bal. in dicta l. Exigere."

21 I have used, with modifications, Alan Watson's translation of *The Digest of Justinian*, vol. 1, 172.

22 Bartolus to *l. Cunctos populos* (Cod. 1. 1. 1), in *Commentaria* (Venice, 1526–9), 4v, no. 18: "Statutum est Assisii ubi est celebratus contractus dotis et matrimonii quod vir lucretur tertiam partem dotis, uxore moriente sine liberis. In hac vero civitate Perusii, unde est vir, est statutum quod vir lucretur dimidiam: quod spectabitur certe statutum terre viri."

23 Baldus de Ubaldis, *Repetitio* to *l. Cunctos populos*, in *Tractatus duo de vi*, 33–4, no. 78.

24 Kirshner, "Women Married Elsewhere," chap. 7 in this volume.

25 *Consilium*, 294r–v: "Sed [MS: quod *post* sed *del.*] hiis non ostantibus, in casu proposito puto de iure dici posse et esse contrarium. Et primo, quia sicut est in casu nostro, quando diversa est consuetudo lucri dotis domicilii viri a domicilio uxoris, servatur consuetudo loci, ubi contrahitur matrimonium, ut xii distin., c. Illud [D. 12 c. 4], viii di., c. Que contra mores [D. 8 c. 2], et xli di., c. Quisquis [D. 41 c. 1]. Et ita sententialiter concludit Io. An. et sequitur post Fran. in dicto c. i, extra, de spon. [X 4. 1. 1] ... At hic, in civitate Florentie, fuit contractum matrimonium et etiam contractus dotis factus: ergo consuetudo civitatis Florentie fuit et est sequenda." See Johannes Andreae to *c. De Francia* (X 4. 1. 1), in *Commentaria* (Venice, 1581), 2r.

26 Antonius de Butrio to *c. De Francia*, in *Commentaria* (Venice, 1575–8), 3r, no. 12; Petrus Ancharanus to *c. De Francia*, in *Commentaria* (Bologna, 1580–1), 2r, no. 9; Abbas Panormitanus (Niccolò de' Tedeschi) to *c. De Francia*, in *Commentaria* (Venice, 1617), 2v–3r.

27 *Consilium*, 294v: "Nec obstat dicta l. Exigere cum aliis supra in contrarium allegatis et doctores de quibus supra, quia primo dico quod intelligendo dictam l. Exigere, prout supra primo loco dixi, prout comuniter intel<l>igitur, non habet aliquid spetialitatis in dote, cum et idem sit in aliis contractibus, ut locus contractus non [MS: non *suprascr.*] inspiciatur quando fit contractus per advenam de proximo recessurum, per dictam l. Heres absens, § i."

28 Dinus Mugellanus to *l. Contraxisse* (Dig. 44. 7. 21), Bologna, Collegio di Spagna, MS 272, 105rb.

29 Bartolus to *l. Cunctos populos*, 4v, nos. 16–17.

30 *Consilium*, 294v: "quia sic in dote maritus non possit conveniri in loco contractus pro dote, sed in loco domicilii sui tantum. Set in aliis contractibus quod possit conveniri tam in loco contractus, ut dicta l. Heres absens."

31 *Consilum*, 296v: "Preterea in casu isto, iste Pisciatinus promisit et destinavit solutionem dicte dotis, in casum restituende dotis, in pluribus locis, scilicet Florentie, Pisis, et inter nominatos et expressos in dicto instrumento promissionis dotis non reperitur quod fuerit nominatus locus domicilii ispsius viri. Ex quo clare colligitur, quod non videtur destinata solutio in

loco ipsius domicilii, et sic nec tacita destinatio hoc casu colligi potest, unde non videtur hoc casu habere locum dispositio dicte legis Exigere."

32 *Lex Qui ex vico* (Dig. 50. 1. 30), in Watson, ed. and trans., *The Digest of Justinian*, vol. 4, 906.

33 *Consilium*, 295r: "Preterea dictus vir non est advena in civitate Florentie, ymmo civis, ut l. Qui ex vico, ff. ad municipal. [Dig. 50. 1. 30], facit l. 1 [Dig. 50. 1. 1], et quod ibi per Bar. ff. eo. ti., sicut et quilibet liber est civis civitatis Romane, que est etiam communis patria, ut l. Roma, ff. ad municipal. [Dig. 50. 1. 11], facit Insti. de patria po., in prin. [Inst. 1. 9 pr], et l. Nam civium, ff. de his qui sunt sui vel alieni iuris [Dig. 1. 6. 4]. Preterea dictus vir non contraxit cum dicta sua uxor ut advena, cum sit civis loci contractus, ut dixi." On the juridical fiction *Roma communis patria*, see Thomas, "*Origine" et "commune patrie*," 1–23; Prosdocimi, "'Roma communis patria'"; Coppens, "Roma communis nostra patria."

34 *Consilium*, 295r: "Preterea cotidie conversatur et habitat in civitate Florentie, ut in facto est veritas. Unde etiam ratione solius assidue conversationis in civitate Florentie forum sortitur et posset conveniri."

35 *Consilium*, 295v "Preterea et alia ratione esto, quod theorica Bartoli et sequacium esset vera in locis preallegatis, actamen non obviat huic decisioni in contrarium, quia Bartolus et alii [MS: de quibus *post* alii *del.*] locuntur in consuetudine diversa loci domicilii viri a domicilio [MS: a domicilio *ex* et domicilii *corr.*] uxoris, quando unus locus non subalternatur alteri, nec sortitur vir forum in domicilio uxoris. Et hoc castrum Piscie est subditum et de districtu Florentie, quo casu dictus vir, licet Pisciatinus, potest tam ex expresa forma statutorum civitatis Florentie in civitate Florentie exigi et conveniri ad instantiam civis, comitatini e districtualis Florentie, sicut est dicta uxor et eius heredes cives florentini, posito quod affecta est de cive districtualis et de comitatu per contractum dicti matrimonii, per l. Imperatores, § Item rescripserunt [MS: Idem responderunt], et quod ibi plene per Bartolum, ff. ad munici., et per ea que not. glo. in dicta l. Exigere, quam etiam ex forma iuris comunis, per quod dato quod sine preiudicio veritatis, vir non possit conveniri nisi in domicilio sue vigore dotis, ut dicta l. Exigere, actamen hoc fallit nisi conveniretur in comuni patria sicut est civitas Florentie quo ad suum districtum ex forma dicti statuti, quam etiam de iure comuni, ut l. Roma, ff. ad munici. [Dig. 50. 1. 33]." For the text of Bartolus's commentary to § *Item rescripserunt*, see my "*Mulier Alibi Nupta*," 173–5.

36 Angelus de Ubaldis of Perugia came close, however. He argued that the customs of the husband's domicile determined the *lucrum dotis* if the dowry contract was made there. On the other hand, the customs of the wife's domicile were looked to if the contract was made there. He reasoned that

this solution was exceedingly advantageous regarding Tuscany, where the local statutes regulating the portion of the dowry to which the husband was entitled on the predecease of his wife were in conflict ("hoc est valde utile et maxime in partibus Tuscie, in qua sunt diversa statuta in lucro dotis uxoris premortue"). See Angelus de Ubaldis to *l. Exigere* (Dig. 5. 1. 65), BAV, Vat. lat. 2612, 160v. Curiously, Ambrosini neglected to cite Angelus's commentary, which, I believe, was a prime source for several arguments in his *consilium*.

37 On jurisdictional pluralism in Florence's territorial state, see Brown, *In the Shadow of Florence*, 19–21; J. Black, "Constitutional Ambitions"; Zorzi, "The 'Material Constitution'"; and Tanzini, *Alle origini*, 82–99.

38 Najemy, "Politics and Political Thought," 283.

39 *Consilium*, 297v–98r.

9. Pisa's "Long-Arm" *Gabella Dotis* (1420–1525)

1 On *confessio dotis*, see Kirshner, "The Morning After," chap. 4 in this volume. The Florentine new year began on 25 March. For the sake of readability, all dates between 1 January and 25 March cited in the text have been modernized. Similarly, I have modernized all dates in the text originally recorded in Pisan style (*more Pisano*), which was one year ahead of modern (and Florentine) usage for the period 25 March–31 December.

2 See Costa's *Iurisdictio*. The reprint of this classic work includes an illuminating introduction by Bartolomé Clavero. See also Grossi, *L'ordine giuridico*, 95. On the relationship between jurisdiction and the making of territorial boundaries, see Marchetti, "*De iure finium*." On the organization of territorial states in central and northern Italy, with a focus on the strategies and material techniques mediating jurisdictional powers, see Chittolini's influential *La formazione dello Stato*. For an overview, see Isaacs, "Changing Layers."

3 Lorenz, *Das Dotalstatut*; Kirshner, "Dowry, Domicile, and Citizenship," chap. 5 in this volume.

4 For a balanced sketch of the *ius commune*, see Caravale, *Alle origini*; Conte, *Diritto comune*; on the intertwined relationship between the *ius commune* and the statutes of Pisa during the period of Florentine domination, see Celli, *Studi sui sistemi*, vol. 1, 133–44.

5 For a first-rate example of such a study, see Cavallar, "Francesco Guicciardini and the 'Pisan Crisis.'"

6 Jayme, *Pasquale Stanislao Mancini*. International law scholars traditionally credit Charles Dumoulin (1500–66), advocate at the Parlement of Paris, with

hatching in embryonic form the concept of party autonomy, in reaction to Bartolus de Saxoferrato and his followers, who had privileged the *lex loci contractus*. See Gamillscheg, *Der Einfluß*.

7 Chittolini, "A Comment," 342.

8 See Valente's comprehensive manual, *Convenzioni internazionali*; and Kofler and Mason, "Double Taxation."

9 Petralia, "'Crisi' e emigrazione," 324, n. 124; Corazzini, *L'assedio di Pisa*, 145. I have been unable to ascertain the relationship between Agapito's branch of the dell'Agnello and that of Giovanni dell'Agnello, who was elected doge of Pisa in 1364. On whom see Tangheroni, "Dell'Agnello, Giovanni."

10 ASLu, Corte de' Mercanti 95 (Libro dei Sensali 1413), 69r, 72r, 73r–v, 74r, 112r; Corte de' Mercanti 96 (Libro dei Sensali 1417), 53r. I owe these references to the generosity of Professor Christine Meek.

11 Casini, "Patrimonio e consumi"; and his *Il Catasto di Pisa*, 373–4. Petralia, "'Crisi' e emigrazione," 330, argues persuasively that the total value of Maggiolini assets was nearer to 30,000 florins. On the family's origins, see also Cristiani, *Nobiltà e popolo*, 50, 352, 463–4. On Maggiolini's commercial activities in Lucca and Milan, see Scharf, "Amor di patria."

12 Pareri dei Savi, 3, 421r–28r. On 31 December 1412, Ridolfo Peruzzi, the Florentine *capitano di custodia* of Pisa, ordered Giovanni di Piero Maggiolini to appear in court to answer charges of fomenting rebellion, mainly by speaking with the condemned rebel Nofri del Moscha, also of Pisa. Maggiolini ignored the summons, was pronounced contumacious, and was confined to Venice, Siena, or Florence for three years. In July 1413 Maggiolini sought and received cancellation of his sentence from the *camera del comune* in Florence. The *camera* made a series of inquiries into whether the various statutes on banishment enacted in the 1370s, 1380s, and 1390s could be enforced against Maggiolini. Six jurists – Philippus de Corsinis, Stephanus de Bonaccursiis, Nellus de Sancto Geminiano, Torellus Torelli, Alexander Salvii de Bencivennis, and Dominicus Sermini – were asked to advise. They were unanimous in supporting the cancellation of the sentence on the grounds of *ex carentia iurisdictionis*, namely, that Florentine laws and statutes did not authorize the *capitano del popolo* of Florence, let alone a lesser official, the *capitano di custodia* of Pisa, to confine someone to a specific locality.

13 Giovanni di Piero Maggiolini, his son Baldassarre, and five nephews were awarded Lucchese citizenship on 21 October 1424. See Romiti, *Le concessioni*, 182–3, no. 168. I am grateful to Professor Michele Luzzati for permitting me to consult Romiti's thesis. The decree granting citizenship is preserved in ASLu, Comune, Governo di Paolo Guinigi, Decr. 2, 678r.

14 My search for Agapito's *confessio dotis* in notarial archives of Lucca, Pisa, and Florence proved fruitless. As far as I can determine, ser Eustachio's registers are lost.

15 On the magistracies Florence established to administer Pisa, see Guidi, *Il governo*, vol. 3, 45–57, 172–5, 241–3.

16 On the organization and extent of Pisa's territorial jurisdiction during the fifteenth century, see Banti, *Iacopo d'Appiano*, 125; and Potenti, *Uomini, villaggi, terreni*, 27–40.

17 Interestingly, unlike Giovanni Maggiolini, who, though residing in Lucca (his home away from home), remained subject to Pisa's jurisdiction and was included in the *catasto* of 1428, Agapito dell'Agnello (assuming he was still alive) was not included in the *catasto*, another sign that his ties to Pisa had become at best tenuous.

18 CRS, 98, no. 240, s.f., *Consilium* XII (hereafter cited as *Consilium* XII): "Agabitus de Agnello civis pisanus habitans ad presens Ianue et a duodecim annis citra, et tempore quo in dicta civitate habitabat duxit in uxorem dominam Tommasiam, filiam Iohannis Maggiolini civis pisani, iam sunt X anni vel circa, in civitate Lucana prope civitatem Pisarum minus quinquaginta miliaria. Deinde mortua dicta domina Tommasia aliam duxit uxorem in civitate Ianue, que distat a civitate Pisarum per 150 [*sic*] miliaria, nomine Catherinam, filiam Luce Spinola, civis Ianue, iam sunt duo anni, et de predicta uxore habuit dotem et eas [*sic*] habuisse confessus fuit in civitate Lucana manu ser Stagii de Montefoscoli, civis et notarii pisani ac etiam civis lucani tunc habitantis in civitate Lucana, et similiter de 2[a] uxore fuit confessus dotem per cartam manu notarii ianuensis publici. De quibus quidem dotibus solute fuerunt gabelle in civitatibus prefatis et nulla soluta gabella de dictis dotibus comuni Florentie, set fuerunt solute gabelle in locis in quibus contracta fuerunt matrimonia. Modo offitiales pro comuni Florentie deputati super exactione gabellarum in civitate Pisana volunt quod dictus Agabitus solvat in civitate Pisana gabellas dictarum dotium secundum formam statuti civitatis Pisane de quibus patet superius, pro eo quia dicitur quod dictus Agabitus est civis pisanus et dicta prima uxor est de civitate Pisana et contractus fuit celebratus per notarium pisanum et prope civitatem Pisarum per quinquaginta miliaria; et similiter dicendum de secunda uxore debere gabellam ratione civilitatis dicti Agabiti, non obstante quod gabelle fuerint solute in civitatibus prefatis. Dictus vero Agabitus respondet quod dicta gabella vel gabelle solvi non debent, cum nec promissio nec confessio dotis nec etiam matrimonium fuerit celebratum in loco subdito dictis statuentibus, et quia statutum simpliciter loquens intelligi debet

ligare subditos in suo territorio et non extra territorium contraentis. Et <queritur> an de ambobus vel saltim altera ex dictis dotibus gabella debeatur nec ne."

19 On Nellus, see Martines, *Lawyers and Statecraft*, 499; Mooney, *The Legal Ban*; Park, "The Readers," 276–7, 279. Nellus was appointed *sapiens communis* seven times: in 1410, 1412, 1413, 1416, 1420, 1423, and 1424. See Tratte 576, 70v, 71r, 72r–v, 73r–v.

20 Urbanus de Cevoli's name appears in the margin of the manuscript alongside the second submitted *consilium*. For his doctorate in civil law, see Davies, "The Studio Pisano," 212, 221, 235, n. 108. For Urbanus's service as Pisa's advocate, see ASPi, Comune di Pisa, div. B. no. 80, 24r (29 July 1423), and as ambassador, ibid., 12r (3 Sept. 1427); 24r (15 Nov. 1428). For references to his private activities in Pisa, see ASPi, Gabella dei contratti, no. 4, 55r (7 June 1423), 126r (14 Feb. 1425/6), 163r (24 Dec. 1424), 262v (12 Aug. 1426), 262r (9 May 1426), 270r (12 Sept. 1426); and Casini, *Il catasto di Pisa*, 90–1, no. 394.

21 Neither law is included in Bonaini, ed., *Statuti inediti*; or Era, ed., *Statuti pisani*.

22 For the rubric of the contract tax, see Accoltus's *consilium* at 171r cited below (n. 45): "nam in dictis reformationibus pisanis habetur in rubrica *De instrumentis ex quibus,* quod in civitate Pisana debet solvi gabella de instrumentis omnibus factis infra 50 miliaria a civitate Pisarum." The rubric of the law making the contract tax applicable to dowries is given in *Consilium* XII: *De dotibus mulierum et quicunque uxorem cepit et eam duxerit.*

23 Silva, "Pisa sotto Firenze"; Brucker, *The Civic World*, 202ff.; Petralia, "Fiscality, Politics and Dominion."

24 Petralia, "Fiscality, Politics and Dominion," 77. See also ASPi, Gabella dei contratti, no. 4, 1r, where it is stated that the *gabella* is owed to the commune of Florence.

25 Meek, *The Commune of Lucca*, 81–3.

26 Dig. 2.11.1, *Vicena milia*. For a penetrating analysis of this *lex*, see Baldus, *Commentaria* (Venice, 1599), 100r–v.

27 See also Dominicus de Sancto Geminiano's introduction (*casus*) to *c. Praesenti*: "quod in isto casu illa loca appellamus vicina curiae Romanae, quae distat a loco ubi est Papa cum sua curia per duas dietas legales: hoc est per xx leucas, nam dieta in iure accipitur pro decem leucis, l. Vicena milia, ff. de cautionibus"; *Commentaria* (Lyon, 1584), col. 440. For other references to *dietae duae*, see also Ottenthal, ed., *Regulae cancellariae apostolicae, ad indicem*; and Meyer, *Zürich und Rom*, 34.

28 In Florentine statutes and laws, a distance of fifty to sixty miles was sometimes used to mark the city's nominal outer territorial boundary encompassing communities under its control or vulnerable to its power. Thus, to qualify for appointment to the office of *podestà* in Florence around 1400, the candidate had to come from a foreign place, meaning at least sixty miles from the city. See Guidi, *Il governo*, vol. 2, 158. Again, a monetary commission was appointed in 1371 to curb the minting of debased coinage anywhere within fifty miles of the city. See La Roncière, *Prix et salaires*, 498.

29 See Bowsky, *The Finance*, 153. Bowsky's informative discussion fails to raise and address the question of the difficulties that undoubtedly confronted Sienese tax officials attempting to track tax contracts made by "every husband of the city, contado and district of Siena," even if the marriage took place outside Sienese jurisdiction. I have not found the law enacted by Pistoia that made its *gabella dotis* enforceable anywhere in the world. It was, however, discussed in a *consilium* attributed to the Florentine jurist Agnolo Niccolini, but it is not clear whether it was Agnolo di Matteo (1473–1542) or Agnolo di Carlo (1474–1509), both jurists. The *consilium* is in CRS, 98, no. 252, 172r: "Preterea et tertio respondeo quod licet statutum simpliciter et indistincte disponat quod in quacunque parte mundi contractus celebratus sit, debet solvi gabella in civitate Pistorii, tamen tale statutum intelligendum est quando in ea parte mundi celebratur dictus contractus in qua nulla ghabella de tali contractu solvebatur, ut in plerisque partibus mundi existit." Niccolini's *consilium*, with variants, was published in Bartholomaeus Socinus, *Consilia*, vol. 2 (Lyon, 1546), 167r–68r, cons. 302.

30 ASPi, Gabella dei contratti, no. 4 (1423–7), 1r: "et cedule dictorum contractuum qui ad dictam gabellam erunt transmisse tam per notarios pisanos etiam per alios quoscumque notarios."

31 I have found only one instance of notification by a third party, in this case of a Pisan husband who received a dowry in Livorno. Ibid., 213r (1 Oct. 1425): "Aghabitus Pauli civis contraxit matrimonium cum domina Antonia, filia Puccini de Luberno, et habuit in dotem dicte domine Antonie a Jacobo dal Ponte florenos centum. Michael Benenati de Sancto Geminiano notificavit Sandro de Altovitis et Nicolo Luce de Albizis provisoribus gabelle dictum contractum, die primo octobris MCCCCXXV, more Florentie." For payment of the *gabella*, ibid., 258r.

32 On the logistical impediments, see Molho, *Marriage Alliance*, 56; and Kirshner, "The Morning After," chap. 4 in this volume. Another difficulty was providing nonresidents adequate notice of the order issued by the officials requiring them to pay the *gabella*.

33 Molho, *Marriage Alliance*, 56; Bongi, ed., *Inventario*, 24. The Florentine Goro Dati reported a *gabella dotis* of 3⅓ percent in 1402. See Pandimiglio, *I libri di famiglia*, 106.

34 Pecchiai, "Il libro di ricordi," 331. In the *Capitoli* of 1509 establishing the terms of Pisa's reincorporation into Florence's dominion, the *gabella dei contratti* payable by inhabitants of the *contado* was limited to 8 denarii for each lira, or 3⅓ percent. Benvenuti, *Storia dell'assedio*, 143, n. 40.

35 The calculation of *gabelle* was based on the valuation of the florin at 4 lire. Some examples, all from ASPi, Gabella dei contratti, n. 4: Antonio di Bacciomeo paid a *gabella* of 30 lire for a dowry valued at 225 florins, a rate of 3⅓ percent: 5r (30 June 1423); Pardo di Andrea paid a *gabella* of 6 lire, 13 soldi, 4 denarii for a dowry of 30 florins, a rate of 3⅓ percent: 20r (31 July 1423); Angelo di Piero, a German residing in Pisa, paid a *gabella* of 8 lire for a dowry, conveyed to him by Corradina di Cambio of Florence, valued at 60 florins, a rate of 3⅓ percent: 87r (30 Oct. 1426).

36 Onclin, "La doctrine de Bartole"; Storti Storchi, *Ricerche sulla condizione*, 29–66.

37 Mayali, "La notion"; Lorenz, *Das Dotalstatut*, 88–92.

38 *Consilium* XII: "Et quia res est clara, ulterius me non extendo, concludens dictum Agabitum ad solutionem dictarum gabellarum nullatenus teneri, attento quod promissiones dotium, solutiones et confessiones ipsarum dotium fuerent facte extra territorium pisanum et attento quod dicte uxores fuerunt ducte ad civitatem Ianue et ibi fuerunt solute gabelle istarum dotium."

39 The foreigners who resided, married, received their dowries, and paid the *gabella dotis* in Pisa hailed from north and central Italy (Genoa, Siena, Florence, San Miniato al Tedesco, Perugia, Todi, Bologna, Piemonte, Cremona, Verona, Venice) and from Germany and Constantinople. See ASPi, Gabella dei contratti, no. 4, 32r, 36r, 42v, 50v, 53v, 87r, 107r, 109v, 120v, 126r, 182r, 192r, 201r, 240r, 245r–v.

40 *Consilium* XII: "Et quicunque uxorem ceperit et eam duxerit, teneatur et debeat solvere communi Pisarum pro gabella denariorum duorum pro libra pro dote, donamentorum et corredorum et valentis possessionum." The tax rate, 2 denarii for each lira, was substantially lower than the mid-Trecento rate of 8 denarii per lira cited by Castiglione, "Gabelle e diritti," 65.

41 *Consilium* XII: "Sola ergo promissio dotis et confessio non faciunt deberi gabellam communis Pisarum, set captio et ductio, et iste actus captionis et ductionis debet expleri in territorio statuentis."

42 Dig. 1. 1. 9, *Omnes populi*; Cod. 1. 1. 1, *Cunctos populos*; Dig. 50. 9. 6, *Municipii lege*; Cod. 4. 63. 4, *Mercatores*. See also Leicht, "Cino da Pistoia";

Stein, "Bartolus"; Hatzimihail, "Bartolus," 29–30; and Kirshner, "'Made Exiles.'" This *ius commune* norm also extended to nonoriginal citizens, that is, newcomers to whom the government granted privileges of citizenship. On this point, see Kirshner, "Citizen Cain of Florence."

43 *Consilium* XII: "Et sic concludo quod de prima dote debetur gabella, quia recepta intra quinquaginta miliaria per subditum statuto. De secunda non, quia recepta extra quinquaginta milaria, licet sit subditus statuto. Laus Deo. Ego Nellus etc. Florentie die 16 aprelis 1423."

44 R. Black, *Benedetto Accolti*, 41ff.; Martines, *Lawyers and Statecraft*, 105–6, 502–3; Park, "The Readers," 296, 300, 301, 302; Davies, *Florence*, 177.

45 CRS, 98, no. 252, 210r–12r (hereafter cited as Accoltus).

46 Other standard pseudonyms were Titius, Petrus, and Martinus, as in a case involving four Pisan citizens exiled to Genoa: "Questio super qua consilium petitur, ponitur esse talis: Quattuor homines, videlicet Petrus, Martinus, Titius et Sempronius origine Pisani." This is the beginning of the *punctus* preceding a *consilium* written by the jurist "Petrus domini Albisi de Pisis legum doctor." A copy of the *consilium* is preserved in BAV, Barb. lat. 1399, 123r–v.

47 In 1426 the duties of the *provveditori* passed to the Florentine Consoli del Mare. From the 1440s onwards, the duties of the Consoli del Mare passed to other magistracies, the Cinque Governatori e Conservatori della Città di Pisa and Florence's Capitani di Parte Guelfa, any one of which could have commissioned Accoltus's *consilium*.

48 See also Bartholomaeus Socinus, *Consilia* (Venice, 1579), vol. 1, 217v, cons. 129, no. 3: "dico quod ex sola longa habitatione de iure communi efficitur quis civis." On the legal doctrines regarding the acquisition of citizenship through residence and payment of taxes, see Kirshner, "*Civitas sibi faciat civem.*" On *cives ex privilegio* and foreigners residing in Genoa, see Casarino, "Stranieri a Genova"; and idem, "Rappresaglie o privilegi?"

49 Accoltus, 170r: "Dubitatur an dictus Sempronius, qui origine est pisanus et habitatione et domicilio civis ianuensis, possit cogi ad solvendam gabellam in civitate Pisarum dotis sibi solute respectu matrimonii initi in dicta civitate Ianuae cum puella ianuensi, attenta forma statuti civitatis Pisarum per quod in effectu disponitur quod si quis contraxerit matrimonium debeat solvere tantum pro dote loco ghabelle, et quod per instrumentum alicuius contractus initi infra 50 miliaria debeat solvi ghabellam."

50 Accoltus, 170r: "Et notatur hoc per Bartolum et Baldum in l. 1., C. de sum. Trin. [Cod. 1. 1. 1], et precipue videtur utrum in proposito, quia dictus Sempronius origine est pisanus, quamquam domicilio sit ianuensis et constitutus, et ideo in dubio debet preferri ad imponendum sibi onus,

locus originis loco domicilii et civitatis. Nam originis locus nobilior est, l. Relegatorum, § Interdicere [Dig. 48. 22. 7. 10], et ibi per Bart., ff. de interdict. et releg., et l. Libertus, § Prescriptio, ff. ad munici. [Dig. 50. 1. 17. 3]; et ita voluit glo. expresse in l. Cives, C. de incol. [Cod. 10. 40[39]. 7], et ibi per Bart. Et idcirco sine dubio est concludendum ut supra." See Bartolus to Dig. 48. 22. 7. 10, in *Commentaria* (Venice, 1526–9), 222, no. 5; to Cod. 10. 40[39]. 7, ibid., 20r.

51 Accoltus, 170r: "Set prefatis non obstantibus, contrarium reputo verius de iure. Et circa hoc primo adverto quod regulariter locus ibi fit contractus attendi debet quantum ad ea que debent servari in dicto contractu vel pro eo, ut in l. Si fundus, ff. de evic. [Dig. 21. 2. 6], et l. Quaero, ff. de solut. [Dig. 46. 3. 100], et not. per Bartolum in d. l. 1, de sum. Trinita." See Bartolus to *l. Cunctos populos* (Cod. 1. 1. 1), in *Commentaria* (Venice, 1526–9), 4v, no. 16.

52 Accoltus, 173r–v: "Item quod sponte est in contractu dotis vel matrimonii quod illis attendi locus ubi vir uxorem ducit et ubi domicilium habet, l. Exigire dotem, et ibi per Bart., ff. de iudi. [Dig. 5. 1. 65], et not. per eundem in dicta l. 1 [Cod. 1. 1. 1]. Et facit quod habetur in l. fin., § Idem rescripserunt, ad munici. [Dig. 50. 1. 38. 3]. Et ideo quia presuponitur quod matrimonium in civitate Ianuae <contraxit> et ibi Sempronius habitat et subiit honera, tam respectu contractus quam respectu habitationis viri, dictum matrimonium debet regulari secundum leges et consuetudines ianuenses." On the *dictum* "forum domicilii est potentius quam sit forum originis," see Rolandus a Valle, *Quaestiones de lucro dotis,* 360r, nos. 15–24.

53 Accoltus, 170v: "Insuper consuetudo est in omnibus partibus Italiae quod gabelle solvantur etiam a forensibus pro contractibus vel rebus asportatis in civitate in qua reperiuntur."

54 Accoltus, 170v: "Preterea onus ghabelle est stricti iuris et odiosum precipue quando imponuntur ab inferiore a principe, per ea que not. per Bar. in l. Locatio [MS: Licitati], § fin. [Dig. 39. 4. 9. 8], et l. Vectigalia, de public. [Dig. 39. 4. 10] ... Et ideo inpositio sit stricti iuris, non debet comprehendere solutionem gabelle super existentibus in alieno territorio." See also Bartolus to *l. Cunctos populos* [Cod. 1. 1. 1], 6r, no. 35: "nam actus quod etiam spectat ad iurisdictionem voluntariam, quandocunque conceduntur ab alio inferiore a principe, non possunt exerceri extra territorium."

55 Accoltus, 170v. See Baldus to *l. Cunctos populos*, in *Commentaria* (Venice, 1599), 8r, no. 76: "quia ubi agitur de iure noviter inducendo per statutum, statutentes nihil possunt ultra limites quibus iurisdictio realiter limitatur, id est, ultra territorium, ut infra, de decurionibus, lex Duumvirum impune, libro 10 [Cod. 10. 32[31]. 53]."

56 Accoltus, 170v.

57 Accoltus, 170v: "Set si esset verum quod dictus Sempronius posse cogi ad solvendum in dicta civitate Pisarum, resultaret magna absurditas quod ipse solveret Ianuae et Pisis gabellam pro eadem re ... Et ideo ut talis absurditas evitetur, reformationes pisanae simpliciter loquentes debent restringi."

58 Accoltus, 170v–71r: "Insuper, ut supra dictum est, gabella solvitur pro rebus a persona, et idcirco ex quo dictus Sempronius est civis ianuensis et ibi habitat et ibi accipit uxorem et ibi accipit dotem de bonis ibi existentibus, sequitur manifesta conclusio quod onus ghabelle quod solvitur per dotem est solvendum Ianuae et non Pisis, quantum etiam sit pisanus civis, ut determinat expresse Bartolus in simili casu post glossam in l. 1, de mulieribus [Cod. 10. 64[62]. 1], in versiculo 'Quero aliquis est civis et alibi,' ubi concludit quod si quis est civis in utrabus civitatibus et in utraque habet bona, collectam que imponitur personis pro bonis debet solvere separatim secundum bona sita in diversis locis, et in uno quoque loco pro portione solvenda est. Igitur cum dictus Sempronius sit civis pisanus et ianuensis et receperit dotem de bonis existentibus Ianuae, ibi debet solvere gabellam pro illis, non in civitate Pisarum." See Bartolus to *l. Eam quae aliunde* (Cod. 10. 64[62]. 1), in *Commentaria* (Venice, 1526–9), 23r (*additio*).

59 Accoltus, 171r: "Preterea presuponitur mihi in facto quod pro dicta dote fuit soluta gabella Ianuae, quo casu stat regula quod licet in casu pari quando quis vocatur ad onera in civitate originis et in loco domicilii, preferatur civitas originis, et prius loco dictum est; tamen si iam una civitas preoccupavit, quia in illa solutum est, non potest quis cogi ad solvendum in civitate originis: et ita determinat glossa in dicta l. Cives, expresse, circa medium, C. de incolis, libro X [Cod. 10. 40[39]. 7]. Ergo sequitur ex predictis, ex eo <quod> semel Ianuae gabella soluta est pro dicto contractu dotis et matrimonii, non potest amplius cogi prefatus Sempronius ad solutionem Pisis."

60 Accoltus, 171r: "Unde cum statutum permittat gabelle exactionem usque ad 50 miliaria, ultra ea videtur prohiberi."

61 On Sallustius Gulielmi, see Kirshner, "Bartolo of Sassoferrato's 'De tyranno'"; on Benedictus de Barzis, see Treggiari, "Barzi, Benedetto"; Park, "The Readers," 292–9; and Abbondanza, "Una nuova fonte"; on Johannes Geronimi de Eugubio, see Martines, *Lawyers and Statecraft*, 501; Kuehn, *Illegitimacy*, 185ff.

62 Accoltus, 171r: "Et inducit Baldus punctualiter ad decisionem thematis nostri, dicens quod si statutum cavetur quod de contractu debet solvi gabellam, tale statutum non vendicat sibi locum in contracto facto per subditum extra territorium statuentis, cum huiusmodi statuta gabellarum sint contra ius commune."

63 Philippus Decius, *Consilia* (Venice, 1580–1), vol. 2, 117v–18r, cons. 457 (hereafter cited as Decius). The *consilium* was cited by Tuschus, *Practicarum conclusionum* (Lyon, 1634–70), vol. 4, 72, concl. 4 (*Gabella de quibus contractibus solvatur multis locis et de quibus non*); 6, 142, concl. 356 (*Pisarum civitas, statuta, consuetudines et privilegia*).

64 On the office and jurisdiction of the Sea Consuls of Florence, see Mallett, "The Sea Consuls," and his *The Florentine Galleys*; Fasano Guarini, "Città soggette," 23; and Addobbati, "La giurisdizione marittima."

65 Decius, 117v: "In causa gabellae, quae tractatur coram Magnificis Consulibus Maris, quaeritur an dominus Vitalis hebraeus et civis pisanus teneatur solvere gabellam dotis pro matrimonio contracto et consumato in civitate Venetiarum. Et pro vera resolutione videndum est de duobus. Primo, an tanquam civis pisanus attento iure communi et statuto pisano hic Pisis teneatur gabellam solvere. Secundo, dato quod non debeat solvere, an per capitula quae habent hebraei cum excellenti republica Florentinorum adstringatur ad solutionem dictae gabellae."

66 The explicit of Decius's *consilium* ("ut notat Bartolus in l. 1, ad munic., Philippus Decius, Pisis") makes clear that it was composed in Pisa. In fact, Decius was present at the Studio in Pisa through 1528, when he moved to Siena. Verde, "Dottorati a Firenze," 714–28. For bio-bibliographic profiles of Decius, see Lange and Kriechbaum, *Römisches Recht im Mittelalter*, 874–81, quote on 877 ("eine glanzvolle Persönlichkeit mit hoher Ausstrahlungskraft"); Belloni, *Professori giuristi*, 190–3; and Mazzacane, "Decio, Filippo."

67 The reliance on *consilia* in cases involving Pisan citizens adjudicated before the Sea Consuls represented a long-standing practice dating from the fifteenth century. See the reference to one such case (*apud Consules Maris*) regarding Pisans residing in Florence in Tomas Jacobi de Salvettis's commentary on the second book of the *Statutorum Florentinorum* of 1415: BNCF, Fondo Principale, II, IV, 434, 13r. Pisan citizens routinely requested *consilia* as part of their pleadings before Florentine magistrates. For example, in 1439, the patrician Battista di Bondo Lanfreducci of Pisa paid the Florentine Gulielmus Francisci de Tanaglis for a *consilium* that the jurist had written on his behalf with regard to a debt he was trying to collect from the estate of Niccholaio Zoppo. The estate had come under the control of the Florentine Ufficiali di Torre, who were authorized to adjudicate claims against the goods and properties confiscated by the government from rebels and citizens condemned to banishment. See Pecchiai, "Il libro di ricordi," 310.

68 On the differences between *consilia sapientis* and *pro parte*, see Ascheri, "Le fonti"; and Kirshner, "*Consilia* as Authority."

69 Luzzati remarks that the da Pisa family "had close connections with university teachers, such as the lawyer Bartolomeo Sozzini": Luzzati, *Ebrei ed ebraismo*, 23. In 1493, Socinus was commissioned by Isacco and Simone for a *consilium* in their dispute with the treasury officials of Lucca. See Lonardo, *Gli ebrei a Pisa*. In 1509, Isacco commissioned several jurists, including the Florentine jurist Antonius de Stroziis and Johannes Crottus of Casale Monferrato, who was at that time teaching at the University of Bologna, to submit *consilia* in support of his claim to the properties that had been confiscated in 1494 by the Pisan government; for which see Cavallar and Kirshner, "Jews as Citizens." Later, in 1515, Isacco's sons engaged Francesco Guicciardini to be their "advocato" in a dispute before the *Otto di Guardia* in 1515. See Cavallar, *Francesco Guicciardini, giurista*, 84, 350, no. 557.

70 On the da Pisa family, see Cassuto, *La famiglia Da Pisa*; Luzzati, "L'insediamento ebraico"; idem, "Matrimoni e apostasia"; idem, *Ebrei ed ebraismo*, 17–28. On Simone's and Vitale's activities in the Veneto, see Luzzati, "I legami"; and Jacoby, "Les Juifs à Venise," 198–9. On Vitale di Simone's scholarship and intellectual standing, see Bonfil, *Rabbis*, 253, 255, 284–9, 292–3; and Guetta, "Religious Life." On Vitale's economic ethics, see Rosenthal, ed. and trans., *Banking and Finance*. See Raymond de Roover's critical "Review of Rosenthal."

71 The exact date of Vitale di Simone's birth is unknown. Luzzati, "I legami," 250, states that Vitale was probably born around 1507 (a date that, on further reflection, he relates in a private communication, now appears to be improbable), while Guetta, "Religious Life," 86, conjectures that Vitale was born "1493?" but offers neither documentary evidence nor an argument in support of his conjecture.

72 Cassuto, *La famiglia Da Pisa*, 26; and his *Gli ebrei*, 55–8; Luzzati, "I legami," 249.

73 Luzzati, *Ebrei ed ebraismo*, 23.

74 Luzzati, "I legami," 254, n. 97; and his "Caratteri dell'insediamento," 38–40; Cavallar, *Francesco Guicciardini, giurista*, 81–5.

75 Luzzati, "Caratteri dell'insediamento," 40, n. 28. See also Cooperman, "A Rivalry of Bankers," 41–50.

76 On the bank of Asher Meshullam and his son Jacob, see Pullan, "Jewish Moneylending."

77 Luzzati, "I legami," 251, n. 88; Muzzarelli, "I banchieri ebrei," 153; Veronese, *Una famiglia*, 45–6.

78 Sestieri, *David Reubeni*, 122–9.

79 Kedar, "Toponymic Surnames"; Kirshner, "A *Consilium* of Rosello."

80 Stow, *Catholic Thought*, 102; Bartolus to *l. Iudaei* (Cod. 1. 9. 8), in *Commentaria* (Venice, 1526–9), 30r.

81 Cod. 1. 19. 18, *Hac victura*; *Decretum Gratiani*, C. 17 q. 4 c. 31, *Constituit*. On barring Jews from public dignities, honors, and offices in the *ius commune*, see Colorni, *Gli ebrei*, 22ff.; Margiotta-Broglio, "Il divieto per gli ebrei"; Pakter, *Medieval Canon Law*, 221–47.

82 In his commentary to *l. Municipem* (Dig. 50. 1. 1), in *Commentaria* (Venice, 1526–9), 249r, no. 8, Bartolus pointedly denied that temporal citizenship, that is citizenship in this world, could be acquired or contracted through baptism: "videte non credo quod quantum ad temporalia quod per baptismum contrahatur civilitas, quia certi sunt modi per quos civilitas, ut hic et l. Cives, C. de inco. [Cod. 10. 40[39]. 7], inter quos non est iste, sed quantum ad spiritualia relinquo canonistis." Pertinent, too, is Alexander Tartagnus's view that "Iudaei dicuntur esse de eodem popolo et corpore civitatis, quamvis non sint de corpore spirituali." See his *Consilia* (Venice, 1590), vol. 6, 52v, cons. 99, no. 2. This was a common view: see Marquardas de Susannis, *De Iudaeis* (Venice, 1584–6), vol. 14, pars 2, cap. II, 41v, no. 1. On this theme, see also Colorni, *La legge ebraica*, 86–94; idem, *Gli ebrei*, 15ff.; Toaff, "*Judei cives*?" 17ff.; Bornstein, "Law, Religion, and Economics," 245–6.

83 This distinction was fairly common and employed in fourteenth-century Marseille. See Smail, *Imaginary Cartographies*, 200. As far as I can tell, there was no juridical category in Umbrian and Tuscan sources of this period signifying "Jewish citizenship," equivalent, say, to the public designations "israelitische Burger" and "judische Burger" employed in Frankfurt am Main before the Jews were granted citizenship rights equal to other citizens in 1864. "*Judei cives*?", the confrontational title of Toaff's otherwise admirable study, is therefore as misleading as it is anachronistic.

84 Decius, 117v, no. 1: "Circa primum de iure communi, res clara videtur quod non teneatur, quia gabella est onus consecutivum contractus, et ideo ubi contractus celebratur, ibi in consequentiam gabella solvi debet."

85 Decius, 117v, no. 3. See Alexander Tartagnus, *Consilia* (Lyon, 1547–9), vol. 6, 68v, cons. 143, no. 6: "Quarto, quero si de isto contractu, etc., et sic sequeretur quod Robertus teneretur de iure ad solvendum gabellam in civitate Bononie et etiam ad solvendum gabellam in civitate Cesene pro eodem contractu dotis, quod non est dicendum, quia res ista regulari debet ut pro eodem facto vel pro eodem re non solvatur bis gabella." To be clear, although Decius implied that Vitale had paid the contract tax on the dowry he presumably received in Venice, I have no corroborating evidence that he did. Moreover, unlike Pisa and Florence, Venice, to my knowledge, did not levy a specific *gabella* on dowries.

86 Decius, 117v, no. 4: "quod maritus qui solvit gabellam extra territorium in loco ubi matrimonium contraxit et consumavit, si postea ducat uxorem ad locum domicilii eius, non tenetur iterum solvere gabellam, et ita casu nostro contingit, et idem concludit Socinus in consilio 302." See Bartholomaeus Socinus, *Consilia* (Venice, 1579), vol. 2, 167r–v, cons. 302, no. 2. Similarly, Petrus Philippus Corneus, *Consilia* (Venice, 1572), vol. 4, 111r–v, cons. 109, no. 2. In another *consilium* printed in the same volume, Corneus argued that a husband who consummated his marriage and paid a contract tax on his dowry in Fossombrone was thereby released from the obligation to pay the *gabella dotis* in his own locality, Borgo Sansepolcro (*de terra Burgi*). See cons. 97, 109r–v, nos. 3–4: "Insuper ex alio dicendum est quod dicta gabella solui non debeat per dictum Martinum, quia in themate praesupponitur quod ipse Martinus [de terra Burgi] pro dicta dote soluit gabellam in civitate Forimsempronii, ubi duxit uxorem, matrimonium cum ea consumando, ubi coactus fuit solvere gabellam ex forma statuti. Ideo dictam gabellam iterum solvere non tenetur, quia pro eadem re seu pro eodem contractu non debeat pluries solvi gabella."

87 Decius, 117v, nos. 7 and 8.

88 Cassuto, *Gli ebrei*, 83; Stephens, *The Fall*, 73.

89 For citizenship clauses in the *Capitoli* between Florence and the Jews of 1437, 1448, and 1481, see Ciardini, *I banchieri*, i–x, at vii (doc. I), xxi–xxxv, at xxviii (doc. VI), lvii–lxxxi, at lxvi and lxviii (doc. XXI); and Gow and Griffiths, "Pope Eugenius IV," 290–2. See also Siegmund, *The Medici State*, 140ff. On the *Capitoli* and enactments granting Jews the privileges of local citizenship, see Colorni, *La legge ebraica*, 33–94, esp. 92, n. 78. On the juridical construction of citizenship-conferring enactments in Florence, see Kirshner, "*Ars imitatur naturam.*"

90 Simonsohn, "La condizione giuridica," 108–16; Bonfil, "Società cristiana," 255–6; Toaff, "*Judei cives?*" 17ff.; Traniello, *Gli ebrei*, 47–55; idem, "Tra appartenenza ed estraneità" (also at http://rm.univr.it/rivista/atti/Ebrei.htm; Mueller, "Lo status degli ebrei"; and his "The Status."

91 For similar positive assessments regarding the citizenship status of Jews in fourteenth-century Worms and Cologne, see Kisch, "Die Rechtsstellung," 126–31; Schmandt, *Judei*, 64ff. The enforceability of these privileges and the actual security experienced by the Jews were in fact variable and dependent on local political and religious circumstances. As is all too well known, the privileged status and citizenship of the Jews in north and central Italy were battered by the feral denunciations and crude libels of Franciscan Observants preachers, especially San Bernardino da Siena (d. 1444), San Giovanni da Capestrano (d. 1456), and Blessed Bernardino da Feltre (d. 1494).

92 Decius, 117v, no. 8: "quod Florentiae observatur quod cives Florentini qui extra territorium contrahunt matrimonium et consumant matrimonium et recepta dote extra territorium, si cum uxore postea revertiantur Florentiam, ibi etiam coguntur gabellam solvere, sive hoc fit de consuetudine sive ex forma statuti."

93 Decius, 117v, no. 10: "quod si concessum sit alicui privilegium civilitatis in suum favorem, certe iste tenebitur ad datia seu collectas tanquam civis, quia hoc est onus civilitatis existentia rei." See Baldus to *l. Cum ex oratione* (Dig. 27. 1. 44), 36v, in *Commentaria* (Venice, 1599), no. 1, where he gives the example of inhabitants of the countryside (*comitativi*) who received the privilege of citizenship: "quod comitativi sunt ad civilitatem recepti, eo ipso in poenis et favoribus debeant tractari ut veri cives, et non solum favoribus, sed in odiis, quod est verum, ut hic in fine, unde dispensatio super statu habet se pariter ad favorem et odium."

94 Decius, 117v–18r, nos. 11–12. On the doctrinal points discussed in this paragraph, see Kirshner, "'Made Exiles,'" 184–6. Female citizens who married elsewhere and became citizens in their husband's towns were similarly said to enjoy the benefits of original citizenship while being released from its burdens. See Kirshner, "Women Married Elsewhere," chap. 7 in this volume.

95 Decius, 118r, no. 13: "Non obstante allegatione supra in contrarium, et primo dum dicitur quod hebraei debent tractari in gabellis ut cives Florentini, quia hoc est verum respectu immunitatis in ipsorum favorem, secus est in eorum odium."

96 Engelmann, *Die Wiedergeburt der Rechtskultur*, 151–2; Stow, *Catholic Thought*, 149ff.

97 Decius, 118r, no. 13: "Non obstat quod onus gabelle veniat in consequentiam civilitatis secundum Baldum in locis in contrarium supra allegatis, quia loquitur Baldus in eo, qui efficitur civis ex privilego, [in] dicta l. Quod favore [Cod. 1. 14. 6], et pariter in dicta l. Cum ex oratione [ED: Cum ratione] loquitur de receptis ad civilitatem. Nam tali casu cum sit civis absolute, tenetur subire onera civium; secus est, quando quis non efficitur civis, sed debet ut civis tractari, prout in casu isto dicitur, quia tunc talis praerogativa concessa in favorem non debet in odium resultare." Decius's distinctions were conventional; they are found in earlier discussions of the tax obligations of those "qui habeantur pro civibus": see, for example, Johannes Bertachinus (d. 1506), *De gabellis*, 65v, nos. 40–1. See also Julius Ferrettus (d. 1547), *De gabellis*, 84v, no. 208.

98 Decius, 188r, no. 15: "quia potest quis creari civis absque onore, ut notat Bartolus in l. 1, ad munic." Bartolus to *l. Municipem* (Dig. 50. 1. 1), 149r,

no. 17: "Quero utrum statuta que loquuntur de civibus locum habeant in illis civibus qui munera non subeunt." Bartolus's *dictum*, as Decius was assuredly aware, had been employed in a *consilium* of 1509 by the Florentine jurist Antonius de Stroziis, his former student and then colleague at the Pisan Studio, in defending the status of Vitale's uncle, Isacco, as an original citizen of Pisa: CS, ser. 3a, 41, vol. 14, 253v–55r, 253v: "In primis, Isac potest dici civis pisanus origine propria, quia in dicta civitate natus est, in qua pater eius constituerat domicilium, ut habetur in l. 1, et l. Assumptio, in principio, ff. ad municipalem [Dig. 50. 1. 1. and 6], et habetur per Bar. in d. l.1, ubi etiam in fine dicit quod, dato quod non subeat munera, tamen dicitur esse civis, licet forte non deberet vocari tunc municipes illius loci, quin munera et honera participans." This *consilium* and another by Johannes Crottus relating to this case are now critically edited and discussed by Cavallar and Kirshner ("Jews as Citizens").

99 This point similarly applies to the early modern period. See De Benedictis, "Citizenship and Government."

Appendix 1

1 The dates recorded in this document are all in the Florentine style.

Appendix 2

1 Lapa *ms.*

2 singulia *ms.*

3 Lapa *ms.*

4 Lape *ms.*

5 singulia *ms*

6 singulia *ms.*

7 contitetur *ms.*

Appendix 3

1 punctus est *ed.*

2 dissimulatione *ed.*

3 extortum *om. ed.*

4 vitij *ed.*

5 ASF, Statuti di Firenze, Podestà (1355), n. 18, 140r–v, lib. II, rubr. VIII, *De precepta guarentigie*.

6 utrum *om. ed.*

7 dicte *om. ed.*
8 meretur *ed.*
9 In-amen *om. ed.*
10 tam *om. ed*
11 etiam *om. ed.*
12 ad *V*
13 Johannes Andreae ad *c. Non est obligatorium* (VI 5. 13. 58), in *Commentaria* (Venice, 1581), 49r–v; Dinus Mugellanus ad *c. Non est obligatorium* (VI 5. 13. 58), in *De regulis iuris* (Venice, 1505), 23r.
14 a *ed.*
15 debitum *cor. ex* delic<t>um *V*
16 contracta *ed.*
17 et honest<at>i contradicens· resultet; contrarium contineat *ed.*
18 si *cor. ex* sic *V*
19 et *om. ed.*
20 amplectemur *ed.*
21 et *om. ed.*
22 ascendentes vel descendentes *ed.*
23 aut *suprascr. V*
24 a *V*
25 civili *ed.*
26 Innocentius IV ad *c. Gemma* (X 4. 1. 29), in *Commentaria* (Frankfurt am Main, 1570), 446r–v.
27 vult *ed.*
28 Glossa *Stipulatio* ad *c. Gemma* (X 4. 1. 29), in *Decretales* (Venice, 1572), 849, col. a.
29 sic *V*
30 sicut *V*
31 est simpliciter *ed.*
32 vel *ed.*
33 vel *ed.*
34 indifferentes *ed.*
35 vtique *ed.*
36 non *post* civilis *add. ed.*
37 sed *ed.*
38 assendere *om. ed.*
39 novam matrimonia: nova iura matrimonialia *ed.*
40 intermittitur *ed.*
41 stipulationem *ed.*

42 ex *om. ed.*
43 in transensu: transgressu *ed.*
44 possunt *ed.*
45 vel civili *om. ed.*
46 debet intelligi *ed.*
47 evaquantur *ed.*
48 apparet-confitendi: arras et ideo confiteri *ed.*
49 non *ms.*
50 ideo *suprascr. V*
51 non *ed.*
52 firmantur *ed.*
53 mutatas *ed.*
54 sunt *ed.*
55 valet *ed.*
56 Innocentius IV ad *c. Que in ecclesiarum* (X 1. 2. 7), in *Commentaria* (Frankfurt am Main, 1570), 3v.
57 Johannes Andreae ad *c. Statutum* (VI 1. 3. 11), in *Commentaria* (Venice, 1581), 12r–14r.
58 vel *ed.*
59 maleficium *ed.*
60 statuto: propter statutum *ed.*
61 disponi *cor. ex* dispositioni *V*
62 municipiali *ed.*
63 si *cor. ex* sit *V*
64 vel *ed.*
65 ut *om. ed*
66 ubi *ed.*
67 casu et *ed*
68 est *post* similibus *add. ed*
69 mores *om. ed.*
70 prescriptum *ed.*
71 possunt *ed.*
72 exceptiones obiectum *ed*
73 et-doctor: Angelus de Perusio *ms.*
74 Punctus *om. ed.*
75 licentia *ed.*
76 Eusepio *ed.*
77 completa *ed.*
78 ab incarnatione *om. ed.*

79 Eusepii *ed.*
80 illius *ed.*
81 quem *ms.*
82 Antonii et Lau. *ed.*
83 et curaturum *repet. V*
84 completorum *ed.*
85 consentient *ed.*
86 scilicet *ed.*
87 24 ms., *sed vide* BAV, Vat. lat. 2540, 209va, cons. 25.
88 malicitia *V*
89 non erat-suplesset etatem *om. ed.*
90 obligatio *ed.*
91 saltem *ed.*
92 saltem *ed.*
93 ita *ed.*
94 senserunt *om. ed.*
95 igitur *om. ed.*
96 quod *ed.*
97 significet *ed.*
98 per quem: alias *ed.*
99 recipiendo *ed.*
100 videtur *ms.*
101 gerebat *corr. ex* gerebant *V*
102 adiecta *ed.*
103 l. iii. V *ed.*
104 ratione *ed.*
105 dicto *om. ed.*
106 determinat *ed.*
107 et sinu. et *V*
108 de forma, nulla mora: dote, mora, nulla forma *ed.*
109 iur. *ed.*
110 quia *ed.*
111 quod *om. ed.*
112 Et ita-et cet.: Angelus de Perusio *V*

Appendix 4

1 Giovanni *ms.*
2 Uxor *ms.*

Appendix 5

1 In 1485, for example, Piero di Covero di Niccolò collected interest on 26 January (two days before Pitti), 1 June (three days after Pitti), and 26 September (the same day as Pitti); Piero di Bartolomeo di Puccio collected interest on 5 February (seven days after Pitti), 3 June (five days before Pitti), and 13 October (eighteen days after Pitti); Salvestro di Domenico di Iacopo Federighi collected interest on 29 January (one day after Pitti), 28 May (the same day as Pitti), and 24 September (two days before Pitti). Source: MG, 956, 243r–44r, 255r.

References

Manuscripts Cited

Bologna
  - Archivio di Stato
  Statuti (1357)
  - Collegio di Spagna
Castiglion Fiorentino
  - Archivio Comunale
  Statuti (1384)
Chicago
  - University of Chicago, Regenstein Library
  MS 6
  Rosenthal MS 310
Florence
  - Archivio di Stato (ASF)
  Acquisti e Doni
  Archivio Cerchi
  Archivio della Gherardesca
  Arte dei Giudici e Notai (AGN)
  Balìe
  Capitani di Parte Guelfa
  Carte del Bene
  Carte Strozziane (CS)
  Catasto (1427, 1433, 1480)
  Consiglio del Cento
  Conventi Soppressi
  Corporazioni Religiose Soppresse (CRS)

Manoscritti
Monte Comune
Monte delle Graticole
Notarile Antecosimiano
Notificazioni di atti di emancipazione
Pareri dei Savi
Podestà
Provvisioni-Registri
Santa Maria Nuova
Statuti delle comunità autonome e soggetti
Statuti di Firenze
Tratte 576
– Archivio Guicciardini
– Archivio Niccolini da Camugliano
– Biblioteca Nazionale Centrale (BNCF)
Fondo Panciatichiano
Fondo Principale
Magliabechiano
Lucca
– Archivio di Stato (ASLu)
Corte de' Mercanti
Governo di Paolo Guinigi Decr. 2
Statuti del Comune di Lucca 6
Milan
– Biblioteca Ambrosiana
M107 suss.
Perugia
– Archivio di Stato
Notarile
Ospedale di S. Maria della Misericordia
Pisa
– Archivio di Stato (ASPi)
Comune di Pisa
Gabella dei contratti
Rome
– Biblioteca del Senato
Statuti 765
Turin
– Biblioteca Nazionale Universitaria
Cod. H, I, 13

Vatican City
- Biblioteca Apostolica Vaticana (BAV)
Barb. lat.
Urb. lat.
Vat. lat.
Vicenza
- Biblioteca Bertoliana
Gonzati 566
Viterbo
- Biblioteca degli Ardenti
Statuti (1469)

Sources for *Ius Commune*

Abbas Panormitanus (Niccolò de' Tedeschi). *Commentaria in quinque libros Decretalium*. Lyon: Mareschal, Moylin, and Petit, 1520–1.

– *Commentaria*. Venice, 1617 (= *Abbatis panormitani commentaria … Decretalium libri*. 5 vols. Venice: Giunta, 1617).

– *Consilia*. Venice, 1578 (= *Abbatis Panormitani consilia, tractatus, quaestiones …* Venice: Dominicus & Ioannes Baptista Guerreus, [fratres]), 1578).

Albericus de Rosate. *Commentarii*. Venice: n.p., 1585–6; repr., 9 vols., Bologna: Arnaldo Forni, 1974–82.

– *Dictionarium juris tam civilis quam canonici*. Venice: Dominicus & Ioannes Baptista Guerreus (fratres), 1573.

Alexander Tartagnus. *Commentaria*. Venice, 1570 (= *Alexandri Tartagni Imolensis iuriscon.: Celeberrimi in primam & secundam Infortiati partem commentaria*. Venice: Giunta, 1570).

– *Commentaria*. Venice, 1595 (= *Alexandri Tartagni Imolensis … commentaria in primam & secundam Infortiati partem*. Venice: Giunta, 1595).

– *Consilia*. Lyon, 1547–9 (= *Consiliorum seu responsorum clarissimi omnium iuris utriusque doctoris et consummatissimi iureconsulti Domini Alexandri Tartagni Imolensis* … Lyon: Georgius Regnault; Compagnie des libraires, 1549).

– *Consilia*. Venice 1590 (= *Consiliorum seu responsorum Alexandri Tartagni … liber primus* [*-septimus*]. Venice, Felix Valgrisius, 1590).

Angelus de Ubaldis. *Commentaria*. Venice, 1579 (= *Angeli Ubaldi Commentaria in Digestum, Codicem, et Authenticam eruditissimorum hominum adnotationibus illustrata*. Venice: n.p., 1579–80).

– *Consilia*. Lyon, 1551 (= *Consilia D. Angeli De Ubaldis Perusini …: Varias decisiones legum studiosis utilissimas complectentia* … Lyon: n.p., 1551).

– *Lectura*. Lyon, 1548 (= *Lectura super prima* [*- secunda*] *Infortiati*. Lyon: Georgius Regnault, 1548).

Antonius de Butrio. *Commentaria*. Venice, 1575–8 (= *Super prima primi Decretalium commentarii*. 8 vols. Venice: Giunta, 1575–8; repr., 5 vols., Turin: Bottega d'Erasmo, 1967).

– *Consilia*. Venice, 1575 (= *Consilia seu responsa D. Antonii de Butrio Bononiensis* ... Venice: Christophorus Zanettus, 1575).

Archidiaconus (Guido de Baysio). *Commentaria*. Venice, 1601 (= *Guidonis a Baisio archidiaconi Bononiensis* ... *In Decretorum volumen commentaria*. Venice: Giunta, 1601).

Azo. *Summa aurea*. Lyon, 1557 (= *Azonis summa aurea recens pristinae suae fidei restituta, ac archetypo collata*. Lyon: Petrus Fradin, 1557).

– *Summa Azonis*. Venice, 1581 (= *Summa Azonis, locuples iuris ciuilis thesaurus: Hactenus deprauatissima, nunc autem summa fide emendata, ac exquisito studio, suo pristino nitori recens restituta* ... Venice: sub signo Angeli Raphaelis, 1581).

Baldus de Ubaldis. *Commentaria*. Lyon, 1498 (= *Lectura super Digesto novo*. Lyon: Siber, 1498).

– *Commentaria*. Lyon, 1548 (= *Commentaria subtilia, nec non copiosa, D. Baldi Ubaldi Perusini* ... Lyon: Georgius Regnault, 1548).

– *Commentaria*. Venice, 1577 (= *In* [*Corpus iuris civilis*] *Baldi Ubaldi Perusini* ... *commentaria*. 9 vols. Venice: Lucas Antonius Giunta, 1577).

– *Commentaria*. Venice, 1595 (= *In Decretalium volumen commentaria*. Venice: Giunta, 1595; repr., Turin: Bottega d' Erasmo, 1971).

– *Commentaria*. Venice, 1599 (= *Commentaria omnia*. 8 vols. Venice: Giunta, 1599; repr., Goldbach: Keip, 2004).

– *Consilia*. Venice, 1575 (= *Baldi Ubaldi Perusini iurisconsulti omnium concessu doctissimi pariter et acutissimi consiliorum sive responsorum volumen primum* [*-sextum*]. 6 vols. Venice: Francesco de' Franceschi senese, Gaspare Bindoni il vecchio, eredi di Nicolò Bevilacqua e Damiano Zenaro, 1575; repr., 3 vols., Turin: Bottega d'Erasmo, 1970).

– *Tractatus duo de vi et potestate statutorum*, edited by Eduard M. Meijers. Haarlem: H.D. Tjeenk Willink & Zoon, 1939.

Bartholomaeus de Saliceto. *Commentaria*. Lyon, 1515 (= *Eximii profundissimique juris utriusque interpretis et doctoris D. Bartholomei de Salyceto Lecture prima* [*-quarta*] *pars super Codicis* ... Lyon: Mareschal, 1515).

Bartholomaeus Socinus. *Consilia*. Lyon, 1546 (= *Prima* [*-secunda*] *pars consiliorum Mariani et Bartholomei de Socinis senensium*. Lyon: Giunta, 1546).

– *Consilia*. Venice, 1571 (= *Consiliorum sive malis responsorum Mariani Socini iunioris iurisconsultissimi* ... *volume* ... Venice: Dominicus & Ioannes Baptista [fratres]), 1571).

– *Consilia*. Venice, 1579 (= *Consiliorum seu potius responsorum Mariani Socini ac Bartholomaei filii Senensium … volumen*. 5 vols. Venice: Franciscus Zillettus, 1579).

Bartolus de Saxoferrato. *Commentaria*. Venice, 1526–9 (= *Commentaria cum additionibus Thomae Diplovatatii aliorumque excellentissimorum doctorum*. Venice: Baptista de Tortis, 1526–9; repr., 9 vols., Rome: Il Cigno Galileo Galilei, 1996).

– *Commentaria*. Venice, 1570–1 (= *Bartoli a Saxoferrato opera*. 12 vols. in 10. Venice: Giunta, 1570–1).

– *Consilia*. Venice: 1570–1 (= *Bartoli a Saxoferrato opera*. Venice: Giunta, 1570–1).

– *Consilia*. Venice, 1585 (= *Consilia, quaestiones, et tractatus*. Venice: Giunta, 1585).

Blume, Fred H., trans., and Timothy Kearley, ed. *Annotated Justinian Code*. George William Hopper Law Library. University of Wyoming. http://www.uwyo.edu/lawlib/blume-justinian/ajc-edition-2/.

Bonellus de Barulo, Andrea. *Commentarii in tres libros Codicis*. Venice: Sessa, 1601; repr., Bologna: Arnaldo Forni, 1975.

Bonifatius VIII. *Liber sextus Decretalium D. Bonifacii VIII*. Lyon: n.p., 1584.

Cinus de Pistorio, *Commentaria*. Frankfurt am Main, 1578 (= *Cyni Pistoriensis in Codicem et aliquot titulos primi Pandectarum tomi, id est Digesti veteris, doctissima commentaria*. 2. vols. Frankfurt am Main: Sigismundus Feyerabend, 1578; repr., Turin: Bottega d'Erasmo, 1964).

Conte, Emanuele, and Sara Menzinger. *La Summa Trium Librorum di Rolando da Lucca (1195–1234): Fisco, politica, scientia iuris*. Rome: Viella, 2012.

Corpus iuris canonici. Edited by Emil Freidberg. 2 vols. Leipzig: B. Tauchnitz, 1879; repr., Graz: Akademische Druck- u. Verlagsanstalt, 1959.

Corpus iuris civilis. Edited by Theodor Mommsen, Paul Krueger, Rudolph Schoell, and Wilhelm Kroll. 3 vols. Berlin: Weidmann, 1872–95; repr., 1954.

Decretales. Venice, 1572 (= *Decretales Gregorii noni Pontificis Maximi, cum glossis ordinariis*. Venice: n.p., 1572).

Derrer, Felix, ed. *Lo Codi: Eine Summa Codicis in provenzalischer Sprache aus dem 12. Jahrhundert: Die provenzalische Fassung der Handschrift A (Sorbonne 632): Vorarbeiten zu einer kritischen Textausgabe*. Zurich: Juris Verlag, 1974.

Dinus Mugellanus (de Rossonis). *Commentarius in regulas iuris pontifici*. Cologne: Theodorus Baumius, 1578.

– *De regulis iuris: Lib. VI* … Venice: Benedictus Fontana, 1505.

– *De regulis iuris commentaria*. Lyon: Bartholomaeus Vincentius, 1577.

Dominicus de Sancto Geminiano. *Commentaria* (= *Liber sextus Decretalium D. Bonifacii VIII*). Lyon: Compagnie des Libraires, 1584).

Federicus de Senis. *Consilia et questiones*. Rouen, 1513 (= *Consilia et questiones domini Frederici de Petruciis Senensis famosissimi decretorum doctoris*. Rouen: Petrus Olivier, 1513).

Fitting, Hermann, ed. *Lo Codi, in der lateinischen Übersetzung des Ricardus Pisanus herausgegeben*. Halle: Max Niemeyer, 1906.

– ed. *Summa Codicis des Irnerius*. Berlin: J. Guttentag, 1894.

Franciscus Accoltus de Aretio. *Commentaria*. Venice, 1589 (= *In primam et secundam Digesti novi partem commentaria*. Venice: Giunta, 1589).

– *Consilia*. Venice, 1572 (= *Francisci Accolti iurisconsulti Aretini longe omnium ingenij praestantissimi Consilia, seu responsa*. Venice: Nicolaus Beuilaqua & socii, 1572).

Franciscus de Zabarellis. *Commentaria*. Venice, 1502 (= *Commentum seu lectura cardinalis Francisci de Zabarellis super V libris Decretalium*. Venice: Simon de Leure pro Andrea Torresano de Asula, 1502).

Glossa ordinaria. Lyon, 1562 (= *Corpus iuris civilis cum glossa*. 5 vols. Lyon: Ioannes Ausultus, 1562; Venice: n.p., 1569; Venice: Hieronymus Polus, 1591).

Goffredus de Trani. *Summa super titulis Decretalium*. Lyon, 1519 (= *Summa perutilis et valde necessaria doctoris Goffredi* ... Lyon: Moylin de Cambray, 1519; repr. as *Summa super titulis Decretalium*, Aalen: Scientia, 1968).

Gulielmus Durandus. *Speculum iudicale*. Basel, 1574 (= *Gulielmi Durandi Episcopi Mimatensis iuris utriusque doctoris Speculum iuris, Ioannis Andreae, Baldi, reliquorumque praestantissimorum iuris utriusque doctorum theorematibus illustratum* ... Basel: Ambrosius & Aurelius Frobenius [fratres], 1574).

– *Speculum iudicale*. Frankfurt am Main, 1592 (= *Speculum iuris: Cum Ioannis Andreae, Baldi reliquorumque ... doctorum visionibus hactenus addi solitis* ... Frankfurt am Main: Andreaa Wechel [haeredes], 1592).

Hostiensis (Henricus de Segusio). *Commentaria*. Venice, 1581 (= *Henrici de Segusio, Cardinalis Hostiensis ... in primum* [*-sextum*] *Decretalium librum Commentaria* ... Venice: Giunta, 1581).

– *Summa aurea*. Venice, 1574 (= *Cardinalis Hostiensis Summa aurea*. Venice: Jacobus Vitalis, 1574).

Innocentius IV. *Commentaria*. Frankfurt am Main, 1570 (= *Commentaria Innocentii Quarti Pont. Maximi super libros quinque Decretalium*. Frankfurt am Main: Sigismundus Feyerabend, 1570).

Jacobus Butrigarius. *Commentaria*. Paris, 1516 (= *Super Codice lectura*. Paris: Ioannes Petit, 1516; repr., Bologna: Arnaldo Forni, 1973).

Jacobus de Arena. *Commentaria*. Lyon, 1541 (= *Doctoris Iacobi de Arena Parmensis, Super iure civili* ... Lyon: Hugo a Porta, 1541; repr., Bologna: Arnaldo Forni, 1971).

Jacobus de Belvisio. *Commentarii in Authenticum et consuetudines feudorum.* Lyon: Sachon, 1511; repr., Bologna: Arnaldo Forni, 1971.

Jacobus de Ravanis (Jacques de Revigny). *Lectura.* Paris, 1519 (= *Lectura super Codice.* Paris: Petrus Gromorsius, 1519; repr., Bologna: Arnaldo Forni, 1967).

Jason de Mayno. *Commentaria.* Turin, 1573 (= *Iasonis Mayni Mediolanensis iurisconsulti clarissimi commentaria.* Turin: Nicolaus Bevilaqua, 1573).

Johannes Andreae. *Commentaria.* Venice, 1581 (= *In quinque Decretalium libros novella commentaria.* 6 vols. Venice: Franciscus de Franciscis, 1581; repr., 4 vols., Turin: Bottega d'Erasmo, 1963).

– *Commentaria.* Venice, 1581 (= *In sextum Decretalium librum novella commentaria.* Venice: Franciscus de Franciscis, 1581; repr., Turin: Bottega d'Erasmo, 1966).

– *De sponsalibus et matrimoniis.* Venice, 1584 (= *Tractatus compendiosus ... de sponsalibus et matrimoniis* ... In *TUI*, vol. 9, 2ra–3vb. Venice: Franciscus Zillettus, 1584).

Johannes Bertachinus. *De gabellis.* Venice, 1584 (= *Io. Bertachini, De gabellis, tributis, et vectigalibus.* In *TUI*, vol. 12, 51vb–76ra. Venice: Franciscus Zillettus, 1584–6).

Johannes de Erfordia. *Summa confessorum* (= *Die Summa confessorum des Johannes von Erfurt.* 3 vols. Edited by Norbert Brieskorn. Frankfurt am Main: Lang, 1980).

Johannes de Imola. *Commentaria.* Lyon, 1547–9 (= *Commentariorvm iuris vtriusque monarchae domini Ioannis Imolensis* ... 5 vols. Lyon: Gaspar Trechsel, 1547).

Johannes Petruccius de Montesperello. *Consilia.* Venice, 1590 (= *Consiliorum, seu mavis responsorum praeclarissimi ac celeberrimi iurisconsulti Iohannis Petrutii de nobilibus de Monte Sperello* ... Venice: Franciscus de Franciscis, 1590).

Julius Ferrettus. *De gabellis.* Venice, 1584 (= *Iulii Ferretti Ravennatis, De gabellis, publicanis, muneribus, et oneribus.* In *TUI*, vol. 12, 76rb–95vb. Venice: Franciscus Zillettus, 1584–6).

Lapus de Castiglionchio Senior. *Allegationes.* Venice, 1571 (= *Allegationes iuris utriusque monarcae domini Lapi de Castiglionchio* ... Venice: Franciscus Zilletus, 1571).

Ludovicus Pontanus (Romanus). *Commentaria.* Lyon, 1547 (= *D. Ludovici Pontani Romani* ... *in primam Digesti veteris partem* ... Lyon: Hugo & haeredes Aemonis à Porta, 1547).

– *Commentaria.* Venice, 1580 (= *Ludovici Pontani vulgo Romani* ... *in primam atque secundam Digesti veteris partem commentaria* [etc.]. Venice: n.p., 1580).

– *Consilia.* Lyon, 1565 (= *Consilia Ludovici Romani: Nunc recens multis mendis repurgata* ... Lyon: Compagnie des libraires, 1565).

Mansi, Joannes Dominicus, ed. *Sacrorum conciliorum, nova et amplissima collectio*. 54 vols. in 58. Paris: H. Walter, 1901; repr., Graz : Akademische Druck-u. Verlagsanstalt, 1960–1.

Marianus Socinus and Bartholomaeus Socinus. *Consilia*. Venice, 1579 (= *Consiliorum seu potius responsorum Mariani Socini ac Bartholomaei filii Senensium … volumen*. 5 vols. Venice: Franciscus Zillettus, 1579).

Marquardus de Susannis. *De Iudaeis et aliis infidelibus*. In *TUI*, vol. 14, 27rb–77a. Venice, Franciscus Zillettus, 1584–6.

Mommsen, Theodor H., Rudolf Schöll, and Wilhelm Kroll, eds. *Corpus iuris civilis*. 3 vols. Berlin: Weidmann, 1928–9.

Nellus de Sancto Geminiano. *De bannitis*. Venice, 1584 (= *Tractatus insignis ac praeclarissimus editus ab … Nello de Sancto Geminiano … de bannitis*. Venice: Franciscus Zillettus, 1584–6).

Odofredus, *Commentaria*. Lyon, 1550 (= *Odofredi iuris utriusque peritissimi dicaearchi, super tribus libris Codicis praelectiones* … Lyon: Franciscus & Claudius Marchant [fratres], 1550).

– *Commentaria*. Lyon, 1552 (= *Domini Odofredi inter iureconsultos facile primi, elaboratae praelectiones in undecim primos; postremum Pandectarum Iustiniani tomum*. Lyon: Blasius Guido, 1552).

Paulus de Castro. *Commentaria*. Venice, 1582 (= *Commentaria, cum multis tum D. Francisci Curtii, tum etiam aliorum quorundam* … 10 vols. Venice: Lucas Antonius Giunta, 1582).

– *Commentaria super Digesto veteri II*. Lyon, 1553 (= *Pauli Castrensis in secundam Digesti veteris partem Patavinae praelectiones*. Lyon: Compagnie des libraires, Petrus Fradin, 1553).

– *Commentaria super Infortiato*. Lyon, 1553 (= *Pauli Castrensis in primam et secundam Infortiati partem Patavinae praelectiones*. Lyon: Compagnie des libraires, 1553).

– *Consilia*. Venice, 1581 (= *Consiliorum siue responsorum praestantissimi iuris consulti Pauli Castrensis volumen primum* [*-tertium*]. 3 vols. Venice: n.p., 1581).

– *Consilia*. Frankfurt am Main, 1584 (= *Consilia Pauli de Castro eminentissimi et acutissimi iuris interpretis volumen*. Frankfurt am Main: Sigismundus Feyerabend, 1582–4).

Petrus Ancharanus. *Commentaria*. Bologna, 1580–1 (= *In quinque Decretalium libros facundissima commentaria*. 5 vols. Bologna: Societas Typographiae Bononiensis, 1580–1).

Petrus de Bellapertica. *Commentaria*. Frankfurt am Main, 1571 (= *Petrus a Bella Pertica commentaria in Digestum novum* … Frankfurt am Main: Christophorus Corvinus, 1571).

Petrus Philippus Corneus. *Commentarius*. Lyon, 1553 (= *Petri Philippi Cornei Perusini in secundam Codicis partem [In secundam Digesti veteris partem] commentarius* ... Lyon: Jacobus Giunta (heredes), 1553).

– *Consilia*. 4 vols. Venice, 1572 (= *Consiliorum sive responsorum ... volumen quartum*. Venice: Nicolaus Bevilacqua, 1572.

Philippus Decius. *Consilia*. 2 vols. Venice, 1580–1 (= *Consiliorum sive responsorum tomus primus [-secundus]*. Venice: Hieronymous Polus, 1580–1).

Rainerius de Forlivio. *Lectura super Digesto novo*. Lyon, 1523 (= *Utilis et fecunda lectura ... super prima et secunda parte ff. novi ... cum eiusdem Raynerii ...* Lyon: Vincentius de Portonariis, 1523).

Raphael de Raymundis (Cumanus). *Commentaria*. Lyon, 1554 (= *Raphaelis Cumani commentationes in eius Pandectarum partis primam et secundam*. Lyon: Blasius Guido, 1554).

– *Consilia*. Lyon, 1548 (= *Consilia Raphaelis Cumani et Raphaelis Fulgosii*. Lyon: Iacobus Giunta (haeredes), 1548).

– *Consilia*. Venice, 1576 (= *Consilia, sive responsa acutissimorum iuris interpretum, Raphaelis Cumani* ... Venice: Gaspar Bindonus, 1576).

Rolandus a Valle. *Questiones de lucro dotis*. In *TUI*, vol. 9, 351va–95ra. Venice: Franciscus Zillettus, 1584–6.

Theodosiani libri XVI cvm Constitvtionibvs Sirmondianis et Leges novellae ad Theodosianvm pertinentes. Edited by Th. Mommsen and Paul Meyer. Berlin: Weidmann, 1905.

Tuschus, Dominicus. *Practicarum conclusionum*. Lyon: 1634–70 (= *Practicarum conclusionum iuris in omni foro frequentiores ... tomus primus [-octavus]*. Lyon: Ioannes Pillehotte, 1634–70).

Watson, Alan, ed. and trans. *The Digest of Justinian*. 4 vols. Philadelphia: University of Pennsylvania Press, 1985.

Ziletti, Giovanni Battista, ed. *Matrimonialium consiliorum ex clarissimis iureconsultis tam veteribus, quam recentioribus, diligentia d. Io. Baptistae Ziletti i.u.d. veneti collectorum, primum volumen*. Venice: Iordanus Zilettus, 1563.

Statutes

Angelini, Lorenzo, ed. *Lo statuto di Barga del 1360*. Lucca: Accademia Lucchese di Scienze, Lettere ed Arti, 1994.

Ascheri, Mario, ed. *L'ultimo statuto della Repubblica di Siena (1545)*. Siena: Accademia Senese degli Intronati, 1993.

Ascheri, Mario, and Fulvio Mancuso, eds. *Abbadia San Salvatore: Una comunità autonoma nella Repubblica di Siena: Con edizione dello statuto (1434–sec. XVIII)*. Siena: Il Leccio, 1994.

Bacchetti, Enrico, ed. *Statuti di Belluno del 1392 nella trascrizione di età veneziana*. Corpus statutario delle Venezie, 16. Rome: Viella, 2002.

Balletto, Laura, ed. *Statuta antiquissima Saone (1345)*. 2 vols. Collana storica di fonti e studi, 8 and 9. Bordighera: Istituto Internazionale di Studi Liguri-Museo Bicknell, 1971.

Betto, Bianca, ed. *Gli statuti del comune di Treviso (sec. XIII–XIV)*. 2 vols. Rome: Istituto Storico Italiano per il Medio Evo, 1984–6.

Bonaini, Francesco, ed. *Statuti inediti della città di Pisa dal XII al XIV secolo*. 3 vols. Florence: Vieusseux, 1854–70.

Buzzi, Corrado, ed. *Lo statuto del comune di Viterbo del 1469*. Rome: Istituto Storico Italiano per il Medio Evo, 2004.

Caggese, Romolo, ed. *Statuti della Repubblica fiorentina del l'anno 1325*. 2 vols. Florence: Comune di Firenze, 1910–21.

Caprioli, Maria, ed. *Lo statuto della città di Rieti dal secolo XIV al secolo XVI*. Rome: Istituto storico italiano per il Medio Evo, 2008.

Caprioli, Severino, ed. *Statuto del Comune di Perugia del 1279*. Perugia: Deputazione di Storia Patria per l'Umbria, 1996.

Egidi, Pietro, ed. *Statuti della provincia romana.* Fonti per la storia d'Italia pubblicate dall'Istituto storico italiano. Rome: Forzani, 1930.

Era, Antonio, ed. *Statuti pisani inediti dal XIV al XVI secolo*. Sassari: Galluzzi, 1932.

Fugazza, Emanuela, ed. *Lo statuto di Piacenza del 1323*. Pavia: Pavia University Press, 2012.

Ius municipale vincentinum cum additione partium illustrissimi dominii. Venice: Bartholomaeus Contrinus, 1567.

Liber statutorum Civitatis Castelli. Città di Castello: A. de Mazochis et Nicolaus & Bartholomaeus (fratres) de Gucciis, 1538.

Lo Conte, Antonio, and Elena Vannucchi, eds. *Lo statuto di Massa e Cozzile del 1420: Le norme giuridiche medievali in uso in un Comune rurale della Valdinievole*. Florence: Polistampa, 2006.

Magi, Beatrice, ed. *Radicofani e il suo statuto del 1441*. Siena: Cantagalli, 2004.

Mangini, Marta Luigina, ed. *Statuta civitatis et episcopatus Cumarum (1458)*. Varese: Insubria University Press, 2008.

Marri Camerani, Giulia, ed. *Statuto di Arezzo, 1327*. Florence: Deputazione di storia patria per la Toscana, 1946.

Menichetti, Antonio, ed. *Lo statuto vecchio del comune di Gubbio con le aggiunte del 1376*. Gubbio: Petruzzi, 2002.

Morandi, Ubaldo, ed. *Statuto del comune di Montepulciano (1337)*. Florence: L.S. Olschki, 1966.

Onori, Alberto M, ed. *Lo statuto di Pescia del 1339*. Pistoia: Società pistoiese di storia patria, 2000.

Pepe, Iolanda, ed. *Codice Civile (1865), Codice di Commercio (1882): Testi non commentati*. Naples: Esselibri-Simone, 2008.
Regni, Claudio, ed. *Bevagna e il suo statuto dell'anno 1500*. Perugia: Deputazione di storia patria per l'Umbria, 2005.
Salem Elsheikh, ed. *Statuto del Comune e del Popolo di Perugia del 1342 in volgare*. 3 vols. Perugia: Deputazione di storia patria per l'Umbria, 2000.
Santini, Pietro, ed. *Documenti dell'antica costituzione del comune di Firenze*. Florence: L.S. Olschki, 1895.
Statuta civitatis Forolivii (1504). Forlì: Franciscus Surianum, 1616.
Statuta civitatis Pisauri noviter impressa. Pesaro: Balthassar de Carthularis, 1530–1; repr., Bologna: Arnaldo Forni, 1985.
Statuta magnificae civitatis Asisii. Perugia: Hieronymus Carthularus, 1534–43.
Statuta Pallavicinia (1429–1570). Parma: Erasmus Viottus, 1582.
Statuta populi et communis Florentiae ... anno salutis MCCCCXV. 3 vols. Freiburg [Florence]: Kluch, 1778–83.
Statutorum et reformationum magnifice civitatis Senogallie volumen. Pesaro: Balthassar de Carthularis, 1537.
Statutorum magnificae civitatis et communis Feltriae (1439). Venice: Leonardus Tivanus, 1749.
Statutorum magnificae civitatis Spoleti ... Spoleto: L. Bini, 1542.
Storti Storchi, Claudia, ed. *Lo statuto di Bergamo del 1331*. Milan: Giuffrè, 1986.
Trombetti Budriesi, Anna Laura. *Lo Statuto del Comune di Bologna dell'anno 1335*. 2 vols. Rome: Istituto Storico Italiano per il Medio Evo, 2008.
Vannucchi, Elena, and Antonio Lo Conte, eds. *Lo statuto di Uzzano del 1389*. Pescia: Edimedia, 2004.

Other Primary Sources

Alberti, Leon Battista. *Dinner Pieces: A Translation of the Intercenales*. Translated by David Marsh. Binghamton, NY: Medieval & Renaissance Texts & Studies, 1987.
– *I libri della Famiglia*. Edited by Ruggiero Romano and Alberto Tenenti. Turin: Einaudi, 1969.
Altieri, Marco Antonio. *Li nuptiali*. Edited by Enrico Narducci. Rome: C. Bartoli, 1873.
Andreas Capellanus. *De Amore* [*Andrea Capellanus on Love*]. Translated by Patrick G. Walsh. London: Duckworth, 1982.
– *Trattato d' amore*. Edited by Salvatore Battaglia. Rome: Perella, 1947.
Angelus Carletus de Clavasio. *Summa angelica.* Lyon, 1520 (= *Summa angelica reuerendi patris fratris Angeli de Clavasio*. Lyon: Antoine du Ry, 1520).

– *Summa angelica.* Venice, 1569 (= *Summa angelica de casibus conscientalibus.* Venice: Iacobus Sansovinus, 1569).

Antoninus (sant'Antonino of Florence). *Summa theologica.* Venice, 1581–2 (= *Summa sacrae theologicae, iuris pontificii, et caesarei* ... Venice: Giunta, 1581–2).

Barbaro, Francesco. *Francesci Barbari De re uxoria liber.* Edited by Attilio Gnesotto. Padua: Accademia Patavina di Scienze, Lettere ed Arti 1915.

Bartholomaeus Fumus. *Summa Armilla.* Venice: Aldine press, 1554.

Battista Trovamala de Salis. *Summa casuum conscientiae.* Venice: Paganinus de Paganinis, 1499.

Boccaccio, Giovanni. *Genealogie deorum gentilium libri.* Edited by Vincenzo Romano. Bari: Laterza, 1951.

Bruni, Leonardo. *History of the Florentine People.* Edited and translated by James Hankins. Cambridge, MA: Harvard University Press, 2001.

Buonaccorsi, Biagio. *Libro di ricordi.* In *Biagio Buonaccorsi: Sa vie – son temps – son oeuvre.* Edited by Denis Fachard. Bologna: Massimiliano Boni, 1976.

Cammelli, Antonio. *Rime edite ed inedite di Antonio Cammelli detto il Pistoia.* Edited by Antonio Cappelli and Severino Ferrari. Livorno, 1884.

– *I sonetti del Pistoia, giusta L'Apografo Trivulziano.* Edited by Rodolfo Renier. Turin: Loescher, 1888.

Castellani, Francesco di Matteo. *Ricordanze A (1416–1459).* Edited by Giovanni Ciappelli. Florence: L.S. Olschki, 1992.

Cenci, Cesare, ed. *Documentazione di vita assisana, 1300–1530.* 3 vols. Grottaferrata: Aquas Claras, 1974.

Compagni, Dino. *Cronaca.* Edited by Gino Luzzatto. Turin: Einaudi, 1968.

Corazzini, Giuseppe O. *L'assedio di Pisa (1405–6): Scritti e documenti inediti.* Florence: Diligenti, 1885.

Covini, Maria Nadia, ed. *Il libro di ricordi di Bartolomeo Morone, giureconsulto milanese (1412–1455): Edizione e commento.* Milan: Unicopoli, 2010.

De Angelis, Laura, Elisabetta Gigli, and Franek Sznura, eds. *I notai fiorentini dell'età di Dante: Biagio Boccadibue (1298–1314).* 4 vols. Florence: Università di Firenze, 1978–86.

Della Casa, Giovanni. *Prose di Giovanni della Casa.* Edited by Arnaldo Di Benedetto. Turin: Unione Tipografico-Editrice Torinese, 1970.

Dominici, Giovanni. *Il libro d'amore di carità del fiorentino B: Giovanni Dominici.* Edited by Antonio Ceruti. Bologna: Romagnoli-dall'Acqua, 1889.

Festus, Sextus Pompeius. *Sexti Pompei Festi De verborum significatu quae supersunt cum Pauli epitome.* Edited by Wallace M. Lindsay. Leipzig: Teubner, 1933.

Formularium diversorum contractuum. Venice: Giorgio Rusconi, 1506.

Guicciardini, Francesco. *Ricordi, diari, memorie*. Edited by Mario Spinella. Rome: Riuniti, 1981.

Jacobus de Voragine. *The Golden Legend: Readings on the Saints.* Translated by William G. Ryan. Princeton, NJ: Princeton University Press, 1993.

Kohl, Benjamin G., Ronald G. Witt, and Elizabeth B. Welles, eds. *The Earthly Republic: Italian Humanists on Government and Society*. Philadelphia: University of Pennsylvania Press, 1978.

Landucci, Luca. *Diario fiorentino*. Edited by Iodoco Del Badia. Florence: G.C. Sansoni, 1883.

Lapus de Castiglionchio, Junior. *Vitae illustrium virorum Lapo fiorentino interprete.* Venice, 1491 (= Plutarch. *Virorum illustrium vitae ex Plutarcho graecho in latinum versae, solertique cura emendatae*. Venice: Ioannes Rigatius de Monteferrato, 1491).

Machiavelli, Niccolò. *Florentine Histories.* Translated by Laura F. Banfield and Harvey C. Mansfield, Jr. Princeton, NJ: Princeton University Press, 1988.

– *Opere*. Edited by Mario Bonfantini. Milan: Riccardo Ricciardi, 1954.

– *The Portable Machiavelli.* Edited and translated by Peter Bondanella and Mark Musa. New York: Penguin, 1979.

Macinghi Strozzi, Alessandra. *Lettere di una gentildonna fiorentina ai figluoli exuli.* Edited by Cesari Guasti. Florence: Sansoni, 1877.

Martelli, Ugolino di Niccolò. *Ricordanze dal 1437 al 1483.* Edited by Fulvio Pezzarossa. Rome: Edizione di Storia e Letturatura, 1989.

Meyer, Andreas, ed. *Ser Ciabattus, Imbreviature lucchesi del Duecento: Regesti, I, anni 1222–1232.* Lucca: Istituto Storico Lucchese, 2005.

Morelli, Giovanni di Pagolo. *Ricordi.* Edited by Vittore Branca. Florence: Le Monnier, 1956.

Moschetti, Guiscardo, ed. *Il cartularium veronese del Magister Ventura del secolo XIII.* Naples: Edizioni Scientifiche Italiane, 1990.

Mosiici, Luciana, and Franek Sznura, eds. *Palmerio di Corbizo da Uglione notaio: Imbreviature, 1237–1238*. Florence: L.S. Olschki, 1982.

Palmieri, Matteo. *Ricordi fiscali (1427–1474).* Edited by Elio Conti. Rome: Istituto Storico Italiano per il Medio Evo, 1983.

Paolo da Certaldo. *Libro di buoni costumi, documento di vita trecentesca.* Edited by Alfredo Schiaffini. Florence: Le Monnier, 1945.

Perosa, Alessandro, ed. *Giovanni Rucellai ed il suo zibaldone*. Pt. 1, *Il zibaldone quaresimale.* London: Warburg Institute, 1960.

Petrarca, Francesco. *Remedies for Fortune Fair and Foul: A Modern English Translation of De Remediis Utriusque Fortune, with a Commentary.* Edited and translated by Conrad H. Rawski. Bloomington: Indiana University Press, 1991.

Petrucci, Armando, ed. *Il libro di ricordanze dei Corsini (1362–1457).* Rome: Istituto Storico Italiano per il Medio Evo, 1965.

Petrus Aldobrandinus. *Summa totius artis notarie.* Venice, 1546 (= addition to Rolandinus de Passageriis. *Summa totius artis notariae Rolandini Rodulphini.* Venice: Giunta, 1546).

Plautus. *Plautus.* Edited and translated by Paul Nixon. London: Heinemann, 1928.

Rainerius de Perusio. *Die Ars Notariae des Rainerius Perusinus.* Edited by Ludwig Wahrmund. In *Quellen zur Geschichte des römisch-kanonischen Prozesses im Mittelalter.* Innsbruck: Wagner, 1917.

Rinuccini, Filippo di Cino. *Ricordi storici di Filippo di Cino Rinuccini dal 1282 al 1460.* Edited by Giuseppe Aiazzi. Florence: Dalla Stampa Piatti, 1840.

Rolandinus de Passageriis Bononiensis. *Summa totius artis notariae Rolandini ...* 2 vols. Venice: Giunta, 1546; repr., Bologna: Arnaldo Forni, 1977.

Rosenthal, Gilbert S., ed. and trans. *Banking and Finance among Jews in Renaissance Italy: A Critical Edition of The Eternal Life (Haye olam) by Yehiel Nissim da Pisa.* New York: Bloch, 1962.

Sacchetti, Franco. *Il trecentonovelle.* Edited by Valerio Marucci. Rome: Salerno Editore, 1996.

Salatiele. *Ars notarie.* Edited by Gianfanco Orlandelli. 2 vols. Milan: Giuffrè, 1961.

San Bernardino. *Opera Omnia. Quaracchi, 1950* (= *S. Bernardini Senensis ordinis Fratrum Minorum Opera omnia.* 5 vols. Florence: Ad Claras Aquas, 1950).

– *Le prediche volgari: Predicazione del 1425 in Siena.* 2 vols. Edited by Ciro Cannarozzi. Florence: Rinaldi, 1958.

– *Prediche volgari sul Campo di Siena, 1427.* Edited by Carlo Del Corno. Milan: Rusconi, 1989.

Scalfati, Silio P.P., ed. *Un formulario notarile fiorentino della metà del dugento.* Florence: EDIFIR, 1997.

Sercambi, Giovanni. *Novelle.* Edited by Giovanni Sinicropi. 2 vols. Scrittori d'Italia, 250–1. Bari: Latenza, 1972; Florence: Le Lettere, 1995.

Tarlazzi, Antonio. *Appendice ai monumenti ravennati dei secoli di mezzo.* Ravenna: G. Angeletti, 1869–76.

Villani, Giovanni. *Nuova cronica.* Edited by Giuseppe Porta. Parma: Fondazione Pietro Bembo, 1990.

Vitale, Marcella, ed. *Il quaderno di ricordi di messer Filippo de' Cavalcanti (1290–1324). Studi di filologia italiana* 29 (1971): 5–112.

Zaccaria di Martino. *Summa artis notarie.* Edited by Roberto Ferrara. Bologna: Istituto per la Storia dell'Università di Bologna, 1993.

Secondary Works

Abbondanza, Roberto. "Ambrosini, Pietro." In *DBI*, vol. 2, 729–30. Rome: Istituto della Enciclopedia italiana, 1960.

– "Una nuova fonte per la biografia di Benedetto Barzi da Perugia (1379–ca. 1459): Con precisazioni su Benedetto da Piombino." *Index* 22 (1994): 512–28.

Abouçaya, Claude. "Les différents conceptions de la *donatio mortis causa* chez les romanistes médiévaux." *RHDF* 44 (1966): 378–431.

Abrahams, Israel. *Jewish Life in the Middle Ages* (1896). Philadelphia: Jewish Publication Society of America, 1993.

Addobbati, Andrea. "La giurisdizione marittima e commerciale dei Consoli del Mare in età medicea." In *Pisa e il Mediterraneo: Uomini, merci e idee dagli Etruschi ai Medici*, edited by Marco Tangheroni, 311–15. Milan: Skira, 2003.

Ago, Renato. "Oltre la dote: I beni femminili." In *Il lavoro delle donne*, edited by Angela Groppi, 164–82. Bari: Laterza, 1996.

Albini, Giuliana. "Una reciproca e collettiva concessione di cittadinanza: Parma e Reggio all'inizio del Quattrocento." *Nuova rivista storica* 96 (2012): 115–44.

Alexandre-Bidon, Danielle. "La dent et le corail ou la parure prophylactique de l'enfance à la fin du Moyen Âge." *Razo* 7 (1987): 5–35.

Allerston, Patricia. "Wedding Finery in Sixteenth-Century Venice." In *Marriage in Italy, 1300–1500*, edited by Trevor Dean and Kate J.P. Lowe, 25–40. New York: Cambridge University Press, 1998.

Amati Canta, Antonietta. *Meffium, morgincap, mundium: Consuetudini matrimoniali longobarde nella Bari medievale*. Bari: Palomar, 2006.

Angelini, Piero. *Il "procurator."* Milan: Giuffrè, 1971.

Anné, Lucien. *Les rites des fiançailles et la donation pour cause de mariage sous le Bas-Empire*. Louvain: Desclée, de Brouwer, 1941.

Aquino, Marco, and Roberto Tallarita. "La promessa di matrimonio." In *Manuale del nuovo diritto di famiglia*, edited by Giuseppe Cassano, 69–102. Piacenza: La Tribuna, 2000.

Arena, Marta, Bruno Nascimbene, and Giovanna Zincone. "Italy." In *Acquisition and Loss of Nationality*, edited by Rainer Bauböck et al., vol. 2, 329–36. Amsterdam: Amsterdam University Press, 2006.

Arjava, Antti. *Women and Law in Late Antiquity*. Oxford: Clarendon Press, 1996.

Armstrong, Lawrin. "Usury, Conscience, and Public Debt: Angelo Corbinelli's Testament of 1419." In *A Renaissance of Conflicts: Visions and Revisions of Law and Society in Italy and Spain*, edited by John A. Marino and Thomas Kuehn, 173–240. Toronto: Centre for Reformation and Renaissance Studies, 2004.

Arrow, Kenneth Joseph. *Essays in the Theory of Risk-Bearing*. Amsterdam: North-Holland, 1976.

Ascheri, Mario. "Le fonti e la flessibilità del diritto comune: Il paradosso del *consilium sapientis*." In *Legal Consulting in the Civil Law Tradition*, edited by Mario Ascheri, Ingrid Baumgärtner, and Julius Kirshner, 11–54. Studies in Comparative Legal History. Berkeley: Robbins Collection, 1999.

Astolfi, Riccardo. *Il fidanzamento nel diritto romano*. Padova: CEDAM, 1989.

Astuti, Guido. "Cessio (premessa storica)." In *Enciclopedia del diritto*, vol. 6, 805–22. Milan: Giuffrè, 1959.

– "Il Code Napoléon in Italia e la sua influenza sui codici degli Stati italiani successori." In *Atti del convegno Napoleone e l'Italia (Roma, 9–13 ottobre 1969)*, 192–216. Rome: Accademia Nazionale dei Lincei, 1973.

Aznar Gil, Federico Rafael. "El consentimiento paterno o familiar para el matrimonio en la legislación eclesiástica ibérica bajomedieval (ss. XII–XVI)." *RIDC* 6 (1995): 127–51.

Baldwin, John W. *Masters, Princes, and Merchants: The Social Views of Peter the Chanter & His Circle*. Princeton, NJ: Princeton University Press, 1970.

Balestracci, Duccio. "Il testamento di Giacomo Galganetti, mercante lucchese: Una fonte per lo studio della povertà nella Lucca di metà Trecento." In *La Toscane et les Toscans autour de la Renaissance: Cadres de vie, société, croyances: Mélanges offerts à Charles-M. de La Roncière*, 161–9. Aix-en-Provence: Université de Provence, 1999.

Bancarel, Jean. "Le mariage entre absents en droit canonique." PhD diss., Université de Toulouse, 1919.

Banti, Ottavio. *Iacopo d'Appiano: Economia, società e politica del comune di Pisa al suo tramonto (1392–1399)*. Pisa: Università di Pisa, 1971.

Barassi, Lodovico. "Le *fictiones juris* in Baldo." In *L'opera di Baldo, per cura dell' Università di Perugia nel V centenario della morte del grande giureconsulto*, edited by Oscar Scalvanti, 113–38. Perugia: Unione Tipografia Cooperativa, 1901.

Barbero, Alessandro. *Un'oligarchia urbana: Politica ed economia a Torino fra Tre e Quattrocento*. Rome: Viella, 1995.

Barbieri, Gino. "Donne ed affari a sostegno della signoria viscontea: Il caso di Donina de Porris." *Economia e storia* 1 (1973): 483–91.

Bargagli, Roberta. "Documenti senesi per la biogafia di Bartolomeo Sozzini (1436–1506)." *Bullettino senese di storia patria* 99 (1992): 266–323.

Bariatti, Stefania. *La disciplina giuridica della cittadinanza*. Vol. 2, *Legge 5 febbraio 1992 n. 91*. Milan, Giuffrè, 1996.

Bartoli Langeli, Attilio. "Après la 'Morgengabe': Donations nuptiales et culture juridique dans l'Italie communale." In *Dots et douaires dans le haut Moyen*

Âge, edited by François Bougard, Laurent Feller, and Régine Le Jan, 123–30. Collection de l'École Française de Rome 295. Rome: École Française de Rome, 2002.

– "Parole Introduttive." In *Margini di libertà: Testamenti femminili nel medioevo*, edited by Maria Clara Rossi, 9–19. Verona: Cierre, 2010.

Baskins, Cristelle L. *Cassone Painting, Humanism and Gender in Early Modern Italy.* Cambridge: Cambridge University Press, 1998.

– "*La Festa di Susanna*: Virtue on Trial in Renaissance Sacred Drama and Painted Wedding Chests." *Art History* 14 (1991): 329–45.

Battaglia, Salvatore, ed. *Grande dizionario della lingua italiana.* Turin: Unione Tipografico-Editrice Torinese, 1961.

Bauböck, Ranier, et al., eds. *Acquisition and Loss of Nationality: Policies and Trends in 15 European States.* 2 vols. Amsterdam: Amsterdam University Press, 2006.

Baum, Hans-Peter. "Annuities in Late Medieval Hanse Towns." *Business History Review* 59 (1985): 24–48.

Baumgärtner, Ingrid, ed. *Consilia im späten Mittelalter: Zum historischen Aussagewert einer Quellengattung.* Schriftenreihe des deutschen Studienzentrums in Venedig 13. Sigmaringen: Thorbecke, 1995.

Baumgärtner, Ingrid, Mario Ascheri, and Julius Kirshner, eds. *Legal Consulting in the Civil Law Tradition.* Studies in Comparative Legal History. Berkeley: Robbins Collection, 1999.

Baxendale, Susannah Foster. "Exile in Practice: The Alberti Family In and Out of Florence, 1401–1428." *Renaissance Quarterly* 44 (1991): 720–56.

Beaucamp, Joelle. "Le vocabulaire de la faiblesse féminine dans les textes juridiques romains du IIIe au VIe siècle." *RHDF* 54 (1976): 485–508.

Beck, James. "Desiderio da Settignano (and Antonio del Pollaiuolo): Problems." *Mitteilungen des Kunsthistorischen Institutes in Florenz* 28 (1984): 203–24.

Behrends, Okko. "Die Prokurator des klassischen römischen Zivilrechts." *ZRG (RA)* 88 (1971): 215–99.

Bellavitis, Anna, and Linda Guzzetti, eds. *Donne, lavoro, economia a Venezia e in Terrafirma tra medioevo ed età moderna.* Special issue, *Archivio veneto* 143 (2012).

Bellomo, Manlio. *The Common Legal Past of Europe, 1000–1800.* Translated by Lydia G. Cochrane. Washington, DC: Catholic University Press, 1995.

– *La condizione giuridica della donna in Italia: Vicende antiche e moderne.* Turin: ERI, 1970.

– "Dote (Diritto Intermedio)." In *Enciclopedia del diritto*, vol. 16, 8–32. Milan: Giuffrè, 1965.

– *Problemi di diritto familiare nell'età dei comuni: Beni paterni e "pars filii."* Milan: Giuffrè, 1968.

– *Quaestiones in iure civili disputatae: Didattica e prassi colta nel sistema del diritto comune fra Duecento e Trecento*. Rome: Istituto Storico Italiano per il Medio Evo, 2008.

– *Ricerche sui rapporti patrimoniali tra coniugi: Contributo alla storia della famiglia medievale*. Milan: Giuffrè, 1961.

– "La scienza del diritto al tempo di Federico II." *RIDC* 3 (1992): 173–96.

– "Tracce di *lectura per viam quaestionum* in un manuscritto del *Codex* conservato a Rovigo." *RIDC* 8 (1998): 217–73.

Belloni, Annalisa. *Professori giuristi a Padova nel secolo XV: Profili bio-bibliografici e cattedre*. Frankfurt am Main: V. Klostermann, 1986.

Bender, Tovah. "Negotiating Marriage: Artisan Women in Fifteenth-Century Florentine Society." PhD diss., University of Minnesota, 2009.

Benvenuti, Gino. *Storia dell'assedio di Pisa (1494–1509)*. Pisa: Giardini, 1969.

Berger, John. *Ways of Seeing*. London: British Broadcasting Corp., 1972.

Berti, Luca. "I capitoli *De vestibus mulierum* del 1460, ovvero 'status' personale e distinzioni sociali nell'Arezzo di metà Quattrocento." In *Studi in onore di Arnaldo d'Addario*, 5 vols., edited by Luigi Borgia et al., vol. 4, 1171–214. Lecce: Conte, 1995.

Bertran, Martin. "Mittelalterliche Testamente: Zur Entdeckung einer Quellengattung in Italien." *Quellen und Forschungen aus italienischen Archiven und Bibliotheken* 68 (1988): 509–45.

Bestor, Jane F. "The Groom's Prestations for the *Ductio* in Late Medieval Italy: A Study in the Disciplining Power of *Liberalitas*." *RIDC* 8 (1997): 129–77.

– "Marriage Transactions in Renaissance Italy and Mauss's *Essay on the Gift*." *Past and Present* 164 (1999): 6–46.

Biagi, Guido. *Due corredi nuziali fiorentini, 1320–1493, da un libro di ricordanze dei Minerbetti.* Florence: Carnesecchi, 1899.

Biancalana, Joseph. "Testamentary Cases in English Chancery." *RHD* 76 (2008): 283–306.

Biggart, Nicole W., and Richard P. Castanias. "Collateralized Social Relations: The Social in Economic Calculation." *American Journal of Economics and Sociology* 60 (2001): 471–500.

Birks, Peter. "The Roman Law Concept of Dominium and the Idea of Absolute Ownership." *Acta Juridica* (1985): 1–37.

Bizzarri, Dina. *Studi di storia del diritto italiano.* Edited by Federico Patetta and Mario Chiaudano. Turin: Lattes and Co., 1937.

Black, Jane. "Constitutional Ambitions, Legal Realities and the Florentine State." In *Florentine Tuscany: Structures and Practices of Power*, edited by William J. Connell and Andrea Zorzi, 48–64. Cambridge: Cambridge University Press, 2000.

Black, Robert. *Benedetto Accolti and the Florentine Renaissance*. Cambridge: Cambridge University Press, 1985.

Blomeyer, Arwed. "Aus der Consilienpraxis zum kanonischen Zinsverbot." *ZRG* (*KA*) 66 (1980): 317–35.

Bolmont, Mylene, John T. Cacioppo, and Stephanie Cacioppo. "Love is in the Gaze: An Eye-Tracking Study of Love and Sexual Desire." *Psychological Science* published online 16 July 2014, DOI: 10.1177/0956797614539706. The online version of this article can be found at: http://pss.sagepub.com/content/early/2014/07/15/0956797614539706.

Bonfil, Roberto. *Rabbis and Jewish Communities in Renaissance Italy*. Washington, DC: Littman Library, 1993.

– "Società cristiana e società ebraica nell'Italia medievale e rinascimentale: Riflessioni sul significato e sui limiti di una convergenza." In *Ebrei e cristiani nell'Italia medievale e moderna: Conversioni, scambi, contrasti: Atti del VI Congresso internazionale dell'AISG, S. Miniato, 4–6 novembre 1986*, edited by Michele Luzzati, Michele Olivari, and Alessandra Veronese, 231–60. Rome: Carucci Editore, 1988.

Bongi, Salvatore, ed. *Inventario del R. Archivio di Stato in Lucca*. Lucca, 1876.

Böninger, Lorenz. *Die deutsche Einwanderung nach Florenz im Spätmittelalter*. Leiden: Brill, 2006.

Bornstein, Daniel. "Le donne di Giovanni Dominici: Un caso nella recezione e trasmissione dei messaggi religiosi." *Studi medievali* 36 (1995): 355–61.

– "Law, Religion, and Economics: Jewish Moneylenders in Christian Cortona." In *A Renaissance of Conflicts: Visions and Revisions of Law and Society in Italy and Spain*, edited by John A. Marino and Thomas Kuehn, 242–56. Toronto: Centre for Reformation and Renaissance Studies, 2004.

Børreson, Kari Elisabeth. *Subordination and Equivalence: The Nature and Role of Women in Augustine and Thomas Aquinas*. Kampen: Kok Pharos, 1995.

Bors, Marc. *Bescholtene Frauen vor Gericht: Zur Rechtsprechung des Preussischen Obertribunals und des Zürcher Obergerichts auf dem Gebiet des Nichtehelichenrechts*. Frankfurt am Main: V. Klostermann, 1998.

Botticini, Maristella. "A Loveless Economy? Intergenerational Altruism and the Marriage Market in a Tuscan Town, 1415–1436." *Journal of Economic History* 59 (1999): 104–21.

Botticini, Maristella, and Aloysius Siow. "Why Dowries?" *American Economic Review* 93 (2003): 1385–98.

Bourdieu, Pierre. *Distinction: A Social Critique of the Judgement of Taste*. Translated by Richard Nice. Cambridge, MA: Harvard University Press, 1984.
– *La domination masculine*. Paris: Seuil, 1998.
Bowd, Stephen D. *Venice's Most Loyal City: Civic Identity in Renaissance Brescia*. Cambridge, MA: Harvard University Press, 2010.
Bowsky, William M. *The Finance of the Commune of Siena, 1287–1355*. Oxford: Clarendon Press, 1970.
Braccia, Roberta. "*Uxor gaudet de morte mariti*: La *donatio propter nuptias* tra diritto comune e diritti locali." *Annali della Facoltà di Giurisprudenza di Genova* 30 (2000–1): 76–128.
Brandileone, Francesco. "Contributo allo studio della *subarrhatio*." In *Saggi sulla storia della celebrazione del matrimonio in Italia*, 401–502. Milan: Hoepli, 1906.
– *Scritti di storia del diritto privato italiano*. 2 vols. Bologna: Zanichelli, 1931.
Bredbenner, Candice L. *A Nationality of Her Own: Women, Marriage, and the Law of Citizenship*. Berkeley: University of California Press, 1998.
Brettel, Caroline B. "Property, Kinship, and Gender: A Mediterranean Perspective." In *The Family in Italy from Antiquity to the Present*, edited by David I. Kertzer and Richard P. Saller, 340–54. New Haven, CT: Yale University Press, 1991.
Briegleb, Hans K. *Geschichte des Executiv-Prozesses: Über executorische Urkunden und Executiv-Prozess*. Stuttgart: Liesching, 1845.
Briganti, Antonio. *La donna e il diritto statutario in Perugia: La donna commerciante (secc. XIII–XIV)*. [Perugia, 1911].
Brizio, Elena. "La dote nella normativa statutaria e nella pratica testamentaria Senese (fine sec. XII–metà sec. XIV)." *Bullettino Senese di Storia Patria* 111 (2004): 9–39.
– "In the Shadow of the Campo: Sienese Women and their Families (14th–16th Centuries)." In *Across the Religious Divide: Women, Property, and Law in the Wider Mediterranean (ca. 1200–1800)*, edited by Jutta Sperling and Shona Kelly Wray, 122–36. New York: Routledge 2010.
Brown, Judith. *In the Shadow of Florence: Provincial Society in Renaissance Pescia*. Oxford: Oxford University Press, 1982.
Brucker, Gene A. *The Civic World of Early Renaissance Florence*. Princeton, NJ: Princeton University Press, 1977.
– "Ecclesiastical Courts in Fifteenth-Century Florence and Fiesole." *Mediaeval Studies* 53 (1991): 229–57. Reprinted in Gene A. Brucker, *Renaissance Florence: Society, Culture, and Religion*, no. 16. Goldbach: Keip, 1994.
– *Firenze nel Rinascimento*. Translated by Sergio Bertelli. Florence: La Nuova Italia, 1980.

– "Florentine Voices from the *Catasto*." *I Tatti Studies* 5 (1993): 22–32. Reprinted in Gene A. Brucker, *Renaissance Florence: Society, Culture, and Religion*, no. 6. Goldbach: Keip, 1994.

– *Giovanni and Lusanna: Love and Marriage in Renaissance Florence*. Berkeley: University of California Press, 1986.

– *Renaissance Florence*. New York: Wiley, 1969.

– *Renaissance Florence: Society, Culture, and Religion*. Goldbach: Keip, 1994.

– *The Society of Renaissance Florence: A Documentary Study*. New York: Harper & Row, 1971.

Brundage, James A. "Implied Consent to Intercourse." In *Consent and Coercion to Sex and Marriage in Ancient and Medieval Societies*, edited by Angeliki E. Laiou, 245–56. Washington, DC: Dumbarton Oaks Research Library and Collection, 1993

– *Law, Sex, and Christian Society in Medieval Europe*. Chicago: University of Chicago Press, 1987.

– "Sumptuary Laws and Prostitution in Late Medieval Italy." *Journal of Medieval History* 13 (1987): 343–56.

Buettner, Brigitte. *Boccaccio's "Des cleres et nobles femmes": Systems of Signification in an Illuminated Manuscript.* Seattle: University of Washington Press, 1996.

Bullough, Vern I. "Medieval Medical and Scientific Views of Women." *Viator* 4 (1973): 485–501.

Bulst, Neidhart. "Kleidung als sozialer Konfliktstoff: Probleme kleidergesetzlicher Normierung im sozialen Gefüge." *Saeculum* 44 (1993): 32–46.

Burrus, Virginia. "Reading Agnes: The Rhetoric of Gender in Ambrose and Prudentius." *Journal of Early Christian Studies* 3 (1995): 25–46.

Cadden, Joan. *Meanings of Sex and Difference in the Middle Ages: Medicine, Science, and Culture.* Cambridge: Cambridge University Press, 1993.

Cadogan, Jean K. *Domenico Ghirlandaio: Artist and Artisan*. New Haven, CT: Yale University Press, 2000.

Cagnin, Giampaolo. *Cittadini e forestieri a Treviso nel medioevo (secolo XIII–XIV)*. Verona: Cierre Edizioni, 2004.

Callmann, Ellen. *Apollonio di Giovanni*. Oxford: Clarendon Press, 1974.

Cammarosano, Paolo. "Aspetti delle strutture familiari nelle città dell'Italia comunale: Secoli XII–XIV." In *Famiglia e parentela nell'Italia medievale*, edited by Georges Duby and Jacques Le Goff, 109–24. Bologna: Il Mulino, 1977.

Campitelli, Adriana. *Precetto di guarentigia e formule di esecuzione parata nei documenti italiani del secolo XIII*. Milan: Giuffrè, 1970.

– "Una raccolta di *quaestiones* in tema di documenti guarentigiati e il *Tractatus de guarentigiato instrumento* attribuito a Guido da Suzzara." In *Studi sulle "quaestiones" civilistiche disputate nelle università medievali*, edited by Giuliana D'Amelio et al., 57–96. Catania: Tringale, 1980.

Cannata, Carlo A. "Dote (dir. rom.)." In *Enciclopedia del diritto*, vol. 16, 1–8. Milan: Giuffrè, 1965.

Canning, Joseph. *The Political Thought of Baldus de Ubaldis.* Cambridge: Cambridge University Press, 1987.

– "A State like Any Other? The Fourteenth-Century Papal Patrimony through the Eyes of Roman Law Jurists." In *The Church and Sovereignty, c. 590–1918: Essays in Honour of Michael Wilks*, edited by Diana Wood, 243–60. Oxford: Blackwell, 1991.

Caravale, Mario. *Alle origini del diritto europeo: Ius commune, droit commun, common law nella dottrina giuridica della prima età moderna*. Bologna: Monduzzi, 2005.

Carnesecchi, Carlo. "Niccolò *delle Grillande*." *Rivista d'arte* 4 (1906): 56–61.

Casarino, Giacomo. "Rappresaglie o privilegi? Dai debiti mercantili alla copromozione industriale: I Lucchesi a Genova tra Tre e Quattrocento." In *Comunità forestiere e "nationes" nell'Europa dei secoli XIII–XVI*, edited by Giovanna Petti Balbi, 299–324. Naples: Liguori, 2001

– "Stranieri a Genova tra Quattro e Cinquecento: Tipologie sociali e nazioni." In *Dentro la città: Stranieri e realtà urbane nell'Europa dei secoli XII–XVI*, edited by Gabriella Rossetti, 137–50. Pisa: GISEM, 1989.

Casini, Bruno. *Il catasto di Pisa del 1428–29*. Pisa: Tip. editrice Giardini, 1964.

– "Patrimonio e consumi di Giovanni Maggiolini mercante pisano nel 1428." *Economia e storia* 7 (1960): 37–62.

Caso, Anna. "Per la storia della società milanese: I corredi nuziali dell'ultima età viscontea e nel periodo della Repubblica Ambrosiana (1433–1450), dagli atti del notaio Protaso Sansoni." *Nuova rivista storica* 65 (1981): 521–51.

Cassandro, Giovanni. *Le rappresaglie e il fallimento a Venezia nei secoli 13 e 14: Con documenti inediti.* Turin: S. Lattes, 1938.

Cassuto, Umberto. *Gli ebrei a Firenze nell'età del Rinascimento*. Florence: Galletti e Cocci, 1918.

– *La famiglia Da Pisa*. Rome: Galletti e Cassuto, 1910.

Castelli, Patrizia. "Le virtù delle gemme: Il loro significato simbolico e astrologico nella cultura umanistica e nelle credenze popolari del Quattrocento." In *L'oreficeria nella Firenze del Quattrocento*, 307–64. Florence: SPES, 1977.

Castello, Carlo. "Lo strumento dotale come prova del matrimonio." *Studia et documenta historiae et iuris* 4 (1938): 208–24.

Castiglione, Roberto. "Gabelle e diritti comunali nel Trecento a Pisa." *Bollettino storico pisano* 71 (2002): 41–80.

Cattaneo, Enrico. "La celebrazione delle nozze a Milano." *Archivio Ambrosiano* 29 (1976): 142–80.

Cavalca, Desiderio. *Il bando nella prassi e nella dottrina giuridica medievale.* Milan: Giuffrè, 1978.

Cavallar, Osvaldo. "Francesco Guicciardini and the 'Pisan Crisis': Logic and Discourses." *Journal of Modern History* 65 (1993): 245–85.

– *Francesco Guicciardini, giurista: I ricordi degli onorari.* Milan: Giuffrè, 1991.

Cavallar, Osvaldo, and Julius Kirshner. "Jews as Citizens in Late Medieval and Renaissance Italy: The Case of Isacco da Pisa." *Jewish History* 25 (2011): 269–318.

– "*Licentia navigandi ... prosperis ventibus aflantibus*: L'esenzione dei *doctores* e delle loro mogli da norme suntuarie." In *A Ennio Cortese*, vol. 1, 204–27. Rome: Galileo Galilei, 2001.

Cavallo, Sandra. "O padre o figlio? Ruoli familiari maschili e legami tra uomini nel mondo artigiano in età moderna." In *Pater familias*, edited by Angiolina Arru, 59–100. Rome: Biblink, 2002.

Cavina, Marco. "Carlo Ruini consulente: Autorità del giurista e *communis opinio* nel secolo XVI." *Clio* 20 (1984): 663–90.

Cazzetta, Giovanni. "*Praesumitur seducta*"*: Onestà e consenso femminile nella cultura giuridica moderna.* Milan: Giuffrè, 1999.

Cecchi, Dante. "Disposizioni statutarie sugli stranieri e sui forestieri." In *Stranieri e forestieri nella Marca dei secoli XIV–XVI, Atti del XXX convegno di studi maceratesi (Macerata, 19–20 novembre 1994)*, 29–91. Studi Macertatesi 30. Macerata: Centro di studi storici maceratesi, 1996.

– "Il matrimonio-contratto dall'Ostiense ai canonisti tre-cinquecenteschi." *RSDI* 40/41 (1967/68): 35–69.

Celata, Giuseppe. "La condizione contadina in una signoria e in un comune rurale autonomo fra il Duecento e il Trecento." *Rivista di storia dell'agricoltura* 19 (1979): 65–103.

Celli, Roberto. *Studi sui sistemi normativi delle democrazie comunali: Secoli XII–XV*. Florence: Sansoni, 1976.

Ceppari Ridolfi, Maria A., and Patrizia Turrini. *Il mulino della vanità: Lusso e cerimonie nella Siena medievale*. Siena: Il Leccio, 1993.

Chabot, Isabelle. "*A proposito* di 'Men and Women in Renaissance Venice' di Stanley Chojnacki." *Quaderni storici* 118 (2005): 203–29.

– "La beneficenza dotale nei testamenti del tardo medioevo." In *Povertà e innovazioni istituzionali dal medioevo ad oggi*, edited by Vera Zamagni, 55–76. Bologna: Il Mulino, 2000.

– *La dette des familles: Femmes, lignage et patrimoine à Florence aux XIVe et XVe siècles*. Collection de l'École Française de Rome 445. Rome: École Française de Rome, 2011.

– "Lineage Strategies and the Control of Women in Renaissance Florence." In *Widowhood in Medieval and Early Modern Europe*, edited by Sandra Cavallo and Lyndan Warner, 127–44. Harlow, Essex: Longman/Pearson Education, 1999.

–"La loi du lignage: Notes sur le système successoral florentin (XIVe–XVe–XVIIe siècles)." *Clio: Femmes, histoire et sociétés* 7 (1998): 51–72.

– "La reconnaissance du travail des femmes dans la Florence du bas Moyen Âge: Contexte idéologique et réalité." In *La donna nell'economia, secc. XIII–XVIII*, edited by Simonetta Cavaciocchi, 563–76. Florence: Le Monnier 1990.

– "Widowhood and Poverty in Late Medieval Florence." *Continuity and Change* 3 (1988): 291–311.

Chabot, Isabelle, and Massimo Fornasari. *L' economia della carità: Le doti del Monte di Pietà di Bologna (secoli XVI–XX)*. Bologna: Il Mulino, 1997.

Charageat, Martine. "Cópula carnal: La preuve de mariage dans les procès à Saragosse au XV siècle." *Mélanges de la Casa de Velázquez* 33 (2003): 47–63.

Chareyon, Nicole. "De l'histoire à la chanson: Les fiançailles rompues de Louis de Male." *Moyen* Âge 103 (1997): 545–59.

Cherry, David. "Gifts between Husband and Wife: The Social Origins of Roman Law." In *Speculum Iuris: Roman Law as a Reflection of Social and Economic Life in Antiquity*, edited by Jean-Jacques Aubert and Boudewijn Sirks, 34–45. Ann Arbor: University of Michigan Press, 2002.

Cherubini, Giovanni. "I *libri di ricordanze* come fonte storica." In *Scritti toscani: L' urbanesimo medievale e la mezzadria*, 269–87. Florence: Salimbeni, 1991.

Chiantini, Monica. *Il Consilium sapientis nel processo del secolo XIII: San Gimignano, 1246–1312*. Siena: Il Leccio, 1997.

Chiappelli, Luigi. "Un *consilium* inedito di Angelo da Perugia." *Archivio giuridico* 36 (1886): 102–15.

Chiodi, Giovanni. "Scelte normative degli statuti di Spoleto del 1296." In *Gli statuti comunali umbri*, edited by Enrico Menestò, 123–305. Spoleto: Centro di Studi sull'Alto Medioevo, 1997.

– "Tra la *civitas* e il *comitatus*: I suburbi nella dottrina di diritto comune." In *Dal suburbium al faubourg: Evoluzione di una realtà urbana*, edited by Mariavittoria Antico Gallina, 225–320. Milan: Edizioni Et., 2000.

Chittolini, Giorgio. "A Comment." In *Florentine Tuscany: Structures and Practices of Power*, edited by William J. Connell and Andrea Zorzi, 333–45. Cambridge: Cambridge University Press, 2000.

– *La formazione dello Stato regionale e le istituzioni del contado: Secoli XIV e XV*. Turin: Einaudi, 1979.

Chojnacki, Stanley. "Dowries and Kinsmen in Early Renaissance Venice." In *Women in Medieval Society*, edited by Susan M. Stuard, 173–98. Philadelphia: University of Pennsylvania Press, 1976. Reprinted in Chojnacki, *Women and Men in Renaissance Venice*, no. 6.

– "From Trousseau to Groomgift." In *Medieval and Renaissance Venice*, edited by Ellen E. Kittell and Thomas F. Madden, 141–65. Urbana: University of Illinois Press, 1999. Reprinted in Chojnacki, *Women and Men in Renaissance Venicety*, no. 3.

– "Getting Back the Dowry: Venice, c. 1360–1530." In *Time, Space, and Women's Lives in Early Modern Europe*, edited by Anne Jacobson Schutte, Thomas Kuehn, and Silvana Seidel Menchi, 77–96. Sixteenth Century Essays and Studies 57. Kirksville, MO: Truman State University Press, 2001. Reprinted in Chojnacki, *Women and Men in Renaissance Venice*, no. 4.

– "Patrician Women in Early Renaissance Venice." *Studies in the Renaissance* 21 (1974): 176–203. Reprinted in Chojnacki, *Women and Men in Renaissance Venice*, no. 5.

– *Women and Men in Renaissance Venice: Twelve Essays on Patrician Society*. Baltimore: Johns Hopkins University Press, 2000.

Ciappelli, Giovanni. *Una famiglia e le sue ricordanze: I Castellani di Firenze nel Tre-Quattrocento*. Florence: L.S. Olschki, 1995.

– "I processi matrimoniali: Quadro di raccordo dei risultati della schedatura (Venezia, Verona, Napoli, Feltre e Trento, 1420–1803)." In *I tribunali del matrimonio (secoli XV–XVIII)*, edited by Silvana Seidel Menchi and Diego Quaglioni, 67–100. *Annali dell'Istituto storico italo-germanico in Trento*, Quaderni 68. Bologna: Il Mulino, 2006.

Ciardini, Marino. *I banchieri ebrei in Firenze nel secolo XV e il Monte di Pietà fondato da Girolamo Savonarola*. Borgo San Lorenzo: Tipografia Mazzocchi, 1907.

Ciccarelli, Anna, ed. *Donne e testamenti a Stroncone tra il XIV e il XV secolo: Mostra foto-documentaria dall'Archivio storico e notarile comunale*, Stroncone, 18 agosto–5 settembre 1999, Sala consiliare Palazzo Municipale. Arrone: Thyrus, 1999.

Cicchetti, Angelo, and Raul Mordenti. *I libri di famiglia in Italia*. Vol. 1, *Filologia e storiografia letteraria*. Rome: Edizioni di storia e letteratura, 1985.

Clerici, Roberta. *La cittadinanza nell'ordinamento giuridico italiano*. Padua: CEDAM, 1993.

– "Gleichheit im Familienrecht: Einfluß der Verfassung und italienischer Verträge." In *Gleichheit im Familienrecht*, edited by Bea Verschraegen, 103–24. Bielefeld: Gieseking, 1997.
– "La nuova legge organica sulla cittadinanza: Prime riflessioni." *RDIPP* 29 (1992): 741–76.
– "Nuove prospettive in tema di cittadinanza della donna maritata." *RDIPP* 11 (1975): 678–714.
– "Problemi in tema di cittadinanza nella giurisprudenza italiana." *RDIPP* 8 (1972): 22–75.
Cline, Ruth H. "Heart and Eyes." *Romance Philology* 25 (1972): 263–97.
Cochrane, Eric, and Julius Kirshner. *The Renaissance*. Chicago: University of Chicago Press, 1986.
Cohn, Samuel K., Jr. *The Cult of Remembrance and the Black Death: Six Renaissance Cities in Central Italy*. Baltimore: Johns Hopkins University Press, 1992.
– "Donne e Controriforma a Siena: Autorità e proprietà nella famiglia." *Studi storici* 30 (1989): 203–24.
– *The Laboring Classes in Renaissance Florence*. New York: Academic Press, 1980.
– "Women and Work in Renaissance Italy." In *Gender and Society in Renaissance Italy*, edited by Judith C. Brown and Robert C. Davis, 107–26. Harlow, Essex: Longman, 1998.
Colli, Vincenzo. "Il Cod. 351 della Biblioteca Capitolare Feliniana di Lucca: Editori quattrocenteschi e *Libri consiliorum* di Baldus de Ubaldis (1327–1400)." In *Scritti di storia del diritto offerti dagli allievi a Domenico Maffei*, edited by Mario Ascheri, 255–82. Padua: Antenore, 1991. Reprinted in Vincenzo Colli, *Giuristi medievali e produzione libraria: Manoscritti, autografi, edizioni*, no. 11. Stockstadt am Main: Keip, 2005.
Colliva, Paolo. "Angelo degli Ubaldi e le *Constitutiones Aegidiane*." *Archivio giuridico* 184 (1973): 103–20.
Colorni, Vittore. *Gli ebrei nel sistema del diritto comune fino alla prima emancipazione*. Milan: Giuffrè, 1956.
– *La legge ebraica e leggi locali: Ricerche sull'ambito d'applicazione del diritto ebraico in Italia dall'epoca romana al secolo XIX.* Milan: Giuffrè, 1945.
Conte, Emanuele. *Diritto comune: Storia e storiografia di un sistema dinamico*. Bologna: Il Mulino, 2009.
– *Tres Libri Codicis: La ricomparsa del testo e l'esegesi scolastica prima di Accursio*. Frankfurt am Main: Vittorio Klostermann, 1990.
Contessa, Maria Pia. "La costruzione di un'identità familiare e sociale: Un immigrato cipriota nella Firenze del secondo Quattrocento." *Annali di Storia di Firenze* 4 (2009): 151–92. http://www.dssg.unifi.it/SDF/annali/annali2009.htm.

Conti, Elio. *L'imposta diretta a Firenze nel Quattrocento (1427–1494).* Rome: Istituto Storico Italiano per il Medio Evo, 1984.

Coombs, Mary. "Agency and Partnership: A Study of Breach of Promise Plaintiffs." *Yale Journal of Law and Feminism* 1 (1989): 1–23.

Cooperman, Bernard D. "A Rivalry of Bankers: *Responsa* Concerning Banking Rights in Pisa in 1547." In *Studies in Medieval Jewish History and Literature*, edited by Isadore Twersky, vol. 2, 41–82. Cambridge, MA: Harvard University Press, 1984.

Coppens, Chris. "Roma communis nostra patria." In *Iuris Historia: Liber Amicorum Gero Dolezalek*, edited by Vincenzo Colli and Emanuele Conte, 177–91. Studies in Comparative Legal History. Berkeley: Robbins Collection, 2008.

Corbett, Percy E. *The Roman Law of Marriage*. Oxford: Clarendon Press, 1930.

Cornil, Georges. "Die *Arrha* im justinianischen Recht." *ZRG* (*RA*) 48 (1928): 51–87.

Cortese, Ennio. *Il diritto nella storia medievale*. Vol. 2, *Il basso medioevo.* Rome: Il Cigno Galileo Galilei, 1995.

– *La norma giuridica: Spunti teorici nel diritto comune classico*. Milan: Giuffrè, 1962.

– "Per la storia del mundio in Italia." *RISG* 8 (1955–6): 323–474. Reprinted in Cortese, *Scritti*, vol. 1, 1–154.

– *Scritti*, edited by Italo Birocchi and Ugo Petronio. 2 vols. Spoleto: Centro Italiano di Studi sull'Alto Medioevo, 1999.

Costa, Pietro. *Civitas: Storia della cittadinanza in Europa*. Vol. 1, *Dalla civiltà comunale al Settecento*. Bari: Laterza, 1999.

– *Iurisdictio: Semantica del potere politico nella pubblicistica medievale, 1100–1433*. Milan: Giuffrè, 1969; repr., 2002.

Cott, Nancy F. "Marriage and Women's Citizenship in the United States, 1830–1934." *American Historical Review* 103 (1998): 1440–74.

Coulet, Noël. *Affaires d'argent et affaires de famille en haute Provence au XIVe siècle: Le dossier du procès de Sybille de Cabris contre Matteo Villani et la compagnie des Buonaccorsi*. Rome: École Française de Rome, 1992

Couliano, Ioan P. *Eros and Magic in the Renaissance*. Translated by Margaret Cook. Chicago: University of Chicago Press, 1987.

Courtemanche, Andrée. *La richesse des femmes: Patrimoines et gestion à Manosque au XIVe siècle*. Montréal: Bellarmin; Paris: J. Vrin, 1993.

Cozzi, Gaetano. "Padri, figli e matrimoni clandestini (metà secolo XVI–metà secolo XVIII)." *La Cultura* 14 (1976): 169–213.

Crabb, Ann Morton. *The Strozzi of Florence: Widowhood and Family Solidarity in the Renaissance*. Ann Arbor: University of Michigan Press, 2000.

Craig, Randall. *Promising Language: Betrothal in Victorian Law and Fiction.* Albany: State University of New York Press, 2000.

Cristellon, Cecilia. *La carità e l'eros: Il matrimonio, la Chiesa, i suoi giudici nella Venezia del Rinascimento (1420–1545).* Bologna: Il Mulino, 2010.

– "Marriage and Consent in Pretridentine Venice: Between Lay Conception and Ecclesiastical Conception, 1420–1545." *The Sixteenth Century Journal* 39 (2008): 389–418.

Cristiani, Emilio. *Nobiltà e popolo nel comune di Pisa dalle origini del podestariato alla signoria dei Donoratico.* Naples: Istituto Italiano per gli Studi Storici, 1962.

Crook, John A. "Feminine Inadequacy and the *Senatusconsultum Velleianum.*" In *The Family in Ancient Rome: New Perspectives*, edited by Beryl Rawson, 83–92. Ithaca, NY: Cornell University Press, 1986.

Cuturi, Torquato. "Angelo degli Ubaldi in Firenze." *Bollettino della R. Deputazione di Storia Patria per l'Umbria* 7 (1901): 189–221.

– "Baldo degli Ubaldi in Firenze." In *L'opera di Baldo, per cura dell'Università di Perugia nel V centenario della morte del grande giureconsulto*, edited by Oscar Scalvanti, 365–95. Perugia: Università di Perugia, 1901.

D'Alatri, Mariano. "Donne di ieri a Roma e nel Lazio." *Lunario romano* 7 (1978): 182–95.

Dauvillier, Jean. *Le mariage dans le droit classique de l'église, depuis le Décret de Gratien (1140) jusqu'à mort de Clément V (1314).* Paris: Sirey, 1933.

Davide, Miriam. "La cittadinanza (secoli XIII–XV): Modalità di acquisizione, diritti e doveri nelle terre nordorientali d'Italia." In *Identità cittadine e aggregazioni sociali in Italia, secoli XI–XV, convegno di studio, Trieste, 28–30 giugno 2010*, edited by Miriam Davide, 31–54. Trieste: CERM, 2012.

– *Lombardi in Friuli: Per la storia delle migrazioni interne nell'Italia del Trecento.* Trieste: CERM, 2008.

– "La permanenza degli assegni nuziali di origine germanica nel Friuli tardo medievale e di prima età moderna." In *La condizione giuridica delle donne nel medioevo: Atti del convegno di studio-Trieste, 23 novembre 2010*, edited by Miriam Davide, 95–116. Trieste: CERM, 2012.

Davies, Glenys. "The Significance of the Handshake Motif in Classical Funerary Art." *American Journal of Archaeology* 89 (1985), 627–40.

Davies, Jonathan. *Florence and Its University during the Early Renaissance.* Leiden: Brill, 1998.

– "The Studio Pisano under Florentine Domination, 1406–1472." *History of Universities* 16 (2000): 197–235.

Davis, John. *The People of the Mediterranean: An Essay in Comparative Social Anthropology.* London: Routledge and Kegan Paul, 1977.

Davis, Robert C. "The Geography of Gender in the Renaissance." In *Gender and Society in Renaissance Italy*, edited by Judith C. Brown and Robert C. Davis, 19–38. New York: Addison Wesley Longman, 1998.

d'Avray, David L. "Marriage Ceremonies and the Church in Italy after 1215." In *Marriage in Italy, 1300–1500*, edited by Trevor Dean and Kate J.P. Lowe, 107–15. New York: Cambridge University Press, 1998.

– *Medieval Marriage: Symbolism and Society*. Oxford: Oxford University Press, 2005.

Dean, Trevor. "Fathers and Daughters: Marriage Laws and Marriage Disputes in Bologna and Italy, 1200–1500." In *Marriage in Italy, 1300–1500*, edited by Trevor Dean and Kate J.P. Lowe, 85–106. New York: Cambridge University Press, 1998.

De Benedictis, Angela. "Citizenship and Government in Bologna (Sixteenth–Seventeenth Centuries): Privilege of Citizenship, Right of Citizenship, Benefice of the *Patria*, Honor of the Magistrates." In *Privileges and the Rights of Citizenship: Law and the Juridical Construction of Civil Society*, edited by Julius Kirshner and Laurent Mayali, 127–46. Studies in Comparative Legal History. Berkeley: Robbins Collection, 2002.

Del Gratta, Rodolfo. *Giovan Battista De Luca e gli statuti di Piombino*. Naples: Edizioni Scientifiche Italiane, 1985.

D'Elia, Anthony F. "Marriage, Sexual Pleasure, and Learned Brides in the Wedding Orations of Fifteenth-Century Italy." *Renaissance Quarterly* 60 (2002): 379–443.

Della Misericordia, Massimo. *Divenire comunità: Comuni rurali, poteri locali, identità sociali e territoriali in Valtellina e nella montagna lombarda nel tardo medioevo*. Milan: UNICOPLI, 2006.

Demoulin-Auzary, Florence. *Les actions d'État en droit romano-canonique: Mariage et filiation (XIIe–XVe siècles)*. Paris: L.G.D.J., 2004.

Denholm-Young, Noel, and Hermann Kantorowicz. "*De ornatu mulierum*: A *Consilium* of Antonius de Rosellis with an Introduction on Fifteenth-Century Sumptuary Legislation." *La Bibliofilia* 35 (1933): 1–40.

Denifle, Heinrich. *Die Entstehung der Universitäten des Mittelalters bis 1400*. Berlin: Weidmann, 1885.

De Stefano, Francesco Paolo. *Romani, longobardi e normanno-franchi della Puglia nei secoli XV–XVII: Ricerche sui rapporti patrimoniali fra coniugi fino alla prammatica "De antefacto" del 1617*. 2 vols. Naples: Jovene, 1979.

Deutsch, Christina. *Ehegerichtsbarkeit im Bistum Regensburg (1480–1538)*. Cologne: Böhlau, 2005.

Dilcher, Gerhard. "Zum Bürgerbegriff im späteren Mittelalter: Versuch einer Typologie am Beispiel von Frankfurt am Main." In *Bürgerrecht und Stadtverfassung im europäischen Mittelalter*, 115–82. Cologne: Böhlau, 1996.

Dilonardo Buccolini, Gabriella. "Note sul popolazionismo a Viterbo nel secolo XV: La concessione della cittadinanza." In *Studi in onore di Amintore Fanfani*, vol. 2, 477–90. Milan: Giuffrè, 1962.

Di Renzo Villata, Maria Gigliola. "Il volto della famiglia medievale tra pratica e teoria nella *Rolandina*." In *Rolandino e l'ars notaria da Bologna all'Europa: Atti del convegno internazionale di studi storici sulla figura e l'opera di Rolandino: Bologna, città europea della cultura, 9–10 ottobre 2000*, edited by Giorgio Tamba, 377–458. Milan: Giuffrè, 2002.

Di Renzo Villata, Maria Gigliola, and Gian Paolo Massetto. "La facoltà legale: L'insegnamento del diritto civile (1361–1535)." In *Almum Studium Papiense: Storia dell'Università di Pavia*, vol. 1, *Dalle origini all'età spagnola*, edited by Dario Mantovani, 429–66. Milan: CISALPINO, 2102.

Di Simplicio, Oscar. *Peccato, penitenza, perdono, Siena 1575–1800: La formazione della coscienza nell'Italia moderna*. Milan: FrancoAngeli Storia, 1994.

Dixon, Suzanne. "*Infirmitas sexus*: Womanly Weakness in Roman Law." *Tijdschrift voor Rechtsgeschiedenis* 52 (1984): 343–71.

Dolezalek, Gero. *Das Imbreviaturbuch des erzbischöflichen Gerichtsnotars Hubaldus aus Pisa: Mai bis August 1230*. Cologne: Böhlau, 1969.

Donahue, Charles, Jr. "The Case of the Man Who Fell into the Tiber: The Roman Law of Marriage at the Time of the Glossators." *American Journal of Legal History* 22 (1978): 1–53.

– "*Ex Officio* Cases in the Officiality of Paris 1384–1387." In *Mélanges en l'honneur d'Anne Lefebvre-Teillard*, edited by Bernard d'Alteroche et al., 393–412. Paris: Éditions Panthéon-Assas, 2009.

– "Female Plaintiffs in Marriage Cases in the Court of York in the Later Middle Ages: What Can We Learn from the Numbers?" In *Wife and Widow in Medieval England*, edited by Sue Sheridan Walker, 181–213. Ann Arbor: University of Michigan Press, 1993.

– *Law, Marriage, and Society in the Later Middle Ages: Arguments about Marriage in Five Courts*. Cambridge: Cambridge University Press, 2007.

– "Lyndwood's Gloss *propriarum uxorum*: Marital Property and the *Ius Commune* in Fifteenth-Century England." In *Europäisches Rechtsdenken in Geschichte und Gegenwart: Festschrift für Helmut Coing zum 70. Geburtstag*, edited by Norbert Horn, Klaus Luig, and Alfred Söllner, 19–37. Munich: C.H. Beck, 1982.

– "Was There a Change in Marriage Law in the Late Middle Ages?" *RIDC* 6 (1996): 49–80.

– "What Causes Fundamental Legal Ideas? Marital Property in England and France in the Thirteenth Century." *Michigan Law Review* 78 (1980): 59–88.

Donaldson-Evans, Lance K. *Love's Fatal Glance: A Study of Eye Imagery in the Poets of the École Lyonnaise*. University of Mississippi Romance Monographs 39. Oxford, MS: Romance Monographs, 1980.

Dondarini, Rolando, ed. *La libertà di decidere: Realità e parvenze di autonomia nella normativa locale del medioevo*. Ferrara: Deputazione Provinciale Ferrarese di Storia Patria, 1993.

Dondorp, Harry, and Eltjo J.H. Schrage. "The Sources of Medieval Learned Law." In *The Creation of the "Ius Commune": From "Casus" to "Regula,"* edited by John W. Cairns and Paul J. du Plessis, 7–56. Edinburgh: Edinburgh University Press, 2010.

Donkin, Robin A. *Beyond Price: Pearls and Pearl-Fishing: Origins to the Age of Discoveries*. Philadelphia: American Philosophical Society, 1998.

Duby, Georges. "Structures de parenté et noblesse dans la France du Nord au XIe et XIIe siècles (1967)." In *Hommes et structures du Moyen Âge: Recueil d'articles*, 267–85. Paris: Mouton, 1973.

Dumont, François. *Les donations entre époux en droit romain*. Paris: Sirey, 1928.

Edigati, Daniele, and Lorenzo Tanzini. *Ad Statutum Florentinum: Esegesi statutaria e cultura giuridica nella Toscana medievale e moderna*. Pisa: ETS, 2009.

Edler, Florence. *Glossary of Medieval Terms of Business: Italian Series, 1200–1600*. New York: Mediaeval Academy of America, 1934.

Edler de Roover, Florence. "Andrea Banchi, Florentine Silk Manufacturer and Merchant in the Fifteenth Century." *Studies in Medieval and Renaissance History* 3 (1966): 223–85.

– *L'arte della seta a Firenze nei secoli XIV e XV*, edited by Sergio Tognetti. Florence: L.S. Olschki, 2000.

– "Restitution in Renaissance Florence." In *Studi in onore di Armando Sapori*, 775–89. Milan: Istituto Editoriale Cisalpino, 1957.

Elliot, Dyan. "Bernardino of Siena versus the Marriage Debt." In *Desire and Discipline: Sex and Sexuality in the Premodern West*, edited by Jacqueline Murray and Konrad Eisenbichler, 168–200. Toronto: University of Toronto Press, 1996.

Emigh, Rebecca J. "Property Devolution in Tuscany." *Journal of Interdisciplinary History* 33 (2002): 385–420.

– *The Undevelopment of Capitalism: Sectors and Markets in Fifteenth-Century Tuscany*. Philadelphia: Temple University Press, 2009.

Engelmann, Woldemar. *Die Wiedergeburt der Rechtskultur in Italien durch die wissenschaftliche Lehre: Eine Darlegung der Entfaltung des gemeinen italienischen Rechts und seiner Justizkultur im Mittelalter unter dem Einfluss der herrschenden Lehre der Gutachtenpraxis der Rechtsgelehrten und der Verantwortung der Richter im Sindikatsprozess*. Leipzig: Koehlers, 1938.

Epstein, Steven. "The Family." In *Italy in the Central Middle Ages, 1000–1300*, edited by David Abulafia, 183–96. Oxford: Oxford University Press, 2004.

– "Labour in Thirteenth-Century Genoa." *Mediterranean Historical Review* 3 (1988): 114–40.

– *Wills and Wealth in Medieval Genoa, 1150–1250*. Cambridge, MA: Harvard University Press, 1984.

Ercole, Francesco. "La dote romana negli statuti di Parma." *Archivio storico per le provincie parmensi* 8 (1908): 15–146.

– "L'istituto dotale nella practica e nella legislazione statuaria dell'Italia superiore." *RISG* 45 (1908): 191–302; 46 (1910): 167–257.

– "Vicende storiche della dote romana nella practica medievale dell'Italia superiore." *Archivio giuridico* 80 (1908): 393–490; 81 (1908): 34–148.

Esmein, Adhemar. *Le mariage en droit canonique*. Paris: Sirey, 1929.

Evans Grubbs, Judith. "Abduction Marriages in Antiquity: A Law of Constantine and Its Social Context." *Journal of Roman Studies* 79 (1989): 59–83.

– *Law and Family in Late Antiquity: The Emperor Constantine's Marriage Legislation*. Oxford: Clarendon Press, 1995.

– *Woman and the Law in the Roman Empire: A Sourcebook on Marriage, Divorce and Widowhood*. London: Routledge, 2002.

Fabbri, Lorenzo. *Alleanza matrimoniale e patriziato nella Firenze del '400: Studio sulla famiglia Strozzi*. Florence: L.S. Olschki, 1991.

Faini, Enrico. "Il convito del 1216: La vendetta all'origine del fazionalismo fiorentino." *Annali di Storia di Firenze* 1 (2006): 7–36.

Falcón-Pérez, Maria I. "Le mariage en Aragon au XV siècle." In *La femme dans l'histoire et la société méridionales (IXe–XIXe s.): Actes du 66e congrès de la Fédération Historique du Languedoc Méditerranéen et du Roussillon organisé à Narbonne les 15 et 16 Octobre 1994 à l'occasion du VIIIe centenaire de la fin du gouvernement de la vicomtesse Ermengarde*, 151–84. Montpellier: La Fédération, 1995.

Falsini, Aliberto B. "Firenze dopo il 1348: Le conseguenze della peste nera." *ASI* 129 (1971): 425–503.

Fasano Guarini, Elena. "Città soggette e contadi nel dominio fiorentino tra Quattro e Cinquecento: Il caso pisano." In *Ricerche di storia moderna*, vol. 1, edited by Mario Mirri, 1–94. Pisa: Pacini, 1976.

Feci, Simona. *Pesci fuor d'acqua: Donne a Roma in età moderna: Diritti e patrimoni*. Rome: Viella, 2004.

Feldner, Birgit. "Der Ausschluss der Frau vom römischen *officium*." *Revue internationale des droits de l'antiquité* 47 (2000): 381–96.

Feller, Laurent. "Morgengabe, dot, tertia: Rapport introductive." In *Dots et douaires dans le haut Moyen Âge*, Collection de l'École Française de Rome 295, edited by François Bougard, Laurent Feller, and Régine Le Jan, 1–25. Rome: École Française de Rome, 2002.

Ferrante, Lucia. "Marriage and Women's Subjectivity in a Patrilineal System: The Case of Early Modern Bologna." In *Gender, Kinship, Power: A Comparative and Interdisciplinary History*, edited by Mary Jo Maynes, 115–29. New York: Routledge, 1996.

– "Gli sposi contesi: Una vicenda bolognese di metà Cinquecento." In *Matrimoni in dubbio: Unioni controverse e nozze clandestine in Italia dal XIV al XVIII secolo, Annali dell'Istituto storico italo-germanico in Trento*, Quaderni 57, edited by Silvana Seidel Menchi and Diego Quaglioni, 329–62. Bologna: Il Mulino, 1998.

Ferrari, Giannino. "Diritto matrimoniale secondo le Novelle di Leone il Filosofo." *Byzantinische Zeitschrift* 18 (1909): 159–75.

Ferraro, Joanne M. *Marriage Wars in Late Renaissance Venice*. Oxford: Oxford University Press, 2001.

Figliuolo, Bruno, "Lo spazio economico dei mercanti messinesi nel XV secolo (1415–1474)," *Nuova rivista storica* 97 (2013): 757–800.

Finch, Andrew John. "Sexual Morality and Canon Law: The Evidence of the Rochester Consistory Court." *Journal of Medieval History* 20 (1994): 261–75.

– "Sexual Relations and Medieval Marriage in Normandy." *Journal of Ecclesiastical History* 47 (1996): 236–56.

Fingerlin, Ilse. *Gürtel des hohen und späten Mittelalters*. Munich: Deutscher Kunstverlag, 1971.

Finocchiaro, Alfio, and Mario Finocchiaro. *Riforma del diritto di famiglia: Commento teorico pratico alla legge 19 maggio 1975, n° 151*. Milan: Giuffrè, 1975.

Finucci, Valeria. "The Virgin's Body and Early Modern Surgeons." In *Masculinities, Childhood, Violence: Attending to Early Modern Women – and Men*, edited by Amy E. Leonard and Karen L. Nelson, 195–222. Newark: University of Delaware Press, 2011.

Fiore, Pasquale. *Della cittadinanza e del matrimonio*. Naples: Marghieri, 1909.

Forcheri, Giovanni. "I rapporti patrimoniali fra coniugi a Genova nel secolo XII." *Bollettino ligustico per la storia e la cultura regionale* 2 (1970): 3–20.

Fossier, Robert. "Les structures de la famille en Occident au Moyen Âge." In *XVe Congrès International des Sciences Historiques, Rapports*, vol. 2, 115–32. Bucharest: Editura Academiei Republicii Socialiste Romania, 1980.

Foster, Susannah Kerr. "The Ties That Bind: Kinship Association and Marriage in the Alberti Family 1378–1428." PhD diss., Cornell University, 1985.

Fraher, Richard M. "Conviction According to Conscience: The Medieval Jurists' Debate Concerning Judicial Discretion and the Law of Proof." *Law and History Review* 7 (1989): 23–88.

Freccero, Carla. "Economy, Woman, and Renaissance Discourse." In *Refiguring Woman: Perspectives on Gender and the Italian Renaissance*, edited by Marilyn Migiel and Juliana Schiesari, 192–208. Ithaca, NY: Cornell University Press, 1991.

Freud, Sigmund. *On Sexuality.* Edited by Angela Richards. Pelican Freud Library. Harmondsworth: Penguin, 1977.

Frick, Carole Collier. *Dressing Renaissance Florence: Families, Fortunes, & Fine Clothing*. Baltimore: Johns Hopkins University Press, 2002.

Frost, Ginger Suzanne. *Promises Broken: Courtship, Class, and Gender in Victorian England.* Charlottesville: University Press of Virginia, 1995

Frova, Carla, Maria Grazia Nico Ottaviani, and Stefania Zucchini, eds. *VI centenario della morte di Baldo degli Ubaldi, 1400–2000.* Perugia: Università degli studi, 2005.

Fubini Leuzzi, Maria. "*Condurre a onore*": *Famiglia, matrimonio e assistenza a Firenze in età moderna.* Florence: L.S. Olschki, 1999.

Fugazza, Emanuella. *Diritto istituzioni e giustizia in un comune dell'Italia padana: Piacenza e i suoi statuti (1135–1323).* Padua: CEDAM, 2009.

Gamillscheg, Franz. *Der Einfluß Dumoulins auf die Entwicklung des Kollisionsrechts.* Berlin: Mohr Siebeck, 1955.

Ganz, Margery A. "Paying the Price for Political Failure: Florentine Women in the Aftermath of 1466." *Rinascimento* 34 (1994): 237–57.

García Garrido, Manuel Jesús. *El patrimonio de la mujer casada en el derecho civil.* Vol. 1, *La tradición romanística.* Barcelona: Grupo Editorial CEAC, 1982.

Gardner, Jane F. *Being a Roman Citizen.* London: Routledge, 1993.

– *Family and "Familia" in Roman Law and Life*. Oxford: Oxford University Press, 1998.

– "The Recovery of the Dowry in Roman Law." *Classical Quarterly* 35 (1985): 449–53.

– *Women in Roman Law & Society*. London: Croom Helm, 1986.

Garlati, Loredana. "La famiglia tra passato e presente." In *Diritto della famiglia*, edited by Salvatore Patti and Maria Giovanna Cubeddu, 1–48. Milan: Giuffrè, 2011.

Garnsey, Peter. "Roman Citizenship and Roman Law in the Late Empire." In *Approaching Late Antiquity: The Transformation from Early to Late Empire*, edited by Simon Swain and Mark Edwards, 133–55. Oxford: Oxford University Press, 2006.

Garufi, Carlo Alberto. *Il matrimonio per verba de futuro di un siciliano studente leggi in Bologna nel 1349*. Il circolo giuridico 28. Palermo: Stabilimento Tipografico Virzi, 1897.

Gaudemet, Jean. *Le mariage en Occident: Les mœurs et le droit*. Paris: Cerf, 1987.

– *Sociétés et mariage*. Strasbourg: Cerdic, 1980.

Gaulin, Jean-Louis. "Affaires privées et certification publique : La documentation notariale relative au crédit à Bologne au XIIIème siècle." In *Notaires et crédit dans l'Occident méditerranéen médiéval*, Collection de l'École Française de Rome 343, edited by François Menant and Odile Redon, 55–95. Rome: l'École Française de Rome, 2004.

Gauvard, Claude. "La *fama*, un parole fondatrice." *Médiévales* 24 (1993): 5–13.

Gavitt, Philip. *Gender, Honor, and Charity in Late Renaissance Florence*. New York: Cambridge University Press, 2011.

Gentile, Giovanni. "Le leggi suntuarie nel comune di Pisa nei secoli XIII e XIV." In *La vita e il pensiero*, vol. 4, 185–211. Florence: Sansoni, 1972.

Gerner, Erich. *Beiträge zum Recht der Parapherna*. Munich: C.H. Beck, 1954.

Ghizzi, Giuseppe. *Storia della terra di Castiglione Fiorentino*. Arezzo, 1883–6; repr., Bologna: Arnaldo Forni, 1972.

Giardina, Andrea. "L'egualianza dei coniugi nel diritto internazionale privato." *RDIPP* 10 (1974): 5–31.

Gilbert, Creighton. "The Archbishop on the Painters of Florence, 1450." *Art Bulletin* 41 (1959): 75–87.

Girard, Paul Frédéric. *Manuel élémentaire de droit romain.* 8th ed. Paris: Rousseau, 1929.

Giustiniani, Vito R. "Il testamento di Leonardo Bruni." *Rinascimento*, n.s., 4 (1964): 259–64.

Goitein, Shelomo D., and Paula Sanders. *A Mediterranean Society: The Jewish Communities of the Arab World As Portrayed in the Documents of the Cairo Geniza*. Vol. 3, *The Family*. Berkeley: University of California Press, 1978.

Goldberg, Peter J.P. *Women in England, c. 1275–1525: Documentary Sources.* Manchester: Manchester University Press, 1995.

Goldthwaite, Richard A. *Banks, Palaces and Entrepreneurs in Renaissance Florence*. Aldershot: Ashgate/Variorum, 1995.

– *The Building of Renaissance Florence.* Baltimore: Johns Hopkins University Press, 1980.

– *L'economia della Firenze rinascimentale.* Bologna: Il Mulino, 2013.

– "Local Banking in Renaissance Florence." *Journal of European Economic History* 14 (1985): 5–55. Reprinted in Richard A. Goldthwaite, *Banks, Palaces and Entrepreneurs in Renaissance Florence*, no. 4. Aldershot: Ashgate/Variorum, 1995.

– *Private Wealth in Renaissance Florence: A Study of Four Florentine Families.* Princeton, NJ: Princeton University Press, 1968.

– *Wealth and Demand for Art in Italy, 1300–1600.* Baltimore: Johns Hopkins University Press, 1993.

Goody, Jack. "The Evolution of the Family." In *Household and Family in Past Time*, edited by Peter Laslett and Richard Wall, 103–24. Cambridge: Cambridge University Press, 1972.

Gordley, James. "*Ardor quaerens intellectum*: Sex within Marriage according to the Canon Lawyers and Theologians of the 12th and 13th Centuries." *ZRG* (*KA*) 114 (1997): 305–32.

– *The Philosophical Origins of Modern Contract Doctrine.* Oxford: Clarendon Press, 1991.

Goria, Fausto. "*Romani*, cittadinanza ed estensione della legislazione imperiale nella costituzione di Giustiniano." In *Da Roma alla terza Roma*, vol. 1, *La nozione di "romano" tra cittadinanza e universalità*, 277–342. Naples: Edizioni Scientifiche Italiane, 1984.

Gow, Andrew, and Gordon Griffiths. "Pope Eugenius IV and Jewish Money-Lending in Florence: The Case of Salomone di Bonaventura during the Chancellorship of Leonardo Bruni." *Renaissance Quarterly* 47 (1994): 289–329.

Grbavac, Branka. "Testamentary Bequests of Urban Noblewomen on the Eastern Adriatic Coast in the Fourteenth Century: The Case of Zadar." In *Across the Religious Divide: Women, Property, and Law in the Wider Mediterranean (ca. 1200–1800)*, edited by Jutta Sperling and Shona Kelly Wray, 67–80. New York: Routledge 2010.

Gregory, Heather. "Daughters, Dowries and Family in 15th-Century Florence." *Rinascimento* 27 (1987): 217–37.

– *Selected Letters of Alessandra Strozzi.* Berkeley: University of California Press, 1997.

Grossberg, Michael. *Governing the Hearth: Law and the Family in Nineteenth-Century America.* Chapel Hill: University of North Carolina Press, 1985.

Grossi, Paolo. "*Dominia* e *Servitutes*: Invenzioni sistematiche del diritto comune in tema di servitù." In *Il dominio e le cose: Percezioni medievali e moderne dei diritti reali*, 57–122. Milan: Giuffrè, 1992.

– *L'ordine giuridico medievale.* Rome-Bari: Laterza, 1995.

Grubb, James S. *Provincial Families of the Renaissance: Private and Public Life in the Veneto.* Baltimore: Johns Hopkins University Press, 1996.

Guerra Medici, Maria Teresa. *L'aria di città: Donne e diritti nel comune medievale.* Naples: Edizioni Scientifiche Italiane, 1996.

– *I diritti delle donne nella società altomedievale.* Rome: Edizioni Scientifiche, 1986.

– "L'esclusione delle donne dalla successione legitima e la *Constitutio super statutariis successionibus* di Innocenzo XI." *RSDI* 56 (1983): 261–94.

Guetta, Alessandro. "Religious Life and Jewish Erudition in Pisa: Yehiel Nissim da Pisa and the Crisis of Aristotelianism." In *Cultural Intermediaries: Jewish Intellectuals in Early Modern Italy*, edited by David B. Ruderman and Giuseppe Veltri, 86–108. Philadelphia: University of Pennsylvania Press, 2004.

Guidi, Guidubaldo. *Il governo della città-repubblica di Firenze del primo Quattrocento*. 3 vols. Florence: L.S. Olschki, 1981.

Guzzetti, Linda. "Le donne nello spazio urbano della Venezia del Trecento." In *Donne a Venezia: Vicende femminili fra Trecento e Settecento*, edited by Susanne Winter, 1–22. Rome: Edizioni di Storia e Lettura, 2004.

– "Dowries in Fourteenth-Century Venice." *Renaissance Studies* 16 (2002): 430–73.

– *Venezianische Vermächtnisse: Die soziale und wirtschaftliche Situation von Frauen im Spiegel spätmittelalterlicher Testamente*. Stuttgart: J.B. Metzler, 1998.

– "Women's Inheritance and Testamentary Practices in Late Fourteenth- and Early Fifteenth-Century Venice and Ghent." In *The Texture of Society: Medieval Women in the Southern Low Countries*, edited by Ellen E. Kittell and Mary A. Suydam, 79–108. London: Palgrave Macmillan, 2004.

Haas, Louis. *The Renaissance Man and His Children: Childbirth and Early Childhood in Florence, 1300–1600*. New York: St. Martin' s Press, 1998.

Hacke, Daniella. "*Non lo volevo per marito in modo alcuno*: Matrimoni forzati e conflitti generazionali a Venezia fra il 1580 e il 1680." In *Tempi e spazi di vita femminile tra medioevo ed età moderna*, *Annali dell'Istituto storico italo-germanico in Trento*, Quaderni 51, edited by Silvana Seidel Menchi, Anne Jacobson Schutte, and Thomas Kuehn, 195–224. Bologna: Il Mulino, 1999.

Hajnal, John. "European Marriage Patterns in Perspective." In *Population in History*: *Essays in Historical Demography*, edited by D.V. Glass and D.E.C. Eversely, 101–43. London: E. Arnold, 1965.

Hall, Edwin. *The Arnolfini Betrothal: Medieval Marriage and the Enigma of Van Eyck's Double Portrait*. Berkeley: University of California Press, 1994.

Hamza, Gábor. "Les motifs de la prohibition de la donation entre époux en droit romain et l'hypothèse sur son origine." In *Le droit de la famille en Europe: Son évolution depuis l'Antiquité jusqu'à nos jours*, edited by Roland Ganghofer, 481–90. Strasbourg: Presses Universitaires de Strasbourg, 1992.

Harke, Jan Dirk. "Zum römischen Recht der Forderungsübertragung." *RHD* 76 (2008): 1–18.

Hatzimihail, Nikitas E. "Bartolus and the Conflict of Laws." *Revue hellénique de droit international* 60 (2007): 11–79.

Helmholz, Richard H. *Marriage Litigation in Medieval England*. London: Cambridge University Press, 1974.

Henderson, John. *Piety and Charity in Late Medieval Florence*. Oxford: Clarendon Press, 1994.

Herlihy, David. *Cities and Society in Medieval Italy*. London: Variorum, 1980.

– "Deaths, Marriages, Births, and the Tuscan Economy (ca. 1300–1500)." In *Population Patterns in the Past*, edited by Ronald D. Lee, 135–64. New York: Academic Press, 1977. Reprinted in Herlihy, *Cities and Society*, no. 12.

– "Family and Property in Renaissance Florence." In *The Medieval City*, edited by Harry A. Miskimin, David Herlihy, and Abraham L. Udovich, 3–24. New Haven, CT: Yale University Press, 1977. Reprinted in Herlihy, *Cities and Society*, no. 13.

– "The Florentine Merchant Family of the Middle Ages." In *Studi di storia economica Toscana nel medioevo e nel Rinascimento in memoria di Federigo Melis*. Pisa: Pacini, 1987. Reprinted in Herlihy, *Women, Family and Society*, no. 10.

– "The Making of the Medieval Family: Structure, Symmetry and Sentiment." *Journal of Family History* 8 (1983): 116–30. Reprinted in Herlihy, *Women, Family and Society*, no. 7.

– "The Medieval Marriage Market." *Medieval and Renaissance Studies* 6 (1976): 3–27. Reprinted in Herlihy, *The Social History*, no. 14.

– *Pisa in the Early Renaissance: A Study of Urban Growth*. New Haven, CT: Yale University Press, 1958.

– *The Social History of Italy and Western Europe, 700–1500*. London: Variorum, 1978.

– *Women, Family and Society in Medieval Europe: Historical Essays, 1978–1991*. Edited by Anthony Molho. Providence: Berghahn Books, 1995.

Herlihy, David, and Christiane Klapisch-Zuber. *Les Toscans et leurs familles: Une étude du catasto florentin de 1427*. Paris: Foundation Nationale des Sciences Politiques, 1978.

– *Tuscans and Their Families: A Study of the Florentine Catasto of 1427*. New Haven, CT: Yale University Press, 1985.

Hersch, Karen K. *The Roman Wedding: Ritual and Meaning in Antiquity*. Cambridge: Cambridge University Press, 2010.

Hicks, John. "Liquidity." *Economic Journal* 72 (1962): 787–802.

Hilaire, Jean. *Le régime des biens entre époux dans la région de Montpellier du début du XIIIe siècle à la fin du XVIe siècle: Contribution aux études d'histoire du droit écrit*. Montpellier: Causse, Graille & Castelnau, 1957.

– "Vie en commun, famille et esprit communautaire." *RHDF* 51 (1973): 8–53.

Hind, Arthur M. *Nielli, Chiefly Italian, of the XV Century*. London: British Museum, 1936.

Hoareau-Dodineau, Jacqueline. "*Vir est caput mulieris?*" In *Auctoritas: Mélanges offerts à Professeur Olivier Guillot,* edited by Giles Constable and Michel Rouche, 595–613. Paris: Presses Universitaires de la Sorbonne, 2006.

Horn, Norbert. *Aequitas in den Lehren des Baldus.* Cologne: Böhlau, 1968.

– "Philosophie in der Jurisprudenz der Kommentatoren: Baldus philosophus." *Ius Commune*: *Zeitschrift für europäische Rechtsgeschichte* 1 (1967): 104–49.

Hoshino, Hidetoshi. *L'arte della lana in Firenze nel basso medioevo: Il commercio della lana e il mercato dei panni fiorentini nei secoli XIII–XV*. Florence: Leo S. Olschki, 1980.

– "Francesco di Iacopo Del Bene cittadino fiorentino del Trecento." *Annuario dell'Istituto Giapponese di Cultura* 4 (1966–7): 29–119.

Howard, Vicki. "A 'Real Man's Ring': Gender and the Invention of Tradition." *Journal of Social History* 36 (2003): 837–56.

Howell, Martha C. "Citizenship and Gender: Women's Political Status in Northern Medieval Cities." In *Women & Power in the Middle Ages*, edited by Mary Erler and Maryanne Kowaleski, 37–60. Athens: University of Georgia Press, 1988.

– "Fixing Movables: Gifts by Testament in Late Medieval Douai." *Past and Present* 150 (1996): 3–45.

– *The Marriage Exchange: Property, Social Place, and Gender in Cities of the Low Countries, 1300–1550.* Chicago: University of Chicago Press, 1998.

Hughes, Diana Owen. "Domestic Ideals and Social Behavior: Evidence from Medieval Genoa." In *The Family in History: Lectures Given in Memory of Stephen Allen Kaplan under the Auspices of the Department of History at the University of Pennsylvania*, edited by Charles E. Rosenberg, 115–43. Philadelphia: University of Pennsylvania Press, 1975.

– "La famiglia e le donne nel Rinascimento fiorentino." *Quaderni storici* 24 (1989): 629–34.

– "From Brideprice to Dowry in Mediterranean Europe." *Journal of Family History* 3 (1978): 262–96.

– "Il matrimonio nell'Italia medievale." In *Storia del matrimonio*, edited by Michela De Giorgio and Christiane Klapisch-Zuber, 5–61. Bari: Laterza, 1996.

– "Sumptuary Law and Social Relations in Renaissance Italy." In *Disputes and Settlements: Law and Human Relations in the West*, edited by John Bossy, 69–99. Cambridge: Cambridge University Press, 1983.

Iglar, Richard F. "The Rules of Engagement." *New Jersey Law Journal* 190 (8 October 2007): 189–90.

Ingram, Martin. "Spousal Litigation in the English Ecclesiastical Courts c. 1350–c. 1640." In *Marriage and Society: Studies in the Social History of Marriage*, edited by R.B. Outhwaite, 35–57. New York: St. Martin's Press, 1982.

Isaacs, Ann Katherine. "Changing Layers of Jurisdiction: Northern and Central Italian States in the Late Middle Ages and Early Modern Times." In *Communities in European History: Representations, Jurisdictions, Conflicts*, edited by Juan Pan-Montojo and Frederik Pedersen, 133–50. Pisa: Pisa University Press, 2007

Ius Mediolani: Studi di storia del diritto milanese offerti dagli allievi a Giulio Vismara. Milan: Giuffrè, 1996.

Izbicki, Thomas M. *Friars and Jurists: Selected Studies*. Goldbach: Keip, 1997.

– "*Ista questio est antiqua*: Two *Consilia* on Widows Rights." *Bulletin of Medieval Canon Law* 8 (1978): 47–50. Reprinted in Izbicki, *Friars and Jurists*, no. 15.

– "Pyres of Vanities: Mendicant Preaching on the Vanity of Women and Its Lay Audience." In *De ore Domini: Preacher and the World in the Middle Ages*, edited by Thomas L. Almos, Eugene A. Green, and Beverly M. Kienzle, 211–34. Kalamazoo: University of Western Michigan Press, 1989. Reprinted in Izbicki, *Friars and Juristss*, no. 9.

Izbicki, Thomas M., and Julius Kirshner. "*Consilia* of Baldus of Perugia in the Regenstein Library of the University of Chicago." *Bulletin of Medieval Canon Law* 15 (1985): 95–115. Reprinted in Izbicki, *Friars and Jurists*, no. 28.

Jacks, Philip, and William Caffero. *The Spinelli of Florence: Fortunes of a Renaissance Merchant Family*. University Park: Pennsylvania University Press, 2001.

Jacoby, David. "Les Juifs à Venise du XIVe au milieu du XVIe siècle." In *Recherches sur la Mediterranée orientale du XIIe au XVe siècle*, 163–216. London: Variorum Reprints, 1979.

Jayme, Erik. *Pasquale Stanislao Mancini: Internationales Privatrecht zwischen Risorgimento und praktischer Jurisprudenz*. Ebelsbach: Gremer, 1980.

Jehel, Georges. "Le rôle des femmes et du milieu familial a Gênes dans les activités commercials." *Revue de l'histoire économique et sociale* 53 (1975): 193–215.

Kamenaga Anzai, Yoko. "Attitudes towards Public Debt in Medieval Genoa: The Lomellini Family." *Journal of Medieval History* 29 (2003): 239–63.

Kantorowicz, Hermann. *Rechtshistorische Schriften.* Edited by Helmut Coing and Gerhard Immel. Karlsruhe: Müller, 1970.

Kaser, Max. *Das römische Privatrecht*. 2 vols. Munich: C.H. Beck, 1971.

Kedar, Benjamin. "Toponymic Surnames as Evidence of Origin: Some Medieval Views." *Viator* 4 (1973): 123–9.

Kelleher, Marie A. *The Measure of Woman: Law and Female Identity in the Crown of Aragon*. Philadelphia: University of Pennsylvania Press, 2010.

Kelly, Henry Ansgar. *The Matrimonial Trials of Henry VIII*. Stanford, CA: Stanford University Press, 1976.

Kent, Francis W. "La famiglia patrizia fiorentina nel Quattrocento: Nuovi orientamenti nella storiografia recente." In *Palazzo Strozzi metà millennio,*

1489–1989, Atti del convegno di studi, Firenze, 3–6 luglio 1989, edited by Daniela Lamberini, 70–91. Rome: Istituto della Enciclopedia Italiana, 1991.

– *Household and Lineage in Renaissance Florence: The Family Life of the Capponi, Ginori, and Rucellai.* Princeton, NJ: Princeton University Press, 1977.

Kieckhefer, Richard. "Erotic Magic in Medieval Europe." In *Sex in the Middle Ages*, edited by Joyce E. Salisbury, 30–55. New York: Garland, 1991.

Kirshner, Julius. "*Ars imitatur naturam*: A *Consilium* of Baldus on Naturalization in Florence." *Viator* 5 (1975): 289–331.

– "Baldo degli Ubaldi's Contribution to the Rule of Law in Florence." In *VI centenario della morte di Baldo degli Ubaldi, 1400–2000*, edited by Carla Frova, Maria Grazia Nico Ottaviani, and Stefania Zucchini, 313–64. Perugia: Università degli Studi, 2005.

– "Bartolo of Sassoferrato's 'De tyranno' and Sallustio Buonguglielmi's *consilium* on Niccolò Fortebracci's Tyranny in Città di Castello." *Mediaeval Studies* 68 (2006): 303–31.

– "Children, Betrothal and Marriage of." In *Women and Gender in Medieval Europe: An Encyclopedia*, edited by Margaret Schaus, 126–8. New York: Routledge, 2006.

– "Citizen Cain of Florence." In *La Toscane et les Toscans autour de la Renaissance: Cadres de vie, société, croyances: Mélanges offerts à Charles-M. de La Roncière*, 175–89. Aix-en-Provence: Publications de l'Université de Provence, 1999.

– "*Civitas sibi faciat civem*: Bartolus of Sassoferrato's Doctrine on the Making of a Citizen." *Speculum* 48 (1973): 694–713.

– "*Consilia* as Authority in Late Medieval Italy: The Case of Florence." In *Legal Consulting in the Civil Law Tradition*, edited by Mario Ascheri, Ingrid Baumgärtner, and Julius Kirshner, 107–40. Berkeley: Robbins Collection, 1999.

– "A *Consilium* of Rosello dei Roselli on the Meaning of *Florentinus, de Florentia*, and *de populo*." *Bulletin of Medieval Canon Law* 6 (1976): 87–91.

– "A *Consilium* of Torello di Niccolò Torelli of Prato on *dos aestimata*." In *Iuris historia: Liber Amicorum Gero Dolezalek*, Studies in Comparative Legal History, edited by Vincenzo Colli and Emanuele Conte, 355–68. Berkeley: Robbins Collection, 2008.

– "Custom, Customary Law, and *Ius Commune* in Francesco Guicciardini." In *Bologna nell'età di Carlo V e Guicciardini*, edited by Emilio Pasquini and Paolo Prodi, 151–79. Bologna: Il Mulino, 2002.

– "Encumbering Private Claims to Public Debt in Renaissance Florence." In *The Growth of the Bank as Institution and the Development of Money-Business Law*, edited by Vito Piergiovanni, 19–75. Berlin: Duncker & Humblot, 1993.

– "Genere e cittadinanza nelle città-stato del Medioevo e del Rinascimento," In *Innesti: Donne e genere nella storia sociale*, edited by Giulia Calvi, 21–38. Rome: Viella, 2004.

– "'Made Exiles for the Love of Knowledge': Students in Late Medieval Italy." *Mediaeval Studies* 70 (2008): 163–201.

– "*Maritus lucretur dotem uxoris sue premortue* in Late Medieval Florence." *ZRG* (*KA*) 77 (1991): 111–55.

– "Messer Francesco di Bici degli Albergotti d'Arezzo, Citizen of Florence (1350–1376)." *Bulletin of Medieval Canon Law* 2 (1972): 84–90.

– "*Mulier Alibi Nupta*." In *Consilia im späten Mittelalter: Zum historischen Aussagewert einer Quellengattung*, Schriftenreihe des deutschen Studienzentrums in Vendig, no. 13, edited by Ingrid Baumgärtner, 147–76. Sigmaringen: Thorbecke, 1995.

– "Privileged Risk: The Investments of Luchino Novello Visconti in the Public Debt (*Monte Comune*) of Florence." *RIDC* 14 (2003): 83–117.

– *Pursuing Honor While Avoiding Sin: The Monte Delle Doti of Florence.* Quaderni di Studi Senesi 41. Milan: Giuffrè, 1978.

– "Question of Trust: Suretyship in Trecento Florence." In *Renaissance Studies in Honor of Craig Hugh Smyth*, edited by Andrew Morrogh, vol. 1, 129–45. Florence: Giunti Barbera, 1985.

Kirshner, Julius, and Anthony Molho. "The Dowry Fund and the Marriage Market in Early Quattrocento Florence." *Journal of Modern History* 58 (1978): 403–38.

– "Niccolò Machiavelli's Marriage." *Rinascimento* 18 (1978): 293–5.

Kirshner, Julius, and Jacques Pluss. "Two Fourteenth-Century Opinions on Dowries, Paraphernalia and Non-dotal Goods." *Bulletin of Medieval Canon Law* 9 (1979): 64–77.

Kisch, Guido. "Die Rechtsstellung der Wormser Juden im Mittelalter." *Zeitschrift für die Geschichte der Juden in Deutschland* 5 (1934): 122–33.

Kittell, Ellen. "Women, Audience, and Public Acts in Medieval Flanders." *Journal of Women's History* 10 (1998): 74–96.

Klapisch-Zuber, Christiane. "Childhood in Tuscany at the Beginning of the Fifteenth Century." In *Women, Family, and Ritual in Renaissance Florence*, translated by Lydia G. Cochrane, 94–116. Chicago: University of Chicago Press, 1985.

– "Il complesso di Griselda: Dote e doni di nozze nel Quattrocento." In *La famiglia e le donne nel Rinascimento a Firenze*, 151–91. Bari: Laterza, 1988.

– "Le complexe de Griselda." *Mélanges de l'École Française de Rome* 94 (1982): 7–43. Reprinted in Christiane Klapisch-Zuber, *La maison et le nom*, no. 9.

– "The 'Cruel Mother': Maternity, Widowhood, and Dowry in Florence of the Fourteenth and Fifteenth Centuries." In *Women, Family, and Ritual in*

Renaissance Florence, translated by Lydia G. Cochrane, 117–31. Chicago: University of Chicago Press, 1985.
– *La famiglia e le donne nel Rinascimento a Firenze*. Bari: Laterza, 1988.
– "The Griselda Complex: Dowry and Marriage Gifts in the Quattrocento." In *Women, Family, and Ritual in Renaissance Florence*, translated by Lydia G. Cochrane, 213–46. Chicago: University of Chicago Press, 1985.
– *La maison et le nom: Stratégies et rituels dans l'Italie de la Renaissance.* Paris: EHESS, 1990.
– "Les noces feintes: Sur quelques lectures de deux thèmes iconographiques dans les *cassoni* florentins." *I Tatti Studies* 6 (1995): 11–30.
– "'Parenti, amici, e vicini': Il territorio urbano d'una famiglia mercantile nel XV secolo." *Quaderni storici* 33 (1976): 953–82.
– *Retour à la cité: Les magnats de Florence 1340–1440*. Paris: EHESS, 2006.
– "State and Family in a Renaissance Society: The Florentine *Catasto* of 1427–30." In *Women, Family, and Ritual in Renaissance Florence*, translated by Lydia G. Cochrane, 1–22. Chicago: University of Chicago Press, 1985.
– *Women, Family, and Ritual in Renaissance Florence*, translated by Lydia G. Cochrane. Chicago: University of Chicago Press, 1985.
– "Zacharias, or the Ousted Father: Nuptial Rites in Tuscany between Giotto and the Council of Trent." In *Women, Family, and Ritual in Renaissance Florence*, translated by Lydia G. Cochrane, 178–212. Chicago: University of Chicago Press, 1985.
– "Zacharie, ou Le père évincé: Les rites nuptiaux toscans entre Giotto et le Concile de Trente." In *La maison et le nom: Stratégies et rituels dans l'Italie de la Renaissance*, 151–84. Paris: EHESS, 1990.
– "Le *zane* della sposa: La donna fiorentina e il suo corredo nel Rinascimento." In *La famiglia e le donne nel Rinascimento a Firenze*, 193–211. Bari: Laterza, 1988.
Kofler, Georg W., and Ruth Mason. "Double Taxation: A European 'Switch in Time.'" *Columbia Journal of European Law* 14 (2008/9): 63–97.
Korpiola, Mia. *Between Betrothal and Bedding: Marriage Formation in Sweden, 1200–1600.* Leiden: Brill, 2009.
– "Marriage Causes in Late Medieval Sweden: The Evidence of Bishop Hans Brask's Register (1522–27)." In *Regional Variations in Matrimonial Law and Custom in Europe, 1150–1600*, edited by Mia Korpiola, 211–49. Leiden: Brill, 2011.
– ed. *Regional Variations in Matrimonial Law and Custom in Europe, 1150–1600.* Leiden: Brill, 2011.
– "An Uneasy Harmony: Consummation and Parental Consent in Secular and Canon Law in Medieval Scandinavia." *Nordic Perspectives on Medieval Canon*

Law, edited by Mia Korpiola, 125–50. Saarijàrvi: Publications of Matthias Calonius Society, 1999.

Koschaker, Paul. "Zur Geschichte der *arrha sponsalicia.*" *ZRG* (*RA*) 33 (1912): 383–416.

Kovesi Killerby, Catherine. "*Heralds of a Well-Instructed Mind*: Nicolosa Sanuti's Defence of Women and Their Clothes." *Renaissance Studies* 13 (1999): 255–82.

– "Practical Problems in the Enforcement of Italian Sumptuary Law, 1200–1500." In *Crime, Society and the Law in Renaissance Italy*, edited by Trevor Dean and Kate J.P. Lowe, 99–120. Cambridge: Cambridge University Press, 1994.

– *Sumptuary Law in Italy 1200–1500*. Oxford: Oxford University Press, 2002.

Kreutz, Barbara M. "The Twilight of *Morgengabe*." In *Portraits of Medieval and Renaissance Living: Essays in Honor of David Herlihy*, edited by Samuel K. Cohn and Steven A. Epstein, 131–47. Ann Arbor: University of Michigan Press, 1996.

Kriechbaum, Maximiliane. "Philosophie und Jurisprudenz bei Baldus de Ubaldis: 'Philosophi legum imitati sunt philosophos naturae.'" *Ius Commune* 27 (2000): 299–343.

Kuehn, Thomas. "Contracting Marriage in Renaissance Florence." In *To Have and to Hold: Marrying and Its Documentation in Western Christendom, 400–1600*, edited by Philip L. Reynolds and John Witte, Jr., 390–420. Cambridge: Cambridge University Press, 2007.

– "*Cum consensu mundualdi*: Legal Guardianship of Women in Quattrocento Florence." *Viator* 13 (1982): 309–33. Reprinted in Thomas Kuehn, *Law, Family, & Women: Toward a Legal Anthropology of Renaissance Italy*, no. 9. Chicago: University of Chicago Press, 1991.

– *Emancipation in Late Medieval Florence*. New Brunswick, NJ: Rutgers University Press, 1982.

– "*Fama* as a Legal Status in Renaissance Florence." In *Fama: The Politics of Talk and Reputation in Medieval Europe,* edited by Thelma Fenster and Daniel Lord Smail, 27–46. Ithaca, NY: Cornell University Press, 2003.

– "Family Solidarity in Exile and in Law: Alberti Lawsuits of the Early Quattrocento." *Speculum* 78 (2003): 421–39.

– *Heirs, Kin, and Creditors in Renaissance Florence*. Cambridge: Cambridge University Press, 2008.

– "Honor and Conflict in a Fifteenth-Century Florentine Family." *Ricerche storiche* 10 (1980): 287–310. Reprinted in Thomas Kuehn, *Law, Family, & Women: Toward a Legal Anthropology of Renaissance Italy*, no. 4. Chicago: University of Chicago Press, 1991.

– *Illegitimacy in Renaissance Florence*. Ann Arbor: University of Michigan Press, 2002.

– "Inheritance and Identity in Early Renaissance Florence: The Estate of Paliano di Falco." In *Society and Individual in Renaissance Florence*, edited by William J. Connell, 137–54. Berkeley: University of California Press, 2002.

– "*Multorum Fraudibus Occurrere*: Legislation and Jurisprudential Interpretation Concerning Fraud and Liability in Quattrocento Florence." *Studi senesi* 93 (1981): 309–50.

– "Person and Gender in the Laws." In *Gender and Society in Renaissance Italy*, edited by Judith C. Brown and Robert C. Davis, 87–106. New York: Addison Wesley Longman, 1998.

– "Social Processes and Legal Processes in the Renaissance: A Florentine Inheritance Case from 1452." *Quaderni fiorentini per la storia del pensiero giuridico moderno* 23 (1994): 365–96.

– "Some Ambiguities of Female Inheritance Ideology in the Renaissance." In *Law, Family, & Women: Toward a Legal Anthropology of Renaissance Italy*, 238–58. Chicago: University of Chicago Press, 1991.

– "Women, Marriage, and *Patria Potestas* in Late Medieval Florence." In *Law, Family, & Women: Toward a Legal Anthropology of Renaissance Italy*, 197–211. Chicago: University of Chicago Press, 1991.

Lafon, Jacques. *Régimes matrimoniaux et mutations socials: Les époux bordelais: 1450–1550*. Paris: SEVPEN, 1972.

Lally, Patrick J. "Baldus de Ubaldis on the 'Liber Sextus' and 'De Regulis Iuris': Text and Commentary." 2 vols. PhD diss., University of Chicago, 1992.

Lanaro, Paola, and Gian Maria Varanini. "Funzioni economiche della dote nell'Italia centro-settentrionale (tardo medioevo / inizi età moderna)." In *La famiglia nell'economia europea, secoli XIII–XVIII = The Economic Role of the Family in the European Economy from the 13th to the 18th Centuries*, Atti della "Quarantesima Settimana di Studi," Fondazione Istituto Internazionale di Storia Economica "F. Datini," Prato, 6–10 April 2008, edited by Simonetta Cavaciocchi, 81–102. Florence: Firenze University Press, 2009.

Lanconelli, Angela. "Autonomie comunali e potere centrale nel Lazio dei secoli XIII–XIV." In *La libertà di decidere: Realità e parvenze di autonomia nella normativa locale del medioevo*, edited by Rolando Dondarini, 83–102. Ferrara: Deputazione Provinciale Ferrarese di Storia Patria, 1993.

Landès-Mallet, Anne-Marie. *La famille en Rouergue au Moyen Âge, 1269–1345: Ètude de la pratique notariale*. Rouen: Publications de l'Université de Rouen, 1985.

Lane, Frederic C. "Public Debt and Private Wealth, Particularly in Sixteenth-Century Venice." In *Mélanges en l'honneur de Fernand Braudel*, vol. 1, 317–25. Toulouse: Privat, 1973.

Lange, Hermann, *Römisches Recht im Mittelalter.* Vol. 1, *Die Glossatoren.* Munich: C.H. Beck, 1997.

Lange, Hermann, and Maximiliane Kriechbaum. *Römisches Recht im Mittelalter.* Vol. 2, *Die Kommentatoren.* Munich: C.H. Beck, 2007.

Lansing, Carol. "Poisoned Relations: Marital Conflict in Medieval Bologna." In *Bologna: Cultural Crossroads from the Medieval to the Baroque: Recent Anglo-American Scholarship*, edited by Gian Mario Anselmi, Angela De Benedictis, and Nicholas Terpstra, 129–41. Bologna: Bononia University Press, 2013.

Larner, John. *Italy in the Age of Dante and Petrarch, 1216–1380.* London: Longman, 1980.

La Roncière, Charles-M. de. *Prix et salaires à Florence au XIVe siècle (1280–1380).* Rome: École Française de Rome, 1982.

Laurent-Bonne, Nicolas. "Why Prohibit Donations between Husband and Wife in Medieval Europe?" *Frontiers of Law in China* 7 (2012): 644–55.

Lefebvre-Teillard, Anne. "*Ad matrimonium contrahere compellitur.*" *RDC* 28 (1978): 210–17.

– "Règle et réalité dans le droit matrimonial à la fin du Moyen Âge." *RDC* 30 (1980): 41–54.

Leicht, Pier S. "Cino da Pistoia e la citazione di Re Roberto da parte d'Arrigo VII." *ASI* 112 (1954): 313–20.

– *Storia del diritto italiano: Il diritto privato.* Milan: Giuffrè, 1960.

Leisching, Peter. "Eheschliessungen vor dem Notar im 13. Jahrhundert." *ZRG (KA)* 84 (1997): 20–46.

– "'Et teneat eam per dexteram manum in sua manu dextera …': Zur Handgestik mittelalterlicher Trauungen." *Studia Gratiana* 27 (1996), 311–30.

Lepsius, Susanne. "Die Ehe, die Mitgift und der Tod." In *Fälle aus der Rechtsgeschichte*, edited by Ulrich Falk, Michele Luminati, and Mathias Schmoeckel, 129–46. Munich: C.H. Beck, 2008.

– "Paolo di Castro as Consultant: Applying and Interpreting Florence's Statutes." In *The Politics of Law in Late Medieval and Renaissance Italy*, edited by Lawrin Armstrong and Julius Kirshner, 77–105. Toronto: University of Toronto Press, 2011.

– *Von Zweifeln zur Überzeugung: Der Zeugenbeweis im gelehrten Recht ausgehend von der Abhandlung des Bartolus von Sassoferrato.* Frankfurt am Main: Vittorio Klostermann, 2003.

Le Roy Ladurie, Emmanuel. *Montaillou: Cathars and Catholics in a French Village, 1294–1324.* Translated by Barbara Bray. Harmondsworth: Penguin, 1990.

Lett, Didier. "Genre et paix: Des mariages croisés entre quatre communes de la Marche d'Ancône en 1306." *Annales: Histoire, sciences sociales* 67 (2012/13): 629–55.

Levi Pisetzky, Rosita. *Il costume e la moda nella società italiana*. Turin: Einaudi, 1995.

Lévy, Jean-Philippe. "L'officialité de Paris et les questions familiales à la fin du XIVe siècle." In *Études d'histoire du droit canonique dédiées à G. Le Bras*, 1265–94. Paris: Sirey, 1960.

Lightfoot, Dana Wessell. "Family Interests? Women's Power: The Absence of Family in Dowry Restitution Cases in Fifteenth-Century Spain." *Women's History Review* 15 (2006): 511–20.

Lombardi, Daniela. "Fidanzamenti e matrimoni dal Concilio di Trento alle riforme settecentesche." In *Storia del matrimonio*, edited by Michela De Giorgio and Christiane Klapisch-Zuber, 215–50. Bari: Laterza, 1996.

– "Intervention by Church and State in Marriage Disputes in Sixteenth- and Seventeenth-Century Florence." In *Crime, Society and the Law in Renaissance Italy*, edited by Trevor Dean and Kate J.P. Lowe, 142–56. Cambridge, MA: Harvard University Press, 1994.

– "Il matrimonio: Norme, giurisdizioni, conflitti nello Stato fiorentino del Cinquecento." In *Istituzioni e società in Toscana nell'età moderna: Atti delle giornate di studio dedicate a Giuseppe Pansini: Firenze, 4–5 dicembre 1992*, edited by Claudio Lamioni, 787–805. Rome: Ministerio per i Beni culturali e ambientali, 1994.

Lombardo, Maria Luisa, and Mirella Morelli. "Donne e testamenti a Roma nel Quattrocento." In *Donne a Roma tra medioevo e età moderna*, 23–130. Rome: Centro di Ricerca, 1993.

Lonardo, Pietro M. *Gli ebrei a Pisa alla fine del secolo XV*. Benevento: D'Alessandro, 1899; repr., Bologna: Arnaldo Forni, 1982.

Lopez, Robert. "Familiari, procuratori e dipendenti di Benedetto Zaccaria." In *Su e giù per la storia di Genova*, 329–70. Genoa: Università di Genova, 1975.

– "Proxy in Medieval Trade." In *Order and Innovation in the Middle Ages: Essays in Honor of Joseph R. Strayer*, edited by W.C. Jordan, B. McNab, and T.F. Ruiz, 187–94. Princeton, NJ: Princeton University Press, 1976.

Lorenz, Egon. *Das Dotalstatut in der italienischen Zivilrechtslehre des 13. bis 16. Jahrhunderts.* Cologne: Böhlau, 1965.

Lorenzen-Schmidt, Klaus-Joachim. "Umfang und Dynamik des Hamburger Rentenmarkts zwischen 1471 und 1570." *Zeitschrift des Vereins für Hamburgisches Geschichte* 65 (1979): 21–52.

Luig, Klaus. *Zur Geschichte der Zessionslehre*. Cologne: Böhlau, 1966.

Lumia, Gianna. "Morire a Siena: Divoluzione testamentaria, legami parentali e vincoli affettivi in età moderna." *Bullettino senese di storia patria* 103 (1997): 103–285.

Lumia-Ostinelli, Gianna. "'Ut cippus domus magis conservetur': La successione a Siena tra statuti e testamenti (secoli xii–xvii)." *ASI* 161 (2003): 3–51.

Luzzati, Michele. "Caratteri dell'insediamento ebraico medievale." In *Gli Ebrei di Pisa (secoli IX–XX): Atti del convegno internazionale (Pisa, 3–4 ottobre 1994)*, edited by Michele Luzzati, 1–44. Pisa: Pacini, 1998.

– *La casa dell'Ebreo: Saggi sugli Ebrei a Pisa e in Toscana nel medioevo e nel Rinascimento*. Cultura Storia Pisana 7. Pisa: Nistri-Lischi, 1985.

– *Ebrei ed ebraismo a Pisa: Un millennio di ininterrotta presenza*. Pisa: ETS, 2005.

– "L' insediamento ebraico a Pisa." In *La casa dell'Ebreo*, 17–34.

– "I legami fra i banchi ebraici toscani ed i banchi veneti e dell'Italia settentrionale: Spunti per una riconsiderazione del ruolo economico e politico degli Ebrei nell'età del Rinascimento." In *La casa dell'Ebreo*, 235–64.

– "Matrimoni e apostasia di Clemenza di Vitale da Pisa." In *La casa dell'Ebreo*, 61–106.

Luzzatto, Gino. *Il debito pubblico della repubblica di Venezia: Dagli ultimi decenni del XII secolo alla fine del XV*. Milan: Istituto Editoriale Cisalpino, 1963.

Magagna, Mara. *I patti dotali nel pensiero dei giuristi classici: Per l'autonomia privata nei rapporti patrimoniali tra i coniugi*. Padua: Cedam, 2002.

Mainoni, Patrizia. "Il potere di decidere: Testamenti femminili pugliesi nei secoli XIII–XIV." In *Con animo virile: Donne e potere nel Mezzogiorno medievale, secoli XI–XV*, edited by Patrizia Mainoni, 197–262. Rome: Viella, 2010.

Malanima, Paolo. *I Riccardi di Firenze: Una famiglia e un patrimonio nella Toscana dei Medici*. Florence: Leo S. Olschki, 1977.

Mallett, Michael E. *The Florentine Galleys in the Fifteenth Century*. Oxford: Oxford University Press, 1967.

– "The Sea Consuls of Florence in the Fifteenth Century." *Papers of the British School of Rome* 27 (1959): 156–68.

Manfredi, Mario, and Ada Mangano. *Alle origini del diritto femminile: Cultura giuridica e ideologie*. Bari: Dedalo, 1983.

Marchetti, Paolo. "*De iure finium*": *Diritto e confini tra tardo medioevo ed età moderna*. Milan: Giuffrè, 2001.

Marchetto, Giuliano. *Il divorzio imperfetto: I giuristi medievali e la separazione dei coniugi*. Bologna: Il Mulino, 2008.

– "Matrimoni incerti tra dottrina e prassi: Un *consilium sapientis* iudiciale di Baldo degli Ubaldi (1327–1400)." In *Matrimoni in dubbio: Unioni controverse e nozze clandestine in Italia dal XIV al XVIII secolo, Annali dell'Istituto storico italo-germanico in Trento*, Quaderni 57, edited by Silvana Seidel Menchi and Diego Quaglioni, 83–105. Bologna: Il Mulino, 1998.

Margiotta-Broglio, Francesco. "Il divieto per gli ebrei di accedere alle cariche pubbliche e il problema della giurisdizione ecclesiastica sugli infedeli nel sistema canonistico fino alle decretali di Gregorio IX: Appunti e ricerche." In *Études d'histoire du droit canonique dédiées à Gabriel Le Bras*, vol. 2, 1070–85. Paris: Sirey, 1965.

Marks, Louis F. "The Financial Oligarchy in Florence under Lorenzo." In *Italian Renaissance Studies: A Tribute to the Late Cecilia M. Ady*, edited by Ernest F. Jacob, 123–47. New York: Barnes & Noble, 1960.

Marshall, Richard K. *The Local Merchants of Prato: Small Entrepreneurs in the Late Medieval Economy*. Baltimore and London: Johns Hopkins University Press, 1999.

Martelozzo Forin, Elda "Note sulla famiglia del giurista pisano Benedetto da Piombino († 1410)" *Quaderni per la storia dell'Università di Padova* 33 (2000): 45–68.

Martines, Lauro. *Lawyers and Statecraft in Renaissance Florence.* Princeton, NJ: Princeton University Press, 1968.

– "The Renaissance and the Birth of a Consumer Society." *Renaissance Quarterly* 51 (1998): 197–203.

– *The Social World of the Florentine Humanists, 1390–1460*. Princeton, NJ: Princeton University Press, 1963.

Martino, Federico. "Umanisti, giuristi, uomini di Stato a Firenze fra Trecento e Quattrocento. Lorenzo d'Antonio Ridolfi." In *Studi in memoria di Mario Condorelli*, 177–200. Milan: Giuffrè, 1988.

Masi Doria, Carla. *Civitas operae obsequium: Tre studi sulla condizione giuridica dei liberti.* Naples: Jovene, 1993.

Massetto, Gian Paolo. "Il lucro dotale nella dottrina e nella legislazione statutaria lombarda dei secoli XIV–XVI." In *Ius Mediolani: Studi di storia del diritto milanese offerti dagli allievi a Giulio Vismara*, 189–364. Milan: Giuffrè, 1996.

Mayali, Laurent. *Droit savant et coutumes: L' exclusion des filles dotées XIIème–XVème siècles*. Ius commune, Studien zur europäischen Rechtsgeschichte 33. Frankfurt am Main: V. Klostermann, 1987.

– "*Due erunt in carne una* and the Medieval Canonists." In *Iuris Historia: Liber Amicorum Gero Dolezalek*, Studies in Comparative Legal History, edited by Vincenzo Colli and Emanuele Conte, 161–75. Berkeley: Robbins Collection, 2008.

– "La notion de *statutum odiosum* dans la doctrine romaniste au Moyen Âge: Remarques sur la fonction du docteur." *Ius commune: Zeitschrift für europäische Rechtsgeschichte* 12 (1984): 57–69.

Mazzacane, Aldo. "Decio, Filippo." In *DBI*, vol. 32, 554–60. Rome: Istituto della Enciclopedia Italiana, 1987.

Mazzi, Maria Serena, and Sergio Raveggi. *Gli uomini e le cose nelle campagne fiorentine del Quattrocento.* Florence: L.S. Olschki, 1983.

McLaughlin, Terence P. "The Teaching of the Canonists on Usury (XII, XIII, & XIV Centuries)." *Mediaeval Studies* 1 (1939): 81–147.

Meek, Christine. *The Commune of Lucca under Pisan Rule, 1342–1369*. Cambridge, MA: Harvard University Press, 1980.

– "Il matrimonio e le nozze: Sposarsi a Lucca nel tardo medioevo." In *I tribunali del matrimonio (secoli XV–XVIII), Annali dell'Istituto storico italo-germanico in Trento*, Quaderni 68, edited by Silvana Seidel Menchi and Diego Quaglioni, 359–73. Bologna: Il Mulino, 2006.

– "Un'unione incerta: La vicenda di Neria, figlia dell'organista, e di Baldassino, merciaio pistoiese (Lucca 1396–1397)." In *Matrimoni in dubbio: Unioni controverse e nozze clandestine in Italia dal XIV al XVIII secolo, Annali dell'Istituto storico italo-germanico in Trento*, Quaderni 57, edited by Silvana Seidel Menchi and Diego Quaglioni, 107–21. Bologna: Il Mulino, 1998.

– "Women between the Law and Social Reality in Early Renaissance Lucca." In *Women in Italian Renaissance Culture and Society*, edited by Letizia Panizza, 182–93. Oxford: Legenda, 2000.

– "Women, the Church, and the Law: Matrimonial Litigation in Lucca under Bishop Niccolao Guinigi (1394–1435)." In *Chattel, Servant, or Citizen: Women's Status in Church, State, and Society*, edited by Mary O'Dowd and Sabine Wichert, 82–90. Belfast: Institute of Irish Studies, 1995.

Melis, Federigo. "Sulla non-astrattezza dei titoli di credito del basso medioevo." In *Studi in onore di Giuseppe Chiarelli*, vol. 4, 3687–3701. Milan: Giuffrè, 1974. Reprinted in Federigo Melis, *La banca pisana e le origini della banca moderna*, edited by Marco Spallanzani, no. 7. Florence: Le Monnier, 1987.

Menzinger, Sara. "La donna medievale nella sfera pubblica: Alcune riflessioni in tema di cittadinanza nel panorama degli studi storico-giuridici." In *La condizione giuridica delle donne nel medioevo: Atti del convegno di studio-Trieste, 23 novembre 2010*, edited by Miriam Davide, 117–43. Trieste: CERM, 2012.

Metz, René. "L'enfant dans le droit canonique médiéval: Orientations de recherche." In *L'enfant*, vol. 2, *Europe médiévale et moderne*, Recueils de la Société Jean Bodin 36, 9–96. Brussels: Société Jean Bodin, 1976. Reprinted in René Metz, *La femme et l'enfant dans le droit canonique médiéval*, no. 1. London: Variorum, 1985.

Meyer, Andreas. "Hereditary Laws and City Topography: On the Development of the Italian Notarial Archives in the Late Middle Ages." In *Urban Space in the Middle Ages and the Early Modern Age (Fundamentals of Medieval and Early Modern Culture* 4), edited by Albrecht Classen, 225–44. Berlin: Walter de Gruyter, 2009.

– *Zürich und Rom: ordentliche Kollatur und päpstliche Provisionen am Frau- und Grossmünster 1316–1523*. Tübingen: Niemeyer, 1986.

Michaud, Francine. *Un signe des temps: Accroissement des crises familiales autour du patrimoine à Marseille à la fin du XIIIe siècle*. Toronto: Pontifical Institute of Mediaeval Studies, 1994.

Milani, Giuliano. *L'esclusione dal comune: Conflitti e bandi politici a Bologna e in altre città italiane tra XII e XIV secolo*. Rome: Istituto storico italiano per il Medio Evo, 2003.

Mineo, E. Igor. *Nobilità di stato: Famiglie e identità aristocratiche nel tardo medioevo: La Sicilia*. Rome: Donzelli Editore, 2001.

Misera, Karlheinz. "Die Zeugnisse zum Grund des Schenkungsverbots unter Ehegatten." In *Festschrift für Max Kaser zum 70. Geburtstag*, edited by Dieter Medicus and Hans Hermann Seiler, 407–35. Munich: C.H. Beck, 1976.

Modigliani, Anna. *I Porcari: Storie di una famiglia romana tra Medioevo e Rinascimento*. Rome: Roma nel Rinascimento, 1994.

Molà, Luca. "Le donne nell'industria serica veneziana del Rinascimento." In *La seta in Italia dal Medioevo al Seicento: Dal baco al drappo*, edited by Luca Molà, Reinhold C. Mueller, and Claudio Zanier. 423–59. Venice: Marsilio, 2000.

Molho, Anthony. "L'amministrazione del debito pubblico a Firenze nel quindicesimo secolo." In *I ceti dirigenti della Toscana del Quattrocento*, edited by Riccardo Fubini, 191–207. Florence: Francesco Papafava, 1987. Reprinted in Molho, *Firenze nel Quattrocento*, vol. 1,no. 6.

– *Firenze nel Quattrocento*. Vol. 1, *Politica e fiscalità*. Rome: Edizioni di Storia e Letteratura, 2006. Vol. 2, *Famiglia e società*. 2008.

– *Florentine Public Finances in the Early Renaissance, 1400–1433*. Cambridge, MA: Harvard University Press, 1971.

– "Investimenti nel Monte delle doti di Firenze: Un'analisi sociale e geografica." *Quaderni storici* 61 (1986): 147–70. Reprinted in Molho, *Firenze nel Quattrocento*, vol. 2, no. 5.

– *Marriage Alliance in Late Medieval Florence.* Cambridge, MA: Harvard University Press, 1994.

–"Visions of the Florentine Family in the Renaissance." *Journal of Modern History* 50 (1978): 304–11.

Molho, Anthony, and Franek Sznura, eds. "*Brighe, affanni, volgimenti di Stato*": *Le ricordanze di Luca di Matteo di messer Luca del Firidolfi da Panzano.* Memoria Scripturarum 5; Testi in volgare 2. Florence: Sismel, Edizioni del Galluzzo, 2010.

Molina Meliá, Antonio. *La disolución del matrimonio inconsumado: Antecedentes históricos y derecho vigente*. Salamanca: Universidad Pontifica de Salamanca, 1987.

Mooney, Anthony Michael Christopher. "The Legal Ban in Florentine Statutory Law and the 'De Bannitis' of Nello da San Gimignano, 1373–1430." PhD diss., University of California, Los Angeles, 1976.

Morandini, Francesca. "Statuti e ordinamenti dell'Ufficio dei pupilli et adulti nel periodo della Repubblica fiorentina (1388–1534)." *ASI* 113 (1955): 521–51; 114 (1956): 92–117.

Mordenti, Raul. "Les livres de famille en Italie." *Annales: Histoire, sciences sociales* 59 (2004): 785–804.

Moreno, Paola. "Guicciardiani, Jacopo." In *DBI* 61 (2004): 118–21.

Mueller, Reinhold C. *Immigrazione e cittadinanza nella Venezia medievale.* Rome: Viella, 2010.

– "The Status and Economic Activity of Jews in the Venetian Dominions during the Fifteenth Century." In *Wirtschaftsgeschichte der mittelalterlichen Juden: Fragen und Einschätzungen*, Schriften des Historischen Kollegs, Kolloquien 71, edited by Michael Toch and Elisabeth Müller-Luckner, 63–92. Munich: Oldenbourg, 2008.

– "Lo status degli ebrei nella Terraferma veneta del Quattrocento: Tra politica, religione, cultura ed economia: Saggio introduttivo." In *Ebrei nella Terraferma veneta del Quattrocento: Atti del convegno di studi Verona (14 novembre 2003)*, edited by Gian Maria Varanini and Reinhold C. Mueller, 9–24. Florence: Firenze University Press, 2005.

– *The Venetian Money Market.* Vol. 2, *Banks, Panics, and the Public Debt, 1200–1500.* Baltimore: Johns Hopkins University Press, 1997.

Muir, Edward. "In Some Neighbours We Trust: On the Exclusion of Women from the Public in Renaissance Italy." In *Florence and Beyond: Culture, Society and Politics in Renaissance Italy: Essays in Honour of John M. Najemy*, edited by Daniel Bornstein and David S. Peterson, 271–90. Toronto: Centre for Reformation and Renaissance Studies, 2008.

Müller, Daniela. "*Vir caput mulieris*: Zur Stellung der Frau im Kirchenrecht unter besonderer Berücksichtigung des 12. und 13. Jahrhunderts." In *Vom mittelalterlichen Recht zur neuzeitlichen Rechtswissenschaft*: *Bedingungen, Wege und Probleme der europäischen Rechtsgeschichte*, edited by Norbert Brieskorn, Paul Mikat, Daniela Müller, and Dietmar Willoweit, 223–46. Paderborn: F. Schöningh, 1994.

Musacchio, Jacqueline M. *The Art and Ritual of Childbirth in Renaissance Italy.* New Haven, CT: Yale University Press, 1999.

– *Art, Marriage, & Family in the Florentine Renaissance Palace.* New Haven, CT: Yale University Press, 2008.

– "The Bride and Her *Donora* in Renaissance Florence." In *Culture and Change: Attending to Early Modern Women: Gender, Culture, and Change*, edited by Margaret L. Mikesell and Adele F. Seeff, 177–202. Newark: University of Delaware Press, 2003.

– "The Rape of the Sabine Women on Quattrocento Marriage-Panels." In *Marriage in Italy, 1300–1500*, edited by Trevor Dean and Kate J.P. Lowe, 66–84. New York: Cambridge University Press, 1998.

Musson, Anthony. "Images of Marriage: A Comparison of Law, Custom, and Practice in Medieval Europe." In *Regional Variations in Matrimonial Law and Custom in Europe, 1150–1600*, edited by Mia Korpiola, 117–46. Leiden: Brill, 2011.

Muzzarelli, Maria Giuseppina. "I banchieri ebrei e la città." In *Banchi ebraici a Bologna nel XV secolo*, edited by Maria G. Muzzarelli, 89–157. Bologna: Il Mulino, 1994.

– "La disciplina delle apparenze: Vesti e ornamenti nella legislazione suntuaria bolognese fra XIII e XV secolo." In *Disciplina dell'anima, disciplina del corpo e disciplina della società tra medioevo ed età moderna*, edited by Paolo Prodi, 757–84. Bologna: Il Mulino, 1994.

– *Guardaroba medievale: Vesti e società dal XIII al XVI secolo*. Bologna: Il Mulino, 1999.

– *Gli inganni delle apparenze: Disciplina di veste e ornamenti alla fine del medioevo*. Turin: Scriptorium, 1996.

Najemy, John M. "Politics and Political Thought." In *Palgrave Advances in Renaissance Historiography*, edited by Jonathan Woolfson, 271–97. Basingstoke, Hampshire: Palgrave Macmillan, 2004.

Nardi, Paolo. *Mariano Sozzini, giureconsulto senese del Quattrocento*. Milan: Giuffrè, 1974.

Niccolai, Franco. *La formazione del diritto successorio negli statuti comunali del territorio lombardo-tosco.* Milan: Giuffrè, 1940.

Niccoli, Ottavia. "Baci rubati: Gesti e riti nunziali in Italia prima e dopo il Concilio di Trento." In *Il gesto: Nel rito e nel cerimoniale dal mondo antico ad oggi*, edited by Sergio Bertelli and Monica Centanni, 224–44. Florence: Ponte alle Grazie, 1995.

Niccolini di Camugliano, Ginevra. *The Chronicles of a Florentine Family, 1200–1470*. London: Cape, 1933.

Nico Ottaviani, Maria G. "De glie ariede e fregiature: Alcune considerazioni sulla legislazione suntuaria tra Tre e Quattrocento." In *Studi sull'Umbria medievale e umanistica*, edited by Mauro Donnini and Enrico Menestò, 335–66. Spoleto: Centro Italiano di Studi sull'Alto Medioevo, 2000.

– "*De vanitate mulierum:* Donne, lusso, moderazione e stile di vita nel tardo medioevo." In *"Visibilità" delle donne tra Medioevo ed Età moderna: Carte private e pubbliche apparenze, lusso, e prescrizioni*, edited by Maria Grazia Nico Ottaviani, Università degli Studi di Perugia, *Annali della Facoltà di*

Lettere e Filosfia 2, Studi Storico-Antropologici 34–5 (= n.s., 20–1; 1996/97–1997/98): 39–56.
– "La practica testamentaria femminile a Perugia (secoli XV–XVI)." In *Margini di libertà: Testamenti femminili nel medioevo*, edited by Maria Clara Rossi, 355–80. Verona: Cierre, 2010.
– "*Res sit magni momenti et concernet statum civitatis*: La legislazione suntuaria tra pubblico e privato (secoli XIII–XVI)." In *Famiglie e poteri in Italia tra medioevo ed età moderna*, Collection de l'École Française de Rome 422, edited by Anna Bellavitis and Isabelle Chabot, 373–82. Rome: École Française de Rome, 2009.
Noonan, John Thomas. *The Scholastic Analysis of Usury*. Cambridge, MA: Harvard University Press, 1957.
Nörr, Dieter. "Origo." In *Realencyclopädie der classischen Alterumswissenschaft*, edited by Georg Wissowa, *Supplementband* 10, 433–73. Stuttgart: A. Druckenmüller, 1965.
Nörr, Knut Wolfgang. *Romanisch-kanonisches Prozessrecht: Erkenntnisverfahren erster Instanz in civilibus*. Berlin, Heidelberg: Springer, 2012.
Novarese, Daniela. "Un *consilium* maltese di Giovanni da Imola e la disciplina della comunione dei beni fra coniugi in Sicilia." *RSDI* 60 (1987): 205–54.
Oberto, Giacomo. *La promessa di matrimonio tra passato e presente*. Padua: CEDAM, 1996.
O'Donnell, Cletus Francis. *The Marriage of Minors: An Historical Synopsis and Commentary*. Washington, DC: Catholic University of America Press, 1945.
Oldfield, Paul. "Citizenship and Community in Southern Italy c.1100–c.1220." *Papers of the British School at Rome* 74 (2006): 323–38.
O'Malley, Michelle, and Evelyn Welch, eds. *The Material Renaissance*. Manchester: Manchester University Press, 2007.
Onclin, Willy. "L'âge requis pour le mariage dans la doctrine canonique médiévale." In *Proceedings of the Second International Congress of Medieval Canon Law*, edited by Stephan Kuttner and J.J. Ryan, 237–47. Vatican City: Vatican Library, 1965.
– "La doctrine de Bartole sur les conflicts de lois et son influence en Belgique." In *Bartolo da Sassoferrato: Studi e documenti per il VI centenario*, edited by Danilo Segoloni, 373–98. Milan: Giuffrè, 1962.
Orlandi, Stefano. "Il convento di S. Domenico di Fiesole." *Memorie Domenicane* 4 (1960): 3–180.
Orlando, Ermanno. *Sposarsi nel medioevo: Percorsi congiugali tra Venezia, mare e continente*. Rome: Viella, 2010.
Ottenthal, Emil von, ed. *Regulae cancellariae apostolicae: Die päpstlichen Kanzleiregeln von Johannes XXII. bis Nikolaus V*. Innsbruck, 1888; repr., Aalen: Scientia, 1968.
Pakter, Walter. *Medieval Canon Law and the Jews*. Ebelsbach: Gremler, 1988.

Pampaloni, Guido. "Prato nella Repubblica fiorentina." In *Storia di Prato, secolo XIV–XVI*, vol. 2, 1–218. Prato: Edizioni Cassa di Risparmi e Depositi, 1980.

Pandimiglio, Leonida. *Famiglia e memoria a Firenze*. Vol. 1, *Secoli XIII–XVI*. Rome: Edizioni di Storia e Letteratura, 2010.

– "Giovanni di Pagolo Morelli e la continuità familiare." *Studi medievali*, ser. 3, 22 (1981): 129–81. Reprinted in Pandimiglio, *Famiglia e memoria*, vol. 1, no. 10, 3.

– *I libri di famiglia e il "libro segreto" di Goro Dati*. Alessandria: Edizioni dell'Orso, 2006.

Paoli, Baldassarre. *Del matrimonio rispetto ai beni*. Turin: Fratelli Bocca, 1887.

Park, Katharine. "The Readers at The Florentine Studio according to Communal Fiscal Records." *Rinascimento* 20 (1980): 249–310.

Passerini, Luigi. *Gli Alberti di Firenze: Genealogia, storia e documenti*. 2 vols. Florence: M. Cellini, 1869.

Payer, Pierre J. *The Bridling of Desire: Views of Sex in the Later Middle Ages*. Toronto: University of Toronto Press, 1993.

Pazzaglini, Peter Raymond. *The Criminal Ban of the Sienese Commune, 1225–1310*. Quaderni di Studi Senesi 45. Milan: Giuffrè, 1979.

Pecchiai, Pio. "Il libro di ricordi d'un gentiluomo pisano del secolo XV." *Studi storici diretti da A. Crivellucci* 14 (1905): 297–345.

Pederson, Frederik. "Did the Medieval Laity Know the Canon Law Rules on Marriage? Some Evidence from Fourteenth-Century York Cause Papers." *Mediaeval Studies* 56 (1994): 111–52.

Pene Vidari, Gian Savino. "Dote, Famiglia e patrimonio fra dottrina e pratica in Piemonte." In *La famiglia e la vita quotidiana in Europa dal '400 al '600: Fonti e problemi, Atti del convegno internazionale, Milano, 1–4 dicembre 1983*, 109–22. Rome: Ministero per i Beni Culturali e Ambientali, 1986.

– *Ricerche sul diritto agli alimenti*. Turin: Giappichelli, 1972.

– "Il trattato sugli alimenti di Martino di Fano." In *Medioevo notarile: Martino da Fano e il Formularium super contractibus et libellis*, Fonti e strumenti per la storia del notariato italiano 10, edited by Vito Piergiovanni, 83–112. Milan: Giuffrè, 2007.

Pennington, Kenneth. "Allegationes, Solutiones, and Dubitationes: Baldus de Ubaldis' Revisions of His *Consilia*." In *Die Kunst der Disputationen: Probleme der Rechtsauslegung und Rechtsanwendung im 13. und 14. Jahrhundert*, Schriften des Historischen Kollegs, Kolloquien 38, edited by Manlio Bellomo, 29–72. Munich: Oldenbourg, 1997.

Perelman, Chaim, and Lucie Olbrechts-Tyteca. *The New Rhetoric: A Treatise on Argumentation*. Translated by John Wilkinson and Purcell Weaver. Notre Dame: University of Notre Dame Press, 1969.

Pertile, Antonio. *Storia del diritto italiano: Dalla caduta dell'impero romano alla codificazione*, 6 vols. in 8. Turin: Unione Tipografica-Editrice Torinese, 1892–1902; repr., Bologna: Arnaldo Forni, 1965.

Petralia, Giuseppe. "'Crisi' e emigrazione dei ceti eminenti a Pisa durante il primo dominio fiorentino: L'orizzonte cittadino e la ricerca di spazi esterni (1406–1460)." In *I Ceti Dirigenti nella Toscana del Quattrocento: Atti del V et VI convegno del comitato di studi sulla storia dei ceti dirigenti in Toscana (Firenze, 10–11 dicembre 1982; 2–3 dicembre 1983)*, edited by Donatella Rugiadini, 291–352. Monte Oriolo, Impruneta: Papafava, 1987.

– "Fiscality, Politics and Dominion in Florentine Tuscany at the End of the Middle Ages." In *Florentine Tuscany: Structures and Practices of Power*, edited by William J. Connell and Andrea Zorzi, 65–89. Cambridge: Cambridge University Press, 2000.

Petti Balbi, Giovanna, and Paola Guglielmotti, eds. *Dare credito alle donne: Presenze femminili nell'economia tra medioevo ed età moderna. Atti di convegno internazionali di studi, Asti, 8–9 ottobre 2010.* Asti: Centro di Studi Renato Bordone, 2012.

Piccinni, Gabriella. "Le donne nella mezzadria toscana delle origini: Materiali per la definizione del ruolo femminile nelle campagne." *Ricerche storiche* 15 (1985): 127–82.

Piergiovanni, Vito. "Banchieri e falliti nelle 'Decisiones de mercatura' della Rota Civile di Genova." In *Diritto comune, diritto commerciale, diritto veneziano*, edited by Karin Nehlsen-von Stryk and Dieter Nörr, 17–38. Venice: Centro Tedescho di Studi Veneziani, 1985.

Pierro, M. "Le leggi suntuarie e il problema demografico nel medioevo." *Politica sociale: La legislazione sociale del regime fascista e la più avanzata del mondo* 1 (1930): 13–23.

Pinto, Giuliano. "Forme di conduzione e rendita fondiaria nel contado fiorentino: Le terre dell'ospedale dì San Gallo." In *La Toscana nel tardo medioevo*, 247–330. Florence: Sansoni, 1981.

Pinzi, Cesare. *Storia della città di Viterbo, illustrata con note e nuovi documenti in gran parte inediti.* 4 vols. Rome: Tipografia della Camera dei Deputati; Viterbo: Tipografia Sociale Agnesotti, 1887–1913.

Pistarino, Geo. "La donna d'affari a Genova nel secolo XIII." In *Miscellanea di storia italiana e mediterranea per Nino Lamboglia*, edited by G. Pistarino, 155–69. Genoa: Università di Genova, 1978.

Pluss, Jacques Anthony. "Baldus de Ubaldis of Perugia on *Dominium* over Dotal Property." *RHD* 52 (1984): 399–411.

– "Baldus de Ubaldis on Dowry Law." PhD diss., University of Chicago, 1983.

– "Baldus of Perugia on Female and Male: The Case of Allumella." *Thought* 64 (1989): 221–30.

– "Reading Case Law Historically: A *Consilium* of Baldus de Ubaldis on Widows and Dowries." *American Journal of Legal History* 30 (1986): 241–65.

Polizzotto, Lorenzo, and Catherine Kovesi, eds. *Memorie di Casa Valori*. Florence: Nerbini, 2007.

Polonio, Valeria. "'Consentirono l'un l'altro': Il matrimonio in Liguria tra XI e XIV secolo." *Serta antiqua et mediaevalia* 5 (2001): 23–53.

Pommeray, Léon. *L'officialité archidiaconale de Paris aux XV–XVIe siècles: Sa composition et sa compétence criminelle*. Paris: Sirey, 1933.

Postan, Michael M. "Private Financial Instruments in Medieval England." In *Medieval Trade and Finance*, 29–64. Cambridge: Cambridge University Press, 1973.

Potenti, Alessandra. *Uomini, villaggi, terreni: Aspetti economici e demografici delle campagne pisane del Quattrocento.* Pisa: Pacini, 2002.

Pratt, John W. "Risk Aversion in the Small and in the Large." *Econometrica* 32 (1964): 122–36.

Prodi, Paolo. *Il sacramento del potere: Il giuramento politico nella storia costituzionale dell'Occidente*. Bologna: Il Mulino, 1992.

– *Il sovrano pontifice.* Bologna: Il Mulino, 1982.

Prosdocimi, Luigi. "'Roma communis patria' nella tradizione giuridica della cristianità medievale." In *Da Roma alla terza Roma*, vol. 2, *La nozione di "romano" tra cittadinanza e universalità*, 43–8. Naples: Edizioni Scientifiche Italiane, 1984.

Pryor, John H. "The Origins of the Commenda Contract." *Speculum* 52 (1977): 5–37.

Pullan, Brian. "Jewish Moneylending in Venice: From Private Enterprise to Public Service." In *Gli Ebrei e Venezia: Secoli XIV–XVIII: Atti del convegno internazionale organizzato dall'Istituto di storia della società e dello Stato veneziano della Fondazione Giorgio Cini, Venezia, Isola di San Giorgio Maggiore (5–10 giugno 1983)*, edited by Gaetano Cozzi, 671–86. Milan: Edizioni Comunità, 1987.

Quadri, Rolando. "Cittadinanza." In *Novissimo digesto italiano*, vol. 3, 306–35. Turin: Unione Tipografica-Editrice Torinese, 1959.

Quaglioni, Diego. "Legislazione statutaria e dottrina della legislazione: Le *Quaestiones Statutorum* di Alberico da Rosciate." In "*Civilis sapientia*": *Dottrine giuridiche e dottrine politiche fra medioevo ed età moderna*, 35–75. Rimini: Maggioli, 1989.

– "Le radici teoriche della dottrina bartoliana della cittadinanza." In "*Civilis sapientia*": *Dottrine giuridiche e dottrine politiche fra medioevo ed età moderna*, 127–44. Rimini: Maggioli, 1989.

– "Segni, rituali e simboli nuziali nel diritto." In *I tribunali del matrimonio (secoli XV–XVIII), Annali dell'Istituto storico italo-germanico in Trento*, Quaderni 68, edited by Silvana Seidel Menchi and Diego Quaglioni, 43–66. Bologna: Il Mulino, 2006.

– "*Standum canonistis*?" In *Credito e usura fra teologia, diritto e amministrazione: Linguaggi a confronto (sec. XII–XVI)*, Collection de l'École Française de Rome 346, edited by Diego Quaglioni, Giacomo Todeschini, and Gian Maria Varanini, 247–64. Rome: École Française de Rome, 2005.

Radke, Gary M., ed. *The Gates of Paradise: Lorenzo Ghiberti's Renaissance Masterpiece*. Atlanta: High Museum of Art; New Haven, CT: Yale University Press, 2007.

Rainey, Ronald E. "Dressing Down the Dressed-Up: Reproving Feminine Attire in Renaissance Florence." In *Renaissance Society and Culture: Essays in Honor of Eugene F. Rice, Jr.*, edited by John Monfasani and Ronald G. Musto, 217–37. New York: Italica Press, 1991.

– "Sumptuary Legislation in Renaissance Florence." 2 vols. PhD diss., Columbia University, 1985.

Randolph, Adrian W.B. "Performing the Bridal Body in Fifteenth-Century Florence." *Art History* 21 (1998): 182–200.

Rasi, Piero. "La conclusione del matrimonio prima del Concilio di Trento." *RSDI* 16 (1943): 233–321.

– "Il diritto matrimoniale nei glossatori." In *Studi di storia e diritto in onore di Carlo Calisse*, vol. 1, 129–58. Milan: Giuffré, 1939.

Reid, Charles J., Jr. *Power over the Body, Equality in the Family: Rights and Domestic Relations in Medieval Canon Law.* Grand Rapids, MI: Eerdmans, 2004.

Reyerson, Kathryn. *The Art of the Deal: Intermediaries of Trade in Medieval Montpellier*. Leiden: Brill, 2002.

Reynolds, Philip Lyndon. *Marriage in the Western Church: The Christianization of Marriage during the Patristic Medieval Periods*. Leiden: Brill, 1994.

Rheubottom, David. *Age, Marriage, and Politics in Fifteenth-Century Ragusa*. Oxford: Oxford University Press, 2000.

Ricci, Armando. "Storia di un comune rurale dell'Umbria." *Annali della Scuola Normale Superiore di Pisa* 25 (1913): 2–184.

Ricci, Simona. "*De hac vita transire*": *La pratica testamentaria nel Valdarno superiore all'indomani della peste nera*. Figline Valdarno: Comune di Figline Valdarno, Opus Libri, 1998.

Riemer, Eleanor S. "Women, Dowries, and Capital Investment in Thirteenth-Century Siena." In *The Marriage Bargain: Women and Dowries in European History*, edited by Marion A. Kaplan, 59–79. New York: Institute for Research in History and Haworth Press, 1985.

– "Women in the Medieval City: Sources and Uses of Wealth by Sienese Women in the Thirteenth Century." PhD diss., New York University, 1975.

Rinaldi, Evelina. "La donna negli statuti del comune di Forlì, sec. XIV." *Studi storici* 18 (1909): 185–200.

Rinaldi, Rosella. "Figure femminili nel sistema produttivo bolognese (secc. XIII–XIV)." In *Dare credito alle donne: Presenze femminili nell'economia tra medioevo ed età moderna, Atti di convegno internazionali di studi, Asti, 8–9 ottobre 2010*, edited by Giovanna Petti Balbi and Paola Guglielmotti, 101–20. Asti: Centro di Studi Renato Bordone, 2012.

Robinson, Olivia F. "The Historical Background." In *The Legal Relevance of Gender: Some Aspects of Sex-Based Discrimination*, edited by Sheila McLean and Noreen Burrows, 40–60. Atlantic Highlands, NJ: Humanities Press International, 1988.

– "The Status of Women in Roman Private Law." *Juridical Review* 22 (1987): 143–62.

Rocke, Michael. *Forbidden Friendships: Homosexuality and Male Culture in Renaissance Florence*. Oxford: Oxford University Press, 1996.

– "Gender and Sexual Culture in Renaissance Italy." In *Gender and Society in Renaissance Italy*, edited by Judith C. Brown and Robert C. Davis, 150–70. London: Addison Wesley Longman, 1998.

Rollo-Koster, Joëlle, "The Women of Papal Avignon: A New Source: The *Liber Divisionis* of 1371." *Journal of Women's History* 8 (1996): 36–59.

Romano, Andrea. *Famiglia, successioni e patrimonio familiare nell'Italia medievale e moderna*. Turin: G. Giappichelli. 1994.

Romiti, R. "Le concessioni del privilegio della cittadinanza a Lucca dal 1369 al 1448." Tesi di laurea, Facoltà di Lettere e Filsofia, Università di Pisa, 1983–4.

Roover, Raymond de. "Review of Rosenthal, Gilbert S., ed. and trans., *Banking and Finance among Jews in Renaissance Italy: A Critical Edition of The Eternal Life (Haye olam) by Yehiel Nissim da Pisa*." *Business History Review* 37 (1963): 458–9.

Rosenthal, Elaine. "The Position of Women in Renaissance Florence: Neither Autonomy nor Subjection." In *Florence and Italy: Renaissance Studies in*

Honour of Nicolai Rubinstein, Westfield Publications in Medieval Studies, vol. 2, edited by Peter Denley and Caroline Elam, 369–81. London: Westfield College, University of London, 1989.

Rosier-Catach, Irène. *La parole efficace: Signe, rituel, sacré*. Paris: Seuil, 2004.

Rossi Caponeri, Marilena. "Nota su alcuni testamenti della fine del secolo XIV relativi alla zona di Orvieto." In *Nolens intestatus decedere: Il testamento come fonte della storia religiosa e sociale*, 105–11. Perugia: Regione dell'Umbria–Editrice Umbra Cooperativa, 1985.

Roumy, Franck. *L'adoption dans le droit savant du XIIe au XVIe siècle*. Paris: L.G.D.J., 1998.

Ruggiero, Guido. *The Boundaries of Eros: Sex Crime and Sexuality in Renaissance Venice*. New York: Oxford University Press, 1985.

Rugolo, Carmela Maria. "Donna e lavoro nella Sicilia del basso medioevo." In *Donne e lavoro nell'Italia medievale*, edited by Bruno Andreolli, Paola Galetti, and Maria Giuseppina Muzzarelli, 67–82. Turin: Rosenberg & Sellier, 1991.

Rupp, Leila J. *Worlds of Women: The Making of an International Women's Movement.* Princeton, NJ: Princeton University Press, 1997.

Rusconi, Roberto. "St. Bernardino of Siena, the Wife, and Possessions." In *Women and Religion in Medieval and Renaissance Italy*, edited by Daniel Bornstein and Roberto Rusconi, trans. M.J. Schneider, 182–96. Chicago: University of Chicago Press, 1996.

Saller, Richard P. "*Pietas*, Obligation and Authority in the Roman Family." In *Alte Geschichte und Wissenschaftsgeschichte: Festschrift für Karl Christ zum 65. Geburtstag*, edited by Peter Kneissl and Volker Losemann, 393–410. Darmstadt: Wissenschaftliche Buchgesellschaft, 1988.

Salonen, Kirsi. "Marriage Disputes in the Court of Freising." In *Regional Variations in Matrimonial Law and Custom in Europe, 1150–1600*, edited by Mia Korpiola, 189–210. Leiden: Brill, 2011.

Salvemini, Gaetano. *Magnati e popolani in Firenze dal 1280 al 1295*. Florence: Carnesecchi, 1899.

Santarelli, Umberto. *Per la storia del fallimento nelle legislazioni italiane dell'età intermedia*. Padua: CEDAM, 1964.

Sapiro, Virginia. "Women, Citizenship, and Nationality: Immigration and Naturalization Policies in the United States." *Politics and Society* 13 (1984): 1–26.

Sapori, Armando. "Il libro di amministrazione dell'eredità di Baldovino Iacopi Riccomanni (1272–1274)." *ASI* 106 (1938): 88–113.

Saraceno, Chiara. "Women, Family, and the Law, 1750–1942." *Journal of Family History* 15 (1990): 427–42.

Saradi-Mendelovici, Helen. "A Contribution to the Study of the Byzantine Notarial Formulas: The *Infirmitas Sexus* of Women and the *Sc. Velleianum.*" *Byzantinische Zeitschrift* 83 (1990): 72–90.

Sastre Santos, Eutimio. "Sobre el aforismo: *Adulter est in suam uxorem amator ardentior* allegado en el Decreto: C. 32 q.4 c.5." *Apollinaris* 57 (1984): 587–626.

Sbriccoli, Mario. *L'interpretazione dello statuto: Contributo allo studio della funzione dei giuristi nell'età comunale*. Milan: Giuffrè, 1969.

Scalvanti, Oscar. "Notizie e documenti sulla vita di Baldo, Angelo e Pietro degli Ubaldi." In *L'opera di Baldo, per cura dell'Università di Perugia nel V centenario della morte del grande giureconsulto*, edited by Oscar Scalvanti, 279–98. Perugia: Università di Perugia, 1901.

Schanbacher, Dietmar. *Die Konvaleszenz von Pfandrechten im klassischen römischen Recht*. Berlin: Duncker & Humblot, 1987.

Scharf, Gian Paolo G. "Amor di patria e interessi commerciali: I Maggiolini da Pisa a Milano nel Quattrocento." *Studi storici* 35 (1994): 943–76.

Schmandt, Matthias. *Judei, cives et incole: Studien zur jüdischen Geschichte Kölns im Mittelalter.* Hannover: Hahnsche Buchhandlung, 2002.

Schmid, Karl. "Heirat, Familienfolge, Geschlechterbewusstsein." In *Il matrimonio nella società altomedievale*, vol. 2, 103–37. Spoleto: CISAM, 1977.

Schmitt, Pauline. "Athéna Apatouria et la ceinture: Les aspects féminins des Apatouries à Athènes." *Annales économies sociétés civilisations* 32 (1977): 1059–73.

Schupfer, Francesco. "L'autorizzazione maritale: Studi sugli statuti municipali italiani." In *Pel cinquantesimo anni d'insegnamento del professore Francesco Pepere*, 5–11. Naples: Società Anonima Cooperativa, 1900.

Schwinges, Rainer Christoph, ed. *Neubürger im späten Mittelalter: Migration und Austausch in der Städtelandschaft (1250–1550)*. Berlin: Dunker und Humblot, 2002.

Sechi, Orazio. "Cittadinanza: Diritto italiano e legislazione comparata." In *Digesto italiano*, vol. 7, pt. 2. 221–305.Turin: Unione Tipografica-Editrice Torinese, 1897–1902.

Seidel, Linda. *Jan Van Eyck's Arnolfini Portrait: Stories of an Icon*. Cambridge: Cambridge University Press, 1993.

Seidel Menchi, Silvana. "Percorsi variegati, percorsi obbligati: Elogio del matrimonio pre-tridentino." In *Matrimoni in dubbio: Unioni controverse e nozze clandestine in Italia dal XIV al XVIII secolo, Annali dell'Istituto storico italo-germanico in Trento*, Quaderni 57, edited by Silvana Seidel Menchi and Diego Quaglioni, 17–60. . Bologna: Il Mulino, 2001

Sestieri, Lea. *David Reubeni: Un ebreo d'Arabia in missione segreta nell'Europa del '500*. Genoa: Marietti, 1991.

Shaw, Christine. *The Politics of Exile in Renaissance Italy*. Cambridge: Cambridge University Press, 2000.

Sheehan, Michael M. "The Formation and Stability of Marriage in Fourteenth-Century England: Evidence of an Ely Register." In *Marriage, Family, and Law in Medieval Europe*, edited by James K. Farge, 37–76. Toronto: University of Toronto Press, 1996.

– "The Influence of Canon Law on the Property Rights of Married Women in England." In *Marriage, Family, and Law in Medieval Europe*, edited by James K. Farge, 16–30. Toronto: University of Toronto Press, 1996.

Siegmund, Stefanie B. "Division of the Dowry on the Death of the Daughter: An Instance in the Negotiation of Laws and Jewish Customs in Early Modern Tuscany." *Jewish History* 16 (2002): 73–106.

– *The Medici State and the Ghetto of Florence: The Construction of an Early Modern Jewish Community*. Stanford, CA: Stanford University Press, 2006.

Signorelli, Giuseppi. *Leggi e costumi di Viterbo nel medioevo*. Viterbo: Monarchi, 1887.

Signori, Gabriela. "Family Traditions: Moral Economy and Memorial 'Gift Exchange' in the Urban World of the Late Fifteenth Century." In *Negotiating the Gift: Pre-modern Figurations of Exchange*, Veröffentlichungen des Max-Planck-Instituts für Geschichte 188, edited by Gadi Algazi, Valentin Groebner, and Bernhard Jussen, 285–318. Göttingen: Vandenhoeck & Ruprecht, 2003.

– "Similitude, égalité et réciprocité: L'économie matrimoniale dans les sociétés urbaines de l'Empire à la fin du Moyen Âge." *Annales: Histoire, Science Sociales* 67 (2012): 657–78.

Silini, Giovanni. "Famiglia, società e patrimonio a Lovere negli atti dotali e testamentari (secoli XV e XVI)." *Archivio Storico Bergamasco* 11 (1991): 68–126.

Silva, Pietro. "Pisa sotto Firenze dal 1406 al 1433." *Studi storici* 35 (1909): 133–83, 285–323, 529–79.

Simmel, Georg. *On Individuality and Social Forms*. Edited by Donald N. Levine. Chicago: University of Chicago Press, 1971.

Simonsohn, Shlomo. "La condizione giuridica degli ebrei nell'Italia centrale e settentrionale (secoli XII–XVI)." In *Storia d' Italia, Annali 11: Gli ebrei in Italia*, edited by Corrado Vivanti, 97–120. Turin: Einaudi, 1996.

Smail, Daniel Lord. "Démanteler le patrimoine: Les femmes et les biens dans la Marseille médiévale." *Annales: Histoire, Sciences Sociales* 52 (1997): 343–68.

– *Imaginary Cartographies: Possession and Identity in Late Medieval Marseille*. Ithaca, NY: Cornell University Press, 2000.

Smith, Alison A. "Locating Power and Influence within the Provincial Elite of Verona: Aristocratic Wives and Widows." *Renaissance Studies* 8 (1994): 339–448.

Smith, Susan L. *The Power of Women: A Topos in Medieval Art and Literature.* Philadelphia: University of Pennsylvania Press, 1995.

Spagnesi, Enrico. "Dominus Lapus, iuris utriusque monarcha." In *Antica possessione con belli costumi: Due giornate di studio su Lapo da Castiglionchio il Vecchio (Firenze-Pontassieve, 3–4 ott. 2003)*, edited by Franek Sznura, 121–42. Florence: ASKA, 2005.

– *Utiliter edoceri: Atti inediti degli ufficiali dello Studio fiorentino (1391–96).* Milan: Giuffrè, 1979.

Spallanzani, Marco. "A Note on Florentine Banking in the Renaissance: Orders of Payment and Cheques." *Journal of European Economic History* 7 (1978): 145–68.

Spicciani, Amleto. *Capitale e interesse tra mercatura e povertà nei teologi e canonisti dei secoli XIII–XV.* Rome: Jouvence, 1990.

Starn, Randolph. *Contrary Commonwealth: The Theme of Exile in Medieval and Renaissance Italy.* Berkeley: University of California Press, 1982.

Stein, Peter. "Bartolus and the Conflict of Laws and the Roman Law." In *The Character and Influence of the Roman Civil Law: Historical Essays*, 83–90. London: Hambledon Press, 1988.

Stephens, John N. *The Fall of the Florentine Republic, 1512–1530.* Oxford: Clarendon Press, 1983.

Stevenson, Kenneth. *Nuptial Blessing: A Study of Christian Marriage Rites.* New York: Oxford University Press, 1983.

Storti Storchi, Claudia. "La condizione giuridica delle donne della famiglia nelle strategie testamentarie di Alberico da Rosciate (1345–1360)." In *La condizione giuridica delle donne nel medioevo: Atti del convegno di studio-Trieste, 23 novembre 2010*, edited by Miriam Davide, 53–94. Trieste: CERM, 2012.

– *Intorno ai Costituti pisani della legge e dell'uso (secolo XII).* Europa Mediterranea Quaderni 11. Naples: Liguori, 1998.

– "The Legal Status of Foreigners in Italy (XIVth–XVIth Centuries): General Rules and Their Enforcement in Some Cases Concerning the *Executio Parata.*" In *Of Strangers and Foreigners (Late Antiquity–Middle Ages)*, Studies in Comparative Legal History, edited by Laurent Mayali and Maria M. Mart, 97–135. Berkeley: Robbins Collection, 1993.

– *Ricerche sulla condizione giuridica dello straniero in Italia dal tardo diritto comune all'età preunitaria: Aspetti civilistici.* Milan: Giuffrè, 1989.

– "La tradizione longobarda nel diritto bergamesco: I rapporti patrimoniali tra coniugi (secoli XII–XIV)." In *Diritto comune e diritto locali nella storia dell'Europa (Atti del convegno di Varenna (12–15 giugno 1979)*, 481–553. Milan: Giuffrè, 1980.

Stow, Kenneth R. *Catholic Thought and Papal Jewry Policy, 1555–1593.* New York: Jewish Theological Seminary of America, 1977.

– "Marriages Are Made in Heaven: Marriage and the Individual in the Roman Jewish Ghetto." *Renaissance Quarterly* 48 (1995): 459–91. Reprinted in Kenneth R. Stow, *Jewish Life in Early Modern Rome: Challenge, Conversion, and Private Life*, no. 16. Aldershot: Ashgate/Variorum, 2007.

Strasser, Ulrike. *State of Virginity: Gender, Religion, and Politics in an Early Modern Catholic State*. Ann Arbor: University of Michigan Press, 2004.

Strocchia, Sharon T. "Death Rites and the Ritual Family in Renaissance Florence." In *Life and Death in Fifteenth-Century Florence*, edited by Marcel Tetel, Ronald G. Witt, and Rona Goffen, 120–45. Durham, NC: Duke University Press, 1989.

Stuard, Susan Mosher. "Dowry and Other Marriage Gifts." In *Women and Gender in Medieval Europe: An Encyclopedia*, edited by Margaret Schaus, 229–31. New York: Routledge, 2006.

– "Gravitas and Consumption." In *Conflicted Identities and Multiple Masculinities: Men in the Medieval West*, edited by Jacqueline Murray, 214–42. New York: Garland, 1999.

– *A State of Deference: Ragusa/Dubrovnik in the Medieval Centuries*. Philadelphia: University of Pennsylvania Press, 1992.

Studer, Barbara. "Frauen im Bürgerrecht: Überlegungen zur rechtlichen und sozialen Stellung der Frau in spätmittelalterlichen Stadten." In *Neubürger im späten Mittelalter: Migration und Austausch in der Städtelandschaft (1250–1550)*, edited by Rainer Christoph Schwinges, 169–200. Berlin: Dunker und Humblot, 2002.

Subotnik, Dan. "Sue Me, Sue Me, What Can You Do Me? I Love You: A Disquisition on Law, Sex, and Talk." *Florida Law Review* 47 (July 1995): 311–409.

Superbi, Silvia. "'In dotem pro dote et dotis nomine': Il sistema dotale tra norma e prassi nella Ferrara del XIV secolo." Dottorato di ricerca in modelli, linguaggi e tradizioni nella cultura occidentale, ciclo XXIII, Università degli Studi di Ferrara, 2008/10.

Taddei, Gabriele. *Castiglion Fiorentino fra XIII e XV secolo: Politica, economia e società di un centro minore toscano*. Biblioteca Storica Toscana 60. Florence: L.S. Olschki, 2009.

Tamba, Giorgio. *Una corporazione per il potere: Il notariato a Bologna in età comunale*. Bologna: CLUEB, 1998.

Tangheroni, Marco. "Dell'Agnello, Giovanni." In *DBI*, vol. 37, 47–55. Rome: Istituto della Enciclopedia Italiana, 1989.

Tanzini, Lorenzo. *Alle origini della Toscana moderna: Firenze e gli statuti delle comunità soggette tra XIV e XVI secolo*. Florence: L.S. Olschki, 2007.

Thomas, Yan. "*Fictio Legis*: L'empire de la fiction romaine et ses limites médiévales." *Droits: Revue française de théorie juridique* 21 (1995): 17–63.

– *"Origine" et "commune patrie": Étude de droit public romain (89 av. J.-C.–212 ap. J.-C.)*. Rome: École Française de Rome, 1996.

Timoteo, Marina. "Family Law in Italy." In *Family Law in Europe*, edited by Carolyn Hamilton and Kate Standley, 264–98. London: Butterworths, 1995.

Tintori, Guido. "Naturalization Procedures for Immigrants: Italy." EUDO Citizenship Observatory; NP 2013/13; Naturalisation Procedures Reports, European University Institute, Florence. http://eudo-citizenship.eu.

Toaff, Ariel. "*Judei cives*? Gli ebrei nei catasti di Perugia del Trecento." *Zakhor: Rivista di storia degli ebrei in Italia* 4 (2000): 11–36.

– *Love, Work, and Death: Jewish Life in Medieval Umbria*. Translated by Judith Landry. London: Littman Library of Jewish Civilization, 1996.

Tocci, Mirella. "Il *consensus parentum* alle nozze nella canonistica e nel pensiero dei teologi tridentini: Un caso di obbligo *de honestate*?" *Archivio giuridico* 120 (2000): 541–80.

Todescan, Franco. *Diritto e realità: Storia e teoria del "fictio iuris."* Padua: CEDAM, 1979.

Tognetti, Sergio. *Il Banco Cambini: Affari e mercati di una compagnia mercantile-bancaria nella Firenze del XV secolo*. Florence: Leo S. Olschki, 1999.

Tomas, Natalie R. "Did Women Have A Space?" In *Renaissance Florence: A Social History*, edited by Roger J Crum and John T. Paoletti, 311–28. Cambridge: Cambridge University Press, 2006.

– *The Medici Women: Gender and Power in Renaissance Florence*. Aldershot: Ashgate, 2003.

Torelli, Pietro. *Lezioni di storia del diritto italiano: Diritto privato*. Vol. 2, *La famiglia*. Milan: Giuffrè, 1947.

Toxé, Philippe. "La *copula carnalis* chez les canonistes médiévaux." In *Mariage et sexualité en Moyen Âge: Accord ou crise?* 123–33. Cultures et civilisations médiévales 21. Paris: 2000.

Tracy, James D. *A Financial Revolution in the Habsburg Netherlands: Renten and Renteniers in the County of Holland, 1515–1565*. Berkeley: University of California Press, 1985.

Traniello, Elisabetta. *Gli ebrei e le piccole città: Economia e società nel Polesine del Quattrocento*. Rovigo: Minelliana, 2004

– "Tra appartenenza ed estraneità: Gli ebrei e le città del Polesine di Rovigo nel Quattrocento." In *Ebrei nella Terraferma veneta del Quattrocento: Atti del convegno di studi Verona (14 novembre 2003)*, edited by Gian Maria Varanini and Reinhold C. Mueller, 163–76. Florence: Firenze University Press, 2005.

Treggiari, Ferdinando. "Barzi, Benedetto." In *Dizionario biografico dei giuristi italiani*, edited by Italo Birocchi et al., vol. 1, 187–9. Bologna: Il Mulino, 2013.

Treggiari, Susan. *Roman Marriage: "Iusti Coniuges" from the Time of Cicero to the Time of Ulpian*. Oxford: Clarendon Press, 1991.

Trexler, Richard C. *Synodal Law in Florence and Fiesole, 1306–1518*. Studi e testi 268. Vatican City: BAV, 1971.

Tripoldi, Claudia. *Gli Spini tra XIV e XV secolo: Il declino di un antico casato fiorentino*. Florence: L.S. Olschki, 2013.

Tushnet, Rebecca. "Rules of Engagement." *Yale Law Journal* 107 (June 1998): 2583–618.

Ulivi, Elisabetta. "Su Pietro Di Niccolò Da Filicaia autore del libro di giuochi matematici." Technical Report (2012.07.19, no. 1), Dipartimento di Matematica "Ulisse Dini," Università di Firenze. http://eprints.unifi.it/archive/00002423/.

Valente, Piergiorgio. *Convenzioni internazionali contro le doppie imposizioni*. Milan: Ipsoa, 2008.

Valentini, Vittorio. "L'ordine degli apparati accursiani in una notizia di Angelo degli Ubaldi." *RHD* 53 (1985): 99–134.

Vallaro, Anna Margherita. "*Considerans fragilitatem humanae naturae ...*": *Testaments et pratique testamentaire à San Gimignano de 1299 a 1530*. Bern: Peter Lang, 2005.

Vallerani, Massimo. "*Consilia iudicialia*: Sapienza giuridica e processo nelle città comunali italiane." *Mélanges de l'École Française de Rome* 123 (2011): 129–49.

– *Medieval Public Justice*. Translated by Sara Rubin Blanshei. Washington, DC: Catholic University of America Press, 2012.

Vallone, Giancarlo. "La raccolta Barberini dei *consilia* originali di Baldo." *RSDI* 52 (1989): 3–63.

Valsecchi, Chiara. "'Causa matrimonialis est gravis et ardua': *Consiliatores* e matrimonio fino al concilio di Trento." In *Studi di storia del diritto*, vol. 2, 407–513. Milan: Giuffrè, 1999.

Van Caenegem, Raoul C. "History of European Civil Procedure." In *International Encyclopedia of Comparative Law*, vol. 16, 2, 16–23. New York: Oceana, 1973.

Vanel, Marguerite. *Histoire de la nationalité française d'origine: Evolution historique de la notion de français d'origine du XVIe siècle au code civil*. Paris: Ancienne imprimerie de la Cour d'Appel, 1945.

Varanini, Gian Maria. "*Società cristiana e minoranza ebraica a Verona nella seconda metà del Quattrocento: Tra ideologia osservante e vita quotidiana.*" In *Ebrei nella Terraferma veneta del Quattrocento, Atti del convegno di studi, Verona, 14 novembre 2003*, edited by Gian Maria Varanini e Reinhold C. Mueller, 1–22. Florence: Firenze University Press, 2005.

Veblen, Thorstein. *The Theory of the Leisure Class* (1899). New Brunswick, NJ: Transaction Publishers, 1992.

Verde, Armando Felice. "Dottorati a Firenze e a Pisa 1505–1528." In *Xenia medii aevi historiam illustrantia oblata Thomae Kaeppeli O.P.*, 607–785. Rome: Edizione di Storia e Letteratura, 1978.

Vernelli, Carlo. "Note sulla condizione femminile negli statuti comunale dell'Italia centrale." *Proposte e ricerche* 31 (1993): 187–202.

Veronese, Alessandra. *Una famiglia di banchieri ebrei tra XIV e XVI secolo: I da Volterra: Reti di credito nell'Italia del Rinascimento*. Pisa: Edizione ETS, 1998.

Viale, Vittorio. "Cinture nuziali del XV secolo." *Bollettino della Società Piemontese di Archeologia e di Belle Arti*, n.s., 1 (1947): 44–60.

Vincenzi Amato, Diana. "La famiglia e il diritto." In *La famiglia italiana dall'Ottocento a oggi*, edited by Piero Melograni, 629–96. Rome: Laterza, 1988.

Violante, Cinzio. "Alcune caratteristiche delle strutture familiari in Lombardia, Emilia e Toscana durante i secoli IX–XII." In *Famiglia e parentela nell'Italia medievale*, edited by Georges Duby and Jacques Le Goff, 1–51. Bologna: Il Mulino, 1977.

– "Imposte dirette e debito pubblico nel basso medioevo." In *Economia, società, istituzioni a Pisa nel medioevo: Saggi e ricerche*, 101–69. Bari: Dedalo, 1980.

Vismara, Giulio. "I patti successori nella dottrina di Bartolo." In *Bartolo da Sassoferrato: Studi e documenti per il VI centenario*, vol. 2, 755–83. Milan, Giuffrè 1962.

– "I rapporti patrimoniali tra coniugi nell'alto medioevo." In *Il matrimonio nella società altomedievale*, vol. 2, 633–91. Spoleto: CISAM, 1977.

Vleeschouwers-Van Melkebeek, Monique. "Aspects du lien matrimonial dans le *Liber sentenciarum* de Bruxelles (1448–1459)." *RHD* 53 (1985): 50–61.

Volterra, Edoardo. "Sponsalia." *Nuovissimo digesto italiano* 18 (1971): 34–7.

– "Studio sull'*arrha sponsalicia*." *RISG*, n.s., 2 (1927): 581–615; n.s., 4 (1929): 3–33; n.s., 5 (1930): 155–245.

Wacke, Andreas. "Die Konvaleszenz von Pfandrecht nach römischem Recht." *ZRG* (*RA*) 115 (1998): 438–61.

Waley, Daniel. *The Italian City-Republics.* London: Longman, 1988.

– "Viterbo nello Stato della Chiesa nel secolo XIII." In *Atti del convegno di studio: VII centenario del 1° conclave (1268–71)*, 97–111. Viterbo: Azienda Autonoma di Cura, Soggiorno e Turismo di Viterbo, 1975.

Waltz, Waldo Emerson. *The Nationality of Married Women: A Study of Domestic Policies and International Legislation*. Illinois Studies in the Social Sciences 22, no. 1. Urbana: University of Illinois, 1937.

Watson, Paul F. *The Garden of Love in Tuscan Art of the Early Renaissance*. Philadelphia: Art Alliance Press, 1979.

Weaver, Elissa. "Dietro il vestito: La semiotica del vestire nel *Decameron*." In *La novella italiana: Atti del convegno di Caprarola, 19–24 Settembre 1988*, 701–10. Rome: Salerno, 1989.

Weigand, Rudolf. "Ehe- und Familienrecht in der mittelalterlichen Stadt." In *Liebe und Ehe im Mittelalter*, no. 15, 343–87. Goldbach: Keip, 1993.

– "Liebe und Ehe bei den Dekretisten des 12. Jahrhunderts." In *Liebe und Ehe im Mittelalter*, no. 3, 59–76. Goldbach: Keip, 1993.

– "Zur mittelalterlichen kirchlichen Ehegerichtsbarkeit." In *Liebe und Ehe im Mittelalter*, no. 14, 307–42. Goldbach: Keip, 1993.

Wells, Charlotte C. *Law and Citizenship in Early Modern France*. Baltimore: Johns Hopkins University Press, 1995.

Werckmeister, Jean. "L'apparition de la doctrine du mariage contrat dans le droit canonique du 12e siècle." *RDC* 53 (2003): 5–25.

Wieling, Hans Josef. *Interesse und Privatstrafe vom Mittelalter bis zum bürgerlichen Gesetzbuch*. Cologne: Böhlau, 1970.

Winer, Rebecca Lynn. *Women, Wealth, and Community in Perpignan, c. 1250–1300: Christians, Jews, and Enslaved Muslims in a Medieval Mediterranean Town*. Burlington, VT: Ashgate, 2006.

Witthoft, Brucia. "Marriage Rituals and Marriage Chests in Quattrocento Florence." *Artibus et Historiae* 5 (1982): 43–59.

– "Riti nuziali e loro iconografia." In *Storia del matrimonio*, edited by Michela De Giorgio and Christiane Klapisch-Zuber, 119–48. Bari: Laterza, 1996.

Wolff, Hans Julius. "Zur Geschichte der Parapherna." *ZRG* (*RA*) 72 (1955): 335–47.

Wray, Shona Kelly. *Communities and Crisis: Bologna during the Black Death*. Leiden: Brill, 2009.

Wrigley, Anthony. "Fertility Strategy for the Individual and the Group." In *Historical Studies of Changing Fertility*, edited by Charles Tilly, 135–54. Princeton, NJ: Princeton University Press, 1978.

Wyke, Maria. "Woman in the Mirror: The Rhetoric of Adornment in the Roman World." In *Women in Ancient Societies: An Illusion of the Night*, edited by Léonie J. Archer, Susan Fischler, and Maria Wyke, 134–51. New York: Routledge, 1994.

Young, Bruce W. "Haste, Consent, and Age of Marriage: Some Implications of Social History for Romeo and Juliet." *Iowa State Journal of Research* 62 (1988): 459–74.

Zanetti, Ginevra. "Sul valore giuridico della *subharrhatio anulo* nei riti nuziali del medioevo italico." *RISG* 18 (1943): 3–134.

Zarri, Gabriella. "Il matrimonio tridentino." In *Recinti: Donne, clausura e matrimonio nella prima età moderna*, 203–50. Bologna: Il Mulino, 2000.

Zdekauer, Lodovico. "La confessione di legge nei patti dotali di Firenze." *RISG* 3 (1887): 1–8.
– "Le donne nella Lira senese del 1297." *Bullettino senese di storia patria* 10 (1903): 91–106.
– "Le doti in Firenze nel dugento." In *Miscellanea fiorentina di erudizione e storia*, edited by Iodoco Del Badia, 97–104. Florence: Bonsignori, 1902.
– *La vita privata e pubblica dei senesi nel Dugento*. Siena: Reale Accademia dei Rozzi, 1896.
Zimmermann, Reinhard. *The Law of Obligations: Roman Foundations of the Civilian Tradition*. Cape Town: Juta, 1992.
Zincone, Giovanna. "Citizenship Policy Making in EU States: Italy." Working paper (2010), European University Institute, Florence, EUDO Citizenship Observatory. http://eudo-citizenship.eu.
Zincone, Giovanna, and Marzia Basili. "Report on Italy." Working paper (revised and updated January 2013), European University Institute, Florence, EUDO Citizenship Observatory. http://eudo-citizenship.eu.
Zordan, Giorgio. "I vari aspetti della comunione familiare di beni nella Venezia dei secoli XI–XII." *Studi veneziani* 8 (1966): 127–94.
Zorzi, Andrea. "The 'Material Constitution' of the Florentine Territorial Dominion." In *Florentine Tuscany: Structures and Practices of Power*, edited by William J. Connell and Andrea Zorzi, 6–31. Cambridge: Cambridge University Press, 2000.
Zucca Micheletto, Beatrice. "À quoi sert la dot? Aliénations dotales, économie familiale et stratégies des couples à Turin au XVIIIe siècle." *Annales de Démographie Historique* 121 (2011): 161–86.
– "Reconsidering the Southern Europe Model: Dowry, Women's Work and Marriage Patterns in Pre-industrial Urban Italy (Turin, Second Half of the 18th Century)." *The History of the Family* 16 (2011): 354–70.

Index

Toronto Studies in Medieval Law

1. *The Politics of Law in Late Medieval and Renaissance Italy*, edited by Lawrin Armstrong and Julius Kirshner
2. *Marriage, Dowry, and Citizenship in Late Medieval and Renaissance Italy*, Julius Kirshner

www.ingramcontent.com/pod-product-compliance
Lightning Source LLC
LaVergne TN
LVHW090758070826
844660LV00022B/1023
* 9 7 8 1 4 4 2 6 1 4 2 1 5 *